AMERICAN PHILANTHROPY
ABROAD

Society and Philanthropy Series
Richard Magat, Series Editor

American Philanthropy Abroad

With A New Introduction By The Author

Merle Curti

Transaction Books
New Brunswick (USA) and Oxford (UK)

New material this edition copyright © 1988 by Transaction, Inc., New Brunswick, New Jersey 08903.
Original Edition © 1963 by Rutgers, The State University

Library of Congress Catalog Number: 87-25533
ISBN: 0-88738-711-X
Printed in the United States of America

Library of Congress Cataloging in Publication Data

Curti, Merle Eugene, 1897-
    American philanthropy abroad.

    Reprint. Originally published: New Brunswick, N.J.:
Rutgers University Press, 1963.
    Bibliography: p.
    Includes index.
    1. Charities—United States—History.   2. Disaster relief—United States.   3. Voluntarism—United States—History.   I. Title.
HV91.C87   1987   361.7′0973   87-25533
ISBN 0-88738-711-X

For
Arthur M. Schlesinger in
gratitude and friendship.

Preface

Nations make themselves felt in the world in a variety of ways. Historians have described the influence that nations have exerted through the writings of their intellectuals, through their economic institutions, through diplomacy, and through wars. But scholars have largely overlooked another source of international contact: voluntary giving by one people to another for the relief of suffering in catastrophe, for the improvement of living standards, and for strengthening cultural life. An important part of modern civilization, this concern of man for his fellow man is an outgrowth of values and behavior deeply rooted in human history.

One of the first Americans to call explicit attention to the sentiment and action which any great calamity—plague, flood, fire, or famine—produces among people of other nations as well as among those in the country where the disaster occurred was Elihu Burritt. "The Learned Blacksmith," as this leading social reformer was familiarly known in America and Europe a hundred years ago, contended that "one of the first and most distinctive fruits of Christianity was the production of international sympathy." Resting on the doctrine of the universal brotherhood of man, international sympathy, as he saw it, transcends all national and racial barriers. In holding that God tests the depth and extent of sympathy at the same time that He widens and enriches it by "the mission of great sufferings," Burritt was expressing an ancient Christian precept which owed much to an even older Hebraic tradition. *The Mission of Great Sufferings in the Development of International Sympathy and Benevolence*, as Burritt called his tract, noted the neglect by historians of this sentiment and action. It was also a thoughtful appeal for the conscious extension of international benevolence.

vii

In the century since Burritt wrote, catastrophes of the kind he had in mind have continued to add to man's sorrows and misery. They have also continued to evoke from countries far and wide aid to the hungry and homeless wherever disaster struck. War and revolution, which have taken an unprecedented toll of suffering, have also enlisted compassionate efforts to lessen the suffering that man has caused his fellow man. But, except for studies of limited scope, historians have neglected this story.

I have brought together here much that has been known and a good deal of fresh knowledge about non-government efforts in America to serve humanity in other countries in time of trouble. I have also described and interpreted similar efforts to help other peoples find ways of controlling disease, reducing ignorance, increasing economic productivity, and achieving a higher standard of living. This account is part of the history of American philanthropy undertaken at the University of Wisconsin under a grant from the Ford Foundation.

The term philanthropy has been understood in different ways. Until well toward the end of the nineteenth century the most common meaning in America was "love of man" as expressed in altruism, meliorism, and humanitarianism. With the rise of social work in the last decades of the century, the word was associated with the professionalization of charity and welfare. Increasingly in our own time, philanthropy has implied large-scale giving, whether by well-to-do individuals or by foundations. I have used the term in what may be regarded as its simplest and most comprehensive sense: private giving for public purposes. It includes the traditional concept of charity— giving to meet individual needs. It also includes the broader idea of giving substance and services for education, research, health, the arts, and the attainment of a higher level of living. In this later sense philanthropy implies giving as a kind of "social investment" which promises to better, not only today but tomorrow, the lot of individuals through the improvement of the society of which they are a part.

Thus understood, philanthropy has a long history in European institutions and culture. From Great Britain in particular, colonial Americans derived the values, the impulses which stimulated philanthropy and the laws and institutions through which it found expression. Indeed, for a considerable part of their history Americans received help from the voluntary gifts of men and women in Europe for the establishment and maintenance of the agencies of cultural life and for meeting unusual disasters. Moreover, American philanthropy overseas has been influenced by what people elsewhere have done for the needy in lands other than the United States. Since 1930, and especially since the Second World War, American voluntary aid abroad, like that extended by many countries, has intertwined with the activities of international agencies, official and nonofficial. Thus to understand American philanthropy beyond American borders it is necessary to take into account the world context of which it has been a part. This would be easier if historians had paid more attention to the philanthropic impulse in other countries. Until this has been more largely done, it would be foolish to try to determine whether, in relation to its resources, America has been more or less "philanthropic" than other peoples.

What Americans have done through nonofficial efforts to help peoples abroad has been closely related to what has been done at home for disadvantaged members of the population of the United States. The structure and functioning of the voluntary agencies engaged in foreign relief and rehabilitation resembles that of similar organizations for helping people at home. In a sense, overseas aid is an extension of the social gospel, the techniques of the social worker in the urban slum, the program and methods of the county agent and the director of the 4-H clubs in rural areas in the United States.

By the requirements of our definition of philanthropy this study is concerned with nongovernment as opposed to government programs for relief and technical aid abroad. Yet almost from the start government has had a hand in voluntary efforts. In the interest of national policy or in response to pressure of public opinion or interested groups, the government sometimes transported relief contributed by voluntary effort. Since 1948 it has also allocated a considerable part of its agricultural surplus stores to voluntary agencies for overseas distribution. To prevent conflicts and duplication of effort, the government exerted regulatory control over agencies engaged in foreign relief during the Second World War. Since that time the acceptance of government surpluses and transport has involved meeting specifications determined by law or an official agency. Now and then the government has used the personnel of voluntary agencies in large-scale relief programs. A new type of partnership between voluntary associations and government has lately developed in connection with the financial support the Point 4 program has given to many private agencies. A still newer partnership may be taking shape in the Peace

Corps. It is, in short, impossible to draw a sharp line between official and nonofficial foreign aid.

I have organized the material in terms of chronology and leading themes. This may have led to some overlapping, but the gain in understanding has, I think, warranted it. Attention to situations over time which were both similar and different has also been helpful in understanding the complex nature of motives for giving. A sense of religious duty dominated those who supported missionaries in their role as almoners and as pioneers of technical aid. Religion has also been a major factor in the support given to many nonmissionary agencies with overseas programs. Yet secular motives have also been important. In some cases, overseas giving seems to have been prompted by disinterested humanitarianism, a benevolent concern for people in other lands. At other times, especially in the twentieth century, Americans may have been coaxed to give aid abroad by a sense of guilt over the contrast between abundance in their own country and the misery and poverty in other areas. In still other cases, political sympathy has fed the springs of international philanthropy. At various times, one group or another—Greek patriots, Cuban rebels, Spanish loyalists—have been identified by sympathetic groups in the United States with American democracy. Motivation has also included the obligation which individuals have felt to help needy kinsfolk and related ethnic groups in other parts of the world. As in giving for domestic charities at home, social pressure and sheer habit have also played their part. No effort has been made to measure the relative strength of these varied and intermingled motives. The organization by chronology and theme has also enabled me to analyze more clearly changing methods of providing aid. These have included public meetings to arouse interest and to collect funds and relief in kind, appeals from pulpit and platform, the organization of *ad hoc* and of more permanent agencies and, of course, the organized "drive" with its use of public relations techniques and the mass media.

One of the hardest problems has been that of assessing the accomplishments of American overseas philanthropy. Since the records of many nineteenth-century relief committees have not survived, it was often necessary to rely for amounts collected in a given campaign on newspaper reports. Many of these seem only roughly to have approximated reality. Quantification has, however, been feasible in the period since the First World War, thanks to the fact that the Department of Commerce from that time has systematically tabulated year by year individual and institutional remittances overseas. In assessing achievements in receiving countries the problem of judging the impact of American philanthropy has been even harder. It is often impossible to separate the effects of American donations from those of other countries. Testimonials of appreciation on the part of recipients are abundant, but these cannot always be taken at face value. The reports of foundations are helpful in gauging the achievements of these increasingly important institutions in the field of overseas rehabilitation and technical aid. But foundation archives, which might provide more relevant information than published reports are usually closed to investigators. The reluctance of many voluntary agencies to conduct self-evaluations is understandable but, from the point of view of the historian, regrettable. In 1957 a subcommittee of Congress in comparing the operations and impacts of official and nonofficial aid pointed to the advantages and limitations of both. Helpful though this is, the evaluation was limited in scope and confined mainly to the immediately preceding years. Finally, to assess the impact of overseas philanthropy on the reputation of America or, to use an overworked phrase, the American image, is an even more ticklish problem.

In view of the wealth of available material, especially for the last fifty years, no claim can be made to an exhaustive treatment of every theme. Yet much that took place has been described in considerable detail, particularly when it was possible to work with abundant documentation and when detailed analysis illuminated larger problems involved in the voluntary efforts of Americans to help other peoples in time of special need. A more intensive study of some of the philanthropic endeavors might yield a better understanding of the whole story, and I hope that such investigations may be made by other scholars. We also need studies of philanthropic efforts made in other countries to help peoples overseas both in catastrophes and in the achievement of long-run improvement in living conditions. It goes without saying that intensive studies in the receiving countries of the effects of outside philanthropy are also desirable. I hope, again, that this account of American overseas philanthropy may encourage scholars elsewhere to undertake such studies. Meantime, this account offers an interpretation of the motives, methods, and general achievements of American voluntarism in its overseas errands of mercy, rehabilitation, and technical aid.

Acknowledgments

My indebtedness to the many scholars, research assistants, public and private agencies, and libraries that have made this book possible is so considerable that it cannot be overstated.

The materials on which this study rests are widely scattered. The American Foundation Library Center in New York has collected a good deal of material relevant to what I have done. But it was necessary to use the printed and manuscript records of several government and of many voluntary agencies. Abundant though this material is, it would have been impossible to complete this study without the sustained and generous help of many voluntary agencies which provided out of the way material and enlightened my understanding of problems in time-taking interviews.

I want first of all to acknowledge my indebtedness to the officers and staffs of several religious-oriented voluntary agencies: especially to Mr. A. Klaupiks, Coordinator of the Baptist World Alliance Relief, and Miss Nell Stanley of the Foreign Missions Board of the Southern Baptist Convention; to the Rev. R. T. McGlasson, Foreign Missions Secretary of the Assemblies of God; to Mr. Earle H. Ballou of the Congregational Christian Service Committee Inc.; to Mr. Ove R. Nielson of the Lutheran World Relief, Inc., Dr. Paul C. Empie of the National Lutheran Council, Mr. Raymond Kissam, Lutheran Immigration Services, and Pastor Hans Diehl; to Miss Betty D. Richardson and Mr. John C. Abbott of Church World Service; to Dr. Frank W. Price, director of the Missionary Research Library; to Dr. Frank S. Glick and Miss Norma N. Sherry of the Unitarian Service Committee and especially to Miss Helen Fogg and Mrs. Curtice Hitchcock, of the same agency, who read relevant parts of my manuscript; to the officers and staff of the American Friends Service Committee, especially to Mr. Colin Bell, Miss Barbara Hinchcliffe, Mrs. Nancy Smedley, Mrs. Louis W. Schneider, and, above all, to Professor Lewis M. Hoskins, of Earlham College. Let me also at this point express my gratitude to Dr. J. V. G. Forbes who generously made available to me his own unpublished work on the overseas work of the AFSC. I am likewise indebted to Mr. Willard E. Roth and to Mr. William T. Snyder of the Mennonite Central Committee, and to Miss Hazel Peters of the General Brotherhood Board, Church of the Brethren. Miss Catherine R. O'Connor of Catholic Relief Services-National Catholic Welfare Conference provided useful material, and Mr. James Norris and Miss Eileen Egan of the same agency spared neither time nor effort to be helpful. Mr. Jack Rader, Mr. Paul Bernick, and their colleagues of American ORT Federation deepened my understanding of many aspects of overseas Jewish philanthropy. The officers of Hadassah were equally generous, and I want especially to thank Miss Hannah L. Goldberg for 'ier help. Miss Deborah I. Offenbacher of United Israel Appeal gave me useful material. To the officers and staff of the American Jewish Joint Distribution Committee Inc. I owe a special debt, especially to Mr. Irving R. Dickman, Mr. Edward M. M. Warburg, Miss Henrietta K. Buckman, and Dr. Boris Sapir. Mr. Herbert A. Friedman, Executive Vice-Chairman of United Jewish Appeal, Mr. Sidney Shore of HICEM, Mr. James Rice of United HIAS Service, Dr. Solomon Schwartz, and Mr. Lazar M. Pistrak, Soviet Orbit Librarian, U. S. Information Agency, were all helpful, as were Dr. I. S. Wechsler and Miss Rita Blume of the American Friends of the Hebrew University, Inc. Mr. James N. Rosenberg answered many questions and gave me otherwise inaccessible information. Dr. David J. Kaliski of the American Jewish Physicians Committee similarly provided useful data. Mr. Agmad Kamal of Jami 'at al Islam sent me the reports of the agency with which he is associated.

The officers of many agencies concerned with aid to overseas ethnic groups who provided me with material unavailable in most libraries include Mr. F. X. Swietlik of American Relief for Poland, Mr. S. M. Saroyan of American National Committee to Aid Homeless Armenians, Mr. L. J. de Gatterburg of Romanian Welfare Inc., Mr. Walter Gallan of United Ukrainian American Relief Committee, Mr. B. C. Maday of Coordinated Hungarian Relief Inc., Mr. James McCracken of the Tolstoy Foundation (presently with Church World Service), and Mr. C. G. Michalis of American Relief for Holland.

Dr. Clyde E. Buckingham, Special Projects Officer of the American National Red Cross, and his associates introduced me to the archives of this historic and important agency and generously shared their knowledge of its programs and problems.

CARE Inc. could not have done more to help me. Its officers opened its archives, gave a great many hours in oral interviews, and read pertinent parts of my manuscript. I want especially to express my appreciation to Mr. Gordon Alderfer, Mr. A. Becker, Miss Margaret Ford, and Mr. Richard W. Reuter. My former student, Mr. Stanford Cazier of Utah State University, who is writing a doctoral dissertation on CARE Inc. gave me the benefit of his criticism based on his extensive research in CARE archives.

The officers and staffs of several other secular agencies deserve thanks for their cooperation: Miss Julia M. Stern of the United States Committee for Refugees, Dr. J. S. Noffsinger of International Voluntary Services Inc., and Mrs. Eleanor Kaplan of the United States Committee for UNICEF.

It is no exaggeration to say that this study is indebted above all to the staff of the American Council of Voluntary Agencies in New York. In addition to making its files available, Miss Charlotte E. Owen, the executive director, Mrs. Elizabeth Clark Reiss, Mrs. Margaret Littke, Miss Etta Deutsch, and Dr. Wayland Zwayer spared neither time nor pains in making suggestions and in providing information from their own long and rich experience with voluntary agencies engaged in overseas activities.

Mr. Arthur C. Ringland, formerly ex-officio Executive Director of the Advisory Committee on Voluntary Foreign Aid, was helpful in the early stages of our investigation. I also want to acknowledge my deep gratitude to Mr. William H. McCahon and Miss Joan E. Kain of the Advisory Committee on Voluntary Foreign Aid in Washington. Mr. McCahon's understanding of the agencies and their relations with the federal government is very great, as is that of Miss Kain: both were very generous.

In my efforts to understand the frequently complicated stories of American agencies concerned with education overseas I learned a great deal from and owe a considerable debt to Mrs. Barney Girden of the Near East College Association, Inc., and to my former student, Professor Robert Daniel, of the Ohio University, who did his doctoral dissertation on Near East Relief and the Near East Foundation; to Messrs. Walter S. Rogers and John Crane of the Institute of Current World Affairs; to the late Mr. Wynn C. Fairfield; to Dr. Y. S. Lee of the Yonsei University Medical School and Severance Hospital in Seoul; to Mr. Sherwood Eddy, Ambassador Edwin O. Reischauer, Miss Margaret H. Leonard of the Oberlin Shansi Memorial Association, Mr. Alexander W. Allport of the American Farm School in Salonica, Mr. Eric T. Boulter of the American Foundation for the Overseas Blind, Miss Alice Dulany Ball of United States Book Exchange, Inc., Mr. Finley Dunne Jr., of the International Schools Foundation Inc., Mr. A. H. Washburn of New Hope, Pennsylvania, and Msgr. John Patrick Carroll-Abbing of Boys' Town of Italy, Inc.

I want also to take occasion to thank Mr. Harold Rosenberg of the Advertising Council Inc., Mr. Henry P. McNulty of Free Europe Committee Inc., Mr. Fred G. Taylor of the American Embassy in Prague, Mr. George Hunderston of the American Embassy in Seoul, and Mr. John Flynn of Senator Hubert Humphrey's staff. Former President Harry S. Truman in an interview with my research assistant, Mr. Charles Wetzel, clarified some points regarding the refugee program.

To foundation officials and staffs I am also in debt. Miss Isabel J. Mason of the Iran Foundation Inc., sent me materials, as did Mr. Horace B. Powell of the W. K. Kellogg Foundation. Dr. Raymond Fosdick, former president of the Rockefeller Foundation, was especially helpful in discussing the difficult problem of the impact of the overseas programs of the Rockefeller Foundation; and Mr. John Marshall of the same foundation was also generous in sharing his information and judgment on the same problem. Miss Nanet Paine of the Rockefeller Foundation answered several specific questions. Mr. Robert W. Chandler and Dr. George F. Gant of the Ford Foundation permitted me to read some of the manuscript records in the Foundation's archives. Dean Carl Spaeth of Stanford University Law School, who has had close association with the Foundation, has at all times been helpful.

It is impossible to express fully my debt to many libraries and librarians, but I want especially to mention Mrs. Virginia Downes of the YMCA Historical Library, Dr. Philip C. Brooks and Mr. Philip Lagerquist of the Harry S. Truman Institute and Library, Dr. Herman Kahn of the Franklin D. Roosevelt Library, Mr. Gilbert C. Rich of the Holyoke (Massachusetts) Public Library, Miss Evelyn Nelson of the New York State Library in Albany, and Miss Mary Hoffman Forbes of the Corcoran Gallery of Art. I owe special debts for innumerable courtesies at the hands of the staffs of the Baker

Library of Dartmouth College, the Memorial Library of the University of Wisconsin, the Wisconsin State Historical Society, and the National Archives where Mr. Buford Rowland was most helpful.

Mrs. Basil Hall of Cambridge, Massachusetts, generously sent me the large collection of the manuscripts of her father, which throw much light on American educational activities in the Near East, and Dr. John Baker, Jr., of Gridley, California, answered many questions regarding the disaster relief work of his father in China.

Mrs. Harley C. Stevens of San Francisco and Mrs. Mildred Adams Kenyon of New York, who have studied many aspects of American overseas philanthropies, graciously shared materials and information with me. So did Mrs. Delia W. Kuhn of Washington, D. C.

I am indebted to many scholars in many ways. For taking notes on materials in the Ford Foundation I am grateful to Dr. T. H. Vail Motter. Dr. Kleinert of Hessisches Staatsbad, Bad Nauheim, Germany, and Dr. Erwin H. Ackerknecht of the Medizinhistorisches Institute of Zurich supplied needed information on American support to German medical programs. Professor John Munroe of the University of Delaware, Professor I. L. Kandel of Columbia University and Professor Sheperd Clough of the same University, Professor George Mowry of the University of California at Los Angeles, Sir Hector Heatherington, of Glasgow University, Mr. F. Emerson Andrews, Dr. Fulmer Mood, Dr. Georg Federer, Consul-General of the German Federal Republic in New York City, Dr. Harlan Cleveland, Assistant Secretary of State, and Dr. Robert H. Hamlin of the Harvard School of Public Health all helped in one way or another. I am especially indebted to Mrs. Jessie C. Adams of the Balance of Payments Division of the United States Department of Commerce for putting at my disposal carefully assembled and evaluated official data. Dr. Frank Dickinson, Dr. Ralph Nelson, and Miss Natalie Taylor of the National Bureau of Economic Research, who have been studying recent economic trends in American philanthropy, likewise shared with me results of their researches.

Several scholars have read this manuscript in whole or in part, in one or another version. I am grateful to Dr. Louise W. Holborn of Connecticut College for her comments on my treatment of the refugee problem; to President James Read of Wilmington College, for detailed, careful, and immensely helpful criticisms of my exposition of the same problem; to Professor Lewis M. Hoskins of Earlham College, for similarly helpful criticisms of the last three chapters; to

Professor Robert Bremner of Ohio State University who read the entire manuscript. My colleagues, Professor Scott Cutlip and Professor Irvin G. Wyllie have read parts of the manuscript and constantly given me help too considerable to specify; and my late wife, Dr. Margaret Wooster Curti, read the entire manuscript before her death.

Several research assistants associated with the History of Philanthropy Project at the University of Wisconsin collected material for one or another part of this study: Mr. Rudolph Vecoli, Mrs. Gretchen Kreuter, Miss Sharon Smith, Miss Judith Green, and Mr. Frank Wong plowed through newspaper files or gathered data in public depositories and in private hands in several places. Mrs. Charles Strickland kindly assisted with some translation. To three research assistants I am very heavily indebted: Mr. Raymond J. Wilson did invaluable work in government documents in connection with my treatment of the Second World War and postwar period; Mr. Charles J. Wetzel did the initial study of the principal voluntary agencies in the same period, helped me with intelligence and devotion in the research I did in New York and Washington, and proved a superb collaborator in the many interviews we had with officers and staff members of voluntary agencies and government officials. Roderick W. Nash, David Allmendinger and Miss Judith Green have checked names, dates, titles in the text as well as footnotes, a long and laborious task done with great care and dedication. Mr. Nash has also, in the last stages of the work on this book, helped in various other aspects of the final revision.

Dr. Leslie H. Fishel, Jr., Director of the Wisconsin State Historical Society, provided us with an ample room in which to work, a courtesy the more appreciated in view of the great need for space for the work of the Society. I am grateful to the University of Wisconsin, and especially to President Fred H. Harrington, for the administration of the grant from the Ford Foundation which has made possible not only the work for this book, but that for the several related studies which the codirector of the project, Dr. Irvin G. Wyllie and our associates, have done. To the Ford Foundation I am of course under special obligation. Mrs. Mildred Lloyd, secretary of the History of Philanthropy Project, has been of great help in innumerable ways, including the patient and skillful typing of the manuscript in its original and in its revised forms. I am grateful to Miss Emilie M. Wallace for preparing the index.

Introduction to the Transaction Edition

It is not often that a historian has a chance twenty-five years after the publication of a specialized study to comment on what he had hoped for in subsequent research in the field and on how the story he had told bears on what has happened since. *American Philanthropy Abroad: a History* was published in 1963 and has been out of print for years. It is now reissued, and the sponsors of the reprint series of which it is a part, have asked me to add something to the original preface.

In that Preface I expressed the hope that the hitherto untold story about the efforts of individuals and groups from the early years of the Republic to help victims of natural and manmade disasters beyond our borders might stimulate scholars to explore, more deeply, problems seemingly inherent in gifts and giving. That preface asked for deeper analyses of the many complex impulses behind giving and of its effects on recipients. Disclaiming any specific influence of my book, it is pleasant to report that the scholarly evaluations of continuing American philanthropies overseas have in some part fulfilled that hope.

Before noting some of the continuities as well as new emphases in voluntary aid to the needy in other countries, it may be interesting to summarize the assessments of *American Philanthropy Abroad* when it appeared a quarter of a century ago.

I have not examined reviews by writers in the Third World. Those in England and the United States used such words as "impressive," a "pioneer" undertaking, a "pilot" study, and a "monumental survey." The Literary Supplement of *The Times of London* spoke of the debt of gratitude owed to the author for "ably and unemotionally charting what the still developing world owes to its most generous and imaginative of peoples. His will prove a seminal study, a classic of the 'nicely calculated more or less,' a memorial of his compatriots' munificence." Other reviews in England made similar comments.

The most welcome assessment came from Kenneth S. Latourette of Yale in the *American Historical Review*. As a lifelong observer of and the leading authority on the history of American missions in foreign lands, this scholar had impressive qualifications for reviewing the book. "This is a superbly done and much needed contribution," he wrote, "So thorough has been the coverage that one may be tempted to apply the adjective 'definitive.'. . . . Not for many years, if ever, will it be superceded."

Opinions did, of course, vary and a reviewer sometimes contradicted points made by another. Thus one spoke of its "prosaic prose." Another began by saying "here, with grace and learning lightly deployed . . ." Positions also differed on the author's objectivity. A scholar writing in *The Saturday Review* saw *American Philanthropy Abroad* as a "political" book. On the other hand *The Economist* used the term "always impartial." Reviewers also differed on the question of generalizations. A writer in *The Annals of the American Academy of Political and Social Science* regretted what he saw as the author's reluctance to draw major conclusions and lessons. On the other hand, the *Virginia Quarterly* found the book "meaningful for the questions it raises as well as those that it answers."

Without benefit of research on post-1963 philanthropy abroad and with gratitude for that of other scholars, I am struck by the continuities between what has happened since my book appeared and what had happened earlier. As then, aid has in the main reflected religious and humanitarian concerns. In giving, Americans have likewise responded to a perceived need without thought of repayment. In a familiar vein the resources of private voluntary organizations (PVOs)—Jewish, Catholic, Protestant and secular— have seemed inadequate to tasks in hand. To be sure they have increased, though not as much as might be expected in terms of increasing personal and corporate incomes. By rough estimates budgets went up from $4,222 million in 1964 to $1,084 billion in 1979. Sheila Arvin McLean reported that Protestant churches in 1979 spent $1.1 billion on international programs, of which at least 30 percent might be thought of in secular terms. In 1980 some 732 corporations gave about $17.4 million to groups mainly concerned with overseas aid; this was only 1.7 percent of the total corporate donations in that year, a sum hardly proportionate in view of their business with Third World countries.

With such resources and a larger, more professionalized personnel force the voluntary organizations have, as before, supplied food and medicine to victims of disaster whether earthquakes, drought, famine, political persecution, uprootedness and seemingly endless wars. PVOs have also followed precedents in expanding programs for better education, public health, and a more efficient agriculture in less fortunate places in the world. In continuing to offer services PVOs found an important ally in the volunteers in the government-funded Peace Corps launched in 1961. Most PVOs have, as earlier, tried to play nonpolitical roles. Increasing support from corporations and especially from Washington and recipient governments complicated the observance of the traditional desire for neutrality.

If continuities characterized overseas philanthropy in recent decades so have emphases related to changes in the economy, public policy, and the culture.

On the level of communication the mass media, with more reporters and camera people on the scene, have brought home the plight of the distressed in ways hitherto unavailable. Charged with emotion, vivid images of helpless sufferers from natural disaster, war, revolution and political oppression appeared on television all over the country, as did celebrities in the entertainment world appealing for compassion and generosity. Some have suggested that this may have heightened a sense of global interconnectedness. Others have suggested that Americans have thus, at least dimly, become aware that national security and general well-being are endangered by the bitter distress of poverty, uprootedness and turmoil in countries beyond our borders. In any case, it is at least clear that the computer revolution has expanded the range of personal appeal for funds by direct-mailing networks.

Whatever the influence of such cultural trends on private voluntary organizations there is no question about the ongoing conflict between the two superpowers. American perceptions of national interests and security explain the increasing, if fluctuating, contributions of the public sector to foreign aid in the interest of strengthening allies and of enhancing strategic and economic advantages. In doing so Washington found ways of increasing its ties with PVOs. The established arrangement of having PVOs distribute surplus government food was extended to include further services on their part in publicly-funded programs for health and education.

Several PVOs have also become more closely involved with government policy by taking part in projects for increasing economic productivity of Third World countries and for speeding modernization. As *American Philanthropy Abroad* indicated, the Rockefeller philanthropies initiated development policy. In the early 1960s the Ford Foundation joined in the effort. In substantive terms development greatly extended earlier efforts to lessen the need for direct aid by increasing agricultural yields through genetically improved strains and breeds and through drainage and irrigation projects. It also involved helping recipient countries build an infrastructure of transportation and marketing systems, as well as plants for producing fertilizer, power, and processing. The program further involved loans to small businesses and the training of a technocratic and managerial elite. It depended not only on government aid directly or through loans and credits from the World Bank but also on support from the recipient governments and from the PVOs and the Peace Corps. In short, the development program emphasized the free-enterprise concept of helping others help themselves as the only practicable way of narrowing the alarming gap between the uneasy hungry and the better off.

Such innovative and far-reaching projects for social and economic change sharpened problems philanthropies had long faced and created new ones in the economy, natural environment, and culture of receiving countries.

These problems in turn invited and led to evaluation of goals and achievements. To be sure, foundations themselves had supported in-house estimates of the effectiveness of their programs. The new assessments, however, proved to be more comprehensive, open-ended and public oriented. In a careful statistical study, *The Politics of Altruism* (1977), a Danish scholar, Jørgen Lissner, compared voluntary and official giving of the United States with that of Canada and European countries and showed how the intricate problems of generosity and self-concern were trans-Atlantic. Two years earlier, in 1975, the Filer Commission on Private Philanthropy and Public Needs published a five-volume report which gave some attention to overseas programs. Seven years later Independent Sector, a newly formed coalition representing hundreds of charitable organizations, broke new ground in making available its extensive and thorough-going working papers. Under its vice-president, Dr. Virginia A. Hodgkinson, such research papers continued to expand and deepen understanding of current issues in charitable giving. At the same time government or quasi-government agencies, including the Agency for International Aid and the Institute for Food and Development Policy carried out thorough investigations by forthright and well-trained social scientists. Summaries and critical comment on all these findings yielded useful syntheses such as *Philanthropy and Cultural Imperialism*, edited by Robert F. Arnove (1980) and Landrum R. Bolling's *Private Foreign Aid* (1982). William Shawcross's *The Quality of Mercy* (1984), an independent investigation by a talented observer, reached a wide audience. This assessed the results, often mixed and ironical, of the international response to the plight of Cambodia in the dreadful years following American intervention in Vietnam. All of my comments are deeply indebted to these and other studies.

The context within which PVOs worked included many unpredictable factors over which they had neither control nor much influence: the contributions and their allocation from governments and the voluntary agencies of countries other than the United States; the uncertainties about American official contributions; the shifting value of dollars and credits in relation to varying monetary policies, trade balances, and market conditions; and arbitrary and unpredictable policies of recipient governments.

Assessments of programs and results seem generally to accept much of the self image that voluntary organizations themselves created and publicized. Little serious doubt has been expressed about the claim to represent American values and traditions, such as pluralism and pragmatic flexibility. PVOs, in contrast to government agencies, have been able to handle small but needed allocations. Morever, unlike government agencies, PVOs could often work with local groups in developing countries whose governments have been suspicious of American public policy.

On the other hand scholarly evaluations have by no means been uncritical. In supporting the thesis of philanthropy as cultural imperialism a scholar accused the Rockefeller philanthropies in pre-Communist China of having adminstered excellent medical training to an elite few while ignoring the health of the masses. In somewhat the same way a student of education in Great Britain's African colonies argued that the representatives of the Phelps-Stokes Fund and Carnegie Corporation were mainly responsible for the transfer of the pattern of schooling in the American South, which assumed that inherent deficiencies in intelligence and in capacity for self-direction justified training blacks for subordinate roles.

Explanations for the many failures to improve agricultural efficiency ascribed them to varied factors. When drainage and irrigation projects damaged the ecology the outcome was explained in terms of poor planning, indifference to foreseeable changing conditions and inadequate supervision of the work force. Zest for quick results was also seen as a cause for ignoring hazards. Some felt that mishaps might have been avoided had local leaders been asked to take part in planning and administration. This, of course, hardly explained failures when such cooperation was involved.

Several assessments focused on reasons for failing to narrow the gap between rich and poor or even to get food to those most needy. Recipient governments sometimes allocated supplies and trucks to their own military forces. Material aid in whatever form too often turned up in the black market. Experience, according to some, proved that it was foolish to assume that benefits to governments and favored elites would trickle down to the needy people. One writer vigorously insisted that without change in the power structure outside aid could never shrink the enormous gulf between those who had plenty and those who had nothing.

Such criticisms and suggestions had been heard in the 1950s and early 1960s. The scholarship of the 1970s and early 1980s, however, went more deeply and extensively into the issues. Assessments more frequently stressed the continuing need for further research, new ways of attacking problems, and new leadership. Probing and scrutinizing not only the record but exploring its implications and coming up with new approaches differentiated these assessments from earlier ones. Yet the story of the beginnings of overseas philanthropy and its course to 1963 anticipated much that has taken place and thus provides needed background for what has happened since. This may be the main advantage to reissuing *American Philanthropy Abroad*.

Contents

AMERICAN
PHILANTHROPY
ABROAD

I

Beginnings

Voluntary giving by individuals and groups in one country to those in another, to meet the needs of sufferers in disaster and to build and strengthen agencies for the long-range improvement of mankind, is a complex and little emphasized chapter in the history of international relations.

In giving for these purposes Americans, as in so many other things, followed Old World precedents. Before taking the first steps in helping peoples beyond the seas they themselves had received from Old World donors charity in time of catastrophe and aid in developing educational and welfare institutions.

A long-remembered example of voluntary aid from overseas to Americans in distress occurred at the end of King Philip's War in 1676. Nathaniel Mather, the brother of Increase Mather and a graduate of the Harvard class of 1647, at the time a pastor of a congregational society in Dublin, initiated among the Protestants of that city a fund for the purchase of food to be sent to Massachusetts Bay, Plymouth, and Connecticut. The letter of gift, which Nathaniel Mather no doubt wrote, was specific in directions and generous in spirit. The good ship *Katherine of Dublin* was stored with meal, wheat, malt, butter, and cheese, to be distributed, after enough had been sold to pay transportation costs, "to the poor distressed by the late war with the Indians; wherein wee desire that an equall respect bee had to all godly psons agreing in fundamentals of faith & order though differing about the subject of some ordinances & pticularly that godly Antipedo-baptists bee not excluded: wch wee the rather thus perticularly insert because sundry reports have come hither suggesting that godly persons of the pswasion have been severly dealt withall in New England, & also because divers of the pswasion of this Citty have freely & Con-

3

siderably concurred in advanceing this releif." [1] Further, the donors made clear their desire to have included in the bounty the Indians who had clung to the English in the war, "particularly if they had been Christianized."

The letter of gift consigned the food to three well-known men to be divided among the colonies. On January 4, 1677, the Council of Massachusetts informed the Connecticut authorities that it had sent orders to the several towns in Massachusetts, "by which wee finde six hundred & sixty families, consisting of twenty two hundred sixty five persons in distresse; and yet want returnes from thirteen Townes, which will augment the number of our distressed inhabitants. Wee want such account from yourselues," continued the Bay officials, "by which wee may proportion what is divisible amongst us." In May, 1677, the Connecticut General Court with a handsome gesture of generosity declared that "this Court upon good reason moueing them thereunto, *doe remitt theire* part of the Irish *charaty* (sic) to the distressed persons in the *Massachusetts* Colony and Plymouth Colony." [2] Just what happened is not clear; but the food seems to have been distributed to the needy with efficiency and to have evoked general feelings of gratitude. "The Irish Donation," as the gift was called, lived in New England tradition and was cited in later times when the hungry of Ireland turned to America for help in great distress.

As Europeans contributed to the relief of their own needy in times of epidemics and in the ravages of fire, flood, and earthquake, so too, long after the establishment of independence, they gave to American communities when disaster of unusual proportions struck. It was also natural for Europeans to help ease the rough path of their fellow countrymen and coreligionists who had fled to America to escape intolerable burdens in the Old World. A notable example was the trust fund created by Baron de Hirsch in the later nineteenth century to help Russian-Jewish immigrants start a new life in America.

The chief voluntary giving in the eighteenth and nineteenth centuries on the part of the Old World to the New went to struggling colleges, libraries, and missionary enterprises, many of which could neither have been established nor continued to exist without such

[1] Quoted in Charles Deane, "The Irish Donation in 1676," *The New England Historical and Geneological Register* II (1848), 247.

[2] J. Hammond Trumbull, ed., *Public Records of the Colony of Connecticut* (15 vols.; F. A. Brown, 1852), II, 483.

gifts. Thomas Coram, for example, a British merchant and colony promoter who lived for a time in Massachusetts in the latter part of the seventeenth century, persuaded the associates of Dr. Thomas Bray to send books for New England missionaries to the Indians. Coram's projects also included schemes for the relief of distressed New England seamen in foreign ports and the colonization of Britain's needy and disadvantaged in the Kennebec-St. Croix country.[3] The most notable example of British philanthropic support of colonial enterprises—apart from the establishment of Georgia—was the achievement of the Anglican Society for the Propagation of the Gospel in Foreign Parts. This energetic agency maintained missionaries and provided books and schools for Indians, Negroes, and poor whites.[4]

With such examples of benevolence it was natural for Americans to respond to the needs of victims of calamities in other lands and to return at least in some small part the great debt to Europe for the help American agencies of cultural life had received and continued to receive well into the nineteenth century. To be sure, the needs of America's own institutions of learning and social welfare were so great that giving to those in Europe long remained exceptional. Yet even episodical giving provided increasing links in a chain that in time was to become strong and significant. It testified to the fact that Americans shared the same religious and humanitarian values that inspired the much greater flow from Europe. It also gave support to Tocqueville's thesis that democracy, by weakening the barriers of class and privilege, fostered a feeling of compassion for all members of the human race.

Benjamin Thompson, born and reared in New England and a pioneer investigator of heat and light, was an early example of an individual who gave ideas, service, and funds for welfare and scholarship in Europe. A Tory, Thompson sought refuge and a career in

[3] H. F. B. Compston, *Thomas Coram, Churchman, Empire Builder and Philanthropist* (London: Society for the Promotion of Christian Knowledge, 1918); Hamilton A. Hill, "Thomas Coram in Boston and Taunton," *Amer. Antiquarian Soc. Proc.*, n.s. VIII (April, 1892) 133-48; Worthington C. Ford, "Letters of Thomas Coram," *Mass. Hist. Soc. Proc.* LVI (Oct. 1922) 15-56.

[4] David Humphreys, *An Historical Account of the Incorporated Society for the Propagation of the Gospel in Foreign Parts* (London: J. Downay, 1730); Frank T. Klingberg, *Anglican Humanitarianism in Colonial New York* (Philadelphia: The Church History Society, 1940); Henry Paget Thompson, *Into All Lands; the History of the Society for the Propagation of the Gospel in Foreign Parts* (London: Society for the Promotion of Christian Knowledge, 1951).

Great Britain, but in European eyes he remained an American. Entering the service of the Elector of Bavaria in 1784, Thompson, as Count Rumford, became councillor as well as superintendent of police and minister of war. The beggars of Munich—one out of every twenty-nine in the population was in this category—were said to be more bold and mendacious than those in any city except Rome. One or more of these rascals would engage in bloody brawls with competitors for the possession of a given street. Often worshipers in church could not continue their devotions until they had met the demands of the supplicants. Thompson concluded that these wretches, who extorted charity from the public, might be made self-supporting at less cost than indiscriminate almsgiving involved.

On January 1, 1790, Rumford summoned all beggars, to inform them that henceforth it would be illegal to beg. Those unable to work might receive regular allowances, living in the homes of relatives or friends if they had any, or finding shelter and keep in the newly established Institute for the Poor. Maintenance in both cases was to rest on voluntary contributions to the Institute. This simplification and coordination of voluntary giving anticipated, in some ways, the community chest of our own day. Those beggars able to work were to spend their days at the new House of Industry where they were to learn various skills. The first work program involved making clothing for the Bavarian army. Through sustained experiments in the improved use of fire in cooking and in devising a cheap but nutritious diet, the former beggars were fed at low cost. Thanks to the new efficiency methods it was possible for three women to cook dinner for a thousand persons, with only nine pennies' worth of food being burned in the process! (Later Count Rumford built an even more efficient kitchen in the hospital Della Pieta in Verona, heating it by steam.)

In one week, 2,500 beggars entered the House of Industry, the whole number being stabilized in a few years at 1,400. As a result of the new policy, thousands of Bavarian beggars were redeemed from vice and uselessness to live decent and self-respecting lives. Rumford reported that not only was rehabilitation effected, but that this was done at greatly lowered cost to the public, which was, in addition, no longer plagued by indiscriminate begging.[5]

[5] Benjamin Count of Rumford, *Essays, Political, Economical and Philosophical* (5th ed., 3 vols.; London: T. Cadell Jun. and W. Davies, 1800) I, 21 ff. See also G. E. Ellis, *Memoir of Sir Benjamin Thompson, Count Rumford, with Notices of His Daugh-*

In reporting the experiment to the Institute of France in 1815 the renowned naturalist, Georges Leopold Cuvier, paid high tribute to its efficiency and success. Yet he insisted that Count Rumford did what he did without any love for mankind and without belief in the capacity of men and women to be entrusted with their own welfare.[6] If there was some truth in this, it is also to be noted that Rumford was forward-looking in his repudiation of the lady-bountiful notion of charity and realistic in his insistence that the poor must be made happy before they could be made good. Rumford's sensible approach to philanthropy influenced Sir Thomas Bernard, the Harvard-educated son of the Massachusetts governor, who installed Rumford's food and fuel innovations in London's Foundling Hospital, one of his major interests, from which it spread into all the workhouses of the kingdom.[7]

Count Rumford's arbitrary yet practical handling of Bavarian beggars did not exhaust his philanthropic contributions to the Old World. He presented the Royal Society of Great Britain with one hundred pounds for establishing the Rumford prize and medal "for the most important discovery, or useful improvement, in any part of Europe during the preceding two years, on Heat and Light." This was apparently the first notable gift from an American for the encouragement of learning and science in Europe. The Rumford prize became a coveted honor which distinguished physicists in years to come received with pride. As if to remind the world of his American birth and upbringing, Rumford established in the same year, 1796, a similar prize to be given by the American Academy of Arts and Sciences for outstanding work in the field of heat and light, to which he himself had made such significant contributions. In his will Rumford also provided for a professorship at Harvard College "to teach by regular courses of academical and public Lectures, accompanied by proper experiments, the utility of the physical and mathematical sciences for the improvement of the useful arts, and for the extension of the industry, prosperity and well-being of society." The Rum-

ter (Philadelphia, 1871) and James Clark Easton, "The Social and Economic Reforms of Count Rumford in Bavaria" (unpublished Ph.D. dissertation, University of Wisconsin, 1937).

6 "Memoir of Benjamin Count Rumford, read at the Institute of France, Jan. 9, 1895, by M. Couvier," in *Boston Weekly Messenger*, Oct. 20, 1815. For another contemporary evaluation by a visitor to Munich, see Anne Carey Morris, ed., *The Diary and Letters of Gouverneur Morris* (2 vols., New York: C. Scribner's Sons, 1888), II, 339.

7 James Baker, *The Life of Sir T. Bernard* (London: John Murray, 1819), *passim*.

ford professorship has honored many of Harvard's distinguished scientists.[8]

The transatlantic philanthropies of Count Rumford did not stand alone. An early and little known effort to aid the handicapped in Great Britain is associated with the name of Francis Green. This descendant of one of the early families of Massachusetts served as an officer in the French and Indian War after his study at Harvard. Later he did well as a Boston merchant. Like Thompson, Green took the Tory side in the Revolution, which led to his proscription by the provincial government. In Great Britain he became an authority on methods of instructing the deaf, an interest occasioned by the fact that his son was a deaf mute. Green wrote a dissertation on the subject, translated the forward-looking writings of the Abbé de l'Épée in this field, and helped establish a charitable school for teaching the deaf. This school, located near London, was the first of its kind in the English-speaking world and remains a silent testimonial to the zeal of its American-born promoter. Green returned to Massachusetts and, from 1803 to his death several years later, wrote articles in the *New England Palladium* and other journals on the problems of the deaf and on ways of opening the world of sound to them. His efforts to found a school similar to the one he had helped establish in England failed, however.[9]

A humanitarian interest in the disadvantaged of other lands also inspired William Maclure, Scottish-born scientist best known for his contributions to the geological knowledge of the United States and for his educational work at the New Harmony community in Indiana. In 1819 Maclure bought 10,000 acres of land near Alcante in Spain for the purpose of founding an agricultural school along Pestalozzian lines, to help the needy people of the area. With the collapse of the favorably disposed liberal regime, the new reactionary government confiscated the land and buildings that Maclure had put up, turning them over to the Church. Undaunted by this failure, Maclure in 1828 went to Mexico with the idea again of uplifting the impoverished and backward masses through education. He planned this time to send Indians to New Harmony to be educated to "a knowledge of the

[8] American Academy of Arts and Sciences, *The Rumford Fund* (Boston: The Academy, 1905); Samuel Eliot Morison, *Three Centuries of Harvard* (Cambridge: Harvard University Press, 1936), 147.

[9] Alexander Graham Bell, "A Philanthropist of the Last Century Identified as a Boston Man," Amer. Antiquarian Society, *Proceedings*, n.s., XIII (April, 1900), 383-93; obituary in the *Columbian Sentinel* (Boston), April 22, 1809.

useful arts and the habits that may fit them to rule and to obey." The plan was not carried out. One can suspect that Maclure knew too little about Mexican Indians and the pull their own culture had for them, and that he underestimated other difficulties facing so ambitious an enterprise.[10]

In contrast with philanthropies designed to advance man's welfare through useful knowledge and specialized training of the handicapped, several charities, occasioned by disasters and turmoil overseas, provided short-term relief.

In the summer of 1793 thousands of Santo Domingans, fleeing from revolutionary turmoil in their island home, poured into Baltimore, Norfolk, Philadelphia, New York, and other cities. These men and women had for the most part been well-to-do planters and, as monarchists and conservatives, looked with horror on the republicanism and racial egalitarianism of the French Revolution. Some were able to earn a living by teaching French, dancing, and other arts, but thousands were penniless and completely dependent on American help.

To the first call for aid Philadelphians, despite the yellow fever pestilence wracking their city, responded with a subscription of $14,600. In the following years smaller amounts were also raised. New Yorkers provided a hospital and subscribed $11,000. Baltimoreans responded with an initial subscription of $12,000, later raising another $8,000. The legislatures of Massachusetts, New York, Pennsylvania, Maryland, Virginia, and the Carolinas also voted relief funds. This generous response of private and public philanthropy was heightened by the widespread vogue for French culture. It was the more remarkable since the presence of so many refugees, some of whom took part in American politics, complicated the government's already tender relations with the revolutionary French Republic.[11]

In response to memorials pleading that individuals, cities, and states could no longer carry the burden, the House of Representatives in January, 1794, named a committee to look into the situation. Re-

[10] *American Journal of Science* XV (1829), 15; S. G. Morton, *A Memoir of William Maclure* (Philadelphia: Academy of Natural Science, 1841).

[11] For details see Mary Treudley, "The United States and Santo Domingo, 1789-1866," *Journal of Race Development* VII (July, 1916), 111 ff. and Frances Sergeant Childs, *French Refugee Life in the United States, 1790-1800* (Baltimore: Johns Hopkins Press, 1940), chap. 3.

porting that the need was in truth great, the committee recommended an appropriation of $15,000. Several members feared that such action was unconstitutional. Madison warned that it might provide a dangerous precedent "which might hereafter be perverted to the countenance of purposes very different from those of charity." But Congress passed the appropriation, charging the money provisionally to the debit of the French Republic. On the basis of an inventory of needs the President allocated the appropriation to 1,950 hard pressed refugees in ten states.[12] When the sum was used up, the burden of caring for the refugees again fell to the communities and to private charity.

In providing relief for the Santo Domingan refugees on the ground of the general welfare clause of the Constitution, Congress set a precedent for another step in international philanthropy. The earthquake in Venezuela on March 26, 1812, was the occasion for the first American public aid in an overseas disaster to victims at the scene of the catastrophe. News of this horrible event reached the United States with the arrival at Baltimore of the schooner *Independence* on April 23rd, 1812. Two years earlier the first revolts in Latin America against Spain had quickened the growing interest of merchants and scholars in the United States in the affairs of their southern neighbors. Without giving up the policy of neutrality, the Madison administration sent agents to the trouble spots, and both Congress and the President had expressed interest in and sympathy with the Latin-American patriotic rebels. Now, two days after the *Independence* brought its report, the people of Baltimore read in the *Weekly Register* that more than 5,000 houses had been destroyed in La Guayra, that at least 2,500 men, women, and children in that city had perished, and that the number of victims in Caracas reached perhaps 10,000. The account described heaps of corpses in the debris and the pitiful wails of children separated from parents—an appalling picture of fear, misery, and disease.[13]

Only a short time after this account appeared in the public print Alexander Scott, who had been named American representative at Caracas and who was still in Baltimore, urged Secretary of State Monroe to initiate in Congress a measure for appropriate relief.[14] At about the same time Telésforo de Orea, commissioner to the

[12] *Debates and Proceedings in the Congress,* 3d Cong., 1st Sess., 1794, IV, 153, 169-73, 1418.
[13] *The Weekly Register,* II, April 25, 1812.
[14] E. Taylor Parks, *Colombia and the United States 1775-1934* (Durham: Duke University Press, 1935), 79.

United States from the revolutionary regime in Venezuela, in writing to Monroe about the disaster, expressed the conviction that if only communication with his country were less difficult, compassion and generosity would make Americans spring to the relief of his countrymen. He asked, as a minimum, that the embargo be lifted for outgoing ships to all Venezuelan ports.[15]

Congress was preoccupied with relations with England at this moment. It seemed likely that war was in the offing. The problem of financing such a struggle was a matter of grave concern. Yet within a week Congress had passed An Act for the Relief of the Citizens of Venezuela. In the discussion, John C. Calhoun proposed, successfully, that the initially suggested sum of $30,000 be increased to $50,000. The act authorized the President to have purchased such provisions as seemed advisable and to tender these to Venezuela in the name of the government of the United States.[16] Scott was chosen to administer this fund, being instructed to intimate in suitable terms that the relief was "strong proof of the friendship and interest which the United States . . . [took] in their welfare . . . [and] to explain the mutual advantages of commerce with the United States." [17] In offering aid the government was not forgetting the promotion of national interest in the Caribbean area, toward which maritime interests had been looking with anticipation of a future brisk trade.

The donation of Congress reached La Guayra in May. In pursuance of his instructions, Robert Lowry, United States consul at this port, presented the cargo to the Venezuelan government, at the time dominated by a military clique under Miranda.[18] Scott, the special agent of the United States for the relief of earthquake sufferers, arrived at La Guayra on June 27th. "Never," he wrote later to Monroe, "was any Country in a more deplorable state than this at that period; and the subsequent ocurences have rather augmented, than diminished its calamities." The royalists had spread the idea that the earthquake had been God's way of punishing the rebels for defying the authority

---

[15] Telésforo de Orea to Monroe, Washington, April 28, 1812, William R. Manning, *Diplomatic Correspondence of the United States Concerning the Independence of the Latin-American States* (4 vols.; New York: Oxford University Press, 1940-1945), II, 1157.

[16] *Debates and Proceedings in the Congress*, 12th Cong., 1st Sess., 1812, XXIV, 1366, 1378, 2294.

[17] Monroe to Scott, Washington, May 14, 1812, Parks, *Columbia and the United States*, 80.

[18] Robert Lowry to John Graham (Chief Clerk, Dept. of State), Caracas, Nov. 30, 1816, Manning, *Diplomatic Correspondence*, II, 1170.

of King Ferdinand VII. Thanks to what Scott regarded as the shameful capitulation of Miranda, the royalists were about to regain control. Ironically, the royalists seized upwards of 3,000 barrels of the flour Congress had sent, and otherwise behaved in a way which "by no means corresponded with the generosity and benevolence displayed by the States." [19] It took months to secure the release of the prisoners and when at last the vessels which had brought the flour were returned, the American authorities found that they had been so looted and damaged as to be of little value to their owners.

Yet it would be wrong to regard this American action as a fiasco. The republicans received the relief, according to Scott, "with the gratitude it deserved." It certainly "averted the horrors of famine, which the country must have experienced without it." It would, Scott went on, "make a lasting impression on the people of the country." [20] Nor was the American alone in this view. The great German geographer and student of the American hemisphere, Alexander von Humboldt, declared that this "manifestation of national interest, of which the overflowing civilization of old Europe offers few examples, appears a precious pledge of the mutual benevolence which should forever unite the nations of the two Americas." [21]

Ten years after the gift reached Venezuela, Captain Bache of the United States Army met in Bogota an officer who expressed much gratitude for the "timely offering." Another Latin American, Manuel Palacio, wrote that "it was only by the liberality of the Congress of the United States that the few whom the earthquake spared did not perish by famine." [22] These may have been mere graceful afterthoughts. But despite the misfortunes connected with the reception of the gift, the donation itself suggested that the professions of friendship on the part of the United States, however rooted in national interest, represented more than mere words. On later occasions the gift to Venezuela provided an argument for like appropriations by Congress, but at the time it did not sink into the consciousness of the American people.

During the discussions in the House of Representatives of Vene-

[19] *Idem;* Scott to Monroe, Caracas, Nov. 16, 1812, Lowry to Monroe, La Guayra, June 5, 1812, *ibid.,* 1158-60.

[20] Scott to Monroe, Caracas, Nov. 16, 1812, *ibid.,* 1160.

[21] Quoted in Jane Lucas de Grummond, *Envoy to Caracas: The Story of John G. A. Williamson, Nineteenth Century Diplomat* (Baton Rouge: Louisiana State University Press, 1951), 12-13.

[22] Charles Lyon Chandler, *Inter-American Acquaintances* (Sewanee: The University of the South Press, 1915), 49.

zuela's need for help, Nathaniel Macon of North Carolina submitted a resolution committing Congress to include in the aid to Caracas the purchase and sending of flour to some port in Teneriffe, Canary Islands, in view of the famine that had resulted from the locust pestilence. John Rhea declared that while he favored sending help to Venezuela, he did so because our national interest suggested the desirability of promoting better relations with Latin America. Since national interest was not involved in the Canary Islands, he opposed extending any aid. Others felt that the information from Teneriffe was inadequate, that probably vessels had left our ports for the Canaries with food before the embargo had been enacted. In the vote to include the Canaries in relief aid, forty-seven were in favor, fifty-seven against. John Randolph of Roanoke then submitted a resolution instructing the Committee on Commerce and Manufacturers to inquire into the need for relief in the Canaries. This was agreed to, and shortly after, on May 22, Thomas Newton of Virginia, on behalf of the committee, reported that in its opinion the evidence was not sufficient to justify legislative intervention.[23]

Two disasters in nearby Canada, one in 1816 and one nine years later, did lead to a benevolent response. Just a year after peace was made with England following the War of 1812, when New Englanders were claiming the right to fish on the banks of Newfoundland and Britishers were denying such a right, a fire destroyed a large part of St. Johns. The very day that the news of the disaster arrived in Boston, merchants chartered the *Good Hope* and within three days its hold was loaded with food and clothing contributed by men and women moved by sympathy for fellow creatures burned out of their homes amid the fogs and snows of a Newfoundland winter. Porters and carmen at the wharfs gave their labor, as did the master and his men. The ship, after constant battles with a fierce northeaster, arrived at St. Johns, discharged the cargo, and returned with "the overflowing thanks and benedictions of many a grateful heart."[24]

This episode set the pattern for what was done in 1825 when Boston received reports that at least 1,500 men, women and children were

[23] *Journal of the House of Representatives*, 12th Cong., 1st Sess., 1812, 318-21; *Debates and Proceedings in the Congress*, 12th Cong., 1st Sess., 1812, 1348-52, 1434-35.

[24] John M. Duncan, *Travels Through Part of the United States and Canada in 1818 and 1819* (2 vols.; Glasgow: University Press, 1923), I, 86; Elihu Burritt, "The Mission of Great Suffering," in Charles Northend, ed., *Elihu Burritt: a Memorial Volume*, 221-223.

suffering as a result of the devastating forest fires in New Brunswick.[25] On November 7th a meeting in Boston's Merchants Hall appointed a committee to raise funds and to charter a vessel to take provisions to New Brunswick. The appeal of the committee for contributions struck both a religious and a secular note. The reason for this "dispensation" of God, the public statement declared, was "not knowable." But the "dispensation" might well be meant to arouse sympathy and charity "that the blessings of those who are ready to perish may descend upon their benefactors, so that givers and receivers may harmonize in the sentiments of peace and goodwill." The situation appealed, the framers of the declaration observed, "with uncommon force to the good principles which ought to regulate international friendliness and courtesy of neighboring countries, and to the higher and nobler motives which should influence the conduct of Christian communities." The meeting itself raised $4,000 for relief.[26]

The following Sunday nineteen Boston churches contributed about the same amount that the business men had given. The largest donation came from William Ellery Channing's church—$529. On November 19th the schooner *Billows* sailed for Halifax with food, clothing, and bedding. The funds at hand enabled the *Billows* to make a second errand of mercy.[27] Some communities beyond New England felt called on to help. At about the time that the Boston merchants met to organize relief, a similar meeting in New York raised $6,248. Citizens of Philadelphia and Germantown also sent contributions.[28]

From time to time, in later years, reports of disasters abroad reached an American port, but the response was understandably not always as quick and generous as in the case of calamities nearer home. Early in June, 1832, a letter from Consul William C. Merrill was published in the Newburyport *Herald* telling of a three year drought that had reduced the Cape Verde Islands to near starvation. Vegetation on the parched land had withered. Most of the animals had died. Survivors on one island, the population of which had been

---

[25] *Independent Chronicle and Boston Patriot*, Oct. 22, 1825.

[26] *Boston Courier*, Nov. 7, 9, 1825.

[27] *Boston Courier*, Nov. 16, 18, 20, 1825; *Independent Chronicle and Boston Patriot*, Nov. 30, Dec. 7, 1825.

[28] *Boston Courier*, Nov. 22, 1825; *Independent Chronicle and Boston Patriot*, Dec. 7, 1825; *Niles' Weekly Register*, Nov. 19, 1825. When a fire destroyed two million dollars' worth of property in St. Johns in 1837, no effort at organized relief was reported, possibly because the need was not great enough, possibly because of the depression at home. *Boston Evening Transcript*, Jan. 20, 27, 28, March 3, 4, 1837.

about 1,200, were too weak to bury the dead. The report indicated that the Portuguese government, distraught over an internal crisis, was "too wretched to afford any aid." The commander of the U. S. *Peacock*, the letter reported, had left a few provisions at St. Jago.[29]

This information seems to have led to no action. The mariners of Salem, Newburyport, and other New England towns were accustomed to reports of chronic food shortages on the Cape Verde Islands. Communications being infrequent, they may have thought that the situation had improved. Moreover, the eastern seaboard cities and, increasingly, other parts of the country, were in the midst of a severe cholera epidemic. The lists of the dead in New York and reports of efforts of philanthropic-minded citizens to whitewash and clean tenements at Five Points and to provide charity for the families of survivors, indicated a preoccupation with tragedy at home.[30]

But early in October, Captain Ryder of the *Fredonia*, which had returned from Cape Verde to Salem, brought even more appalling news. Men and women had been seen in the streets gnawing at discarded bones. One gentleman had to stand constant guard to safeguard his small supply of provisions against the desperation of his own slaves. Mr. Gardner, acting consul, computed that from twelve to fourteen souls were dying every day at Port Prayda. The Governor of the Islands sent a plea by Captain Ryder: "For God's sake, tell them to send us something." In printing this report, the *Boston Evening Transcript* simply asked, "Shall we send something?"[31]

In response the Messers C. and P. Flint and Company offered to carry free five or six hundred barrels of flour in a ship that was about to touch at the Cape Verde Islands, if these were forthcoming. "We could spare from our abundance ten times this quantity," declared the *Transcript*, "and then we should scarcely give a sufficient earnest of our gratitude for the unmerited mercy and kindness we have received and enjoyed, at the hands of our common Father, the great source of beneficence."[32]

On October 11, 1832, a large number of Bostonians attended a public meeting presided over by William Thorndike, a prominent merchant. The chairman read a letter from Captain Ryder, describing conditions and reporting the opinion that no help could be expected

[29] Quoted in the *New York American*, June 13, 1832.
[30] *New York American*, July 31, 1832.
[31] *Boston Evening Transcript*, Oct. 8, 1832.
[32] *Ibid.*, Oct. 10, 1832.

from Portugal or from any country other than the United States. The chairman of the meeting appointed a committee of twenty well-known men and a smaller committee to buy and ship the provisions so desperately needed. The committee also agreed to wait on the ministers and priests of the city and to ask them to take up Sunday collections.[33]

People gave. Newburyport contributed $585.87, Charlestown, $250, Portland, $1,200, Boston, $6,800. Cotton factory workers in Ipswich contributed $32.20. The purchasing committee bought and loaded in the hold of the *Charles* a large store. The Messers C. and P. Flint kept their promise of charging no freight for 600 barrels—and asked very little for the rest. The cargo included 150 barrels of potatoes, fifty-nine barrels of rye flour, forty-five barrels of bread, 146 barrels of flour, twenty-two casks of rice, and 3,370 bushels of corn. The provisions were consigned to the American Consul and the Governor, to be distributed as exigency required.[34]

New York, Philadelphia, Baltimore and other cities also responded. The *Boston Evening Transcript*, quoting the New York *Journal of Commerce*, estimated that New York and Philadelphia contributed $7,000 each, Baltimore, $5,000, and Norfolk, $1,000.[35] Wilmington contributed 200 barrels of corn meal. Richmond collected $607. Ships with relief sailed not only from Boston, but from Portland, New York, Philadelphia, and perhaps, other cities.[36] Estimates placed the value of the seven to eight thousand barrels of meal and other provisions at $25,000.[37]

The need was not exaggerated. On the Island of San Antonio, 11,000 died out of a population of 26,000. A ship arriving at Hampton Roads in mid-November brought the news that a belated vessel from Lisbon, laden with provisions, had been described as a cruiser and had been run over in the night by another vessel and sunk. The same information revealed that starvation had reached ghastly proportions. The *Boston Courier*, declaring that the horrors depicted by Dante seemed the only appropriate description, said that "our home

---

[33] *Idem.*, Oct. 12, 1832.
[34] *Boston Evening Transcript*, Oct. 22, 23, 1832.
[35] *Ibid.*, Nov. 21, 1832.
[36] *Niles' Weekly Register*, Oct. 27, 1832; Emerson Davis, *The Half Century* (Boston: Tappan and Whittemore, 1851), 436-37.
[37] *Boston Evening Transcript*, Nov. 21, 1832.

is not confined to our hearths; the earth is our home, and all men are brothers." [38]

The Cape Verde Islands were far away, trade with them was limited, and the responsibility of Portugal for relief seemed apparent. None of these considerations nor the demands of charity at home kept the Americans from giving, largely through churches, and from sending relief ships for the islanders. One of the chief men in the Islands, when told that the food cargoes represented the voluntary gifts of American men, women, and children, spoke for his people: "Magnanimous citizens of the United States! Souls of the most refined philanthropy! May Heaven, with a liberal hand, pour upon you its choicest blessings! Far from us you did hear the doleful accents of our groans; the bitter cries of our deep lamentations penetrated to the bottom of your hearts. O benefactors of the people of the Cape Verds [sic], what a sweet change you have brought in our condition." [39]

But unfortunately the sweet change was not permanent. Dry seasons came periodically, and the Islands were overpopulated. The government of Portugal extracted a small revenue from the Islands and did little or nothing to improve the economy or to encourage colonization in Brazil. Late in November, 1855, the *New York Weekly Herald* published the correspondence between Antonio Martens, vice-consul of the United States at Porto Grande, and Commodore Crabbe, commander-in-chief of the African Squadron. The correspondence revealed the pitiful condition of the citizens in the island of San Antonio. Thirty thousand people were living on banana stalks and the carcasses of dead animals. The complete failure of the crops at St. Nicholas, from which help had been expected, indicated that an additional 10,000 sufferers might be counted on as a certainty. Such a report would probably have evoked a sympathetic response except for the fact that the dreadful ravages of a scourge at Norfolk and Portsmouth were at the same time laying a heavy burden on American benevolence. [40]

In late April and early May, 1856, details of the plight of the islanders came to the attention of the American public through a pitiful letter from Patrico, Bishop of the Cape Verde Islands, to Arch-

---

[38] *Niles' Weekly Register*, Nov. 24, 1832.
[39] Davis, *The Half-Century*, 437.
[40] *National Intelligencer*, April 28, 29, 1856; *New York Weekly Herald*, May 10, 1856.

bishop John Hughes of New York and through the personal reports of Lt. Washington Bartlett of the sloop *Jamestown*, which had visited Porto Praya on March 8th. The Governor, a poor man, had gone without a single cent of his salary in order to send small ships to the African coast to buy grain, but his funds were exhausted. He had persuaded Lisbon to cease taking revenues from the islands, but this meant little. It was clear, he informed Lt. Bartlett, that at least 20,000 people would perish unless help arrived from America.[41]

Several newspapers urged speedy charity. The *National Intelligencer*, reminding its readers of American abundance and of the duty of men, as human beings and as Christians, to relieve such suffering, asked, "will not some generous soul take the lead in starting measures of assistance in this appalling case?" [42] The *New York Daily Times*, in printing Lt. Bartlett's appeal for help, declared that "the crumbs that fall from the wealthy tables of Philadelphia and New York would more than fatten the 120,000 islanders." It also belittled the argument that help would be poorly used by arguing that while this had been true of the succor given to the hungry inhabitants of the Madeira Islands a few years earlier, the despatch of food to Consul Morse at Porto Praya would insure its fair and efficient distribution at the hands of the conscientious and benevolent governor of the Islands.[43]

On May 6th a meeting of less than a dozen Portuguese New Yorkers at the consulate raised $2,185. The consul, M. de Figaniere, of the shipping firm of Figaniere, Reis and Company, offered to take provisions free of cost to the Cape Verdes.[44] Two days later, in part at the instigation of the actor James Hackett, members of the Corn Exchange met and named a committee of twenty-five to collect funds and provisions and to arrange for sending aid.[45] A week later a second meeting of members of the Corn Exchange listened to Lt. Bartlett's moving description of the distress he had seen and to the letter of Bishop Patrico to Bishop Hughes. The Bishop, the meeting learned, had subscribed fifty dollars and collections were to be taken in Catholic churches. Members of the committee of twenty-five reported that over $4,000 had already been collected. A few days later the sum

[41] *New York Daily Times*, April 28, May 3, 1856.
[42] *National Intelligencer*, April 28, 1856.
[43] *New York Daily Times*, April 28, 1856.
[44] *Ibid.*, May 7, 9, 1856; *National Intelligencer*, May 10, 1856.
[45] *National Intelligencer*, May 10, 1856; New York *Journal of Commerce*, May 9, 1856.

had been raised to $5,800.[46] In Washington participants in a meeting at the YMCA rooms appointed a committee to collect funds and to ask ministers to take up offerings in churches. The committee collected over $200. Citizens of Alexandria sent 500 bushels of wheat to New York.[47] In Baltimore, Catholic churches contributed $755 and the Corn Exchange of the city sent $1,045 to the New York group.[48]

Meantime, on May 12, 1856, John Wheeler of New York introduced in the House of Representatives a resolution asking the Navy to provide twenty-five seamen with rations for four months, to enable a privately outfitted ship to carry food to the islands. There was no quorum when a vote was called.[49] A few days later Wheeler's colleague, John Kelley, brought the matter up again at the request of Archbishop Hughes.[50] A spirited debate followed. Protesting that he felt as lively an interest as any gentleman on the floor in the well-being of humanity, William Smith of Virginia opposed the resolution on the ground that the Constitution did not vest the federal government with any such power. Whereupon John Singleton Millson of Virginia asked if there had been any constitutional objection to allowing the *America* to search the Arctic seas for Sir John Franklin when that gallant British explorer had been reported lost. The vote was taken, 123 favoring the proposal, 24 opposing it.[51]

In the Senate, William H. Seward presented a paper indicating that a vessel was ready to sail from New York. Two days later, when the motion was again under consideration in the Committee of the Whole, Senator Fish of New York indicated his desire to have the matter referred to the Committee on Naval Affairs, on the ground that the Navy might not be able to spare twenty-five men for such an errand of mercy. It was so referred, and, apparently, no action was ever taken.[52]

On June 12, the New York committee, in conjunction with the Portuguese consulate and the Portuguese-American merchants, despatched the *New Hand* to the Cape Verde Islands laden with 400

[46] *New York Weekly Herald*, May, 10, 1856; *New York Daily Times*, May 16, 23, 30, 1856.

[47] *National Intelligencer*, May 8, July 15, 1856.

[48] *New York Journal of Commerce*, July 7, 1856.

[49] *Congressional Globe*, 34th Cong., 1st Sess., 1856, XXV, Pt. 1, 1194.

[50] J. Fairfax McLaughlin, *The Life and Times of John Kelley, Tribune of the People* (New York: The American News Co., 1885), 209-10.

[51] *Congressional Globe*, 34th Cong., 1st Sess., 1856, XXV, Pt. 2, 1257-58, 1262.

[52] *Ibid.*, 1257-1258.

barrels of corn and meal and with other provisions. The committee had also chartered the *Claremont* and had begun preparations for loading it.[53]

The supplies came in the nick of time, for on June 30, Consul William Morse, writing to the State Department from Porto Praya, St. Jago, reported that unless the Islands enjoyed quickly a plentiful rain they would be depopulated by starvation and emigration. The islands, he continued, were in a state of utter destitution: immediate action was necessary.[54] On July 24, 1856, Antonio Martens, American vice-consul at St. Vincent, Cape Verde, reported the arrival of the *New Hand*. The vice-consul had circulars written to administrative officers asking them to receive and distribute the food and to call on parish vicars for help. The food came just when existing supplies were all but exhausted, and Martens reported great appreciation for the "disinterested benevolence" of American citizens.[55]

Timely though the cargo of the *New Hand* was, the situation remained dismal. Sufficient rains came during the summer to yield some crops, but cholera and smallpox took 20,000 lives. All in all, what with famine and disease, a fourth of the population perished in less than two years. Consul Morse laconically reported that, salt being the only commodity the Islands now had to export, American trade was very dull. In any case, he added, the supply of hard money had been exhausted in paying for food imported from Europe and America.[56]

What was done was limited largely to certain merchants in New York and Baltimore, to Protestant and Catholic groups in these cities and in Washington. It did not compare with the $11,000 the New York committees collected in the summer of 1856 for the relief of flood sufferers in France.[57] But desperately needed relief was appreciated.

The relief of the Cape Verde Islanders kept alive the idea of responsibility in time of need overseas, and was thus a link in a long

[53] New York *Journal of Commerce*, June 13, 1856. On June 16th the *Journal* reported additional receipts of $274. Among the larger contributors previous to this, William B. Astor, Stephen Whitney, and James Hackett had given $100 each.

[54] William Morse to the Department of State, June 30, 1856, Santiago, Cape Verde, Department of State, National Archives.

[55] Some food was also received from the Canaries, the African coast, and Brazil, New York *Journal of Commerce*, Sept. 1, 1856.

[56] Morse to the Department of State, Santiago, Cape Verde, Jan. 1, July 1, 1856, Department of State, National Archives.

[57] *National Intelligencer*, July 10, 1856.

chain. One link in that chain is an episode that came midway between the first and second disasters in the Cape Verde story. Early in January 1843, *Niles' National Register* reported that tornadoes in the Madeira Islands had swept away bridges, wrecked shipping, prostrated buildings, killed at least half a hundred people, and spread universal dismay. The loss of property was estimated at $2,500,000 and the *Register's* information indicated that "great suffering will be experienced by the inhabitants unless prompt relief is sent to them from other and more fortunate parts."[58] The *Boston Daily Advertiser* announced that the Portuguese vice-consul in that city would receive contributions.[59] Although this newspaper, and other Boston journals did not, apparently, report the immediate outcome, the distinguished historian of maritime Massachusetts has related to us that a cargo of provisions was sent out on the *Nautilus*. The ship, Samuel Eliot Morison continued, returned laden with the choicest madeira, which the grateful people had given, a supply so bountiful that it had at least by rumor not been entirely exhausted as late as 1921.[60]

These American donations to those in need in other countries were in response to a concrete situation which came to the attention of men trading with the area, to government representatives, or to church groups. No systematic or sustained organization was worked out. Despite occasionally successful efforts to enlist government aid, the voluntary pattern of giving predominated. Americans were learning that to give to those in need in foreign lands required even greater effort, greater organization, and more effective leadership, than did fund raising for worthy causes at home. They also learned that the problems of supervising the disbursement of relief abroad created a whole new set of problems not easily solved. But the seeds of the idea that if charity begins at home, it does not end at home, had been planted and had begun to grow.

[58] *Niles' National Register*, Jan. 7, 1843.
[59] *Boston Daily Advertiser*, Jan. 4, 11, 1843.
[60] Samuel Eliot Morison, *The Maritime History of Massachusetts, 1783-1860* (Boston and New York: Houghton Mifflin, 1921), 242.

II

For the Greeks

The first example of popular American enthusiasm and widespread support for a distressed people overseas was the aid given the Greeks in their struggle for freedom. News of the Greek upsurge for independence from the Ottoman Turk, which broke out in 1821, filtered into America through the European press and through reports of Americans who had been in the area—missionaries, merchants and sea captains, travelers on the grand tour, and officers and men in the American Mediterranean Squadron. The leading champion of the Greek cause, Edward Everett, had visited Athens in his student days and was now professor of Greek at Harvard. Everett received from Adamantios Koraes, the great modern Greek scholar, a copy of "The Appeal of the Messenian Senate to the American People," and had it printed in the *Boston Commercial Advertiser* of October 15, 1821.[1]

The Philhellenes, as enthusiasts for Greek freedom called themselves, included, at first, only a few intellectuals besides Everett— the best known being Mathew Carey, book publisher and philanthropist of Philadelphia, William Cullen Bryant, editor of the New York *Evening Post*, and his fellow poets, James Gates Percival and Fitz-Greene Halleck, whose spirited "Marco Bozzaris" became a favorite of orators and school-boy elocutionists. Fourth of July speakers likened the Greek struggle to our own war for freedom from Britain,

[1] The most recent discussion of the American response to the Greek struggle for independence is that of Stephen A. Larrabee, *Hellas Observed: The American Experience of Greece, 1775-1865* (New York: New York University Press, 1957), 65 ff. Earlier accounts are Edward Mead Earle, "American Interest in the Greek Cause, 1821-1827," *American Historical Review* XXXIII (Oct., 1927), 44-63; and Myrtle A. Cline, *American Attitude Toward the Greek War of Independence* (Atlanta, 1930).

and editorials in various newspapers expressed sympathy for the Greek cause.[2]

Nevertheless, widespread interest in and enthusiasm for the Greeks developed slowly. The land of the Hellenes, after all, was a long way off, and reports of the struggle seemed vague and confusing. Secretary of State John Quincy Adams, who was concerned with negotiating a commercial treaty with the Turks and who had no sympathy for sentimentality in foreign relations, insisted on holding the line to our traditional policy of neutrality. Thus President Monroe restricted his reference to the Greek struggle in his annual message of December 3, 1822, to a few general words of goodwill and confidence in the ultimate victory of the Greek revolutionists.[3]

In the autumn of 1822 prominent citizens of Albany assembled in the capitol to devise means of aiding the Greeks. Committees named at the meeting spared no effort to interest citizens in every part of the Union in the cause. Circulars were addressed to distinguished men in Washington, to the governors of the different states, and to the magistrates of the chief cities. An account of this movement in the Albany *Argus* for December 16, 1823, claimed that it inspired the slow but steady awakening of interest in the cause.[4]

Before the end of the year 1822 a meeting similar to the one in Albany was held in Washington, spearheaded by the distinguished architect, Dr. William Thornton. It adopted a memorial to Congress. Citing the aid France had given during the American war for independence, the memorialists asked for an appropriation of two or three millions in "provisions and whatever may be necessary to the Greeks, as an easy and honorable mode of acknowledging the aid, bounty, and obligation received from France in like circumstances." Representative Henry Dwight of Massachusetts, probably at the prompting of Edward Everett, presented the memorial to the House of Representatives and introduced a resolution to implement it. The few in the House who spoke declared that any official aid would violate American neutrality, and Dwight himself moved to lay his resolution on the table.[5]

[2] New York *Evening Post*, Dec. 4, 1824; *Niles' Weekly Register*, Dec. 22, 1822; Larrabee, *Hellas Observed*, 65.

[3] John Quincy Adams, *Memoirs* . . . (12 vols.; Philadelphia: J. B. Lippincott and Co., 1874-77) VI, 227; James D. Richardson, ed., *A Compilation of the Messages and Papers of the Presidents, 1789-1897* (10 vols.; Washington: Govt. Printing Office, 1896-1899), II, 193.

[4] Albany *Argus*, Dec. 16, 1823; *Niles' Weekly Register*, Dec. 7, 1822.

[5] *Debates and Proceedings in the Congress*, 17th Cong., 2d Sess., 1822, XL, 457-60.

By the autumn of 1823, the Greek cause began to excite more general enthusiasm, thanks in part to Edward Everett's eloquently persuasive article in the October issue of the *North American Review*.[6] Men of influence and prestige joined the early Philhellenes (Everett, Carey, Bryant, Halleck, and Percival). The new spokesmen included James Kent, Chancellor of New York, Henry Wheaton, an authority on law, Noah Webster, of dictionary fame, President Jeremiah Day of Yale, and Dr. Samuel L. Mitchell, the well-known scientist at Columbia College. Bishop William White of Pennsylvania, Gregory T. Bedell, rector of St. Andrew's Church in Philadelphia, and Sereno E. Dwight of the Park Street Church in Boston represented the growing number of clergymen who preached and spoke for the Greeks. The Philhellene journalists included, in addition to Bryant, Colonel William L. Stone of the New York *Commercial Advertiser*, Charles King of the New York *American*, Hezekiah Niles, of the *Register* in Baltimore, and Thomas Ritchie of the *Richmond Enquirer*. Figures of prestige and power in the business community who joined in the effort to advance the cause of Greece included Nicholas Biddle, William Bayard, president of the New York Chamber of Commerce and the leading merchant of the metropolis, John Pintard, another prominent New York business leader, John C. Coster, merchant and banker, and Charles Wilkes of the Bank of New York. Stephen Van Rensselaer added his name and interest to the growing group. Political leaders with similar sympathy came from both major groups in public life. Gallatin, Madison, Jefferson, Edward Livingston and, in some degree, President Monroe on the one side, and, on the other, John Adams, Daniel Webster, Henry Clay, and General William Harrison wrote, spoke, or gave to the cause.

In articles in magazines and newspapers, in sermons, in addresses at public meetings, and in memorials to legislatures and to Congress, these and other leaders urged the American public to contribute money for munitions and supplies for the Greek armed forces, to volunteer to fight for the sacred cause, and to promote the recognition of the revolutionary regime by the government at Washington.

The arguments set forth for these objectives throw light on the motives to which the Philhellenes sought to appeal. One such motive was emulation. The champions of Greece reminded their fellow Americans that the London Common Council had voted one thou-

6 Edward Everett, "Affairs of Greece," *North American Review*, n.s. VIII (Oct., 1823), 398-424.

sand pounds for Greek relief, that private citizens on the Continent had given generously, that one alone, a Monsieur Bayard of Rouen, had contributed 1,800,000 francs.[7]

Appeals to national self-interest were made, though this sort of appeal was never dominant. Champions of Greek freedom did contend that a free Greece would provide new trading opportunities to American commerce. More important was the appeal to self-esteem. Don't forget, speakers reminded their audiences, that the Hellenes had first appealed in the famous Address of the Messenian Senate, not to the despots of Europe and their underlings, but to the free-men of America. Their struggle was, so the contention ran, very much like the American war for independence. "In the great Lancastrian school of nations," wrote Edward Everett, "liberty is the lesson, which we are appointed to teach. Masters we claim not, we wish not to be, but the Monitors we are of this noble doctrine." Could then, Americans stand by indifferently when the light of their own example was kindling fires in the darkest corners of the world? [8]

But appeals to emulation, national interest, and national esteem did not exhaust the arsenal of arguments. Enthusiasts saw in the Greek struggle a war between Cross and Crescent. Had not the Turks assassinated the Patriarch of Constantinople on the very doorsteps of his cathedral? Had not Turkish swords beheaded countless Greek patriots? Had not Americans on the scene themselves reported that it was not uncommon to run into whole baskets full of the ears of men, women, and children ruthlessly cut from helpless heads? [9]

The pro-Greeks also appealed to Americans on the score that our own civilization owed an incalculable debt to the ancient Hellenes, whose offspring were now fighting for freedom. Classical and romantic enthusiasm merged in the assumption that the illiterate peasants, the ignorant soldiers, the shrewd merchants of modern Greece were the lineal descendants of Homer, Demosthenes, Plato, and Pericles.[10]

Such were the arguments that the Philhellenes repeated again and

[7] *Niles' Weekly Register*, Oct. 1, 1825, Aug. 12, 19, 1826.
[8] Everett, *North American Review*, n.s. VIII, 423.
[9] *Address of the Committee Appointed at a Public Meeting Held at Boston, Dec. 19, 1823, for the Relief of the Greeks* (Boston, 1823); *Address of the Committee of the Greek Fund of the City of New York to their Fellow-Citizens Throughout the United States* (New York, 1823).
[10] *Address of the Committee of . . . New York.*

again, and such were the motives to which they appealed in their quest for support for the Greek cause. In the later years of the contest the friends of Greece shifted the emphasis to an appeal to the humanitarian sympathies of Americans for a people faced by famine and pestilence, but the whole battery of arguments for aid never disappeared in the discussion.

At the public meetings the assembled citizens listened to letters from American volunteers in Greece which provided a sense of reality and immediacy that no general arguments could give. The volunteers included George Jarvis, a young American living in Europe, the first of his fellow countrymen to offer his services in 1822, and soon to become a general in the Greek army; Jonathan Miller, a restless Vermonter who, after serving in the War of 1812, studied the classics at Dartmouth and the University of Vermont; and, most important of all, Dr. Samuel Gridley Howe,[11] who went to Greece in 1825 fresh from Harvard Medical School to organize hospital services and to become chief surgeon in the Greek Navy. In 1827 and in 1828 Miller and Howe returned to America to raise funds for the Greek cause and to stimulate enthusiasm by speaking at innumerable meetings as well as by writing vivid accounts of their experiences.

These public meetings were arranged by the Greek committees in leading cities, the most active being those in Albany, Boston, New York, and Philadelphia. On January 6, 1824, the New York *Commercial* reported "we cannot keep the record of the numerous meetings called in every part of the country, to procure aid for the Greek cause. It is sufficient to say that the feeling is universal."[12] This was something of an exaggeration, but the refusal of Congress early in 1824 to recognize Greek independence stimulated voluntary and unofficial efforts. And the enthusiasm for Lafayette on his visit during the year, reenforced the "Greek fever," for the popular French leader was a vigorous Philhellene, and his very presence reminded Americans of the debt their country owed to France in the war for independence.

Various groups fell into line on their own. Students at Rutgers raised $177, those at Yale, $500; and the cadets at West Point in sending their $515 to the New York Committee, wrote that their charity had been limited only by their circumstances. Andover Theological Seminary, Hamilton College, the University of Georgia, Tran-

---

[11] Laura E. Richards, ed., *Letters and Journals of Samuel Gridley Howe* (2 vols.; Boston: Dana Estes, 1906-1909), I, chaps. 2-10.
[12] Earle, *American Historical Review* XXXIII, 50.

sylvania, and many other institutions sent their offering. By March, 1827, factory workers in Pittsburgh contributed $405; churches in the city, $361; and the committee raised, in addition to these sums, $800.[13] In New York a barber, not to be outdone by college students and factory employees, gave all his proceeds from his shop for two days—$14.50 in all.[14] The ladies of Baltimore held a fair in Masonic Hall, specially fitted for the occasion and "only surpassed in beauty by the ministering spirits at the shrine of charity and patriotism, whose bright smiles were a sufficient incentive even to the most luke-warm in the cause, to give, and freely too, that the women and children of 'the land of story and song' may be preserved from the horrors of starvation." The ladies on this occasion raised $1,600 and, not to rest on their laurels, held an oratorio benefit the following month.[15] Elsewhere, too, theatricals, musicals and fairs provided means of opening purses for the cause. A favorite fund-raising device was the ball, which led one wit to remark that what Greece really needed was fewer balls and more lead.

Yet it would be wrong to imagine that the "Greek fever" of 1823 and early 1824 met with no opposition. On the contrary. Many conservatively-minded Americans insisted that it was dangerous to excite popular emotions by mass meetings and mass appeals, that such matters had best be left in the hands of the knowing and the competent. Some feared that the Greek excitement might force Congress to endanger the traditional policy of neutrality. And some frankly based their opposition to the whole thing on commerical considerations. This was true of Thomas H. Perkins, leading Boston merchant who was to become a patron of the education of the blind and a great friend of Dr. Howe. Perkins enjoyed a profitable trade with Smyrna, the only Turkish port open to American ships. This wealthy merchant feared that aid to the Greeks, whether from government or from voluntary subscriptions, might so alienate the Porte as to lead to reprisals on American commerce.[16] This view was in striking contrast to that of leading business men in New York, who took active parts in organizing and sustaining the Greek committee.

[13] Cline, *American Attitude toward the Greek War of Independence*, 104 ff.; Larrabee, *Hellas Observed*, 152.
[14] *Niles' Weekly Register*, Jan. 10, 1824.
[15] *Niles' Weekly Register*, Apr. 21, May 5, 1827.
[16] Edward Everett to Thomas H. Perkins, December 19, 1823, in Thomas H. Perkins Papers, Box No. 2, 1812-53, Massachusetts Historical Society; Samuel Eliot Morison, "Forcing the Dardanelles in 1810," *New England Quarterly*, I (April, 1928), 208-25.

In general, the sums gathered in 1823 and 1824 were sent in the form of drafts to Baring and Brothers in London, to be handed over to the Greek authorities in that city, or were used to purchase munitions which went directly to Greece. It is impossible to determine the volume of giving in the first phase. We know that two New York merchants, William Bayard and Charles King, dispatched in May, 1824, on behalf of the Greek committee, $32,000, a remission followed presently by an additional $5,000 which the New York committee got together. In addition, one thousand muskets, rifles, pistols, and swords were presented to the Greeks, together with several boxes of medicine and other supplies. On December 4, 1825, the New York *Evening Post* reported that a copy of the London *Morning Chronicle*, which had just been received, declared that the 8,000 pounds from America was more than the British committee had raised in eighteen months. All the early American contributions, whether in money or in kind, found their way to the Greek leaders without any strings.[17]

The high tide of enthusiasm of 1823 and 1824 waned. Misunderstandings and quarrels between the Greek leaders and European and American Philhellenes on the ground led to tension and frustration. Even the stouthearted Dr. Howe all but lost faith in the ability of the Greeks to manage their own affairs, and deprecated the tendency in America to glorify the Greeks and denounce the Turks by attributing all virtue to the one and all evil to the other.[18] Furthermore, some of the Greek warriors misused American funds and supplies.

This human tendency to appropriate that which was meant for others found a counterpart in America which unfortunately involved the firm of one of the leading members of the New York Greek Committee. This firm, together with another, agreed to build two first class frigates for the Greek government, and after interminable delays, it turned out that the cost of the unfinished ships far exceeded that stipulated in the contract. A pamphlet warfare of charges and countercharges flooded the press. In reviewing six brochures published on one or the other side of the controversy, a writer in the *American Quarterly Review* for March, 1827, summarized its evalua-

[17] *Niles' Weekly Register*, April 24, May 1, Nov. 6, 1824; New York *Evening Post*, Dec. 4, 1824.
[18] Samuel Gridley Howe, *An Historical Sketch of the Greek Revolution* (New York: White, Gallaher and White, 1828), 376-83; *Letters and Journals of Samuel Gridley Howe*, 1, 121.

tion of the messy story: "We believe we hazard nothing in asserting, that the general sentiment of our country is that of *disapprobation and regret.* . . . The only instance in which we could render the Greeks any substantial service, has manifestly been perverted by private cupidity to unwarrantable emolument; a profit of 80,000 dollars made out of their distresses, by their mercantile correspondents, the 'diplomatic agents' of the arbitrators; 50,000 dollars extorted for the use of shipyards and personal services of the owner without expending any of their own money; 10,000 dollars, the *sine qua non* of a captain of the United States' Navy, for superintending an operation in 'a just and sacred cause'; 45,000 dollars imposed on them by arbitrators, for the dedication of a few days to the dispensation of justice."[19]

The publicity given to the scandal had something to do initially with the falling off in enthusiasm for contributions to the Greek cause. But its subsequent effect seems to have been to arouse conciousness of guilt in the public mind and to have stimulated a new crusade of giving. At least a leading figure in the New York campaign for relief funds declared that the Greek people, among many others, had no reason to think well of American merchants. "We may consider ourselves fortunate if all the donations sent from the United States have removed the stain, or compensated for the loss of character which the whole country sustained by the baseness of that transaction. Let those who say the Greeks are worse than the Turks, beware, lest it be said that the Americans are worse than the Greeks."[20]

In the late autumn and early winter of 1826-1827 two of the most ardent friends of Greece, Congressman Edward Everett of Massachusetts and Mathew Carey,[21] inaugurated a new movement for aid to Greece. This was designed, not to supply the Greeks with arms and munitions, but with bread, for the condition of starvation among the civilian population had become desperate. In the new campaign hu-

[19] *American Quarterly Review* I (March, 1827), 285-86. In writing of the affair to Lafayette, an ardent Philhellene, Madison declared that the episode was a mortifying one, that the indignation of the public was highly excited, and that Greece was bleeding in consequence of it. Gaillard Hunt, ed., *Writings of James Madison* (9 vols.; New York: G. P. Putnam's Sons, 1900-1910), IX, 264.

[20] Col. Jonathan P. Miller of Vermont, *The Condition of Greece in 1827-1828* (New York: Harper, 1828), editor's note, 170.

[21] E. L. Bradsher, *Mathew Carey, Editor, Author, and Publisher* (New York: Columbia University Press, 1912), 76-78; Mathew Carey, *Miscellaneous Essays* (Philadelphia: Clark and Raser, 1830).

manitarian arguments outweighed all others. The idea was to move on two planes, the official and the unofficial.

It seemed best for strategic reasons to have someone other than Everett take the lead in Congress. On the second of January, 1827, Edward Livingston of Louisiana introduced a resolution for an appropriation of $50,000. The great jurist and humanitarian supported his proposal with ability and eloquence. He vividly pictured the dire suffering of the Greeks and urged the duty of our government "to clothe the naked, to feed the hungry, to comfort the despairing—to do that which a civilized enemy would himself do." He insisted that such aid could not be regarded as a violation of neutrality and cited the similar appropriation Congress had made in 1812 for the relief of the survivors of the earthquake in Venezuela. When several members of Congress agreed with George McDuffie of South Carolina that such an appropriation, even if used for nonmilitary relief, would make the United States a party to the Turko-Greek war, the motion was tabled. Livingston tried, a few days later, to have his proposal reconsidered. By a vote of 109 to 54, with the votes crossing party lines, the House gave its final "no." [22] The failure of a similar effort in the New York legislature shifted the responsibility of raising funds for Greek relief to volunteer givers.

On December 11, 1827, the Philadelphia committee organized by Mathew Carey issued an appeal to the public. The address included a copy of the letter Carey had just received from Everett, a letter telling the melancholy story of the situation in Greece based on reports from American and Greek friends on the ground. George Jarvis in particular, writing to Everett, emphasized the fact that the committees for the relief of the Greeks in France, Holland and Switzerland had sent twelve cargoes of provisions and that these, distributed by an agent dispatched by the committees, had literally "prevented the final starvation of the country. Let not the United States," Jarvis added, be "indifferent to the sufferings of this dreadful but not desperate conflict." [23] In the address to the public that incorporated the letter from Everett, Carey took note of the fact that Americans annually sent tens of thousands of dollars to support missionaries to convert Hindoos, Chinese, Burmese, and Japanese to Christianity, with problematic success and at an enormous expense per man, when success-

[22] *Register of Debates in Congress*, 19th Cong., 2d Sess., 1827, III, 578-80, 654; *Journal of the House of Representatives*, 19th Cong., 2d Sess., 1827, 146-48.
[23] Carey, *Miscellaneous Essays*, 297.

ful. "Would it not be meritorious to direct this zeal into another channel for a year or two, and let its overflowings be devoted to interpose
a shield for the preservation of the Greeks from impending destruction?" [24]

This appeal, followed at intervals by equally fervent ones setting
forth again and again reasons why Americans ought to dig into their
pockets, aroused some response. So did the special sermon that the
committee induced the Reverend Gregory T. Bedell of St. Andrew's
Church, an old Greek enthusiast and an eloquent orator, to deliver
in Philadelphia's largest house of worship. On March 1, however,
Carey, in a new communication to the public, took to task his fellow
citizens of the City of Brotherly Love for their poor showing. The
Committee at this time had in hand only $11,177, of which but
$5,824 had been collected in Philadelphia. Yet the campaign was in
its eleventh week and had been pushed with an energy and a sacrifice
unknown in any comparable earlier effort in Philadelphia. This, Carey
argued, was shocking, especially when it was remembered that Philadelphia was a city of 140,000 inhabitants, many of whom were men
and women of wealth. Only three citizens had given as much as
$100; and thousands well able to contribute, had given nothing at all.
What a contrast, he went on in his scolding criticism, with nearby
Chester, and with Pittsburgh, a much smaller place which had given
almost a third as much as Philadelphia, the contributors being, in
large part, operatives.[25]

The committee renewed its efforts, issuing 20,000 copies of forty-
three different appeals and arguments. Contributions did come in,
and fifteen months after the campaign opened, the committee had
received $24,056 in cash from Pennsylvanians, and $1,429 in clothing,
medicines, and surgical instruments. On the 23rd of March the
Tontine, and, a month later, the *Levant* set forth for Greece with
cargoes consisting of 1,265 barrels and 254 half barrels of flour, 503
barrels of corn meal, 1,692 of navy bread, forty-five of beef and pork,
200 of fish, thirty-nine of beans, forty tierces of rice, and numerous
articles of clothing and medication.[26]

Meantime, in mid-February, 1827, a public meeting in Boston
named a committee headed by Henderson Inches, a respected merchant. The committee issued an address which declared that it was

[24] *Ibid.,* 298.
[25] *Ibid.,* 304-5, 307.
[26] *Ibid.,* 307, 309.

proper for America to give to the cause of Greek freedom in return for the generous aid the thirteen colonies had received during their struggle. It was also a human duty to relieve suffering, to save the lives of helpless victims. "When it is considered that the subjugation of this people will be accomplished only by their almost entire extinction, and that with their extinction will perish all hopes of the revival of civilization, of learning, and of Christianity in one of the finest portions of the globe, we feel a confidence in presenting this as a cause of benevolence and Christian charity, which is deserving of the deepest consideration of those to whom we appeal." [27] In due course the committee despatched the brig *Statesman* for Greece, laden with a cargo valued at $11,500.42.[28]

Meanwhile, the New York Greek Committee was pushing its fund-raising operations. On January 6, 1827, after Mathew Carey had taken the initiative in Philadelphia but well before anyone in Boston had done anything, New Yorkers issued a call for a public meeting at City Hotel on Broadway. In addition to issuing an address, the meeting named a committee of fifty which in turn appointed an executive committee, including Lynde Catlin, Stephen Allen, Preserved Fish, George Griswold, and Silas Holmes. The newspapers published the address and later statements from the committee. All these made a special point of the determination of those in charge to see that all distributions be carefully supervised by a responsible American on the ground, that nothing designed to save the lives of broken old men, helpless widows, and starving children, be diverted to the military.[29]

The appeal did its work. In the remaining weeks of January, New Yorkers gave more than $6,000 in money. The *Chancellor* was chartered and stored with a cargo including 1,040 barrels of flour, 356 barrels of Indian meal, 435 barrels of hard bread, 154 casks of rice, salted provisions, and twenty-one boxes of clothing and dry goods. The committee declared that the value of the cargo was $13,766. It asked Jonathan Miller, the Vermonter who had soldiered for freedom in Greece but who was now in the States, to sail with the *Chancellor* as supercargo and to distribute its gifts. He accepted and, at the instruction of the executive committee, kept a detailed, factual report,

[27] *Boston Daily Advertiser*, Feb. 20, 22, 1827. The *Advertiser* charged that Boston was lagging behind the other major cities, as was the case.
[28] Miller, *The Condition of Greece*, 195.
[29] *Ibid.*, 11-12, 266-68.

day by day, a document so revealing and so inspiring that the committee in due course arranged for its publication. The *Chancellor*, with the sturdy, shrewd, and humane Miller aboard, sailed on March 10, to be followed in May by the brig *Six Brothers* and in September by the *Jane*, with John R. Stuyvesant and Henry A. V. Post as supercargoes and distributors.

The chartering and supplying of the three New York ships virtually exhausted the funds that the committee had collected in the first half of 1827. The contributions can be summarized: [30]

Individual donations in New York City, cash	$ 7,856.67
Collections in churches, schools, etc. in New York City	3,291.34
Donations in produce and goods, New York City	1,082.00
Donations from other places in New York State	26,965.91
Donations from Connecticut	3,264.71
Donations from New Jersey	3,067.66
Donations from other states	793.32
	$46,321.61

In May 1828, the Committee dispatched the *Herald* with a cargo to be distributed by Judge Samuel Woodruff of Granby, Connecticut, and the Reverend Jonas King of Amherst College, who was to become a celebrated educational missionary. New York's record was, even when population is taken into account, better than that of either Boston or Philadelphia. Other parts of the country at this time showed little interest in the new humanitarian crusade.

The *Chancellor*, after severe damage by storm some 400 miles out, had to return to New York for repairs; but at length, on May 23rd, she arrived at Napoli di Romania in Greece. Miller rejoiced to find his old friend, Dr. Samuel Gridley Howe, on hand; the two men worked together in the hard task before them. They also gave invaluable aid to their fellow Americans who accompanied the later ships from New York, Philadelphia, and Boston.

The first problem confronting Miller was to protect the cargoes, on arrival and during reshipment on small boats to various points on the mainland and the islands, against the ruthless and greedy pirates that infested the Greek seas. It was a stroke of great good fortune when Captain Patterson of the U. S. frigate *Constitution* agreed to escort the *Chancellor* part way to Poros. This famous ship proved helpful on other occasions, but its example was not always followed by other American commanders, of whom at least one made the ex-

[30] *Ibid.*, 290.

cuse that such convoying might jeopardize our neutrality. Greek military chieftains often did not hesitate to seize American cargoes, even
when those in charge explained that the donors had stipulated that
these were to be used only for the relief of needy civilians. Thus local
authorities convinced the supercargo of the Philadelphia committee's
brig *Tontine*, which arrived before Miller, to hand it over to them
to dispose of, with the result that they sold the cargo for their own
benefit and, in Dr. Howe's words, "at a most shameful price," selling
flour which in Philadelphia had cost $12,000, for $2,500. On one
occasion Dr. Howe felt it necessary to surrender a large part of a
cargo to prevent the entire lot from being seized. On another, the
timely return of Captain Patterson with the *Constitution* compelled
local officials to return the keys of the magazines which stored the
supplies pending distribution. On still another occasion local authorities surrendered supplies to soldiers to keep them from pillaging the
town. Miller protested, and the Secretary of State, informing him
that his own house had been plundered, begged the American to
have patience with and compassion for the mistaken conduct of his
countrymen. When the soldiers were starving, they would not listen
to the argument that the provisions had been given by Americans
solely for civilian relief.[31]

Another problem involved making sure that those most needing
aid got it. Miller quickly found out, if he had not known it before,
that many who were able to fight or work, and many of wealth, expected to share in the bounty. Used to the long oppression by the
Turks, many among the higher class of Greeks knew no method of
acquiring riches, as Miller put it, save by chicanery, and had not the
faintest ideas of the disinterested benevolence that prompted the
American donations.[32] Sometimes, in dispensing clothing to almost
naked human beings Miller posted soldiers around his quarters, who
scrutinized each face to make sure that, having once got garments,
he or she did not line up again for a second handout. His journals frequently tell of deceits and frauds perpetrated despite all his precaution. So, too, do those of his co-worker, Dr. Samuel Gridley Howe.[33]

But the chief, and insoluble, problem was that of trying to make
a small supply meet vast and pressing needs. Government officials,
priests, and bishops of the Orthodox Church sent names of families

[31] *Ibid.*, 124-25; *Letters and Journals of Samuel Gridley Howe*, I, 224.
[32] Miller, *The Condition of Greece*, 148.
[33] *Ibid., passim; Letters and Journals of Samuel Gridley Howe*, I, 229.

in especially desperate circumstances and for the most part investigations disclosed that the plight of these unfortunates had indeed not been exaggerated. At times Miller could barely endure what he saw. Here was a girl of eleven, her nose cut off close to her face, her lips completely severed, so that the gums and jaws were left naked, all because, a year before, she had refused the embraces of an Arab. Here was an older woman, who had seen her husband killed before her eyes, who had suffered torture and indignities that Miller could not bring himself to set down in his diary although he had no idea it might some day be published. Or here was a poor wretch, once a soldier, with both hands cut off. And everywhere the sick, the naked, the starving, the dying.[34] Young Henry Post, who distributed the cargo of the *Jane* and the *Six Brothers*, witnessed, on the occasion of drawing up barrels in a square, a confusion and contention utterly inconceivable. "The miserable beings who had been living for months upon no better fare than the beasts of the field, were almost frantic with joy at the unexpected arrival of wholesome and nutritious food. . . . There were old men, gray with years and sinking under the infirmities of age—there were mothers with helpless infants screaming at their breasts— . . . there were children without number, all exhibiting the same emaciated and death-like countenances, all clad alike in rags, and covered with filth and vermin, the unavoidable consequences of their homeless and destitute condition." [35]

Miller, Post, Howe, and Sturtevant did what they could to clothe those completely or almost completely naked, to dole out barrels of flour and bread, to ration the rice to the severely ill. To meet personal expenses and cost of local guards and transport, Miller had to sell some of the provisions. But he found himself handing out a dollar here and a dollar there to someone in extreme need of medical help.

On one occasion when Miller opened a box of clothing from Orange, New Jersey, he found that within half an hour he was surrounded by at least a thousand clamoring women and children. One case struck his fancy as worthy of note. A young woman whose father had been killed and who was penniless as well as naked, received from Miller a garment the tag of which indicated it had been given by

[34] Miller, *The Condition of Greece, passim.*; Henry A. V. Post, *A Visit to Greece and Constantinople in 1827-8* (New York: Sleight and Robinson, 1830), 19-30. See also Samuel Woodruff, *Journal of a Tour to Malta, Greece, Asia Minor, Carthage, Algiers, Port Mahon, and Spain in 1828* (Hartford: Cooke, 1831), 66-67, 70, 89.
[35] Post, *A Visit to Greece and Constantinople*, 19-20.

two young men. "She was indeed beautiful," wrote Miller, "and if the young men who contributed to cover her nakedness, and shield her from the glare of sensuality, had seen her in her new costume, I doubt if there would not have been a contest for her favour." At Ankistri, the sights of misery wrung the American's heart. "To see two thousand people assembled, in rags, with haggard countenances, eagerly watching the little we had to give them and on receiving it, raising their hands to Heaven in thankfulness for this unexpected assistance; while the poor creatures who had not yet received were raising their hands in supplication to us, and begging us for God's sake not to forget them." [36] In helping distribute the cargo of the *Levant* which the Philadelphia committee had sent out, he discovered 400 barrels of bread of such quality and so loathesome to sight and smell, that no human except in an extreme state of starvation could eat of it. Yet this, and a large supply of bread which had been dunked into the sea in a mishap in unloading and which was revolting in its briny and dirty taste and appearance, were avidly seized.

Meantime Dr. Howe was administering a hospital at Napoli, the only one in Greece. In this he was aided by both the supplies Miller spared him and the services of the supercargo who had come from Boston with the *Statesman*, Dr. J. D. Russ, who stayed on when Howe returned to America to raise fresh funds and to write a history of the Greek revolution that Americans might better understand the struggle.

After eight months of trials which can only be imagined even with the aid of the journals he kept, Miller went home. "How far I have executed with justice the confidence reposed in me by the committees in the United States, I shall not pretend to say, but leave it to those who have been witnesses of my conduct to determine and report. I shall not only remark that the campaigns which I made when first in Greece, although attended by trials and privations, were nothing in comparison with the trouble, anxiety, and perplexity with which I have spent the last eight months." [37] According to an English participant in the Greek struggle, George Finlay, "in the present state of the country, the American donations could not be better applied." [38] On the other hand, the President of Greece, Capo d'Istria, while express-

[36] Miller, *The Condition of Greece*, 55-56, 91.
[37] *Ibid.*, 100, 167.
[38] *Ibid.*, 100. See also George Finlay, *History of the Greek Revolution* (2 vols.; Edinburgh and London: Blackwood, 1861), II, 159.

ing deep gratitude for the American contributions, said to Samuel Woodruff, in charge of the cargo of the *Herald*, that, without attaching blame to any one person, former cargoes had brought small benefit to the suffering inhabitants.[39]

Early in February, 1828, a year after the campaign began, the New York newspapers reported the arrival of John R. Stuyvesant and Dr. Samuel Gridley Howe, accompanied by two orphan lads— the first in a series to be adopted in American homes. Howe released the letter of the Supreme Governing Commission of the Greek Republic to the committee which thanked them and all donors and which expressed the hope that the generous aid, so much needed, might continue to be given. Howe himself, in letters to the public, refuted current rumors to the effect that what had been sent had not been appreciated and had in fact done little or no good. That such talk was fairly widespread is suggested by the efforts of other almoners in Greece to make the same point. So far as the imputation that the Greeks were ungrateful, Post admitted that, in the case of the rich and powerful who needed no help, the charge might have some basis. "But as to the poor people," Post continued, "they uniformly evinced the most unaffected and heartfelt gratitude; and I have no doubt, that the friendly aid and sympathy of the American people, has left behind it in Greece, a respect and admiration for the American name, which will not be soon or easily forgotten." [40] Woodruff also reported that the most intelligent Greeks he met often said that the American charities made a far different impression on them than the aid received from any other nation. America was remote from Greece, with no axe to grind; whereas, individuals in England, France, Italy and Russia, who had also contributed, belonged to powers that seemed to have ulterior motives.[41]

In publicizing the continuing need for help, Howe pictured a land laid waste, with olive orchards and vineyards uprooted or in ashes. He told of tens of thousands of refugees from battle and from burned villages, leading a precarious existence in mountain caves and maintaining life on wild roots and snails. Howe urged continued support and pled especially for further aid for the hospital at Poros he had opened and for the ones he hoped would be established.[42]

39 Woodruff, *Journal of a Tour*, 60.
40 Post, *A Visit to Greece and Constantinople*, 86-87.
41 Woodruff, *Journal of a Tour*, 90-91.
42 New York *Evening Post*, Feb. 6, 14, 16, 1828.

Howe also undertook a speaking campaign despite the fact that such activity at such a time was not to his taste. It began in New York City and included many towns and cities upstate. The plan to carry this to the West and the South fell through. But the places that Howe did visit threw off the prevailing lethargy.[43] On May 28, 1828, the New York committee was able to send out the *Herald* with a cargo insured at $49,800.[44] On this occasion the committee reported that it had received $59,890.43 in the campaign. New York headed, as before, the list of states:

New York	$38,573.46
Connecticut	11,869.89
Massachusetts	3,152.54
Maryland	2,459.80
Rhode Island	1,948.25
New Jersey	1,127.17
Vermont	517.12
Virginia	75.00
Ohio	67.00
Upper Canada	10.00
	$59,890.43 [45]

Meantime the Boston committee had collected enough to charter the *Suffolk*, the eighth and last relief ship to sail, with a cargo valued at $12,000, making the total American contribution in cash and provisions approximately $138,000. In effect, the campaign was at an end. Apathy again set in, increased by the preoccupation with the election of 1828 and home issues, and by the virtual recognition of the independence of Greece in 1828.

Howe returned on the *Suffolk* to continue the work of relief which he knew was still greatly needed. He sensed that the misery at hand arose from the want of employment. "Why, then," he asked, "should I give away these donations to be consumed in idleness, when by a proper use of them I can give employment to hundreds in some ways that keep them out of idleness and result in some permanent public good, making a road, draining a marsh, building a hospital, school, or something of the kind?"[46]

The enterprising pioneer in modern methods of charitable relief forthwith undertook a work project involving the building of a quay and improvement of the debris-blocked harbor of Aegina. The Temple

[43] *Letters and Journals of Samuel Gridley Howe*, I, 278-82.
[44] Miller, *The Condition of Greece*, 194.
[45] *Niles' Weekly Register*, June 7, 1828.
[46] *Letters and Journals of Samuel Gridley Howe*, I, 286.

of Venus was excavated. The men lugged the stones to the water-front, the older, hardened peasant women, dirt in their aprons. (With a delicate feeling for the situation Howe arranged to have the refugee girls from Athens work at home, instead of being exposed to the attentions of unscrupulous men.) The men received as pay three pounds of Indian meal, the women two and a half pounds. "For this did they set to work with a hearty shout of joy at finding the means of living." Thus more than six hundred men and women, instead of begging Howe for help, addressed him in such terms as "Welcome among us, sir!" or "Long life to the Americans!" At the same time under Howe's constant direction they did useful work the advantages of which were clear to everyone.[47]

At Hexamilion in the Corinthian peninsula Howe developed on government-granted lands a colony of hopeless and impoverished men and women who had no homes. Huts of wood and stone were built, the colonists being paid for the work merely as much bread as was necessary to sustain life. Howe, using the receipts of sales of American provisions and cash sent from the States, bought for the colonists cotton and corn seed, oxen and simple farming tools. "If Providence smile upon them, and they get in but a moderate crop, the surplus, after enough has been taken for their own subsistence, will serve for establishing several other families, and paying the yearly expenses of a hospital for fifty beds." Howe, finding a native teacher who had learned the Lancastrian methods of instruction in England, opened a school. The colony, called "Washingtonia," did not succeed on as large a scale as he intended. For this he blamed the failure of the chief civilian authority, Capo d'Istria, to keep his promises. But it gave fifty families a new start in life. It offered a model of improved agricultural methods. It also provided a new mode of charity less open to abuse than former methods. Howe heard "on every side, from Greeks, from foreigners, and even from Americans, such expressions of disapprobation of the plan pursued by former agents, and such conclusive evidence of its comparative inutility," that he was more and more content with his innovation, which put relief on a more permanent basis of self-help than mere handouts. Howe admitted that formerly the most pressing need was to allay hunger; but he reflected that the hungry, being unemployed, were in consequence idle, that they contracted "vicious habits." Certainly the work projects

[47] *Ibid.*, 309-314, 330.

met with widespread approval.[48] Keeping his contacts in Greece, Howe returned in 1844 to find that he was still warmly remembered, and, again, after the Civil War, to lead a campaign for aid to Crete.

The American response to the struggle of the Greeks was the first major episode in a series of separate, scattered, and limited disasters abroad that occasioned only local efforts to provide emergency relief. For the first time a relief effort was intertwined with big issues. These included conflicting values and purposes on the part of those who favored aid for victory in a military struggle for freedom and justice and those who wanted to confine what was done to the relief of suffering. Further, the struggle brought American relief efforts into an international orbit, pointed to the need for quasi-national organization for fund raising, and focused the attention of the principal American almoner on the importance of rehabilitation as well as on emergency relief. Most important of all, perhaps, was the fact that the campaign for aid awakened Americans to the problems and needs of another people.

[48] *Ibid.*, 316 ff., 347 ff.

III

The Great Irish Famine

No event in the first half of the nineteenth century—not even the Greek struggle for freedom—led to such widespread and intensive American giving as the Great Famine in Ireland. At the close of the wet, cold, sunless summer of 1845 the failure of the potato crop, Ireland's staple food supply, brought severe suffering. The next year the failure of the crop was even more disastrous. The strange blight spread to Germany and other countries. In Ireland itself the British Government, between October, 1846, and March, 1847, spent £9,250,000 on grain depots, soup kitchens, and public works programs.[1]

When, at the end of November, 1846, it was clear that the measures taken by government had proved inadequate, the Society of Friends in Dublin issued a circular setting forth the need of prompt action, and a plan. A few copies of this widely distributed circular, which brought immediate action on the part of Quakers in England, reached the United States early in December, 1846. This report, followed by others from varied sources, left no doubt of the appalling conditions. Accounts came of the dying and the dead, lying helpless in huts, of corpses strewn on the highways, corpses buried with-

---

[1] The first comprehensive report of the Irish famine to be published in America was Mrs. Asenath Nicholson's *Annals of the Famine in Ireland in 1847, 1848, and 1849* (New York: French, 1851). Mrs. Nicholson, a native Vermonter, had kept a famous boarding house in New York where a vegetarian diet was served to "hundreds of choice spirits from all parts of the country, including most of the names of those engaged in measures of social reform." Mrs. Nicholson had visited Ireland prior to the Great Famine and shared her experiences in *Ireland's Welcome to the Stranger* (New York: Baker and Scribner, 1847). Mrs. Nicholson's second book recounts the sorrows she witnessed in Ireland as she dispensed relief sent by the New York Ireland Relief Committee. The most recent scholarly study of the catastrophe is R. Dudley Edwards and T. Desmond Williams, eds., *The Great Famine: Studies in Irish History, 1845-47* (Dublin: Browne and Nolan, 1956).

out coffins in shallow graves, which starving dogs clawed up and devoured. Before it was all over, the famine and the pestilence it fostered killed over a million human beings. Within a decade, it drove another million and a half to emigrate.

In America everyone knew that the potato blight and failure of the staple food crop in 1845 and 1846 was the immediate cause of the disaster. Here any common agreement stopped. British reports emphasized the extensive relief measures the government sponsored from the moment the gravity of the situation was apparent. Sometimes by implication, sometimes explicitly, reports from England suggested that the indolence of the Irish people had much to do with their sad plight. On the other hand, spokesmen of the Irish immigrants in America and many Americans themselves laid the blame at British doors, an easy enough thing to do in view of the continuing suspicion and dislike of the mother country in many quarters and of edgy feelings that the still unsettled dispute over Oregon stirred in patriotic breasts.

The *New York Tribune* expressed a widely held view in maintaining that much of Ireland's trouble stemmed from the fact that the majority of farms were no larger than three acres and that it was thus impossible to lay in a backlog of foodstuffs; that the land tenure system separated absentee owners from the actual cultivators of the soil; that the population was too large for the island's resources; and that Ireland lost in 1846 the protected position she had enjoyed in the British markets when the corn laws were repealed. Others emphasized the injustice of a tax-supported state church rejected by the great majority of the people and the refusal of England to grant home rule. Some no doubt agreed with the *New York Tribune* in holding that God's hand was manifest in Ireland's calamity: the history of the world proved that great improvements had resulted from great calamities. Horace Binney, Philadelphia's leading lawyer, echoed the same idea regarding the cause of the famine in declaring that God had sent it to enable those not afflicted to act in the true spirit of Christian Brotherhood.

Aroused by reports of prevailing conditions rather than by comment on the causes of the famine, public men in leading cities initiated meetings for arousing opinion and for speeding help to the needy. The first to attract national attention was held in Merchants Exchange in New Orleans on February 4, 1847. Seargent Smith Prentiss, after giving "a thrilling description of death by hunger" electrified the audience by declaring, "Oh, it is terrible, that in this beautiful world, which the good God has given us, and in which there is plenty for us all, that men should die of starvation." Henry Clay also spoke, rising to his well known oratorical heights. The New Orleans *Delta* described Clay's address as "pure and nervous," and full of kind-heartedness. His speech, according to the same source, was received with "the most rapturous expressions of delight and satisfaction by the audience." Both addresses found their way into print in many parts of the land.

Five days later, on February 9, 1847, an impressive meeting took place at Odd Fellows' Hall in the nation's capital. Justices of the Supreme Court and members of Congress, Vice-President George Mifflin Dallas and others of the executive branch of government graced it by their appearance. Robert Dale Owen, Senator John J. Crittenden and Daniel Webster, among others, delivered addresses. The meeting issued an "Appeal to the People of the Nation." This spirited call to action urged citizens in every city and town to hold public meetings, to appoint committees to canvass the community for funds, and to speed contributions in kind and in gold to starving Ireland.

In New York a preliminary meeting took place in Wall Street, attended, in the words of the wealthy, cultivated, and civic-minded Philip Hone, by "the right sort of folks." The venerable merchant Myndert Van Schaick presided. The meeting issued an appeal to the clergy, asking to have special collections taken in the churches. It made plans to collect funds and to fill a ship with provisions. It also decided to call a great public meeting to promote this end.[2] This meeting took place at the Tabernacle on February 16, with Van Schaick in the chair and with a host of well-known men on the platform. The building, Hone noted in his diary the next day, was filled with a "respectable male audience, and exceedingly good feeling was evinced." [3] The *New York Tribune*, in describing the affair, declared that it was "one of the most enthusiastic gatherings ever assembled in New York City" with the Tabernacle "densely filled with men of every class and condition, eager to do their part." The organizing committee resolved to have meetings in every ward, with ward com-

[2] Bayard Tuckerman, ed., *The Diary of Philip Hone, 1825-1851* (2 vols.; New York: Dodd, Mead, 1889), II, 297.
[3] *Ibid.*, 298.

mittees charged with collecting provisions and funds, to report to the standing committee at headquarters in Prime's Building in Wall Street.[4]

Philadelphia did not lag behind. The Society of Friends, in fact, was on the job even before the great meeting of February 16th at the Chinese Salon. Speakers included William Duane, Horace Binney, and Joseph Chandler. Here also committees set about canvassing the city ward by ward.[5]

In Boston the members of the executive and legislative departments of the state government met unofficially on February 19, 1847, with Governor George Briggs in the chair. The officials urged authorities in cities and towns to take subscriptions. Boston also carried through a huge meeting at Faneuil Hall, which 4,000 people attended. Leading men spoke and took on the task of organizing the wards.[6]

Meetings quickly followed in almost every city and in innumerable towns. The *New York Tribune* of February 20, 1847, reported such gatherings in Albany, Troy, Utica, Syracuse, Rochester, New Haven, Cambridge, Norfolk, Richmond and Charleston.[7] The meeting at Andover, Massachusetts, raised $1,000; that at Northampton, a town of but 4,000, attended by washerwomen and woodcutters as well as by leading citizens, collected $5,000.[8] In Montgomery, Alabama, a meeting gave $1,000.[9] And so it went. The committees in Boston, New York, Philadelphia, Baltimore, and New Orleans acted as receiving agents for donations from towns and cities in their regions. Some communities, however, sent their donations directly to the American Minister in London or to the Relief Committee of the Society of Friends in Dublin.

During most of February, 1847, efforts were made to induce Congress to appropriate funds for the relief of Ireland, or of Ireland and Scotland, where the food shortage was also acute. Petitions and memorials and editorials in the press indicate that the movement for such aid found its chief support among the Whigs. This was natural, in view of the party's commitment to a broad interpretation of the Constitution and the fact that its leaders were glad to seize the op-

4 *New York Tribune*, Feb. 20, 1847.
5 *New York Spectator*, Feb. 20, 1847.
6 *Boston Daily Journal*, Feb. 20, 1847.
7 *New York Weekly Tribune*, Feb. 20, 1847.
8 *Boston Daily Journal*, Feb. 26, 1847; *New York Weekly Tribune*, Feb. 27, 1847.
9 *Niles' National Register*, March 13, 1847.

portunity to contrast government spending for destruction in the war with Mexico, to which they were opposed, with spending public funds for saving life. True, a leading Whig, Horace Greeley, confessed, somewhat inconsistently, that he did not sign a petition asking Congress to make the appropriation, as he doubted its constitutionality. "Yet we are very sure it *ought* to be constitutional and ardently hope for its passage." [10]

How abhorrent it was, Greeley added, that our government has undoubted authority to send all our national vessels abroad to dash out children's brains and mangle the bodies of inoffensive men, women, and children, and yet was without a clear mandate to send a single ship loaded with grain for a friendly and famishing people! On the other hand, Thomas Ritchie of the Washington *Daily Union*, organ of the Polk administration, voiced the prevailing view of the Democrats in holding that "our sympathy with her (Ireland's) noble and suffering people should not mislead us into any violation of our constitution." [11]

The editorial debate paralleled that in the legislature of New York, where a resolution urging Congressional action was under consideration. Some members favored "all manner of expressions" of sympathy but doubted the power of Congress to act. Another recalled the aid given to the Greeks in their struggle. Robert Denniston reminded his colleagues that on that occasion high political considerations were at stake, that it was not a question of charity alone. Thomas Barlow hoped that no constitutional barrier would be found. If we cannot relieve suffering under the Constitution, "then it was not right to live under such a constitution." Other Whigs took jibes at the Democrats' readiness to use public moneys to purchase "peace" with Mexico in what in their own eyes was a mere land grab while standing on constitutional grounds against the relief of great suffering.[12]

In this general context Congressman Washington Hunt, a wealthy Whig landowner from Lockport, New York, on February 10, 1847, introduced a bill in the House for the purchase and transportation of foodstuffs to Ireland. The bill was read the first and second time

[10] *New York Weekly Tribune*, March 3, 1847.

[11] Washington *Daily Union*, Feb. 27, 1847. Ritchie noted that he had been almost alone in 1812 in opposing, on constitutional grounds, the appropriation of $50,000 for the relief of sufferers from the Venezuela earthquake.

[12] *New York Spectator*, Feb. 24, 1847.

and then committed to the Whole House.[13] No further action seems to have been taken on this bill.

Two weeks later John J. Crittenden, a Whig from Kentucky, introduced in the Senate a bill appropriating $500,000 for the relief of both Ireland and Scotland.[14] In supporting his proposal Crittenden spoke of the extraordinary character of the calamity, which could be regarded only as "one of those inscrutable dispensations of Providence." He made much of the aid Congress had given in 1812 to Venezuela, noting that the bill had been on that occasion introduced by Nathaniel Macon, a strict constructionist, that it had passed unanimously in the House and met with no opposition in the Senate. How much more important was it to act now, for the Irish famine was a national, not a local, calamity. Moreover, the Irish had not only the claims of humanity on our compassion; they also had the claims of brothers. It would be strange if the Constitution were so fashioned that government could not act. "We can do what individual charity cannot do." And what a spectacle government aid would be, what an influence on the whole world![15] In the course of the discussion Webster indicated that he would vote for the bill but that he would be happier if it were not strictly an offer from one government to another but, rather, a gift of the people. Crittenden gladly accepted this change. Calhoun felt that France ought also to be included in the bounty.

Senator Bagby of Alabama denied the constitutionality of the whole proposal. Such a precedent was dangerous; where would such a system of charity end? Senator Hannegan, a Democrat of Indiana with Irish background, spoke of our obligations to Ireland, and declared that he could find no clause in the Constitution preventing such an act of charity. The highest law of our nature, he said, includes the law of charity. Calhoun, as the archchampion of strict construction, felt called on to explain why he had no hesitation in supporting the proposal. The South Carolinian drew a distinction between the foreign and the domestic policy of the federal government. Entertaining this distinction, he had voted for aid to the Caracas people in 1812; and though he realized that the appropriation Crittenden was asking

---

[13] *Journal of the House of Representatives*, 29th Cong., 2d Sess., 1847, 324; *New York Weekly Tribune*, Feb. 20, 1847.

[14] *Journal of the Senate*, 29th Cong., 2d Sess., 1847, 233.

[15] *Congressional Globe*, 29th Cong., 2d Sess., 1847, XVI, 512.

for imposed a heavy burden in the midst of the war with Mexico, he would gladly vote for it.[16]

On February 27 Senator Mason of Virginia, after explaining why he did not agree with some of his fellow Democrats in holding that the proposal was constitutional, offered an amendment which would have stricken the appropriation from the bill by merely authorizing the President to employ public ships to carry voluntary contributions to Ireland. The vote on this amendment was the real test of the strength of the measure. Seventeen senators voted for the amendment (sixteen Democrats, one Whig), while twenty-four voted against it (eighteen Whigs, six Democrats). The six Democratic votes, one each from South Carolina, Pennsylvania, Ohio, Indiana, Michigan, and Illinois, saved the Crittenden bill, which was then, on the same day, passed by a vote of 27 to 13. Again, ten Democratic yeas from the states just listed, together with votes from Texas, Louisiana, and Missouri, saved the Crittenden measure. On the whole the vote, with notable exceptions, reflected party lines.[17]

The House was then asked to concur in the Crittenden bill. George W. Jones, a Tennessee Democrat, moved to lay the bill on the table; his motion met with defeat in a close vote—84 to 74. Then Congressman Lewis C. Levin, an ardent Native American of Pennsylvania, proposed an amendment allocating the $500,000 for overseas relief to the suffering poor at home, since the influx of foreign paupers and criminals left no room in our almshouses for the American poor. The whole proposal, Levin insisted, was not only unconstitutional. It was "designed to afford *food* for party vultures to feed upon, rather than bread for the starving people of Ireland." [18] The Speaker ruled the proposed amendment out of order and the House affirmed the ruling. A motion to commit the bill to the Whole House was defeated—yeas 68, nays 107. This vote was the decisive action since it prevented the Crittenden bill from coming to a vote. Of the sixty-eight votes for the motion, fifty-one were those of Whigs, seventeen those of Democrats. Of the one hundred seven who voted against it, ninety were Democrats, thirteen were Whigs, and four were Native Americans.

Thus the division was clearly along party lines, 80 per cent of

16 *Ibid.*, 533-35.
17 *Journal of the Senate*, 29th Cong., 2d Sess., 1847, 241-43.
18 *Journal of the House of Representatives*, 29th Cong., 2d Sess., 1847, 452-53.

the Whigs voting for the bill and 84 per cent of the Democrats voting against it. The minority in each party that did not act with the majority may have been moved by personal convictions or by pressure from Irish and other relief-minded constituents. An analysis along regional lines shows that the break in the Whig ranks came in New England, with about one-third of its representatives defecting. The Democratic support for the measure came largely from the band of states from New York to Iowa.[19]

On March 3, the last day of the session, Congressman Robert C. Winthrop of Massachusetts moved the suspension of the rules to allow him to bring the pigeon-holed Crittenden bill to a vote. Winthrop's motion was defeated (57 yeas, 102 nays) with a division of the vote similar to the crucial one of March 1.[20]

The discussion of the proposals in the Congress provided no explicit evidence to explain the predominantly party lines of division. It is possible in view of the political complexion of the times and of editorial comment in the press, that the Whigs sought in part to embarrass the administration by adding another half-million to the already swollen war budget and to provide a dramatic contrast between their own benevolence and the "bloody lust" of their opponents. Possibly the Whigs were also seeking the Irish vote, which had traditionally been Democratic. But this does not explain the votes of those Congressmen from regions where the Irish element was insignificant, any more than it explains the predominant Democratic opposition.

The concern of President Polk lends some support to the thesis that the position of the Democrats in truth did rest in large part on constitutional scruples. Worried lest the House pass the Crittenden bill which had already been approved by the Senate, Polk informed his Cabinet that should it pass the lower chamber he would veto it on the ground that the Constitution did not authorize appropriation of public moneys for charity, whether at home or abroad. Members of the Cabinet expressed no dissent. Polk added that he had expressed his personal sympathy with the starving Irish by contributing his little mite of fifty dollars to the voluntary relief fund.[21]

[19] *Ibid.*, 454.
[20] *Ibid.*, 496; *New York Weekly Tribune*, Feb. 28, March 8, 1847; Washington *National Intelligencer*, March 2, 1847.
[21] Milo M. Quaife, ed., *Diary of James K. Polk During His Presidency, 1845 to 1849* (4 vols.; Chicago: A. C. McClurg, 1910), II, 396-97.

Yet the line between constitutional scruples and the desire in Congress to make some gesture of aid did not prove to be impassable in the matter of lending government war vessels to private groups in New York and Boston for transmitting to Ireland provisions contributed or bought with funds in the hands of the relief committees. In Boston the idea found its leading supporters in the mercantile community—Robert B. Forbes, John F. Forbes, and Abbott Lawrence took the initiative in circulating petitions to this end.[22] In urging Congressman Robert Winthrop to present the petitions, Robert Forbes wrote that the idea "may be considered *absurd* at Washington; but it is *here a very popular idea.*" [23]

At about the same time, On February 24th, Senator Dix, a New York Democrat, presented in the upper house a memorial from Commodore George De Kay, sometime chief of the Argentine Navy and a well-known shipbuilder, praying for the loan of the federal warship *Macedonian* for carrying food from New York to Ireland. Inevitably some questioned the wisdom of such a course when the country was at war with Mexico.[24] But the Senate Committee on Naval Affairs reported favorably the resolution providing for De Kay's use of the *Macedonian*. At the same time the sloop of war *Jamestown* was offered to the Boston group. The Senate vote, 23 against 12, was less clearly along party lines than the crucial one on the Mason amendment of the Crittenden bill, as twelve Whigs were joined by eleven Democrats to make the majority, while four Whigs and eight Democrats made up the minority.[25] In general the press, regardless of party, seems to have approved of this decision.[26] [We shall see, in discussing the problems involved in raising funds and gathering provisions and in transporting foodstuffs to Ireland, how the *Macedonian* and *Jamestown* ventures turned out.] Certainly the discussion in Congress was not unrelated to the desire of many political figures to strengthen themselves among Irish-American voters. In the mind of the wise and

[22] *Boston Daily Journal*, Feb. 22, 1847; Robert B. Forbes, *Personal Reminiscences* (3d rev. ed.; Boston: Little, Brown, 1892), 188 ff.

[23] R. B. Forbes, *The Voyage of the Jamestown on Her Errand of Mercy* (Boston: Eastburn's Press, 1847), iii.

[24] *Congressional Globe*, 29th Cong., 2d Sess., 1847, XVI, 505, 559, 572-73; *Journal of the Senate*, 29th Cong., 2d Sess., 1847, 223, 245, 255.

[25] *Journal of the Senate*, 29th Cong., 2d Sess., 1847, XVI, 255-56.

[26] *New York Spectator*, March 10, 1847; *New York Weekly Tribune*, March 15, 1847; *Washington Daily Union*, Feb. 27, 1847.

fair-minded Philadelphia Quaker, James Luther Mott, this was an important if unmeasurable factor.[27]

The refusal of Congress to grant a substantial sum for Irish relief threw the whole burden of raising funds and of buying and transporting provisions on voluntary efforts. It is impossible to be sure about the motives that led Americans to give; but the appeals made do reflect what leaders and workers in the fund-raising campaign thought would move the public. There is no way, of course, of giving any precise weight to the several motives to which appeals were made; one can only suggest the frequency with which one or another appeal was set forth in public meetings, sermons, and the press.

Certainly the Christian duty of charity figured in many such appeals. In the official proclamations this may have been merely a matter of custom. In any case, the tone of these is well represented in the words of Governor Briggs of Massachusetts, who issued in early March 1847 a Proclamation for a Day of Public Fasting, Humiliation, and Prayer: "that He will animate our hearts with Christian benevolence, keeping ever present the word of the SAVIOUR, 'the poor ye have always with ye' and dispose us cheerfully to discharge then the duty which that truth inculcates!" [28] The Reverend F. D. Huntington, of the South Congregational Society in Boston, to cite a single example from scores of sermons, developed and illustrated the Christian duty of charity in his sermon based on Jeremiah xiv 16, "The Famine and the Sword." [29] Bishop Fitzpatrick of the Catholic diocese of Boston declared in a typical statement that "Christian charity dictates the sharing of what is superfluous with the needy. . . . Whatever you possess beyond the wants of your condition belongs to the poor, and cannot be withheld from them without injustice." [30]

Horace Greeley added another dimension to appeals based on the Christian duty to give by asking the question, "Can Christian charity, essential though it be, divided as it is, work a cure of the appalling evils we now contemplate?" Charity there must be, but even greater was the need for opportunity and for justice. Sending corn to Ireland, he went on, might be practicable for the moment, but it was no last-

[27] James Mott to Richard Webb, Feb. 21, 1847, in "Anti-Slavery Letters," Garrison Manuscripts, XVII, Boston Public Library.
[28] *Boston Daily Journal*, March 10, 1847.
[29] *Ibid.*, March 5, 1847.
[30] The *Boston Pilot*, Feb. 13, 1847, cited in Robert H. Lord, *et al.*; *History of the Archdiocese of Boston* (3 vols.; New York: Sheed and Ward, 1944), II, 434-35.

ing solution. The only permanent answer, as far as Greeley could see, was the recognition of the imminent need "not merely in church but in state of the practical recognition of the Christian Law of Love, the Christian realization of Universal Brotherhood." [31]

Public professions of and appeals to the religious motivation found parallel expression in letters and diaries, representative of which is the comment of the well-to-do Boston merchant, Amos A. Lawrence, "Let us thank God that He has given us the means to exercise our charity in this manner. It is the poorest and cheapest offering that we can make. Let us not grudge that. In his infinite mercy may He open the hearts of all men to feel for these suffering brethren and in his own time give them deliverance." [32] What effect all these public and private appeals had, no one can say; but it is clear that religious groups took a leading part in collecting funds.

Often the appeal to Christian motivation for giving was linked with the humanitarian. The resolutions adopted by the meeting in Faneuil Hall called on individuals to give in response to "the promptings of a common humanity and the dictates of Christian duty." [33] In many instances, however, no explicit reference to Christian duty accompanied humanitarian appeals. Thus in his speech at the Odd Fellows' Hall in Washington Daniel Webster declared that our object was merely "to do a deed of effectual charity, and do it promptly, that the objects of our compassion may bear tidings of kindness and relief from across the ocean before death shall terminate their sufferings." [34] In urging a big turnout at the Tabernacle meeting in the metropolis, the *New York Spectator* begged those attending it to concentrate solely on the fact that children were perishing, to lay aside every consideration of religion, nationality, politics and conduct in reference to the sufferers. "There is starvation in Ireland—that is all we have to know or think of." [35]

Occasionally the discussion suggested what might now be regarded as the beginnings of a rational attack on suffering. In the meeting at Washington that many-sided reformer, Robert Dale Owen, brushed aside the excuse that charity begins at home by declaring that in a

[31] *New York Weekly Tribune*, Feb. 13, 1847.
[32] A. A. Lawrence to T. R. Hazard, Feb. 2, 1847, Lawrence Papers, Massachusetts Historical Society.
[33] *Boston Daily Journal*, Feb. 20, 1847.
[34] *National Intelligencer*, Feb. 11, 13, 1847; *History of the Archdiocese of Boston*, II, 434-35.
[35] *New York Spectator*, Feb. 3, 1847; A. A. Lawrence to T. R. Hazard, Feb. 2, 1847, Lawrence Papers.

world in which neighborhoods were being enlarged all the time by steamships and telegraphs, charity could not end at home. If one felt that relief was useless as long as reform was not uprooting the causes of famine, Owen asked whether one would refuse to alleviate sickness because he could offer no cure.[36]

In appealing to humanitarian motives, many took pains to give concrete illustrations, believing that the personal, the homely, the intimate, stirs feelings as abstractions never can. At the Washington meeting in Odd Fellows' Hall, Orville Dewey, a leading Unitarian minister, did not shrink from sentimentality in telling the story of a child's response to what she heard about the sufferings of boys and girls in Ireland. She saved some of the corn she had for her chickens, that it might be sent to Ireland to save the life of some child.[37] Letters from Ireland with appeals to the women of America similarly gave graphic pictures of misery, pestilence, starvation, and death. The *United States Gazette* published one such appeal: "Oh that our American sisters could see the laborers in our roads, able bodied men scarcely clad, famishing with hunger, with despair on their once cheerful faces. . . . Oh that they could see the dead father, mother, or child lying coffinless, and hear the screams of the survivors around them, caused, not by sorrow, but in the agony of hunger—they, whose hands and hearts are ever open to compassion, would unite in one mighty effort to save Ireland from such misery." [38]

Especially noteworthy were the *Olive Leaves*, tiny once-folded sheets, which Elihu Burritt printed and circulated throughout New England. The "Learned Blacksmith," who was in England in 1846, determined to go to Ireland, to see the disaster with his own eyes, to help in the relief, and to report to his fellow Americans on the extent of the catastrophe and the nature of the need. His sensitive descriptions of human misery, of what the famine, the plague, the spell of death did to this man, to that woman, to these children, must have moved many hearts.[39]

If the appeals for giving reflect the motives presumed to lead to action, pride, in the frequency with which it was mentioned, ranked high in the minds of speakers and writers concerned with the cam-

[36] *New York Weekly Tribune*, Feb. 13, 1847.
[37] *Boston Daily Journal*, Feb. 20, 1847.
[38] *New York Spectator*, Feb. 3, 1847; Allan Nevins and Milton H. Thomas, eds., *The Diary of George Templeton Strong* (4 vols.; New York: Macmillan, 1952), I, 228.
[39] Charles Northend, ed., *Elihu Burritt: A Memorial Volume* (New York: D. Appleton, 1879), 34-35, 217-34.

paign. Sometimes it was a matter of local civic pride, as when S. S. Prentiss, a Kentuckian, spoke of the proverbial generosity of the people of New Orleans, or when the *Boston Daily Journal*, before anything had been done in "the Hub of the Universe," declared that surely some of the city's leading citizens should move in order that "the high character of our city for public philanthropy may not be obscured by discreditable indifference and fatal delay.[40] Again, a region was the focus of appeals to pride, a good example being Robert Dale Owen's declaration that he was sure the appeal would not be made in vain to the generous west.[41]

Admirable though it was for individuals to dig into their pockets, Owen observed, a great national gift would be even more impressive. "It belongs to our national character, particularly as a free people, to tell by a great national benefaction to all the world the superabundance of the bountiful gifts which we enjoy under our happy institutions." [42] An editorial in the *National Intelligencer* struck a related key in holding that giving generously was an answer to "those persons in foreign lands whose habit it is to represent Brother Jonathan (as they style us) as a sordid and mercenary personage, who, never acting but in a spirit of calculation can afford to be generous only when reckoning that he is to gain by being so." [43] It would be easily possible to cite dozens of similar examples. One of the most memorable was an editorial in the Washington *Daily Union:* "We trust that the whole country will rise up, and that America . . . will present the full bosom of her plenty and luxuriance to the lips of the famished Irishman." [44]

Traditional anti-British feeling ran high during the first six months of 1846, to be eased somewhat in June when the governments of the two countries effected a compromise over the long-disputed Oregon country. Meantime letters from correspondents to various newspapers coupled vivid descriptions of the starving Irish with bitter indictments of Lord John Russell. Editorials in the press of both political parties condemned Great Britain for having failed to develop a true federal system in which an Irish parliament might sense and correct existing evils before catastrophe struck, or denounced the government at Westminster for neglect and exploitation of the Irish

[40] *New York Weekly Tribune*, March 3, 1847; *Boston Daily Journal*, Feb. 4, 1847.
[41] Washington *Daily Union*, Feb. 13, 1847.
[42] *Idem.*
[43] *National Intelligencer*, Feb. 22, 1847.
[44] Washington *Daily Union*, Feb. 18, 1847.

peasantry, or for acting in the matter of relief too late and too meagerly.[45] One cannot of course say that such anti-British sentiments were intended to evoke American giving by further appealing to well-known prejudices, but such an inference is not unreasonable.

Appeals for contributions often expressed the idea that Americans ought to give out of a sense of indebtedness. Sometimes such expressions had nothing to do with any idea of obligation to Ireland, as when the people of Nantucket, who had received generous help when a fire destroyed much of their commercial district, contributed $1,900 for the Irish with the message "in gratitude, would we do somewhat to others, as others have done to us." [46] But more often appeals for funds reminded Americans of the help Ireland had given to America, after the devastating King Philip's War, and during the struggle for independence, when Burke, Barre, Montgomery and others of Irish birth or background had sprung to America's defense.[47] The motive of indebtedness was also reflected in the occasional mention of the contribution Irish immigrants had made to the digging of canals and the building of railroads.

Appeals to fear were more frequently and vigorously expressed than those to some sense of indebtedness. Irish immigrants in a desperate plight were pouring into the main seaports, crowding the poorhouses, and threatening to increase the tax burden. "It is becoming a question of vital importance, which is asked by all our citizens, 'How can this flood of pauper emigration be stopped?'" This was a characteristic expression of the fear of Irish immigrant inundation. "The brand of infamy should be affixed to those who are instrumental in flooding our city with pauperism and disease," declared the *Boston Daily Journal*.[48] Meetings protested the further admission of poverty-stricken refugees from pestilence and famine. The proximity in the press of anti-immigration sentiment with appeals for relief of suffering in Ireland suggests that the two may well have been associated in the minds of some who asked for contributions and some who gave.

Some evidence suggests that giving was related to feelings of guilt. Since even the poorest Irish among us are giving, why, asked the *Boston Daily Journal*, should those who live in comfort and abundance, fail to open their purses? What a shame and disgrace that there

---

[45] *Idem; Boston Daily Journal*, Jan. 26, Feb. 4, 1847.
[46] Nathaniel Barney to Richard D. Webb, Nantucket, Feb. 21, 1847, Garrison Manuscripts.
[47] Washington *Daily Union*, Feb. 18, 1847.
[48] *Boston Daily Journal*, April 3, June 7, 1847.

should be starvation when the earth produces every year more than enough to feed and clothe the whole population! How could America, the "cornucopia of the world," stand back enjoying its abundance while others perished? [49]

If benevolence was not a sufficient motive for action, if common decency was an inadequate one, then, S. S. Prentiss reminded his New Orleans listeners, let it be remembered that Americans were adding millions to their fortunes out of this famine which had already doubled the value of our food exports.[50] Philip Hone admitted in his diary a feeling of guilt in participating in a luxurious and expensive dinner while twelve starving Irish wretches had died on a ship that had just docked. He also pondered on the fact that many Americans had grown rich in supplying the wants of starving Ireland as the prices of food and freight shot up.[51] George Templeton Strong, a fellow New Yorker, suspected that a slight fall in the price of grain would "damp the enthusiasm of the Irish relief movement some-what." [52] Even though grain dealers and exporters denied in public statements that prices and freight had shot up because of hoarding, speculation, and profiteering, the impression that this was the case was expressed now and again. Thus, for example, a Boston ship-owner gave $300 as his "debt to starvation" because of the rise in freight rates.[53]

For those who opposed the War with Mexico—and many Whigs of course did—giving to the starving Irish seemed in some part a com-pensation for what in their minds was a great national wrongdoing. Amos Lawrence, Boston merchant and philanthropist, noting that "we are in deep disgrace on account of this wicked Mexican business," expressed satisfaction that the *Jamestown*, a ship of war, was carrying bread to the hungry instead of powder and ball to inflict more suffer-ing on mankind.[54] Philip Hone, another critic of Polk's war policy, on hearing that the New York Irish Relief Committee had received a $5,000 contribution from Corcoran and Riggs, Washington bankers, wrote in his diary that these gentlemen had made a princely fortune by taking the whole of the government's six per cent war loan. "The

[49] *Ibid.*, Feb. 26, 1847.
[50] *New York Weekly Tribune*, March 3, 1847.
[51] *Diary of Philip Hone*, II, 293-95.
[52] *The Diary of George Templeton Strong*, 289.
[53] *Boston Daily Journal*, March 6, June 23, 1847.
[54] William R. Lawrence, ed., *Extracts from the Diary and Correspondence of the Late Amos Lawrence* (Boston: John Wilson and Son, 1855), 241, 238.

capture of la Vera Cruz and the battle of Buena Vista," he continued, "furnished the means of sending a thousand barrels of corn to Ireland; and Scott and Taylor, whilst employed in knocking out the brains of Mexicans, were unconsciously the instruments of saving the lives of Irishmen." [55] These and similar comments suggest that one of the arguments for giving for famine relief, and one of the motives for contributing, were compensatory, designed in some degree to alleviate a sense of personal and national guilt.

The motives for giving to Irish famine relief—the first truly national organized campaign for helping the distressed in a foreign land—were, of course, related to categories of donors and to their place in the social structure. Amos Lawrence, in pondering the whole matter, noted that "the value of the offering to suffering Ireland from our city will be enhanced by the numbers contributing, as the offering will do more good as an expression of sympathy than as a mere matter of relief." [56] Looking beyond Boston, it seems clear that in most parts of the country gifts in money or in kind were contributed from every rank of society.

The *Arkansas Intelligencer* reported that the Choctaws at Choctaw Agency met on the twenty-third of March and subscribed $710 to their white brethren in Ireland. "The poor Indian sending his mite to the poor Irish!" commented *Niles' Weekly Register* in reporting the incident.[57] The slaves of Morgan Smith of Lowndes County, Alabama, sent fifty dollars.[58] Workers in factory and mill in many towns and cities swelled the contributions from the humbler ranks in society. Thus the operatives of the Chelsea Laundry gave fifty dollars, those in the Boot and Shoe factory in the same Massachusetts community, seventy-five dollars. The overseers and operatives in Stark Mills in Manchester, New Hampshire, sent a check to the Boston committee for $625, representing a day's labor and given "most cheerfully and with almost entire unanimity." [59] The "warmhearted laborers" in Honesdale, Pennsylvania, the great depot of coal mined by the Delaware and Hudson Canal Company, sent $1,000 as a freewill offering.[60] The workers of Carmichel, Conder and Company,

55 *Diary of Philip Hone*, 309.
56 *Extracts from the Diary and Correspondence of the Late Amos Lawrence*, 237.
57 *Niles' National Register*, May 1, 1847.
58 *Boston Daily Journal*, April 23, 1847.
59 *Ibid.*, March 13, 1847.
60 *Niles' National Register*, May 1, 1847.

contributed each one dollar, a day's pay. "Poor generous men," commented a newspaper editor in Boston; "they began with a scanty breakfast by candlelight, a poor and hasty meal by noon, and a poorer one by night; and then laid down on their hard beds, in cold shanties, warmed only by the consciousness that they had done all they could." [61] These are merely representative examples of many reports of similar offerings.

In some cases the newspaper press specified the Irish identity of humble givers. The *Brooklyn Advertiser* reported that a servant girl in the family of H. B. Dwight sent her total earnings, thirty dollars, to Ireland only to hear a few days later that her father, mother, brothers, and sisters, eight in all, had died of starvation. [62] Apart from contributions given to relief funds, Irish immigrants in New York, Boston, Philadelphia and Baltimore remitted to relatives and friends approximately $623,193 in the two months of January and February, 1847. [63] In Boston, to take a single important center, Bishop John Fitzpatrick decided, after initial appeals from Catholic pulpits in the diocese, that a permanent organization was needed. This decision led to the formation in February of the Relief Association for Ireland which, by June 23, 1847, had sent $150,000 to Ireland.

When, at about this time, two Franciscan brothers came to Boston from Ireland to raise funds for the starving in Connemara, Bishop Fitzpatrick permitted them to make only private collections. The people, he explained, were exhausted: "Our own streets are filled with the most destitute poor, with parentless children exposed to perversion, and our own orphan asylums are at this moment without funds." [64]

The record of contributions of the 30,000 Irish in Boston, largely newcomers and poorly paid, was, in view of prevailing poverty, indeed impressive. A few Irish-born who had been in the country for longer periods and who had done well, gave in good measure. We do not know the amount given by Andrew Carney, Boston's wealthiest Irish immigrant, who, arriving penniless, had made a fortune in the men's clothing business. But his reputation for charity was impressive,

---

[61] *New York Spectator*, March 3, 1847.
[62] *Ibid.*, March 6, 1847.
[63] *Niles' National Register*, March 20, 1847.
[64] Lord *et al.*, *History of the Archdiocese of Boston*, II, 438.

and he no doubt was the largest single giver among the Boston Irish.[65] And what the Irish of Boston did, their brothers in other places also did. On a single Sunday the parishioners of St. Joseph's Church in New York gave $800, those in the Church of the Nativity, $2,000.[66]

It is hard to be specific in the matter of contributions by farmers for most reports of gifts in kind fail to say whether these were contributed outright by the men who had grown the corn, wheat, and meal, or whether these were bought from the funds gathered by the relief committees. We do know that James Wadsworth, a wealthy farmer in Genesee County in New York, gave a thousand bushels of corn and that Malcolm Bruce of Fayetteville, North Carolina, shipped six hundred bushels of corn to his needy Scotch countrymen.[67] Evidence also suggests that a good part of the produce filling the many ships that sailed from New Orleans, Baltimore, and Philadelphia had been given by those who had grown it.

One paper in reporting that the police of Boston subscribed two days' pay exclaimed, "if the capitalists devoted like them two days of income to the cause, how large a sum would be raised!" [68] Yet many businessmen did a great deal. Amos A. Lawrence reported that two of the wealthiest Boston merchants, Peter Chardon Brooks and Colonel Perkins, sent in $2,000 each; he was inclined to think that a number more would give $1,000, and still more, $100.[69] At the initial small meeting in Wall Street, merchants and bankers contributed $9,000. Businessmen in Philadelphia, Baltimore, Washington, and Louisville also made contributions considered by those reporting them to be liberal. The *National Intelligencer* declared that even railroad corporations which were said to have no souls were offering to carry produce free of toll.[70] A Philadelphia manufacturer offered to provide free all the sacks needed for contributions from Pennsylvania. Millers and flour dealers were often mentioned in accounts of gifts in kind.[71]

At least in Boston, some money found its way into the treasuries

[65] Gerald C. Treacy, "Andrew Carney, Philanthropist," United States Catholic Historical Society, *Historical Records* XIII (May, 1919), 101-105.

[66] *New York Spectator*, March 10, 1847. By mid-March Catholic churches in Albany contributed $5,000. *Niles' National Register*, March 13, 1847.

[67] *Boston Daily Journal*, Feb. 23, March 10, 1847.

[68] *Ibid.*, Feb. 24, 1847.

[69] A. A. Lawrence to T. R. Hazard, Feb. 22, 1847, Lawrence Papers.

[70] *National Intelligencer*, Feb. 22, 1847.

[71] *Niles' National Register*, March 20, 1847.

of the relief committee through the gifts school children made of their pennies.[72] The pupils of the Blind Institution and the members of the Choir of Holy Cross in Boston gave a benefit for the cause.[73] But, apart from the great public meetings, the churches seem to have been the chief agency through which giving was done. Sometimes collections were taken on Sunday. Often the ladies of a church took responsibility for raising funds. Catholic donations naturally bulked large. But Protestant groups also responded to religious and humanitarian appeals. The Jewish Congregation in New Orleans contributed $300, that in New York raised "a large collection." As might be expected, the Quakers were active in giving. The orthodox Friends in Philadelphia had raised $10,000 by February, 1847, and though the Hicksites, less well to do, were unable to match this, their meeting spared no effort in doing all it could.[74] The New Jersey meeting collected $10,000, and those in other Quaker centers gave in correspondingly generous amounts.[75]

The problem of estimating the total giving is complicated. It is not always possible to be sure whether the amounts listed in the later months included sums already reported. Moreover, the chief relief committees in Boston, New York, and Philadelphia received contributions in money and kind from many states, yet reports sometimes indicated what particular cities and states gave without making it clear whether these were included in the overall reports of the sums in the hands of the seaboard relief committees. A few figures in widely scattered communities may help drive home the point that this was, in any case, a truly nationwide campaign. Citizens of Rockingham County, Virginia, sent $500 to the Baltimore Committee; Montgomery, Alabama, contributed $1,000; New Orleans, over $25,000; Louisville, $6,500; the citizens of an Illinois county with a population of 600, raised $226; and the people of Michigan contributed 2,349 barrels of provisions and packages of clothing.[76] In Washington, Senators gave $349, members of the House, $972. Perhaps another way of visualizing the extent of giving is to recall that gift-laden vessels sailed from New Orleans, Alexan-

---

[72] *Extracts from the Diary and Correspondence of the late Amos Lawrence*, 237-38.
[73] *Boston Daily Journal*, Feb. 22, April 2, 1847.
[74] James Mott to Richard Webb, Feb. 21, 1847, Garrison Manuscripts.
[75] *National Intelligencer*, Feb. 17, 1847, *Niles' National Register*, March 13, May 29, 1847; *Boston Daily Journal*, Feb. 12, 17, 1847.
[76] *Niles' National Register*, March 20, Aug. 22, 1847.

dria, Baltimore, Philadelphia, and Jersey City; that New York sent out nine such vessels, and Boston, seven. O. C. Gardiner, in an article published in the *American Review* for December, 1847, estimated that the total amount of donations between December, 1846, and mid-July, 1847, could not have been less than $1,000,000 in money and provisions. He based this on the statement of the Central Relief Committee in Dublin that it had received, by July 10, $545,105 from America. Gardiner added to this the probable amounts sent to other receiving agencies and those that American families sent directly to kinfolk in Ireland. "Where," he asked, "in the history of the world has there been found charity like this?" [77]

The British might well have answered, the British themselves. By February 1847, the London *Times* reported that notwithstanding proverbial English government generosity, private contributions had already been unprecedented.[78] It is hard to be on firm ground when one tries to estimate totals, for the reports are somewhat conflicting. By one estimate British private gifts, to August, 1847, when the worst was over, totaled £425,286. This included the offerings of the churches of England and Scotland and the total given to the British Relief Association.[79] Other estimates were considerably higher. The British Friends alone were reported as giving £35,000 and the Wesleyan Methodists £13,000. Mrs. Nicholson estimated that the British Relief Association dispensed about £400,000, and that the relief given by other associations might be put down at fully £200,000. Local committees in Ireland were said to have given something above £300,000.[80] None of these estimates included the £10,000,000 sterling that Parliament voted for public works and other kinds of relief.

Getting funds and provisions to Ireland presented problems. Early in the campaign Harnden and Company in Boston offered to accept and distribute money and provisions gratuitously through its agents in Ireland, and both were sent through this channel.[81] The Catholic

---

[77] O. C. Gardiner, "Foreign Immigration," *The American Review: A Whig Journal* VI (Dec., 1847), 646. This may be compared with the $1,562,449 contributed during the year 1846 by the various American benevolent societies that held annual meetings in Boston in April, 1847: *Boston Daily Journal*, April 15, 1847.

[78] Cited in the *New York Spectator*, Feb. 24, 1847.

[79] *Niles' National Register*, Aug. 7, 1847.

[80] Nicholson, *Annals of the Famine in Ireland*, 54. Mrs. Nicholson put the total, including remittances from emigrants and private benevolence, at not less than one million and a half sterling, exclusive of government relief.

[81] *Boston Daily Journal*, Feb. 23, 1847.

bishops often sent the funds of their flock to Catholic bishops in Ireland.[82] Elihu Burritt, thanking Lord Russell for his offer to transport in British ships contributions from American Friends, asked if the British Government would also carry without cost contributions from other American sources. The reply was in the affirmative, provided the goods were purchased from private subscriptions and were solely for charitable purposes.[83]

Even after this offer, some relief committees continued to send provisions in ships they had chartered or that offered them a certain amount of free freightage. By the end of May, 1847, thirteen vessels had been chartered and dispatched. One was provided by A. T. Stewart, who had arrived in America from Ireland in 1823 and who built up a great retail and wholesale drygoods business.[84] The most widely publicized ventures were the sending of the two United States warships, lent to the relief committees of Boston and New York, the *Jamestown* and the *Macedonian*. Captain R. B. Forbes commanded the one, Captain George De Kay of New York, a former officer in the Argentine Navy, the other. The novel use of war vessels for such an errand of mercy captured the imagination of both Americans and Britishers. So did the decision to send as chaplain of the *Macedonian*, the picturesque, epigrammatic, and powerful Boston preacher to sailors, Father Edward Taylor, whom Emerson admired and who still lives as Father Mapple in *Moby Dick*. Father Taylor's friends bought him "quite a splendid personal outfit"; but when he returned home he had barely the clothing to keep himself decent and warm; he had characteristically given all he had, piece by piece, to needy sufferers.[85]

The Central Relief Committee of the Society of Friends in Dublin became the almoner of almost all the voluntary aid apart from that dispensed by the Catholic hierarchy and by government officials. It did its work with "great sagacity and prudence." [86] Americans also learned that British authorities had cooperated efficiently and cheerfully in the distribution of voluntary relief offerings. Supplies found

---

[82] Lord *et al.*, *History of the Archdiocese of Boston*, 437.

[83] Elihu Burritt, "An Olive Leaf for the American People: Friends of Humanity!" Reprinted in *Niles' National Register*, May 1, 1847.

[84] Charles Haswell, *Reminiscences of an Octogenarian of the City of New York* (New York: Harper, 1896), 419, 432.

[85] Sarah Forbes Hughes, *Letters and Recollections of John Murray Forbes* (2 vols.; Boston and New York: Houghton Mifflin, 1899), I, 120-21; Forbes, *The Voyage of the Jamestown on her Errand of Mercy; Personal Reminiscences*, 188 ff.; Robert Collyer, *Father Taylor* (Boston: American Unitarian Association, 1906), 33.

[86] *The American Whig Review*, VI (Dec., 1847), 648.

their way without undue delay from the depots to those to whom the Central Committee had issued orders allocating food.[87]

It is impossible to estimate the effect of American relief in terms of suffering mitigated or lives saved, for it was enmeshed with aid from Britain and the colonies. But Dublin's *Nation*, the organ of Young Ireland, a group of chauvinistic patriots, declared that American aid had saved the lives of nearly 1,000,000 by assistance to Ireland or to Irish emigrants.[88]

British opinion about American relief varied. Only occasionally was a sour note heard. A London paper, for example, betrayed its class consciousness by expressing fear that all the charity, American and British, would keep the lower orders of peasantry from returning to work.[89] In commenting on the exuberant Irish praise of America for its sympathy and relief, the London *Enquirer*, with some point, wrote that it was lamentable "that this gratitude to America cannot be publicly expressed in Ireland without insult to England, where both Government and people are making all possible sacrifices to lessen the calamity which has befallen a portion of our countrymen."[90] More typical was the editorial in *The Times* of London which confessed to "a sensation of wounded pride when we hear of our own fellow subjects becoming objects of republican benevolence and our social sores being exposed in the cities of New England." But if the British could not rescue the Irish themselves, then, continued the *Times*, it was hardly becoming to resent the assistance of generous kinsmen and friends.[91]

British officials and other spokesmen often expressed appreciation without reservation and in the warmest terms. At a festival given by the Lord Mayor of London, Lord John Russell spoke "in handsome, nay grateful and enthusiastic terms of the kind and sympathizing aid sent by the generous Americans to the distressed Irish in their hour of need."[92] Lord Palmerston sent to Secretary of State Buchanan the thanks of the government and nation. At about the same time an immense meeting in London unanimously and with loud cheers adopted a resolution of appreciation for American generosity.[93]

[87] New York *Evening Post*, May 19, 1847.
[88] Cited in *Niles' National Register*, May 7, 1847.
[89] *Boston Daily Journal*, May 7, 1847.
[90] *Ibid.*, May 10, 1847.
[91] *Niles' National Register*, May 1, 1847.
[92] *Ibid.*, June 12, 1847.
[93] *Ibid.*, May 1, 1847.

The lot of the beneficiary is not always an easy one, for there is a temptation to look somewhat critically on the giver. And there were indeed some circumstances which might have provoked some edginess. Thus Captain Forbes, in receiving the grateful deputations when he handed over the *Jamestown's* cargo to the authorities at Cork, tactlessly spoke of the necessity of raising the moral standard of the people. What the Irish may have felt was not reported in the American press which spoke of the incident.[94] The *Cork Constitution* somewhat later did, to be sure, think that damaged Indian corn brought to Ireland, teeming with swarms of little insects, was bound to inflict mischief in the provisions in the storehouses not so tainted.[95] But this was the exception which proved the overwhelmingly grateful response to American aid. It is to be matched by the reports Mrs. Nicholson made regarding the valiant efforts of the Irish to master American recipes for Indian corn. These, she remarked, were accepted as "the one thing needful, for they possessed these redeeming qualities: first, they were from America, the land which they loved, for many of their 'kin' were there; next, that though they thought that nobody but negroes ate it—yet negroes *lived* on that food; and 'sure the Americans wouldn't hurt em.' "[96]

In commenting on the enthusiasm shown at Cork when the *Jamestown* docked, the London *Times* declared that the people were "in ecstasies."[97] Typical of the general response was the letter of the Council of the Irish Federation to the American Vice-President, George Mifflin Dallas. The Irish, the Council declared, did not feel humbled at receiving the aid of the American people, however it might reflect on the character of an empire, ostentatious in its pretension to superior wealth, power, and civilization.[98] The Dublin *Freeman's Journal* glowed with enthusiasm for America, contrasting her benevolence with the "slander and abuse" the British heaped on the Irish. "We write with hearts of overflowing gratitude and love, gratitude and love not springing so much from the sense of benefits received, as from a respect for the manner in which they have been rendered."[99] *The Nation*, the organ of Young Ireland, declared that while English journals indulged in invective against Ireland and

94 New York *Evening Post*, May 18, 1847.
95 Cited in *Niles' National Register*, Aug. 7, 1847.
96 Nicholson, *Annals of the Famine in Ireland*, 54-55.
97 *Boston Daily Journal*, May 3, 1847.
98 *Niles' National Register*, May 1, 1847.
99 *Ibid.*, May 7, 1847.

while the English clung to the food supplies they might have shared, American periodicals emphasized Irish merit in order to speed the aid Americans so generously gave.[100] Perhaps as good a summary of Irish feelings about American aid were the remarks of Father Meehan at a public meeting in Dublin, when he declared that "should any calamity threaten America, we who have escaped the famine and pestilence produced by England, would assist her." [101]

The Irish famine called forth the most impressive, and in a sense, the first truly national campaign to relieve suffering in another land without respect to political and nationalistic considerations. It is true that the "Greek fever" of the 1820's did, in its last stages, direct attention to the relief of suffering, but the individual American response was by and large based on other feelings. It is also true that the Greek relief campaign used the big meeting, the benefit, the church collection, to raise money. But the Irish relief campaign carried these methods much further.

The failure of the movement to enlist government aid for purposes other than helping in the transport of a small part of the produce collected for the starving encouraged reliance on voluntary contributions. The Greeks had expressed gratitude for American aid, but now, in the case of the Irish, this sense of gratitude was more readily expressed, for the two countries had many ties. If no one knows just how many lives American aid saved in Ireland, one can say that it helped soften bad feelings on the part of many British toward Americans, that it evoked a great national response in Ireland, and that in some measure it encouraged emigrants and would-be emigrants to think of America as a place of refuge, as offering a chance to share in an abundant society. The Irish relief campaign also fixed fairly well the main pattern of American giving for the relief of a disaster abroad—at least for many decades.

[100] Cited in *Niles' National Register*, May 7, 1847.
[101] *Ibid.*, June 5, 1847.

IV

Renewal

Not until a full three decades after the Irish famine of 1847 did American efforts to relieve suffering abroad reach proportions comparable to those at the time of that great disaster. For one thing, nothing so dramatic or far-reaching as the Irish famine took place in any land with close ties to Americans. For another, the plight of America's own disadvantaged and needy attracted ever greater attention. In the 1850's the plight of the Negro and of the poor in the growing cities led to a more accented response. During the Civil War the ordinary charitable and missionary activities were not only kept up: they actually expanded. This was of course during the very years when the care of sick and wounded soldiers and the succor of their widows and children made unprecedented demands on compassion.[1] Both during and after the War the administration of charity also shifted increasingly from local groups to national organizations. In view of the scope of benevolence on the home front the wonder is that distress in foreign lands aroused the interest and sympathy of so many American donors.

What was done abroad must be put not only in the context of the demands which the Civil War and its aftermath made on American charity but also in that of a series of natural catastrophes in various parts of the nation. In the 1860's, 1870's, and 1880's fires and floods resulted in havoc on a vast scale. The record of a single organization, the New York Chamber of Commerce, is suggestive. In 1856 it contributed to the sufferers from a fire in Troy; in 1865, it responded to needs directly related to the War by giving $56,000 for

---

[1] Linus Pierpont Brockett, *The Philanthropic Results of the War in America* (New York: Sheldon, 1863), *passim*. See also J. M. Ludlow, "War-Charities—National and International, *Good Words* VI (1865), 213-220.

relief in Savannah and East Tennessee. Again, in 1866, it gave $106,-
000 to survivors of a dreadful fire in Portland, Maine. It gave $57,000
to the uprooted men, women, and children in the disastrous Johnstown flood and $1,044,000 for victims of the Chicago fire.[2] The Johns-
town flood and the Chicago disaster called out generous help not
only from the New York Chamber of Commerce; from all over the
country contributions poured into funds for helping those in need.

During the Civil War itself, Ireland's potato crop failed again. In
some places conditions seemed to be almost as bad as they had been
in 1846 and 1847. Americans again responded. In the autumn of 1861
the legislature of Kentucky, a slave state torn by divided loyalties,
by an overwhelming vote instructed its delegation in Washington
to use all appropriate means to induce Congress to give immediate
relief for the distressed in Ireland. The resolution stressed not only
the claims of humanity, but the special claims of the Irish, so many
of whose kinsmen were bravely risking their lives on the battlefield
in defense of the American government and of liberty in time of
great trial.[3] The joint resolution from Kentucky was referred to the
Committee on Foreign Affairs where, apparently, it was pigeon-
holed.[4]

The government again taking no action, voluntary efforts found
expression in New York and in other cities with large Irish-American
populations. At a meeting in the metropolis, held at the Astor
House on May 21, 1862, leading Irish-Americans organized the Committee for the Relief of Ireland. At a later meeting Judge Charles
Patrick Daly, the chairman, summed up what had been done in the
Great Famine: in New York, within a very short time, $171,272 had
been raised in money, together with provisions and clothing valued
at $70,000. Judge Daly noted that leading merchants had taken the
initiative in that crisis and borne the chief burden, and that donations
had been made without respect to religious conviction.

But now the case was different. The $8,000 so far collected had
come largely from Irish maidservants and working people. It was
decided to ask the Vicar General to call for collections in all Catholic

[2] Joseph Bucklin Bishop, *A Chronicle of One Hundred and Fifty Years: The Chamber of Commerce of New York, 1768-1918* (New York: Scribner, 1916), 169 ff.
[3] *Journal of the Senate of the Commonwealth of Kentucky,* 1861, 246, 255, 262;
Journal of the House of Representatives of the Commonwealth of Kentucky, 1861, 337.
According to the Eighth Census of the United States (1860), 22,249 persons in a total
population of 930,201 in Kentucky were born in Ireland.
[4] *Congressional Globe,* 37th Cong., 2d Sess., 1861, XXXII, Pt. 1, 158.

churches, to issue an address to the general public setting forth the conditions in Ireland, and to seek the aid of leading merchants. In naming merchants to the committee and in passing over politicians who saw publicity value in serving on it, Judge Daly infuriated several Tammany men.[5] From time to time special efforts were made to collect funds. In the spring of 1863, for instance, Richard O'Gorman gave a benefit lecture on Edmund Burke at the Cooper Union.[6] Efforts to raise money in places other than New York were made, apparently with indifferent success. Irish-Americans in the Union Army, however, sent funds from their meager pay. According to Linus Pierpont Brockett, $100,000 had been raised for Irish Relief by 1863, but this sum may have been considerably less. Despite some complaints from Ireland about the distribution of American bounty, the Lord Mayor of Dublin in thanking Judge Daly for a recent gift of £500 from the New York committee, assured the donors that their "liberality would bring timely relief to thousands of families in the last stages of want and misery" and that Irish-American sympathy would "render the name of America, ever dear to the Irish people, even dearer."[7]

Even more dramatic was the plight of some 400,000 textile workers in Lancashire. The shutdown of its cotton factories was generally laid at the door of the federal blockade which largely cut off imports of raw cotton from the Confederacy. Goldwin Smith, the Oxford historian, merely summed up a widely held view when, writing in 1864 in the *Atlantic Monthly* about the textile workers, he declared "your civil war paralyzed their industry, brought ruin into their houses, deprived them and their families not only of bread, but, so far as their vision extended, of the hope of bread."[8] But Northern propagandists in England, eager for support in their efforts to dissuade the British government from recognizing the Confederacy, encouraged the workers to believe that the War was a struggle for freedom, and that the sacrifices they were making were in the end

5 *New York Daily Tribune*, May 23, 26, 1862; Harold Earl Hammond, A *Commoner's Judge: The Life and Times of Charles Patrick Daly* (Boston: Christopher Publishing House, 1954), 162.
6 *New York Daily Tribune*, May 4, 5, 7, 1863.
7 Brockett, *The Philanthropic Results of the War in America*, 26; Hammond, A *Commoner's Judge*, 171; C. Knox to Daly, April 6, 1863, Michael Corcoran to Daly, May 13, 1863, Lord Mayor of Dublin to Daly, May 21, 1863, Charles P. Daly Papers, New York Public Library.
8 Goldwin Smith, "England and America," *Atlantic Monthly* XIV (Dec., 1864), 759.

bound to advance the cause of free labor everywhere. In great public meetings spokesmen of the English textile operatives expressed sympathy for the North, opposed the effort of British public figures to bring about recognition of the Confederacy, and agreed to endure as long as possible the hardships the War had brought to their homes.

British response to the sufferings of the Lancashire cotton workers was slow in getting under way. The Poor Law Guardians finally increased the benefits to the needy, but public-spirited citizens saw the pressing need for supplementing this meager relief by private charity. The London Mansion House Committee received contributions not only from British but from Canadian, Australian, Indian and American donors. By midsummer, 1863, Lord Derby reported that about £2,000,000 had been promised or placed in the hands of the various relief committees by voluntary beneficence.[9]

Cotton textile areas in France as well as in England also suffered. According to the New York *Journal of Commerce* the French press was apathetic to the plight of the factory hands. Comparatively few voluntary contributions from the French, it was said, were forthcoming to relieve the distress of workers in Rouen, Dieppe, and Le Havre.[10]

By mid-November, 1862, New Yorkers, particularly leaders in the Chamber of Commerce, were suggesting the need of organized relief of sufferers from the cotton famine. On learning of this, John Bright, an outspoken champion of the Northern cause, wrote to Senator Charles Sumner of his pleasure at the report that "some one in the States has proposed to send something to our aid. If," he added, "a few cargoes of flour could come, say 50,000 barrels, as a gift from persons in your Northern States to the Lancashire working man, it would have a prodigious effect in your favor here." [11]

Such a movement was, in fact, already under way. A circular addressed to the merchants of New York, signed by such eminent leaders as W. E. Dodge, A. A. Low, J. J. Phelps, S. B. Ruggles, and John Taylor Johnson, issued a call for a general meeting. According to the *New York Times*, the speeches and resolutions were humane and businesslike, the proceedings grand and thrilling. On behalf of his

---

[9] *The Economist* XXI (July 11, 1863), 760.

[10] New York *Journal of Commerce*, Jan. 1, 1863; W. Reed West, *Contemporary French Opinion on the American Civil War* (Baltimore: Johns Hopkins Press, 1924), 59-60.

[11] Charles Francis Adams, Jr., *Charles Francis Adams* (Boston and New York: Houghton Mifflin, 1900), 276.

mercantile firm William E. Dodge offered $5,000; John Taylor Johnson, railroad executive, art collector, and patron of New York University, subscribed $2,500. Captain Marshall offered $2,000 and the Babcock brothers pledged an equal amount. Within a few minutes, $26,000 had been raised. Six other firms or individuals gave $1,000 each.[12]

The next day A. T. Stewart, New York's fabulously rich drygoods merchant, sent a check for $10,000 for the suffering operatives "whose return to their usual avocations can be secured by no means other than the complete ascendency of the Union over the rebellious states." He added that "the people of the United States are *certain* to accomplish their object." [13] A well-known firm offered to transport 1,800 tons of supplies to the Lancashire sufferers in its new ship, the *George Griswold*.[14] Within a few days pledges of provisions came in from several points in the North and West, including the 1,000 barrels of flour offered by the New York upstate philanthropist, Gerrit Smith.

The American International Relief Committee for the Suffering Operatives of Great Britain which resulted from the meeting, fused with the Committee of 31 of the New York Chamber of Commerce, several of whose members were also serving on the International Committee. The president and treasurer of the new committee, John C. Green and A. A. Low, were well-to-do China merchants.

The Committee's eloquent *Address to the American People* spelled out the great need of the textile workers. The London *Times* was cited to the effect that conditions were worse than they had ever been since the great Irish famine. "Common humanity," the *Address* continued, "would be the first reason for responding" to such distress. "Common origin, common religion, common language, common hopes, and a common destiny attach us closely to Old England." But there were special reasons for acting in this situation. The American struggle for national existence brought hardship to the operatives of Europe. The obligation to give was thus the greater because the condition that giving was designed to remedy sprang from our struggle for existence. The recipients were strong opponents of the Con-

---

[12] Washington *National Intelligencer*, Dec. 8, 9, 1862; *New York Daily Tribune*, December 6, 7, 1862; *New York Times*, Dec. 5, 1862; American International Relief Committee for the Suffering Operatives of Great Britain, *Report*, 1862-1863 (New York, 1864), 7-8.

[13] *National Intelligencer*, Dec. 9, 1862.

[14] New York *Journal of Commerce*, Dec. 7, 8, 1862.

federacy and of the movement for British recognition of it. The agricultural resources and efforts of America, moreover, made it the
granary of the nations. The appeal continued: "Let us not at this
moment of responsibilities imposed on us by the munificence of the
Ruler, permit our sorrows and burdens to harden us to the peculiar
duties belonging to our position." Let corn be forwarded "with the
generosity that becomes a people who have undergone the greatest
trial that can befall a nation, and who know the value of sympathy
tendered in the moment of suffering." [15]

The *Address* was praised by the London *Times* for its good taste
and feeling.[16] The wording accompanying gifts was important, for
certain donors had given in such a way as to minimize the effects of
their action. Thus one Bostonian had publicly expressed the hope
that the munificence of the New York merchants would shame
Lancashire's callous and selfish millionaires into emulating the superior sense of responsibility of their American counterparts.[17] And
A. T. Stewart, in sending his $10,000 to the Committee, accompanied
it by a letter which the London *Times* found highly offensive. He
only made it manifest, the *Times* observed, that his political and
economic foresight were not equal to his benevolence. On the other
hand, many like Thurlow Weed, who contributed $1,000, echoed
the general sentiments of the framers of the *Address*.

In addition to the International Relief Committee, two other
groups raised money for provisions. By mid-December, 1862, the
Produce Exchange Fund reached $20,825, and the British Residents'
Fund, $18,327. These figures brought the total which all agencies
at this time had raised to $119,327.[18] It is impossible to be certain
of the final amount contributed by the American groups. But it is
likely that the International Relief Committee of the Chamber of
Commerce collected close to $150,000. This, with the other New
York funds, may well have approximated the $265,000 which Lucius
Pierpont Brockett, a careful writer in summing up the Civil War
philanthropies in 1865, thought to be a fair estimate.[19]

On the morning of January 9, 1863, the International Relief Committee assembled at Pier No. 10, East River, to see the *George*

[15] New York *Journal of Commerce*, Dec. 8, 1862; *National Intelligencer*, Dec. 9,
1862; American International Relief Committee, *Report*, 16-17.
[16] *The Times* [London], Dec. 23, 1862.
[17] New York *Journal of Commerce*, Dec. 9, 1862.
[18] *National Intelligencer*, Dec. 13, 1862.
[19] Brockett, *The Philanthropic Results of the War in America*, 25-26; American International Relief Committee, *Report*, 71.

Griswold off on her maiden voyage to Liverpool. Amid the vociferous shouts and cheers of her well-wishers and the salutes of British vessels in the harbor, the ship set forth. "A nobler spectacle was never seen in our beautiful bay," commented the *New York Times*. The cargo, which included 13,236 barrels of flour and other provisions valued at $100,000, had been largely purchased by the International Relief Committee, although the Corn Exchange had loaded into the ship 1,000 barrels of provisions.[20] In the latter part of January the *Arkwright* and the *James Adger Jr.* transported 3,000 barrels of flour supplied by the International Relief Committee.[21] The R. B. Buck Company provided free transit in the *Hope* of provisions donated by Ichabod Washburn, Gerrit Smith, Joseph Shipley and others.[22] Not to be outdone, Philadelphians contributed 5,020 barrels of foodstuffs valued at $35,000. The provisions were loaded into the hold of the *Achilles* which took off after a religious ceremony.[23] Other ships carried similar donations.

These gifts were made when relations between Washington and London were severely strained. Englishmen remembered the *Trent* affair—the legally dubious removal by an American naval officer of two Confederate agents from a British steamer. In the United States, bad blood had been stirred up by the openly friendly attitude of the British official class toward the Confederacy. Moreover, in July, 1862, the British-built *Alabama* had been allowed to slip out of Liverpool harbor to hoist the Stars and Bars and to embark on its course of sinking Northern ships, an act which seemed a particularly unfriendly violation of British neutrality to almost everyone in the Union. That American generosity was shown in the midst of so much ill feeling toward British policy was the result of several factors. The sense of responsibility that many Americans felt for the unemployment of the Lancashire textile workers reflected genuine humanitarian sympathy. But giving was also regarded as a means of cementing the ties between the Lancashire working people and the British middle classes on the one hand, and the Northern cause on the other. Many also hoped that the donations would improve the strained relations between the two countries. Under the caption "Columbia Brings Substantial Blessings to Her Poor Relations over the Sea" a cartoonist in the sophisticated Boston magazine, *Vanity Fair*, took full satiric

[20] *New York Times*, Jan. 9, 10, 1863; *New York Daily Tribune*, Jan. 9, 12, 1863.
[21] New York *Journal of Commerce*, Jan. 24, 1863.
[22] *The Times* [London], Dec. 23, 1862.
[23] New York *Journal of Commerce*, Jan. 21, 1863; *National Intelligencer*, Jan. 22, 1863.

advantage of the incongruities in the whole situation: he depicted a bulldog barking at Columbia as she handed a stocking of gifts to a British workingman, with American bags of grain in the foreground, an American relief ship in the background, and framed reminders of "intervention" and *Alabama* on the walls.[24]

The British working and middle classes greatly appreciated the American donations. Even the London *Times*, so often severely critical of the North, declared that the general spirit animating the generosity of the American bankers and merchants might well, if extended to the press, the politicians, and the bulk of the people, replace existing chilly relations between the two countries with a cordiality that would make war impossible not only in the immediate future but forever.[25]

One need not claim that American gifts changed materially the course of Anglo-American relations during the war, but there was point to the comment by the son of the American Minister in London. "That in the midst of such stress—carnage, wounds, and devastation," wrote Charles Francis Adams Jr., "food by the cargo was forthcoming as a gift from those involved in the real agony of war to those for whom that war had occasioned distress, passing though sharp, was neither unnoticed nor barren of results." [26]

Even on the Continent the story of the American gifts to the Lancashire workingmen was heard. In speaking at a meeting in Paris early in 1866 to collect funds for American freedmen, the Protestant clergyman, M. Grandpierre, did not mention the trifling help the Americans had given to the needy cotton operatives in France. But he made much of the disinterested and magnanimous generosity to the English workingmen, even representing the gifts as amounting to three or four million dollars! [27]

The American government did not supplement the private contributions for relief in Ireland, England, and France. In view of the pressure of the Civil War this was understandable. But also in the decades that followed, the government did not resume even the limited role it had on earlier occasions played in the relief of distress in foreign lands. Consular and diplomatic officials did, to be sure, report disasters in countries to which they were accredited. In some

[24] *Vanity Fair* VI (Dec. 20, 1862), 295.
[25] *The Times* [London], Dec. 23, 1862.
[26] Adams, *Charles Francis Adams*, 277.
[27] John Bigelow, *Retrospections of an Active Life* (5 vols.; New York: Baker and Taylor, 1909-1913), III, 343.

cases suggestions that relief contributions would be welcome were made in general terms, as when our Minister to Switzerland, in reporting in 1868 the disastrous floods in Tessin, observed that there seemed no indication of an intention to appeal especially to Swiss Americans, but that "this cry of distress appeals with equal force to the benevolent of our countrymen of whatever origin or nationality they may be." [28]

If the Swiss could take care of their own, this was not the case of less fortunate peoples. In the same year as the Tessin floods, 1868, earthquakes, tidal waves and fires destroyed large parts of leading Peruvian cities—Callao, Arica, Arequipa, and Iquique, and great areas in Ecuador. The American Minister to Peru, Judge Alvin Hovey, who had served as a brigadier general in the Civil War, urged the commander of our South Pacific fleet to rescue the ruined and starving people insofar as his resources permitted. "The generosity of our country, in days gone by," Hovey wrote to Secretary of State Seward, "has left a record that will never be forgotten—Greece, Poland, Hungary, and Ireland, with no greater, if not far less claims for aid or charity, have found that in the United States there were feeling hearts and open hands for those who deeply suffer. Will not our generous-hearted countrymen add Peru and Ecuador to their noble list?" To Hovey's request for an appeal to the American people for aid, Seward replied that the disasters had deeply moved the sympathies of the President and the people of the United States. Hovey later reported that every article in the American press expressing sympathy had been translated and published in Peruvian newspapers. But his pleas for private and Congressional relief did not, apparently, lead to any organized fund-raising campaign. [29]

Meanwhile, a crisis in North Africa was brought to America's attention. Late in 1867 and early in 1868 the consulate in Tunis

[28] George Harrington to William Seward (Secretary of State), Berne, Oct. 10, 1868, *Papers Relating to Foreign Affairs* (Washington: Govt. Printing Office), 1868, Pt. II, 226-27.

[29] Alvin Hovey to Seward, Lima, August 22, Sept. 14, Oct. 1, 28, 1868, Seward to Hovey, Washington, Sept. 30, Oct. 1, 1868, *ibid.*, 870-71, 874-75, 885-88. The *New York Times* reported the earthquakes in detail, emphasizing not only the horrible destruction and suffering, but trying to explain the causes and role in nature of these phenomena. *New York Times*, Sept. 13, 14, 15, 19, 1868. Henry Meigs, an American builder of railroads in Peru and other South American countries, who spent money lavishly in breaking down opposition to those opposing the lucrative government contracts he sought from the Peruvian government, was reported to have given $75,000 for immediate relief and to have offered a draft for $200,000 additional relief if needed. *National Intelligencer*, Sept. 17, Oct. 16, 1868.

reported widespread death by famine and pestilence. In the city of Tunis alone, 142 died on a single day. Rural roadsides were strewn with dead bodies. By February 27, 1868, Consul Heap was reporting that an average of 200 were dying each day. He noted that Christians and Jews received some aid from their coreligionists, but that Arab Mohammedans were left by their brethren to die with a stoical apathy that seemed incomprehensible. Although it was clear, Heap noted, that the Arabs had no such claims on Americans as had the Irish, still, they did have the claim of a common humanity, and he appealed to the State Department to put the Tunisian cause before the American public. Many, Heap continued, looked to the United States for help, having heard of its reputation for generosity to nations in distress. The situation became truly grim when typhus struck the country. Americans in the United States and several who were traveling abroad sent to the Tunis consulate donations which enabled Heap to clothe and feed a considerable number of women and children.[30]

The post-Civil War years saw one fairly well organized campaign, largely the result of the leadership of Dr. Samuel Gridley Howe and the memory of what had been done almost half a century earlier for the Greeks. When the Cretans, who had remained under Turkish rule at the time Greece won her freedom, struck for their independence in 1866, Howe heard the old call of the Hellenes. At his initiative a committee was formed in Boston to collect funds. At the first public meeting Howe, Oliver Wendell Holmes, Wendell Phillips, Edward Everett Hale, and other notables spoke. The speeches emphasized the claims of Crete on the sympathies of the civilized world. The struggle was presented, as that of the Greeks had been, as a contest between Christianity and Mohammedanism, between freedom and despotism. Governor Andrews addressed one meeting and amidst great applause introduced resolutions calling for aid. New England women's societies provided some 10,000 garments. Within a few weeks after the campaign began, Boston and its neighbors had raised $37,000. New York also bestirred itself.[31] The press, both

[30] George Heap to William H. Seward, Secretary of State, Tunis, Dec. 20, 1867, Jan. 4, Feb. 27, April 24, 1868, Department of State, National Archives.
[31] Laura E. Richards, ed., *Letters and Journals of Samuel Gridley Howe* (2 vols.; Boston: Dana Estes, 1906-1909), II, 537 ff.

secular and religious, taking vigorous positions in behalf of the Cretans, asked for American benevolence toward them.[32]

Two months later Dr. Howe was on his way, with a young seventeen-year-old daughter, to administer relief much as he had embarked on a similar errand of mercy forty-five years before. Thanks to home support, he was able to distribute clothing, provisions, and supplies.

The immediate problem was to help some 12,000 Cretan refugees in Greece. Uprooted, without clothing, in a state of near starvation, these women, children, and old men stood in great need of aid. With the help of American missionaries Howe distributed clothing and food. Determined to make the refugees in part self-supporting, he provided the women with material for making commercial bags. Since many of them did not know how to use the needle, wives of American missionaries opened work schools to teach them needed skills. But the flow of new refugees went on. In an effort to stem the tide Howe, with the help of Cretan rebels, engaged in the risky venture of transporting food and clothing to the interior of Crete, where civilians were in a desperate plight. But what he had to give was too little to check the flights to Greece.

The Howes returned to America to urge further giving. A fair at Music Hall in Boston resulted in contributions of clothing and food valued at $30,000. Through *The Cretan*, a little newspaper, and through addresses at public meetings, Howe urged Americans to stimulate the government to use its influence with the Powers to intervene in behalf of the Cretans.[33] But this was not to be; the Turks did not withdraw from the island until 1898 and Crete did not become a part of Greece until 1913. Frustrated in his efforts to secure political action, Howe kept at the job of relief. He had harsh words for the reluctance of American naval vessels to transport Cretan refugees to Greece, especially after Russia, France, Italy, and Austria had begun to aid in the task. Howe reassured donors that their gifts had gladdened the hearts and strengthened the hands of the Cretans, the more so because American aid was the first substantial sign of

[32] *The Nation* III (Oct. 4, 1866, 275-77; IV (Jan. 24, 1867), 70; IV (Apr. 18, 1867), 318-19; VII (July 2, 1868), 10-11; *The Monthly Religious Magazine* XXXIX (May, 1868), 379-87; *Hours at Home* IV (April, 1867), 554-561; *Letters and Journals of Samuel Gridley Howe*, II, 548 ff.

[33] Samuel G. Howe, *The Cretan Refugees and their American Helpers* (Boston: Lee and Shepard, 1868), 45.

sympathy for the insurgents. Howe also felt that American voluntary contributions far exceeded those from England.[34]

In view of proximity and many other ties, British relief both preceded and exceeded that from America during the dark days of France in her war with Prussia in 1870 and 1871. On February 6, 1871, British provision trains were unloaded in Paris. Three days later fifty more carloads of relief arrived, for which desperate citizens queued up.[35]

It was with great satisfaction that E. B. Washburne, the American Minister in Paris, learned that the New York Chamber of Commerce had decided to aid the needy French.[36] At a meeting on February 5th a committee of the Chamber of Commerce decided to cable $10,000 immediately to the American Legation. At the same meeting the committee adopted a resolution which declared that America ought to aid the French, not for political reasons, but as "a Christian nation" acting "in the sacred name of charity." In three days the New York committee collected, chiefly from large givers, $12,650.[37] Following the example of the Chamber of Commerce, the New York Producer's Exchange issued an appeal urging that even though France had foolishly provoked the war, aid should be given and quickly. The appeal reminded members of the Exchange that France had generously helped the Americans during their struggle for independence. Several speakers at the meeting which initiated the Exchange's movement emphasized the Christian obligation of charity. The Reverend Dr. Henry Bellows of the Unitarian Church of All Souls noted that the Exchange was "a graniverous, not a carniverous creature" and challenged the group to make its place of business "a House of God." Archibald Baxter, who offered the resolution, declared that the Exchange was obligated to give because the war which had been so disastrous to France had been "immensely profitable to the Exchange." Some $6,600 was collected at the meeting, a sum later augmented to $15,905.[38]

The New York Chamber of Commerce, in a second appeal issued in early March, expressed the hope that in the "rivalry" of England,

34 *Ibid.*, 12.
35 *New York Times*, Feb. 6, 9, 1871; E. B. Washburne, *Recollections of a Minister to France, 1869-1877* (2 vols.; New York: Scribner, 1887), II, 1.
36 Washburne, *Recollections*, II, 1-2.
37 *New York Times*, Feb. 5, 8, 1871.
38 *Ibid.*, Feb. 10, 1871.

Belgium, and America to aid France, America "will not be out-distanced." It asked for contributions of grain and seed for the farmers of northern and central France and promised to pay freight costs on any consignment to New York over 100 bushels. The Chamber of Commerce sent out two ships, the *Supply* and the *Relief*. The total New York contribution, $124,782.72, had come from the two commercial groups, from associated firms, and from well-to-do individuals. It was in no sense a popular "drive." [39]

Other cities also bestirred themselves. Chicago held a large meeting at the Opera House. Cleveland was the center of the Northern Ohio Relief Association, which numbered fifty vice-presidents in important northern Ohio towns and which asked for funds for the needy in both France and Germany. [40] On February 11 the San Francisco Stock Exchange wired $1,000 to the New York fund. Ten days later the San Francisco Chamber of Commerce sent $10,000 to New York. An independent San Francisco effort was the collection for French relief on St. Patrick's day by the city's Irish societies. San Jose and Santa Clara collected $1,500. [41]

The most picturesque movement originated in Boston. Citizens subscribed $81,000 to French relief, and undertook entertainments and clothing collections to sustain their drive. Theatrical and musical performances were held and Julia Ward Howe gave a reading. A large fair also proved a successful fund-raising device. Bostonians also supported the ambitious scheme of Captain Robert B. Forbes to send an entire ship filled with relief supplies for the French. Forbes had conceived the idea of the relief ship for Ireland in 1847; he and his friends now hoped to gain nationwide support for their venture by securing a government ship. [42]

Meantime in Washington Senator Samuel Pomeroy, a leading Republican who had been president of the relief committee during the famine in Kansas in 1860 and 1861, introduced a joint resolution authorizing Navy vessels to transport donations of food from Boston for the suffering people of France and Germany. Senator Jacob Howard of Michigan failed to see the propriety of including Germany

[39] *Ibid.*, Feb. 15, 20, March 2, 21, 24, 1871.

[40] *Ibid.*, Feb. 5, 11, 1871. It is worth noting that in Cincinnati the German victory was celebrated and that no funds were raised for the needy French. This was also true of other cities with large German populations.

[41] *Ibid.*, Feb. 11, 19, March 3, 4, 1871.

[42] *Ibid.*, Feb. 3, 4, 9, 11, 12, 15, 1871; Francis Greenwood Peabody, "An Episode in International Philanthropy," *New England Quarterly* VI (March, 1933), 85-97.

inasmuch as its people were "tolerably well supplied just now." But others noted the presence in America of German-Americans who had relatives in need, and still others, including Carl Schurz, emphasized the aid Germany had given the North in the Civil War in taking federal loans and in providing German soldiers. Charles Sumner gracefully remarked that both France and Germany had befriended us on different occasions and that it was better to give in the spirit of true Christian charity than to try to weigh the value of French and German contributions to America. The House concurred in the Senate's action after amending the joint resolution to permit naval vessels to transport donations from New York and Philadelphia as well as from Boston.[43]

By a fortunate coincidence, the *Worcester*, a brand new steam-and-sail-propelled sloop of war was ready in the Charlestown Navy Yard to make her maiden voyage. The Navy received without enthusiasm the plea of the Boston committee to designate the *Worcester* as the ship of transport. But social and political pressure induced the Secretary of the Navy to consent. The ship was loaded with flour, beef, peas and pilot bread, and officered by Commander William D. Whiting and Lieutenant Commander Alfred T. Mahan. Young Francis Peabody was sent with the *Worcester* as a supercargo, while two prominent Bostonians took a steamer to England to oversee the transit across the Channel and the distribution of the gifts. A violent explosion in the boiler of the *Worcester* the third day out made it necessary to depend on sails through heavy gales. When the *Worcester* finally docked at Plymouth it was learned that the French Commune had replaced the Republican government and that there was no responsible government to whom the cargo could be assigned. So the cargo was sold in the London market and the commissioners took the cash to France to distribute through the international relief committee and the American Legation. Edmund Dwight, one of the commissioners, reported that he found "the French to be in no need of provisions generally, and that the few who were willing to receive the supplies sent out from Boston were not able to pay the transportation to its destination."

Young Peabody, later to become a distinguished Harvard professor and pioneer in social ethics, was deeply disappointed, as he had pictured himself handing out food to famishing French youngsters.

[43] *Congressional Globe*, 41st Cong., 3d Sess., 1871, XLIII, Pt. 2, 953-56, 1000, 1043, 1072.

"Thus this movement," he wrote almost sixty years later, "undertaken with such enthusiasm and generosity, may be regarded as an illustration of the ill-advised sentimentalism in which the history of philanthropy abounds. It was a hasty and precipitate expression of generous emotion, offering what was not wanted in an extravagant and futile way." Yet the French received what they most needed, a substantial sum of money, and, as Peabody concluded, "the French temperament is fed by sentiment as truly as by bread." [44]

Upon receiving the initial $10,000 from the New York Chamber of Commerce, Minister Washburne sought French advice on how to distribute the relief. A commission was set up headed by the Finance Minister, Ernest Pickard. Minister Washburne named to sit on it an American gentleman of "honor, intelligence, and respectability," Joseph Karrick Riggs, long a resident of Paris. In addition to the funds that Washburne turned over to the commission, he asked Stephen Lee and other Americans to distribute funds among the poor in the Loire valley, and he himself dispensed part of the American gift. Minister Jules Fabre wrote to Washburne that he was "infinitely touched by the striking mark of sympathy which France had received from free America." He begged the American Minister to convey his gratitude to those who had aided France in the hour of her cruel trial.[45]

What was said about American aid ranged from the eloquent expression of Jules Fabre to the mellow disillusionment of Francis Peabody in his last years. But the episode had its own special significance. It was the first substantial philanthropy from America to war-harassed Europeans since the Greek struggle for independence. It introduced Clara Barton to Europe and gave her first-hand experience with the recently formed Red Cross movement. Leaving the retreat in which she was recuperating, she did some work in the field for which her work in the Civil War stood her in good stead; she also used contributions from New York, Boston, and other places to set up workshops in which needy civilians sewed garments as a means of tiding themselves through an emergency.[46] American participation in relieving victims of the Franco-Prussian war also reflected the mixture of voluntary giving and government aid. It combined giving in kind with giving in cash. It stemmed only in slight degree from political

[44] Peabody, *New England Quarterly* VI, 94-96.
[45] Washburne, *Recollections of a Minister to France*, II, 2-3; *New York Times*, March 22, 25, 1871.
[46] William E. Barton, *The Life of Clara Barton, Founder of the American Red Cross* (2 vols.; Boston and New York: Houghton Mifflin), II, 10-54.

considerations or conscience of obligation; it was chiefly a mark of Christian charity and of humanitarianism.

Proximity made reciprocal aid between American and Canadian cities in time of disaster natural, and much easier than the sending of succor across the Atlantic. St. John in New Brunswick generously sent help to Boston and Chicago when these cities were struck by devastating fires. In June, 1877, a horrible conflagration destroyed two-thirds of the area of St. John. Property damage was estimated at $12,000,000. Victims were homeless, hungry, and in desperate need of clothing. The mayor of Portland, Maine, at once cabled that citizens were forwarding by "this evening's steamer, all the cooked provisions we could gather. Please telegraph me what you need most—whether provisions, blankets, and the like, or money." Mayor Prince of Boston telegraphed at once $5,000, and Boston's relief committee raised in all about $50,000 in cash and supplies, dispatching immediate help in the United States Revenue cutter *Gallatin*. Philadelphia's leading banker, A. J. Drexel, telegraphed $3,000 with the welcome words "more coming." Chicago, Detroit, New York, and other cities also sent contributions. Church groups, lodges, YMCA's, and other organizations forwarded clothing. Thus the relief effort took on something of a national character even though each city or group acted more or less independently.[47]

Three years later the failure of the wheat crop in many places in Central Europe and of the potato crop in Ireland, presented the American people with a far greater and more complex problem than had any of the preceding claims on their benevolence. By the end of the year 1879 Europe was short an estimated 200,000,000 bushels of wheat. According to a contemporary champion of benevolence, the Reverend T. De Witt Talmage, American speculators cornered the wheat market, stacked the warehouses, and demanded fifty cents a bushel. Europe retaliated by importing grain from Russia, South America, and Australia. In one week the markets of the American Northwest bought over 15,000,000 bushels, of which only 4,000,000 were exported. The "kings of the wheat market said to Europe, 'Bow down before us, and starve.'" Suddenly America was startled to find that flour was selling in London for two dollars less a barrel than in New York. Lying idle in New York Harbor were hundreds

[47] George Stewart, *The Story of the Great Fire in St. John, N. B., June 20, 1877* (Toronto: Belford, 1877).

of vessels waiting for cargoes.[48] The market reacted, and by February, 1880, prices were sufficiently reduced to admit of free shipments. In that month the *Trade List* promised a ready sale of the entire surplus of the country at figures very satisfactory to producers.[49] But taking such advantage of the Old World's misfortune was not characteristic of American attitudes. In the end what was done enhanced the American reputation for generosity.

The ethnic and cultural tie figured prominently among the varied motives for giving. New York German-Americans, for example, contributed to the relief of needy Silesian peasants.[50] It was even more marked in the case of Ireland where the situation in 1879-1880 was far worse than anywhere else. The press fed readers with vivid examples of suffering as reported by special correspondents and letters from priests, landlords, and tenants. Moreover, New York was now second to Dublin in the number of Irish-born residents. In other cities, too, those born in Erin or of Irish parents made up an appreciable part of the population. These facts were stressed in appeals for charity. As in the campaigns of 1847 and 1862 for Irish relief, speakers again emphasized common language and religion, the sweat of Irish immigrants in building American canals, railroads, and factories, and the contributions of the Irish to the American wars for independence and self-preservation.[51]

The simple desire to help starving fellow human beings was evident in countless appeals and actions. After drinking to Ireland with "a glass of pure water," the Reverend Jeremiah Rankin declared at a Washington rally that the audience was on hand less in their roles as Irishmen than as Americans, and more as Christians than either as Irishmen or Americans. When calamity strikes, Joseph Hawley remarked at the same meeting, race and religion make no difference.[52]

American experience with want and the paradoxical sense of Amer-

---

[48] Rev. and Mrs. T. De Witt Talmage, *T. De Witt Talmage as I Knew Him* (New York: E. P. Dutton, 1912), 102-03.

[49] *New York Daily Tribune*, Feb. 25, 1880.

[50] *Ibid.*, Feb. 21, 1880.

[51] All these reasons for giving were emphasized at a mass meeting in Washington, D. C., which was addressed by such prominent figures as Chief Justice Carter of the District Court, Senators Thurman, Conklin, and Eaton, Congressmen Randall, Hawley, Loring, Ellis and others, and by such leading business men as Corcoran and Riggs and by such clergymen as Father Boyle and Dr. Rankin, Washington *Evening Star*, Jan. 21, 1880 and *Washington Post*, Jan. 21, 1880.

[52] *Washington Post*, Jan. 21, 1880; Washington *Evening Star*, Jan. 21, 1880.

ican abundance also figured in thought and deed. In contributing $425, the people of Falls City, Nebraska, expressed satisfaction in giving out of an abundance when only a few years earlier the town was itself the object of charity during a drought and grasshopper plague.[53] In similar vein a large meeting at Chattanooga subscribed several hundred dollars on the spot out of gratitude to Ireland for having been the first country to send relief to the city during the yellow fever epidemic of 1878.[54] But the most frequently struck note can be illustrated by an editorial in the *New York Herald* in the spring of 1880: "with our granaries full, with our well-fed children frolicking and laughing in their new outdoor life, their voices as cheerful as the carolling birds, it would seem like a sin, a sin to smite the conscience, if we sent no kindly and commiserating thought and no efficient aid to the desolate hovels to which the season brings no joy, and where wan and wasted mothers gaze in agony upon their pining, moaning, dying babes." [55]

Organized efforts for relief began with Irish-Americans in New York. On December 19, 1879, the Fenian Brotherhood assured Judge Charles Patrick Daly of support in any initiative he might take to help the homeland. Daly summoned some of the colleagues who had served with him on the Committee for the Relief of Ireland in 1862.[56] A new committee was organized. Judge Daly accepted the chairmanship, Richard O'Gorman was named secretary and H. L. Hoguet, president of the Emigrant Industrial Savings Bank, treasurer. The committee decided to study the whole matter before issuing a public appeal. It met on January 7th and its members subscribed $7,365, sending the sum, with the approval of Cardinal McCloskey, to the Mansion House Committee in Dublin, which enjoyed the support of Catholic as well as Protestant bishops of Ireland.[57] As reports of the increasing distress crossed the Atlantic, the Committee issued 40,000 copies of "An Address to the People of the United States."

[53] *New York Herald*, Feb. 23, 1880.

[54] *Washington Post*, Feb. 6, 1880.

[55] *New York Herald*, March 10, 1880.

[56] *New York Daily Tribune*, Jan. 18, 1880; Harold Earl Hammond, A *Commoner's Judge*, 297; H. L. Hoguet, Emigrant Industrial Savings Bank, to Charles Daly, Feb. 12, 1880, Adolph Sanger (attorney for Daly) to Daly, Feb. 18, 1880, Eugene B. Murtha to Daly, Feb. 28, 1880, Charles Daly Papers. The volume for 1878-79 also has pertinent material on the relations of the Fenian Brotherhood of the District of Manhattan to the relief movement.

[57] *New York Daily Tribune*, Jan. 18, 1880; *New York Herald*, Jan. 1, 7, 31, 1880.

Directed particularly to Americans of Irish descent, the appeal also called on the whole public for help.

Meantime public meetings were organized in various cities, collections taken, and committees named. Leading members of Congress addressed a meeting in Washington, which raised over $3,000 on the spot. In Philadelphia the sponsors included such prominent men as John Wanamaker, George W. Childs, A. J. Drexel, and John Welch. Although the response was at first disappointing, within little more than a month the committee had over $11,000 in hand. The principal speaker at the public meeting in Boston was Wendell Phillips, who denounced England as responsible for Ireland's ills. Seven hundred dollars was collected. By early February Boston's central relief committee had $5,000, a sum to rise to $63,793 by late March. In St. Louis a public meeting at the Exchange raised $5,000 in provisions and cash. Galveston's relief committee reported $1,412, that of Sioux City, $3,000. The San Francisco committee raised $2,000.[58]

The work of these more or less representative committees was supplemented by contributions of the Irish societies. The Irish-American organizations in New York responsible for the St. Patrick's Day parade and celebrations raised considerable sums. In Boston the twenty-nine Irish societies could not agree on many matters, including proper channels of fund raising, but one, the Charitable Irish Society, gathered $1,000 by late February. In Brooklyn the St. Vincent de Paul Society subscribed $2,000, sending the sum directly to the parent organization in Ireland with the request it was to be given to the needy without respect to creed.[59]

Through church collections Catholics also contributed. Early in January Archbishop Wood of Philadelphia instructed priests to receive contributions. Over $7,000 was given at masses in the Scranton churches. Cardinal McCloskey of New York met with a remarkable response to his request for contributions. On the first Sunday after he had made it, $28,000 were given in New York churches. By mid-February, 1880, $52,711 had been sent from the archdiocese of New York to Catholic bishops in Ireland. Archbishop Gibbons of Baltimore and other members of the hierarchy made similar appeals. At the end of January Catholic churches in the Boston diocese re-

---

[58] *New York Herald*, Jan. 7, 11, 21, 31, Feb. 3, 5, 21, 22, 1882; *Boston Daily Advertiser*, Feb. 13, 1880, March 5, 26, 1880.
[59] *New York Herald*, Jan. 27, 1880; *Boston Daily Advertiser*, Feb. 21, 1880.

ported $4,117. The Hartford diocese contributed $23,764; that of St. Louis, $4,814; the Buffalo diocese, $15,101; Chicago, $15,000.[60] Eugene Kelley and Company, New York bankers, reported in early March that the firm had sent to Ireland $136,700, chiefly the contributions of Catholic churches.[61]

Protestant clergymen also appealed for contributions. No doubt many Protestants did give, though the newspaper press seldom reported collections in Protestant churches.[62] On the other hand, even though many Protestants shared nativist prejudices, the outspokenness of Dr. Wild of the Union Congregational Church in Brooklyn was, judging from the newspaper accounts, exceptional: Dr. Wild urged from the pulpit that not a cent be given to "political Roman Catholic agitators," that, if one wanted to give, he had best do it through the committee of the Duchess of Marlborough.[63] The Yorkville Citizens Association, speaking as nativists, declared that Americans had best take care of their own, letting the Irish send contributions to the Pope and the English feed the Irish poor.[64] By contrast Jewish congregations seem to have been more generous than Protestant ones. The *American Hebrew*, in reporting the initiative of the Young Men's Hebrew Association in fund raising for the Irish needy, declared that the Israelites should demonstrate that "under the sacred banner of charity we can join hands with every race and labor for a common end." [65] Commending the general response to the cries of Ireland, the *New York Daily Tribune* declared that "no sect or class among our fellow-citizens . . . has contributed more generously or with more hearty good will than the Hebrews." It was high time, the *Tribune* added, that the public should examine its long cherished views of this race which, next to Quakers, managed its charities with more skill and wisdom than any other group. "The poor despised Jew is now in a position to retaliate for the hate and injustice with which his Gentile brother pursued him for centuries. We now see how he chooses to act." [66]

---

[60] *New York Herald*, Jan. 7, 12, 22, 25, 26, 27, Feb. 13, 14, 22, March 9, 13, 18, 21, 1880; *Boston Daily Advertiser*, Feb. 2.

[61] *New York Herald*, March 3, 1880. A few days later the *Herald* reported that the Brooklyn diocese had contributed a total of $20,335.69. *New York Herald*, March 9, 1880.

[62] *Ibid.*, Feb. 13, 1880.

[63] *Ibid.*, Jan. 26, 1880.

[64] *Ibid.*, March 13, 1880.

[65] *Ibid.*, Feb. 14, 1880.

[66] *New York Daily Tribune*, Feb. 25, 1880.

The contributions of Catholics and other religious groups, of well-to-do members of the business community, including Irish-Americans, and of the general public, were substantial. But in view of the prevailing prosperity of the country and the great need of the 300,000 Irish men, women, and children suffering from lack of food, what was given in the early weeks of 1880 seemed to some observers insufficient. One reason was a disagreement about the causes of the famine and the most effective relief.

Some Americans held that the only solution for what seemed to be a chronic problem was emigration. Under the leadership of Robert A. Johnston, a New York merchant, the Fermanagh Relief Association was organized to assist tenant farmers in northern Ireland in emigrating to the States. But collecting funds was not easy. As late as February 8, the Association had been able to raise only $5,420. Two weeks later it reported that it had forwarded 200 steamship tickets to northern Ireland.[67] Much more successful was the Irish Emigrant Society. Between November 1, 1879, and February 28, 1880, it remitted to Ireland drafts in small amounts totaling $221,114, and, in larger sums, an amount equalling $23,000.[68] Most of the emigrants aided by the Society received free passage and railway fare. Sometimes additional aid was given. The Catholic bishop of Minnesota, John Ireland, donated or provided lands enabling a hundred families to come to that state. Steamship lines paid the passages and railways paid the fares.[69]

In view of the nativist tradition such means of alleviating the lot of the Irish were sure to arouse criticism. The editorial policies of three newspapers, each representing a special emphasis, are characteristic of this opposition. The *New York Daily Tribune* declared that America had endured too many pauper immigrants, that it wanted only those able to establish themselves on western farms. "We could almost better afford to feed the Irish at home than to have them thronging our eastern cities, overtaxing our charities, and overflowing our market for unskilled labor."[70] The *Boston Daily Advertiser*, representing the older business community in a heavily populated Irish-American area, attributed Ireland's ills to dishonest leadership,

---

[67] *New York Herald*, Jan. 7, 10, Feb. 8, 22, 1880.
[68] *Ibid.*, Feb. 28, 1880.
[69] *Ibid.*, March 13, 1880.
[70] *New York Daily Tribune*, March 18, 1880.

general sloth, refusal to encourage British capital for the development of industry and, above all, overpopulation. Admitting that an exodus seemed to be the most likely remedy, the *Daily Advertiser* favored emigration to Canada, not to New England.[71] And the *Chicago Tribune* felt that the British, by exploiting the Irish people, had driven them to America against their will, and that Americans were thus bearing a burden that was properly England's.[72]

Further emigration to the United States seemed to many Americans of Irish background, as well as to old stock, an unsatisfactory solution. In their minds the cause of the chronic famines was not sloth, nor bad leadership, nor the accidents of weather, but the prevailing system of absentee landlordism, together with the other ties that subordinated Ireland to England. This view was publicized by the National Irish Land League. Its spokesmen insisted that charity sent to Ireland for food or for emigration found its way into the pockets of the landlords. The Land Leaguers also held that two large relief funds, those of the Mansion House Committee and of the Duchess of Marlborough, were dominated by men and women who had neither understanding of nor true sympathy for the Irish people. Both funds, it was maintained, were used to bolster an unjust land tenure system. Relief was refused to tenants who could not or would not pay their rents. The whole controversy was sharpened when Charles Stewart Parnell and his lieutenant, John Dillon, arrived in the later part of 1879 to arouse sympathy for the Land League and to collect funds.

At first Parnell declared, in both interviews and speeches, that he had not come to America to collect money for famine relief, for he was convinced in view of American generosity in 1847, that it was unnecessary for him now to ask for money to keep Ireland's starving people alive.[73] He found, however, that many Irish-Americans were unwilling to give to the political activities of the Land League when their kinfolk were starving. He also quickly discovered that native Americans resented the interjection of Irish political controversies when the pressing need was for food. An influential section of the press took Parnell severely to task for contributing to the further starvation of his countrymen by confusing the American public and thus deterring it from giving for famine relief. The *New York Daily*

[71] *Boston Daily Advertiser*, Jan. 6, 10, 24, Feb. 12, 1880.
[72] *Chicago Tribune*, Jan. 2, 15, 1880.
[73] *New York Herald*, Jan. 2, 1880.

Tribune declared that less money had been given for relief than would have been the case had Parnell not mixed politics with philanthropy. "In Europe," the *Tribune* added, "America is regarded as a fat cow among nations, but she is not lacking in intelligence and does not submit to being milked by foreign politicians as readily as of old."[74] Other papers, including the *New York World*, the *New York Herald*, the *Boston Transcript*, the *Boston Daily Advertiser*, the Philadelphia *Press*, and the *Washington Post*, took a like stand. As a result of these criticisms Parnell, early in January, 1880, set up a separate Irish Famine Relief Fund to be administered in Ireland by the National Land League.[75]

It is hard to evaluate the effects of Parnell's activities on American giving for Irish relief. In Washington the Congress invited him to speak in the chamber of the House and he called on the President and members of the Cabinet. During his two month's stay, Parnell traveled almost 11,000 miles and spoke in 62 cities. In many of these, as in Brooklyn, Newark, Albany, Philadelphia, Baltimore, Pittsburgh, Chicago, Springfield, Illinois, and Madison, Wisconsin, he met with enthusiastic receptions. The Irish *Times* sent glowing accounts to Dublin of the ovations he received. One of his most influential supporters was the *Chicago Daily Tribune*, which, in addition to being anti-British, held that the abolition of the feudal land tenure in Ireland and the substitution of the American type of individual freehold was the only realistic remedy for Ireland's sick economy.[76]

On the other hand, some hostile papers, such as the *Boston Daily Advertiser*, a staunch defender of property rights, gave credence to the talk which in dubbing Parnell a "communist" confused Irish-Americans and others as well. Some papers, such as the *New York Daily Tribune*, questioned the alleged popularity of his reception. The *New York Herald*, whose feud with Parnell degenerated, on both sides, into downright indecency, belittled his tour and impact. The *Chicago Daily Tribune*, incidentally, ascribed the anti-Parnell rancor of the *New York Herald* to the snobbish desire of its editor, James Bennett Jr., to break into the social circles of the British aristocracy by "toadying" to its lords and ladies.

[74] *New York Daily Tribune*, Jan. 12, 1880.
[75] *Washington Post*, Jan. 5, 1880; *Boston Daily Advertiser*, Jan. 12, 14, 16, 1880.
[76] *Evening Star*, Feb. 3, 1880. The *New York Daily Tribune* in its issue of Feb. 22, reported that the English reaction to the decision of Congress to put the chamber of the House at Parnell's disposal for a public address, was one of good-natured amusement rather than of pique or anger. See also the *Chicago Daily Tribune*, Jan. 3, 5, 15, 1880.

Parnell's path was a rough one quite apart from the harsh criticisms he met for "interjecting Irish politics" into American public discussion. The Fenians in his audiences were hostile when in his first Madison Square Garden address he repudiated revolutionary violence. Under pressure from these "fire-eaters" he seemed on other occasions to bow to their position. To audiences in which there were few or no Fenians, he emphasized the overweening importance of land reform and intimated that this could be achieved by parliamentary action if enough funds to sustain the Land League's campaign were forthcoming.

A telling test of Parnell's success or failure is the amount of money that he collected. Until early February, Drexel, Morgan and Company acted as the agent for receiving and transmitting contributions to Parnell's cause. Apparently under pressure to break this connection, the firm did so. Parnell insisted that its action was the result of misrepresentations of the use to which the donations were to be put.[77] In any case, the decision hampered the success of Parnell's financial campaign. He himself claimed, in late February, 1880, that nearly $100,000 had been given to the Irish Famine Relief Fund.[78] His critics put the figure at no more than $70,000. Parnell's biographer estimated that $200,000 was given in all, for the famine relief fund and for the political activities of the League.[79] It is in any case clear that Parnell and Dillon gave a great stimulus to the work of Patrick Ford, the immigrant editor of the *Irish World*, who in 1880 and 1881 organized nearly 2,500 branches of the Irish Land League and sent to Ireland $300,000 for its activities, a sum that was later doubled.[80]

During the later part of January the *New York Herald* announced that while plenty of meetings were being held in behalf of the starving Irish, contributions thus far were but as a drop in the bucket in relation to the rapidly mounting crisis. With food supplies in Ireland reaching the point of exhaustion, the time had come, the *Herald* insisted, to regard the discussion of the land question, and even emigration, as irrelevant. What was needed was food, and food at once.[81]

[77] *New York Herald*, Feb. 5, 1880; *Washington Post*, Feb. 16, 1880.
[78] *New York Herald*, Feb. 27, 1880; *Washington Post*, Feb. 23, 1880.
[79] R. Barry O'Brien, *The Life of Charles Stewart Parnell, 1846-1891* (2 vols.; London: Smith, Elder, 1899), I, 204.
[80] *Dictionary of American Biography* VI, 518; P. H. Bagenal, *The American Irish* (London: Kegan, Paul, Trench, 1882).
[81] *New York Herald*, Jan. 22, 1880.

Thus it was no surprise when on February 4th the *Herald* announced the opening of a special fund under its own auspices. It asked for small as well as for big contributions; it promised to list the names of all who gave twenty-five cents or more; it called on newspapers throughout the land to cooperate by printing the names of contributors and to send these funds through any one of the national express agencies, all of which agreed to provide such services free of charge. The *Herald* urged Irishmen "to bury, or at least postpone, their differences, and join heart and soul for the relief of suffering to which they are best qualified to understand." It promised not only to conduct a nonpolitical campaign but to take every precaution to see that contributions were fairly and efficiently administered in Ireland.[82]

The *Herald* itself started off the fund by a contribution of $100,000 on the part of the owner and publisher, James Gordon Bennett, Jr. The prominent Brooklyn preacher, the Reverend T. De Witt Talmage, declared that "the effect of Mr. Bennett's gift of this week has been electric beyond all description."[83] The *Washington Post* took advantage of the occasion to jibe: "When Queen Victoria decided to give $2,500 to relieve her starving subjects, a private citizen of this Republic saw her and decided to go her $97,500 better. Her Majesty will have to put in a letter of sympathy to make up the deficit."[84]

The reaction of other newspapers varied. Some, of which the *Boston Daily Advertiser* was representative, looked on the *Herald's* campaign as vulgar and as furnishing publicity seekers a means of parading their wealth and generosity. In a similar tone, the *Chicago Daily Tribune*, a pro-Parnell organ, noted that Bennett was a bachelor with an income of $200,000 a year and that by standing with the landlords and denouncing Parnell, he had disappointed and even alienated many Americans. "Whether Bennett gave this money as a politic act or in order merely to undo his previous exploits, it was certainly," the *Tribune* conceded, "an act of amazing generosity, which ought to have, though it will not, many imitators on the other side of the water."[85]

Many other papers had no reservations at all in hailing the *Herald's* fund-raising activities. The *Journal of Commerce* announced that an incidental benefit of the *Herald's* lead would be the suppression of

---

[82] *Ibid.*, Feb. 4, 1880.
[83] Unidentified clipping dated Feb. 7, 1880, T. De Witt Talmage Papers, Library of Congress.
[84] *Washington Post*, Feb. 9, 1880.
[85] *Chicago Tribune*, Feb. 5, 1880.

Parnell, who had discouraged many Americans from giving because of his mixing of philanthropy with politics. Papers in Providence, Philadelphia, Washington and other cities cooperated with the campaign. Before it was over the *Times-Picayune* of New Orleans sent in $2,619 and the *Daily Democrat* of the same city, $1,096.[86]

The *New York Herald* spared no pains to reach the public. All over the metropolitan area it scattered subscription blanks and collection boxes. It enlisted the support of clubs, trade organizations and the theatrical profession. The names of contributors, with amounts given, appeared daily in ever longer lists. The *Washington Post* reported ten days after the campaign opened that "all hands appear to be giving, the little children and the aged, the fireman, the policeman, the actor and actress, the rich leaders and the poor working girls, all tell the story of love and compassion in the subscription lists." [87]

Stephen English, of the *Insurance Times*, volunteered to approach the well to do, "to draw their attention from absorbing temporal matters to the propriety and virtue of charitable works and to the demands upon their benevolence, ignored by them in the hurry and pressure of business affairs." [88] And the rich did respond, with and without special solicitation. Two weeks after the fund was begun, the *Herald* listed five $1,000 contributions from wealthy New York firms and individuals, including E. A. Buck, publisher of the *Spirit of the Times*, leading sports magazine, and John Jacob Astor. August Belmont, of the great Rothschild private banking firm, gave $500. An anonymous donor sent $5,000 with a letter expressing confidence in the *Herald's* nonpolitical approach to the cry of hunger. Another man who also preferred to remain anonymous gave $10,000. "Modesty and munificence," remarked the *Herald*, upon a scale like this are not only extremely rare but are almost without a parallel in the annals of charity. As Americans we feel pride in the fact that this precedent of silent charity is entirely American.[89]

The larger donations included $1,000 from the Ballantine Brewers and $5,000 from Tracy and Russell, brewers, and $5,000 from a "Resident Spaniard." The Irish-born bonanza king, John Mackay of Virginia City, Nevada, forwarded $10,000. He also shared in the

[86] New York *Journal of Commerce*, Feb. 5, 1880; *New York Herald*, Feb. 28, 1880.
[87] *Washington Post*, Feb. 10, 1880.
[88] *New York Herald*, March 20, 1880.
[89] *Ibid.*, Feb. 14, 18, 19, 20, 1880.

magnificent $25,000 gift of the Nevada Bank of San Francisco, whose directors included, besides himself, his compatriots, James C. Flood and Louis McLane.[90]

The lowly and poor, as well as the well-to-do and middling groups, also gave. The day after the campaign opened one man collected, in twenty-five cent sums, $5.75 from humble associates. "God knows," he wrote, "some of them cried when they read the *Herald*." [91] A boy sent $1.75 with a note: "I had saved this to buy a pair of skates. It will feed a little boy for a week, and I'll do with my old pair." [92] Workers in the Lucy Furnace Company in Pittsburgh gave $222.50, mostly in one and two dollar contributions. Operatives of many other plants also gave. The employees of the New York, Pennsylvania, and Ohio railroad sent, mostly in contributions of one dollar or less, $817.70. Reminiscent of 1847, the barbers in one shop sent their earnings for a week, and "an artist in shines" contributed a quarter.[93]

Occasionally letters accompanying gifts betrayed special motives and excited piquant reactions. Thus "Yankee Doodle" in sending a contribution confessed: "I have one idiosyncrasy sure. It was born in me. I dont like the Irish. I enclose $5.00 as I dont believe—when a man is starving—in stopping to ask where he was born until after I have fed him." The next day the *Herald* published a reply: "For God's sake send that man, Yankee Doodle, back his $5. He is no American. An Irishman would die before he would take bread from such a hand, as it would sure poison him. Enclosed is $10." [94]

To an extent greater than in earlier campaigns, benefits, theatricals, and auctions augmented the relief funds. Concerts, entertainments, billiard, boxing, and bicycle tournaments were held in New York. At the Stock Exchange public auctions of donated poultry, Irish greyhounds, and other items swelled the treasury. Approximately a thousand dollars came in from a sale of paintings donated by American artists. Mayo's Olympic Theater contributed ten per cent of gross receipts for each evening's performance over a considerable period. Managers of theaters arranged special benefit performances on St. Patrick's day. On another occasion $2,410.48 was raised at a special benefit performance of an Edwin Booth play. E. H. Southern and Joseph Jefferson each contributed $500. Dion Boucicault, an Irish

90 *Ibid.*, Feb. 10, 12, 1880.
91 *Ibid.*, Feb. 5, 1880.
92 *Ibid.*, Feb. 6, 1880.
93 *Ibid.*, Feb. 24, 29, April 30, 1880.
94 *Ibid.*, Feb. 6, 7, 1880.

actor, playwright, and impresario, spared no effort to mobilize the theater.[95] "When the history of the present relief movement comes to be written no class of the community will hold a higher place than members of the theatrical profession," wrote the editors of the *Herald* in a flush of gratitude.[96]

In less than a week after the campaign began, the *Herald* reported that the fund was growing at about $7,000 a day and that within the first six days eight times as much had been collected as during a similar period in the 1847 famine. On April 1, 1880, the *Herald* reported a total of $321,000. At the height of the campaign, on February 23, the paper published a table indicating that about 20,000 persons had thus far contributed. The distribution ranged from over 6,000 contributions of a dollar to a single gift of $25,000.[97]

Except for Parnell, few seem to have been especially suspicious or critical of the *Herald's* enterprise. The Irish orator insisted that the fund was started "to support the landlords in Ireland in attempting to put down the land movement."[98] If the *New York Herald* was so appalled by the toll the famine was taking, why did it sustain the Irish landlords and the British government, and not the Irish people? In a moment of special bitterness, Parnell suggested that the United States send several warships to Ireland to transport the Irish landlords to New York where, since Bennett was so concerned about their welfare, he might convert the *Herald* offices into poor-houses for them. But Parnell also insisted that the *Herald's* fund-raising campaign was a mere advertising device comparable to Bennett's sensational expedition to Africa to rescue Livingston. Having alienated Irish-American readers by his opposition to Parnell and the land tenure reform, Bennett, according to Parnell, was merely investing $100,000 in an effort to increase the sales of his paper. For, Parnell

[95] *Ibid.*, Feb. 7, 8, 17, March 7, 1880.

[96] *Ibid.*, Feb. 26, 1880.

[97] *Ibid.*, Feb. 23, 1880. The frequency of contribution for a particular amount followed an interesting pattern. Column one represents the number of contributors; column two, the amount given:

One	Two	One	Two	One	Two
2,881	25¢	392	$10	15	$250
3,404	50¢	179	$25	10	$500
6,380	$1	117	$50	5	$1,000
1,455	$2	125	$100	2	$5,000
254	$3	2	$150	2	$10,000
1,387	$5	8	$200	1	$25,000

[98] *Ibid.*, Feb. 7, March 3, 1880.

asked, who could be so credulous as to believe that Bennett personally cared "two straws whether the whole Irish people died of famine tomorrow or not." As the *Herald's* fund swelled despite the attacks of Parnell, he insisted that his criticisms had at least made Bennett more circumspect in his plans for distributing the take.[99]

That Parnell had a point in viewing the *Herald's* enterprise as a publicity stunt was undoubtedly true. But the more significant thing about it was summed up by John Graff of the Philadelphia *Press*. "The *Herald*," Graff wrote, "has discovered a still more important field in the capabilities of the journalist, to wit, its power to enlist popular sympathy in behalf of the suffering." [100]

The *Herald* rejected the offer of the Duchess of Marlborough's committee to act as almoner and also decided against turning over its assets to the Dublin Mansion House committee. Instead, Bennett organized a committee of his own. It included Colonel King-Harman, said to represent the best class of Irish landlords, Mr. Shaw, MP., home rule leader, Professor Baldwin, a specialist on Irish affairs, Cardinal McCloskey of New York, whose proxy the *Herald* found acceptable, and the Reverend George Hepworth, a popular New York evangelical preacher. Parnell was initially invited to serve on the committee, but the *Herald* professed to view his suggestion that Patrick Egan serve in his stead as proof of bad faith.

Once in Ireland the committee faced an almost overwhelming task. Except in Donegal, there were no efficient local committees, so it had to work directly through the parishes. At first the members of the committee, in examining applications and in investigating cases, labored until three o'clock in the morning. "The money of all the committees combined," the group reported, "only succeeds in keeping the people just above the starvation point." [101]

Increasingly the committee turned its attention to the needs of Ireland's children, victims of a situation over which they had no control and for which they had no responsibility. If these youngsters grew up malnourished, they would be "unfit for equal competition in the struggles of life." So the *Herald* set up a special Children's Fund. By the end of the first week in April it was providing a daily "wholesome meal" for 15,345 children. A week later 22,000 were getting free breakfasts. To help the impoverished Irish help them-

[99] *Ibid.*, Feb. 11, 1880, March 3, 1880.
[100] *Ibid.*, Feb. 11, 1880.
[101] *Ibid.*, March 18, 1880.

selves, arrangements were made by which Dublin seamstresses sewed 4,000 children's suits. In appealing for further help, the *Herald* declared that the "greater sensitivity" to the sufferings of children was an "American peculiarity." [102]

The *Herald* reassured the donors that the committee was not only working hard and efficiently, but that the books, kept by a professional accountant, would be available for inspection in New York at the end of the operation. The committee continued at its work through the spring. Cooperation with other relief committees presented no unusual snarls, and the program was successfully carried through.[103]

Meantime, as in 1847, efforts were made to supplement voluntary famine relief by Congressional action. On December 9, 1879, Richard Graham Frost, a St. Louis lawyer and a Democrat, and Edward Hooker Gillette, an Iowa Greenbacker, introduced similar resolutions in the House of Representatives expressing sympathy for the suffering people of Ireland in their struggles for self-government and, in the case of the Gillette resolution, asking the President to urge the British government to provide relief from landlord rule.[104] In the latter part of January and in early February, 1880, John Ellis of Louisiana, a former Confederate officer and a Democrat, and James Phelps of Connecticut, prominent in judicial circles and also a Democrat, introduced joint resolutions requesting Congressional appropriations for famine relief. These resolutions were all referred either to the Committee on Foreign Affairs or to the Committee on Appropriations.[105]

On March 15, 1880, the House received the report of the Committee on Foreign Affairs, the work largely of its chairman, Samuel Cox, Ohio-born, a Brown University graduate, a lawyer and editor who represented a New York City Democratic district. His report recommended as a substitute for several resolutions a joint resolution (No. 238) providing national aid for relief and appropriating $300,000. It

[102] *Ibid.*, March 19, 20, April 7, 8, 9, 17, 1880.
[103] Susan Hayes Ward, *George H. Hepworth, Preacher, Journalist, Friend of the People* (New York: E. P. Dutton, 1903), 189 ff.
[104] *Congressional Record*, 46th Cong., 2d Sess., 1879, X, Pt. 1, 41, 43.
[105] *Ibid.*, 418, 649. The *Chicago Daily Tribune* did not doubt the benevolence of Phelps' intentions, but felt that he was going about the matter in the wrong way. Congress, it maintained, had no power to make such an appropriation which, even if granted, would barely feed the starving for a day. The wiser course, the *Tribune* argued, would have been the introduction of a resolution asking the State Department to use its good offices in persuading the British government to reform its Irish policy, and to protest against landlordism. *Chicago Daily Tribune*, Feb. 5, 1880.

emphasized the authentic evidence at hand for the persisting great
need of Ireland's people and recommended the distribution of the
money through the several relief organizations in that country. The
report spoke of the contributions the Irish had made in the American
war for independence and in the building of canals, railroads, and
factories. It reminded the Congress of the some 15,000,000 Americans
of Irish birth or descent. The report also appealed to the dictates
of humanity. "The divine injunction to move in charitable works is
not limited by the lines of patriotism or the boundaries of empires."
But the chief reliance was put on precedent. The report gave a detailed account of the unanimous support in Congress and in the administration for the relief of Venezuelans in the 1812 earthquake and
of the aid given to Ireland in 1847 through the provision of a national
vessel for transporting food. In view of all this, Cox asked, how
could aid now, in a period of prosperity, with an opulent surplus, be
refused? [106]

But, as the press pointed out, the proposal had little chance in
view of the extreme strict constructionists among the Southerners
and of the Republicans who did not believe in giving aid out of the
Treasury to people abroad while the colored people were oppressed
in the South.[107]

Another movement in Congress did, however, succeed. William
Ward, a graduate of Girard College, a lawyer, a representative from
the Chester, Pennsylvania, district, and a Republican, introduced a
resolution authorizing the Secretary of the Navy to designate a vessel
to carry, free of charge, contributions for relief to the people of Ireland.[108] A similar resolution in the upper house, introduced by two
Republican senators, Samuel McMillan of Minnesota and John A.
Logan of Illinois, was ardently supported by the Irish-born Charles
William Jones of Florida, chairman of the Committee on Naval
Affairs.[109] The Committee on Naval Affairs recommended favorable
action. President Hayes approved the joint resolution, which had
found House support, on February 25, 1880.[110]

For the time it looked, as the Washington *Evening Star* put it, as if
the authorization for the Navy to transport supplies would be "only

[106] U. S., Congress, House, Committee on Foreign Affairs, *Report on Relief for the Irish People*, 46th Cong., 2d Sess., 1880, H. Rept. 465, X, Pt. 2, 1571-72.
[107] *New York Herald*, March 6, 1880.
[108] *Congressional Record*, 46th Cong., 2d Sess., 1880, X, Pt. 1, 763.
[109] *Ibid.*, 938, 963.
[110] *Ibid.*, Pt. 2, 1046, 1065, 1076, 1175.

ornamental," for no supplies were forthcoming.[111] Thereupon Representative Levi Morton, who represented the Murray Hill district in New York City, and who had been charged in the election of 1878 with being an enemy of the Irish, anonymously offered through the *New York Herald* to provide one fourth of the cargo if others made up the balance. Morton's biographer claimed that the anonymity of the offer proved that there was no intent to make political capital.[112] In any case, the name of the donor was presently public knowledge. The Irish-born William Russell Grace, international merchant, capitalist, steamship owner, and concessionaire, who was later to be the first Catholic mayor of New York City, gave another fourth, the *New York Herald* a third, and the final portion was made up from smaller gifts.[113]

With a cargo of 3,315 barrels of flour, meal, potatoes, and sundry provisions, the *Constellation*, a sailing vessel built in 1798 and now commanded by Edward E. Potter left New York on March 30. "After an anxious and boisterous passage" the ancient ship reached Queenstown on April 20th. The offer of the Duke of Edinburgh to help distribute the cargo with his emergency relief fleet was accepted. The mayor, the Duke of Edinburgh, and other notables received the *Constellation's* officers and crew. Balls and dances were also given the officers at Queenstown. Cork officials tendered an impressive banquet. One awkward note was struck when the Irish National Land League presented to Commander Potter an address which he refused to receive until its political sentiments were deleted. It ended with the injunction "God Save Ireland" which took the Commander with such surprise that he merely replied curtly, "Thank you." [114] The British government expressed its "high appreciation" of so generous an act of "international comity" as the fitting out of a national vessel on a mission of benevolence. As Commander Potter noted in his report, not only the British government and officials in Ireland, but "all classes and conditions of people" extended the Americans remarkable "civilities and kindnesses." [115]

[111] Washington *Evening Star*, March 8, 1880.
[112] *Ibid.*, March 16, 1880; Robert McElroy, *Levi Parsons Morton, Banker, Diplomat and Statesman* (New York: G. P. Putnam's Sons, 1930), 92. McElroy states that Morton had decided to provide the whole cargo if others did not respond quickly.
[113] *New York Herald*, March 18, 1880.
[114] *New York Herald*, April 26, 1880.
[115] U. S., Congress, Senate, *Letter from the Secretary of the Navy Transmitting Report of the Commander of the Relief-ship Constellation*, 46th Cong., 2d Sess., 1880, Sen. Exec. Doc. 215.

This ended American efforts to relieve the Irish famine of 1880. If the federal government's gesture of good will was hardly comparable with the $100,000 that the Canadian government appropriated for relief,[116] it was, as the British authorities indicated, an act of extraordinary "comity." Even if the larger population and greater wealth of the United States in 1880 in comparison with the situation in 1847 is given due weight, what was done by voluntary initiative was still impressive. This is the more true in view of the rumors of grain speculation as a contributory cause of distress and confusion over competing funds, a competition which disgusted such conservative and lukewarm journals as the *Boston Daily Advertiser*. Much that was collected resulted from persistent publicity and sustained organizational effort, a fact on which many newspapers commented.

The campaigns reflected at least three fairly well defined attitudes toward giving, though of course one merged into another. The first was expressed by a generous donor, Irish-born Eugene Kelley, who said at the start that the "idea America is always to feed millions of people in times of famine is preposterous." The *New York Daily Tribune* expressed essentially the same idea in declaring that Irish demands on American charity must be met but that things in Ireland should be so managed that such demands ended.[117]

Another view was phrased by the *New York Herald*. "We think it important to be noted that the growth of wealth has not been attended with a growth of selfishness; that the character of our people has not degenerated; that habits of luxury have not dried up the fountains of generous human sympathy; that increase of riches is not accompanied by any signs of moral deterioration." [118]

Related to this, but stressing the idea that such giving to peoples abroad had political as well as humanitarian implications, was a statement by ex-Governor Horatio Seymour of New York. "We can make evil minister to good," Seymour said. He urged that the question was not merely shall starving men be fed; it was, also, shall those who give be made more happy by acts of charity. "May we not hope," Seymour went on, "if there shall be here a grand exhibition of man's sympathy for his fellow-man, one that shall reach from continent to continent, across the Atlantic—that it will make monarchs hesitate before they wantonly destroy the lives and happiness of

116 *Washington Post*, Feb. 23, 1880.
117 *New York Daily Tribune*, Feb. 17, 1880.
118 *New York Herald*, Feb. 19, 1880.

those separated from them by a mere line?" In brief, to Seymour American giving had been based on a benevolent sentiment that might "bind peoples more closely together into a true brotherhood, thus serving the cause of peace." [119]

Many givers, well known and humble, no doubt gave with none of these noble thoughts in mind. They gave without thinking much about either the causes of the famine, despite all that Parnell and Dillon did to bring this home to the public, nor about the effects of giving, save that lives were at stake, and that America had something to give. But at least in a period of civil war and heavy demands for charity at home in the years that followed, giving to those in need abroad was sustained. That giving was affected, in part adversely, by the controversies over domestic issues in the needy countries. But precedents, a new type of publicity, the existence of surplus foods, and the generosity of countless Americans accounted for an impressive overseas philanthropy in the period of renewed demands.

[119] *Ibid.*, March 16, 1880.

V

The Widening Circle

"The present famine," wrote Charles Emory Smith, American Minister in St. Petersburg in 1891 and 1892, "is one of those stupendous catastrophes which almost baffle description." [1] It was, in fact, one of the worst of the eleven major famines that scourged Russia between 1845 and 1922. Minister Smith, well known as editor of the Philadelphia *Press* and highly regarded in Republican circles, reported to the State Department on October 21, 1891, that crop failures had put some 13,700,000 people in desperate need. With the harvest ten months off, two million pounds of bread, costing upwards of $25,000,000, could hardly prevent widespread death. In later reports Smith added grim details. He recounted sympathetically the efforts of the Russian government to ease the situation by remitting taxes, making direct appropriations for relief, establishing work projects, and importing some food from the Caucasus. But he made it clear that even these efforts, supplemented by the relief work of Tolstoy, the Grand Duchess Elizabeth, and other well known Russians, were failing to stem the mounting disaster. [2]

Neither the reports of Minister Smith nor his article in the *North American Review* showed more than a superficial understanding of the famine, which he attributed merely to drought. Actually, the peasants in many areas suffered even in normal times for lack of food. The shortage was related to the steady increase of rural population and to the policy of the mirs in parceling out units of land too small to give farmers an opportunity to store a surplus, as well as to primitive agricultural methods and poor transportation. To make matters

[1] Charles Emory Smith, "The Famine in Russia," *North American Review* CLIV (May, 1892), 541-51.
[2] *Papers Relating to the Foreign Relations of the United States*, 1891 (Washington: Govt. Printing Office, 1891), 362-69; *Foreign Relations*, 1892, 746-56.

worse, the government required one tenth of the crop for payment on foreign debts. Thus general conditions, political as well as economic, figured in the situation.

Political images of Russia played both a positive and a negative role in American philanthropic response to the emergency. On the one hand, some Americans felt a sentimental obligation to give because Russia had shown sympathy with the North during the Civil War. But on the other, the pogroms of 1881 and 1882 had caused the tradition of friendship to deteriorate. These had aroused bitter protests. Pro-Jewish petitions had more than once been presented to Congress. On August 20, 1890, just a year and a half before the call for aid to Russia's starving peasants, the House of Representatives had asked the President for information regarding "the harsh treatment and sad conditions" of Jews in Russia.[3] Russian-American relations had also sagged during the pending negotiations over the status of Russian-born American citizens who returned to the homeland on business or for visits. Finally, in 1891 George Kennan's *Siberia and the Exile System,* which painted a dark picture of the Russian government, aroused hostility in all parts of America.

It was in this setting that the first voices were raised for American aid to the Russian peasants. At the annual meeting of the Red Cross in Boston on November 13, 1891, Clara Barton appealed for a Thanksgiving collection in the churches: the $200 raised at the convention itself was forwarded to the Countess Tolstoy. But the main call to action came, not from religious groups or eastern commercial organizations or even immigrants from the disaster area, but from editors and millers of the Middle West. At the suggestion of William O. McDowell of *Home and Country* the Siberian Exile Petition Association asked for a bushel of corn from each of its 1,000,000 members for famine relief. On December 6, the Davenport *Democrat,* edited by Benjamin Franklin Tillinghast, urged that relief work be hastened, broadened, and systematized. Already in Davenport the Unitarian minister, as well as Arthur M. Judy, Colonel George W. French and Alice French ("Octave Thanet") had been discussing what might be done. This group approached Governor Boies, who appointed the Iowa Russian Famine Relief Commission, consisting of a prominent person in each Congressional district.

[3] *Congressional Record,* 51st Cong., 1st Sess., 1891, XXI, Pt. 9, 8882. See also the resolutions introduced by Rep. Hobart Hitt of Illinois and Sen. Wilkinson Call of Florida, *ibid.,* 51st Cong., 2d Sess., 1891, XXII, Pt. 3, 2219, 2663.

Two days before Tillinghast's appeal, the editor of the *North-western Miller*, published in Minneapolis, had noted that the grain crops were almost paralyzing the transportation system, that Americans had far more wheat, corn, and flour than they could possibly eat. The editor, William C. Edgar, declared that in such circumstances it was hard to think of Russian peasants being forced to eat bread made of bark and ferns, flavored with ground peas. "It seems like a grim, gaunt fairy tale, of years long passed; of conditions which advancing civilization have made impossible. The poorest dog which hangs about the city streets of America can pick up better food than the Russian peasant clamors for."⁴ Edgar proposed that every reader give, out of his plenty, a few sacks of low-grade flour to relieve distress in Russia. If one stops to think of it, there was, he went on, enough flour on the floor of every mill into which the *Northwestern Miller* entered to lift a starving Russian peasant from misery to joy. If a peasant fed on "hunger bread" were to ask at any American mill for a bag of flour he would get it straight off. Was there any reason for not giving just because the ocean stood between America and Russia? "We do not," Edgar finished, "appeal to the millers of the United States as Protestants or Catholics, as Christians or Hebrews, but we simply ask them, in the name of humanity if, in such distress as this, they can not show a sense of the benefits which the good God has showered upon them, by taking from their stock a small portion to send across the ocean to these starving people."⁵

In asking for enough flour to load a ship with 6,000,000 pounds of cargo, Edgar insisted on the practicality as well as the humanitarianism of his proposal. He did, to be sure, want the millers to show the world that they had hearts as well as pocketbooks; but he also urged that there were good business reasons for giving. "Philanthropy and business may properly walk hand in hand in this instance." In later charities that might be suggested by this initial movement, the question would come up, Edgar said, what to give. Peasants being unable to eat money and needing bread, and the United States being the only country with an exportable surplus of flour, it was clear that one free shipload would simply call worldwide attention to America's plenteous store. Many a paid shipload would follow it and these, in

⁴ *Northwestern Miller*, Dec. 4, 1891. See also John W. Hoyt, *Report of the Russian Famine Committee of the United States* (Washington: Rufus J. Darby, 1893), 7; and B. F. Tillinghast, "A Far Reaching Charity," *Midland Monthly* I (April, 1894), 325-38.
⁵ *Northwestern Miller*, Dec. 4, 1891.

all probability, would be loaded with flour bought at the very mills that gave away a free sample cargo.[6]

To prove further the practicability of the scheme the *Northwestern Miller* proposed that the railroads carry the flour free to New York, and that the Russian government provide freight across the ocean. To give official sanction to a private enterprise, Edgar got the backing of Governor W. R. Merriam of Minnesota, who named a commission to supervise operations. Edgar, of course, was made a member. Governor Merriam also gave statewide publicity to the movement and asked fellow governors in the Middle West to push the movement forward, as several did.

To meet in advance every possible objection to giving, Edgar declared that if, as some thought, gifts had been inefficiently, even dubiously, handled in the Irish famine and in the Johnstown flood disaster, every precaution would now be taken. An official of the American Red Cross, he announed, would accompany a member of the staff of the *Northwestern Miller* to Russia, personally to check on the distribution by the Russian Red Cross and by czarist officials. In dealing with the argument that the Czar was at fault for Russia's sufferings, Edgar did not mention the initial effort of the ruler to minimize the disaster and to regard the publicity about it as a thrust on the part of his critics. He insisted that the monarch was deeply concerned for the peasants, as, somewhat belatedly, he indeed was. If blame were to be laid, Edgar went on, it had better be put at the door of "the peculiar methods of government, the long-continued abuses of officials, and the generally unfortunate situation of the peasantry, which is the result of years of peculiar habits and customs which it will take generations of progress to change." In any case, this was a question not of politics, but of humanity.[7]

In addition to emphasizing the humanitarianism and the practicality of the program, Edgar appealed to the trade-consciousness of millers. Urging speed, he pointed to the desirability of having the millers exclusively contribute the first shipload. "We want to be the first on the spot and to carry the name of the millers of the United States proudly in the van to those who are lifting their hungry faces toward our country."[8] The shrewd editor appealed further to indi-

[6] *Ibid.*, Dec. 11, 1891.
[7] *Ibid.*
[8] *Ibid.*, Dec. 18, 25, 1891.

vidual pride and emulation by listing each week the names of donors and the amounts given.

The response was magnificent. Within an hour of the time that the Minneapolis millers were approached, the Pillsbury-Washburn Flour Mills offered 800 sacks of their product, and eight other mills offered lots varying from 100 to 600 sacks. Minnesota led the way, not only because it was a center of wheat growing and flour milling, but also because of the businesslike and enthusiastic cooperation of Governor Merriam. The Governor named commissions in each county to canvass every town and solicited the cooperation of businessmen and the local press. In St. Louis the Bemis Bag Company offered to provide bags. By the first of January the pledge exceeded 1,500,000 sacks and each day the responses to special telegrams raised the totals.[9]

At this point Senator William Drew Washburn, a leading Minnesota figure in lumbering, real estate, railroad building, and management, and the founder of the great milling firm of W. D. Washburn and Company, entered the story. Before the Christmas holidays he learned from the Secretary of the Navy that the venerable *Constellation*, currently being used at Annapolis as a training ship, could be made available for transporting donations. But when the Congress convened he was surprised to find out that the *Constellation* could at best carry not more than a fourth or fifth of the flour already pledged. In the Senate on January 5th, 1892, Washburn, declaring it proper for Congress to do what it had done in 1880, introduced a resolution authorizing the Secretary of the Navy to arrange transportation. If the Navy did not have facilities at hand it might charter private vessels. An amendment put a ceiling of $100,000 on the appropriation.

During the brief discussion Vice-President Levi Morton read a communication from President Harrison which declared that the response to the initiative of the millers justified the belief that a ship's cargo could very soon be delivered to the seaboard through the generosity of transportation lines. "It is most appropriate," the message continued, "that a people whose store houses have been so lavishly filled with all the fruits of the earth by the gracious favor of God should manifest their gratitude by large gifts to His suffering chil-

[9] In addition to the files of the *Northwestern Miller*, this account rests on William C. Edgar's *The Russian Famine of 1891 and 1892* (Minneapolis, 1893).

dren in other lands." Harrison recommended that the Navy charter a suitable ship since it had no steam vessel at its disposal, and that the donations be sent under the charge of a naval officer to convenient Russian ports.[10] Without referring the Washburn resolution to a standing or special committee, the Senate, in Committee of the Whole, approved the proposal by a vote of 40 to 9. Of the 35 Senators not voting, several who paired with colleagues indicated that had they voted, it would have been in the affirmative. The opponents were all Southern Democrats except for James H. Kyle, a Congregationalist minister chosen by a fusion of Populists and Democrats in the South Dakota legislature. Meanwhile, petitions from various parts of the country were being presented, asking for such government assistance. The next day, January 6, the Vice-President read a communication from Clara Barton, head of the American Red Cross, urging the government to insure the expeditious transit of large donations of grain for the relief of the famine-stricken Russians.[11]

On January 5, the day that the Senate took action, three resolutions were introduced in the House by members from Shreveport, Baltimore, and Canton, Massachusetts, expressing sympathy with Russian Jews in their suffering, protesting against their treatment, asking for an inquiry into the causes for their continued persecution, and calling on the government to use its good offices in securing amelioration of their lot. These resolutions were referred to the Committee on Foreign Affairs while the President's message was sent to the Committee on Naval Affairs. When the Senate Joint Resolution was presented, William C. Breckinridge, a Kentucky Democrat, expressed the hope that the House would endorse this quickly in view of the starving state of twenty million Russians and the contributions of American grain and flour for which no transportation was available. That there was apt to be debate was suggested by the remark of Constantine B. Kilgore of Texas that Congress appeared to look out for everybody's people but its own, and that he meant to oppose the resolution.[12]

The next day, January 6, the House spent several hours in debating the Senate's joint resolution. Several members insisted that it be referred to a committee. It was unseemly, the argument went, to take

[10] U. S., Congress, Senate, *Message from the President of the United States Recommending that the Secretary of the Navy be Authorized to Charter a Vessel for the Transportation of Supplies to the Suffering People of Russia*, 52d Cong., 1st Sess., 1892, Sen. Exec. Doc. 12; *Congressional Record*, 52d Cong., 1st Sess., 1892, XXIII, Pt. 1, 110.
[11] *Congressional Record*, 52d Cong., 1st Sess., 1892, XXIII, Pt. 1, 110-11, 139.
[12] *Ibid.*, 121, 125-6, 129-30.

so important an action without careful consideration. The intent to kill the resolution was obvious but the House continued to discuss it in Committee of the Whole.

One argument repeated again and again by Democrats was that this Congress had been elected on a promise to reduce federal expenses and that it therefore could not approve such an appropriation for aid of a foreign people. Democrats also argued that there was no evidence that the Russian government was unable to take care of its own. Thus John Pendleton of West Virginia pointed to an article in the *Washington Post* presumably by a highly placed official to the effect that everything was under control. And why, asked Pendleton, shouldn't everything be under control in a country of vast territorial expanse, great wealth and military power, and abundant gold reserves for future wars in the banks of western Europe?

Pendleton and others denied that Russia was the traditional friend that proponents of official aid contended she was. It was impossible, Pendleton insisted, for the United States to clasp the hand of a country which was a menace to modern civilization. The Tartar must mend his ways before the two countries could be friends. Above all, the Russians must cease persecuting the Jews and driving them into exile. Elijah Morse of Massachusetts offered an amendment to the effect that there must be no discrimination against Jews in the dispensation of American food in Russia. The amendment was defeated, partly on the ground that Russian officials could not be trusted to distribute food fairly, and partly on the score that approval of such an amendment would place conditions on the gift that the donors themselves had not put.[13]

The most frequent argument against approval of the Senate's joint resolution to authorize Navy transport of voluntary food contributions was that Congress had no power to spend taxpayers' money for such purposes. A few years back, declared Kilgore, when his own people in Texas were suffering from a horrible drought, his state asked Congress for $10,000 with which to buy seed. The request was rightly turned down on the ground that Congress had no such authority.

---

[13] Fearing that Jews might not contribute to the funds that the New York Chamber of Commerce was soliciting for Russian relief, Jacob Schiff, leading banker and philanthropist, urged his fellow religionists to give in view of the pressing need. Schiff hoped that contributions might be distributed through Tolstoy rather than through officials he regarded as "corrupt, unreliable, and tyrannical." Schiff was contributing to the publication of a journal called *Free Russia*, issued in both London and New York, which took a similar position. Cyrus Adler, *Jacob H. Schiff: His Life and Letters* (2 vols., Doubleday, Doran, 1928), II, 116.

Young William Jennings Bryan of Nebraska made the same point—at greater length and with more oratory. In the summer of 1890, when private charity and state funds for relief of hard-pressed Nebraska farmers were exhausted, Bryan related, an appeal was made to Congress for help. Bryan agreed that the refusal of Congress to give aid was based on sound constitutional principles.

This position was given many twists. J. Logan Chipman of Detroit said that the proposal was really only one for being generous with money not belonging to Congress. Walt Butler, an Iowa Democrat, declared that the proponents of aid came chiefly from states which, unlike his own, had done little or nothing for the Russians through voluntary efforts. He favored charity, but was it charity to give from someone else's pockets? The upshot of all these arguments was expressed by Kilgore of Texas who rejected the precedent of Congressional aid to the Irish in 1880 on the ground that this was mere pandering to the Irish-American vote and by Josiah Patterson of Memphis who declared that "the government of the United States is not an eleemosynary institution."

One Democrat, Oates of Alabama, did not accept the constitutional argument against tendering government transport for food. Having. reviewed the debates of 1812, 1846, and 1880, he held with Calhoun that while in its domestic relations the federal government being a compact, could not dispense charity, it might do so in its relations with other powers, for in this role it was a sovereign agent. At the same time Oates opposed the resolution: he saw no convincing evidence that the Russian government could not take care of its own. Actually, only one Democrat, William Breckinridge of Kentucky, argued for the Senate's proposal. He noted that Clara Barton of the Red Cross had conveyed to Congress the information that the suffering was very great and that the Russian government would welcome aid. Breckinridge also urged that if relief were to be furnished, it be done as became a great nation, without higgling over so small a matter. Shall it be said a government with power to wage war is powerless to help, out of American abundance, a suffering people?

The burden of the debate in favor of government aid in transporting voluntary gifts was carried by Republicans. These insisted that if the Democrats had discovered that the federal government could not aid Texans, Nebraskans, and Russians, the discovery had not after all been patented. The quality of mercy is not strained, insisted Charles Boutelle of Maine: let it not now be strained by constitutional quibbling. Others insisted that the need for aid had been abundantly verified not only by the Red Cross but by the press and by the President himself. Some speakers distinguished between the Russian government, at whose door blame was laid for so much that was regrettable, including persecutions of the Jews, and the sorry plight of the people themselves.

When the arguments had been repeated again and again the Speaker, somewhat reluctantly, yielded to the demand for a yea-nay vote on the amendment of Representative William Holman of Indiana, to strike out the provision for an appropriation of $100,000 for the transport of donations to Russia. The amendment won the support of 165 members of the House, all being Democrats or Populists except one. Of the seventy-two voting against the amendment, only one was a Democrat. Ninety-four members of the House did not vote.[14]

It is hard to gauge the relative weight of several arguments against the official transport of food to Russia. The well-informed editor of the *Review of Reviews,* who did much to keep the Russian need of help before the American public, reported that the action of the House in turning down the Senate proposal was totally unexpected even by the Democrats voting against it. The opponents in the House, according to the *Review of Reviews,* voted as they did "more with a mistaken idea of going on record in favor of retrenchment and reform than with any serious objection to the measure." The writer added that many of the Democrats, in the face of censure from constituents and the press, regretted their action.[15]

One might expect that the press would have reacted according to party affiliations, but such was not always the case. The *Chicago Daily Tribune,* a Republican paper, did not condemn the Democrats who voted against the proposal for government aid. It held that the United States was already doing enough in caring for the 50,000 Jews expelled from Russia by persecution; it argued that quite possibly the Russians would prefer gifts in money to those in kind; it contended that while in many respects praiseworthy, the movement for collecting flour was hardly a business-like one, and that, in any case, Russian ships or vessels chartered through American philanthropy would no doubt carry the donations across the Atlantic.[16]

14 *Congressional Record,* 52d Cong., 1st Sess., XXIII, Pt. 1, 157-76.
15 *Review of Reviews* V (Feb., 1892), 37-39.
16 *Chicago Daily Tribune,* Jan. 8, 10, 1892.

On the other hand, the *New York Daily Tribune* probably spoke for a larger segment of Republican opinion in declaring that there was no financial stringency sufficient to justify the House in refusing a modest sum for a worthy cause; that constitutional barriers did not stand in the way; and that probably the disapproval of the Russian treatment of the Jews loomed large in the minds of many who voted against federal aid. Clearly sympathetic with government transport of food, the *New York Daily Tribune* held that the American people as a whole knew that the persecutions of the Jews stemmed from a tyrannical regime.[17]

Several things, however, suggested the importance of the argument against aiding a country in which anti-Semitism was so rampant. During the negotiations over an extradition treaty, under way for some years and still continuing, many members of Congress insisted on assurances against the persecution of citizens of Russian birth returning to the homeland. On June 10, 1892, Representative Dungan of Ohio introduced a joint resolution asking for the severance of diplomatic relations with Russia. Although this did not win much support, the platforms of both major parties in the summer of 1892 expressed sympathy for the persecuted Jews.[18]

In any case the outcome meant that the program had to be carried through entirely by voluntary efforts such as those already under way. Those most concerned redoubled their efforts. First of all, potential donors had to be convinced that the inaction of Congress, however unfortunate, was only a challenge to voluntary giving. It was also necessary to counteract the efforts of an ambiguous committee in Washington which discouraged giving on the score that famine relief would only relieve an unjust Russian regime from shouldering responsibility and effecting reforms. For many must have believed, with Alexander Johnson, director of the Indiana State Board of Charities, that relief was unwise altruism. In writing to Clara Barton, Johnson asked, "Why should we spend our strength and give our money to prolong the wretched lives of these poor miserable creatures? Every dollar we send to Russia means a dollar given to help the worst possible government in the world." [19] Finally, it was also necessary to bring some degree of cooperation between the several

[17] *New York Daily Tribune*, Jan. 10, 1892.

[18] *Congressional Record*, 52d Cong., 1st Sess., 1892, XXIII, Pt. 6, 5228; William T. Page, *Platforms of the Two Great Political Parties* (Washington, 1928), 83, 89.

[19] Alexander Johnson to Clara Barton, Feb. 22, 1892, Clara Barton Papers and Correspondence, 1891-92, Library of Congress.

movements in the middle west and those under way in Boston, New York, Philadelphia, and Washington.

In the months that followed it proved difficult, however, to effect a national organization despite several steps taken in that direction. Just after the House turned down the Senate proposal for transport of food to Russia, Clara Barton urged on the American people the great importance of giving help, adding that her organization would act as a medium for effecting distribution in Russia.[20] Working in cooperation with the Red Cross, John W. Hoyt, former editor of the *Wisconsin Farmer and Northwestern Cultivator*, recent governor of Wyoming Territory, and a man of broad international experience including travel in Russia, took the lead in organizing the Russian Famine Committee of the United States. Designed to awaken greater public interest and to facilitate cooperation between the local movements, the Committee publicized the slogan "Grain from the West, money for the cost of transportation from the East." It included fifteen senators, the Speaker of the House, the Chief Justice, thirteen bishops and archbishops, as well as many highly placed clergymen and charity workers. The Committee urged the governors of all states to follow the example of Iowa, which had an effective state commission at work, to enlist the support of the press, and to stimulate the raising of funds through public meetings. The address noted that many railroads had agreed to transport free of charge all grain and flour and that the Red Cross had arranged for reduced freight across the sea and for placing all supplies in the Russian branch of the Red Cross. Similar addresses appealed to chambers of commerce, boards of trade, editors, farmers, and other organizations.[21] If no preference was expressed, the Committee handed over contributions, which ran upwards to $10,000, to the Red Cross.

Meantime various governors and private organizations got into action. Governor Russell of Massachusetts appealed for generous contributions and named a committee, including Edward Everett Hale, with Bishop Phillips Brooks as chairman. Massachusetts donors sent several thousand dollars to Minister Smith in St. Petersburg

---

[20] *New York Daily Tribune*, Jan. 14, 1892; Clara Barton to Lenora Halstead, no date, Barton Papers; Clara Barton, *The Red Cross* (Washington: American National Red Cross, 1898), 175-76.

[21] John Hoyt to the Governors of the Several States, Washington, Jan. 27, 1892, in Russian Famine Correspondence, Citizens Permanent Relief Committee Papers, Historical Society of Pennsylvania; Hoyt, *Report of the Russian Famine Committee of the United States*.

for distribution. The governors of Rhode Island and Maryland took similar steps. In New York City the Chamber of Commerce, stimulated by an article of N. Shishkoff in the *Nineteenth Century Review*, held a meeting at which several spoke of earlier contributions to similar emergencies—the Irish famines, the labor troubles in Lancashire, the floods in France, and the siege of Paris in the Franco-Prussian War. Note was taken of the fact that in the previous thirty years $2,000,000 had passed through the Chamber's treasurer for "the relief of suffering humanity."

Charles S. Smith, president of the organization, named a committee of fifty to appeal for funds to be distributed through reliable channels. J. Pierpont Morgan, Abram S. Hewitt, and other prominent New Yorkers subscribed liberally, but smaller sums also swelled the fund, including the $7,000 raised at a concert at Music Hall. By mid-April the Committee had more than $50,000, some of which was spent for food to complete the cargoes other groups had sponsored and some of which was sent in bank drafts to the American Minister in St. Petersburg for distribution through the Anglo-American Church in the capital, the Tolstoy fund, the Jewish Committee, and the Red Cross.[22]

The movement in Philadelphia was the most vigorous of any on the east seaboard. Mayor Edwin S. Stuart appointed a committee of prominent Philadelphians including Frederick W. Taylor, Robert C. Ogden, A. J. Drexel, and John H. Converse. The International Navigation Company offered on liberal terms the *Indiana* which the Committee planned to fill with grain, corn, and flour from the commissions in Iowa and Minnesota that had been gathering these stores. But the Iowa and Minnesota commissions reported that arrangements had already been made with the New York committee. The Minnesota millers were eager to have the flour accumulated under the leadership of Edgar move to Russia as one unit in one ship. Thus the Philadelphia committee had to raise additional money to buy produce.

It was not easy for the Philadelphians to break down general indifference and some opposition. The campaign included appeals through the press, the holding of small meetings in private homes of key leaders as well as public gatherings, the naming of special committees to canvass every trade, and enlistment of the clergy in

[22] *New York Daily Tribune*, Jan. 30, Feb. 2, 5, 6, 7, 13, 18, 21, March 13, April 15, 1892.

raising funds through churches. The problem of buying large quantities of flour at reasonable prices and in getting it quickly to the Philadelphia docks proved a hard one. Here Washburn Crosby of Minnesota was helpful in expediting the transit of thirty cars of flour. Despite all these difficulties and a not unnatural tension between some of the parties to the campaign, within three weeks of the original initiative, over $100,000 was raised and a cargo purchased.

When the *Indiana* was being loaded crowds gathered at the dock, prayers were offered by Archbishop Ryan, Rabbi Jastrow, Protestant Episcopal Bishop Whitaker and other leaders of the clergy. American and Russian flags flew in the brisk breeze, the national anthems of the two countries were played, and the anchor was lifted. A committee of Philadelphians, Rudolph Blankenburg, A. J. Drexel, Jr., and Oliver Biggle, hurried by a faster steamer to Libau to supervise the distribution.[23]

The urgent appeals for further help from the Philadelphians once they got to Russia spurred the home committee to new efforts. Contributions came not only from the City of Brotherly Love and from many Pennsylvania towns, but from scattered points throughout the country, including New Haven, Washington, D. C., Massilon, Ohio, Vincennes, Indiana, Portland, Oregon, and Vancouver, Washington. The *Conemaugh* was chartered and stored with 188,000 pounds of rice and 6,000,000 pounds of flour. After simple taking off ceremonies conducted by members of the Society of Friends, the *Conemaugh* in the last week of April set sail for a Baltic port.[24]

A group of new donors helped fill the *Conemaugh's* hold by providing 5,000 sacks of flour. These donors were readers of the *Christian Herald*, the organ of a popular Brooklyn preacher, T. De Witt Talmage, and his editor and friend, Louis Klopsch, a man who combined great talents in journalism and business with practical idealism. The inclusion in the *Christian Herald* of Talmage's sermons, of interesting and highly moral fiction, and of homely and appealing anecdotes, made the paper the most widely circulated religious organ in the English-speaking world. The paper printed graphic accounts of the horrors of the Russian famine together with photographic illustrations designed to wring the heart. The names of the donors,

[23] Russian Famine Correspondence; *Harper's Weekly* XXXVI (March 5, 1892), 223; Francis B. Reeves, *Russia Then and Now, 1892-1917* (New York: G. P. Putnam, 1917), 3-5.
[24] Russian Famine Correspondence; *Philadelphia Public Ledger*, April 25, 1892.

who sent sums from a nickel to a dollar, were printed conspicuously. The *Christian Herald* told its readers that a barrel of sound, wholesome flour could be bought for $3.50 and that ten dollars would buy the equivalent of 570 five cent loaves of bread. "It is gratifying to be assured," continued the editor, "that all contributions coming from this country will be certain to reach the afflicted people direct, instead of passing into the hands of Russian officials, as the Czar's government has consented that Americans shall manage the distribution of their country's benevolence." [25]

The *Christian Herald* announced that Talmage and Klopsch would go to Russia themselves. When the $20,000 mark was reached, Klopsch and his associates chartered the steamer *Leo*. A cargo of 3,000,000 pounds, including seventeen hundred sacks of flour, bought from the New York Chamber of Commerce and the Chicago Board of Trade, together with medicine and delicacies for the sick, were loaded into the *Leo*. The contribution was valued at $31,884. "Probably," wrote Klopsch, "there has never been a more remarkable spectacle of disinterested Christian charity than this: no more beautiful and complete obedience to the command of the Master." [26]

Meantime the movement launched in the Middle West gained momentum. On February 12, 1892, the *Northwestern Miller* joyfully announced that through the foreign freight agent of the New York Central, William James, the Atlantic Transport Lines had offered the millers the use of the steamer *Missouri*. The Terminal Warehouse Company promised free storage in New York, and F. Hogan and Sons' stevedores agreed to load the ship as their contribution. F. C. Williams of Buffalo secured free insurance. "We congratulate the givers of this food," Edgar wrote. "We have demonstrated that nowhere else but in America could such an undertaking be successfully carried out in eight short weeks. Furthermore, it is a pleasure to add that we have, from start to finish, carried out our project without government aid, and, relying purely upon business men and business methods, have succeeded in opening up a channel through which the generous-minded in America can extend aid to suffering humanity in Russia." [27]

A cargo of flour and corn, estimated at 5,600,000 pounds and

[25] *Christian Herald* XV (March 23, 1892), 181.
[26] *Ibid.* (May 4, 1892), 296. The *Herald* listed the following items as composing the cargo: 14,485 bags of flour; 35 bags of meal; 55 barrels of flour; 510 bags of corn; 8 bags of beans; 38 packages of crackers, milk, etc.: *Ibid.* (June 29, 1892), 406.
[27] *Northwestern Miller*, Feb. 12, 1892.

representing 800 subscriptions from twenty-five states and territories, was loaded into the *Missouri*. Each package of corn meal, processed by Ferdinand Schumacher of the American Cereal Company in Cleveland, included circulars in Russian giving directions for its use. The New York *World* estimated the value of the millers' contribution at $100,000, that of the donors of transport, coal, telegraphic services, insurance, and other items, $67,000, or a total of $167,000.[28] But, as Edgar noted, this figure did not include the $12,000 worth of additional flour contributed by the New York Chamber of Commerce at the last moment to enable the *Missouri* to sail with a full cargo, nor the "great gift" of Nebraska's corn: the value of the whole enterprise edged toward $200,000. The *New York Herald* printed three big pictures of the loading of the *Missouri* and other metropolitan papers gave the project full publicity.[29] On March 15, with no to-do except a toast, a cheer, and the whistle of the tugboat, the *Missouri* set out to sea.

Edgar felt that the Philadelphians had been guilty of bad taste in beating the millers to a head start, but on sober reflection admitted that the important thing was to get the food to Russia as fast as possible. He himself and a colleague sailed for St. Petersburg to oversee the distribution. Some, he reflected, were at each point ready to find fault; but many more were prompt and cheerful in offering aid. "This success," Edgar wrote, "would not be worth winning if it had not been secured in the face of difficulties, at the cost of hard work, and after much effort." It reflected international credit on American millers, he concluded, showing the whole world that they "can feed the hungry, even when the latter have nothing to offer them in return for their flour, and are far removed from them, both geographically and commercially." [30]

The movement in Iowa, begun at the same time that Edgar issued his call, had its own flavor. The crusade, for such it was, combined the energies of Miss Alice French ("Octave Thanet"), of Benjamin Franklin Tillinghast, the remarkable editor of the Davenport *Democrat* and Secretary of the Governor's Russian Famine Relief Commission, and of the newly formed Women's Auxiliary of the Red Cross. These women drove into the country, stopping at every farm to ask for corn, urged townspeople to give money to buy more corn,

28 New York *World*, March 9, 1892.
29 *New York Herald*, March 6, 8, 1892.
30 *Northwestern Miller*, Feb. 26, 1892.

and raised funds by arranging for concerts, light operas, and a mock political convention at the State University. Alice French turned her facile pen from romance to reality, providing much of the enthusiasm and leadership. Tillinghast, who, according to Alice French, was doing the work of fifty men, did not find it easy to overcome a prevailing apathy. "Every personal, social, political and other influence I possess," he wrote to Clara Barton, "is being used with all the judgment and discretion I can give it. I have written a personal letter of thanks to every newspaper in the State which has favorably mentioned our cause and the same to individuals, strangers as well as friends." [31] It was hoped that the railroads, popularly regarded as "soulless corporations," would offer free freight to counteract prevailing hostility: they came through handsomely. In all, the Iowa Russian Famine Relief Committee, with the Ladies' Auxiliary, raised in corn and cash, contributions adding up to $40,000.

Tillinghast oversaw the shelling of the corn which he consigned to Clara Barton in New York. In turn, Miss Barton handed Tillinghast a check for $20,000. This represented the contributions of the people of the nation's capital, including earnings of the children of the White House. The *Tynehead*, chartered for the Iowa-Red Cross contribution, was loaded with 117,000 bushels of corn, 200 tons of flour, and several tons of canned meats, soups, and jellies for the sick. The enterprise cost $83,500. Tillinghast gallantly declared that the *Tynehead* might properly be looked on as the special contribution of American women. The point was all the more well taken since Mrs. Theophilia Kraemer was to set up kitchens in Russia and to teach the peasants how to follow the recipes for corn dishes, and Mrs. Mary Burnett, a well-known Chicago physician, was to give her services in fighting typhus. [32]

It is hard to estimate the total worth of American contributions in view of the overlapping character of a good deal of the work. Moreover, it is hard to compute the cash value of gifts in kind and of services such as those given by the International Navigation Company, the Atlantic Transportation Company, the railroads, express and insurance agencies, the Western Union, the warehouses, the coal

---

[31] Alice French to Clara Barton, Davenport, Jan. 25, 1892, and B. F. Tillinghast, Davenport, to Clara Barton, Jan. 23, 1892, Barton Papers.

[32] Benjamin Franklin Tillinghast, "The Women's Gift to Russia," *Harper's Weekly* XXVI (April 23, 1892), 402, and "A Far Reaching Charity," *Midland Monthly* I (April, 1894), 325-338.

companies that supplied the relief ships, and the stevedores. The Red Cross contributions ran to over $125,000: these included not only the funds raised in Washington but, to cite only a few examples, the $2,500 from Jacksonville, Florida, the $2,100 from Concord, New Hampshire, and the $7,000 from Russian immigrants in Lincoln, Nebraska. In relation to population the largest contribution came from Johnstown where, three years before, the Red Cross had given effective aid in the great flood. The New York Chamber of Commerce contributed $80,000, part of which helped fill the cargoes of the relief ships and part of which was sent directly to the American Legation in Russia for distribution. The American Minister in St. Petersburg received $77,500 from various sources; of this the Boston Committee headed by Phillips Brooks sent $10,396. The Friends of Russian Freedom contributed a much smaller amount; apart from what was given in Massachusetts, $2,013 was sent to Tolstoy from various parts of the country. The value of the cargoes of the five ships was estimated at $750,000. All in all, the American contribution must have edged toward a million dollars.

W. C. Edgar admitted that this was a mere drop in the bucket in relation to the need—a comment in contrast with the ebullient boast of the *Christian Herald* that "we have saved the lives of 125,000 Russians." But Americans contributed in far greater measure than any other people except the Russians themselves. The English Friends sent $165,000. The British Russian Famine Fund reported contributions of £3,000. And the British community in Moscow raised $10,000.[33] One Englishman, the Reverend Alexander Francis of the Anglo-American Church in St. Petersburg, was profoundly impressed by the generosity of the Americans which "exceeded that of all other nations combined." At the time he ascribed this generosity to a greater compassion. But some years later on visiting the United States Francis modified this generalization. Compassion, he then felt, implying as it did a kind of weakness on the part of both giver and receiver, was not, after all, a marked American trait. The Americans gave generously to Russia out of a sense of justice rather than com-

---

[33] *Free Russia* (The organ of the English Society of Friends of Russian Freedom) II (July, 1892), 7. It is worth noting that Gilbert Coleridge, treasurer of the British Russian Relief fund, concluded his summary with this statement: "The helping hand which England has privately extended to the sufferer in a distant land is a factor which has and will have a widespread political significance. He will not look upon England as his natural enemy, and he will remember that there are large masses of people over here who take a keen interest in and deeply sympathize with his hard and poverty-stricken lot."

passion. They gave, in short, because of an unprecedented prosperity, a traditional friendship for Russia, and a belief in "the ideal of a moral order founded on respect for self and other, that is, on personal dignity and worth." [34]

The commissioners accompanying each of the four relief ships agreed that Russia's plight had, contrary to some reports, been in no sense exaggerated. They wrote in detail of the suffering they saw. Much publicity was given to the stringy, smelly, porous, and black-ened "hunger bread" which Edgar brought back with him.

The commissioners also reported hearty and efficient cooperation from Russian officials and the American legation and consulates. Minister Smith approved of the Russian government's proposal to have the cargoes distributed under the auspices of a specially ap-pointed relief committee the members of which enjoyed general confidence. In some cases the Anglo-American Church in St. Peters-burg and Dr. Julian Hubbell of the American National Red Cross took part in the distributions; and all of the American commissioners watched the unloading of the cargoes and the reloading into Russian trains that were given priority over other rolling stock and sped toward the famine areas. The commissioners for the *Indiana*, the first ship to reach a Russian port, cabled to the sponsoring committee in Philadelphia that the system of distribution "disarms all criticism." [35] The other commissioners agreed.

At the ports of debarkation, at the capital cities, and in the villages themselves, the Americans met with every evidence of appreciation. The ships were unloaded in the presence of cheering throngs to the tunes of "The Star Spangled Banner" and "Hail Columbia" which Russian military bands played with great spirit. When the provisions brought by the *Conemaugh* were entrained in thirty-six Russian cars gaily decorated with intertwined flags of Russia and the United States, the Bishop of Livonia made an address "filled to the brim with grateful and earnest Christian sentiment." The Bishop's elo-quence seemed to one of the Philadelphia commissioners to contrast strangely with the failure of the immensely wealthy Orthodox Church to open soup kitchens or to give of its vast treasures for relief. After the address, the Bishop presented the jewelled cross to the Ameri-cans present to be kissed, and the service was concluded with chanting

[34] Alexander Francis, *Americans: An Impression* (New York: Appleton, 1909), 46-48.
[35] Russian Famine Correspondence.

and songs of praise.[36] On similar occasions the provisions were blessed by priests as onlookers crossed themselves. The crews, officers, and commissioners were given official dinners, even when they would have preferred less publicity, speechmaking, and toasting. The *Missouri's* captain received a Russian antique tea service. The committee welcoming the *Missouri* declared that the cornbread prepared for its sampling by the ship's cook was as "good as cake" and everywhere there was much interest in Nebraska's contribution of corn, with its abundant supply of Russian language leaflets giving recipes and exhorting the recipient to "praise God from whom all blessings flow." [37]

In the villages the donations were received sometimes with murmurs of exaltation, sometimes with outright ecstasy.[38] Many peasants, crossing themselves before taking a contribution, wanted to know where the flour came from and the names of the donors. They expressed great appreciation when told that some of these were themselves poor and had made sacrifices in order to contribute to the relief ships.[39] Russian newspapers described in detail the donations and distribution. The *Moscow Gazette* after interviewing Edgar gave a big spread to the story of the millers' contributions. "The gifts of America," wrote Edgar himself, "have been gratefully received. From the highest prince to the lowest peasant, all Russia is deeply touched by what has been done by the United States for her hungry people." [40] Count Bobrinsky, head of the Czarevitch's Relief Committee and responsible for the distribution, wrote that "the names of Indiana, Missouri, Conemaugh, Tynehead and Leo will always remind us of the most beautiful example of international charity and fraternal love that history has, perhaps, ever mentioned." [41] Tolstoy spoke of the American donations as an indication of a dawning universal brotherhood.[42] A prominent St. Petersburg artist presented to the Corcoran Gallery in Washington his painting of a troika carrying

---

[36] Reeves, *Russia Then and Now*, 31-33.

[37] *Northwestern Miller*, May 6, 1892.

[38] Jonas Stadling, "Relief Work of the Younger Tolstoy," *Century*, n.s. XXIV (August, 1893), 568. See also Stadling's first hand impression in his "With Tolstoy in the Russian Famine," *ibid.* (June, 1893), 249-63.

[39] *Christian Herald* XV (Oct. 19, 1892), 658-59. See also Rev. and Mrs. T. De Witt Talmage, *Talmage as I Knew Him* (London: John Murray, 1912), 264 and Charles M. Pepper, *Life-Work of Louis Klopsch: Romance of a Modern Knight* (New York: The Christian Herald, 1910), 26.

[40] *Northwestern Miller*, August 12, 1892.

[41] B. F. Tillinghast, "Far-reaching Charity," *Midland Monthly* I (May, 1894), 425.

[42] *Northwestern Miller*, June 10, 1892.

American supplies at the dockside in Feodosiya as a token of the hearty appreciation of the people of his country for "the generous and timely assistance rendered by the United States during the recent famine in Russia." In 1961 the picture was hanging in a White House conference room, a reminder, perhaps, of a time when happier relations existed between the two countries.[43]

Accounts in the American press ranged from the ecstatic and almost obsequious praise by the *Christian Herald*[44] to Edgar's diagnosis of the famine as a result of the communal rather than the individual system of land ownership.[45] To be sure, the press on rare occasions criticized the Russian handling of the whole famine problem.[46] But apparently little or no publicity was given to the report of George W. Wurts, chargé d'affaires, to the effect that the collapse in grain prices in the late spring of 1892 revealed vast quantities of grain hoarded by speculators and that Russian newspapers were saying that American aid should cease as it was depressing the grain market.[47]

Whatever the truth in these reports and innuendoes, the new Minister to Russia, Andrew D. White, informed the State Department that in 1893 the famine was in many ways more trying than it had been the year before. Peasants had eaten draught animals and burned for fuel everything not absolutely needed for shelter. Exhibits of "hunger bread" from Finland, correspondence with the Tolstoy family, and other proof showed the situation was indeed bad for millions of peasants. White distributed an additional 40,000 rubles from Philadelphia, but this did not go far. When he spoke of the matter to the Czarevitch, who was president of the Imperial Relief Commission, he was shocked at the offhand, easygoing way in which the heir to the throne remarked that he was no longer giving any heed to the matter since the famine was now worthy of no attention.[48] Despite the amazed anxiety of Andrew D. White, things apparently drifted along until 1897 when famine and disease again

---

[43] E. M. Halliday, "Bread upon the Waters," *American Heritage* XI (August, 1960), 64-65; Mary Hoffman Forbes, The Corcoran Gallery of Art, August 7, 1961, to Merle Curti.

[44] *Christian Herald* XV (Oct. 19, 1892), 658-59.

[45] W. C. Edgar, "Russia's Land System: The Cause of the Famine," *The Forum* XIII (July, 1892), 575-82.

[46] Murat Halstead, "Politics of the Russian Famine," *The Cosmopolitan* XIII (May, 1892), 80-83.

[47] *Papers Relating to the Foreign Relations of the United States*, 1892, 384.

[48] *The Autobiography of Andrew D. White* (2 vols., New York: Century, 1905) II, 9-10.

reached serious proportions in parts of Russia. A call for funds from a Wall Street broker was publicized in *The Outlook* but met with little response.[49]

The experience with Russian famine relief widened the circle of American effort geographically and contributed to the growing interest in the needs of other peoples. It showed that helping others was a highly complex problem. It brought home the importance of the recipient country's internal political and ethical system, especially the treatment meted out toward the Jewish minority. American democratic emotions had been stirred during the Greek struggle and the Irish famines: but the experience with Russia heightened these in a setting that anticipated the troubled decades ahead. The Russian experience also brought the Red Cross into foreign relief. It involved new groups of donors as well as of organizers. Humanitarian motives were dominant here as in previous relief crises, but this experience pointed up the importance of an existing situation in the economy—this time a surplus of corn and wheat—which figured in the decision of what and how much to give.

The failure of the Americans to respond in 1897 to new Russian needs was closely tied to demands for help in other quarters, demands presented with greater emotional appeal by a small but highly influential group of Americans. Beyond the southern reaches of Russia, in the heart of Asiatic Turkey, lay hundreds of Armenian towns and villages which became the focus of American philanthropic attention only two years after the Russian famine had widened the American circle of large-scale giving to the furthest point it had yet reached. Eager to unify the empire, the Turkish sultan, Abdul Hamid, had for some time been encouraging the land-hungry and fanatical Kurds to wipe out all villages of Christian Armenians that refused to embrace Islam. But the bloody massacre at Sasun in August, 1895, exceeded in extent and horror anything that had yet happened. The livestock, homes, and shops of the Armenian victims were seized by the Kurds or by Turkish officials as the survivors, naked and hungry, sought refuge in the centers of American missionary activity.[50] The *New York Tribune* reported that according

---

[49] *The Outlook* LXII (August 12, 1899), 829-30.

[50] Contemporary American accounts include Edwin M. Bliss, *Turkey and the Armenian Atrocities* (London: T. Fisher Unwin, 1896); H. Allen Tupper, Jr., *Armenia: Its Present Crisis and Past History* (Baltimore and New York: John Murphy, 1896) and Frederick D. Greene, *The Armenian Crisis in Turkey* (New York: G. P. Putnam, 1895).

to the American Minister in Constantinople 10,000 Armenians had been killed in thirty days. Americans read, almost week by week, of further massacres, of mutilated children, of ravished women.[51]

At this time the Americans dominated Protestant missions in Turkey. This resulted from the early initiative of the American Board and from the fact that the Sublime Porte evidently felt less apprehensive of American designs on the Empire, via missionary intrusion, than in the case of European missions. American colleges were in operation at Constantinople, Smyrna, Scutari, Harpoot, Marsovan, Beyrut, and Aintab, hospitals in the latter city, at Mardin and Caesarea, and schools for boys and for girls at Broussa, Afana, Trebizond, Sivas, Mosul, Van, and other places.[52] The one hundred and fifty-odd American missionaries insisted that their role in the political and nationalistic tensions was a neutral one, that, in fact, they inculcated among the Armenians the duty of obeying authority. But the Turks suspected that the missionaries stirred up political unrest.[53] In 1893 a Moslem mob burned the missionary girls' school at Marsovan. Within three years, approximately a million dollars of American property had been destroyed. In the increasing chaos that accompanied the massacres of the Armenians, the missionaries were often terrorized into keeping within their compounds. But they could and did report to the outside world what was happening. This, of course, only increased the Turks' resentment.[54]

Writing in *The Outlook* of December 7, 1895, the Reverend Cyrus Hamlin, founder and first president of Robert College in Constantinople, provided context for a better understanding of the shocking atrocities that threatened the extinction of a people and aroused mounting indignation. Hamlin noted the reluctance or refusal of the European Powers to intervene, despite promises which they had earlier extracted from Turkey for the fair treatment of the Armenian Christian minority. He made it clear that the Sultan's denial of any responsibility for the massacres rested on foundations too flimsy to be taken seriously. At least 250,000 people, Hamlin continued, were

---

[51] *New York Tribune*, Nov. 13, 1895; Philadelphia *Record*, March 13, 1896. The estimates of the total number of Armenians massacred in 1895 and 1896 varied from 20,000 to 50,000.

[52] Bliss, *Turkey and the Armenian Atrocities*, 310 ff; Tupper, *Armenia*, 97-98.

[53] George P. Knapp, an American missionary, was expelled from Bitlis in March, 1896, on the charge of sedition. *Appleton's Annual Encyclopedia*, 1896 (New York: Appleton, 1897), 736.

[54] For examples of missionary reports of the atrocities, see the *New York Tribune*, Nov. 13, 17, 18, Dec. 6, 1895.

bound to die of cold, hunger, typhus, and other diseases before the winter was over unless help on a large scale could be rushed to Armenia and administered by reliable American almoners. If the American government, he concluded, was unwilling to step in and play the role that the European Powers ought to play in protecting the Armenians against further outrages, at least Americans out of their abundance ought to give a million dollars for relief.[55]

Three months before this appeal was made Louis Klopsch of the *Christian Herald* had begun collecting funds. W. W. Howard, who had recently come back from Armenia, was named commissioner of the *Christian Herald's* relief movement. Thanks to these funds, Dr. Grace Kimball, a medical missionary at Van, was able to augment the relief she was dispensing by contributions from British and American friends. In December, 1895, Dr. Kimball in acknowledging receipt of $10,000 from the *Christian Herald* fund reported that she was feeding about 1,500 people daily as well as distributing clothing to villagers in the direst need. The hardest part of the job, she continued, was to turn away needy claimants, for it was impossible to do more than a little for the 15,000 refugees in and around Van. On Christmas day Dr. Kimball reported that 8,000 were now actually being helped and that untold suffering was being relieved. The total contributions to the *Christian Herald* fund from the first subscription on September 4, 1895, to the first of June, 1898, when the books were closed, was $73,867.98. "There was hardly a mission from Van to the Bosphorus," Klopsch wrote, "in which the readers of the *Christian Herald* were not remembered with blessings and gratitude." Often those who received bread knelt and kissed the feet of the giver. Not least of the causes for gratitude was the work of Commissioner Howard in rescuing terrified fugitive Armenians and helping them find a haven in Persian border villages.[56]

In addition to the funds raised by the *Christian Herald*, *The Outlook* and *Lend a Hand*, the organ of the well-known Unitarian minister of Boston, Edward Everett Hale, sent contributions to be distributed by American missionaries on the ground. In the course of her work Dr. Kimball employed needy victims in spinning and weaving raw wool, in knitting and sewing, in baking and carpentering. During March, 1896, she spent $2,000 in maintaining the indus-

[55] Cyrus Hamlin, "The Armenian Massacres," *The Outlook* LII (Dec. 7, 1895), 944-45.
[56] Charles M. Pepper, *Life-Work of Dr. Klopsch*, 28 ff, 49.

trial department, reporting that of 19,230 persons that had been helped, 10,857 were beneficiaries of the self-help industrial department. The effort to help the refugees rehabilitate themselves and reestablish communities supplemented the giving of food to keep the victims of persecution alive.[57]

As account after account from eyewitnesses filled the newspaper and periodical press indignation mounted. Great meetings in dozens of towns and cities protested the massacres and asked the government at Washington to check the slaughter. Bills and joint resolutions, accompanied by memorials and petitions, were introduced into both houses of Congress asking the government to protect the Christian inhabitants of Turkey, to condemn the cruelty of the Turkish officials, to insure the safety of American citizens in Turkey, and to guarantee the rights of Americans of Armenian background.[58] Looking back on all the public meetings, petitions, resolutions, speeches, and articles in the press a few years after the movement reached its crest, Talcott Williams, born of missionary parents in Turkey and at the time a nationally known editorial writer for the *Philadelphia Press*, summed things up in telling words: "Our hearts burned within us as we saw Christian Europe turning back from a clear duty for selfish reasons and a sense of the risks that might come from war, as if history knew any risk greater than unredressed justice and duty disregarded."[59]

Local relief committees were organized in several cities. In New York the committee included Bishop Alonzo Potter, Archbishop Corrigan, and such prominent business leaders as Morris K. Jessup, Jacob Schiff, Spencer Trask, and Everett P. Wheeler, who solicited funds and entered into correspondence with similar groups in other places in the interest of forming a national organization. The New York Chamber of Commerce, true to its traditions, joined the initiating group in promoting such a nation-wide organization.[60] Among the local groups with which the New York committee entered into correspondence was the Citizens Permanent Relief Committee of Philadelphia, established in 1893, and led by such well-known in-

---

[57] Edward G. Porter, "The Distribution of Relief in Armenia," *Lend a Hand* XVI (March, 1896), 188-92; Dr. Grace Kimball, "Van Industrial Bureau," *ibid.* (June, 1896), 446-51; Bliss, *Turkey and the Armenian Atrocities*, 515.

[58] See, for example, *Congressional Record*, 54th Cong., 1st Sess., 1895, XXVIII, Pts. 1-2, 108, 725, 854, 897, 1639.

[59] Talcott Williams, "Cuba and Armenia," *Century*, n.s. XXXV (Feb., 1899), 634-35.

[60] Spencer Trask to Robert Ogden, New York, Dec. 5, 1895, Leonard Bacon to Robert Ogden, New York, Dec. 12, 1895, Robert C. Ogden Papers, Library of Congress.

dustrialists, bankers, and professional men as John Converse, Rudolph Blankenburg, Charles J. Harrah, John Y. Huber, Dr. M. S. French, and Robert Ogden.[61] In Boston the American Board of Commissioners of Foreign Missions played a key role. Out of the leadership given by the New York Armenian Relief Committee the local groups developed the National Armenian Relief Committee, a loosely federated organization. Its executive committee included Supreme Court Justice David J. Brewer, Spencer Trask, Chauncy Depew, Dr. Leonard Woolsey Bacon, and the Reverend Frederick D. Greene, of New York. Operations centered at the Bible House in New York, and Brown Brothers in Wall Street served as treasurer.[62]

The National Armenian Relief Committee gave directions on how to form local committees. In due course such committees, some formed earlier, some later, carried on fund-raising activities in Springfield and Worcester in Massachusetts, in Syracuse, Harrisburg, Baltimore, Washington, Detroit, Cleveland, Columbus, Indianapolis, Chicago, St. Paul, and other cities. The national organization provided literature and arranged for speakers for affiliated committees. It suggested as effective procedures at the public meetings the reading of letters from missionaries in Armenia describing atrocities and what was being done to help the victims. But it warned against overreaching the mark. "Much harm has been done," wrote the secretary of the National Committee to a Philadelphia correspondent, "by painting the subject in colors so black as to paralyze all effort to relieve it and even to make such an effort absurd." [63] It was well, the National Committee advised, to introduce Armenians as speakers if they spoke briefly and did not seize the occasion to turn the meeting into one of mere protest rather than for relief. The praiseworthy zeal of some Armenians had, the national leadership warned, led to "very serious waste and complications." Above all, the scattering and dividing of relief effort must be avoided by every possible means.[64]

Notwithstanding the indignation expressed in memorials, petitions, resolutions, in articles and editorials in the press, and in

---

[61] "Armenian Massacres," in Citizens Permanent Relief Committee Papers, Historical Society of Pennsylvania.

[62] *New York Tribune*, Jan. 4, Feb. 17, 1896; Spencer Trask to Robert Ogden, New York, Dec. 6, 1895, Robert Ogden to John H. Converse, Dec. 6, 1895, Dr. M. S. French to Robert Ogden, Dec. 9, 1895, Talcott Williams to Robert Ogden, Dec. 12, 1895, Leonard Bacon to Robert Ogden, Dec. 12, 17, 1895, Ogden Papers.

[63] Frederick D. Greene to Herbert Welsh, Jan. 16, 1896, Herbert Welsh Collection, Historical Society of Pennsylvania.

[64] *Ibid.*, L. W. Bacon to Herbert Welsh, Jan. 8, 16, 1896.

speeches at public meetings, the raising of money proved to be hard work. Economic depression still gripped the country. The cry for relief of the starving Russians still echoed in many ears; the movement for aid to the Cubans proved a competing factor. Moreover, some accepted the official Turkish view that there had been much exaggeration in reports of the massacres and that in any case the Turkish government and relief committee had the matter in hand. F. Hopkinson Smith took this position while F. Marion Crawford publicized a dim view of the Armenians as the sharpest, shrewdest and trickiest of eastern peoples.[65] Many Americans honestly doubted whether contributions, however much needed, could be effectively used in view of the difficulties imposed by the Turkish authorities on distributing agencies.

The list of contributions contained some sizable gifts. John D. Rockefeller, for example, gave $1,000. But generally speaking the sums were small. The plan of enlisting school children met with varying response. In Philadelphia school authorities felt it was unwise to distract children from their daily tasks by confronting them with horror stories and refused to be impressed by the argument that the collection of small contributions in the schools might be made truly educational.[66] On the other hand, 2,500 school children in Minneapolis sent a contribution of over $700.[67]

Toward the end of the campaign Robert Ogden of Philadelphia, summing up the experience of the Permanent Relief Committee in the City of Brotherly Love, wrote that "never in all the history of my connection with the Permanent Committee was so much earnest, energetic, persistent and intelligent work done for any cause as was bestowed upon the Armenians with the result that we secured and forwarded twenty-five thousand dollars, a miserably small and meager sum, and out of all proportion to the success met with on other occasions, with causes far less powerful in their appeal to the benevolent."[68] The Philadelphians on another occasion contrasted the sluggishness of giving in their city with the record in New York. On March 17, 1896, the *Philadelphia Inquirer*, in reporting the step-up in effort on the part of the Citizens Committee, noted that thus far only $15,000 had been collected in the city while Boston had sent

---

[65] *Ibid.*, Herbert Welsh to F. Hopkinson Smith, Dec. 5, 1896; *New York Tribune*, Feb. 5, 8, 1896.
[66] Herbert Welsh to Henry Hobart Brown, Jan. 17, 1896, Welsh Collection.
[67] *New York Tribune*, June 7, 1896.
[68] Robert Ogden to Herbert Welsh, Dec. 15, 1896, Welsh Collection.

$40,000 and New York, $95,000.[69] These figures total to a considerably higher amount than other estimates: writing about the same time, Edward G. Porter concluded that somewhat over $100,000 had thus far been sent from the United States to relieve suffering Armenians.[70] An examination of the contribution lists in the newspapers suggests that this was not far out of line. In the end American contributions probably approached the $300,000 mark.[71]

The matter of the appropriate agency or agencies for distribution led to much debate. The normal thing would have been to send contributions to American missionaries. This was done. Dr. Caleb Frank Gates, who had recently become president of Euphrates College in Harput, distributed relief money by March, 1896, to 54,000 people in 160 villages—the money being given to him from English and Turkish as well as American sources.[72] But obstacles thrown in the way of the activities of missionaries suggested that other agencies might be more effective. In early February, 1896, the National Armenian Relief Committee sent $35,000 to the International Committee at Constantinople, a group composed of British consular officials, American missionaries, and other men in whom there was confidence. On March 19, 1896, the National Armenian Relief Committee forwarded another $10,000 to the International Committee in Constantinople.[73] But many questioned the effectiveness of this committee and felt that American contributions ought to be dispensed by an American agency.

On advice from missionaries in Constantinople the American Board of Commissioners of Foreign Missions, with headquarters in Boston, had decided early in December, 1895, that the American National Red Cross was the best possible agency for distribution. It had the experience of working in the recent Russian famine. It belonged to the International Red Cross organization and thus had the advantage of presumable access to Turkey since the Porte had recognized the international agency. Others agreed with the American Board: Pajap Bogigian, a Boston rug dealer and head of the Boston Armenian relief committee; Secretary of State Olney, who sent

---

[69] *Philadelphia Inquirer*, March 26, 1896.

[70] Porter, *Lend a Hand*, XVI, 188.

[71] This estimate is based on the $73,000 collected by the *Christian Herald*, the $107,000 which the Red Cross had to distribute, and the contributions sent through *Outlook*, *Lend a Hand*, and the Philadelphia Citizens' Committee.

[72] Caleb Frank Gates, *Not to Me Alone* (Princeton: Princeton University Press, 1940), 121-123.

[73] Philadelphia *Times*, March 19, 1896.

Bogigian to Clara Barton with the word that the Red Cross was the only body in the country that could cope with the field problems of relief in Turkey; Louis Klopsch of the *Christian Herald*; and the National Armenian Relief Committee in New York.[74] But the Philadelphia group stoutly opposed the idea. Robert Ogden was convinced that the Red Cross had bungled things in the Johnstown flood. Moreover, neither he nor his close associates had any confidence in Clara Barton, whom they regarded as dictatorial, inefficient, and much too old—she was seventy-four.[75]

On her part, Clara Barton had no great desire to assume so heavy a burden. When approached by the Boston and New York people she stipulated that the Red Cross would enter the work only if there was a unanimous desire on the part of the local committees to have it do so, only if the call "be an appeal from people strong, brave, and influential enough to crush all antagonists and fault-finders." Miss Barton further stipulated that her organization would go into the field only if there was an assurance of sufficient funds—the Red Cross at this time was not a fund-raising organization. Finally, the Red Cross agents in Turkey must have complete authority—it was not to be divided with the missionaries. The Boston and New York representatives seemingly agreed on these points.[76]

The response to appeals for funds was sluggish. Feeling that every day was precious, Clara Barton announced that she would start with a small staff of field workers and the minute sum of $50,000 on hand. On January 10, 1896, Justice Harlan presided over a large farewell meeting at the First Congregational Church in Washington. "If I live to come back," Clara Barton said, "judge me not harshly, nor praise me unjustly, for I shall only have done all that I could. I may not meet you again, and therefore bid you good-bye." A rising ovation testified to the admiration of the courage of the grand old lady.[77]

Then trouble began. On the claim that the Red Cross was not truly neutral, that the reports of the massacres had been highly exaggerated for political purposes, and that the Turkish government

[74] L. W. Bacon to Robert Ogden, Dec. 17, 1896, Ogden Papers; *New York Tribune*, Dec. 6, 14, 1896; "Catch Books," Nov. 30, Dec. 2, Dec. 3, Dec. 5, 1895, Barton Papers.

[75] Spencer Trask to Robert Ogden, Dec. 19, 1895, James Barton to Talcott Williams, Jan. 20, 1896, L. W. Barton to Robert Ogden, Jan. 28, 1896, Ogden Papers.

[76] Clara Barton Diary, Nov. 30 to Dec. 14, 1895, in Barton Papers, Library of Congress.

[77] *New York Tribune*, Jan. 12, 1896; Diary, Dec. 5, Dec. 7, Dec. 16, Dec. 18, 1895, "Catch Books," Jan. 28, 1895–Jan. 1, 1896, Barton Papers.

and affiliated Red Crescent were doing all that was necessary, the Sublime Porte forbade the American Red Cross to come into Turkey. Appeals were sent to Congress and to President Cleveland urging that Minister Terrell in Constantinople use pressure on the Turkish authorities to have the prohibition revoked.[78] Without waiting for the result Miss Barton sailed from New York on January 22nd. At Southampton the little party of six, including Miss Barton, received word that the Turkish government would permit Minister Terrell to name individuals for the administration of relief, and that he had named Miss Barton and her associates. In Paris, en route to Constantinople, the group learned at the American Legation of the diatribes that were being made in Congress against Turkey. Miss Barton's diary commented: "America is taking a very foolish stand in this matter and will become involved in European difficulties unless she takes a more conservative view of the situation. Certain it is her attitude will make our work more difficult." [79]

The party arrived in Constantinople on February 16, 1896. During an interview with Tewfik Pasha, Minister of Foreign Affairs, Miss Barton explained the nonpartisan policy of the Red Cross: it would administer relief according to need and without reference to nationality, religion, or politics. She had, she said, brought no newspaper correspondents. All the communications she and her associates sent would go out on the Turkish telegraph. She meant to aid the state by helping those in distress; if she found there was no need, the Red Cross would withdraw. She made it plain that she had brought skilled, practical helpers who would try to get the people back to their deserted fields and provide them with plows, hoes, spades, sickles, scythes, seed corn and wheat, so that they could support themselves. She was also ready to provide them with cattle or other animals. "I shall never counsel nor permit a sly or underhand action with your government, and you will pardon me, Pasha, if I say that I shall expect the same treatment in return—such as I give I shall expect to receive." Immediately Tewfik Pasha replied, "And you shall have it. We honor your position and your wishes will be respected. Such aid and protection as we are able to, we shall render." [80]

The next day an official appeared at the hotel where the Red Cross

[78] Barton, *The Red Cross,* 277 ff.
[79] Clara Barton Diary, Feb. 6, 1896, Barton Papers.
[80] *Ibid.,* Feb. 18, 1896; Barton, *The Red Cross,* 279-80.

staff was staying to tell Miss Barton that she must delay sending the expeditions already in preparation until the government could translate a vast pile of newspapers and documents, just received from America, which seemed to indicate that the national government and the governors of the several states had taken part in a move against Turkey. Miss Barton herself had read some of the inflammatory American newspaper stories and could understand the Turkish anxiety. In the end, she was permitted to send into the interior five expeditions, each escorted by Turkish troops.[81]

Learning from the British ambassador that typhoid, typhus, dysentery, and smallpox had broken out in Marash and Zietoun and that the need for help was desperate, Miss Barton was persuaded to change the course of the expeditions, which had planned to get into the interior by way of the Black Sea routes, and to send them by small coast steamers along the Mediterranean to Alexandretta. This and other necessary changes were misunderstood in America, being interpreted as proof of Miss Barton's incompetence. Cables arrived suggesting that it was obvious she did not know what she was doing. On another occasion an unfounded report that she had agreed to dispense relief only as the Turkish authorities ordered caused hysterical protests. "One cannot fail to see how nearly a misguided enthusiasm, desire for sensational news, vital action without thought or reflection," wrote Miss Barton in retrospect, "came near to the overthrowing of their entire object, the destruction of all that had been or has since been accomplished for humanity, . . ."[82] Thus much of her time and energy at her headquarters in Constantinople went into ironing out misunderstandings and in mending public relations. Much more time, to be sure, went into keeping in touch with Turkish authorities, who were providing the indispensable escorts, and with the five expeditions some thousand miles away in almost incommunicable isolated areas.

With the help of Dr. Ira Harris, a resident American physician in Tripoli, Syria, remarkable results were achieved in the pestilence-ridden Marash and Zietoun areas. Dr. J. B. Hubbell, Ernest Mason, Charles King Wood, and Edward M. Wistar, who led expeditions, achieved equally remarkable results at the cost of hard work, difficult travel, and great exposure. Arrangements were made for the manufacture of household equipment which gave employment to refugees

---

[81] Barton, *The Red Cross*, 280, 283-84.
[82] *Ibid.*, 284-90.

in the Oorfa area. Local committees helped distribute bread, clothing, farm animals, seed, and simple agricultural tools. Wistar, to take a single example, distributed in the Harpoot area 500 beds, 3,500 articles of clothing, 300 farm animals, 1,640 bushels of grain, and 3,000 farm implements. The program as a whole brought help to almost half a million people. In contrast with the Anglo-American committee's use of much greater resources to feed the hungry, the Red Cross helped sufferers by giving them the means to keep alive. The lifting of the spirits of men and women who had sunk into a sluggish apathy through fear and terror meant the awakening of hope and of faith that life might still be worth living.[83] Dr. Caleb Frank Gates of the Euphrates College, who did a great deal of relief work himself and helped the Red Cross agents as well, summed up the larger significance of what was done: "One of the greatest contributions made by the benevolent men and women in distant parts of the world was the assurance brought by their gifts that they cared for these alien sufferers; that their sympathy, their thoughts, and their prayers went with their gifts; and that this afflicted people was not left abandoned of all men." [84]

In view of the colossal difficulties Clara Barton faced, difficulties compounded because of suspicion and criticism at home, her achievement was remarkable. She generously paid full credit to those that helped her, to her staff, to the Turkish authorities who provided military escorts on the relief expeditions, to the American diplomatic and consular officers, to the missionaries in Turkey whose guidance and help was so valuable, to the American press, to the committees at home, and to the donors. Only a few knew the extent to which she had given herself. But she took satisfaction in knowing she had done her best. She also took some pride in the appreciation the Turkish government showed in conferring on her the medals of two orders.[85]

The plight of widows and orphans continued to call for help. By 1900 some 50,000 orphans were housed in asylums built by contributions from Germany, England, America, and elsewhere. One observer, though expressing appreciation for what was being done, noted the

[83] Dr. J. B. Hubbell, "General Field Agent's Report," *ibid.*, 334-49; Dr. Ira Harris, "Medical Report," *ibid.*, 350-56; J. Rendel Harris and Helen B. Harris, *Letters from the Scenes of the Recent Massacres in Armenia* (New York and Chicago: Fleming H. Revell, 1897), *passim*.
[84] Gates, *Not to Me Alone*, 136.
[85] Barton, *The Red Cross*, 299-304.

shortsightedness of the American Protestant missionaries in giving their charges an education ill-suited to life in Turkey, an education the more likely to alienate them from their surroundings since it inculcated Protestanism while their people were Armenian Catholics.[86]

To support the widows and orphans new appeals were launched. Clara Barton herself wrote a Thanksgiving appeal which the National Armenian Relief Committee publicized widely: "Unless the open hands of charity be reached out and across and access be secured, hunger and cold will gather victims by the tens of thousands and bury them like the falling leaves beneath the snow." [87] Clara Barton's friend, Frances Willard, urged the WCTU to contribute to the relief of orphans—a dollar, she reminded her followers, would support a child for a month.[88]

But "the tide of beneficence" could not be expected to flow continuously into relief even if it were desirable to try to support an entirely impoverished people. On the other hand, to rehabilitate the Armenians by self-help programs might merely invite further despoilment unless the Turkish authorities could be made to protect the Christian minority. Two avenues, beyond continuing what must be a dwindling fund for relief and rehabilitation, seemed to be open.

One was colonization and emigration. Frances Willard appealed for funds to help colonize refugees in Bulgaria, a scheme which Lady Henry Somerset was promoting.[89] Other prominent English people were helping Armenian widows and orphans to settle in Cyprus. A few hundred sought admission to the United States. The immigration authorities at Ellis Island required a bond of $500 for each person—a sum not easy to find despite the interest of such prominent social leaders as Mrs. Wistar of Philadelphia (the daughter of Fanny Kemble). Once the bond was raised, there was the problem of looking out for these helpless victims of Turkish persecution. Alice Stone Blackwell found work for some in the farms and kitchens of New England.[90] The Salvation Army, the Christian Endeavor, and

[86] Carl Albert Paul Rohrbach, "A Contribution to the Armenian Question," *The Forum* XXIX (June, 1900), 481-92. On the other hand, an American missionary, Miss Corinna Shattuck, wrote glowing accounts of the industrial programs in operation at the orphanages at Oorfa, Harpoot, Mardin, and Van: Pepper, *Life-Work of Louis Klopsch*, 48.

[87] *New York Tribune*, Nov. 26, 1896.

[88] *Ibid.*, Nov. 28, Dec. 15, 1896.

[89] *Ibid.*, Dec. 24, 1896.

[90] Herbert Welsh to Mrs. I. G. Barrows, Oct. 24, 1896, Welsh Collection.

the Woman's Christian Temperance Union all helped in locating some five hundred refugees. At Summit, New Jersey, an obstacle arose when about a hundred workingmen, unable to get jobs, protested the bringing in of twenty-nine Armenians by well-placed citizens who arranged housing and work for them.[91]

In the other approach the British relief committee headed by the Duke of Westminster pointed the way. Despite the £35,000 the organization sent to the relief committee in Constantinople by early April, 1896, frustration was felt when it was reported that at least another £100,000 was needed to see 200,000 destitute Armenians through the months ahead. The Duke of Westminster's committee as early as October, 1895, had urged the Prime Minister to pressure the Ottoman government into compensating the Armenian peasants for the losses they had suffered at Sasun. When the massacres continued the committee, despairing of the "terrible condition of affairs," urged the importance of administrative reforms in Turkey as well as some form of order to preserve life, property, and religious liberty. Unless genuine stability was secured in Turkey, there seemed little point in continuing palliative measures for the Armenians. As one report put it, "we are only feeding them now for future massacres."[92]

On December 10, 1895, Senator Wilkinson Call of Florida introduced a concurrent resolution calling on the government to prevent by peaceful negotiation or by force of arms if necessary, the cruelties inflicted on the Armenians. He introduced the motion, he declared, in the name of religion, humanity, and the principles on which all civilization rests. To give effect to its intention, he included in the resolution the provision for the establishment of an independent Armenian state the permanence of which the civilized Powers of the world were to guarantee. This was much too sweeping for the Committee on Foreign Relations, to which it was referred. On January 24, 1896, Senator Shelby Moore Cullom of Illinois, chairman of the Committee, introduced a joint resolution assuring the President of the support of Congress in any move he might make to induce the Powers to respect their treaty obligations to the Armenian people by appropriate pressure on the Ottoman government. In supporting his resolutions Senator Cullom, while admitting that the United States

[91] *New York Tribune*, Oct. 22, 30, Nov. 22, 1896.
[92] *The Times* [London], Oct. 24, Nov. 4, 19, 1895, March 12, June 23, July 1, Nov. 27, 1896, April 27, 1897.

could not as a neutral interfere in the affairs of Europe, insisted that the country had an obligation to humanity to which it could not be blind.[93]

The discussion in the Senate indicated, at least on the part of almost everyone who spoke, a feeling that the resolutions did not go far enough. This was the opinion of Senator Newton Blanchard of Louisiana and of Senator Wilkinson Call of Florida. The Cullom resolutions were, Call claimed, tame and insignificant, giving neither relief nor protection. Senator William Frye of Maine, on the Republican side, noted that the American people had invested six million dollars in Turkey for the sole purpose of improving the condition of its people. It had been a work of wonderful benevolence, now brought to an absolute stop. Was the government to do nothing except to exhort the European Powers to do their duty? The only dissident note was sounded by Senator George Frisbie Hoare of Massachusetts. He sympathized not only with the resolutions but with the sentiments of his colleagues. Yet it was unwise, he felt, to hurl extreme statements at Turkey when Clara Barton was on her way to administer relief and when it was not yet clear whether the Porte would permit her to carry out an errand of mercy. The Senate adopted the joint resolution, which was then sent to the House.[94]

In a spirited discussion lasting a full four hours, members of the House expressed a variety of views. Charles Henry Grosvenor of Ohio regarded the resolution as a most inefficient and unworthy utterance of the American people. "They have asked us for bread, and we are giving them a stone. They have asked us for the fish of a Christian nation's powerful protest, and we have given them the serpent of an abject falling down and apology at the feet of the Turkish government." Why, he demanded, abandoning his wonderfully mixed metaphor, should the United States call on other nations to do that which it had a perfect right to do itself? William Peters Hepburn of Iowa took a similar stand: the resolutions just didn't go far enough. On the other hand, Robert Adams of Pennsylvania opposed the resolutions as contrary to the Monroe Doctrine. Henry Turner of Georgia attacked them as an impertinence. The reporter of the *New York Tribune* who heard the debate, felt that at least seven-eighths of the members present in the House favored strong action. When the vote was taken—143 in favor of the Cullom resolu-

[93] *Congressional Record*, 54th Cong., 1st Sess., 1896, XXVIII, Pt. 1, 108, 959-61.
[94] *Ibid.*, 961-965.

tion, 26 against—it was clear that most of the opposition was on the Democratic side.[95]

In these discussions and in the joint resolution adopted by Congress, the emphasis for the first time, in any situation at all comparable, was not on temporary relief, either by voluntary or by government agencies. It was rather on political action to remove the causes of a great and continuing disaster. But the resolution was as far as the matter went. Oscar Straus, a former Minister to Turkey, urged President Cleveland to make no attempt to influence the internal affairs of Turkey, lest the Sultan claim that the Red Cross was interfering and the single opportunity of bringing relief to the suffering be lost.[96] President Cleveland remained noncommittal when a delegation of well-known New York business and professional men including William E. Dodge and Andrew D. White asked for action on the resolutions adopted by Congress.[97]

But a precedent had nonetheless been made when Congress took a stand, regarded by many of its members as far too mild, in recommending government action as the only appropriate means of giving significant and lasting aid to a people in grave distress.

Seldom free from famine in one or another part of the vast subcontinent, India experienced in 1897 and the following years its most disastrous food shortage in the second half of the nineteenth century. The British system of famine relief, worked out over previous decades, proved inadequate to meet the crisis. Before the end of the initial year, 1897, over 4,500,000 people had received aid, either from the Government or from voluntary contributions from England and the Empire, France, Germany, and the United States. Of these, the gifts from England were the largest: the Mansion House Committee in London and the people of Lancashire sent £708,000.[98] The Viceroy informed the American people that voluntary contributions would be welcome. Little wonder, if there was truth in the report of Julian Hawthorne whom the *Cosmopolitan* sent to India, and who reported in the summer of 1897 that at least 3,000,000 men, women, and children had already died of the famine and the pestilence that fol-

[95] *Ibid.*, Pt. 1, 1000, Pt. 2, 1000-1016; *New York Tribune*, Jan. 28, 1896.
[96] Mabel A. Elliott, "American National Red Cross Disaster Series, 1881-1918," American National Red Cross Archives, Washington, 79 ff.
[97] *New York Tribune*, May 16, 1896.
[98] *Appleton's Annual Cyclopedia*, 1897, 399-401.

lowed in its wake.[99] Meantime the *Christian Herald,* from early January, 1897, had been publishing in every issue appalling accounts of rib-protruding, sunken-eyed, starving men, of pitiful child-mothers reduced to skin and bone, and of children with swollen bellies.

In view of the later American response it was ironical that, early in the famine, a shipload of American wheat arrived in Calcutta only to be sent on to England because of the report that prices were much higher there.[100] Yet the American response, once the press publicized conditions, was, unlike that of Great Britain, influenced neither by the responsibilities of empire nor by political considerations. The only consideration other than the dominant humanitarian one was the argument of American missionaries in the field that generous contributions would materially aid the work of conversion.[101]

Several agencies, including the Missionary Society of New York and the Mennonites, appealed for and distributed funds. But none conducted so vigorous, sustained, intensive, and dramatic a campaign as the *Christian Herald.* From early January, 1897, on, every issue contained appeals for generosity. Such headlines as "India's Dying People," "Plague in Bombay is slaying thousands of people," and "India's Bitter Cry" were spelled out with firsthand accounts of the horrible conditions which American missionaries were witnessing and by photographs which they sent of actual men, women, and children in advanced stages of starvation. "Every dollar saves a life. Is your name on the Life-Roll? Have you saved a life today?" As before the magazine listed week by week the name of every contributor, including such telling if anonymous identifications as "A Follower of the Savior," "In His Name," "A Free Will Offering," and "An Old Lady of 87 and Her Granddaughter." Now and again a letter was also shared with readers, "Although I am a poor working girl, I would like to add my mite toward the relief fund for starving India. Enclosed find one dollar." [102]

The response was impressive. But to spur public opinion Klopsch, Talmage, and Margaret Lettsch, a missionary of seventeen years' service in India, took the stump during the spring. As a result of their appeals at a vast meeting at the Chicago auditorium, $10,000 in

---

99 Julian Hawthorne, "The Horrors of the Plague in India," *The Cosmopolitan* XXIII (July, 1897), 232-46; Hawthorne, "India Starving," *ibid.* (August, 1897), 368-84.
100 *Appleton's Annual Cyclopedia,* 1897, 399.
101 Pepper, *Life-Work of Louis Klopsch,* 56.
102 *Christian Herald* XX (Feb. 24, 1897), 147.

cash and twenty-five carloads of corn were pledged.[103] In Omaha Talmage told an audience, packed to near suffocation, that the American people spent millions on chewing gum and might well contribute corn and money to the people of India, where, he added, Christ had once lived.[104] At the meeting in Lincoln, Chancellor MacLean of the University of Nebraska presided. He remarked that Nebraskans hadn't fully recovered from the awful drought but that in the promise of prosperity he was sure they would now give. Klopsch told the same audience that he believed heaven could be found on earth: it consisted of helping one's unfortunate neighbors.[105] In all these and in other meetings, purse strings were opened.

A less idealistic note was struck when Klopsch urged Talmage to go to India in order to give prestige to the begging tour. It would mean, Klopsch admitted, the sacrifice of lucrative returns from a proposed Chautauqua tour, but everyone would know and speak of this. Talmage would certainly be received by the Viceroy and the Prince of Wales, and, on his return, no doubt by Queen Victoria herself.[106] Talmage did not give up the Chautauqua tour, but in the end Klopsch himself went to India.

Meantime the *Christian Herald* was sending substantial funds to a committee of American missionaries in India headed by the renowned Methodist bishop, James Thoburn. Convinced that food as well as other provisions was needed and that many could give corn when they could not afford to give cash, Klopsch induced railroads to carry corn to San Francisco at greatly reduced rates. He also chartered the *City of Everett*, whose cargo of corn, wheat, and beans was insured at $60,000. The Reverend R. G. Hobbs sailed with the cargo and delivered it into the hands of the committee in Calcutta and Madras. It was distributed by the missionaries who reported that it saved thousands of lives. And the donation was received with great appreciation. The Viceroy expressed his warm thanks.[107] So did articulate Indians. "We feel profoundly touched," wrote the Indians associated with the Tamil mission in Madras, "with that love which has prompted you to raise in America such an enormous quantity of grain

[103] *Chicago Times-Herald*, May 4, 1897.
[104] Omaha *Weekly Bee*, April 28, 1897.
[105] *Nebraska State Journal*, April 30, 1897.
[106] Louis Klopsch to T. De Witt Talmage, April 14, 1897, T. De Witt Talmage Papers, Library of Congress.
[107] Pepper, *Life-Work of Louis Klopsch*, 57, 66; *Christian Herald* XX (June 16, 1897), 476; (June 23, 1897), 502.

and a magnificent sum of money to feed the hungry in a foreign land like India."[108] When the *Christian Herald* published the accounts it appeared that $196,561.69 had been contributed in cash and $256,502 in grain and freight charges. In all the *Christian Herald's* contribution amounted to more than $500,000.[109]

With surprising unanimity, Congress in April, 1897, provided for the securing of vessels to transport gifts in kind to India.[110] But the crisis had passed before the Navy could put a ship at the disposal of American donors.

In November, 1899, the Indian government again officially recognized a state of famine. Klopsch persuaded Secretary of State Hay and Secretary of the Navy Long to provide transport and this time the government, at the cost of $40,000, chartered the *Quito*. Its cargo, insured at $100,000, included 200,000 bushels of corn and substantial quantities of seed suitable for sowing in India. With appropriate ceremonies the *Quito* sailed from Brooklyn harbor on May 10, 1900. Meantime the *Christian Herald* had cabled $40,000 to India. On arriving in Bombay in May, Klopsch, after interviews with the Governor and the International Missionary Committee, cabled the sad story of desperate need. Roving into the interior, he sent the *Christian Herald* heartrending accounts of the death and suffering that he saw. In July the *Christian Herald* cabled another $100,000. By the spring of 1901, the total contributions through the agency of this amazing journal had totaled $641,071.97. When actual famine relief ended, the unexpended balance of $173,973 was applied to the support of 5,000 famine orphans at sixty missionary stations.[111]

As the nineteenth century closed, the circle of American giving in foreign lands had reached around the world. Meantime close to home a situation had developed which heralded a new era in which the United States, like Great Britain, was to be confronted with the problems of colonial responsibility and world power. These problems were certain to affect the now well-established pattern of fund raising and provision collecting, of transport of goods and food in

---

[108] Pepper, *Life-Work of Louis Klopsch*, 65.
[109] *Christian Herald* XX (April 14, 1897), 294; (April 21, 1897), 317-18.
[110] *Congressional Record*, 55th Cong., 1st Sess., 1897, XXX, Pt. 1, 561, 706, Pt. 2, 1164, 1391, 1472.
[111] Pepper, *Life-Work of Louis Klopsch*, 68 ff.

government subsidized vessels as well as those chartered through private initiative and support. This kind of overseas philanthropy had made a notable record, not entirely uncolored by selfish considerations, but one which on the whole represented a truly humanitarian impulse.

VI

The Expansion of Religious Benevolence

The major impulse in nineteenth-century philanthropies beyond the seas flowed from the evangelical missionary movement. This was the only cause to inspire constant, sustained giving for a single purpose and to become world-wide in scope before the end of the century. To be sure, the American movement cannot be disassociated from the great Protestant missionary impulse in Great Britain to which, at the start, it owed a deep debt, nor from related missionary movements in Germany, Switzerland, and other continental countries.[1]

In many respects, however, the American story had its distinctive features. These stemmed in part from the greater emphasis on voluntary contributions than in countries with established or state churches. Another distinctive feature lies in the fact that although the American missionary movement, like others, followed the paths of trade, it owed little to commercial and political considerations except in the case of Hawaii and to a lesser degree, China and Japan. In fact, for some time American missionaries in meeting the opposition of governing authorities in China, India, Turkey, Portuguese East Africa and elsewhere abroad, could not count on much help from the diplomatic representatives of their country. Writing in 1838 in the *Chinese*

[1] The monumental work in the field is Kenneth Scott Latourette, A *History of the Expansion of Christianity* (7 vols.; New York, London: Harper, 1937-45). The approach of Professor Latourette is, properly, international rather than American, British, Rhenish, or Swiss. This makes difficult, however, the isolation of the distinctively American contributions to the missionary movement and a comparative evaluation of the contributions of various countries to the financial support and to the personnel of the "expansion."

Repository, a correspondent—probably S. Wells Williams—pointedly declared that scientific travelers, philanthropists, and missionaries, and all other persons whose business it was to impart rather than to acquire, were entitled to the same protection afforded to other Americans. "No citizen can be deemed to have forfeited his country's protection by becoming a philanthropist. Acquisitiveness is no more sacred than benevolence." [2] In time, something like cooperation between merchants, missionaries, and diplomatic representatives became the order of the day, but the missionaries never regarded themselves as agents of national policy or of commerce.

A not uncommon mid-twentieth-century point of view regards the missionaries of the nineteenth century as more or less narrow-minded do-gooders, ignorant of the culture of "the natives," or at least as failing to have understood it. That there was narrowness and lack of adequate understanding among the missionaries is indeed true. But narrowness did not characterize all of them. And even the least of them made some contribution to an important philanthropic movement. American missionaries, together with those of other countries, served as relief workers in time of famine and pestilence. They contributed to the growing impact of Western civilization on Asiatic and African cultures, an impact that quickened the breakdown of traditional institutions, social structures, and value systems and that, in turn, grafted fragments of Western culture on to emerging patterns in these lands. American missionaries, like those from other countries, contributed to, and in many cases played the dominant role in introducing new types of education, the theory and practice of Western medicine, and innovating ideas about the status and role of women. Notable, too, were contributions of American missionaries to the world's knowledge of linguistics, geography, ethnology, and anthropology.

In interpreting other peoples to their constituents at home, American missionaries broadened the horizons of their fellow citizens and helped to prepare the stage for the more positive role America was to play in the larger world. They did more. With all their limitations, the missionaries helped many members of the human family to understand each other.

Even before the overseas missionary movement got under way, the preparation had begun. Cotton Mather and Jonathan Edwards

[2] *Chinese Repository* VII (May, 1838), 21.

had felt that America had a special obligation to evangelize the world. This, combined with the continuing sense of obligation to Christianize the Indians, provided a background for the evangelical awakening the young republic shared in the 1790's with Great Britain. Certainly the crusade that started in the 1790's and early 1800's also owed a good deal to the organization in England in 1792 of the Baptist Missionary Society, and, before the decade was over, of two other missionary societies. American periodicals in the 1790's borrowed liberally, from Scottish and English magazines, story after story about heathen peoples. Add to these examples and influences the conviction that the Christian onslaught against the secularism and skepticism of the Enlightenment must include the aggressive carrying of the Word to heathens everywhere. A millennial sense that the time might be short, added to the urgency of the conviction.

This is the context that helps explain the rise of an organized foreign missionary movement. One cannot specify the first American seriously to nurse the idea that it was his duty to go to foreign lands to convert the heathen. But if action is the test, the finger points to Samuel John Mills. This son of a Congregational minister at Torringford, Connecticut, reported a telling experience that he had in the autumn of 1801. For three years young Mills had been deeply upset about his spiritual state. His mother's piety helped him to believe that God's perfection is such that he need not and ought not be overconcerned about his own destiny. The theology of Hopkins taught him that the true believer must be *willing* to endure eternal torment, having faith in God's disinterested benevolence. In a flash Mills saw that he ought also to be willing to risk everything in this life, and life itself, as a testimony to his faith in the same disinterested benevolence of the Almighty. He ought, he felt, to preach the gospel in heathen lands to those in darkness, whatever the difficulties, whatever the risks. Selling a farm bequeathed to him by a grandmother, Mills entered a nearby academy and in 1806 enrolled in Williams College.

His story is familiar: how he led a student revival, how he gathered a few friends at a haystack and with much fervor and prayer, proposed that they dedicate themselves to foreign missions. The Brethren, as these young men called themselves, accepted the challenge. At first Mills found no support for his idea, but he was persistent. As a student at Andover Theological Seminary he talked foreign missions day and night. As a result of a paper he and three friends presented to the General Association of Massachusetts, the American Board of Commissioners for Foreign Missions took form in 1810.

Mills himself did not go at once to distant points overseas, for he had accepted a call from the Connecticut and Massachusetts home missionary societies to gather information about religious conditions in the Mississippi Valley, to preach, and to leave Bibles and tracts wherever he could. But at last he did go to West Africa to choose a site for a proposed colony for freedmen. On his way back in 1822 he died of fever and was buried at sea.[3]

American Baptists, Congregationalists, and Presbyterians had been giving to the Baptist mission established in India by William Carey, the pioneer British missionary to that little known land. But it did not seem feasible or even possible to the new American Board of Commissioners for Foreign Missions to raise enough money to send out the young men who under the leadership of Mills yearned to go. One of them, Adoniram Judson, went to England to lay before the London Missionary Society a plan for a joint British and American effort to support missionaries from both countries who were eager to embark for India.[4] But the British leaders felt that cooperation presented too many problems and suggested that the Americans strike out on their own in the great enterprise. A desire in the young republic to emulate the mother land encouraged Americans to redouble their efforts to find a way. So did the related desire to show that the United States was now in fact as independent of England in all matters as it was in the political sphere.

It proved easier to enlist young Americans to give themselves than it did to persuade the well to do and the rank and file among the Protestants to donate money. To give to foreign missions, many felt, was to take from needed efforts to evangelize the Indians and the pioneer in our own West. Others argued that if the heathen in foreign lands were given the opportunity to turn to God and refused to do so, He might condemn them to everlasting damnation, whereas, He might extend His grace to those that had never had a chance to

[3] Thomas C. Richards, *Samuel J. Mills, Missionary, Pathfinder, Pioneer, and Promoter* (Boston, New York: The Pilgrim Press, 1906). See also Oliver Wendell Elsbree, *The Rise of the Missionary Spirit in America* (Williamsport, Pa.: Williamsport Printing and Binding Co., 1928), 36, 51, 109-111, 150, 151.

[4] Francis Wayland, *A Memoir of the Life and Labors of the Rev. Adoniram Judson* (2 vols.; Boston: Phillips, Sampson, 1853) and Edward Judson, *The Life of Adoniram Judson by His Son* (New York: A.D.F. Randolph, 1883).

accept His Word. Once missionaries began their labors in the foreign field, reports of failure to make much headway militated still further against giving. Aldin Grout, for example, toiled for eleven years in Africa before making his first convert. In the Marathi mission in west India the number of missionaries who died in a twenty-one year period exceeded the number of converts they made.

The means for attracting and training missionaries and for combating indifference toward fund raising gradually developed on the model of British organizations. The first agency of course was the missionary society itself—the various state missionary societies, the American Board of Commissioners for Foreign Missions, the Missionary Society of the Methodist Episcopal Church, the General Missionary Convention of the Baptist Denomination in the United States for Foreign Missions, and the Foreign Missionary Board of the Protestant Episcopal Church, to cite only a few examples. The annual meetings of these societies made plans for fund raising and for new missionary stations. The societies generally supported a periodical. An early example was *The Panoplist,* founded in 1805 by the Reverend Jedidiah Morse to combat Unitarian tendencies. This evolved into the far-reaching *Missionary Herald.* These magazines printed missionary sermons by home-based clergymen and returning missionaries. They also printed letters from the field.

It would have been hard for sensitive-minded men, women, and children, in an age in which religious orthodoxy was a vigorous force, to remain indifferent to descriptions of idleness, vice, crime, polygamy, and slavery, and of the superstition and depravity in which the heathen walked. For it was not until the later decades of the nineteenth century that missionaries generally began to have a more realistic and compassionate understanding of the cultures of those among whom they worked and of the religious values in many Oriental faiths. Nor could sensitive readers of the magazines close their hearts to the graphic accounts of deprivation and disease, of hairbreadth escapes of missionaries from death, of martyrdom at the hands of inflamed native zealots, including even cases of cannibalism. Such readers were touched by pathetic references to cases of early death in the field, all set in a frame of prayer and transcendent faith in the ultimate success of the missionary cause.[5] Opposition and

[5] This generalization rests on the reading of several score of biographies and autobiographies of nineteenth century American missionaries of several denominations in the Pacific Islands, Asia, Africa, and Europe.

indifference also melted at church services dedicated to the cause at which congregations listened to eloquent pleas and sang spirited missionary hymns, including Bishop Heber's "From Greenland's Icy Mountains" and America's own Bishop George Washington Doane's

> Fling out the banner! Heathen lands
> Shall see from far the glorious sight,
> And nations crowding to be born,
> Baptise their spirit in its light.

Partly because reported figures often failed to distinguish clearly between the closely intertwined home and foreign missionary causes, it is impossible to give more than a rough indication of the resources of the overseas missionary enterprises at various points in the nineteenth century. The oldest and in some ways strongest organization, the American Board of Commissioners for Foreign Missions which included, until 1857, Presbyterian and Dutch Reformed constituents as well as Congregationalists, reported an income for 1849 of $291,705.27—an appreciable increase over the $999.52 it had at its disposal in the inital year ending in September, 1811.[6] The American Missionary Association, at the other end of the scale, received $22,000 in 1849. The General Missionary Convention of the Baptist Denomination in the United States of America for Foreign Missions, organized in 1814, had an income of $88,902 in 1849, the Missionary Society of the Methodist Episcopal Church, active since 1819, reported receipts of $84,405 [7] and the Board of Missions of the Episcopal Church, an outgrowth of the Domestic and Foreign Missionary Society established in 1820, $34,800.[8] Although Emerson Davis, in his survey of the first fifty years of the nineteenth century in America, estimated that the amount contributed by all denominations for the year ending in the summer of 1849 for foreign missions was approximately $650,000, this figure may have been too high. Of interest is his estimate that of this sum, $566,000 was given by churches having 642,000 members, and $84,000 by those with a membership of 1,137,000—he did not specify the denominations.[9]

Annual contributions to all missionary societies varied from year

[6] American Board of Commissioners for Foreign Missions, *Annual Report*, 1849 (Boston: T. R. Marvin, 1849), 234.
[7] Emerson Davis, *The Half Century* . . . (Boston: Tappan and Whittemore, 1851), 310-12.
[8] *The Spirit of Missions* XV (August, 1850), 238
[9] Davis, *The Half Century*, 315.

to year, being especially adversely affected by depressions. For example, just when the missions in India and Ceylon were being enlarged
and the outlook seemed encouraging, the depression of 1837 so diminished contributions that in Ceylon 171 free schools had to be
closed and over 5,000 pupils suddenly dismissed. Recalcitrant and
suspicious "heathen" rejoiced, seeing an abortive end to the arduous
labors of the missionaries who had worked so hard to found the
schools. But the program, though crippled and, in the eyes of missionaries at the time, possibly retarded permanently, picked up with the
return of good times in America.[10]

Despite recurring depressions and the drain of the Civil War, the
annual assets available for foreign missions increased with the growing American population and economy. In 1891 the American Board's
Committee on Extra Gifts set up a plan for raising an additional
$100,000 during the year. In 1892 the receipts reached $840,000
as against $824,000 in 1891 and $762,000 in 1890. But income
did not reach even $750,000 again during the rest of the decade.
Other agencies likewise experienced awkward fluctuations from year
to year. Nevertheless, the overall picture showed great gains. Thus
in the year ending August 31, 1890, total expenditures for all foreign missions sponsored by American constituents were $4,023,005,
$540,789 of which had come from contributions of natives in the
field.[11] The American contributions of 1890 should be seen in the
light of an increase in the population of the country from 23,191,876
in 1850 to 62,947,714 in 1890, and a jump in estimated national
wealth from 7,135 millions of dollars in the earlier year, to 65,037
millions in 1890.

Allied organizations augmented the reach of foreign missions by
contributing religious literature. The most notable example was the
American Bible Society. Launched in 1818 by Elias Boudinot after
the British model, the Society gave an increasing number of Bibles to
foreign missions abroad and aided in the translations of the testa-
ments and other religious literature into native languages. To cite
one example, the Society gave more than $35,000 in its first twenty-
five years for the printing and distribution of Bibles in India and

10 William E. Strong, *The Story of the American Board* (Boston, Chicago, New York: The Pilgrim Press, 1910), 32-33.
11 *Ibid.*, 483; Edwin M. Bliss, *The Encyclopedia of Missions* (2 vols.; New York: Funk and Wagnalls, 1891), II, 606 ff, 625.

Ceylon.[12] In addition to what the American Bible Society did, the Baptist-supported American and Foreign Bible Society had prior to 1848 published 300,000 volumes in foreign lands, containing the Bible or some part of it in which the word "immersion" appeared instead of "baptism." [13]

How was the money raised for the missions themselves? In general, large gifts, whether by living persons or in the form of bequests, were few and, especially in the early years, also far between. It was a godsend when the American Board received in 1813 the bequest of Mrs. Mary Norris of Salem of $30,000, a huge sum for those days.[14] Later bequests included the $100,000 that Anson Greene Phelps left at his death in 1853. This represented one sixth of the philanthropic bequests of this generous New York merchant whose fortune rested on the manufacture of saddles, tin plate and other metals, and on mining and railroads.[15] The largest gift was that in 1879 of Asa Otis, of New London, a quiet, careful reader of the *Missionary Herald*. The news of his legacy of $1,000,000 to the Board of Commissioners, coming as it did at a particularly dark financial moment, was sensational. The Board had barely accustomed itself to the possibilities of this windfall when, in 1884, it inherited nearly $600,000 from the estate of Samuel W. Swett of Jamaica Plain, Massachusetts, who had been impressed in the course of his commercial activities in the Pacific Ocean with the work of the missionaries in the Sandwich Islands. By 1892 returns on legacies to the American Board amounted to nearly $250,000 yearly. To be sure, this was an unusually high return, for in many years the income on investments was far less—it was only $102,200, for example, in 1899.[16]

Such large bequests for a time lessened the rate of annual giving.

[12] Henry O. Dwight, *Centennial History of the American Bible Society* (New York: Macmillan, 1916), 166, 236, 242. During the depression of 1837-38, the Society's program was largely saved by the sale of Pennsylvania lands bequeathed by Elias Boudinot and by an unsolicited gift of £1,000 from James Douglass of Cavors, Scotland.

[13] Davis, *The Half Century*, 328.

[14] Strong, *Story of the American Board*, 13.

[15] G. E. Prentiss, *A Sermon Preached on the Death of Anson G. Phelps with Extracts from His Diary* (New York, 1854); Carlos Martyn, *William E. Dodge; The Christian Merchant* (New York and London: Funk and Wagnalls, 1890), 154. Phelps bequeathed $50,000 for a college in Liberia and an additional $100,000 for home missionaries.

[16] Strong, *Story of the American Board*, 315-16, 325; Chauncy J. Hawkins, *Samuel Billings Capen* (Boston, Chicago: Pilgrim Press, 1914), 147.

Important though income from bequests increasingly became, all missionary societies depended largely on current contributions. Most of these were in small sums, but there were almost always enough large ones to make a world of difference. One of the most cheering early sources of current support was David Washington Cincinnatus Olyphant (1789-1851), a devout New York merchant who might have made an even bigger fortune in the China trade had he indulged in the opium traffic. Olyphant suggested and supported the publication of the *Chinese Repository*, a major vehicle for informing the English-speaking world of the needs and achievements of the missions in the Celestial Empire. Before his death, he had given free passage to and from China for almost fifty missionaries. Beginning in 1831 Olyphant provided a junk, or larger vessel, each year to cruise the Asiatic waters scattering religious literature in one port after another. In 1835 about 18,000 volumes were thus distributed. In 1836 the firm bought the *Himmaleh* and carried through the most extensive enterprise of this sort yet undertaken.[17] Some grumbled that the use of these unread books as wrapping paper proved the futility of the venture, but others testified that many of the books found readers, even if they failed to make converts. When Olyphant was told he could not recover from an illness he had contracted, he replied: "I do not wish to live for the sake of worldly riches or comforts; but for the sake of the missions, I could have desired to remain a little longer."[18] His son continued to give liberally to missionary work in China.

A list of the larger givers would include such men as Arthur and Lewis Tappan, New York merchants who gave generously to a dozen or more benevolent causes until adversity struck them. These causes included the American Board. But when it would not take a stand against slavery, the Tappans withdrew and supported the newly organized American Missionary Association. This society refused to take "tainted" money from slaveowners or to hire slavery sympathizers as missionaries.[19] Or one might cite as another example Elliott

[17] S. Wells Williams, *The Middle Kingdom* . . . (4th ed., 2 vols.; New York: John Wiley, 1871) II, 339-40. For a suggestive study of missionary work in China see James M. McCutcheon, "The American and British Missionary Concept of Chinese Civilization in the Nineteenth Century" (unpublished Ph.D. dissertation, University of Wisconsin, 1959).

[18] *Chinese Repository* XX (July, 1851), 509.

[19] Lewis Tappan, *Life of Arthur Tappan* (New York: Hurd and Houghton, 1870); Phyllis M. Bannan, *Arthur and Lewis Tappan* (Ann Arbor: University Microfilms, No. 1829, 1950); *New York Times*, June 23, 1873.

Cresson, a member of a family of successful Quaker merchants "noted more for distribution of his wealth than for activities in attaining it." Cresson's interest in colonization was expressed in a $10,000 bequest to the Episcopal Mission in Liberia.[20] To move into the later nineteenth century, any list would certainly include Dr. Daniel Kimball Pearsons, who made a fortune in the Middle West in lumber, real estate, and banking. Though the bulk of his $5,000,000 fortune went to forty Christian colleges in the United States, he gave generously to the American Board and to the Presbyterian Women's Board.[21] Outstanding, too, was Henry Allen Tupper, corresponding secretary of the Board of Foreign Missions of the Southern Baptist Convention. In 1883 this former Confederate chaplain, temperance worker, and founder of a girls' school in Coahuila, Mexico, wrote that in the past thirty years he donated $124,541.39 for religious work, including foreign missions, from a total income of $279,500.98, largely earned from the books he wrote for young people for Sunday School libraries, but properly to be regarded as "from the Lord." [22]

Most large donors preferred to give to a specific institution sponsored by one of the missionary boards, such as a school, a hospital, or a college. The desire to provide buildings, scholarships, and professorships for colleges initiated by missionaries can be readily understood in view of the growing popularity of giving to institutions of higher learning on American soil. Such gifts not only yielded immediately visible results but promised to project the memory and influence of the donor into the future.

Of special interest in this connection is John Franklin Goucher, a Methodist minister who married a woman of wealth, and who is best known as the founder, president, and benefactor of the college for women in Baltimore that bears his name. Beginning in the 1880's

[20] Archibald Alexander, *A History of Colonization on the Western Coast of Africa* (Philadelphia: W. S. Martien, 1846); Henry Simpson, *The Lives of Eminent Philadelphians* (Philadelphia: William Brotherhead, 1859), 268-69; American Colonization Society, *Thirty Eighth Annual Report*, 1855 (Washington-Alexander, 1855), 3 ff.

[21] Edward F. Williams, *The Life of Dr. D. K. Pearsons: Friend of the Small College and of Missions* (New York, Boston: Pilgrim Press, 1911), 223; *Congregationalist* XCVII (May 4, 11, 1912), 630.

[22] Henry Allen Tupper, *The Foreign Missions of the Southern Baptist Convention* (Philadelphia: American Baptist Publication Society, 1880) and *A Decade of Foreign Missions 1880-1890* (Richmond: Foreign Mission Board of the Southern Baptist Church, 1891); *Religious Herald* LXXVI (April 3, 1902), 8; *Foreign Missions Journal* LII (May, 1902), 339-40; *Dictionary of American Biography* XIX, 33-34.

Goucher supported vernacular primary schools in India—at one time his list included 120—from which the more promising boys and girls were sent to secondary institutions. Goucher made possible the founding in Korea of its first Christian school, Pail Chai. The Anglo-Japanese Methodist College in Tokyo owed its twenty-four acre campus to his generosity. His benefactions included gifts of land and money which made possible the West China Union University. Listing in 1904 men of wealth who had supported the missionary cause, John R. Mott wrote that Goucher's benefactions already exceeded $250,000.[23]

The larger bequests include gifts for the endowment of the Syrian Protestant College, which came to be the celebrated American University of Beirut. Founded in 1866, the total endowment by 1882 had come to be $179,000, a sum totally inadequate for the program of the college. The endowment was in the decade ahead augmented by several gifts and bequests from Gerald F. Dale, Jr., William E. Dodge, Stuart D. Dodge, and other members of this philanthropic New York merchant family. By 1902 the new plant was valued at $645,000.[24] One of the earliest and most generous friends of Beirut was Morris Ketchum Jesup. This manufacturer of railroad supplies was a benefactor of the American Museum of Natural History, to which he gave $1,000,000 in his lifetime and an equal amount in his will. He was also a benefactor of Union Theological Seminary, Yale, Harvard, Princeton, Williams, Hampton, and Tuskegee. For more than forty years he was a constant supporter of the Syrian Protestant College. His increasingly large and frequent gifts included the establishment of the Maria De Witt Jesup Foundation for the development of the hospital and medical facilities of the institution.[25]

Equally or even better known was Robert College near Constantinople. Christopher Rhinelander Robert, who made a fortune as an importer of sugar, tea, and cotton, as well as in railroads, had given

[23] Charles H. Fahs, "John F. Goucher: Missionary Educator," *Missionary Review of the World* XLV (Nov., 1922), 877-80; *Christian Advocate* XCVII (July 27, 1922), 923-25; Anna Heubeck Knipp and Thaddeus P. Thomas, *The History of Goucher College* (Baltimore: Goucher College, 1938), 48-51; John R. Mott, *The Pastor and Modern Missions: A Plea for Leadership in World Evangelization* (New York, Student Volunteer Movement for Foreign Missions, 1904).

[24] Stephen B. L. Penrose, Jr., *That They May Have Life: The Story of the American University of Beirut, 1866-1941* (New York: Trustees of the American University of Beirut, 1941), 71-72.

[25] William Adams Brown, *Morris Ketchum Jesup: A Character Sketch* (New York: Scribner's Sons, 1910), 23, 86 ff; *The Outlook* [New York] LXXXVIII (Feb. 1, 1908), 242-43.

generously to American colleges and to the Auburn Theological Seminary before he became interested in the plan of J. H. and W. B. Dwight for founding a secular college in Constantinople. A devout man, Robert was convinced that support could only be mustered for a college that was founded on a religious base. So convinced, he threw his strength to the institution which Dr. Cyrus Hamlin, a missionary of the American Board in Turkey, was projecting. Opening its humble doors to a few students in 1863 and meeting seemingly insuperable obstacles, the college, which was named for Robert despite his objections, survived and grew. For many years this New York merchant met an annual deficit of $10,000 or more, and gave unsparingly of his time and interest to further the sound growth of the institution. His will, probated in 1878, designated one sixth of his estate for Robert College, bringing his total gifts to at least $600,-000.[26]

Other representative institutions include the Euphrates College and Anatolia College in Turkey, the Batticotta Seminary in Ceylon, the Christian Forman College at Lahore, St. John's University in Shanghai, Canton Christian College, Rangoon College (Judson University), and the Doshisha University in Kyoto, Japan, to which J. N. Harris, of New London, Connecticut, a merchant, banker, former member of the legislature, and mayor, gave $100,000 in 1889 to establish a scientific department on the graduate level. Most of these institutions were supported from the general missionary funds of the affiliated agency though many also received gifts and bequests of sizable sums.

As the decades passed foreign missions attracted increasing support from the well to do. Yet many felt that the rich gave far less generously, in proportion to means, than did the poor. In discussing the financial situation in 1876 the *Heathen Woman's Friend* reported that Methodist women the year previously had given $76,000 earned at the needle's point and over the washtub. The pennies of poor children likewise went into the fund. The goal of $100,000 for the next year, which the ladies hoped to raise by prayer and effort, was far too little in view of the need. "If the rich gave as liberally as do

[26] Cyrus Hamlin, *My Life and Times* (2d ed.; Boston, Chicago: The Congregational Sunday-School and Publishing Society, 1893); George Washburn, *Fifty Years in Constantinople and Recollections of Robert College* (Boston, New York: Houghton Mifflin, 1909); *Home Missionary* LI (Dec., 1878), 196-98; *New York Observer*, Nov. 7, 1878; Caleb Frank Gates, *Not to Me Only* (Princeton: Princeton University Press, 1940), 159 ff.

the poor, we would not be discussing the possibility of giving $100,000. The question would be, How many millions can we raise?" The concluding note was one to ponder. A Mrs. Miller was quoted as saying in her *Parish of Fair Heaven* that the value of kid gloves imported into New York in a year was ten times as great as the total of funds leaving the country from all the missionary societies.[27]

Samuel Billings Capen, a Massachusetts carpet manufacturer, civic reformer, and president of the American Board of Commissioners for Foreign Missions, joined the women, declaring, early in the twentieth century, that only one male church member in ten was interested in world-wide missions, and that the average gift per member was less than one cent a day for home and foreign missions together. Insisting that individuals must give in relation to their capacity, that the nation itself must contribute in proportion to its wealth, Capen argued that the only thing now necessary for the evangelization of the world was money. In speaking to business men he noted that the evangelical progress in Hawaii and Turkey had increased the demand for American products and had stimulated American commerce. But Capen went beyond such mercenary appeals. As a devout Christian he insisted that commerce was now triumphant and that without God it was a dangerous materialism: business needed to support the foreign missionary movement to save itself spiritually from the American commercial spirit. Capen urged business men and those of wealth to give more generously, to be true stewards in their relations with the missionary movement. At the same time he insisted that business methods be introduced in the conduct of philanthropy.[28]

It would be misleading to imply that all these bequests and substantial gifts to particular educational and medical institutions and to the missionary associations themselves came without special effort on the part of those most deeply concerned. There was the missionary journal with its accounts of overseas sufferings and achievements, the sermon, the collection, and the diligent labor of women who, after the Civil War, often formed their own organizations. Above all there was the missionary home on furlough, tired and often ailing,

[27] *Heathen Woman's Friend* VII (October, 1876), 81-2.
[28] Chauncy J. Hawkins, *Samuel Billings Capen. His Life and Work* (Boston: Pilgrim Press, 1914), 127 ff; Samuel Billings Capen, *Foreign Missions and World Peace* (Boston: World Peace Foundation, 1912); *Missionary Herald* CX (March, 1914), 109-112.

who preached, talked, wrote and visited anyone and everyone that might give to his organization or to the educational or medical institution he had close at heart.

After twelve years of residence in Canton and Macao, S. Wells Williams, to cite one example, came home to lecture on China in New York, Buffalo, Cleveland, and other cities, devoting the proceeds to the manufacture of a font of Chinese type for printing religious literature.[29] The autobiography of another successful missionary fund raiser, John Clough of the Baptist station in south India, gives few details of his campaign of 1873, when he collected $50,000 for founding a theological school for the Telegus. In 1883 he raised $15,000 for mission houses in Ongole and Madras, and in 1890 got together $100,000 for sending missionaries to new stations and for establishing Ongole College.[30] The imagination must help fill in the reference to the "irresistable solicitings" of Dr. C. H. Wheeler and his wife who in 1876 secured the basis of an endowment of $50,000 for a college at Harpoot in Turkey.[31] Bishop James M. Thoburn, the great Methodist missionary, succeeded by his eloquent appeals throughout the United States in raising large sums for the far-flung missionary institutions he nurtured throughout India and southeast Asia.[32]

The story of the fund-raising activities of Cyrus Hamlin, a graduate of Bowdoin and of the Bangor Theological Seminary, is well documented. He opened a school and a theological seminary on the Bosphorus in 1840 which he directed for twenty years under the auspices of the American Board. Much to the disapproval of other missionaries on the ground, Hamlin set up a workshop in which his needy Armenian students made rattraps, iron stoves and pipes. His bakeshop and steam flour mill provided work for the Armenian Christians whom the Turks boycotted. These enterprises expanded during the Crimean War, furnishing bread for British hospitals. This enterprising Yankee also improvised washing machines which cleaned the soldiers' vermin-infested uniforms. In this way Hamlin earned

[29] Williams, *The Middle Kingdom*, I, xiii.

[30] John E. Clough, *Social Christianity in the Orient: The Story of a Man, a Mission, and a Movement* (New York: Macmillan, 1914), 217, 254.

[31] Strong, *Story of the American Board*, 224.

[32] Marvin Henry Parker, *Ecclesiastical Organization and Administration of the Methodist Episcopal Church in India* (Lucknow: The Lucknow Publishing House, 1936), 82; James Mills Thoburn, *My Missionary Apprenticeship* (New York: Phillips and Hunt, 1884) and *The Christian Conquest of India* (New York, Toronto: Young People's Missionary Movement, 1906).

$25,000 for the support of native Protestant churches. In 1860 differences with the Board, which favored replacing the English language with Armenian in missionary schools, led to his resignation.[33]

Returning to the United States, Hamlin proposed raising a subscription of $100,000 for his projected college on the Bosphorus. The American Board did not favor the idea, and the outbreak of the Civil War made fund raising for such a purpose all but impossible. Christopher Robert came to his rescue by digging up $30,000 with which to buy a site and start operations. Against the opposition of the foreign colony in Constantinople and the Turkish government, Hamlin opened the college in 1863 with four students. But the number grew, and the outlook, despite continuing difficulties, seemed promising.[34]

Yielding to the insistence of Robert, Hamlin in 1871 came home to raise an endowment. He was ill, he lacked confidence in his ability successfully to "beg," and he found business conditions unsettled. "To my surprise," he wrote, "I found the rich and benevolent men of New York city, with a few honorable exceptions, wholly disinclined to give the college any aid." [35] One difficulty was that many did not want to give to a college which was not strictly denominational. But some extremely wealthy men took the position that Robert had founded the College, that it was named for him, and that he should endow it. Though very benevolent, Robert was unpopular, and not a single one of the eighty gentlemen who received a letter enclosing a blank check, responded with even so much as a dollar. From New Haven, Hamlin wrote his children that an entire week's work had yielded only $100. He could get subscriptions of $25, $50, $100, but nothing from the rich. "They [the rich] do not like to *unload*. They are prosperous, & they feel *savage* when asked to give. How can a man who has an income of $40,000 give anything when he has been accustomed to spend $45,000 to live? He is already economizing $5,000." [36] In Boston he was received coldly when he called on Henry Mason, manufacturer of pianos. Mason said he had given a large donation to the Board of Commissioners for missions, but even when Hamlin told him that Robert College had nothing to do with the Board, still he would give nothing. "I seem," Hamlin wrote to his

[33] Hamlin, *My Life and Times*, 205 ff.
[34] *Ibid.*, 415 ff.
[35] *Ibid.*, 490.
[36] Cyrus Hamlin to "Dear Children," New Haven, March 7, 1870, Washburn Manuscripts in possession of Mrs. Basil Hall, Cambridge, Massachusetts.

son, "to be endowed from on high with the special talent . . . of calling out the selfishness of men. Others awaken only their benevolence. I cannot yet find out how it is done."[37] Amazed at the number of childless millionaires, he thought it worth trying to solicit from them; but experience proved that they were not necessarily the ones that would give.

As the depression deepened, everyone told him not to open his subscription at that time.[38] So Hamlin had to be content with promises and with the $6,000 he raised in Hartford, the $13,000 he got in Boston and its vicinity, and the $30,000 clause Robert inserted in his will as a future gift to the College. Despite all this, the College continued to grow but Hamlin was shocked and hurt beyond measure when Robert's cordiality changed and when he told him, after seventeen years of association, that it had "been thought best that you should not return to Constantinople!" Dismissed without warning from the presidency at the age of sixty-six, Hamlin found a job at the Bangor Theological Seminary until Middlebury College rescued him by making him president in the hope he might build up a declining institution. Continuing to befriend the cause of missions and of Robert College by speaking and writing, Hamlin lived to see the College recognized as a great institution and, in a sense, as a monument to his efforts.[39]

Hamlin's son-in-law, George Washburn, richly endowed with common sense and realism as well as with Christian piety and intelligence, began his association with Robert College as a teacher. During the twenty-five years that he held the presidency, to which he was appointed in 1878, he saw the College grow in enrollment and improve in scholarship. He also saw it extend and deepen its influence in the Near East.[40] Shortly after taking the presidency, Washburn raised $50,000 in Boston and, during subsequent fund-raising visits, won friends and secured gifts for the College.[41] Among those whose help proved especially valuable were Mrs. Walter Baker, wife of the founder of Baker's Chocolate Company at Dorchester, Massachusetts, who not only maintained an annual scholarship but made

[37] Hamlin to "My dear Son," Boston, March 1, 1872, Washburn Manuscripts.
[38] Hamlin to George Washburn, New York, Jan. 28, 1874, Washburn Manuscripts.
[39] Hamlin, *My Life and Times*, 503 ff.
[40] Washburn, *Fifty Years in Constantinople*, 296 ff.
[41] *Robert College: Appeal Issued by the Trustees*, Oct. 20, 1904, Washburn Manuscripts.

her home a place for Washburn to meet men and women of means and influence.[42]

Some of the larger donors, like Alanson Trask of Brooklyn, contributed toward the endowment of special chairs. Others, like the Stokes' sisters, provided buildings. By special good fortune John Stewart Kennedy visited the campus in 1888 and became president of the board of trustees in 1894. Kennedy gave land to enlarge the campus, built houses for the president and members of the faculty, and met annual deficits. His will, probated in 1909, generously added to his long record of giving.[43] In the early years of the twentieth century donors included Mr. and Mrs. Cleveland Dodge and Mrs. Russell Sage. In writing to Washburn about another donor, John D. Rockefeller, the new president, Caleb Frank Gates, confessed to having no scruples at all about taking the oil millionaire's money. "I know," Gates remarked, "that there is a great moral question as to how money should be *acquired,* but this is a question as to how money should be *spent* and I know that we are on the right side of the question." [44]

Daniel Bliss, another missionary leader of higher education was a poor farm boy who made his way from farms in Vermont and Ohio to Amherst, where he married Abby Wood, a friend of Helen Hunt Jackson and of Emily Dickinson. Assigned by the American Board to a station in Lebanon, the Blisses learned Arabic and, more important, came to understand the people among whom they worked. It was clear to this young couple that education, not mere training, was necessary if native leaders were to be developed. It was also clear that this education should be in the vernacular, that those educated should not be educated out of their culture. Equally plain was the fact that the missionary societies, depending as they did chiefly on small contributions for the direct preaching of the Gospel and for teaching old and young to read it, could not divert their slender funds for education. With the approval of his missionary colleagues, Bliss and his wife in 1862 returned to the United States and pleaded for support for their ideas at the annual meeting of the Board.[45]

[42] Mrs. Walter Baker to Mr. and Mrs. George Washburn, Dorchester, May 5, 1890, Washburn Manuscripts.

[43] Manuscript eulogy of John S. Kennedy, in the handwriting of Washburn, undated, Washburn Manuscripts.

[44] C. F. Gates to George Washburn, Constantinople, May 31, 1905, Washburn Manuscripts. See also Gates, *Not to Me Only,* 168 ff.

[45] Daniel Bliss, *Reminiscences of Daniel Bliss,* edited and supplemented by his eldest son (New York, Chicago: Fleming H. Revell, 1920), 162 ff.

The response was encouraging. William E. Dodge, his wife, and their son, the Rev. D. Stuart Dodge and his wife, all expressed interest. As Bliss put it, "the fountain of benevolence in Mr. Dodge's heart was not enlarged, but a new channel was opened for his benefactions." [46] The Board, the religious press, and certain philanthropists publicized the program and the need, including the emphasis Bliss put on the great desirability of establishing a first-rate medical school in a land where there were so many quacks. As president, Bliss of course had to ask for money. He seldom took up a collection after a sermon or speech. He did not actively "solicit." Rather, he was indefatigable in making calls, sometimes stopping in a day at a dozen offices and homes. He stated the aims of the enterprise and left his little book in which his host might at his leisure read the list of those who had already contributed. Bliss seldom asked directly for a donation. Once, however, he successfully varied from the practice. In a letter introducing him to a well-known donor, the writer remarked that the bearer was a modest man, and that it was to be hoped he would not suffer on that account. After listening to the plan for the College, the philanthropist said, "Well, I will give you two thousand dollars." "Can't you make it five?" Bliss suggested gently. Bringing his fist vehemently down on his desk, the potential giver burst forth, "Good God! I shall write my friend that Mr. Bliss is *not* a modest man!" But he put his name down for $5,000.[47]

Things did not always come out so well. Sometimes a gift was offered with the provision that certain religious observances be promised, or that no vivisection take place in the projected medical school. Bliss refused all such conditional gifts. When someone refused to give he was not discouraged. It seemed unwise, he concluded, to set a particular date for completing the $100,000 endowment at which he aimed. "It will come in God's own time, which is better. . . . The whole course of benevolence in the world is too much dependent upon personal influence. The reputation of the solicitor and his standing have more to do with contributions than the object to be aided. . . ." [48] During the two years of canvassing, Bliss traveled 16,993 miles and made 279 public addresses. At last he had $100,000 in greenbacks. But since the par value of these was low, he went to England to solicit enough pounds sterling to build and to open the

46 *Ibid.*, 169.
47 *Ibid.*, 171-72.
48 *Ibid.*, 173.

College. In England audiences questioned Bliss's faith that his green-backs would in due course be worth their face value. Impressed, however, by his sincerity and ability, those to whom he talked contributed £4,000—and some provided in their wills for the future institution at Beirut. With the British pounds sterling in hand, Bliss returned to Lebanon and in 1866 opened the Syrian Protestant College.[49] Its success is an exciting story.

During the five visits home that Bliss made between 1874 and 1889—with stop-offs in England—he increased the resources of the college and enlarged its endowment. Members of the faculty, especially Dr. Henry H. Jessup and Dr. George E. Post, also effectively contributed to the work while on journeys in America. In addition to the continued support of the Dodge family, new friends were made, many of whom contributed generously to buildings, equipment, and endowment. When Bliss retired from the presidency in 1902, the college plant was valued at $645,000, the endowment at $326,963.[50]

Just as much American secular giving at home rested on the expectation that it would provide the recipient with the means and stimulus to carry on without further help, so the foreign missionary movement looked forward to the time when native churches could support themselves.[51] Save in Hawaii and in Burma this hope was not generally realized in many stations during the nineteenth century despite the growing contributions of native converts to local churches. Much was to be said for the idea of self-help, but it was sometimes overdone. As one great missionary, Dr. Daniel McGilvary, remarked, in looking back on the experiment in Siam and Laos in the 1890's, the native churches were often "asked to walk before they could stand; and the ministers to work, as well as walk, by faith and not by sight." [52]

The most striking effort to develop self-help in foreign missions was that of Bishop William Taylor, a Methodist evangelist of physical vigor and commanding personality. His enthusiasm, faith, and re-

[49] *Ibid.*, 175-86.
[50] Penrose, *That They May Have Life*, 59, 71 ff.
[51] Dr. Pomeroy writing on the missions of the Board of Commissioners in 1849, identified the growing ability of native converts and churches to become self-supporting, with the "law of progress." It was, he insisted, as important for these to provide their own leaders as it was to provide their own funds. American Board of Commissioners for Foreign Missions, *Annual Report*, 1849, 79.
[52] Daniel McGilvary, *A Half Century Among the Siamese and the Lao: An Autobiography* (New York, Chicago: Fleming H. Revell, 1912), 379.

ligious zeal were fortunately tempered by common sense and humor. After evangelical crusades in Africa and Australia, Taylor developed in India in the 1870's the "Pauline system" by which missionaries depended for support on the converts they made, supplemented, if need be, by income earned with their own hands. In the later 1870's Taylor extended his self-help system to Peru and Chile where, he felt, as indeed many Protestants did, that the Catholic Church had failed to check skepticism among the more educated classes and had largely left the masses untouched. Taylor's self-supporting missionaries established several self-supporting schools, the center of the movement being Coquimbo, in Chile. Generally speaking, the self-support system wasted the time of the missionaries, for the teaching they did in schools that could be attended only by tuition-paying children of the well to do or the work they did in business, drained energy as well as time from missionary labor. In some instances the schools, despite inadequate plant and equipment, did well, as for example, the Santiago College (it did even better when Anderson Fowler, an intelligent and generous business man, gave it $50,000). But in general the disadvantages of the system seemed in many eyes to outweigh the advantages.[53]

What did American contributions in money and service accomplish in the missionary field in the nineteenth century? It is hard to say, partly because in many places there was no clear distinction made in reports between the work of the missionaries from the United States and those from other countries, particularly Great Britain. Evaluation is also difficult because the record differed from place to place, whether by reason of the particular native culture, the attitude of the governing power, or the number, resources, personalities, and leadership of the missionaries themselves.

If number of converts be the test, the results were hardly impressive save in the Sandwich Islands where, according to Richard Henry Dana, a leading Episcopalian, lawyer, and writer who visited the Islands in 1860, the missionaries of the American Board in a period of forty years taught the whole people to attend public worship more

[53] O. Von Barchwitz-Krauser, *Six Years with Bishop Taylor in South America* (Boston: McDonald and Gill, 1885); John H. Paul, *Soul-Digger; or, Life and Times of William Taylor* (Upland, Ind.: Taylor University Press, 1928); William Taylor, *Story of My Life* . . . (New York: Hunt and Eaton, 1895); Goodsil F. Arms, *History of the William Taylor Self-Supporting Missions in South America* (New York, Cincinnati: Methodist Book Concern, 1921), 7, 226 ff.

regularly than most people in the United States did.[54] But the population was small, the attitude of the chiefs favorable, and the native culture already crumbling. In some places years of effort yielded slender harvests. Thus in the Gilbert Islands Hiram Bingham and his wife after fourteen years of labor confessed that only fifty converts had been brought to God. At the end of the century, just before the Boxer uprising in China, the Christians numbered a little over 550,000 in a population of some 360,000,000. Moreover, there was much backsliding among those who had been converted in time of famine when the missionaries served as almoners of relief. Only transcendent faith enabled the missionaries to go on, such faith as that recorded by an editor writing about the Reverend Jonas King, who experienced much persecution in Greece: "Perhaps 'the set time' may be near. The night has been long, and dark, and not without storms; but in 'the fourth watch of the night' the Saviour sometimes comes to his faint and weary people, and his coming is the ushering of the day." [55] With such faith, no wonder that one commentator at home could insist that the workers in the field had not failed, that his constituents had failed in giving such meager support.

However disappointing the number of converts, which even faith and confidence could not always conceal, no one can deny the important material and cultural consequences of the missionary movement. These consequences, particularly through most of the nineteenth century, resulted largely from the means used to achieve their end of evangelization.

Being Protestant and thus attaching importance to the ability to read the Bible, it was necessary for the missionaries first of all to teach old and young to read. Sometimes this involved establishing day and evening schools to teach those who came to read in their own language after the Bible and other religious literature was translated. But in many underdeveloped areas, the oral language had never been written down. So the missionaries had to learn it, construct an alphabet, find the grammatical structure of the language, and painfully translate the Bible, hymns, and hortatory tracts. A leading modern scholar of linguistics has paid tribute to the "great part

[54] Rufus Anderson, *The Hawaiian Islands: Their Progress and Condition under Missionary Labors* (2d ed.; Boston: Gould and Lincoln, 1864), 99-100.
[55] American Board of Commissioners for Foreign Missions, *Annual Report*, 1849, 104-05.

played by Christian missionaries in broadening our knowledge of exotic languages." [56]

Let a few examples suggest the story. Beginning in 1822 the first missionaries in the Sandwich Islands, with the encouragement of the native king, fixed on an alphabet of twelve letters and prepared a spelling-book which "the chiefs received . . . with deep interest." William Richards, who later codified the laws, advised the king, organized an educational system, and secured in Washington, London and Paris the recognition of the Islands' independence, was not only a pioneer in reducing the language to written form, but translated the Bible and other religious literature.[57] Another missionary, Oliver Pomeroy Emerson, compiled an English-Hawaiian dictionary when he was not supervising irrigation projects, building roads, surveying land, improving dairy herds, and teaching boys to become government clerks, teachers, and preachers.[58] In the Gilbert Islands Hiram Bingham and his wife amplified an unwritten language with fewer than 4,000 words into a written one of three times that number, made the first Gilbertese dictionary, and after thirty-four years of labor, finished a translation of the Bible.[59] In Burma Baptist missionaries reduced to writing the Sgau-Karen and Pwo-Karen languages, together with many related dialects.[60] Especially memorable in extending knowledge of southeast Asian languages is the towering figure of Francis Mason, whose extensive translations include a Karen version of the Gospel of St. Matthew, a Sgau-Karen New Testament, and a *Synopsis of a Grammar of the Karen Language*.[61] In Africa Lewis Grout performed the herculean task of analyzing the Zulu language, reducing it to writing, preparing a grammar, and making basic translations.[62] Dr. A. Sims made a dictionary of Kiteke and Kiyansi, for

[56] Holger Pedersen, *Linguistic Science in the Nineteenth Century: Methods and Results*, trans. John Webster Spargo (Cambridge: Harvard University Press, 1931), 99.

[57] Samuel Williston, *William Richards* (Cambridge: privately printed, 1938); Lucy Goodale Thurston, *Life and Times of Mrs. Lucy G. Thurston* . . . (Ann Arbor: S. C. Andrews, 1882), 64-65.

[58] Oliver Pomeroy Emerson, *Pioneer Days in Hawaii* (Garden City: Doubleday, Doran, 1928), 127 ff.

[59] *Missionary Herald* CIII (January, 1907), 5-6; Hiram Bingham, *A Residence of Twenty-one Years in the Sandwich Islands* . . . (Hartford: H. Huntington, 1849).

[60] Edmund F. Merriam, *A History of American Baptist Missions* (Philadelphia: American Baptist Publication Society, 1900), 218 ff.

[61] Francis Mason, *The Story of a Workingman's Life* (New York: Oakley, Mason, 1870).

[62] Rev. Lewis Grout, *Zulu-Land; or Life Among the Zulu-Kafirs of Natal and Zulu Land, South Africa* (Philadelphia: Presbyterian Publication Committee, 1864), 204 ff; Lewis Grout, *A Brief Outline of the Rev. Lewis Grout's Eighty Years' Life and Labor*

which he received the Legion of Honor from the French Government and a decoration from the King of the Belgians.[63] In the Congo the Southern Presbyterians, toward the end of the century, reduced to writing one of the leading languages, prepared a dictionary, a grammar, and a body of Christian writing.[64] Bishop John Payne of the Protestant Episcopal Church in West Africa put the Grebo tongue into writing and translated parts of the Old Testament and New Testament, besides liturgies and catechisms.[65] And in Persia Dr. Justin Perkins constructed a modern Syriac literature, giving the Nestorians, a primitive Christian people, a literature in their own spoken language, which they had never before had. These examples by no means exhaust the list.

Nor was it only in the more primitive languages that missionaries contributed to knowledge. In many cases in which the language had an alphabet and a literature, the missionaries in the course of translations constructed dictionaries of great value. Thus in the Dravidian family of languages in south India, Dr. Miron Winslow (1789-1864) began in 1833 his monumental *Comprehensive Tamil and English Dictionary of High and Low Tamil.* It contained 64,450 words with definitions and was hailed as a "noble contribution to Oriental literature." [66] Dr. Lyman Jewett translated the Bible into Telegu. In north India, James C. R. Ewing, the president of Forman Christian College and, ultimately, vice-chancellor of the Punjab University, made a Greek-Hindustani dictionary.[67] The translations of the Bible into Assami, Burmese and other languages all served useful linguistic purposes. Of special note was the first practical manual of Cantonese prepared by Elijah Coleman Bridgman and Samuel Wells Williams,

in Africa and America (Brattleboro, Vt.: Phoenix, 1895); Johannes Du Plessis, *A History of Christian Missions in South Africa* (London, New York: Longmans, Green, 1911), 220 ff.

[63] Merriam, *American Baptist Missions,* 219.

[64] The great figure in this work was W. M. Morrison. See Robert Dabney Bedinger, *Triumphs of the Gospel in the Belgian Congo* . . . (Richmond: Presbyterian Committee of Publication, 1920); William H. Sheppard, *Presbyterian Pioneers in Congo* (Richmond: Presbyterian Committee of Publication, 1917); Samuel P. Verner, *Pioneering in Central Africa* (Richmond: Presbyterian Committee of Publication, 1903).

[65] Anna M. Scott, *Day Dawn in Africa; or, Progress of the Protestant Episcopal Mission at Cape Palmas, West Africa* (New York: Protestant Episcopal Society for the Promotion of Evangelical Knowledge, 1858), 67.

[66] *Missionary Herald* LIX (May, 1863), 130-32. Winslow's dictionary was widely regarded as the most notable work of its kind at that time in any language of India.

[67] Robert E. Speer, *Sir James Ewing* (New York, Chicago: Fleming H. Revell, 1928).

two pioneer American missionaries in China.[68] In Japan Dr. James C. Hepburn translated the Bible into Japanese and prepared a Japanese grammar and the first Japanese-English dictionary.[69] Notable too in the effort and knowledge required was Dr. Nathan Brown's translation of the Bible into Japanese. In the Near East, in addition to Justin Perkins' achievements in Syriac studies, the Arabic version of the New Testament was brought out in 1860 as the joint labor of Dr. Eli Smith and Dr. Cornelius V. A. Van Dyck. This superseded earlier translations.[70]

The contributions of nineteenth century American missionaries were not solely confined to linguistics. Much was done to increase the Western world's knowledge of historic cultures and anticipated the currently fashionable "area studies." Outstanding was Samuel Wells Williams' *The Middle Kingdom*, first published in New York and London in 1848, and which, in the revisions that followed, held its place as a leading authority.[71] Francis Mason, in addition to the philological contributions in the Burmese languages, wrote a remarkable synthesis in *The Natural Productions of Burmah*. Rich in its knowledge of ethnology, flora, fauna, and geography, this book was revised and published by the British government.[72] George Washburn's study of the geology of the Bosphorus was contributed to the leading American scientific journal, and his paper on "Calvert's Supposed Relics of Man in the Miocene of the Dardenelles," with Mason's work on Burma, suggests the range of work in the natural sciences.[73]

In 1859 William McClure Thomson brought out the first edition of *The Land and the Book*. This widely read study of the relationships between Biblical data and the topography, archaeology, and

[68] Eliza J. G. Bridgman, *Life and Labors of Elijah Coleman Bridgman* (New York: A. D. F. Randolph, 1864; Frederick Wells Williams, *The Life and Letters of Samuel Wells Williams* (New York, London: G. P. Putnam's Sons, 1889).

[69] William Elliot Griffis, *Hepburn of Japan . . . a Life Study of Toil for Christ* (Philadelphia: Westminster Press, 1913); *Church at Home and Abroad* XXII (October, 1897), 270.

[70] Strong, *Story of the American Board*, 203.

[71] S. Wells Williams, *The Middle Kingdom* (2 vols.; New York, London: Wiley and Putnam, 1848).

[72] Francis Mason, *The Natural Productions of Burmah . . .* (Maulmain: American Mission, 1850) and *Flora Burmanica . . .* (Tavoy: Karen Mission Press, 1851).

[73] *American Journal of Science and Arts* VI (September, 1873), 186-94; American Association for the Advancement of Science, *Proceedings for the Twenty-second Meeting, August, 1873* (Salem, Mass.: AAAS, 1874), 203-05.

geography of Palestine and Syria is still useful for the descriptions of physical nature and of artifacts before the impact of modern life.[74] Of comparable importance was the contribution of Justin Perkins, the Syriac scholar, who had a genius for discovering manuscripts and other treasures which he generously shared with distinguished European scholars who duly honored him.[75]

Missionaries not only contributed to Western knowledge of many lands but also introduced Western scholarship to the learned men where they labored. A few examples may be taken as representative. W. A. P. Martin, who went to south China in 1859, translated Henry Wheaton's great work on international law as part of his contribution toward training future officials of China.[76] The story of the introduction of Western knowledge in Japan by missionaries is a familiar one. Representatives of the Dutch Reformed and Presbyterian churches led the way. The names of Samuel H. Brown, Guido H. F. Verbeck, and John Hyde de Forest are still remembered in Japan. Of special importance was the American support for the Christian university founded by the Reverend Jospeh Hardy Neesima at Kyoto in 1874, for it became a center for the dissemination of Western knowledge within a Christian setting.[77]

In the Near East, French Catholic missionaries had long been active, and, generally speaking, used French as the medium of instruction. The American Protestant College at Beirut, by contrast, decided from the start to use Arabic as the basic language. Christian Lebanese and other minority groups in the old Turkish Empire who received their education at Beirut, molded classical Arabic into a new

[74] Henry H. Jessup, *Fifty-Three Years in Syria* (2 vols.; New York, Chicago: Fleming H. Revell, 1910) I, 61, 62; William McClure Thomson, *The Land and the Book; or, Biblical Illustrations Drawn from the Manners and Customs, the Scenes and Scenery of the Holy Land* (2 vols.; New York: Harper, 1859); *Church at Home and Abroad* XV (June, 1894), 527.

[75] Rev. Henry Martyn Perkins, *Life of Rev. Justin Perkins, D.D.: Pioneer Missionary to Persia* (Chicago: Woman's Presbyterian Board of Missions of the Northwest, 1887), 40 ff.

[76] Martin was called in 1869 to the presidency of the T'ung Wen Kuan, which grew out of an official Chinese school for interpreters. He later became the first president of the Imperial University in Peking: W. A. P. Martin, *A Cycle of Cathay; or China, South and North* (New York, Chicago: Fleming H. Revell, 1896), 17-76, 293 ff.

[77] William Elliot Griffis, *A Maker of the New Orient, Samuel Robbins Brown, Pioneer Educator in China, America and Japan* (New York, Chicago: Fleming H. Revell, 1902) and *Verbeck of Japan* (New York, Chicago: Fleming H. Revell, 1900); Jerome D. Davis, *A Sketch of the Life of Rev. Joseph Hardy Neesima* (Kyoto, Japan: Doshisha University, 1936); Latourette, *A History of the Expansion of Christianity* VI, 383 ff.

instrument capable of expressing modern thought. These and other intellectuals, many of whom had come under the influence of the American Protestant College, thus helped prepare the way for the awakening of modern Arabic nationalism.[78] George Antonius, a student of Arabic history and culture, attributed to the direct and indirect influence of the Protestant missionaries, in greater degree than to any other factor, the beginnings of an Arab national revival.[79] At Robert College students from the minorities rubbed elbows with each other, softened mutual hatreds and antagonisms, and furnished leaders in the national and democratic movements in several countries, notably in Bulgaria.[80]

In contributing to knowledge in several fields and in founding and maintaining colleges which introduced Western learning, the missionary influence touched only a few, though this few included future scholars and public leaders. But in establishing boarding schools and, especially, village day schools, the missionaries came into contact with people in all walks of life. Their influence was extended by the fact that in some countries, notably Japan, missionaries helped mold the rising system of public education in the 1870's and 1880's. Their impact on Siam was even greater: in 1878 the King appointed Samuel G. McFarland, a member of the Presbyterian mission, as superintendent of public instruction and head of the royal college at Bangkok.[81]

One innovation struck at an established custom in many lands— the restriction of formal education outside the home to boys. Among the early pioneers in opening the windows of knowledge to girls were the Reverend John Henry Hill and his wife. After spending twenty years in business, Hill studied at the Episcopal Seminary in Alexandria, Virginia, took holy orders, and in 1830 went to Greece, where he and Mrs. Hill devoted more than a half century to teaching girls. Generally speaking, the Hills' school attracted daughters of influential,

[78] Philip K. Hitti, *History of Syria, including Lebanon and Palestine* (New York: Macmillan, 1951), 701-02.
[79] George Antonius, *The Arab Awakening: The Story of the Arab National Movement* (4th ed., New York: G. P. Putnam's Sons, 1946), 35-60.
[80] Edgar J. Fisher, *The Meaning of Robert College. Founders' Day Address, March 23, 1926* (n.p.:n.d.), 19-20, 26-27.
[81] George Bradley McFarland, *Historical Sketch of Protestant Missions in Siam, 1828-1928* (Bangkok: Bangkok Times Press, 1928); Arthur Judson Brown, *The Expectation of Siam* (New York: Board of Foreign Missions of the Presbyterian Church in the U.S.A., 1925).

well-to-do Greeks, but many of their students later opened girls' schools that reached larger segments of the population.

The Hills also founded the "American School" in Agora where hundreds of poor children received a free education. Since the Hills made no effort to win their students away from the Greek Orthodox Church, they got along well with the hierarchy and finally came to be looked on by the Greeks as belonging to their country. Hill refused many honors offered by the Greek government but nevertheless received numerous evidences of esteem and appreciation. "If we estimate the greatness of the benefits he conferred," declared A. Diomedes Kymakos at his funeral, "we cannot for a moment hesitate to inscribe the name of Hill among those of the greatest benefactors of our country. He was the first . . . to promote the education of females among us." [82]

In its report for 1848-1849 the Board of Commissioners for Foreign Missions declared, in speaking of Greece and Armenia, that "the operation and influence of the female schools in this mission are highly propitious, and promises much for the elevation of the female character, the best interests of social and domestic life, and the future prosperity of religion. . . ." [83]

To the slow, uphill work of developing educational opportunities for girls and young women in the Near and Middle East many pioneers contributed. Justin Perkins and his wife, reaching Mesopotamia in 1834, opened the way in this ancient land for the education of girls. Another outstanding figure was Fidelia Fiske, a graduate and former member of the faculty of Mount Holyoke Female Seminary, which sent so many young women to foreign lands to open missionary schools for girls. [84]

To launch collegiate education for women was no less an innovation than to establish lower schools. The Constantinople College for Women opened its doors in 1871. The College attracted the support of such donors as Mrs. Albert Bowker and Caroline Borden of Boston, Pauline A. Durant, co-founder of Wellesley, Olivia Phelps Stokes

[82] *The Churchman* XLV (August 5, 12, 26, 1882), 29, 147, 176, 227. For an interesting first-hand account of the Hills' school toward the end of their career see C. Edmund Maurice, ed., *Life of Octavia Hill as Told in Her Letters* (London: Macmillan, 1913), 408-09.

[83] American Board of Commissioners for Foreign Missions, *Annual Report*, 1849, 62.

[84] Justin Perkins, *A Residence of Eight Years in Persia* . . . (New York: M. W. Dodd, 1843); Daniel T. Fiske, *The Cross and the Crown; or Faith Working by Love as Exemplified in the Life of Fidelia Fiske* (Boston: Congregational Sabbath School and Publishing Society, 1869).

and Caroline Phelps Stokes, Mrs. Finley J. Shepard, and, in time, George A. Plimpton and Mrs. Russell Sage. The interest which Grace Dodge developed in the institution was a special godsend. When the President, Dr. Mary Mills Patrick, first asked Miss Dodge for help, she was busy in getting Teachers College on its feet and wrote that she could not do anything for the college in Constantinople. Gradually, however, she was struck by the strategic position of the College in the Near East and sensed the contribution it might make in helping the peoples of this area understand each other. When Miss Patrick visited Miss Dodge, she said she might help, but that she must first see the budget. She was astounded when Miss Patrick, who disliked figures, replied that there was no budget. Grace Dodge became president of the board of trustees and not only gave of her money but of her administrative talents and inspired Miss Patrick to develop similar ones.[85]

In the Far East the foundations for the education of girls and women were also laid by missionaries. Mrs. John Hepburn opened the first schools for girls in Japan. In China American missionaries with colleagues from other lands found there were great odds against establishing educational opportunities for women. Numerous schools did, however, spring up, one of the best known being the McTeire Home and School for girls in Shanghai, which trained many daughters of well-to-do and influential Chinese officials and merchants. In India, Isabella Thoburn, working with Methodists, founded at Lucknow a school which in time became the college bearing her name. It offered an excellent education to young women from every part of India.[86]

Education for girls in non-Western countries often met with much resistance on the ground that missionary boarding schools disqualified girls for life as it was lived in the community. To counteract this impression Ella Marie Holmes, a Baptist missionary in Assam, adopted the village cottage as the unit for her school. Here she taught, initially, the village arts, including cooking, spinning, and sewing.[87] In far off Zululand and in other missions in central Africa, a similar

---

[85] Mary Mills Patrick, *A Bosporus Adventure: Constantinople Woman's College 1871-1924* (Stanford: Stanford University Press, 1934); Abbie Graham, *Grace H. Dodge, Merchant of Dreams* (New York: The Woman's Press, 1926), 291 ff.

[86] James Mills Thoburn, *Life of Isabella Thoburn* (New York: Eaton and Mains, 1903).

[87] Ella Marie Holmes, *Sowing Seed in Assam, Missionary Life and Labours in Northeast India* (New York, Chicago: Fleming H. Revell, 1925).

type of industrial or vocational education for girls seemed the most realistic and promising approach.[88] All this educational work for girls received impetus when American women in the second half of the nineteenth century increasingly formed their own foreign missionary societies.

Vocational education for boys as well as girls increased as the decades of the nineteenth century gave way one to another. This emphasis was as important an educational innovation as the opening of schools for girls. The pioneers were the missionaries in Hawaii. The first group that went out in 1819 included a farmer as well as a printer. The industrial schools at Lahaina and Hilo inspired General Samuel C. Armstrong, whose father was a missionary in Hawaii, to establish a similar program after the Civil War at Hampton Institute in Virginia.[89] Elsewhere industrial training slowly caught on in the mission stations among the more "backward" peoples. Sam Higginbottom developed a famous agricultural school at Allahabad[90] while other industrial schools were established by the missionaries working with the Telugu in south India.[91]

In the Congo, schools for training the indigenous peoples in agriculture and industry had become an accepted part of the program of the Presbyterian missionaries in the last decades of the century.[92] Bishop William Taylor, whose far-ranging labors included Africa, promoted industrial training in Angola.[93] In the early decades of the twentieth century American missionaries in Mexico, Brazil, and other

[88] Gertrude R. Hance, *The Zulu Yesterday and To-day: Twenty-nine Years in South Africa* (New York, Chicago: Fleming H. Revell, 1916), 264 ff; Thomas J. Bowen, *Central Africa: Adventures and Missionary Labors in Several Countries in the Interior of Africa from 1849 to 1856* (Charleston: Southern Baptist Publication Society, 1857); Latourette, *A History of the Expansion of Christianity*, V, 358 ff.

[89] Mary Dillingham Frear, *Lowell and Abigail: A Realistic Idyll* (New Haven: Privately printed, 1934), 67; Rufus Anderson, *A Heathen Nation Evangelized: History of the Sandwich Islands Mission* (Boston: Congregational Publishing Society, 1870); Harold W. Bradley, *The American Frontier in Hawaii: The Pioneers, 1789-1843* (Stanford: Stanford University Press, 1942), 341-42, 350; Edith Armstrong Talbot, *Samuel Chapin Armstrong: A Biographical Study* (New York: Doubleday, Page, 1904), 155.

[90] *Sam Higginbottom, Farmer: An Autobiography* (New York: Scribner's Sons, 1949).

[91] Latourette, *A History of the Expansion of Christianity*, VI, 191-2.

[92] Bedinger, *Triumphs of the Gospel in the Belgian Congo*; Sheppard, *Presbyterian Pioneers in Congo*; Verner, *Pioneering in Central Africa*.

[93] Taylor, *Story of My Life*; Sadie Louise Miller, *In Jesus' Name*; *Memoirs of the Victorious Life and Triumphant Death of Susan Talbott Wengatz* (Upland, Indiana: Taylor University, 1932).

Latin American countries were to do yeoman work in introducing rural education.[94]

In disasters, efforts were sometimes made to do more than sustain life by parceling out food, clothing, and medicines to those in need. The restoration of village life after the brutal devastations in Armenia by setting up temporary workshops and facilitating the restoration of agriculture did not stand alone among efforts to provide long-term aid. A pioneer in a constructive approach to relief was the Baptist missionary in Central India, John E. Clough, who supervised a government supported canal project, thus giving work as well as relief to thousands of helpless human beings caught in the grip of famine. Toward the end of the century, three supporting missionary organizations established and maintained at the University of Nanking in China a department of agriculture and forestry with a program of research into the causes and best methods of preventing famine.[95] But the most characteristic approach beyond the distribution of food and clothing was the establishment of orphan asylums for the children of men and women who had died of hunger or pestilence or who had been massacred by fanatics. After the Sepoy Mutiny in India, the Methodist mission established the first orphanage in Lucknow. The policy spread to other missions in India, and, especially, in Turkey after the Armenian massacres. Whatever the shortcomings of these institutions, they provided homeless waifs with food, shelter, care, and such comforts as Christian teaching offered.[96]

It was in medicine and public health, however, that the missions made their most important contributions to social welfare. Western medicine came to large areas of the world through missionaries, among whom Americans were pioneers. The dispensaries, hospitals, and nurses' training schools which the missionaries built not only offered the benefits of Western medicine to rich and poor alike; they also trained native doctors and nurses. Missionaries at first established dispensaries and hospitals in order to open doors to evangelization, to break down the isolation to which native prejudices subjected them. Effecting cures of diseases which had baffled native practitioners gave the missionaries much needed prestige. At

[94] Latourette, *A History of the Expansion of Christianity*, V, 113-17.
[95] *Ibid.*, VI, 352-54.
[96] Parker, *Ecclesiastical Organization and Administration of the Methodist Episcopal Church in India*, 9; Rev. Andrew Gordon, *Our India Mission, 1855-1883* (Philadelphia: A. Gordon, 1886), vii.

the same time, these agents of Christ believed that it was their duty to heal the sick as a demonstration of the compassion and love inherent in the Master's teachings. Toward the end of the nineteenth century, the missionary movement increasingly emphasized the medical program as something more than a mere adjunct to evangelization, as, in brief, a much-needed Christian service that was its own reward.

Dr. Peter Parker, the first Protestant medical missionary in China, led the way. A year after his arrival in Canton in 1834, he opened a dispensary which quickly came to be known as the Ophthalmic Hospital.[97] With his British associate, Dr. T. R. College, Parker called a public meeting in Canton on February 21, 1838, which resulted in the organization of the Medical Missionary Society in China. At first the dispensary and hospital found their chief support in this Society, made up of foreign residents in the port cities. But gradually help came from American constituents across the Pacific. Other missionary hospitals opened their doors in Macao and Chusan, and by the end of 1840 the three agencies had treated more than 10,000 patients.[98]

The seed planted by Dr. Parker was nourished by Dr. John Glasgow Kerr, a graduate of the Jefferson Medical College in Philadelphia, who came to Canton in 1853 under the auspices of the Presbyterian Board. Dr. Kerr labored for more than forty-five years in China, winning renown for surgery in vesical calculus, for his attack on syphilis and opium addiction, and for providing for the first institutional care of the mentally ill.[99] And all the time, Dr. Kerr preached Christ. When the Canton Hospital finished its first century of service, it had treated over 2,000,000 sick and disabled; it had trained two hundred doctors and many more nurses; and it had achieved creditable results in research. Leading figures in Chinese public life testified to its great contributions to their country.[100]

What Peter Parker and John Kerr did in China, Dr. John C. Hepburn, and especially Dr. John C. Berry, did in Japan. Arriving in 1872, Berry, in addition to his work for prison reform, taught medical

---

[97] George B. Stevens, *The Life, Letters, and Journals of the Rev. and Hon. Peter Parker* . . . (Boston, Chicago: Congregational Sunday School and Publishing Society, 1896); Williams, *The Middle Kingdom*, II, 346 ff.

[98] *Chinese Repository* V (January, 1841), 52-54.

[99] William Warder Cadbury, *At the Point of a Lancet: One Hundred Years of the Canton Hospital, 1835-1935* (Shanghai, Hongkong: Kelly and Walsh, 1935).

[100] *Ibid.*

subjects at the Doshisha University in Kyoto, managed its hospital, and directed a training school for nurses.[101] Since the Japanese government early took a strong hand in medical education, the missionaries did not emphasize the medical program in which Dr. Berry pioneered. But a notable later contribution was made by Dr. Rudolf Bolling Teusler, an Episcopalian from Richmond, Virginia. Arriving in Tokyo in 1900, Teusler took over a rundown, story-and-a-half hospital that had often closed its doors for lack of support, and created St. Luke's Hospital and medical center, one of the great institutions of its kind in the world.[102] In nearby Korea Dr. Horace Newton Allen, who became court physician and at whose suggestion the government opened in 1885 the hospital of which he was put in charge, not only broke the path for modern medicine but played an important role in diplomacy as well.[103] In India women physicians from America, under Methodist auspices, began their work in 1869 when Dr. Clara Swain, trained at the University of Pennsylvania, opened a dispensary and hospital. Her work and that of her associates, helped break down the prejudices of Indian women toward Western medicine, which had been entirely under male direction.[104]

Many other missionary groups, including the Baptists and Lutherans, also worked in the medical field; but special note needs to be made of the thirty-nine years' service of Dr. William James Wanless, a Canadian who developed, under the Presbyterian Board of Foreign Missions, one of the greatest medical centers in Asia.[105] In Siam and Laos Dr. Daniel McGilvary continued the work begun in the middle years of the nineteenth century, combining, as his predecessors did, the health and evangelistic roles of the medical missionary. Laos, in particular, proved an almost ideal place for the medical missionary, for while the field was virtually closed to the preaching of the Gospel, the mission doctor was warmly welcomed.[106]

[101] Griffis, *Hepburn of Japan;* Katherine Fiske Berry, *A Pioneer Doctor in Old Japan: The Story of John C. Berry, M.D.* (New York, London: Fleming H. Revell, 1940).

[102] Howard Chandler Robbins and George K. MacNaught, *Dr. Rudolf Bolling Teusler: An Adventure in Christianity* (New York: Scribner's Sons, 1942), Preface by Joseph C. Grew, vii, 30 ff.

[103] Fred H. Harrington, *God, Mammon, and the Japanese; Dr. Horace N. Allen and Korean-American Relations, 1884-1950* (Madison: University of Wisconsin Press, 1944), 45-48, 79, 86, 94.

[104] Margaret Balfour and Ruth Young, *The Work of Medical Women in India* (London, New York: Oxford University Press, 1929), 15 ff.

[105] Sir William James Wanless, *American Doctor at Work in India* (New York, Chicago: Fleming H. Revell, 1932), 142 ff.

[106] McGilvary, *A Half Century Among the Siamese and the Lao.*

What happened in Asia was repeated in those parts of Africa in which American missions operated and, above all, in the Near East. The American Board was the first to introduce Western medical practice into Turkey. Among the leading figures were Clarence D. Ussher, who entered the most hostile dwellings and prepared the hearts and minds of those whose bodies he cured[107] and Dr. Henry Lobdell, who was somewhat exceptional in refusing to give medicine to a dignitary in the palace until he got written permission that he might preach to the patient.[108] Dr. Asahel Grant taught and practiced medicine among the Nestorians.[109] Dr. Fred Douglas Shepard, who became professor of surgery in 1882 in the newly opened medical department of the Central Turkey College, established a hospital, played a crucial role in quelling cholera in 1895, and deserved his reputation as "one of the outstanding missionaries of his generation, one who practiced both medicine and Christianity."[110] Towering over all other medical centers was the medical school at the Syrian Protestant College of Beirut which, even before the end of the nineteenth century, had achieved an enviable reputation and had wide influence.[111]

Each medical missionary would deserve comment, for each has a story worth telling. Charles S. Dutton of Wisconsin, who gave heroic aid to Father Damien, founder of a sanctuary for lepers in the Sandwich Islands in the later nineteenth century, was only one American who labored in this field.[112] No worker deserves more appreciation than Mary Reed, who went to India in 1884 under the sponsorship of the Methodist Women's Foreign Missionary Society. While on a furlough in Ohio in 1890 to recover from a persistent illness which doctors could not diagnose, Mary Reed herself discovered that she

[107] Clarence D. Ussher and Grace H. Knapp, *An American Physician in Turkey* (Boston, New York: Houghton Mifflin, 1917).

[108] Rev. William S. Tyler, *Memoir of Rev. Henry Lobdell, M.D., Late Missionary of the American Board at Mosul including the Early History of the Assyrian Mission* (Boston: American Tract Society, 1859), 237.

[109] Rev. Thomas Laurie, *Dr. Grant and the Mountain Nestorians* (Boston: Gould and Lincoln, 1853).

[110] Alice Shepard Riggs, *Shepard of Aintab* (New York: Interchurch Press, 1920), 107 ff.; Rev. W. Nesbitt Chambers, "Dr. Shepard, of Aintab," *Missionary Herald* CXII (March, 1916), 115-16.

[111] Penrose, *That They May Have Life*, 27, 28, 31, 45, 57, 100, 108, 110. Mention should also be made of the hospital for the mentally ill founded in Lebanon in the 1890's and supported by American and English Friends: *The Autobiography of Theophilus Waldemeier* (London: Friends Bookshop, 1925), 294 ff.

[112] Charles J. Dutton, *The Samaritans of Molokai: The Lives of Father Damien and Brother Dutton Among the Lepers* (New York: Dodd, Mead, 1932), 220 ff.

had contracted leprosy. She returned to India determined to give whatever years remained to the lepers, becoming superintendent of the Leper Asylum of Pithoragarh in the foothills of the Himalayas. Under her direction the asylum increased its facilities and services. Her much publicized story was the more dramatic since the disease was arrested—she felt through prayer—and her work continued through a ripe age until death.[113]

Finally, missionaries were forerunners in public health education. In Hawaii the pioneers vaccinated virtually the whole native population to stamp out the devastating smallpox. Elsewhere, in schools, dispensaries, and hospitals, the first steps were taken toward introducing Western ideas of sanitation and other preventive measures.

What the American missionaries, in association with their Old World colleagues, did beyond the seas in the nineteenth century fell far short of what they wanted to do, or what their constituents at home felt they should have done. It is also true that, in relation to the need for Western medicine and scientific knowledge, for the uplifting of the masses, including women, and for a distinctively religious program, the accomplishment fell far short of the need. But the record was nonetheless impressive. In their giving for evangelization and human uplift beyond the seas, nineteenth-century Americans found their principal inspiration and agency in the few thousands of missionaries who carried to disadvantaged foreign peoples what they regarded as the best that the Western world in general, and America in particular, possessed.

Among the factors that stimulated in the first two decades of the twentieth century an expansion of what was already under way, the stimulus of America's new role as a world power was, however intangible, nevertheless real. The increasing financial support, so marked in the 1890's, reached new levels, both as a result of broadly based giving and of generous donations of the well to do. The latter included the Cleveland industrialist, Louis Henry Severance, whose fortune, estimated at his death in 1913 at $8,000,000, rested in part on his pioneer association with the Rockefeller oil interests. Severance supported Presbyterian missions, schools, and hospitals in India, Japan, and Korea. The Severance Hospital and Medical College in Seoul, which was to play a continuously important role in the im-

---

[113] John Jackson, *Mary Reed; Missionary to the Lepers* (9th ed.; London: Marshall Brothers, 1909).

provement of medical care and education, was well established before the donor's death. Another well-to-do contributor was Henry J. Heinz, the Pittsburgh pickle manufacturer, whose interest in the international Sunday School movement led him to support various educational enterprises under missionary auspices in Japan, Korea, and China.[114]

The largest benefactor of the American missionary movement was John D. Rockefeller. His advisor, the Reverend Frederick T. Gates, wrote to him in 1905, the year of his two largest gifts to the cause thus far, that in introducing steam and electricity as well as Christianity into the Orient, missions added to American commerce a thousand times the sum given in a single year for the conversion of the heathen. Such a consideration, however, was hardly needed, for Rockefeller's commitment to the stewardship of wealth had long embraced foreign missions. Three years before his gift of $1,000,000 to Baptist missions in 1905, James L. Barton, of the Congregational Board of Missions, had approached Gates on the matter of a Rockefeller donation. After considerable negotiation, the philanthropist on February 11, 1905, approved a gift of $100,000 with the request that it be spent for schools in Japan, India, Ceylon, Bulgaria and Turkey. The Prudential Committee of the American Board of Christian Foreign Missions for the Congregational Church accepted the gift with enthusiastic gratitude. But a group of thirty ministers and laymen, led by the well-known apostle of the Social Gospel, Washington Gladden, insisted that acceptance of the gift would amount to a tacit approval of the methods by which the Rockefeller fortune had been accumulated; "tainted money" offered for a sacred cause, must be rejected. The Prudential Committee replied that for a hundred years gifts had been accepted from all quarters—from Mohammedans, Buddhists, Hindus, and African savages—and that if there was a legal title to funds offered, these could not properly be turned down. In the end the Board, with the overwhelming support of the governing body of the church, maintained its position, accepting the money. Rockefeller, who at first kept silence, was convinced that, in view of the widespread discussion it would be well

[114] *Cleveland Plain Dealer*, June 26, 1913; Y. S. Lee to Gregory Lee, Cultural Attaché, American Embassy, Seoul, Dec. 30, 1959, with enclosures; Gregory Lee to Merle Curti, Jan. 4, 1960; L. George Paik, *Facts about Yonsei University and Severance Medical College* (Seoul, 1960).

publicly to defend Standard Oil, and, through appropriate channels, did so.[115]

During the controversy over the Rockefeller gift Protestants were surprised to learn how small missionary budgets actually were and even more surprised to hear that Americans spent vastly more in a given year on liquor than they did on foreign missions. Thus the controversy gave force to a movement, already under way, to increase the number of relatively small donors. The movement had been spearheaded by the Young People's Society of the Christian Endeavor and the Student Volunteer Movement, which had been organized in the 1880's and 1890's. In 1902 the Laymen's Missionary Movement augmented the campaign for an expansion of foreign missions. In the first two decades of the twentieth century the activities of these and other organizations increasingly widened among people of modest income the base of financial support and available personnel.[116] A windfall also came when, thanks to the pressure of the State Department, the Turkish government paid the American Board $100,000 for the damage done missionary agencies during the Armenian massacres. Part of the Boxer indemnity also enabled the missionary movement in China to rebuild its ruined churches and schools.

Thanks to larger assets, the work of the foreign missions expanded. The schools and colleges in the Near East, in China, in India, and in Africa enlarged their facilities and improved their programs. New

[115] *New York Times*, April 17, 1905; *New York Tribune*, March 31, April 1, 1905; *Congregationalist and Christian World*, XC (March 18, 1905), 349; XC (April 1, 1905), 424-25; LX (April 8, 1905), 465; LX (April 15, 1905), 495; Washington Gladden, *Recollections* (Boston, New York: Houghton Mifflin, 1909), 402 ff.; *Herald of Gospel Liberty* XCVII (April 13, 1905), 225-26, 229-31. For the effect of the controversy on the public relations policy of Standard Oil, see Allan Nevins, *John D. Rockefeller: The Heroic Age of American Enterprise* (2 vols.; New York: C. Scribner's Sons, 1940) II, 534 ff.

[116] For the Student Volunteer Movement, see John R. Mott, *Five Decades and a Forward View* (New York, London: Harper, 1939) and Clarence P. Shedd, *Two Centuries of Student Christian Movements: Their Origin and Intercollegiate Life* (New York: Association Press, 1934); and George Sherwood Eddy, *Eighty Adventurous Years: an Autobiography* (New York: Harper, 1955). For the Laymen's Missionary Movement, see William T. Doherty, "The Impact of Business upon Protestantism," *Business History Review* XXVIII (June, 1954); Gains Glenn Atkins, "The Crusading Church at Home and Abroad," *Church History* I (Sept., 1932), 131-49; William T. Ellis, *Men and Missions* (Philadelphia: Sunday School Times, 1909). The most scholarly and comprehensive treatment of these and related movements is John Lankford, "The Protestant Theology of Giving in the Twentieth Century" (unpublished Ph.D. dissertation, University of Wisconsin, 1961).

educational undertakings, such as Miss E. C. Clark's famous kindergarten school in Sofia, the Gerard Institute in Syria, Dr. J. H. House's Agricultural and Theological Institute in Salonika, to cite only three examples, were launched. In Peking several institutions of higher learning combined into a simple plan of cooperation which led to more efficient administration and enlarged offerings.

In general the early nineteen hundreds witnessed a heightening of the tendency, already under way in the 1890's, to depend more and more on native leaders for purely evangelical work, to specialize in the fields of education and medicine, and to develop the social and community activities of missionary stations. This last development roughly paralleled the growth of social settlements and welfare activity which the growing sense of social responsibility of the churches stimulated at home. As the missionaries became more closely acquainted with the peoples among whom they worked, they came to understand better their customs and faith. Moreover, they came to some appreciation of the religious spirit, crude and mistaken though it seemed, and of the ethical values in the various Oriental faiths, values to which appeal could be made in their own effort to present the claims of Christianity.

VII

For Welfare and Culture

Relief of disasters and aid to foreign missions were only a part of American overseas philanthropy in the late nineteenth century. A growing number of Americans contributed, sometimes conventionally, sometimes creatively, to the establishment abroad of schools, hospitals, art galleries, orphan asylums, and projects for mitigating or even eliminating poverty. That private giving for education and welfare became a more important segment of American philanthropy was in part the result of the accumulation of wealth in the hands of men and women with personal ties to a foreign country, whether by reason of nativity or of residence abroad for long stretches of time. The expansion of the few isolated cases of such giving in the earlier nineteenth century may also have reflected a consciousness on the part of donors of a role to be played as citizens of a country that had somewhat suddenly become recognized as a world power.

Just as donors in America gave to improve the welfare or culture of their local communities or even to purposes national in scope, so American philanthropy abroad was directed toward local, regional and national improvement. Such gifts resembled those made by many men and women of means to their own communities or early homes in America. One of the assumptions underlying overseas giving was the traditional view that any advance in knowledge and the arts must ultimately aid mankind in general. Another was that such a contribution, as well as support of welfare projects, represented an investment in the future, a means of improving the quality of life rather than of merely meeting a temporary need through emergency relief. And personal interest, affection, and desire to be appreciated made giving to a cultural or welfare cause in a particular overseas community or country an appropriate action.

Almost a century passed before Americans followed the example of Count Rumford in giving to an established institution of learning or culture in the Old World. In 1892 Thomas G. Hodgkins, a bachelor who had migrated to the United States from England at the age of twenty-nine and had made a fortune in business in New York, bequeathed $100,000 to the Royal Institute in the country of his birth.[1] At about the same time Dr. Thomas Wiltberger Evans, a self-made American who acquired both a fortune and social position as a renowned dentist in Paris, built the Lafayette House in the Rue de la Pont in that city, a residence for young American girls studying art and music in the French capital.[2] As a token of America's appreciation of her literary heritage, George William Childs, a well-to-do Philadelphia publisher, a few years before his death in 1894, gave the handsome Shakespeare Memorial Fountain in Stratford-on-Avon. To honor Herbert, Cowper, and Milton, he also installed memorial windows in Westminster Abbey and in nearby St. Margaret's.[3]

Two institutions established in Europe primarily in the interest of American classical scholarship were nevertheless to contribute to the world's knowledge of antiquities. The philanthropies which initiated or supported these agencies reflected the conviction that American scholarship in these fields needed the opportunities provided by immediate access to artifacts. Moreover, the promoters and donors felt that America, sharing as she did in the advantages of the republic of knowledge and the arts, had a responsibility to support agencies in the Old World which could make contributions to concerned scholars everywhere.

Support for the American School of Classical Studies in Athens, launched in 1881, was discouragingly slow in developing. Henry G. Marquand gave the School $5,000, one of the larger individual gifts. Especially encouraging was the support of Catherine Lorillard Wolfe, a rich, religious, and social-minded New York maiden lady, whose

---

[1] *New York Times*, Nov. 26, 1892. Hodgkins also bequeathed $200,000 to the Smithsonian Institution in Washington, $100,000 to the Society for the Prevention of Cruelty to Children, and the same amount to the Society for the Prevention of Cruelty to Animals.

[2] *New York Times*, Nov. 16, 1890; *New York Tribune*, Dec. 29, 1890. Dr. Evans' principal philanthropy was the establishment of the Thomas W. Evans Museum and Dental Institute in Philadelphia, now the Dental School of the University of Pennsylvania. For his career see Edward A. Crane, ed., *Memoirs of Dr. Thomas W. Evans: the Second Empire* (2 vols.; New York: D. Appleton, 1905).

[3] George W. Childs, *Recollections* (Philadelphia: J. B. Lippincott, 1891), 187-308.

benefactions were both generous and far ranging. Her contribution to the Wolfe Expedition to Babylonia in 1885, inspired by an interest in the program of the American School, resulted in a worthy increment of knowledge to archaeology and Biblical scholarship through the discovery of tablets, columns, and inscriptions.[4] Only in 1903, however, did the American School of Classical Studies at Athens reach the $100,000 endowment that its founders and early directors regarded as the minimum base for effective work; and only in the 1920's did American foundations insure its future.

A comparable, though in many ways different agency, the American Academy in Rome, was the result of the imagination and effort of Charles Follen McKim, the architect. His own gifts and those he persuaded his friends to make got the Academy off to a promising start. In time it attracted enough support from American institutions of learning, foundations, and individuals to become one of the highest embodiments of training in the fine arts and classical scholarship.[5]

A few nineteenth-century American gifts reflected a desire to improve community life in the village or province in which the donor had been born and from which he had migrated. An example in point is Oswald Ottendorfer, who was born in Swittau in Moravia. After his immigration, he worked for the *New-Yorker Staats-Zeitung*, becoming the proprietor on the death of its founder. Ottendorfer built a fountain in his native town, established charitable institutions, and in 1890 founded a library and endowed it at an expense of $300,000.[6] During the Nazi occupation of Czechoslovakia the value of the library and its collections was reduced by interference of the occupying authorities, but the library, now consisting of 10,000 books, is still in use.[7]

---

[4] *New York Tribune*, April 5, 7, 1887; *The Churchman* LV (April 9, 1887); Louis E. Lord, *A History of the American School of Classical Studies at Athens* (Cambridge: Harvard University Press, 1947), 17.

[5] In 1905 J. Pierpont Morgan and Henry Walters each pledged $100,000 to the endowment of the school. James Stillman, William Vanderbilt, and others also subscribed, and, in time, foundations likewise supported this institution: *The Promise of American Architecture: Addresses at the Dinner of the American Institute of Architecture, Jan. 11, 1905* (Washington, D. C., 1905).

[6] *Zur Erinnerung an Oswald Ottendorfer* (New York: New-Yorker Staats-Zeitung, 1900). Ottendorfer's wife, Anna Behr Uhl Ottendorfer, also European-born, established a reputation for generous giving to the charitable institutions in the New York area and to German-American educational agencies. In 1883, the German Empress, Augusta, decorated her for her charitable and philanthropic activities.

[7] Fred G. Taylor, Press Attache, American Embassy, Prague, to Merle Curti, April 14, 1960.

A notable gift in this category was that of George Munroe. After leaving his home in Nova Scotia in 1856 he made a fortune in New York in publishing Munroe's Ten Cent Novels, *Old Sleuth the Detective*, and *Fireside Companion*, an inexpensive family paper of mass circulation. But Munroe did not give for the support or improvement of popular culture. He seemed to cherish the memory that he had entered adult life as a teacher in the academies of his native province. Beginning in 1879 he gave generously to education, in time establishing five chairs at Dalhousie University in Halifax. To these chairs able scholars were called, some of whom later became renowned professors in the universities of Scotland and England. Munroe also attracted superior students to Dalhousie by establishing bursarships. His benefactions to the University, adding up to $500,-000, were the first large gifts to a Canadian institution of higher learning. Thanks to them, Dalhousie was put on a firm basis.[8]

Like Munroe, Henry Rosenberg was an immigrant who "made good" and remembered the place of his origin. A leading drygoods merchant and banker in Texas, Rosenberg bequeathed nearly two thirds of his fortune to educational and charitable institutions in Galveston, but, before his death in 1893, he renovated and rebuilt the parish church in Bilten, Switzerland, where he had been baptized and confirmed. His will provided for a bequest of $30,000 to the communal government of Bilten for civic purposes and of $50,000 as an endowment for the orphanage. The town fathers and the pastor of Bilten received these gifts with warm appreciation.[9]

Hodgkins, Munroe, and Rosenberg represent the immigrants from Europe who gave to the country of birth. Another type of motivation was that of the American who spent years in a foreign land and became identified with it. Charles Reed Bishop is an interesting example. Early orphaned and brought up by his grandparents in Glens Falls, New York, he went to Hawaii in 1846, married a wealthy chieftainess, and made money. His Hawaiian wife at her death left almost her entire estate to build and endow the Kame-

---

[8] *New York Times*, April 25, 1896; Dalhousie College and University Centenary Committee, *One Hundred Years of Dalhousie* (Halifax, N. S., 1919), 24-30. Francis Donahoe, another immigrant who made money in publishing, contributed generously to Boston Catholic charities and, before the Civil War, to Mill Hill, an English institution for training priests for colored missions. Before his death in 1901 he also contributed to American institutions in Rome: *Boston Evening Transcript*, March 18, 1901.
[9] The Rosenberg Library, *Henry Rosenberg, 1824-1893* (New York: The De Vinne Press, 1918), 13-16.

hameha Schools for Boys and Girls. Bishop himself made handsome gifts to these schools, of which he was trustee for twenty-four years. He also established and endowed in memory of his wife the Bernice P. Bishop Museum, a scientific institution which has collected valuable Polynesian artifacts, flora, and fauna and supported research programs in Pacific studies. Bishop's benefactions, which reached several millions of dollars, were given both during his life and by his will to the educational and charitable agencies of his adopted land.[10]

The tie of residence and sympathetic interest figured in other acts of benevolence. In cooperation with Americans and Englishmen, Una Hawthorne, daughter of the writer, tried to establish in London a "preventive home" in connection with an orphanage. Its object was "the rescue of friendless girls from the sufferings and perils of a vicious life." [11] Little is known about the outcome. In the same year, 1873, Helen Gould was, however, said to have succeeded surprisingly well in the school she founded in Rome to Christianize and to "civilize" poor youth in the Eternal City. The school was reportedly conducted "in a manner not to offend popular prejudice or awaken unnecessary opposition. . . ." [12]

The outstanding example of welfare philanthropy on the part of an American identified with another country was that of George Peabody, whose gift to the poor of London surpassed in magnitude and impact that of any other nineteenth-century American gift in Europe. This self-made man, who began his business career at the age of eleven as an apprentice to a grocer in Danvers, Massachusetts, accumulated his fortune in the wholesale dry goods business in Baltimore, in railroads and, especially, in the London firm he established for dealing in foreign exchange and American securities. Simple in tastes, unmarried, and a devoted American as well as an appreciative long-term resident in England, Peabody began in 1856 to give away the bulk of his fortune. While still active, he gave, in fact, over $10,000,000, a sum making him the most notable philanthropist in the first three quarters of the nineteenth century. In his American philanthropies Peabody showed wide interests. The needs for founding, endowing, and encouraging libraries and museums, for scientific

[10] Mary H. Krout, *Memoirs of the Hon. Bernice Pauahi Bishop* (New York: Knickerbocker Press, 1908); *San Francisco Chronicle*, July 18, 1910; *Dictionary of American Biography* XXI, 82.

[11] *The Christian Union* VII (June 25, 1873), 507.

[12] *Ibid.* (April 2, 1873), 274.

research, and for public education in the South after the Civil War were all apparent. To these causes he gave the great part of his fortune.[13]

British attention to Peabody's generosity was first aroused in 1852 when he gave $10,000 to outfit a ship to search the Arctic seas for the lost explorer, Sir John Franklin. It was not easy for Peabody to know how to give in England. London was a rich city. Its museums, libraries, and educational institutions enjoyed generous support.

In turning to the problem of providing inexpensive and decent living quarters for the working class, Peabody was something of a pioneer. In giving in 1862 the sum of $750,000 for such a venture, Peabody was not motivated solely by a desire to do something that was needed in the country in which he had accumulated a large part of his fortune as a token of his appreciation. He also hoped that his gift would soften the bitter feelings between America and England that had arisen out of the Civil War. His later gifts enlarging the housing project also rested in part on the hope that this philanthropy might tie more closely the two great English-speaking peoples. Peabody supplemented the original gift so that $2,500,000 was available for the tenement project. The tenements were not a gift to the working people, but rather provided much better housing than they could afford to pay from their meager wages. The first units of the Peabody Dwellings opened in 1864 at Spitalfields. Others presently followed in Chelsea, Bermondsey, Islington, and Shadwell. The British public as well as leading citizens testified to their appreciation in many ways. The workingmen of London presented an address. Peabody received the freedom of the city. Oxford gave him an honorary D.C.L. While he was absent in America, the Prince of Wales unveiled a bronze statue of him, executed by William Story. But Peabody

[13] Peabody's principal American philanthropies were the $1,500,000 given to establish the Peabody Institute of Baltimore, with its free library, lectures, art gallery, and academy of music; the $250,000 for the Peabody Institute in Peabody, Massachusetts, which provided for a library and an endowed lectureship; the $140,000 to found at Salem the Peabody Academy of Science; the $150,000 to establish the Peabody Museum of Natural History and Science at Yale; the $150,000 for the Peabody Museum of Archaeology and Ethnology at Harvard; and the $3,500,000 for promoting public education in the post-Civil War South through the Peabody Educational Fund. There is no adequate full-length biography of Peabody—that of Phebe Ann Hanaford, *The Life of George Peabody* . . . (Boston: B. B. Russell, 1870), being slenderly documented and over-eulogistic. Franklin Parker, "George Peabody: Founder of Modern Philanthropy" (unpublished Ph.D. dissertation, George Peabody College, 1956) is exhaustive in its research.

refused the Queen's offer of a baronetcy and the Grand Cross of Bath.[14]

In commenting at the time of his death in 1869 on Peabody's philanthropies, the *Times* of London declared that there had been nothing hard or narrow about his giving; that it had pauperized nobody; that, even more important, it represented his truly original discovery of a new motive for heaping together wealth—the pleasure of giving it away. He might, the editorial went on, have followed convention in his charities by giving to churches and almshouses, or he might have expressed his own vagaries. Instead, he searched for genuine needs and in the search consulted those in a position to know. Thus his gifts marked a high point in charity, for they forfeited the pleasure of being charitable after one's own taste. His London charities, the *Times* continued, met all the major criteria for wise and creative giving and in so doing, set a high example: his gifts expressed a manifest interest in and affection for England, where he had long lived. The gifts also met a real, not a superficial need, and expressed the sound maxim that in giving it is well to help the recipient to help himself, rather than to pauperize him. Moreover, in giving, while he was alive, to trustees to whom he delegated full power, he avoided the chance of miscarriage of his intentions or the corruption of his gifts. "Mr. George Peabody," the editorial concluded, "in abdicating all property in his riches while living, has made it impossible to dissociate his identity from them now that he is dead." [15]

Peabody's philanthropy did more than help change the British image of America and improve relations between the two countries. If interest in cheaper and decent housing for the working classes would have grown even without the Peabody Buildings, these provided a stimulus to the movement in England and, to some extent, in the United States where such philanthropists as James Lenox, A. T. Stewart, Alfred T. White, Robert Treat Paine, Edwin Ginn, Henry Phipps, Kate Gleason, and E. M. Chase, among others, were either pioneering or were to pioneer in this field. On the other hand, it would be easy to overestimate the effects of the Peabody benefaction in England itself. By the 1930's Peabody's name was not

[14] *Dictionary of National Biography* XV, 575-76.
[15] *The Times* [London], November 5, 1869.

mentioned in the Fund's literature and tenants were unaware of the American origin of the quarters in which they lived.[16]

Compassion for the disadvantaged in the Old World also inspired efforts to assist those wanting to come to America or who, having come, needed help. In a sense, of course, these efforts do not strictly belong to a discussion of American philanthropies beyond the seas, yet the line of demarcation is a thin one. Bishop Ireland of St. Paul, with the cooperation of Bishop Spalding of Peoria, took the lead in uniting religion and philanthropy, to use the latter's phrase, by helping Irish Catholic immigrants locate in neighborhoods on western farm lands: many did not have the $400 needed for a family to get a start in the West. A spirited campaign in 1880 and 1881 tried to raise through mass meetings at least $100,000 as a capital fund. The campaign fell $17,000 short of the goal. This did not result solely from the inability of Catholics to give, for during these very months, Irish Catholics in the United States, poor as well as rich, contributed large amounts to Charles Stewart Parnell's campaign for the newly founded Irish Land League.[17] No wonder that Bishop Spalding wrote regretfully of the great difficulties experienced in attempting to raise even $100,000 among Catholics for colonization purposes. Thanks, however, to the zeal of Bishop Ireland, Bishop Spalding and a few helpers, and to the cooperation of some of the land-grant western railroads, colonies took shape in Minnesota and Nebraska. In this way something was done to help impoverished Irish immigrants who had given up the struggle in the homeland to establish farms on the American prairies.[18]

To the west of the great plains the Mormons were contributing to the Perpetual Emigrating Fund. Between its establishment in 1849 and its dissolution by the federal government in 1887, this enabled some 87,000 of the "lord's poor" in Great Britain and northern Europe to reach the Promised Land. In theory those helped paid back into the Fund what they had received. But the spirit of the enterprise was altruistic. In practice the economic hardships that many

[16] Richard H. Heindel, *The American Impact on Great Britain 1898-1914* (Philadelphia, University of Pennsylvania Press, 1940), 377.
[17] See Chapter Four and James P. Shannon, *Catholic Colonization on the Western Frontier* (New Haven: Yale University Press, 1957).
[18] John Lancaster Spalding, *The Religious Mission of the Irish People and Catholic Colonization* (New York: Catholic Publication Society, 1880).

immigrants experienced in Utah led to special consideration for widows, the aged, the infirm, and the truly poor, whose debts were often forgiven.[19]

Irish Catholics and Mormons were not the only ethnic and religious groups to help needy coreligionists in Europe reach inland America. As refugees from the later nineteenth-century persecutions of Jews in eastern Europe flooded into New York, Boston, and Philadelphia, it was only too clear that many stood little chance of making a decent life in unfriendly slums. There were, of course, deep-rooted prejudices against them, even among already established Jews. But coreligionists responded to the plight of the newcomers. The pioneer organizer was Michael Heilprin, an immigrant of Polish-Hungarian background, a poet, an encyclopediast, and a scholar. Heilprin's zealous efforts to raise money for the establishment of farm colonies in New Jersey, the Dakotas, and the far northwest hastened his death.[20] The fortunes of these colonies is another story. But the movement itself, which was finally rescued by the gifts of Baron de Hirsch, not only stimulated the Jewish community in America to expand the scope of its distinctive charities but also to indicate that the Atlantic was no barrier to the claims of compassion.

The patterns of giving for welfare and culture overseas that developed in the nineteenth century showed no marked change in the first decades of the twentieth. To be sure, more frequent and impressive giving was to be expected in view of the increasing number of well-to-do and wealthy Americans and of the growing cosmopolitanism of many men and women of means. It is also likely that the sense of being a citizen of a new world power contributed to an interest in overseas giving.

The mantle of George Peabody as an innovator in social welfare in a sense fell on Joseph Fels, who had made his money in the manufacture of soap. During a stay in England devoted to promoting his export trade, Fels came under the spell of such humanitarians as

[19] Leonard J. Arrington, *Great Basin Kingdom: An Economic History of the Latter-day Saints 1830-1900* (Cambridge: Harvard University Press, 1958), 382; William Mulder, *Homeward to Zion: The Mormon Migration from Scandinavia* (Minneapolis: University of Minnesota Press, 1957), 142-56.

[20] Gustav Pollak, *Michael Heilprin and His Sons: A Biography* (New York: Dodd, Mead, 1912); *The Nation* XLVI (May 17, 1888), 402; *New York Times*, May 11, 1888.

George Lansbury who interested him in the back-to-the-land movement. Fels bought 1,300 acres of land at Hollesley Bay to enable unemployed to earn a living; later he added other tracts to his first acquisition. Such practical enterprises as health centers and boys' and girls' clubs in London also won his support. Keir Hardie, the Scottish labor leader, encouraged Fels' zeal for social improvement.[21]

It was his conversion to the single tax doctrines of Henry George, however, that governed Fels' philanthropy. Giving up his business, he devoted his personal talents and some $100,000 a year to promoting the single tax, both in the United States and abroad. Of the annual $100,000 which he thus spent on educational campaigns, $25,-000 went to England, $5,000 to Denmark, $5,000 to Canada, and lesser sums to the campaigns in Germany, France, Spain and Australasia. Fels played an important role in persuading Lloyd George to include a land-tax provision in the budget of 1909 and in encouraging the Danish parliament a few years later to undertake a nation-wide tax evaluation and tax revision. The Fels Fund, with which Frederic Howe, Tom Johnson, and Lincoln Steffens were associated, underwrote translations of *Progress and Poverty* into Swedish, Bulgarian, Yiddish, Chinese, and other languages. This kind of overseas philanthropy, though aiming to promote welfare by drastic action in the economic sphere rather than by temporary relief measures, had its own limitations. Lincoln Steffens concluded that in some ways it did more harm than good: in releasing disciples from the labor of collecting money, in encouraging them to relax their efforts or to lose sight of the basic purpose in preoccupation with developing machinery, the philanthropic support tended to encourage single-taxers to rely on subsidies rather than on persuasion. Nevertheless the gifts of Fels attracted wide attention to a social cause regarded in Europe and Australasia as a characteristically American program for advancing social welfare.[22]

While Fels was promoting the single tax in Great Britain and Ireland, Walter Vrooman, a well-to-do Kansas liberal, and Charles A. Beard, undertook a philanthropy designed to build solidly on a British base. The scheme they worked out for a labor college at

[21] Mary Fels, *Joseph Fels: His Life-Work* (New York: B. W. Huebach, 1916), 38 ff.

[22] Charles A. Barker, *Henry George* (New York: Oxford University Press, 1955), 627; Heindel, *The American Impact on Great Britain*, 363; George R. Geiger, *The Philosophy of Henry George* (New York: Macmillan, 1933), 446-47; *The Autobiography of Lincoln Steffens* (New York: Harcourt Brace, 1931), 641-44.

Oxford, Ruskin Hall, met with fairly cordial British response and in time played a role of some importance in the labor movement.[23]

Edward Tuck and his wife, Julia Stell, represented still another type of private philanthropy. Graduating with Phi Beta Kappa honors from Dartmouth in 1862, Tuck went abroad seeking a cure for the defective eyesight which had kept him from military service. He was named vice-consul in Paris. Then he joined Munroe and Company, the only American bank in the French capital. Studying financial problems, he won a reputation as a leading authority. On his return to America in 1866, Tuck associated himself with James J. Hill in the Great Northern enterprise, played a part in the development of the Northern Pacific, invested and helped organize utilities and, in 1886, became a director of the Chase National Bank. A man of sound judgment and a friend of leading business men, Tuck saw his fortune steadily grow. In 1890 he and his wife, who had no children, returned to Paris, to settle in the city and in the nearby suburb of Rueil. But Edward Tuck was no ordinary expatriate. He became, as suited a disciple of Benjamin Franklin, an unofficial American ambassador to France.[24]

Sensing the need for a hospital for poorly paid industrial workers, the Tucks in 1903 founded an institution named for Mrs. Tuck's mother—l'Hôpital Stell. Determined to have it second to none, Tuck sent an architect to America to study hospital construction and to provide for the latest equipment. L'Hôpital Stell, with its sixty beds, was sufficiently endowed to care for those unable to pay. It remained under Mrs. Tuck's supervision, but it was deeded to the Department of Seine-et-Oise. The hospital, which developed a visiting nurse service, quickly became an institution of note and influence.[25]

Mrs. Tuck also interested herself in the welfare of children and youth. In the Passy district she and her husband established a home for working girls. In Rueil itself, the Tucks founded the École Ménagere, designed to give girls the education available in French public schools and, in addition, training in the household arts and

[23] Burleigh Taylor Wilkins, ed., "Charles A. Beard on the Founding of Ruskin Hall," *The Indiana Magazine of History* LII (Sept., 1956), 277-84; Harlan B. Phillips, "Charles Beard, Walter Vrooman, and the Founding of Ruskin Hall," *South Atlantic Quarterly* L (April, 1951), 188-91.
[24] Robert Davis, "The Unofficial Ambassador to France," *Dartmouth Alumni Magazine* XX (August, 1928), 789-802.
[25] *Ibid.*

stenography. The need was real, the success remarkable. The École was liberally supported by endowment and, like l'Hôpital Stell, deeded to the Département.[26]

This activity did not conclude the Tucks' philanthropy. Great art collectors, they presented valuable artifacts to the Palais de Malmaison, together with a forty-five-acre park, and an endowment for its upkeep. After the First World War, during which they played an active part in relief activities, these remarkable Americans gave to the City of Paris, to be deposited in the "Tuck Gallery" of the Petit Palace on the Champs-Élysées, a priceless collection of tapestries, paintings, porcelains, and furniture. At the time, this was the most notable artistic gift from America to Europe. In addition to these benefactions, Tuck gave liberally to the American Hospital and to the American Library in Paris. He also provided a dormitory for Americans at the new Cité Universitaire. At about the same time that he and his wife began to give in France, Tuck initiated a series of notable gifts to his alma mater and thus, more than any other benefactor, helped create what President William Jewett Tucker called "the new Dartmouth." [27]

The cosmopolitanism in giving so admirably represented by the Tucks was not, to be sure, a major trend in American philanthropy. But the Tucks and Joseph Fels were not alone in private benefactions overseas. Imbued with something of the same cosmopolitan spirit, James Loeb, the vivid and brilliant New Yorker associated with a famous banking circle, did not confine his philanthropies to any national boundary. Best remembered for inspiring and making possible the famous Classical Library bearing his name, Loeb also gave generously to Harvard and Columbia and to the Museum of Antiker Kleinkunst at Munich, to the Jewish Nurses' Home in Hamburg, and to the Marie Antonie Students' Home in Munich. In 1911 he founded the German Institute for Psychiatric Research at Munich, a decision related to personal problems. With tragic irony, it became a center for the promulgation of anti-Jewish propaganda during the Nazi era.[28]

The advancement of health also interested other donors. Henry

[26] Horatio S. Krans, "Edward Tuck: A Biographical Sketch," *Dartmouth Alumni Magazine* XXIV (June, 1932), 613.

[27] William Jewett Tucker, *My Generation: An Autobiographical Interpretation* (Boston, New York: Houghton Mifflin, 1919), 302 ff., 319 ff.

[28] Frieda Schiff Warburg, *Reminiscences of a Long Life* (New York: privately printed, 1956), 19-20; *New York Times*, May 29, 1933.

Phipps, a one-time associate of Carnegie in the iron and steel business, made possible the holding in Washington of the Sixth International Congress on Tuberculosis in 1908. To be sure, this benefaction was not exclusively directed toward stamping out the white plague in foreign lands alone. But in bringing together leading specialists and authorities from thirty-three countries to share knowledge, to study the pathological, therapeutic, and educational exhibits and to discuss legislative approaches to the problem, the Congress did contribute to the campaign in many countries to control the death-taking scourge.[29] A leading English authority was on sound ground in predicting that the moral and educational effect of the Congress in all places to which its influence reached, was bound to be "enormous."[30]

Nor was medicine the only branch of science to stimulate giving overseas in the years before the Carnegies and the Rockefellers. A contemporary of Phipps, Darius Ogden Mills, benefactor of hospitals, orphan asylums, botanical gardens, and art museums, extended his interest in science to the Southern Hemisphere in financing an expedition under the auspices of the Lick Observatory. Setting up equipment in Chile, the expedition measured over three hundred of the brighter stars in the one-quarter of the sky surrounding the South Pole and provided the world's astronomers with relevant data, including treasured photographs.[31]

The promotion of cultural understanding between nations was not confined to scientific enterprises. The role of successful immigrants in this field has been a touching indication of the strength of national loyalties. A Serbian immigrant and major contributor to electronics, Michael Pupin of Columbia University, made gifts to various cultural agencies in his native land and contributed $10,000 in 1912 to relieve the Balkan peoples during their war with Turkey.[32] Still another immigrant determined to use a large part of his wealth

[29] For a biographical sketch see George F. Redmond, *Financial Giants of America* (2 vols.; Boston: Stratford, 1922), I, 227-29. In 1902 Phipps established in Philadelphia the Henry Phipps Institute for the Study, Treatment, and Prevention of Tuberculosis and, later, gave in all, $1,000,000 for building sanitary tenements as a means of reducing the incidence of tuberculosis: *New York Times*, Sept. 23, 1930; Lawrence F. Flick, "America and the International Congress on Tuberculosis," *Charities and the Commons* XV (Dec. 9, 1905), 353-60, and XXI (Nov. 7, 1908), 185-262.

[30] *Nature* LXXIX (Nov. 12, 1908), 48.

[31] W. W. Campbell, "The D. O. Mills Expedition to the Southern Hemisphere," *Scientific American* LXXXVII (November 29, 1902), 360-61.

[32] Clipping, dated Oct. 21, 1912, in the Michael Pupin Papers in the Columbiana Collection of Columbia University; Pupin to Nicholas Murray Butler, Nov. 12, 1914, Pupin Papers; Columbia University, *Alumni News*, Jan. 14, 1927.

to promote closer relations between Denmark, where he was born, and its neighbors on the one hand, and the United States on the other, was Niels Poulson. Poulson came to America in 1864, worked for a time as a mason, then as a draftsman in an architectural office in Washington, after which he made a substantial fortune in the Hecla Iron Works, of which he became president. The American Scandinavian Society, established in 1908 to support cultural interchange, interested Poulson so much that he provided it with an office and secretary, together with scholarships for study in the United States and Denmark. In 1910 Poulson decided to set aside a trust fund of $100,000 to be administered by the Society, which was thus able to expand its program by arranging for visiting lectureships and for publication in America of Scandinavian classics. Poulson gradually concluded he could make no better use of his money than to leave the bulk of his estate to this cause. The Society merged into the Scandinavian American Foundation. On Poulson's death in 1911, the foundation came into possession of some $400,000. It attracted additional gifts and embarked on a fruitful policy which has resulted in closer cultural ties between the United States and the northern countries.[33]

The overseas benefactions of another immigrant encompassed the whole spectrum of projects and purposes—the advancement of learning, social welfare, world peace, and the related promotion of intercultural understanding. In truth, the philanthropies initiated abroad by Andrew Carnegie overshadowed all others in magnitude and impact. What this amazing self-made industrialist did in this field symbolized in a genuine sense the new and telling role of American world leadership in the period between the Spanish-American War and the First World War. The philanthropic ideology of Carnegie, who not only expounded his ideas in articles and books but spelled out his thought in action, rested on basic conceptions which knew no national boundary. One was that the rich man should give during his own lifetime for public purposes everything not needed by his own family. But he must give in such a way as to encourage self-help, and to that end provide opportunities through which the poor

---

[33] *New York Times,* May 4, 1911; *New York Tribune,* May 4, 1911; *American-Scandinavian Review* III (Jan., 1915), 51, (March-April, 1915), 115; William Hovgaaro, "The American-Scandinavian Movement," *American-Scandinavian Review* III (Sept.-Oct., 1915), 290-302.

man who was ambitious to better himself could do so by taking advantage of agencies not provided for, or inadequately provided for, by public funds. This conviction was reflected in Carnegie's benefactions to educational agencies, both of a liberal and vocational character, and especially by public libraries given on the condition that the recipient communities maintain their support.

Another principle informing Carnegie's philanthropies abroad and at home was that benefactions ought to enrich facilities for the appreciation of art, music, and scientific research, the last being, in his mind, the key to individual and social progress. Finally, the Pittsburgh iron and steel magnate believed thoroughly in the high importance of international peace and understanding. His gifts in this sphere, while designed to promote the larger end, focused especially on the encouragement of rapport between his beloved adopted land and Great Britain, to which he was also passionately devoted, notwithstanding his sharp criticisms of its monarchical and aristocratic institutions. His benefactions, guided by these ideas, reached the monumental sum of $350,000,000, of which $62,000,000 was allotted to the British Empire.[34]

As was so often the case with naturalized Americans, Carnegie cherished a special fondness for the town in which he was born and in which he spent his childhood. His first public gift, in 1873, provided for baths in his birthplace, Dunfermline. Ten years later, when he and his seventy-one-year-old mother crossed the Atlantic to revisit Dunfermline, he watched her with pride as she laid the cornerstone of the public library which he gave to the town at a cost of $90,000.[35] As in the case of all his library benefactions, Carnegie made no effort to interfere with policy. Gifts of organs to Dunfermline's churches followed.

But the library and the organs did not end his liberality to his home town. He bought Pittencrieff Park and Glen and transferred it to the citizens as a recreation center. The gift was accompanied by a deed of trust bestowing on the lucky Dunfermline $2,500,000 in

[34] Carnegie's philosophy of philanthropy was developed on the literary level in two articles: "Wealth," *North American Review* CXLVIII (June, 1889), 653-64, and "The Best Fields for Philanthropy," *North American Review* CXLIX (Dec., 1889), 682-98. See also his *Autobiography* (Boston: Houghton Mifflin, 1920) and Burton J. Hendrick, *The Life of Andrew Carnegie* (2 vols.; Garden City: Doubleday, Doran, 1932). My discussion rests on these materials and on the voluminous Carnegie Papers in the Library of Congress.

[35] Andrew Carnegie, *An American Four-in-Hand in Britain* (New York: Scribner's Sons, 1891), 283-85.

United States Steel securities. The specific object of the gift, which was later supplemented, was set forth in the deed creating the Carnegie Dunfermline Trust: "To bring into the monotonous lives of the toiling masses of Dunfermline, more of 'sweetness and light,' to give to them—especially to the young—some charm, some happiness, some elevating conditions of life which residence elsewhere would have denied, that the child of my native town, looking back in after years, however far from home it may have roamed, will feel that simply by virtue of being such, life has been made happier and better." [36] The trustees carried out the broad intent of the trust by providing for circulating library services, lectures, and musical concerts, for recreational facilities, including new public baths, gymnasiums and playing fields, and for institutes offering training in the technical vocations, in music, in health and hygiene.

The Carnegie Dunfermline Trust also provided for the physical examination of school children and for health care at a clinic until public authorities, convinced of the value of the innovation, took over responsibility for it. It also added another dimension to the economy by reviving the traditional, but somewhat forgotten, arts and crafts. Until his death, Carnegie received innumerable evidences of Dunfermline's appreciation for a liberality that seemingly knew no limit. To be sure, there were those who grumbled that the Trust was not sufficiently democratic to be responsive to public opinion, and that much it did should rather have been provided by the state. But the consensus regarded it as highly successful in bringing some part of "sweetness and light" to the run-down manufacturing town which Andrew Carnegie and his parents had left in 1848 to seek better opportunities in the new world. Dunfermline went on to become a center of considerable influence in Scotland. [37]

An intimate friend of many leading writers and scholars in both the United States and Great Britain, Carnegie was not indifferent to the value of a scholar's library. When Lord Acton, Regius Professor

[36] *Autobiography of Andrew Carnegie*, 289-90.
[37] The Carnegie Dunfermline Trust invited Sir Patrick Geddes to report on the laying out of the park and on the layout of buildings needed to carry out the work of the Trust. The invitation resulted in a significant book by Geddes: *City Development: A Study of Parks, Gardens and Culture Institutes* (Birmingham: Saint George Press, 1904). For other material on the Trust see Hendrick, *The Life of Andrew Carnegie*, II, 248 ff.; John B. Mackie, *Andrew Carnegie: His Dunfermline Ties and Benefactions* (Dunfermline: Dunfermline Journal Printing Works, 1916); and Samuel Harden Church, "Andrew Carnegie's Endowments at Dunfermline," *Survey* XXVIII (May 4, 1912), 211-20; Carnegie Dunfermline Trustees, *Annual Reports*, 1909-1915 (Dunfermline: A. Romanes, 1909-1915).

of History at Cambridge, was threatened with the loss of his library, Carnegie, acting through Gladstone, a mutual friend, provided $50,-000 for its purchase, with the stipulation that Acton use it as long as he lived. On Acton's death Carnegie rejected Andrew D. White's plea that the collection be given to Cornell. He turned it over to one of his own intimate friends, John Morley, who in due course gave it to Cambridge University. Carnegie's part in the episode reflects not only the importance he attached to personal friendships, but also his indifference to privileged academic institutions—as did his refusal at Gladstone's urging to come to the rescue of the Bodleian Library at Oxford.[38]

Convinced that popular enlightenment was the key to social progress and that his giving must broaden opportunities for those on the lower rungs of the economic ladder, Carnegie paralleled his gifts for public library buildings in the United States by similar ones in Canada, Australasia, and Great Britain and Ireland. The handsome structures given to Inverness, Aberdeen, and Edinburgh were only the start. The one hundred and twenty-five buildings presented to Canadian towns and cities cost $2,556,660; the forty-three to other Dominions and colonies, $522,652; and the six hundred and sixty erected in Great Britain and Ireland, added up to a total of $11,-894,457. Thus the benefactions making possible public libraries in the British Empire represented approximately thirty-seven per cent of the total of $56,162,623 given for this purpose.[39]

Gifts to libraries overshadowed those of organs to churches of all denominations. In the United Kingdom and English-speaking countries other than the United States, Carnegie gave 3,285 organs costing $2,566,303. In the Scottish Highlands strict Presbyterians denounced the attempts "to worship God with a kist fu' o' whistels" instead of the God-given human voice, and so the wily philanthropist decided to require a partner in his sin. Each congregation was asked to pay one half of the desired new organ, and the plan worked.[40]

Not only his Scottish birth but his predilection for the less advantaged institutions of higher learning, a predilection reflected in his support of the smaller American colleges rather than those bearing the "ivy league" stamp, explains in part Carnegie's decision to

[38] Hendrick, *The Life of Andrew Carnegie*, I, 352 ff., II, 199.
[39] Durand R. Miller, comp., *Carnegie Grants for Library Buildings 1890-1917* (New York: Carnegie Corporation, 1943), 8.
[40] *The Autobiography of Andrew Carnegie*, 278-79.

do something for the universities of Scotland rather than for Oxford and Cambridge. Articles in the January, 1897, issue of the *Nineteenth Century* and in the December, 1900, issue of the *Fortnightly Review* called attention to the critical state of the Scottish universities and to their pressing need for rehabilitation, especially for laboratories, residence halls, and free tuition. Only some Maecenas, or at least someone willing to play the role that Rockefeller had played at Chicago, could do what was needed, for the state could not manage to provide the needed sum, estimated at $5,000,000.[41]

After reading the first of the articles, Carnegie decided to give $10,000,000 in United States Steel Company bonds, one half of the annual income to be used to pay the fees of deserving students, the other half to improve the universities. The donor named as trustees of the Carnegie Trust for the Universities of Scotland leading men in public and educational life. The proposed deed of trust provided that the trustees, by majority vote, might at some future time change the purposes and modes prescribed for administering the beneficence in case changing conditions seemed to warrant it. The trustees suggested that a two-thirds majority would be wiser, and Carnegie accepted the proposal, which he subsequently incorporated in all his large gifts.[42]

The capital was kept intact, and within a few years after Carnegie's death in 1919 the Trust had contributed $15,000,000 to the Scottish universities. The issue of free tuition proved thorny and brought considerable criticism on the donor and especially on the administrators of the Trust. In reviewing the pros and cons of the controversy the London *Times* declared in 1913 that "the sum of the matter is that the whole Carnegie system of payment of fees is a blunder from first to last." Many needy parents with worthy children regarded acceptance of free tuition as a charity incompatible with self-respect while many youths took free tuition who did not need it. Moreover, the trustees brought criticism for using grants as a means of compelling reform.[43] But there was also appreciation for such constructive achievements as the establishment of chairs in the newer fields of knowledge, the building of laboratories, residence halls, and unions, and the support of research. Thus new life was breathed into

[41] Thomas Shaw, "The Educational Peace of Scotland," *Nineteenth Century* XLI (Jan., 1897), 113-23 and William Wallace, "The Scottish University Crisis," *Fortnightly Review* LXXIV (Dec., 1900), 982-93.

[42] *The Autobiography of Andrew Carnegie*, 269-71.

[43] William Ramsay, "The Carnegie Trust for the Scottish Universities," *Contemporary Review* XCIII (June, 1908), 709-25; *The Times* [London], Sept. 2, 1913.

ancient institutions that had been unable by reason of financial considerations to keep abreast of modern developments in higher education. Carnegie, who was chosen Lord Rector of Aberdeen and of St. Andrews, took pride in the reinvigoration that his philanthropies had been largely instrumental in bringing about and in the influence his example had on men of wealth in the United Kingdom.[44]

Canadian universities also profited, though in much smaller degree, from Carnegie's interest in higher education. Convinced that the institutions of higher learning in the United States and in Canada needed to provide scholars with a greater sense of security if the ablest talent was to be attracted and if research and teaching were to be sustained under the most favorable conditions, Carnegie in 1905 initiated a pioneer program for professors' pensions. The Carnegie Foundation for the Advancement of Teaching, endowed with a fund of $15,000,000, set up a retirement provision for institutions that could qualify by reason of academic standards and secular character. As in the United States, the desire and needs of certain institutions—notably Queens and Victoria—to share in the Carnegie allotment led to readjustments of provisions in the charters for church affiliation. When, after World War I the plan had to be modified by reason of inadequate funds, the adjustments made in the Canadian universities more or less paralleled those in sister institutions in the States: the institutions and the professors contributed to the pension funds. It is difficult to say whether the desire on the part of Canadian universities to share in the initial plan had the effect, as was true in some places in the United States, of raising academic standards. In any case, the inclusion of the Canadian universities pointed to the growing international scope of American philanthropy.[45]

[44] Carnegie Trust for the Universities of Scotland, *Annual Reports*, 1901- (Edinburgh: The University Press, 1902-); J. R. Peddie, *The Carnegie Trust for the Universities of Scotland*, 1901-51 (Edinburgh, 1951).

[45] David Starr Jordan, *The Days of a Man: Being Memoirs of a Naturalist, Teacher and Minor Prophet of Democracy* (2 vols.; Yonkers-on-Hudson, N. Y.: World Book Co., 1922) II, 187 ff.; Joseph Jastrow, "The Endowment of Learning," *The Dial* XXXVIII (May 16, 1905), 343-46; Howard Savage, *Fruit of an Impulse: Forty-five Years of the Carnegie Foundation*, 1905-1950 (New York: Harcourt Brace, 1953); Carnegie Corporation of New York, *Report of the President for the Year ended Sept. 30, 1936* (New York: Carnegie Corporation, 1936), 16 ff.; Rainard B. Robbins, *College Plans for Retirement Income* (New York: Columbia University Press, 1940), 183, 189, 195, 207, 213, 214, 218, 220, 230. The University of Toronto began its retirement system in 1891, though it was not compulsory, and though the University itself contributed nothing to retirement, *Ibid.*, 118; Delano D. Calvin, *Queen's University at Kingston: The First Century of a Scottish-Canadian Foundation, 1841-1941* (Kingston, Ontario: The Trustees of the University, 1941), 145-46; Charles B. Sissons, *A History of Victoria University* (Toronto: The University of Toronto Press, 1952), 266.

But Carnegie's major interest continued to be popular education and welfare. On October 3, 1913, the Carnegie United Kingdom Trust, with an initial endowment of $10,000,000 in United States Steel Company securities, was incorporated, to be administered by trustees centered in Dunfermline. The scope of the new trust was broad. It was designed "for the improvement of the well-being of the masses of people of Great Britain and Ireland by such means as are embraced within the meaning of the word 'charitable' according to Scotch and English law, and which the Trustees may from time to time select [as] best fitted from age to age for securing these purposes, remembering that new needs are constantly arising as the masses advance." [46] The deed of trust further specified that the income was never to be used for purposes countenancing the institution of war. The trustees took over the commitments Carnegie had made for the further giving of library buildings and organs. It moved into the field of rural libraries and special library services, including the provision of books for the blind. Other projects included the building of public baths and washhouses, the establishment of a Central Bureau of Employment for Women, centers to provide welfare services to mothers and children, and subsidies to the United Irish Women, whose program concentrated on rural welfare. The Trust also supported the movement for the revival of Tudor music.[47]

Comments in the British press were, generally speaking, both favorable and appreciative. As was to be expected, *Punch* could not resist a good-natured jibe: ". . . the name of the splendidly generous philanthropist who has subscribed £200,000 to provide all the inhabitants of the Grand Sahara with niblicks has become public property. It is, as was generally apprehended, none other than our old friend ANDREW CARNEGIE. No conditions accompany the gift, except the negligible one that the ratepayers of Timbuctoo shall contribute to the upkeep of a Temple of Arbitration, with Free Library attached, on the banks of Lake Tchad." [48]

Highly individualistic in his outlook on life and setting great store on personal initiative, courage, and readiness to risk self in the service

[46] Carnegie United Kingdom Trust, *First Annual Report*, 1914 (Edinburgh: The University Press, 1915), 3-4.

[47] Carnegie United Kingdom Trust, *Second, Third, and Fourth Annual Reports for the years ending December 31, 1915, 1916, 1917* (Edinburgh: The University Press, 1916-1918), *passim*.

[48] *Punch* CXXXVII (July 14, 1909), 28; *Nature* XCIII (May 14, 1914), 279 and CI (May 2, 1918), 177-78; *New Statesman* XII (March 1, 1919), 473; *The Times* [London], June 24, 1914, May 30, 1916.

of others, Carnegie sometimes felt that the benefaction that gave him the deepest satisfaction was the Hero Fund Commission. Established in 1904 to provide medals and grants of money from a $5,000,000 endowment for those who had suffered injury in heroic deeds involving others and for the widows and children of heroes, the deed of trust included in its scope Canada and Newfoundland as well as the United States. Carnegie made it clear that it was not designed to stimulate heroic action by putting a premium on heroism, for heroes, he insisted, never thought of reward. The Hero Fund was rather an evidence of Carnegie's conviction that whereas the heroes of the barbarian past wounded or killed their fellows, those of our own civilized time served or saved others.[49]

The Hero Fund idea was extended to Great Britain—the trustees of the Carnegie Dunfermline Trust taking over its administration. In due time it was offered to and accepted by France, Germany, Italy, Belgium, Holland, Norway, Sweden, Switzerland, and Denmark. National commissions in each country administered the program. Edward VII of Great Britain thanked Carnegie in an autograph letter for this and for other Carnegie gifts, while Kaiser William II, whose advisors at first expressed hostility or skepticism regarding the idea, conveyed to Carnegie his appreciation of the donor's discrimination and his enthusiastic appreciation of the Fund.[50]

The overseas benefactions of Carnegie, although primarily focused on the British Empire, reached to other countries in two spheres in addition to the hero funds. In his mind there were no national boundaries to the benefits of scientific research to mankind. Thus the Carnegie Institution of Washington, established in 1902 with an initial endowment of $10,000,000, subsequently to be enlarged, did not confine its program to the United States. Its publications in the fields of geophysics, terrestrial magnetism, astronomy, archaeology, embryology, and genetics, and in the historical and social sciences, circulated freely all over the world. And now and again the Institution subsidized special researches conducted by such agencies as the Institute of Geophysical Inquiry at Johannesburg and the famous aquarium in Naples.[51] Nor was this all. Convinced of the importance of investing in gifted scientists, Carnegie enabled Marie Curie, through a grant of $50,000, to probe more deeply into the nature

[49] *The Autobiography of Andrew Carnegie*, 262 ff.
[50] *Ibid.*, 263-65.
[51] Carnegie Institution of Washington, *Yearbook*, 1902 (Washington: Carnegie Institution, 1903), xiii; 1903, xv ff.; 1904, 145; 1908, 18; 1911, 7-8; 1912, 23.

of radioactivity. To Robert Koch he gave $120,000 to enable him to extend his investigations in bacteriology.[52] The most truly international interest that Carnegie supported was, of course, the peace movement. His disapproval of war went back to his boyhood—his parents were disciples of Bright and Cobden and an uncle frequently spoke at peace meetings in Scotland. Possibly his conscience was troubled by the fact that some of his fortune rested on profits derived from the manufacture of armor plate. In any case, during the early years of the twentieth century he poured money into peace and arbitration societies, and supported lecturers, writers, and publications throughout the world. In 1907, at the request of Andrew D. White and the Dutch government, he gave funds for a Temple of Peace which became the celebrated Peace Palace at The Hague. And he vigorously sponsored the idea of a league of nations vested with a police force to keep the peace. Carnegie also contributed generously to the Association for International Conciliation, an organization fathered by the Baron d'Estournelles de Constant and promoted by Nicholas Murray Butler of Columbia University. To the many urgent requests to endow the peace cause with a large sum Carnegie responded with the remark that his money might "taint" the cause: "There is nothing that robs a righteous cause of its strength more than a millionaire's money." At the same time, the man who considered himself a practical realist, hesitated to endow a cause which many whom he admired, including Theodore Roosevelt, regarded as in the control of the "lunatic fringe" of reformers.[53]

Two events probably led to a momentous decision to change his mind about giving more money to the peace cause. One was the example of Edwin Ginn, the Boston textbook publisher, who in 1910 put a million dollars, a third of his entire fortune, into an agency chartered as The World Peace Foundation, which quickly launched a vigorous educational program.[54] The second was the

---

[52] Hendrick, *The Life of Andrew Carnegie*, II, 229; Frederick H. Lynch, *Personal Recollections of Andrew Carnegie* (New York, Chicago: Fleming H. Revell, 1920), 134-37. In 1901 Carnegie also paid the expenses of a group of British professors in order to enable them to visit American institutions before founding the Baker-Street Church of England High School.

[53] Hendrick, *The Life of Andrew Carnegie*, II, 323 ff.

[54] Edwin Ginn, *An International School of Peace: An Address Delivered at the International Peace Congress at Lucerne, September, 1905* (Boston, 1905); Jordan, *Days of a Man* II, 390-93; *The World Peace Movement* III (May 15, 1914), 214; World Peace Foundation, *Annual Report*, 1913, 1914, 1915 (Boston: World Peace Foundation,

position which President Taft took in a startling address in 1910 in which he declared that all controversies, even those allegedly involving national honor, ought to be submitted to international arbitration.[55]

In December, 1910, the world learned that Ginn's example had been followed on a grander scale by the establishment of the Carnegie Endowment for International Peace. Its assets, $10,000,000 in United States Steel Company securities, skyrocketed, ironically, with the outbreak of the First World War. Carnegie chose a distinguished board of trustees in which Nicholas Murray Butler was the guiding hand. Although Carnegie expressed the hope that the trustees would support President Taft's program of unlimited arbitration, he permitted them considerable leeway in what was done with the funds of the Endowment, having confidence in their common sense and being convinced that future action could not be determined with wisdom. He merely stipulated that the trustees should "keep unceasingly in view" the one end, "the speedy abolition of international war between so-called civilized nations." [56]

The Carnegie Endowment for International Peace devoted much attention to the juridical approach to the problem of peace and war. It subsidized the International Law Institute and reissued the great classics on international law. But it also allocated funds to the more popular peace societies in both America and Europe. It disseminated materials designed to increase international understanding and good will, to teach nations to become better friends. The Endowment also promoted international exchanges of lecturers. Severely criticized by the more doctrinaire peace organizations for what appeared to them to be an undue emphasis on juridical procedure and on scholarly literature, the Endowment hewed its own path and in so doing contributed to an increase in knowledge in a sphere in which there was much ignorance and misunderstanding. It also gave prestige to an international movement commonly regarded in every country as either unpatriotic or unrealistic, or both.[57]

1913-15). In addition to Ginn, the peace movement had begun to attract the support of such prominent and wealthy families as the Untermeyers, the Schiffs, the Strausses, the Goulds, the Choates, the Villards, and others.

[55] William Howard Taft, "The Proposed Arbitration Treaties with Great Britain and France," *Judicial Settlement of International Disputes* VII (Baltimore, 1912).

[56] Carnegie Endowment for International Peace, *Yearbook*, 1911 (Washington: Carnegie Endowment for International Peace, 1912), 1-3.

[57] *Ibid.*, 20-28, *Yearbook*, 1915, 25-26, 31 ff.; Merle Curti, *Peace or War: The American Struggle, 1636-1936* (New York: W. W. Norton, 1936), 203-06.

Carnegie did not stop with establishing the Endowment. Sensing the importance of the religious impulse against war, he supported J. Allan Baker, an English Quaker, temperance reformer, and educationist, in organizing the World Alliance for Promoting International Friendship through the Churches. And in 1914 he endowed with two million dollars the Church Peace Union, an organization which included among its trustees Protestants, Catholics, and Jews and which was designed to coordinate and strengthen the religious commitment to peace.[58]

In the same year that Carnegie lent support to the Church Peace Union, the outbreak of the war in Europe struck a blow to his hope for international peace, a hope expressed in the provision in the deed of trust in the Carnegie Endowment that if and when peace became a reality, the funds were to be used to attack "the next most degrading evil or evils." Meantime American philanthropy on the world stage had found continuing opportunities, both in recurrent natural disasters and in a little war which, in retrospect, seemed a curtain raiser to the great drama of 1914.

[58] Curti, *Peace or War*, 205.

VIII

A Little War and New Disasters

American benevolence toward the tens of thousands of Cubans, dying of starvation and disease during the last phase of the struggle for independence from Spain, followed traditional patterns of voluntary giving. But what was done also anticipated emphases that were to become increasingly characteristic, namely, the closer intermeshing of voluntary and official action and the steps taken toward the institutionalization of relief.

Official efforts were at first confined to the plight of American citizens in Cuba. Some of these were native to the island but had taken out citizenship papers during sojourns in the States. In May, 1897, Congress appropriated $50,000 for food, clothing, and medicine for distressed Americans in Cuba. Consular officials administered the relief.[1]

More important were the voluntary, unofficial efforts to help Cuban reconcentrados, civilians confined to military camps fenced in with barbed wire. These private relief efforts were not, however, completely separate from official policy. President McKinley was troubled by the growing pressure of the Cuban juntas in the United States for military intervention in behalf of "Cuba libre," a pressure that mounted as more and more people responded to sensational exposures in the yellow press of Spanish "barbarism" toward reconcentrados. The President did not favor military intervention, but at the same time he sympathized with the sufferings of hundreds of thousands of reconcentrados. He believed that the intervention movement might be held in check by pressure on Madrid for con-

[1] *Congressional Record*, 55th Cong., 2d Sess., 1897, XXX, Pt. 1, 1081, 1120 ff.

cessions to the Cuban rebels and by unofficial relief for the suffering prisoners.[2]

With her field operations in Turkey fresh in mind, Clara Barton was eager, in fact determined, to have the Red Cross control any relief for civilians in Cuba that might be undertaken. To that end, during the summer of 1897, she secured permission of the Spanish government for the Red Cross to distribute relief in Cuba under the terms of the Geneva Convention, to which both Spain and the United States were parties. But she also had to convince the American government and public opinion in the United States that the Red Cross had a rightful claim to an exclusive control over any expeditions for the relief of Cuba. Throughout the summer of 1897 she spared no efforts to quash the efforts of a group of women who were bent on equipping and sending a relief expedition to the Pearl of the Antilles. These ladies assumed the name of the National Relief Fund for Cuba. Miss Barton called them the "court ladies," and in an interview with President McKinley she persuaded him to give these ladies no countenance.[3]

With this potential rival out of the way, with evidence at hand of the increasing need in Cuba and of American interest in relief measures, Clara Barton went to the White House on November 30, 1897. It happened that President McKinley and Assistant Secretary of State Day were at the very moment discussing what could be done in Cuba—and they welcomed Miss Barton's suggestions. She made it clear that the Red Cross would be glad to dispense relief if it had the approval of the administration and if American opinion was back of it. Within a month the President issued an appeal for funds and supplies for Cuban relief.

Wanting to give as broad a base as possible to the fund raising, the State Department put the matter in the hands of a Central Cuban Relief Committee made up of Dr. Louis Klopsch of the *Christian Herald*, Charles A. Schieren of the New York Chamber of Commerce, and Miss Barton. Eager to take the field in Cuba in person, she asked to have the Red Cross represented in the Committee by her nephew, Stephen Barton of New York, second vice-president of the organization. It should be remembered, of course, that at this

---

[2] I am indebted for some of the material used in this account to Raymond Jackson Wilson's "American Relief to Cuba in 1898" (unpublished Master's dissertation, University of Wisconsin, 1959).

[3] Clara Barton Diary, Sept. 10, Nov. 25, 1897, Clara Barton Papers, Library of Congress.

time the American Red Cross was a relief-administering agency, not a fund-raising one, and that it had only a nominal relation to the loosely affiliated local and state auxiliaries.[4]

It was clear that the Central Cuban Relief Committee must play a nonpartisan role in its fund raising and in its dispensation of relief in Cuba. The fact that the Red Cross had a hand in it would alone have made this necessary, for, according to the Geneva Convention, Red Cross field work must be completely neutral *en face* the conflicting parties, and must be governed by human need rather than by any political, religious, or other consideration. In addition, the cooperation of Spanish authorities in Cuba was necessary for any relief work: hence the Committee had to avoid any show of sympathy with the revolutionists. Further, the American government was still following a nonintervention policy. If a relief program in Cuba was to reinforce this policy by lessening the clamor for intervention, then it was all the more necessary for the Committee to be neutral in its attitude toward the strife in the island.

Many Americans accepted the necessity and even the wisdom of a neutral dispensation of relief. Several governors and mayors proclaimed the purely humanitarian nature of the Central Committee's campaign for funds.[5] This was also the position of the *Christian Herald* in its appeals for contributions.[6] At least a few Americans urged their fellow citizens to give on the ground that by so doing they would help President McKinley in his efforts to avoid war.[7]

But the necessity of neutrality was on the whole a handicap in fund raising since American opinion was increasingly prointerventionist. In such a situation appeals for funds for mere relief were found to meet with criticism or apathy. Many Americans argued that if the Committee was to cooperate with Spanish officials in the island no one could be sure that relief would actually reach the suffering reconcentrados. Others insisted that it was foolish to pour money into Cuba for relief when the only sensible thing to do was to remove the cause of suffering—the cruelty of Spanish rule. From the start Clara Barton fully appreciated the difficulties imposed by the need of nonpartisanship. At the time she was asked by the Associated

---

[4] Foster Rhea Dulles, *The American Red Cross: A History* (New York: Harper, 1950), 47-49.

[5] Barton Papers, Box 42.

[6] *Christian Herald* XXI (Feb. 9, 1898), 104-06 and (March 16, 1898), 226-30.

[7] This was the position of Governor Edward Scofield of Wisconsin: *Wisconsin State Journal*, March 29, April 2, 1898.

Press for an endorsement of the appeal for funds made by President McKinley, she wrote in her diary: "the state of political feelings is such that a *strong* endorsement or a touching article might rouse opposition in the form of an accusation that his inaction in the recognition of 'belligerent' rights was the *cause* of that very suffering he is now so anxious to relieve. This would form an excuse for not giving anything and the energies of the people and the press would be spent on smart and vehement criticism." [8]

And so it was not surprising that governors in South Dakota and Washington and the chairmen of many state and local committees reported that relief aroused little enthusiasm since the public felt that justice, rather than charity, was needed.[9] The chairman of the committee in Wisconsin declared that the only way to get relief into Cuba was to shoot it in, and that his committee had not seen fit to bestir itself.[10] No doubt the Cuban juntas in the United States, which had raised considerable money for the struggle in Cuba, encouraged the feeling that relief was only a means for enabling Spain to continue her brutality.[11]

The disadvantages imposed by the nonpartisan policy may, however, have stimulated the Central Cuban Relief Committee to conduct a spirited fund-raising campaign. It sent hundreds of postcards to editors, ministers, school administrators, women's clubs, and business leaders urging the formation of local Cuban relief committees. The Committee replied to endless inquiries about ways of sending food, clothing and medicine to the New York group. The *Christian Herald* on its part printed a special appeal for contributions from the popular evangelist, Dwight L. Moody.[12] Several tons of food, medicine, and clothing were dispatched to Cuba, along with cash remittances. In some cases the United States government aided in the transit by providing shipping facilities. Consul General Lee, who was designated as the recipient, reported that nearly $200,000 in money and supplies reached the sufferers before the declaration of war on Spain on April 25, 1898.[13]

Clara Barton had been asked by the New York Committee and the

8 Clara Barton Diary, Jan. 10, 1898.
9 Barton Papers, Box 33.
10 *Wisconsin State Journal*, April 16, 1898.
11 Edwin F. Atkins, *Sixty Years in Cuba* (Cambridge: privately printed, 1926), 218.
12 Charles M. Pepper, *Life-Work of Louis Klopsch* (New York: Christian Herald, 1910), 115-16.
13 Fitzhugh Lee, *Cuba's Struggle Against Spain* . . . (New York: American Historical Press, 1899), 211.

State Department to go to Cuba to help distribute the shipments of food as these arrived. She gladly left Washington on February 6, 1898, accompanied by J. K. Elwell, who had lived in Santiago while connected with shipping interests and who had agreed to take charge of the warehouses and supplies in Havana. What began as a simple, unobtrusive effort to do the little that could be done to relieve the woes of the Cubans thus grew into a major enterprise.

That enterprise was hampered by friction within the Committee in New York. Dr. Louis Klopsch, proud of his role in the *Christian Herald's* activities during the Russian famine of 1892 and the Armenian massacre, could not understand Clara Barton's insistence that the Red Cross have sole authority in the administration of relief in Cuba. He was perplexed when, after he had personally offered to send a hundred nurses to Cuba, Miss Barton advised the State Department to reject the proposal, which it did.[14] Nor could Klopsch understand Clara Barton's objection to his coming to Cuba to help with the relief operations. On her part, she felt that with her staff of twenty Red Cross workers, and the cooperation of the American consuls, she had the situation well in hand and that Klopsch, with his flair for publicity, would only complicate matters.

But Dr. Klopsch was no one to be set aside easily, and he went to Cuba. In his impulsive way, believing in immediate action, he cut through what he termed red tape and wrote one thousand and two thousand dollar checks for relief in situations that seemed to him imperatively desperate.[15] Consul General Lee, who remained somewhat cold toward Miss Barton, favored Dr. Klopsch. "He was *in* the hotel with the Consul-gen'l and nearly all the *reporters*, and made it headquarters for all the malcontents he could engraft," wrote Clara Barton, "and slung his money about like chips, and used us for a target night and day." [16] He had, she told her nephew, "got his fangs in, and his slime over nearly every department and person. . . . I never saw so complete a ruin of a good thing in so short a time." [17] It is true that Klopsch was openly critical of Miss Barton and that his criticisms, reaching New York, threatened to undermine confidence in the campaign. Stephen Barton on the one hand urged his aunt to give all possible credit to Klopsch and on the other

14 Clara Barton Diary, Jan. 7, 1898.
15 Pepper, *Louis Klopsch*, 115-17.
16 Clara Barton to Stephen Barton, April 14, 1896, Barton Papers, Box 33.
17 *Ibid.*

cabled him private advice: "Your actions displease me. Pray use moderation. Reports detrimental." [18] In a dramatic move Miss Barton went to Washington and persuaded the State Department to give the Red Cross full management of relief. In the end Klopsch was in effect forced to resign from the Committee.

This internal dissension did not, as Miss Barton had feared, ruin the relief efforts in Cuba. This was fortunate, because conditions cried for help.[19] When Miss Barton arrived in Havana on February 9, 1898, she quickly concluded that the massacres of Armenia seemed merciful in comparison with the scenes that here met her eyes: uprooted, starving people in military camps without adequate food, water or sanitation, orphaned children, rampant disease, the shadow of death everywhere. Consul General Lee estimated that at least 200,000 reconcentrados had died of starvation and disease.[20]

Some giving proved ineffective. In two instances shipments of food —one from Kansas City and one from Philadelphia—neither of which had any connection with the New York Committee or with Red Cross, failed to reach the suffering civilian population. The one from Kansas City fell into the hands of Spanish soldiers, the one from Philadelphia was sent back. Clara Barton on the other hand reported that the goods bearing the Red Cross mark were respected everywhere and that she invariably met with courteous treatment from Spanish officials. American consular authorities also reported generally good cooperation on the part of Spanish military and civil authorities in the distribution of milk, flour, rice, and canned goods to those most desperately in need. Part of the 2,000 tons of food and medicine at the disposal of the Red Cross reached the reconcentrados, but most of it went to Havana, where the need was less pressing.

In addition to supervising many of the distributions, Clara Barton established orphan asylums for the children of reconcentrados who had died in military camps. Despite the friction with Klopsch and what she regarded as lack of cooperation on the part of Consul General Lee, this seventy-six-year-old woman succeeded remarkably well in her operations. Senator Redfield Proctor of Vermont, whose first-hand account of conditions was to influence the decision in Washing-

[18] Stephen Barton to Cottrell, March 20, 1898, Barton Papers, Box 33.
[19] Lee, *Cuba's Struggle Against Spain*, 202 ff.
[20] Clara Barton, *The Red Cross: A History of This Remarkable International Movement in the Interest of Humanity* (Washington: American National Red Cross, 1898), 520 ff.; *Christian Herald* XXI (Jan. 26, 1898), 63; U. S., Congress, Senate, *Consular Reports of Conditions of Reconcentrados in Cuba*, 55th Cong., 2d Sess., 1898, Senate Doc. 230, 40; Barton Papers, Box 10; *New York Times*, April 9, 1898.

ton to intervene in the struggle, declared that Miss Barton needed no endorsement from him. "I saw nothing to criticize, but everything to commend," he continued. "The American people may be assured that their bounty will reach the sufferers with the least possible cost and in the best manner, in every respect." [21]

When war between the United States and Spain seemed imminent, Miss Barton reluctantly followed the advice of Consul General Lee and left Cuba. Thus American relief halted. But both she and the New York Committee felt that every effort should be made to resume the work that had been suspended. In Washington she urged this position on the State Department, which consented to the outfitting of a relief ship and to Miss Barton's return to Cuba to supervise distribution. The *State of Texas*, which the New York Committee chartered and which bore 1,400 tons of food, medicines, and hospital supplies, with a Red Cross staff, left its moorings and headed toward Cuba. But two days later war was declared.

It was thus necessary for the *State of Texas* to put in at Tampa, where Miss Barton joined it for most of the period in which it was marooned in that harbor. For several reasons it was unfortunate that she permitted herself thus to be stranded on the *State of Texas*. Her head and hand were needed at national headquarters in Washington; the Committee had paid $15,000 in charter fees and most of the $12,000 spent in costs subsequent to the ship's leaving New York went into maintenance at Key West. Clara Barton in vain tried to persuade Admiral Sampson to permit the *State of Texas* to break through the blockade and precede the American armed invasion in Cuba, in order to administer, immediately, much needed civilian relief. The weeks of tedious waiting at Tampa and at Key West were, it is true, brightened by opportunities to help needy Cuban refugees and almost equally needy crews of captured Spanish prizes.[22] But even these services only partly compensated for the expense, the frustration of waiting, and the problems of dealing with military and naval authorities who did not understand the official status the Red Cross presumably enjoyed since the ratification of the agreement between the American and Spanish governments after war had been declared. "I feel," Clara Barton confided to her diary, "in all this turmoil of ambition and strife for place, as if surrounded by a pack of wolves. Their howls do not terrify, but they make me

[21] Barton, *The Red Cross*, 539; *Congressional Record*, 55th Cong., 2d Sess., 1898, XXXI, Pt. 3, 2917.

[22] Barton, *The Red Cross*, 368 ff.

want to escape." [23] And again: "Am so sore of heart that I can scarcely carry the burden of life." [24]

On June 20th, 1898, with the invasion of Cuba at last under way, the *State of Texas* was authorized to head for Guantanamo. Utterly inadequate provision had been made by the commissary and the medical corps for the armed forces: there was insufficient food for the able-bodied soldiers, insufficient hospital supplies for the sick and wounded. Clara Barton, who had come to succor Cuban civilians, was asked to provide cots, blankets, hypodermic needles, medicine, and food for American combatants. It was no easy thing, given the forbidding surf, to land small boats with provisions. It was still harder to transport them in commandeered mule teams, now under a broiling sun, now in downpouring torrents that made the wretched roads all but impassable. In spite of the difficulties the job was done. Clara Barton herself prepared food for the soldiers who had gone unfed because of the breakdown of the commissary. There would be those to criticize her for this, needed as she was in Washington to direct larger activities and to try to straighten out tangles and misunderstandings. But the story of what was done in Cuba for the American armed forces, though it unfolded on foreign soil, is not properly part of the record of American philanthropies to other peoples. [25]

The staff of the *State of Texas* did not to be sure limit its errand of mercy to first aid and to providing hospital facilities for American casualties in the dreadful days of the invasion. It turned to the work it had come to do. The group fed thousands of Cuban refugees at Siboney, El Cano, and other towns. At Guantanamo fifty thousand Cubans received rations from the seemingly inexhaustible stores of the *State of Texas*. In the first five days after the surrender of Santiago, the Red Cross, in addition to serving hot soup to ten thousand soldiers daily, furnished food in bulk to thirty-two thousand half-starved Cubans. [26] This work done, Miss Barton returned to Washington.

---

23 Clara Barton Diary, May 7, 1898.

24 *Ibid.*, June 8, 1898.

25 Clara Barton tells the story herself in *The Red Cross*, 514 ff. See also William E. Barton, *The Life of Clara Barton* (2 vols.; Boston, New York: Houghton Mifflin, 1922) II, 280-93 and Gustave R. Gaeddert, "History of the American National Red Cross," vol. II, "The Barton Influence, 1866-1905" (mimeographed monograph in the Library of the American National Red Cross, Washington, D. C.), 170 ff.

26 Gaeddert, "The Barton Influence," 174; Barton, *The Red Cross*, 520 ff.; George Kennan, *Campaigning in Cuba* (New York: Century, 1899), 191.

After painful negotiations with Washington officials and with the New York Committee Clara Barton returned to Cuba in April, 1899, to administer relief made possible by the remaining $50,000 in the treasury of the Central Cuban Relief Committee. Many felt that she was much too old for such sustained field work. Ugly rumors circulated to the effect that the financial affairs of the Red Cross were in bad order. Though these things deeply disturbed her, she again showed amazing vitality. Continued help in Cuba was indeed needed: she estimated that at least 50,000 children, unfed, unclothed, unhoused, roamed the streets of Havana. Her orphan asylums cared for at least two thousand of these unfortunate waifs. With the help of her staff and of prominent Cubans, Miss Barton also established a well-equipped hospital in the suburbs of Havana. And she strengthened the local Cuban Red Cross organization. All this was appreciated in Cuba.[27]

Ingratitude stemmed rather from the growing body of critics within the American National Red Cross, who were concerned over the inadequate coordination between the central body in Washington and the state societies, over the tangles with government officials, and over what were regarded as other evidences of faulty leadership. Within a few years the Red Cross was to be reorganized under new leaders, with a closer tie to government. This reorganization was closely related to the experiences during the Spanish-American War and to the new role of world leadership on which the United States was embarking. But the reorganization and the growing work of the Red Cross in overseas benevolence did not entirely obscure the significance of what Clara Barton accomplished against great odds during the Spanish-American War and in the months that followed the armistice.

In that aftermath in Cuba the Red Cross, to be sure, did not play a lone hand in relief activity. Nathan Straus, German-born merchant associated with R. H. Macy and Company and well known for a spirited campaign for compulsory pasteurization of milk and for the establishment of milk stations in American and European cities, provided for pasteurized, refrigerated milk for the needy in Cuba. He was also responsible for transporting to Santiago an ice and water-distillation plant which distilled 20,000 gallons of water and manu-

[27] Clara Barton, *The Story of the Red Cross* (New York: Appleton, 1904), *passim.*; Gaeddert, "The Barton Influence," 175 ff.

factured thirteen tons of ice each day.[28] But the chief American efforts to improve conditions in Cuba, Puerto Rico, and the Philippines were those of government officials associated with the occupation. These efforts, which anticipated the Point Four program, do not properly belong in this story of the growth of private, nonofficial American overseas philanthropies.[29]

Opportunities for the expansion of American giving abroad were not limited to the needs of the new territorial acquisitions. Natural disasters in various parts of the world continued to invite aid. More effective channels of communication, general prosperity in the country, and the growing interest of the State Department in American relief in overseas catastrophes partly explain the steady development of the impulse of benevolence beyond our own shores. The more intimate relations of the Red Cross to the federal government after the reorganization of 1905 augmented the already existing voluntary channels for collecting funds. Prominent among these agencies were the chambers of commerce, the Philadelphia Citizens Permanent Relief Committee and, above all, the *Christian Herald* under the management of the publicity-conscious humanitarian, Louis Klopsch.

In the early years of the 20th century disasters in many places of the earth succeeded each other with breath-taking rapidity. On May 12, 1902, President Roosevelt, in a special message to Congress, informed that body that "one of the greatest calamities of history has befallen our neighboring island of Martinique." The city of St. Pierre, he continued, had virtually ceased to exist. The American consul and his family were among the estimated 30,000 who lost their lives in the eruption of the volcano Pelée. Another 30,000 were homeless and hungry. The French government requested the United States to send as quickly as possible the means of transporting from the stricken island those in danger of starvation.[30] The Island of St. Vincent, a British possession, was also seriously stricken by a volcanic eruption. Before the year was over northern Sweden and, to a

---

[28] Lina Gutherz Straus, *Disease in Milk* (2d ed. rev.; New York: Dutton, 1917), 134.

[29] Merle Curti and Kendall Birr, *Prelude to Point Four: American Technical Missions Overseas, 1838-1938* (Madison: University of Wisconsin Press, 1954), chap. 5; Joseph Van Hise, "American Contributions to Philippine Science and Technology, 1898-1916" (unpublished Ph.D. dissertation, University of Wisconsin, 1958).

[30] *A Compilation of the Messages and Papers of the Presidents* (21 vols.; New York: Bureau of National Literature, 1917-1922) XIV, 6680; *Papers Relating to the Foreign Relations of the United States, 1903* (Washington: Govt. Printing Office, 1903), 412-17 [cited hereafter as *Foreign Relations*].

greater degree, Finland, experienced grave food shortages. As reports continued to come, vivid with harrowing details, the *Christian Herald* summoned its readers to help: "With famine raging in a Christian land, whose unfortunate people are totally unable to help themselves, it becomes the duty of other Christians to give every aid and comfort to the stricken ones." [31] Dr. Klopsch, arriving in Finland on February 6, 1903, sent back reports of desperate need among the sick, the aged, and the children.[32]

What happened in Finland was repeated three years later in Russia on a much larger scale. *The Outlook* reported in its issue of February 23, 1907, that by the most conservative reports 20,000,000 souls were suffering for lack of food and from the diseases that accompany famine.[33] Nicholas Shishkoff, a recent member of the Duma, came to America to lay before the American people the plight of Russia and to stimulate fund raising.[34] Other firsthand accounts, especially that of Leroy Scott, told of silent, empty barnyards, breadless houses and babies sucking vainly at shriveled breasts, of sobbing, desperate villagers prayerfully bowing in the snow and piteously crying out "Don't forget us! Do not forget the hungry ones." [35] The aftermath of the war with Japan and of the revolutionary uprising only added to and complicated the problem.[36] Early in 1912 famine again stalked the Russian land with millions of peasants in the provinces bordering on the Volga and Urals reported as eating weeds and bark and dying of scurvy and typhus.[37] The report of the Chief Medical Inspector of Russia summed matters up: "In short, the Russian famine is rapidly assuming the dimensions of a terrible national calamity." [38]

Meantime floods in China brought famine in gargantuan proportions. Newspapers in the spring of 1901 reported the urgent need of relief. In taking the lead in calling for contributions, Dr. Klopsch reminded American Christians that, if missionaries were being unjustly maligned, deeds, not words, were the best counterarguments. "Our benevolence in India and elsewhere has been an object lesson

---

[31] *Christian Herald* XVI (Jan. 14, 1903), 30.

[32] *Ibid.* (May 13, 1903), 403-04.

[33] *Outlook* LXXXV (Feb. 23, 1907), 397-99.

[34] *Ibid.* and *Outlook* LXXXV (March 9, 1907), 566.

[35] Leroy Scott, "In the Land of the Great Hunger," *Outlook* LXXXV (Feb. 23, 1907), 411-25.

[36] George Kennan, "Russian Despotism," *ibid.* (March 30, 1907), 751-55; Samuel J. Barrows, "In the Track of the Famine," *ibid.* LXXXVIII (Jan. 11, 1908), 87-91.

[37] *Outlook* C (Jan. 6, 1912), 5-6; *ibid.* (Jan. 20, 1912), 110-11.

[38] *Ibid.* (April 6, 1912), 756.

to the Asiatic races," he declared.[39] The American Minister to
China, E. H. Conger, reported that the starving Chinese were de-
vouring grass, leaves, bark, and even each other. Letters and cables
from American missionaries confirmed these reports. In the spring
of 1903 more than a million people in the Kwang Si province were
said to be without any food at all.[40] Francis Nichols, a young journalist whom the *Christian Herald* sent as its representative, wrote
from the remote province of Shensi of the extensive sale of children
and of flesh of human beings that had died of hunger. According
to the best estimates Nichols could make, two and a half millions,
or 30 per cent of Shensi's population, were dead of starvation before
the Empress Dowager took steps to get food over the mountain
fastnesses and desert trails.[41] In 1910 and 1911 Kiangsi and Anhui
provinces were devastated by still another famine, while bubonic
plague swept over Manchuria.[42]

Following in the wake of the Russo-Japanese War, a famine that
resulted from failure of the rice crop led to acute suffering among
three quarters of a million people in the northern provinces of Japan.
News of the calamity first reached America through missionaries,
but the imperial government, sensitive though it was, admitted that
relief from the outside would be a welcome supplement to its own
measures, which included work projects. Despite the exigencies of
war with Russia, the Japanese Red Cross had only recently sent
$110,000 for the relief of San Francisco earthquake sufferers, and
this generosity was now recalled. In addition the Roosevelt administration was eager, in the interest of national policy and international
good-will, to have the American people respond to Japan's need.[43]

The same year, 1906, brought calls for help from Chile where, in
the words of President Theodore Roosevelt, "a dreadful calamity"
had befallen a sister Republic, one, moreover, which had special
claims on American benevolence in view of the interest the United
States had expressed at the Rio de Janeiro Pan-American Congress in

[39] Pepper, *Louis Klopsch*, 167.
[40] *Ibid.*, 168-69.
[41] Francis H. Nichols, *Through Hidden Shensi* (New York: Scribner's Sons, 1905),
228-32; William T. Ellis, "China's Great Famine," *Outlook* LXXXV (March 30,
1907), 755-59.
[42] *Congressional Record*, 61st Cong., 3d Sess., 1911, XLVI, Pt. 3, 2109; *Foreign
Relations*, 1911, 56-62.
[43] *The American National Red Cross Bulletin* I, no. 3 (July, 1906), 3 ff.; Elting E.
Morison, ed., *The Letters of Theodore Roosevelt* (8 vols.; Cambridge: Harvard University Press, 1952) V, 193 ff.; *Foreign Relations*, 1906, Pt. 2, 999 ff.; *New York Tribune*, Feb. 14, 15, 21, 22, March 23, 1906; Pepper, *Louis Klopsch*, 203-09.

Latin America.[44] Reminding the country of the help San Francisco had received in a similar earthquake disaster, President Roosevelt asked his countrymen to give out of their abundance as others had given to us.[45]

The earthquake at Valparaiso evoked far less interest and response than a similar but more far-reaching one in Sicily and Calabria in late January, 1908. Villages, towns, and cities in a fifty-square-mile area were wiped out: there was virtually nothing left of Messina, a city of 150,000. Official Italian estimates put the dead at 77,283: the job of digging out corpses from the debris and of getting rid of them took many months.[46] Contributions and relief poured in from several parts of the globe in a disaster quickly recognized as the major one thus far in the new century.

Other earthquakes, fires and famines nearer home followed one after the other in a never-ending sequence: in Jamaica (1907), in Mexico (1909), in Costa Rica (1910), in Haiti (1915), in Guatemala (1915), and San Salvador (1917).[47] None of these disasters seemed so heart-rending, at least to the people in the northeastern part of the country, as the great fire resulting from the explosion of a munitions ship in Halifax harbor on the evening of December 6, 1917. The horror of a driving blizzard was superimposed on the fire that destroyed thousands of buildings, left homeless at least 8,000 men, women, and children and, according to official estimates, killed 1,900 citizens and sailors. The ravages of pneumonia, which quickly set in, threatened to kill additional hundreds of people.[48]

Floods, as well as earthquakes and fires, added demands for help,

---

[44] *Foreign Relations,* 1906, Pt. 1, 156-58; *New York Tribune,* August 29, 1906.

[45] *New York Tribune,* August 26, 1906; *Independent* LXI (August 23, 1906), 464-65.

[46] Ernest P. Bicknell, "Calabria and Sicily Two Months After the Earthquake," *American Red Cross Bulletin* IV, no. 3 (July, 1909), 11-25 and *Pioneering with the Red Cross: Recollections of an Old Red Crosser* (New York: Macmillan, 1935), 105-33; Maude Howe [Elliott], *Sicily in Shadow and in Sun: The Earthquake and American Relief Work* (Boston: Little Brown, 1910), 1-38; Mabel A. Elliott, "History of the American National Red Cross," vol. XX: "American National Red Cross Disaster Series, 1881-1918" (mimeographed monograph in the Library of the American National Red Cross, Washington, D. C.), 162 ff.

[47] *Independent* LXII (Jan. 24, 1907), 173-75; *New York Times,* August 15, 1915; *Foreign Relations,* 1910, 410-14; *Ibid.,* 1917, 754-59; 1214-1221; Herman Stöhr, *So Half Amerika: Die Auslandshilfe der Vereinigten Staaten, 1812-1930* (Stetin: Ökumenischer Verlag, 1936), 87 ff. American contributions to overseas disasters also included a sealing fleet catastrophe in Newfoundland, a Samoan typhoon, a cholera epidemic in Tripoli, a fire in Istanbul, and the refugee problem of the Balkan wars.

[48] *The Survey* XXXIX (Dec. 15, 1917), 305-07; Elliott, "American National Red Cross Disaster Services," 203 ff.

particularly those in France in 1910.[49] And apart from these vicissi-
tudes incidental to natural disaster, civil war with attending famine
and pestilence struck Nicaragua with resulting calls for aid.[50] The
revolution breaking out in Mexico in 1911 was also attended by widespread suffering that made still further demands on American benevolence.[51]

These disasters did not exhaust the catalogue. Two tragedies,
deeply rooted in history, provided in this period a curtain raiser to
even greater ones that came to a bitter climax in the First World War.
One was the outbreak of anti-Jewish pogroms in 1903 in Kishineff
and, in the following years, in Odessa and other Russian cities. Many
American Jewish leaders, including Oscar Straus, Cyrus L. Sulzberger, Isaac Seligman, Adolph Kraus, Adolph Lewisohn, and Louis
Marshall, spared no efforts in raising relief funds and in joining in
protests to the State Department and to the Russian government itself.

But the name of Jacob Schiff leads all the rest. This devout Jew,
who took seriously the commands of his religion to give to those in
need, had come to New York in 1865 and in due course was a leading
member of the famous banking firm of Kuhn, Loeb and Company.
His philanthropic interests included the Metropolitan Museum, the
free public library movement, the Charity Organization Society, the
Henry Street Settlement, the Young Men's Hebrew Association, the
National Child Labor Committee, the Montefiore Hospital, Jewish
scholarship, Tuskegee, Cornell, Columbia, Barnard, and a struggling
technological institute in Palestine which aroused his interest on a
visit to that land in 1908. He was also a leader in the Red Cross endowment campaign. No wonder that Bishop Potter of the Episcopal
Church characterized him as New York's leading philanthropist and
as the millionaire who had done more than any other to alleviate the
condition of the poor and oppressed.[52] As early as 1878 Schiff had
acted as treasurer of an American committee that raised funds for the
relief of Jews during the Russo-Turkish War.[53]

Now, as the new wave of anti-Semitism broke out in Eastern

[49] *Foreign Relations*, 1910, 508-10.
[50] *Ibid.*, 1912, 1127-31.
[51] *Survey* XXXIV (July 17, 1915), 347-48; *Ibid.* (July 31, 1915), 387.
[52] Cyrus Adler, *Jacob Schiff: His Life and Letters* (2 vols.; New York: Doubleday,
Doran, 1928) II, 356; Frieda Schiff Warburg, *Reminiscences of a Long Life* (New
York: privately printed, 1956), 52 ff.
[53] Adler, *Jacob Schiff* II, 277.

Europe, Schiff joined others in arranging for a public meeting in Carnegie Hall to raise funds for the Kishineff victims.[54] In 1906 he joined Dr. Cyrus Adler in founding the American Jewish Committee to safeguard the civil and religious rights of Jews and to alleviate the consequences of persecution abroad as well as at home. Even before the great troubles of the First World War, succeeding crises, including those associated with the Balkan wars, invited sustained efforts to provide relief for persecuted and dispossessed Jews.

The other tragedy was the renewed outbreak of the persecution of the Armenian Christians in the Ottoman Empire. In 1909 it was estimated that between 20,000 and 30,000 Christians were slaughtered despite the more tolerant attitude of the Young Turks who had come into partial power. Ambassador John G. A. Leishman reported the plight of homeless and penniless widows and orphans entirely dependent on greatly needed charity.[55] But these atrocities were only a prelude to those of 1914-1915 which were to include Turkey, Persia, and the Russian Caucasus, and which possibly claimed more than a million victims.

To meet all these overseas disasters, crowding so closely one on the other as to be virtually endemic, the established agencies for fund-raising and relief activities again swung into action. These included the more or less independent Citizens Permanent Relief Committee in Philadelphia, which was especially alert after the Martinique earthquake and during the Russian famine.[56] Included also were such business organizations as the New York Chamber of Commerce. Its president, Morris Ketchum Jessup, trusting that his action would be confirmed, purchased on his own responsibility several cargoes of grain which he dispatched to Martinique on the occasion of the earthquake and fire in 1902.[57] The New York Merchants Association Committee raised over $8,000 as a contribution for the relief of suffering in the Valparaiso earthquake. Members of the New York business community who contributed to the fund included such well-known banking, mining, and export firms as Spencer Trask and Company ($250), Lanman and Kemp ($1,000), James

[54] *New York Times*, May 29, 1903.

[55] *Foreign Relations*, 1909, 575-77.

[56] Stöhr, *So Half Amerika*, 74; Barrows, *Outlook* LXXXVIII, 87-91. Collection of the Citizens Permanent Relief Committee and the Herbert Welsh Papers, Historical Society of Pennsylvania, *passim*.

[57] William Adams Brown, *Morris Ketchum Jessup* (New York: C. Scribner's Sons, 1910), 121.

Speyer and Company ($2,500), M. Guggenheim Sons ($5,000) and W. R. Grace and Company ($10,000).[58]

For flood relief in France the American Chamber of Commerce raised $38,000, the largest contributor being J. Pierpont Morgan Company.[59] The American Chamber of Commerce sent approximately $25,000 for relief of the Sicilian earthquake victims. After the earthquake in Costa Rica, the United Fruit Company, which had made big profits from its enterprise in this country, contributed the relatively small sum of $11,000 for relief.[60] In the great famine in China in 1906 Edward H. Harriman of the Union Pacific and Marvin Hughitt of the Chicago and Northwestern arranged to have their roads transport freight-free 1,000 tons of produce from the midwest to San Francisco.[61]

During the Mexican troubles of 1911 and the following years, American corporation interests, with investments equalling a billion dollars, formed the National Mexican Relief Committee of the Red Cross. As American property suffered and American lives were lost, and as the clamor for intervention mounted, the Committee was inevitably involved in public discussion, the more so by reason of its composition. Its president was William C. Potter of the Guaranty Trust, who had also been general manager in Mexico City of the American Smelting and Refining Company. Prominent also in the Committee were Joseph Cudahy of Chicago and the Guggenheims. The funds raised by the Committee, supplemented by those contributed in a general Red Cross appeal, seem to have been only a minor factor in the tangled skein of American-Mexican relations.[62]

As in earlier campaigns for funds for overseas disasters, communities having a special proximity or feeling a special obligation, played more active parts than did others. Thus San Franciscans, with their own disaster and the foreign relief which had been so welcome fresh in mind, and with some interest in the west coast of South America,

---

[58] *New York Tribune*, August 25, 26, 1906.

[59] *Foreign Relations*, 1910, 508-10.

[60] *Ibid.*, 411.

[61] Pepper, *Louis Klopsch*, 190.

[62] *Survey* XXXIV (July 17, 1915), 347-48 and *Ibid.* (July 31, 1915), 387; *World's Work* XXX (August, 1915), 388. Total Red Cross expenditures for distressed Americans in Mexico, for refugees, and for the Mexicans themselves were $125,000. The administration of relief taxed greatly the Red Cross personnel—transportation difficulties, rebel seizures of supplies, and anti-Americanism all encumbered the program. Dulles, *American Red Cross*, 127-29.

responded immediately to the cry for help in the Chile earthquake
of 1907 with a contribution of $10,000.[63] New Englanders and
New Yorkers similarly took the lead and carried the main relief burden at the time of the Halifax fire in 1917. Also, as might have been
expected in view of the generous contributions of Irish-Americans
during the famines in their homeland in the 1840's and the 1880's,
immigrant groups often formed special committees for raising funds
when widespread distress was reported in the countries of their nativity. The some 300,000 Finnish-Americans, mostly humble and poor
folk, formed, under the leadership of Dr. Oskar Henrik Sorsen, a
Finnish Central Relief Committee of the Western States which dispatched funds from the slender savings of its constituents. So, too,
Swedish-American groups responded to the cry for help in the famine
which at the same time struck the northern provinces of their mother-
land.[64] In 1906, in much the same way, Japanese-Americans organized to collect funds for the relief of the famine in Japan. The same
year a general Relief Committee of Italian-Americans, in the organization of which William Randolph Hearst took a leading role,
indefatigably collected donations for the relief of sufferers in the eruption of Vesuvius.[65]

The precedent of forming a special committee in a given crisis was
followed in these years, the most notable example being the Russian
Famine Relief Committee of 1908. Its secretary was the Reverend
Samuel J. Barrows, a Unitarian, editor of the *Christian Register*, and
leader in civil service and prison reform movements. Barrows steered
a path made particularly rough by the argument on one hand that
the famine was the result of revolutionary agitation and, on the other,
that it stemmed from the incompetence of a hopelessly reactionary
regime. The Committee, which included prominent business men
and charity leaders, raised approximately $75,000.[66] Most of the sub-
scriptions were in comparatively small amounts. "It was apparent in

---

[63] *Foreign Relations*, 1906, Pt. 1, 157. The gift ultimately rose to over $15,000:
Ibid., 159.

[64] Pepper, *Louis Klopsch*, 121 ff., 141 ff. These committees in general sent the funds
collected directly to relief committees in Finland and Sweden. *Christian Herald* XVI
(Jan. 7, 1903), 3, 14. The periodical *Skandinaven* collected funds which it sent to Dr.
Klopsch: *Christian Herald* XVI (Feb. 4, 1903), 94; Juuso Hirvonen, *Michigania kupari-
alve ja suomalaiset siirtolaiset* (Duluth, 1920), 135.

[65] *New York Tribune*, Feb. 21, 1906, 4; *La Tribuna Italiana*, April 21, 1906.

[66] Isabel C. Barrows, in a biography of her husband, *A Sunny Life* (Boston: Little
Brown, 1913), does not refer to his work for Russian famine relief; *Outlook* LXXXVIII,
87-91; Kennan, *Outlook* LXXXV, 751-55; William English Walling, "How is it with
the Russian Revolution?", *Ibid.* (March 9, 1907), 564-67.

this as in nearly all popular collections," Barrows observed, "that the people who have small fortunes find it easier to part with their money than those who have large ones. Many gifts," he added, "were accompanied by expressions of deep interest for the Russian people." [67]

Two organizations loomed larger than all the others in fund raising and in exerting some measure of supervision over administering the relief. Each brought to the campaigns of the period between the Spanish-American War and the First World War the experience of relief activities in earlier disasters and each cooperated with the other. These were the *Christian Herald*, with its indefatigable, enthusiastic, practical, "twentieth century captain of philanthropy," Dr. Louis Klopsch, who regarded himself as a partner of God in meeting human needs in times of distress; and the reorganized American Red Cross, now more tightly affiliated with the federal government and led by Mabel Boardman and Ernest P. Bicknell.

Even before the death in 1902 of the Reverend De. Witt Talmage, Klopsch had shouldered the main burden of the fund-raising and relief campaigns of the *Christian Herald*. Of the $132,000 sent to Norway, Sweden, and Finland in the famine of 1902-1903, Klopsch's campaign was responsible for $77,000, mostly in small gifts. [68] His efforts in raising relief for the Japanese famine in 1906 were praised by President Roosevelt, who wrote: "You have raised $100,000, and you have rendered a very real service to humanity and to the cause of international good-will." The total of the *Herald's* contributions in the Japanese famine actually added up to $241,822. [69] In the Chinese famine of 1906-1908 the *Christian Herald* collected $427,323 from 149,000 contributors, a substantial proportion of America's contribution which in turn made up two-thirds of the total funds, Chinese and foreign, raised for relief. [70] Expressing appreciation for the gift, a Chinese mandarin told the *Christian Herald's* representative, Moyer B. Duncan, that "Few of these people ever heard of America before this famine relief began. They will always remember it as the land of

[67] Barrows, *Outlook* LXXXVIII, 87.

[68] *Christian Herald* XVI (March 11, 1903), 207; (April 15, 1903), 323; (April 29, 1903), 367-68.

[69] Pepper, *Louis Klopsch*, 209, 212.

[70] *Ibid.*, Missionaries were the chief almoners of American donations although the Central China Famine Relief Fund Committee, composed of prominent Chinese officials and foreign merchants and government officials resident in China, provided guidance and general oversight. *Report of the Central China Famine Relief Fund Committee* (Shanghai: North China Daily News and Herald, 1907), 16 ff.

The Christian Herald." [71] The paper's gifts to famine-ridden India totaled $700,000. When King Victor Emmanuel II of Italy asked Klopsch the average donation making up the $71,000 contribution for relief of the Messina earthquake victims, the fund-raiser replied "$2.75." The king seemed incredulous when Klopsch added that within fifteen years the *Christian Herald* had collected and disbursed over $3,000,000.[72]

In all these campaigns, as in those of the 1890's, Klopsch appealed for donations by giving his readers concrete, graphic, and illustrated accounts of distress and by assuming that they would gladly give sufficiently to cover the sums he had immediately cabled to missionaries or consular officials on learning of pressing need. His relations with contributors remained personal, even intimate. Every name and the amount given, no matter how small, appeared in the paper's columns. Sometimes a special representative was sent to the spot to report details and to supervise the distribution of funds and supplies. Klopsch himself, at his own expense, went to Finland, Sweden, and Italy in connection with the *Herald's* contributions to disaster relief in those lands. If funds were not used up in a given case, what was left was handed to missionaries for the care of orphans or allocated to the orphanage at Nyack, New York, in which Klopsch took a special interest.

All in all, there was little overstatement in the claim of one of his biographers that, more than anyone else, Klopsch taught the American people the lesson of giving dimes and dollars for large-scale overseas disaster relief.[73] Irving Bacheller summed up the significance of Klopsch in memorable, if somewhat purple, words: "Mainly he preached with bread; he prayed with human kindness; he blessed with wheat and corn. His best missionaries were loaded ships; his happiness was in mitigated pain. His week-day was as holy as his Sabbath, his office as consecrated as his church. . . ." [74]

In this period the Red Cross, with which Klopsch had better relations than in the Cuban episode, steadily moved to the front as a major agency in overseas relief despite the fact that its activities were

[71] Pepper, *Louis Klopsch*, 180-81.
[72] *Ibid.*, 238-39. Klopsch added that the weekly circulation of the paper was 246,000: *Ibid.*, 240.
[73] *Dictionary of American Biography* X, 447-48.
[74] Pepper, *Louis Klopsch*, vii.

confined to fund raising, with the exception of the Italian earthquake disaster, when it took the field. Both before and after its reorganization in 1905 its management was free to respond to requests for help in natural disasters, insofar as its resources permitted. Between 1906 and 1909 its smaller contributions included earthquake relief for Kingston, Jamaica ($5,381), the Russian famine sufferers ($9,000), the Chileans at the time of the Valparaiso disaster ($9,844), the survivors from the eruption of Vesuvius ($16,226), and the Armenian victims of Turks and Kurds ($29,500). The larger gifts included the $245,865 for famished Japanese, the $327,897 for the Chinese in the famine of 1906, and the $986,378 for the Sicilian and Calabrian earthquake, the latter being the largest sum that any national Red Cross transmitted to the Italian Red Cross. In all, the American Red Cross contributed $1,640,186 for natural disaster relief abroad in the period. It was a record in part made possible by the reorganization of 1905 which resulted in closer and more effective relations between the central office and the state and local auxiliaries.[75]

But in civil disturbances the Red Cross was less free to act. This resulted from the close tie-up with the federal government which resulted from the reorganization: the President of the United States now became its president and members of the State Department served on key committees. In theory the Red Cross was still committed to serve without reference to religion, race, or national politics and interest. In fact, when national interest was involved in foreign civil disturbances, the Red Cross tended to become an arm of the federal government. This was evident in the Mexican Revolution of 1911 and in disturbances in the Central American and Caribbean countries. Nevertheless, the overseas activities of the American Red Cross were of importance in themselves and by reason of the valuable experience stored up for the services needed and rendered during the First World War.[76]

One innovation in the Red Cross activities in the period between the Spanish-American War and the First World War promised to cut a new path. The endemic aspect of flood and famine in China put a heavy strain on American giving—a million dollars went for relief in China in the pre-World War I period. But what could be given was

[75] *Foreign Relations*, 1909, 7-8. For contributions of the British Friends and the Relief Committee to Russian famine sufferers, see *The Times* [London], Oct. 17, Nov. 25, 1907, Jan. 2, 1908. It is interesting to note that the Red Cross contributed $2,963,200 to California at the time of her earthquake disasters in the same period.
[76] Dulles, *The American Red Cross*, 121-22.

at best a mere drop in the bucket in terms of actual need. In 1911 the Red Cross, with the approval of the State Department and the Chinese government, sent an American engineer, Charles Davis Jameson, to study and report on the feasibility of flood control in the Hwai area. Jameson finished his preliminary survey in the spring of 1913, and the way was open to further planning. With the approval of Congress an army engineer, Colonel William S. Sibert, was lent to continue the work. The Red Cross, with the active cooperation of Paul Reinsch, American Minister in Peking, did what it could to interest international bankers in lending China $30,000,000—the estimated cost of what had come to be known as the Hwai River Conservancy Project. But neither the bankers nor the Rockefeller Foundation, which had been working on health problems in the Philippines and China, were willing to move in. The outbreak of war in 1914 postponed until the 1920's further discussion of what was designed by the Red Cross to be a fundamental approach to the whole problem of flood and famine in China.[77]

Related both to the program of the Red Cross and, more directly, to the new sense of world responsibility, was the enlarged role the government took in overseas relief. Presidents Roosevelt, Taft, and Wilson all responded to disaster abroad by inquiring whether American aid was needed and, if such was the case, by appealing to the American people for funds to enable the Red Cross to move in.[78] Moreover, the government was more liberal than in earlier days in providing both transport for produce to famine and pestilence-stricken areas and in appropriating funds for direct relief. There was little debate in Congress over the propriety of appropriations for such ends.

Thus, when President Roosevelt requested $500,000 for aid for the earthquake sufferers in the 1902 disasters in Martinique and St. Vincent, Congress quickly responded by appropriating $200,000 and by authorizing the use of Army and Navy transports, personnel, and supplies. On May 14, 1902, the USS *Dixie* sailed from New York with rations and cash. Other relief ships followed.[79] At the time of

[77] *Foreign Relations*, 1914, 95-119; Paul Reinsch, *An American Diplomat in China* (Garden City, N. Y.: Doubleday, Page, 1922), 98, 162, 207. After the War the Red Cross decided against any further participation in the project.

[78] *Messages and Papers of the Presidents* XIV, 6680; *Foreign Relations*, 1906, Pt. 1, 155, Pt. 2, 913 ff., 999 ff.

[79] *Congressional Record*, 57th Cong., 1st Sess., 1902, XXXV, 5304-05, 5330 ff.; *Foreign Relations*, 1902, 412-16, 523 ff.

the earthquake in Jamaica in 1907 Congress promptly approved a resolution authorizing the distribution of provisions from Navy stores. The *Missouri* and the *Indiana*, the same ships that carried food to the Russians in 1892 served again in a similar capacity.[80] In the 1907 famine in China the produce collected by the *Christian Herald* and the Red Cross was, by authorization of Congress, dispatched on the *Buford*, the same Army transport that in 1919 was to take 248 reluctant deportees to Russia.[81] In 1911, when famine again ravaged a large area in China, Congress authorized the expenditure of $50,000 for transport services.[82] Aid was also furnished in disasters in Nicaragua and Haiti.

But the appropriation in 1909 of $800,000 for the purchase of building materials to replace some of the homes destroyed by the Messina, Sicily, earthquake and for other relief was on a truly unprecedented scale.[83] In this instance Navy personnel supervised the construction of the 3,000 cottages that testified to American official benevolence.[84] Finally, American consular and diplomatic officials took an increasingly active part in the distribution of funds and other relief, notably after the earthquakes of Chile and Jamaica and in the Chinese famines of 1906 and 1911. The outstanding example of initiative and sustained supervision on the part of foreign service officials was, however, in the Messina earthquake catastrophe, when Consul Bayard Cutting and Ambassador Lloyd Griscom organized resident Americans in relief committees, hastened to the scene of disaster, and directed the use of American unofficial as well as official contributions.[85]

The larger part taken by American government officials in overseas relief activities was paralleled by continued reliance on indigenous organizations at the receiving end. In cases in which the national Red Cross enjoyed a good reputation, as in Japan, funds were

[80] *Foreign Relations*, 1907, 558-69.

[81] *American National Red Cross Bulletin*, II, no. 3 (July, 1907), 5 ff.; Pepper, *Louis Klopsch*, 189 ff.

[82] *Congressional Record*, 61st Cong., 3d Sess., 1911, XLVI, Pt. 3, 2109, 2327, 2389, 2415.

[83] *Ibid.*, 60th Cong., 2d Sess., 1909, XLIII, Pt. 1, 456-57, 468; American Relief Committee at Rome, *Report of Funds Administered for Relief of Earthquake Sufferers in Sicily and Calabria* (Rome: 1909).

[84] Reginald Rowan Belknap, *American House Building in Messina and Reggio, An Account of the American Naval and Red Cross Combined Expedition to Provide Shelter for the Survivors of the Great Earthquake of December 28, 1908* (New York, London: G. P. Putnam's Sons, 1910), 2-4, 10, *passim*.

[85] Howe, *Sicily in Shadow and in Sun*, 20-21, 85 ff.

turned over to and administered by these agencies. Where the national Red Cross was reputed to be partisan, as in Russia, or inefficient, as in Italy, greater reliance was put on other agencies. Such agencies were the Finnish Central Relief Committee, made up largely of Lutheran ministers and local business men, the United Zemstov Relief Association, the Free Russia Economic Society, and the Friends of Russian Freedom. In Italy American officials and the American Red Cross, which on this occasion took the field, cooperated with the Italian government in relief work. In China and Turkey missionaries acted as almoners. To keep an eye on things and to give firsthand reports to donors, Klopsch followed earlier precedents in going to Finland and Italy and in sending representatives to China. Samuel Barrows, a leader in fund raising for the Russian famine sufferers, also went to Russia to give direct reports on conditions and on relief administration.

The records examined contain some evidence of discontent on the part of donors or recipients. The American Minister in Valparaiso reported that Chilean officials handed out relief to individuals and that the method of so doing left a good deal to be desired.[86] In Russia the government, fearful that voluntary organizations might, if permitted to distribute relief funds, disseminate revolutionary propaganda, kept things in its own hands until the ineptitude of the bureaucracy and the demoralization of the Red Cross led to the decision to entrust relief to voluntary agencies. Americans in Russia reported that the well to do gave little to the stricken until they had been made aware of conditions by American contributions.[87] Italian authorities were critical of Katharine Davis's work program on the ground that no one who could get relief without toil would work.[88] Many felt that the Americans in building their own type of cottages with materials sent from the States paid too little attention to Italian tastes and customs. But the chief criticism of the extensive field relief

[86] *Foreign Relations*, 1906, Pt. 1, 159.

[87] Barrows, *Outlook*, 88, Samuel J. Barrows, "Famine Relief Work in Russia," *Charities and the Commons* XX (June 6, 1908), 353-57; *Outlook* C (April 6, 1912), 756. *Punch* informed British contributors that Russian government officials would be allowed to have no part in distributing funds to famine sufferers in Samara, Russia. *Punch*, CXXXII (May 8, 1907), 332.

[88] Katharine Bement Davis, "Relief Work for the Messina Refugees in Syracuse," *Survey* XXII (April 3, 1909), 37-47. Miss Davis, a well-known figure in American prison reform, was vacationing in Sicily when the earthquake took place and in addition to initiating work relief programs, supervised various programs, including the establishment of orphanages.

activities of the Americans in Sicily and Southern Italy was that in maintaining a secular policy in the orphan asylums that were established, Catholic sensibilities were disregarded.[89]

In each relief episode government officials and reigning monarchs expressed deep appreciation for American contributions in produce, gold, and services. Such official expressions must of course be taken at something less than face value. Yet many evidences suggest that appreciation was deeper than surface politeness. The King and Queen of Sweden in the audience given to Louis Klopsch were "moved to tears" on hearing that many thousands of Americans had contributed for the relief work.[90] The King and Queen of Italy were in no sense perfunctory in their expression of appreciation when they received Klopsch. For what he did for the Japanese famine sufferers, he received the order of the Rising Sun and the written thanks of Japanese governors.[91] The governor of Shensi Province in China told Francis Nichols that he had doubted that Christianity taught men to forgive those that wronged them, but that he was inclined to believe this might be true in view of the famine relief sent in so soon after the Boxer attack on westerners. He also asked Nichols' advice as to how famines might be prevented and although he admitted that the proposal—railroads—would bring in more of the foreigners he so much disliked, he was sufficiently impressed by the advice not to oppose new means of transportation.[92]

When the Empress Dowager arrived in this starving land with 10,000 in her retinue she showed her feelings in ways strange to us but definite. She had prominent mandarins who had failed in relief administration beheaded. She also directed that every facility be given the missionaries who had come with funds for buying food for the starving and expressed her gratitude for the generosity of the donors. More meaningful were the expressions of appreciation of those who were actually suffering. Nichols was reasonably sure that two-thirds of the inhabitants of Shensi had never heard of America before American money arrived. "To-day, from one end of the province to the other," he added, "it is known as the one foreign nation that is

[89] Howe, *Sicily in Shadow and in Sun*, 248-50; Mabel A. Elliott, "American National Red Cross Disaster Services," 169-70.
[90] *Christian Herald* XVI (April 8, 1903), 294-95.
[91] Pepper, *Louis Klopsch*, 212 ff., 237 ff.
[92] Nichols, *Through Hidden Shensi*, 195, 231, 236.

really a friend, and whose people, though barbarians, are strangely kind." [93]

Louis Klopsch wrote home from Finland that "wherever we stopped for the night, crowds gathered under our windows, singing songs of welcome, bringing flowers, and on our appearance, telling us, in a strange language, how sincerely they appreciate the great goodness of the American people in the hour of Finland's direst need." [94] The American construction of a hospital, a school, orphanages and 3,000 cottages in Sicily not only afforded desperately needed relief but, in the words of Reginald R. Belknap, former naval attaché at Rome, "was a dashing enterprise, almost spectacular, and it made a great impression. . . ." [95] One handsome old Italian, in expressing gratitude for the American effort not only to relieve immediate want but to help his countrymen help themselves, remarked: "That grand and majestic country, America, is not egotistical; what vibrant sympathy it has shown our country! We are egotists, it is the curse of our people; but I revere America most, for the wondrous new science that has come from there." [96]

What was done in the period between the Spanish-American War and World War I was both inadequate and minor in relation to the need. But voluntary giving and, to a larger extent than ever before, government action, saved the lives of tens of thousands in all quarters of the globe. The value of American aid in keeping up the hope and courage of those in need can not be calculated, any more than can the as yet meager efforts at stimulating self-help. But the nation now had the habit of giving, and organizations with which to meet new emergencies such as those brought by the Great War.

[93] *Ibid.*, 241.
[94] *Christian Herald* XVI (April 15, 1903), 323.
[95] Reginald R. Belknap, "Earthquake Relief Work at Messina and Reggio," *Survey* XXXII (May 2, 1914), 115-19.
[96] Howe, *Sicily in Shadow and Sun*, 371-72.

IX

The Great War

Only a tiny fraction of the philanthropic giving that the First World War evoked in America before the government became a belligerent was channeled into efforts to stop the combat through neutral mediation. The Women's International Committee for Permanent Peace, led by Jane Addams, promoted this idea but found it hard to enlist financial support for publicizing it. The Carnegie Endowment, one of the two foundations committed by its charter to working for a peaceful world, turned down all proposals to embark on any stop-the-war movement. Its directors were convinced that peace was possible only after Germany and her allies had been thoroughly crushed.

But the feeling that something ought to be done did enlist the interest of a great industrialist not hitherto known for philanthropic activities. Henry Ford, believing that the war was senseless and unnecessary, had from the start shown his colors. He had, among other things, given liberal support to the pacifists' widespread circulation of Congressman Clyde Tavenner's exposure of the relationship between munitions interests and preparedness groups. And in the autumn of 1915 Madame Rosika Schwimmer, the Hungarian feminist and journalist who had been active in the Women's Peace Party, and Louis Lochner, an internationally-minded journalist, persuaded him to make a bold, dramatic stroke for peace by giving world-wide publicity to the idea of continuous neutral efforts at mediation.[1]

Ford invited a number of able and prominent Americans to sail with him to the neutral countries of Europe, in order to stir up public

[1] The development of this idea is traced in Marie Louise Degen, *The History of the Women's Peace Party*" (Johns Hopkins University Studies in Historical and Political Science, series LVII, no. 3; Baltimore: Johns Hopkins University Press, 1939), 28 ff. and in Walter Trattner, "Julia Grace Wales and the Wisconsin Plan for Peace," *Wisconsin Magazine of History* XLIV (Spring, 1961), 203-213.

opinion and to pressure neutral governments to offer continuous constructive mediation. The invitation was accepted by a few well-known public figures, including Jane Addams (whom illness eventually prevented from going), S. S. McClure, the publisher, and Judge Ben Lindsey of Denver. But most of the hundred "peace pilgrims" were not widely known to the public: ministers, feminists, socialists, single taxers, lecturers and college students—some of whom later said that they went along "for the ride."

Madame Schwimmer, convinced that the peace cause had been presented in too dull and gray a manner, believed that it could be made as colorful and exciting as war itself. But a skeptical and light-hearted press presented what was intended to be color and drama as a mismanaged crusade of "noisy adventurers and ludicrous dreamers." It exploited to the full the disagreements of participants over the issue of preparedness, for which President Wilson had come out, and played up Ford's decision to leave the peace ship at Christiania as evidence of a complete fiasco.

Actually, the expedition established a Conference for Continuous Mediation which served both as a clearinghouse and a sounding board. It culled from the press of belligerent countries items indicating a desire for peace along liberal, constructive lines and circulated these, in translation, in other belligerent lands. The Conference also publicized such slogans and ideas as peace without victory (before Wilson adopted it), self-determination of peoples, disarmament, and a league of nations.[2]

Ford's attitude toward the affair was curiously ambivalent. On being told that he had spent $465,000 on the expedition, his response was, "Well, we got a million dollars worth of advertising out of it, and a hell of a lot of experience." [3] When David Starr Jordan tried to rekindle his interest, he found Ford unresponsive.[4] Twenty-five years later, however, on the eve of another war, Ford wrote, "It seems to me that with the ocean full of warships, we can afford to remember

[2] This is based largely on the account in Merle Curti, *Peace or War: The American Struggle*, 1636-1936 (New York: Norton, 1936), 236, 241-46 and on the Louis Lochner collection in the Wisconsin State Historical Society.

[3] Allan Nevins and Frank Ernest Hill, *Ford*, vol. II: *Expansion and Challenge*, 1915-1933 (New York: C. Scribner's Sons, 1954-57), 53-54. Ford later confided to Erwin G. Pipp that on the voyage he had discovered potential markets for his tractor and, also, the cause of the War—the Jews—an illusion which, in the words of Nevins and Hill, "He was later to act upon most unhappily." *Ibid.*, 54.

[4] David Starr Jordan, *The Days of a Man . . .* (2 vols.; Yonkers: World Book, 1922) II, 684-85.

that there was once a peace ship. At least we who sailed in 1915 did not decrease the love that was in the world." [5]

The disinclination of Americans to support stop-the-war movements did not mean that they were indifferent to the sufferings resulting from the holocaust. But organized American philanthropy was poorly prepared for large-scale fund-raising and relief programs. The American Red Cross in 1914 had only 150 chapters and 20,000 members despite the progress that had been made since its reorganization. It at once appealed to its constituent chapters to raise funds for relief. In accord with its tradition of neutrality and of providing medical aid and hospitalization to combatants it offered to help its sister societies in all belligerent countries. Mabel T. Boardman, the principal executive officer, proposed the dramatic step of chartering a vessel flying the Red Cross and American flags to transport hospital supplies, doctors, and nurses to each of the belligerent nations. [6]

On September 12, 1914, the *Red Cross*, referred to by the press as "the Mercy Ship," sailed from New York with 170 doctors and nurses and with equipment for establishing hospital bases. A considerable part of the press applauded the undertaking, though some critics declared that it was chiefly a means of advertising the Red Cross and that the aid given would inevitably be too slight to warrant the cost and the headaches involved in fitting American personnel into the medical services of the belligerent armed forces. Between the outbreak of the war and America's entrance in the spring of 1917 the Red Cross made 341 shipments of supplies valued at over a million and a half dollars of which all but $300,000 went to the Allied countries. The sixteen Red Cross hospital units with 75 surgeons and 225 nurses established in England, France, Belgium, Russia, Germany, Austria-Hungary, and Serbia provided aid for over 20,000 seriously sick and wounded. [7] Ernest Bicknell, a highly placed Red Cross official, writing ten years after the experience, suspected that the countries accepting the units found that "the accompanying responsibilities largely outweighed the benefits." [8] The conditions in the improvised hospitals under which the American doctors and

[5] *New York Times*, Dec. 5, 1940.
[6] Foster Rhea Dulles, *The American Red Cross: A History* (New York: Harper, 1950), 130-31.
[7] Herbert Hoover, *An American Epic, vol. II: Famine in Forty-Five Nations. Organization behind the Front, 1914-1923* (Chicago: Regnery, 1960), 190-91.
[8] Ernest Bicknell, *Pioneering with the Red Cross* (New York: Macmillan, 1935), 234.

nurses worked were "cramping and irritating": a former school of technology in Kiev, a theater in Germany, a casino in France, a tobacco warehouse in Serbia. On the other hand, the Red Cross units familiarized European army medical authorities with the high standards of American hospitals. Notwithstanding friction, the units also did something to develop a basis of mutual respect and understanding not only for the Red Cross but for the United States government in its later associations with its allies. And many diaries, letters, and reports of nurses indicate that despite obstacles these women often found their work "deeply satisfying." [9] The hospital units were given up after the first year, partly because the initial generosity of the local chapters had waned and partly because of difficulties imposed by the Allies in permitting the transit of supplies and personnel to the Central Powers.[10]

Meantime it was decided that the Red Cross might appropriately aid civilian sufferers in war-burdened countries. In cooperation with the Rockefeller Foundation the Red Cross undertook to combat a typhus epidemic in Serbia. On March 15, 1915, Dr. Richard P. Strong, professor of tropical medicine at Harvard, with a staff of fifty eminent physicians and sanitarians, sailed from New York on this errand of mercy. The success in checking the scourge was a major victory both for medicine and humanitarianism.[11]

The Rockefeller Foundation, still sensitive because of the suspicion that progressives in and out of Congress felt toward it at the time it sought a federal charter, had entered on a program of relief activity in Europe before the Serbian campaign against typhus. Shortly after the war broke out it chartered a ship and sent a cargo of food to Belgium. Concerned over living conditions among the civilian populations of both allied and central powers, the Foundation, in October, 1914, appointed a War Relief Commission. Its chairman, Dr. Wicklyffe Rose, director of the Foundation's International Health Commission, and its staff, which included Ernest Bicknell of the Red Cross, toured several European countries and reported on conditions and needs. The Commission also interested

[9] Portia B. Kernodle, *The Red Cross Nurse in Action, 1882-1948* (New York: Harper, 1949), 103, 105 ff.

[10] The Red Cross continued, however, to provide supplies to the hospitals of the belligerents. In addition to the Red Cross hospital units, several others, the largest being that organized and supported by Harvard, aided the medical services of the British and French armies.

[11] Ernest Bicknell, *In War's Wake, 1914-1935* (Washington: American National Red Cross, 1936), 178-79.

itself in the support of demonstration hospital units and in the plight of war prisoners. All in all, the Foundation played a significant role in relief activities, allocating a generous portion of the $22,000,000 it was to spend before the war was over, to this part of its war program. Looking back over this feverish early period in which the war took priority over all other activities. Dr. George E. Vincent, President of the Foundation, declared that the long, exhausting and frequently frustrating task was necessary and probably worthwhile. But he could not help thinking of the creative work which the money and effort thus expended might have resulted in had the Foundation been able to work in a world of reason and sanity.[12]

In addition to the Red Cross and the Rockefeller Foundation, three other well-established organizations representing diverse social groups developed overseas relief programs during the years of neutrality. The Daughters of the American Revolution made over 450,-000 items consisting of surgical supplies, hospital garments and knitted wear for the Red Cross and other organizations: American, British, and French. The DAR also contributed in cash more than $400,000 to agencies engaged in relief work. In the autumn of 1914 the Christian Science Church organized a War Relief Committee which raised over $100,000 for the needy, regardless of religious affiliation, in Germany, England, France, and countries in eastern Europe. At the other end of the social spectrum the Salvation Army under the vigorous leadership of Commander-in-Chief Evangeline C. Booth appealed for old linen which was washed, sterilized and rolled into more than a million bandages. Its members operated ambulances in France, set up "huts" for rest and recreation, and established homes for destitute children.[13]

These established organizations which developed relief programs worked closely with the *ad hoc* agencies that were set up to meet pressing needs. Two of these owed their inspiration and success to Myron Herrick, American Ambassador to France. This Cleveland lawyer, banker, and railroad magnate was instrumental in convert-

[12] Raymond B. Fosdick, *The Story of the Rockefeller Foundation* (New York: Harper, 1952), 28; Bicknell, *In War's Wake*, x, xi, 1-2, 12-14; *Commercial and Financial Chronicle* XCIX (Nov. 14, 1914), 1408.

[13] Hoover, *An American Epic*, II, 224-27, 233-35; Herbert A. Wisbey, *Soldiers without Swords: A History of the Salvation Army in the United States* (New York: Macmillan, 1955); Evangeline Booth and Grace Livingston Hill, *The War Romance of the Salvation Army* (Philadelphia: Lippincott, 1919).

ing the American Hospital in Paris into a "military ambulance," the French term for an emergency war hospital. At Herrick's instance well-to-do Americans in Paris shouldered responsibility for contributing or for obtaining from friends in the States the $400,000 necessary to expand and maintain the hospital for a year. It was said that every American in Paris worked, subscribed, and got others to give to the hospital.

The American Ambulance Hospital fathered the American Ambulance Field Service, which attracted such medical leaders as Crile of Cleveland and Cushing of Boston. Impressed by the reputation of the American work, the British ordered that all badly wounded officers be sent to the "Ambulance" to the limit of its capacity.[14] The success of the work depended not only on Herrick and the American colony in Paris, especially the Reverend Samuel N. Watson of the American Church of the Holy Trinity,[15] but on generous contributions including, among others, those of Mr. and Mrs. John Drexel and Mrs. Harry Payne Whitney. James Stillman turned over his large Paris home as an auxiliary to the American Ambulance.[16]

Soon after the outbreak of the war, organizations of almost every imaginable kind were formed in America to send aid to the suffering in Europe, especially in France and Belgium. Relief societies of Americans in France also sprang into action. Confusion threatened as huge sums and thousands of packages reached the American Chamber of Commerce and the American Embassy in Paris, which were unprepared to deal with such matters. Having in mind the need of making sure that the relief funds and supplies reached those most in need of them, that those who had given their money be protected, and that the good name of the United States be safeguarded, Herrick proposed, early in November, 1914, that the Americans who had helped repatriate tens of thousands of stranded fellow countrymen form a clearing house to handle American contributions efficiently. With the approval of the Paris and Washington governments, the group organized the American Relief Clearing House. It secured the promise of the French Line to transport provisions across the

---

[14] Thomas Bentley Mott, *Myron T. Herrick, Friend of France* (Garden City: Doubleday, Doran, 1929), 133-42, 191-92.

[15] Samuel N. Watson, *Those Paris Years: With the World at Cross-Roads* (Chicago, New York: Fleming H. Revell, 1926), 218 ff.

[16] *New York Times*, March 16, 17, 1918. Stillman also sent his check for $200,000 to the French Ambassador in Washington to be used for children of members of the Legion of Honor who had died for France.

seas, of the French government to admit them customs-free, and of the French railroads to transport them to specified distributing points. The Clearing House straightway began to coordinate and systematize relief, to keep careful records and to issue receipts, and to cooperate with local French committees and officials at the receiving end. As the work expanded, the Clearing House operated through special committees, dealing with public relations, transportation, and distribution. On one occasion Mr. Barbour, of the public relations committee, wrote 13,000 personal letters to Americans, especially to manufacturers, who responded with liberal shipments of greatly needed shoes, shirts, lints, and textiles.[17]

Herrick saw that organization in America was as necessary as it was in France. At his suggestion a group of prominent financial and industrial leaders in New York organized the War Relief Clearing House for France and her Allies. A. Barton Hepburn of the Chase National Bank acted as chairman. The officers included such well-known people as R. L. Bacon and Cornelius Vanderbilt, but the big burden was carried by Charles A. Coffin, creator and president of the General Electric Company.[18] The War Relief Clearing House received contributions in cash and kind from over 6,000 American organizations in addition to the 300 chapters of the Red Cross. The New York Farmers Association on one occasion contributed twenty-five plows and the same number of harrows, reapers, horserakes, binders and mowers, as well as 1,500 shovels and hayrakes—not many in view of the need but a welcome gift. Other organizations gave dried fruit, flour, condensed milk, sugar, clothing, linen, blankets, medicines, surgical instruments, artificial limbs, toys, and provisions for the sick and convalescent. In all, the French Line transported across the seas 95,769 cases which, at ordinary freight rates, made the Company's contribution total $1,413,670.

To stimulate giving, groups organized bazaars and theatricals, sponsored lectures on invaded France and Belgium, and showed war films. Every donor received a thank you, even those who gave as little as fifty cents. "Why not?", asked Mr. Scott of the Paris office. "The giver took the trouble to send his half-dollar—and his whole heart." [19] When the committees were absorbed into the Red Cross

[17] Percy Mitchell, *The American Relief Clearing House* (Paris: Herbert Clarke, ca. 1922), 6 ff.; Whitney Warren, *American Charity in France: What Has Been Done, What Remains to Be Done* (Boston: 1916), 8 ff.

[18] Mott, *Myron F. Herrick*, 240.

[19] Mitchell, *The American Relief Clearing House*, 49-50.

and the larger governmental organizations at the time the United States entered the war in the spring of 1917, the Clearing House in Paris had received and distributed in cash some 12,000,000 francs and goods in kind to the value of over 74,000,000 francs.[20]

The Clearing Houses equipped sanatoriums for the tubercular and the maimed, re-established peasants on the land, provided sewing for widows in *ouvroirs*, and took care of orphans. It brought food and clothing to the poor and hungry, medicine and dressings to the sick and wounded, supplies of all sorts for the homeless. And it did this efficiently and without condescension. Its staff was animated by the sense that it was a privilege to give and to serve, that what was done was only a slight counterbalance for the prosperity the war was bringing to an America which, in the eyes of many, ought to be fighting for the cause for which France stood.

Poincaré could with good grace sum up a widely held French attitude. "Never will France forget," he declared, "the bounties she received in the gloomy hours of war from a multitude of American friends. The crusade of Charity preceded the military crusade; benevolence came to our aid even before the birth of our brotherhood of arms. In the first days of hostilities, the United States turned spontaneously to France, attacked and invaded: and never in the world, within memory of man, was there such an outflow of sympathy and solidarity. Neither distance nor the ocean could prevent the hearts of our two peoples from feeling closely drawn together." [21] The French exponent of power politics was in a sentimental mood, but it was nonetheless true that the value of American material contributions, channeled through the Clearing House, was immensely enhanced in French eyes by reason of the spirit of the givers and of the volunteers who stimulated, organized, and administered the program.

The most extensive, ingenious, and statesmanlike relief program during the period of American neutrality was, however, that for Belgium. The plight of 9,000,000 Belgians, subjected to German military rule and unable by reason of the Allied blockade to import the food on which the lives of their highly industrialized economy depended, was indeed desperate. American relief work began as a

[20] *Ibid.*, 61; Watson, *Those Paris Years*, 247.
[21] Foreword by M. Raymond Poincaré in Mitchell, *The American Relief Clearing House*, [ix].

response to the necessity of repatriating Americans, a task performed by Minister Brand Whitlock and three American engineers and business men resident in Brussels, D. Heineman, William Hulse, and Millard Shaler. After taking care of their fellow countrymen, the group turned to the Belgians. A committee which included three Americans, the Spanish Ambassador, and M. Ernest Solvay, Belgium's richest citizen, secured permission from the Germans to bring in an emergency purchase from Holland. The committee then sent Shaler to England to make additional purchases. Finding the British unwilling to permit food to move into Belgium lest it be used to feed the German army of occupation, Shaler turned to Ambassador Walter Hines Page and to Herbert Hoover, who had just finished a volunteer job of supervising the repatriation of his fellow countrymen caught in the war zones. The American government took the matter up with Berlin, which promised to permit food brought into Belgium through Holland to be used for civilians only.

After considerable negotiation the British agreed to permit food to enter Holland on condition that the Americans as neutrals supervise its distribution among Belgian civilians. A new organization for this purpose was formed which in due course became known as the Commission for Belgian Relief. Hoover resigned a $100,000 a year job to take charge of the work, paid for the expenses of the "delegates" out of his own pocket to the extent of $35,000 a year, and gave up the dearest ambition of his life, that of becoming president of Stanford University. The trustees held the post open as long as possible but he did not feel he could desert the work in hand.[22]

On October 16, 1914, Minister Brand Whitlock cabled President Wilson from Brussels that "in two weeks the civil population in Belgium, already in misery, will face starvation." The Commission on Belgian Relief lost no time in appealing to the English-speaking world in general and to the United States in particular for public charity. New relief committees sprang up all over the States. By November 14, 1914, Hoover could report to Brussels that the Commission, with the help of virtually the whole American press, had con-

[22] Brand Whitlock, *Belgium: A Personal Narrative* (2 vols.; New York: Appleton, 1919) I, 398 ff.; Vernon Kellogg, *Fighting Starvation in Belgium* (Garden City: Doubleday Page, 1918), 19 ff. and "The Authentic Story of Belgian Relief," *World's Work* XXXIV (June, 1917), 169-76; Herbert Hoover, *Memoirs, vol. I: Years of Adventure, 1874-1920* (New York: Macmillan, 1951), 152 ff.; Allan Nevins, ed., *The Letters and Journals of Brand Whitlock* (2 vols.; New York: Appleton-Century, 1936), II, 240; Frank Surface and Raymond L. Bland, *American Food in the World War and Reconstruction Period* (Stanford: Stanford University Press, 1921).

ducted an "enormous propaganda" on the subject of the Belgian people. "We have cabled to all associations of whom we could hear, stimulating them as to position. We have cabled to the governors of every state asking them to see that such an association was set up in their territory. . . ." [23]

The response was heartening: the San Francisco and Seattle Chambers of Commerce collected enough money to buy 5,000 tons of foodstuffs and to charter ships to send them to Rotterdam. The Philadelphia Belgian Relief Committee, in cooperation with the *Ladies Home Journal*, dispatched the *Thelma* with a cargo of 2,900 tons of cereals. The Rockefeller Foundation dispatched two vessels each carrying 4,000 tons of food. The publishers organized the Dollar Christmas Fund, which collected $43,000 before the end of 1914 and improved its record so that in 1917 it collected $100,000 for Belgian children. A Woman's Division of the Commission was organized in New York which enlisted the support of women's clubs all over the country. Until the pressure became too great late in the year, railroads shipped contributions eastward free of charge, and the leading express companies gave the Commission a two-thirds reduction of carrying charges.[24] By December 19 the veteran in such matters, William Edgar, editor of the *Northwestern Miller*, had in hand 70,000 barrels of flour. The cargo which sailed on December 28 as a result of Edgar's labors was valued at $500,000.[25]

By the spring of 1915 public interest had sagged but Hoover refused to listen to a suggestion that the appeals for charity be discontinued. The DAR made a wide appeal for funds, raising over $150,000 and receiving the personal thanks of Queen Elizabeth. The mining engineers of the country organized the Belgian Kiddies, Ltd., and collected $98,000 to feed 10,000 Belgian children for a year. In a similar campaign the Rocky Mountain Club, another body of engineers, raised some $280,000. In 1916 a newly organized Commission for Belgian Relief Committee in Greater New York pledged itself for the support of 500,000 children in Liege, Limbourg, Luxembourg, and Namur; a Pennsylvania Committee adopted Antwerp province;

[23] George I. Gay and H. H. Fisher, eds., *Public Relations of the Commission for Relief in Belgium: Documents* (2 vols.; Stanford: Stanford University Press, 1929), I, 12-36.

[24] *Ibid.*, I, 37; II, 282.

[25] William C. Edgar, *The Millers' Belgian Relief Movement 1914-1915: Final Report of Its Director* (Minneapolis: Northwestern Miller, 1915); Edgar, *How Belgium Is Fed: The Work of Saving a Brave Nation from Starvation* (London: National Committee for Relief in Belgium, 1915).

and the New England Belgian Relief Fund undertook to supply an extra daily meal to 20,000 children in Louvain. Similar committees in Michigan, Ohio, and New Jersey adopted Belgian communes. The New York Chamber of Commerce enlisted itself in the Commission's 1917 campaign for Belgian children and collected $69,625. The Commission realized $119,000 as its share from a great Allied Bazaar in New York in June, 1916. Bazaars in Boston and Chicago yielded smaller sums. Catholic children and their parents contributed $77,000 to the Cardinal Gibbons Fund. The *Literary Digest* ultimately added over $600,000 to the Belgian relief campaign.[26]

There were some large contributions of several hundred thousand dollars. Edward S. Harkness gave over $300,000 and the Cameron Forbes Fund was notable not only in munificence but for designating its money for helping families in special need. But most of the contributions, representing millions of individuals, were in small sums. Thus girls in a charity home in Cooperstown, New York, each sent one dollar each month. Children in a country school near Montara lighthouse on the Pacific Coast ripped open their penny savings banks, and brought home-made jams; their teacher, a young girl, took the contribution in a buggy forty miles through a storm in order to deposit it at the California committee's office in San Francisco. In one Indiana town a druggist sent a dollar a week for two years. In another, a country grocer dispatched a fixed percentage of his profits. One man, having no money, sold a gold watch, a family heirloom, in order to help some starving family.[27]

In summing up experiences in fund raising, Hoover wrote that "the only real fruitful method of securing what we want is through strong decentralized committee organization. The thing which produces money and material is the personal interest and solicitation of people of standing in each community."[28] This type of organization was realized increasingly after 1915. When the United States entered the war in the spring of 1917, most organized efforts to raise funds for the Commission ceased, but a few committees continued to be active until the armistice.

The total cash donations contributed in the United States for Belgium totaled $6,051,860. Gifts in kind, principally provisions and clothing, added up to $28,469,167.[29] This amounted to a per-capita

[26] Gay and Fisher, eds., *Relief in Belgium* II, 246, 272 ff., 281 ff., 290-309.
[27] *Ibid.*, II, 235-309.
[28] *Ibid.*, II, 269.
[29] *Ibid.*, II, 309.

contribution of slightly over ten cents. Of the $52,000,000 charity given in all countries, the American share was over $34,500,000. The per-capita contribution of Canada was twenty-two cents, of the United Kingdom, nine cents, and of Australia, $1.34. New Zealand, with a per-capita average of $2.29, held the record.[30]

At first the Commission assumed that the entire Belgian population would have to be supported by publicly subscribed charity. Actually, in the end, this amounted to only 5.8 per cent of the total funds which the Commission handled. The Belgians wanted to help themselves, and Hoover helped them to do it. Subsidies from the British and French governments, the use of Belgian government deposits abroad, and, after 1917, American government loans, together with economic measures of exchange and the stabilization of Belgian currency, greatly narrowed the application of public charity to the Belgians who were too destitute to pay for food and clothing. Thus almost from the start the Commission relied on government subventions and on Belgian assets and loans as well as on world charity to carry on the provisioning of all Belgium and the work of pure benevolence for those unable to buy the food and provisions which the Commission shipped into the occupied country by way of Holland.

Americans often failed to understand that Belgium was standing the great part of Belgian relief, thinking that it all came from American contributions.[31] It is true, however, that Belgium would have starved without the brilliant help of Hoover and his associates. But as Hoover himself realized, Belgian participation in the relief work added immensely to its overall effectiveness. Enabling the Belgians to help themselves and to regain their feet economically was for Hoover a primary objective of the relief.[32]

Stimulating Americans to organize and give, persuading the British Cabinet to grant subventions to the Commission, and enabling the Belgian exile government in Le Havre to assume the great part of costs, were only a few of the things Hoover and the forty Americans associated with him did. It was necessary to buy over five million tons of food and provisions in competition with the Allied and neu-

[30] Kellogg, *Fighting Starvation in Belgium*, 98; Gay and Fisher, eds., *Relief in Belgium*, II, 297. Kellogg, who worked with the Commission from 1915 to 1918, states that the total amount of private charity from all countries was $30,000,000, of which the American contribution was $10,000,000: Kellogg, *Fighting Starvation in Belgium*, 29.

[31] Bicknell, *In War's Wake*, 60 ff.

[32] Gay and Fisher, eds., *Relief in Belgium*, II, 268.

tral governments, and to transport this in chartered ships over mine-ridden seas. It was necessary to be able to assure the British and French that none of the material would reach the German forces. The British were never entirely satisfied that the Americans were actually keeping supplies out of German hands. On one occasion, in the words of Brand Whitlock, Kitchener made to Hoover the "cynical and brutal" proposal that if the Belgians were let to starve it would require more German troops to subdue the revolutions that hunger would prompt. Hoover told Asquith bluntly: "You have America's sympathy only because America feels pity for the suffering Belgians," and threatened to send a cable to America which would end "the last vestige of pity for England" unless authorities cooperated fully with the Commission. After this and a famous interview with Lloyd George, he got what he wanted.[33]

On their part, the Germans were suspicious of the Commission and at times its continued operation in Belgium seemed to be threatened. The military, regarding everyone connected with relief work as an interloper or spy, was utterly incapable of appreciating the work the Americans were doing. "What do you Americans get out of this?" asked one German official of Hoover. The American engineer looked him squarely in the face and replied, "It is absolutely impossible for you Germans to understand that one does anything from pure humanitarian, disinterested motives, so I shall not attempt to explain it to you."[34]

Troubles did not end with the British and the Germans. To make matters worse, the Spanish Ambassador, who was nominally cooperating with the Commission and who did not like Hoover, tried to secure as much credit as he could for himself.[35] Even some of the Belgian officials proved difficult. One official complained that Hoover's "college boys" rode about in Belgian cars, lived in chateaux, and enjoyed themselves, an ungracious and hardly accurate charge. Hoover had also come into conflict years before in China with Emile Francqui, Belgian banker and head of the Comité National. The friction first manifested long ago persisted in the relations of the two men and caused Hoover often to seek out Brand Whitlock, American Minister to Belgium, and there unburden himself of his troubles. "Human nature," Whitlock wrote sadly in his journal after

[33] Nevins, ed., *Brand Whitlock*, I, 226, II, 77-78.
[34] *Ibid.*, II, 98-99.
[35] *Ibid.*, II, 240.

one such visit, "is very rife in the relations between C.R.B. and the Comité National." But he accepted it philosophically with the feeling that "to be sure gratitude is rare, and obligation hard to endure." [36]

Yet the Commission could carry on its work only because of the devotion and competence of most of the local committees of the Belgians and of the officers of the communes, and, as operations were extended into occupied France, of similar committees and officers there. All this involved on the part of Hoover and the forty Americans working with him talents of a high order, including an ability to work with others in a situation making for jangled nerves and sustained tension. Administrative skill was tested on every hand. This latter included the difficult and delicate task of inaugurating and maintaining a rationing system and of getting food to those in need of it. That this was done, on the whole, in such a way as to minimize the sense of shame of the self-respecting citizens who in many cases had no money to pay for what was received, was an achievement of no mean proportion. And on the part of Hoover himself the job involved remarkable skill in balancing humanitarian considerations with tangled international politics. To his credit Hoover emerged from the assignment an important national and world figure.[37]

Testimony on the part of the Belgians and French of appreciation for what the Commission did is abundant. One example must represent a body of opinion from which many instances might be chosen. Madame Saint-René Taillandier emphasized the modesty of both the leadership and personnel of the Commission. "It always touched us when you tried to avoid our thanks and when you told us how well the Belgians and the French in the invaded districts had seconded you, and how during their frightful ordeal they had proved the truth of the proverb, 'Help thyself, and heaven will help thee.' " [38]

During the period of neutrality the Commission for Belgian Relief overshadowed all other American philanthropic enterprises on the war scene, including the Clearing House and the Rockefeller

---

[36] *Ibid.*, II, 261-62.

[37] Vernon Kellogg, "The Authentic Story of Belgian Relief," *World's Work* XXXIV (June, July, August, 1917), 169-75, 264-85, 405-12; Introduction by Herbert Hoover in Charlotte Kellogg, *Women of Belgium: Turning Tragedy into Triumph* (New York, London: Funk and Wagnalls, 1917), vii-xviii.

[38] Madame Saint-René Taillandier, *The Soul of the "C.R.B.": A French View of the Hoover Relief Work*, trans. Mary C. Jones (New York: Scribner's Sons, 1919), vi-vii.

Foundation. But the intense pro-Ally sympathy in many quarters found expression also in more than a score of smaller organizations. Women of means and social position took prominent part in many of these. Others represented a special interest, such as organizations of writers, artists, and actors for the relief of foreign colleagues in need. Many rested on state and local subsidiaries. Some were affiliated with related British, French, and Belgian groups. At least one, the American Women's Hospitals, organized by the war service committee of the National Medical Women's Association, entered the field in France, Serbia, Russia, and Roumania because its members felt that male prejudice against women doctors deprived these of a chance to serve.[39]

Broadly speaking, the relief agencies fell into one of three main groups. One aimed at publicizing the needs of sufferers in the Allied countries and in raising money for general relief purposes. The leading example was the National Allied Relief Committee, organized in New York in July, 1915, which coordinated the activities of various groups by appealing for funds and working with related societies. Shortly after America's entrance into the war the Committee had raised more than $1,000,000.[40]

A second group of relief agencies was aimed especially at providing aid to wounded and maimed soldiers. Examples were California House, a home in London for the re-education of Belgian mutilated war victims and sustained largely by contributions from the state whose name it bore.[41] Another was the Committee for Men Blinded in Battle. Still another, the American Fund for French Wounded, was inspired by Mrs. Benjamin Lathrop who worked, with a personal touch to all she did, in the Paris depot of the agency, early and late, sick or well. This depot was sustained by five hundred branches which shipped a million dollars worth of articles needed in French military hospitals. Among other Americans who helped Mrs. Lathrop were Gertrude Stein and Alice B. Toklas. The Stein version is worth quoting:

"One day we were walking down the rue des Pyrmides and there was a ford car being backed up by the street by an american girl and on the

[39] Esther Pohl Lovejoy, *Certain Samaritans* (rev. ed.; New York: Macmillan, 1933), *passim*.

[40] Ida C. Clarke, *American Women and the World War* (New York, London: Appleton, 1918), 412.

[41] John Van Schaick, *The Little Corner Never Conquered: The Story of the American Red Cross War Work for Belgium* (New York: Macmillan, 1927), 197.

car it said American Fund for the French Wounded. . . . We went over and talked to the american girl and then interviewed Mrs. Lathrop, the head of the organization. She was enthusiastic, and she said, get a car. But where, we asked. From America, she said. But how, we said. Ask somebody, she said, and Gertrude Stein did, she asked her cousin and in a few months the ford car came . . . We had a consultation with Mrs. Lathrop and she sent us off to Perpignan, a region with a good many hospitals that no american organisation had ever visited . . . We did finally arrive at Perpignan and began visiting hospitals and giving away our stores and sending word to headquarters if we thought that they needed more than we had. At first it was a little difficult but soon we were doing all we were to do very well. We were also given quantities of comfort-bags and distributing these was a perpetual delight, it was like a continuous Christmas." [42]

Dominant though France and Belgium were in American philanthropic minds, Serbia, Roumania, and Russia also received help through the Serbian Relief Committee, the American Ambulance in Russia, and the Russian War Relief Committee.

The American Women's Hospitals established dispensaries and hospitals in several allied countries for general medicine and for acute convalescent cases. Other agencies in this category were the National Surgical Dressings Committee which in the first two years of its existence sent 18,000,000 surgical dressings abroad. The list also includes the Lafayette Fund, whose trench kits proved a godsend to many a weary *poilu*, the American Field Service, the War Heroes Fund, and the American Committee supporting *Le Bien-Être du Blessé*.

In addition to general relief and help for specific groups, there was a third category: relief to needy families in Allied countries, particularly to orphans, to civilian refugees, and to victims of tuberculosis. To be sure, some organizations, such as the Roumanian Relief Committee of America and the Serbian Relief Committee, bridged the two categories, ministering to those in need, whether military or civilian. And some organizations, which at first concerned themselves only with the sick and wounded in the armed forces,

[42] Ruth Gaines, *Helping France: The Red Cross in the Devastated Area* (New York: Dutton, 1919), 48 ff., 135; George B. Ford, *Out of the Ruins* (New York, Century, 1919), 96 ff.; Clarke, *American Women and the World War*, 455; Gertrude Stein, *The Autobiography of Alice B. Toklas* (New York: Harcourt Brace, 1933), 207-08, 213, 217. After the war the French Government decorated both Stein and Toklas for their services.

spread their program to include civilians. This was true, for example, of the American Fund for French Wounded, whose Civilian Committee under Mrs. Dike re-established ruined homes in the devastated areas, where Gertrude Stein and Alice B. Toklas gave blankets, underclothing, and babies' booties to refugee families.

Of special importance was the Committee of Mercy established in October, 1914, with the blessing of President Wilson. Shortly after our entrance into the war, it reported having collected more than $2,000,000 which had been used for the relief of noncombatants made destitute by the war. The Guthrie Society, an American agency for the relief of French orphans, began its work at Paris headquarters in 1916 and by the fall of the next year was helping over 18,000. The Fatherless Children of France, the American Aid for Homeless Belgian Children, and Edith Wharton's Children of Flanders, all found work to do and appreciation of work done. The New York Committee of the *Secours National*, the chief French civilian relief agency, raised $400,000. Mrs. Wharton's American Hostels for Refugees and Mrs. Nina Larrey Duryea's Duryea War Relief, which helped 70,000 refugees with money, clothing, and other supplies, owed their successful records to the dedication of their founders.

The Polish Victims Relief Fund Committee managed to raise $2,000,000, thanks in part to the heroic work of the Paderewskis in America. The Serbian and Roumanian relief committees, with smaller resources, found sympathetic donors both in and out of the Serbian-American and Roumanian-American centers. Since many of these agencies continued operations after the United States entered the war and did not report intake periodically, it is impossible to say how much was raised during the period of neutrality: it seems safe to put the estimate at about $10,000,000.

While the plight of Belgium and France brought forth the most extensive relief efforts during the neutral years, the 8,000,000 Americans of German and Austrian-Hungarian descent naturally turned their attention to the needs of the fatherlands. German-language newspapers, churches, and recreational societies took the initiative in arranging concerts, bazaars, sewing bees, and theatrical performances, and individuals of course also gave. It is estimated that $2,000,000 was spent for the relief of war victims, for milk for babies, and for the American hospital in Munich. All the funds were administered by the national Red Cross and other relief organizations in Central Europe.[43]

Before the attention of the two and a half million American Jews was drawn to the plight of their coreligionists in Germany and, especially, in the German-occupied territories of Russia, word came of the desperate situation of some 60,000 Jews in Palestine. In August, 1914, Louis Marshall and Jacob Schiff, prominent officials in the American Jewish Committee and well-known New York philanthropists, received a cable from Ambassador Henry Morgenthau in Constantinople warning that warring armies and the Anglo-French blockade of the eastern Mediterranean were cutting off the opportunities of Palestine Jews to export their fruits and depriving the elderly among them from the remittances from their families in the West. The $50,000 which he declared to be imperatively necessary was quickly speeded to Palestine.[44]

At the same time came news of the desperate situation of millions of Jews in the areas of Poland and Russia occupied by German and Austrian troops. Robbed by the armies of both contestants and driven from their homes, these unfortunates, long accustomed to discrimination and pogroms, were now in danger of annihilation from hunger and disease. Their own charitable organizations and community life were so thoroughly disrupted that their very existence depended on outside help.

It was clear that this was more than a temporary emergency, that substantial and sustained aid was indicated. In October, 1914, the Union of Orthodox Congregations organized the Central Committee for the Relief of Jews. This group represented for the most part the less assimilated and relatively recent Jewish immigrants from Eastern Europe. Shortly thereafter the Ameircan Jewish Committee issued a call for joint action. The American Jewish Committee had been organized in 1906 to defend the civil rights of Jews everywhere and had enlisted the support of well-to-do Jews, largely German in background and given to thinking of themselves as assimilated Amer-

[43] Carl F. Wittke, *German-Americans and the World War* (Ohio Historical Collections, vol. V; Columbus: Ohio State Archaeological and Historical Society, 1936), 3-44.

[44] Henry Morgenthau, *All in a Life-Time* (Garden City: Doubleday, Page, 1922), 211 ff.; Joseph C. Hyman, *Twenty-Five Years of American Aid to Jews Overseas* (rev. ed.; New York: Jewish Publication Society of America, 1939), 9-10; Morris R. Werner, *Julius Rosenwald: The Life of a Practical Humanitarian* (New York, London: Harper, 1939), 174.

icans. The call resulted in the organization of the American Jewish Relief Committee, headed by Louis Marshall, Cyrus Sulzberger, and Felix Warburg. Presently, in the interest of efficiency, the Central Relief Committee and the American Jewish Relief Committee, without giving up fund-raising activities, established the Joint Distribution Committee to dispense funds. A few months later the People's Relief Committee, representing for the most part the new immigrants of a secular and labor orientation, also joined the Joint Distribution Committee. While organized to help Jews, the JDC announced that it stood ready to aid all races and creeds in areas in which it worked, and that its objectives were humanitarian rather than political.[45]

In an organization made up of differing backgrounds and outlook, conflict and overlapping were inevitable. In the words of one participant this was sometimes dramatic, sometimes commonplace. Yet a reasonable degree of cooperation was achieved. This was in large part the result of the leadership of Felix M. Warburg, a cultivated, German-born member of the banking firm of Kuhn, Loeb and Company. Tactful, wise, charming, Warburg possessed an amazing ability to persuade men of different backgrounds to work together.

Despite the deep-rooted tradition in Jewry of mutual aid in time of need, it was not easy to raise among no more than 500,000 Jewish families money to meet in even small part the vast needs of co-religionists abroad. In an article in the *Menorah Journal* in 1915 Jacob Schiff informed readers that it was hardly possible to exaggerate the horrors that Jews were enduring in the war-stricken countries. Three million dollars, Schiff went on, were immediately and desperately needed for rudimentary relief: American Jews had thus far given only a third that much. "We Jews," the great and generous banker concluded, "must give until it hurts, until it really becomes self-sacrifice." [46]

In response to such appeals thousands of men and women gave their energy, time, brains, and money to the task at hand. One of the fund-raisers, Henry H. Rosenfelt, observed that the agonies of detail and conflict seemed overwhelming. On the other hand, there

[45] Herbert Agar, *The Saving Remnant: An Account of Jewish Survival* (New York: Viking, 1960) is a history of the Joint Distribution Committee and its work.
[46] Jacob H. Schiff, "The Jewish Problem Today," *Menorah Journal* I (April, 1915), 75-79.

was also sacrifice and brotherly effort, a spirit which weakened fear, hatred, prejudice, and suspicion.[47]

The drives were nation-wide. In many cities donors contributed sums varying from $5,000 to $25,000. But all eyes looked to New York, the population center of American Jewry. At a great meeting in Carnegie Hall on December 21, 1915, the chairman, Louis Marshall, announced that from the start of the war to the moment at hand, American Jews had contributed to the relief of unfortunate victims of war and persecution a million and a half dollars. But this, he quickly added, was a mere drop in the bucket. Then Dr. Judah L. Magnes, rabbi of the leading Reformed temple in New York, a learned scholar and a pacifist, movingly and graphically described conditions of Jews abroad. His eloquence was magnetic. Never in the history of Carnegie Hall, the *New York Times* reported, had there been such enthusiasm and spontaneous generosity; the whole audience of 2,500 literally jumped up and rushed forward to give cash, jewelry, and personal checks. The announcement that Schiff, Rosenwald, Nathan Straus, and the Guggenheim brothers were subscribing $100,000 each was hailed with an enthusiastic outburst that prompted further pledges among those present. Before the meeting was over nearly a million dollars had been raised.[48]

But this was only a beginning. Under the leadership of the new campaign director Joseph Billikopf, a goal of $10,000,000 was set for 1916. President Wilson proclaimed January 27 of that year as Jewish Relief Day. The take reached a million dollars, Jews and Gentiles contributing. Billikopf persuaded Julius Rosenwald to give $100,000 for every $1,000,000 given up to $10,000,000. The effect was electric. In the 1917 campaign five million dollars was raised in New York in ten days. In Chicago, Rosenwald, who at first favored merging Jewish war relief with the general effort to help war sufferers, contributed a second million dollars. During the war period Cyrus Adler estimated that he himself raised ten million dollars in Philadelphia.[49]

These gifts from wealthy Jews were paralleled by the self-sacrifice of ladies' clubs, professional groups, trade associations and labor unions. The rank and file in the United Hebrew Trades, the Amal-

---

[47] Henry H. Rosenfelt, *This Thing of Giving: The Record of a Rare Enterprise of Mercy and Brotherhood* (New York: Plymouth Press, 1924), 7-9.

[48] *New York Times*, Dec. 22, 1915.

[49] Werner, *Julius Rosenwald*, 174 ff., 183 ff.; Cyrus Adler, *I Have Considered the Days* (Philadelphia: Jewish Publication Society of America, 1941), 303-04.

gamated Clothing Workers of America, the Workmen's Circle, and the International Ladies' Garment Workers Union, some 500,000 individuals, gave one day's pay. The sustained intensity of the fund-raising drives has been vividly preserved in the account of Henry Rosenfelt, who hastened from city to city during the yearly drives and whose story of how $63,000,000 was raised to relieve the war-stricken Jews of Europe during and after the fighting is not only a testimony to the ways in which his venture into philanthropy yielded personal rewards "beyond price" but which also, especially in the account of the great non-sectarian drive opened in the spring of 1918, shows how this campaign did much to reduce prejudice and to change the attitude of Jews toward Gentile neighbors.[50]

Palestine received in war years from the JDC $2,257,000 of the $14,939,000 it disbursed. The first tangible help was the dispatch in 1916, at the suggestion of Henry Bernstein of the Jewish newspapers, *The Day* and the *American Hebrew*, of the USS *Vulcan* with a cargo of food and medicine for the Jews, Christians, and Moslems of the Holy Land. It was a heroic venture successfully accomplished.[51] A year later medical supplies were also sent. By this time local committees established on behalf of the Joint Distribution Committee were granting loans and extending cash relief, particularly to rabbis and scholars, providing aid for religious institutions, giving food to school children, and attempting to solve medical and sanitary problems in Palestine.[52]

In Europe itself the JDC put into the hands of local Jewish agencies the administration of relief in the form of clothing, food, and medical aid to the some 700,000 who fled or were deported from Poland and the Baltic provinces. When the United States entered the war in 1917, the JDC could no longer carry on relief in the fighting zones through indigenous Jewish agencies with which the Joint was affiliated. It did, however, arrange to have an agency in neutral Holland distribute funds. What was done in the war period itself, however inadequate in terms of need, proved a godsend to hundreds of thousands of helpless, hopeless, victimized Jews in central and eastern and southeastern Europe. And what was done was tangible

[50] *New York Times*, Nov. 25, 1918; Rosenfelt, *This Thing of Giving*, 29 ff.
[51] Louis H. Levin, lawyer and secretary of the Federated Jewish Charities of Baltimore, undertook this mission: Adler, *I Have Considered the Days*, 304.
[52] Moses A. Leavitt, *The JDC Story: Highlights of JDC Activities, 1914-1952* (New York: American Joint Distribution Committee, 1953), 7.

evidence of the growing responsibility that American Jews felt for desperate fellow believers across the seas. It was but the beginning of vast efforts in the years ahead.

The Jewish Joint Distribution Committee was not alone in its concern for the plight of victims of the upheavals of war in the Near East. Little information filtered through the Turkish censorship but enough did to give grave concern to those interested in the non-Moslem populations of the empire. The deep-seated suspicion that the Turks had long felt for these peoples—Greeks, Jews, Syrians and above all Armenians—resulted in a policy of deportation without destination, the destruction of villages, and all the old accompanying horrors of rape, famine and pestilence. The five hundred-odd Americans engaged in missionary, medical, and educational work in the Near East continued to operate as best they could the some forty schools, colleges, and hospitals, which became havens of refuge to the uprooted. With the help of natives, of British, German, Swiss, and Danish coworkers, and with the invaluable aid of the United States foreign service officers, American missionaries organized committees. Using money borrowed from fleeing Armenian merchants and what other funds they could lay their hands on, the relief committees provided such food, clothing, and medical treatment as were permitted by limited resources and by the disturbed conditions in Turkey and Persia, into which Armenian and other persecuted refugees had fled.

In the United States itself the first organized efforts, apart from those of the Jewish Joint Distribution Committee, to give succor to the non-Moslem peoples centered on Syria, Palestine, and Persia. The Palestine-Syrian Committee, officered by Talcott Williams, Oscar Straus, Rabbi Stephen Wise, and Stanley White, got under way in December, 1914. By the spring of 1915 the Jews had raised $100,000, earmarked for Palestine, the Syrians $20,000 for their homeland. But the Committee broadened its services by transmitting to Syria some $155,000 which Syrian-Americans had contributed for relatives in the Near East. After the Turks and Kurds invaded Persia early in 1915, the Persian Relief Committee, with Robert Speer as chairman, was formed. Competition with fund-raising agencies for European relief proved sharp, and even with the help of a $20,000 grant from the Rockefeller Foundation, the Committee was able by the following

October to send only $70,000 to alleviate refugee suffering in Persia.[53]

Having protested in vain to the Turkish government against the atrocities, Ambassador Morgenthau on September 2, 1914, cabled to the State Department that the "destruction of the Armenian race in Turkey is progressing rapidly." He urged the formation of a committee to provide means for saving at least a remnant of these unfortunate people.[54]

On September 16 a meeting took place in the New York office of Cleveland Dodge, chairman of the board of trustees of Robert College and a well-known supporter of missionary and philanthropic enterprises in the Levant. The prominent men interested in the Near East who attended this meeting agreed that a temporary relief committee was needed and, adopting the name of the Committee on Armenian Atrocities, decided to raise $100,000, half of which was subscribed on the spot. The officers chosen—James L. Barton, Charles R. Crane, and Samuel Dutton—had no more idea than their associates that out of this *ad hoc* committee was to develop one of the most remarkable, long-term agencies engaged in overseas philanthropies. From the start Cleveland Dodge, who provided administrative costs, devoted time, thought, and resources to the enterprise. He had able and dedicated associates. On November 20, in response to the condition stipulated by the Rockefeller Foundation, the Committee on Armenian Atrocities, the Syrian-Palestine Relief Committee, and the Persian War Relief Fund, amalgamated to form the American Committee for Armenian and Syrian Relief, the name retained until Congress chartered the Near East Relief in 1919.

The Committee organized in Dodge's office authorized its officers to seek permission from the State Department to study the files of its foreign service officers in the Near East, a permission readily given. Sifting this material, the Committee was able to publicize conditions about which even those interested in the Near East had been only vaguely aware. It was clear that hundreds of thousands of women and children were facing death from disease and hunger. One of the cases put before the public, *Ravished Armenia, the Story of Aurora Mardiganian,* made the general story concrete by describing what

[53] James L. Barton, *Story of the Near East Relief, 1915-1920* (New York: Macmillan, 1930), 15-16; Robert L. Daniel, "From Relief to Technical Assistance in the Near East, A Case Study: Near East Relief and Near East Foundation" (unpublished Ph.D. dissertation, University of Wisconsin, 1953), 7 ff.

[54] Henry Morgenthau, *Ambassador Morgenthau's Story* (Garden City: Doubleday, Page, 1918); *Papers Relating to the Foreign Relations of the United States,* 1915 (Washington: Govt. Printing Office, 1915), supplement, 988.

happened to a fourteen-year-old girl whom a military commandant demanded as a concubine: wandering, suffering, imprisonment, escape, recapture and rape, and final rescue by the relief committee. Much of the material in the widely read *Treatment of Armenians in the Ottoman Empire* (1917) by Viscount James Bryce was borrowed from the committee's files. The press gave widespread publicity to the committee's releases. Not always entirely fair to the Turks nor altogether objective, this material provided ammunition for speakers at innumerable mass meetings. Local committees organized to inform the public further and to canvass for funds.[55]

Before the end of the year 1915 the Committee had sent $176,929 for relief work in Persia, Turkey and the Russian Caucasus, into which many desperate Armenians had fled. Between October, 1915, and June, 1916, the Rockefeller Foundation's grants totaled $330,-000. The Red Cross and the Federal Council of Churches also contributed substantial sums, the religious press and the *Literary Digest* launched special fund-collecting programs, and churches, societies, and individuals gave despite the pull of other campaigns for overseas relief. Before the end of the year 1916, receipts amounted to $2,404,-000. Thanks to vigorous promotional campaigns this sum was doubled in 1917.[56]

Despite the anti-Turkish character of its publicity, the Committee made much of its neutral policy in its relations with belligerent governments and in the actual administration of relief. Relief was administered in some cases by American consuls, in most by doctors, nurses, teachers, and native assistants associated with mission hospitals, schools, and stations. Almost all of these men and women knew the languages of the area, were familiar with needs and conditions, and had acquired a good deal of experience in relief work during long residences in Turkey and Persia. Some ruined their health, some died of pestilence. The dedication and self-sacrifice of these relief workers rank them among the world's heroes.[57]

[55] Daniel, "From Relief to Technical Assistance in the Near East," 30 ff.
[56] Barton, *Near East Relief*, 409. In 1918 receipts doubled again, reaching $7,022,000.
[57] See, for examples, Ernest C. Partridge, "Mary Louise Graffam," *Armenian Affairs* I (Winter, 1949-50), 62-65 and "The Pensacola Party and Relief Work in Turkey," *Ibid.* (Summer and Fall, 1950), 293-97; Alice Shepard Riggs, *Shepard of Aintab* (New York: Interchurch Press, 1920); Grace H. Knapp, *The Tragedy of Bitlis* (New York: Fleming H. Revell, 1919); Margaret MacGilvary, *The Dawn of a New Era in Syria* (New York: Fleming H. Revell, 1920); Clarence D. Ussher, *An American Physician in Turkey* (Boston, New York: Houghton Mifflin, 1917), and Lovejoy, *Certain Samaritans*, 34 ff.

What was accomplished? The relief workers harbored starving, mutilated, and pestilence-stricken refugees in their compounds and hospitals and added new dispensaries to those already at hand. They opened refugee camps, set up workshops in which widows contributed to the support of themselves and children by spinning, weaving, and sewing, and operated soup kitchens. Hastily put together "homes" received the helpless aged and the abandoned orphans. Seeds were given to those whose land had been burned over; tracts were provided for the landless to cultivate. And plans took shape for further rehabilitation once the war was over. All these things were carried on in Turkey, Persia, Syria, and the Caucasus prior to America's entrance into the war. What was done was, of course, small in relation to need. But in view of the gargantuan nature of the problem, the achievement was almost superhuman.

With the entrance of the United States into the war in April, 1917, much of the American relief work overseas followed the patterns already worked out. This was true in the Near East. But new agencies, some inspired by deep religious conviction, such as the American Friends Service Committee, some by secular humanitarianism, such as the Smith College Relief Unit, entered the field of relief and rehabilitation.

Most important of all, of course, was the American Red Cross. The old leadership gave way to a new one composed of the great names in finance and industry, the directing body being the newly organized War Council, headed by Henry P. Davison of the J. Pierpont Morgan Company. A drive for membership and funds was undertaken and before the war was over the Red Cross increased its membership from 250,000 to almost a hundred times as many and its assets from $200,000 to a total intake of $400,000,000. In the first great drive the goal of $100,000,000 was readily reached, thanks not only to widespread smaller contributions but to one individual and many corporation gifts of $1,000,000. The Red Cross gave up all pretense of neutrality and became a nationalistic arm of the government.

By June, 1917, a commission, composed of eighteen experts and led by Grayson M. P. Murphy, a gifted organizer and a man able to make others like him, reached France. The commission at once bolstered sagging French morale by giving $1,000,000 to the French Red Cross and by rapidly building along the entire front a series of canteen and rest rooms for the discouraged soldiery. Steps were also taken to extend relief to the families of the French soldiers, to aid war refugees and the repatriated Frenchmen that German authorities had permitted to return to France, and to provide immediate medical help and visiting nurses' service for those among these groups who were in greatest need. Twenty-five civilian hospitals were established, and a program inaugurated for the treatment of the rapidly increasing number of victims of tuberculosis. Emergency hospitals were also built along the front, and base hospitals developed in both France and England. Meantime, warehouses filled with medical supplies, clothing, food, and building materials were strategically located with supporting automobile transport. All this was only the beginning of a vast program which resulted in the expenditure in France of $2,400,000 in the anti-tuberculosis campaign (which the Rockefeller Foundation took over), $3,000,000 for the assistance of needy children, $3,800,000 for the help of families of French combatants, and $9,800,000 for the relief of refugees.[58]

On establishing itself in France in the summer of 1917, the Red Cross took over the functions of the Clearing House. Backed by President Wilson's recommendation that all existing American relief agencies place themselves under the Red Cross, the commission planned to absorb those in the field and in the process of formation. But this plan did not work out. Many agencies which had pioneered in relief work during the neutrality period and which were supported by women of initiative and influence, did not want to lose their identities. A compromise was worked out by which some agencies such as the Secours Anglo-Americaine and the Guthrie Society gave up their names and separate sources of support while others, such as the Fund for French Wounded and the American Committee for Devastated France, became loosely affiliated. The new agencies, notably the Smith College Relief Unit and the American Friends Service Committee, which began active work in France in the early fall of 1917, worked closely with the Red Cross.[59]

In general the Red Cross allocated material to other agencies, to the older and newer American relief organizations, as well as to French and Allied groups. When conditions became acute and morale sank, the Red Cross entered directly into the work of service to the refugees, appointing a committee under Dr. Edward T. Devine and Homer Folks, leading social workers. The Department of Civil

[58] Dulles, *The American Red Cross*, 154, 177.
[59] Gaines, *Helping France*, 44 ff., 92-93.

Affairs, as the new subagency was called, worked with local committees and authorities in distributing food, clothing, utensils, furniture, and tools to refugees, aided in finding work for refugees and in establishing farmers on tracts of land they could cultivate, and located lodging for some 20,000 persons. Where no local committee existed, the Red Cross organized one and then worked through it.[60] The Red Cross itself assumed responsibility for caring for refugees in Paris. A children's bureau concerned itself with the nutritional and health problems of the young. The Reconstruction Research and Propaganda Service, organized by George Ford in March, 1917, and working in close collaboration with French technical authorities, set up standards of improved methods in building, sanitation, and town planning as guideposts for economic reconstruction.[61]

While all this was under way in France, commissions were established in Great Britain (chiefly for service to American troops), Belgium, Switzerland, Russia, Greece, Roumania, Serbia, Palestine and the Near East. The commission to Italy, which arrived during the grim winter of 1917-1918, provided hospital supplies, organized soup kitchens for refugees, distributed clothing and other needed material, and set up work shops that offered employment for needy women and children. The Red Cross mission which reached Petrograd in August, 1917, allocated medical supplies to Russian hospitals and distributed 450,000 cans of condensed milk to children. The job in Switzerland was largely one of helping refugees and prisoners of war. In Palestine and the Near East the relief activities which began in 1918 consisted chiefly of emergency work, providing medical supplies, and laying the groundwork for more extensive programs after the armistice. Some $64,000,000 was spent in the civilian relief work outside of France.[62]

Belief in the worth of the individual, in the importance of saving human lives, was undoubtedly the guiding ideal in all this work. The

[60] Ford, *Out of the Ruins*, 17 ff.; Homer Folks, *The Human Costs of the War* (New York: Harper, 1920), *passim.*

[61] Ford, *Out of the Ruins*, 230.

[62] Dulles, *The American Red Cross*, 187 ff. For special accounts see in addition to titles already cited Edward Hungerford, *With the Doughboy in France* (New York: Macmillan, 1920); Charles M. Bakewell, *The Story of the American Red Cross in Italy* (New York: Macmillan, 1920); Alfred Worcester, *American Red Cross Service in Switzerland, 1918-1919* (Boston: Four Seas, 1925); Henry Rushton Fairclough, *Warming Both Hands: The Autobiography of Henry Rushton including his experiences under the American Red Cross in Switzerland and Montenegro* (Stanford: Stanford University Press, 1941); George Buchanan Fife, *The Passing Legions* (New York: Macmillan, 1920).

paradox of working for this ideal among the Allies, while at the same time rejoicing over each military victory over the enemy, was not unrecognized. But the country was at war and the course seemed clear. Saving lives was thought of not only as a value in itself, but as a means to victory. Thus Lt. Col. John Van Schaick, Commissioner of the Red Cross to Belgium, emphasized the point that "the same reasons which impel us to clean up slums in peacetime impel us to deal effectively with refugees in wartime. Leaving aside all motives of brotherhood and humanity . . . refugees have to be cared for or they will get in the way of armies, block roads, create city slums, breed contagion which spreads to troops, and if maddened by hunger, start riots and take troops needed elsewhere to put them down." [63]

The guiding principles and pattern of organization worked out by the American Red Cross in the several countries in which it administered civilian as well as military relief, reflected the experience gained over the years in catastrophes at home. Every effort was made to reduce overhead expenses—thanks to a large amount of voluntary help, the Red Cross claimed that administrative costs amounted to only one per cent of expenditures. Also, much emphasis was put on organization. But the organization involved cooperation in an efficient way with local groups. It also involved the stimulation of self-help in such a fashion as to minimize a sense of dependency. The policy of helping the unfortunates help themselves so that the humblest person understood the plan which saved him from humiliation was, as one observer put, "recognized as the American way." [64]

With a hastily recruited personnel amounting by the end of the war to well over 6,000 in France alone, it was inevitable that the Red Cross should fail in many points of tact, etiquette, and understanding. To some Frenchmen it seemed to have the aggressiveness and pushing faults of American democracy itself.[65] One American critic, former Mayor Carter H. Harrison of Chicago, attributed much of the inefficiency and callousness he observed in the upper ranks of the personnel to the alleged fact that it was chosen by the big business men running the organization in Washington without reference to any consideration except favoritism or the recommendation of a

[63] Van Schaick, *The Little Corner Never Conquered*, 83-84.
[64] Gaines, *Helping France*, 72.
[65] *Ibid.*, v.

friend or a friend of a friend.[66] There was certainly much confusion resulting from the change of direction or decision at headquarters— tangles that became worse after the armistice. Nor was the ideal of cutting through red tape to meet unexpected emergencies and rapid shifts in a situation always realized.

But whatever complaints could legitimately be made about the Red Cross its work was genuinely appreciated. One must of course allow for rhetoric and public relations in trying to evaluate testimonies to the devotion, industry, efficiency, and humanity of the American Red Cross. Yet the testimonies probably represented appreciation beyond mere politeness or invitations for additional help. Two examples must speak for many others. Premier Orlando in addressing the Italian Parliament declared: "Our soil is stirred again with appreciation and admiration for the magnificent dash with which the American Red Cross has brought us powerful aid in our recent misfortune. We attribute great value to the cooperation which will be given us against the common enemy by the prodigious activity and by the exuberant and consistent force which are peculiar to the American people." [67] And a French woman who gave invaluable service in guiding the American Red Cross declared: "You have come here not only to help us win the war, but to share with us all our burdens, all our sufferings; those of the front and those of the trenches, and those also behind the lines. . . . All the victims of war have laid their problems before you, all our sorrows have found an echo in your hearts." [68]

Probably more weight should be given to what was said by local officials, priests, shopkeepers, and villagers. These did not usually write reports or articles or books. But directly and indirectly they expressed appreciation not only of the Red Cross but of emergency and reconstruction work undertaken by individuals or groups laboring in France either independently or in association with the Red Cross.

The efforts of individuals or small groups, in contrast to the prevailing large scale and organized approach to the problems of war, represented a traditional American type of philanthropy in which only the very well to do could, if so minded, indulge. Mrs. Crocker

[66] Carter H. Harrison, *With the American Red Cross in France* (Chicago: Seymour, 1947), 10, 12, 55-56, 254, 260, 262.
[67] Dulles, *The American Red Cross*, 189.
[68] Gaines, *Helping France*, 20.

and Miss Daisy Polk of California restored the completely destroyed village of Vitrimont in the Meurthe-et-Moselle. When George Ford visited it in October, 1916, half of the former inhabitants had returned to the tottering walls that had been their homes and looked with some amazement at the fifty workmen on the scene. Houses were rebuilt, baths constructed, electricity installed. The Americans had left, but the attitude of the villagers toward them was expressed in naming the principal street "la rue de Californie" and in making over to their benefactors any remuneration the French government might give: a tribute to the success of the Americans in doing what they did without cutting into the self-respect of the villagers.[69] Mrs. Whitney Warren of New York adopted Cocy-le-Chateau. Kate Gleason, who had won engineering honors for the innovations she made in the tool machine factory of her father, sponsored Septmont.[70] Miss Belle Skinner,[71] daughter of a public-spirited philanthropist in Holyoke, Massachusetts, adopted Hattonchâtel, an almost entirely ruined village. As houses were rebuilt she removed the manure piles from the fronts to hygienic storehouses in the rear. At a cost of a million dollars she built a school, town hall, public laundry, and modern water system. And all of this was done modestly and in a way to enlist the affection of those benefited.

Of the groups that volunteered to do needed work in France the Smith College Relief Unit was one of the best known. It developed from the suggestion made by Mrs. Harriet Boyd Hawes at a meeting of alumnae in Boston in April, 1917: let the College extend to a wider stage the concept of service in which it pioneered in founding the College Settlement in New York, let it add to its tradition of individual culture the larger value of public service. Presently the forty-two Smith College Alumnae Clubs scattered over the country were raising money for the Smith College Relief Unit. Its seventeen initial members—two physicians and three nurses, with social workers, chauffeurs, child care experts, and builders—arrived in France in August, 1917. The Unit was given the task of helping

69 Ford, *Out of the Ruins*, 199-200.
70 Helen Christine Bennett, "Kate Gleason's Adventure in a Man's Job," *American Magazine* CVI (Oct., 1928), 42-43, 168-75.
71 Frederick Palmer, "The Best Story in Europe To-day," *Collier's* LXXII (Nov. 17, 1923), 18, 37. Gilbert C. Rich to Merle Curti, July 8, 1959. Miss Skinner also gave to Holyoke a "Coffee House" to serve as a recreational center for the city. Her remarkable collection of old musical instruments is at Yale.

the returning refugees resume normal life in fifteen villages in Picardy, with headquarters in Grécourt.[72]

The spirit that guided the Smith women was expressed by Mrs. Hawes: "To make the French glad we came, that is what we must work for. The most efficient charity organization is a failure if it cannot qualify by this test." [73] The women fed and clothed those in need; they supplied blankets, farm tools, seeds, livestock, chickens, and rabbits, taking minimal fees for these when the villagers had money. They helped rebuild houses. They established a district nursing service and a health program. They developed educational and recreational facilities. Living intimately with those they were helping, the women assisted in dealings with the Ministry of Reconstruction, and in reestablishing agricultural syndicates and cooperative societies. When voices were raised in criticism of sending an independent unit rather than in pooling resources in a centralized effort, Mrs. Hawes replied: "Ask the French." And many testimonies from mayors and villagers bore her out. Part of the success of the Smith College Relief Unit resulted from the modesty and complete absence of the lady-bountiful attitude. The women believed that they had received in fellowship, understanding, and broadened spiritual horizons, far more than they had given.[74] The Smith example was followed by Barnard, Wellesley, Goucher, Vassar and Stanford; and Smith itself developed besides its original unit, a canteen unit, a refugee unit, and a Near East Unit.

Another memorable example of war service, destined to grow into a permanent organization, was that of the Friends. In April, 1917, representatives of three branches of the American Quakers met in Philadelphia to consider how young Quakers might express their love for their country and desire to serve it in constructive work for humanity. Out of the meeting developed the American Friends Service Committee. At first it planned merely to send a few score of relief workers, chiefly young men who could not accept military service for reasons of conscience, into France to cooperate with the relief and

[72] Ruth Gaines, *Ladies of Grécourt: Smith College Relief Unit in the Somme* (New York: Dutton, 1920), 12 ff.

[73] *Ibid.*, 217-18.

[74] See also Ruth Gaines, *A Village in Picardy* (New York: Dutton, 1918). Outside evaluations are to be found in Ford, *Out of the Ruins*, 110 ff. and Fisher Ames, Jr., *American Red Cross Work Among the French People* (New York: Macmillan, 1921), 76-80.

reconstruction work in which British Friends had been engaged from the beginning of the war. The part that the AFSC played in securing alternate service for men whose conscientious religious convictions kept them from taking part in military activities is not, except indirectly, a part of this story. Nor is the advice that members of the Committee gave to troubled young Americans uncertain about their obligations. The story has been told many times, never so effectively as it was by the great moving spirit in the organization, Rufus Jones, who had long sought to promote unity among Friends through constructive humanitarian service. In his mind, Quakerism was or should be a way of life in which service was a natural and integral part, the necessary expression of Christ's spirit of love, the means by which the finite could be transcended and identity with the infinite, with God, approximated.[75]

Unit Number One, made up of some sixty-odd young men who had rigorously trained for service in an overseas unit during the summer in a program at Haverford, reached France in mid-September, 1917. It worked under the civilian branch of the American Red Cross, placing itself at the disposition of the larger organization and in turn augmenting its own limited resources by supplies from Red Cross warehouses. While the main task of the Unit was to cooperate with British Friends in reconstruction work in the region of the Aisne, the Somme, and the Oise, it often took part in emergency operations, such as the evacuation of the Somme area in the spring of 1918. On this occasion and during the drive between Rheims and Soissons in May, the Friends, under heavy fire, evacuated a maternity hospital, convoyed six hundred insane patients to Lourdes, fed refugees in canteens, and rescued the aged, the crippled, and the sick.[76]

But during the period of the war itself the chief work was the reconstruction of designated devastated areas through a program of relief, medical services, building of shelters and homes, and help in getting manufacturing and agriculture again under way. On their arrival in France, J. Henry Scattergood had told the young Quakers, "We are here because we feel that we must do something, not ex-

[75] Rufus M. Jones, *A Service of Love in War Time: American Friends Relief Work in Europe, 1917-1919* (New York: Macmillan, 1920), Elizabeth Gray Vining, *Friend of Life: The Biography of Rufus M. Jones* (Philadelphia, New York: Lippincott, 1958), 156 ff., 168 ff.; Mary Hoxie Jones, *Swords into Ploughshares: An Account of the American Friends Service Committee, 1917-1937* (New York: Macmillan, 1937), 3 ff.

[76] Charles Evans, *First Annual Report of the Chief of Friends' Unit in France to the American Red Cross* (Philadelphia, 1918), 11.

pecting an easier life than the millions of men who are following their light in other ways, and we are ready to do the hardest and lowliest kind of work. It is not that our blood is any less red or our patriotism any less real; it is that we are conscious that we are servants of a King who is above all nations—the King of Love and that we must live out his gospel of love." [77]

And so the Quaker men sawed boards, built and repaired houses, put up window shades, hung doors for destitute peasants in destroyed villages in the Marinne and Somme areas. They felled trees in the Jura Mountains, sawed lumber, made portable houses, rebuilt burned villages, and ran tractors, plows and reapers. They helped peasants sow the seed provided them and reap the harvests. Also, these men fought contagion, made artificial limbs, cared for the tubercular, operated maternity hospitals, and helped in schools for the mutilated. And all this they tried to do in such a way as to make the French return their friendship.

The young Quakers did not do what they did without conflict. One of them felt his blood boil when he read of babies spitted on bayonets and felt impelled to join the army and "take it out on somebody." Only after a struggle with his conscience did he reassure himself that neither military defeat nor victory by any nation would insure an autocratic or a democratic world, persuade himself again that violence could only add to existing tragic realities, that helping the French to restore their life was not the chief thing, that it was rather to help them see that "kindness really can be given out for nothing" and that love alone yields "absolute results." [78]

Non-Quakers associated with relief and reconstruction spoke and wrote enthusiastically about the spirit and labors of the American Friends Service Committee. "No organization in Europe," declared Lt. Col. John Van Schaick, "surpassed the Quakers in quick adaptability and hard common sense. They did the thing needed and did it with unusual intelligence. And they all fell to with their hands as well as their heads." [79] Dr. Richard Cabot was no less eloquent. And Homer Folks testified that he and his immediate associates in the Red Cross learned more from the Quakers than from anyone else. In the Quakers' own reports one gets now and then glimpses of the

---

[77] Van Schaick, *The Little Corner Never Conquered*, 162.

[78] Daniel Owen Stephens, *With Quakers in France* (London: C. W. Daniel, 1921), 187, 214-15, 303.

[79] Van Schaick, *The Little Corner Never Conquered*, 163.

appreciative response of the French people to what was done, but it is necessary to look in places other than the modest Quaker accounts for tributes to the Friends.

Other agencies played some part in work abroad which was philanthropic in greater or less degree. As early as 1915 the YMCA, which met with considerable criticism in its ministrations to "doughboys," undertook to help prisoners of war, the work in the belligerent powers being conducted by local YM agencies, the money coming from America. The program nowhere was adequate, but classes were organized in languages, commercial subjects, handicrafts and branches related to the life of the prisoner. Conducted as far as could be by the prisoners themselves and by prisoners' organizations, these classes were both useful in a practical sense and beneficial from the point of view of therapy. Something like $2,000,000 was spent on this program.[80] The YWCA, like its counterpart, was chiefly concerned with Americans abroad, but it supported thirty-one foyers or centers of rest and recreation which a French organization had inaugurated on a limited scale in an effort to help women working in war plants.[81]

The wide base of American overseas philanthropy was further expressed in helping orphans. In the United States 150,000 school children pledged themselves to send $36 a year for two years to each of the 150,000 French children who had lost his father in the war. In France itself the *Stars and Stripes*, the official paper of the armed forces abroad, suggested that soldiers provide means for maintaining fatherless French children for a year. In the first week of the campaign only five children were "adopted." But the idea caught on. By Christmas, 1917, money was in hand for nearly 3,500 orphans.

The administration of the program proved to be too much for the *Stars and Stripes*. It asked the Red Cross to take over and manage

[80] National War Work Council, Summary of World War Work of the American YMCA (n.p.: International Committee of YMCAs, 1920), *passim.*; William Howard Taft, et al., *Service with Fighting Men: An Account of the Work of the American Young Men's Christian Associations in the World War* (2 vols.; New York: Association Press, 1922), II, 230-42, 507-40. The $14,000,000 which the Knights of Columbus raised during the war for work at home and abroad was chiefly used in the interest of religion and patriotism for Catholic members of the armed forces: Maurice Frances Egan and John B. Kennedy, *The Knights of Columbus in Peace and War* (2 vols.; New Haven: Knights of Columbus, 1920), I, 222 ff.

[81] *Report of the Overseas Committee of the War Work Council of the Y.W.C.A.* (New York: National Board of the Y.W.C.A., ca. 1921), 5-68.

details. The Red Cross provided lists of names and photographs of orphans in special need. From these the doughboys made selections. Money kept coming in and a Continuation Fund was opened. The Paris edition of the *Chicago Tribune* gave the profits it made during the war to General Pershing, to be used at his discretion. He presented 114,000 francs to the *Stars and Stripes* War Orphans Continuation Fund. Finally, the *Stars and Stripes* petitioned Congress to permit it to turn over the 2,184,640 francs profit from the enterprise for continuing aid to orphans. All in all, this movement, however sentimental and casual, was a magnanimous and much appreciated gesture on the part of men who had fought in France.[82]

To sum up, in the period before America's entrance into the First World War, giving for overseas emergencies reflected not only humanitarianism but, even more markedly, sympathies with particular groups—Jews, the distressed peoples of the Near East, one or more or all of the Allied nations and, to a much lesser extent, on the part of those of German and Austrian backgrounds, the Central Powers. After America's entrance into the war, individual initiative still played a large part in organizing, supporting, and administering many relief and reconstruction projects. This was particularly true of the American resident in Paris possessing leisure and means.

The most characteristic feature of American giving in the first years of the war, however, was the increasing reliance on large-scale, highly organized, businesslike approaches to the problem. Also, the role of members of the American foreign service in philanthropies overseas was greater and more sustained than ever before. In scale of magnitude, what was done exceeded any earlier overseas effort. It was ironical that a vast war, highly destructive of life, brought forth such devoted efforts in providing money, supplies, and services to lessen the force of the disaster. What Americans did, however much appreciated by recipients, was, after all, insignificant in view of the need which was to continue and become even greater.

[82] Ames, *American Red Cross Work Among the French People,* 8, 149-51.

X

The Aftermath

During a United War Chest drive in the autumn of 1918 many were surprised to hear John R. Mott of the YMCA declare that peace was only a little less demanding of aid than war. America's allies, especially France and Italy, did indeed stand in great need. The late enemies in Central Europe, with new and unstable regimes, were struggling with starvation and epidemics. In Poland and southeast Europe the situation was even worse. In many parts of the Continent transportation had broken down, currencies were in chaotic fluctuation, and the threat of Bolshevism stalked over the land. The plight of uprooted and persecuted Jews in Central Europe and in Poland and Russia was no less than tragic. In Soviet Russia starvation and pestilence threatened untold millions of lives. Nationalistic strivings and racial tensions had increased in the Near East. In this turbulent area food shortage was desperate, brigands roamed the land, and the refugee problem seemed hopeless. With the war at an end, constructive aid could now reach the needy nations.

Many thoughtful Americans, sensitive to these vast needs and complex problems, asked two leading questions: Would their fellow-countrymen, weary of the war effort and eager to return to "normalcy," be willing to sustain the generous giving of the war period? Would America herself give leadership to the Allies and neutrals in a concerted effort to provide relief, to undertake rehabilitation, and to build constructively an order in which peace might become a reality?

One of the Americans who pondered these things was Henry P. Davison of the House of Morgan, head of the American Red Cross War Council which had mobilized voluntary support for the war effort at home and abroad on a scale hitherto unimaginable. He hoped that the practical idealism that had inspired the voluntary sacrifice of giving during the war might be directed toward a continuing service to humanity as a means of building peace. Such an effort must, as Davison saw it, be a cooperative one, including at first the national Red Cross societies of the Allied nations and, in time, all nations. He proposed that the national Red Cross societies be coordinated in a peacetime effort to take over the whole relief effort in Europe, to help those in distress wherever they might be, and to emphasize public health.

In establishing the League of Red Cross Societies, Davison enlisted the support of President Wilson and well-known men in the United States and Great Britain. The chief financial support came from the American Red Cross (over $2,000,000 by 1923). Nevertheless, many older leaders in this organization favored a return to the limited prewar operations. This, together with the initial opposition of the International Red Cross Committee, a self-perpetuating all-Swiss group that had long regarded itself as the special guardian of the Red Cross principle, militated against the full realization of the vision of Davison and his associates. Even more important, the growing isolationism, both in the United States and among the Allies, hampered the development of the new League of Red Cross Societies. Nevertheless the League stimulated national Red Cross societies in the field of public health and prodded governments to take comprehensive action. By the time of the Second World War it succeeded in effecting a measure of cooperation on the part of the various national Red Cross societies in the anti-Fascist countries with telling results.[1]

Meantime, the task of aiding former Allies in rebuilding their devastated cities and countryside, feeding their hungry, and combating tuberculosis and more formidable epidemics, enlisted American individuals and voluntary agencies.

War-torn Belgium was a happy exception to the dismal plight of the Allies on the Continent. The little country showed a surprising power of recovery. But many Americans felt a special sympathy for this first victim of the war and wanted to help in its restoration. The Red Cross bought needed laboratory equipment for the Uni-

[1] Clyde E. Buckingham, "The Golden Moment: Henry P. Davison and American Influence in the Founding of the League of Red Cross Societies" (unpublished manuscript, 1961).

versity of Brussels. Liberal gifts from the Rockefeller Foundation enabled the medical faculty of the University to meet the high standards the Foundation had set as a condition for helping similar institutions in other parts of the world. At Louvain, the library was a stark ruin. Nicholas Murray Butler, president of Columbia University and an official of the Carnegie Endowment for International Peace, sponsored a movement for building a new one for the University. Eager to have it testify to the generosity not only of the Endowment but of American education, Butler, with the help of a professional publicity agent, solicited gifts from American college students and school children. When these sources proved inadequate for completing the new structure, Herbert Hoover stepped in to preserve the national face by finishing the job with funds from the Belgian Relief Commission. The plaque on the new library bearing the words "Destroyed by German fury, restored by American generosity," stirred up an unpleasant discussion. Some thought it unduly vindictive. No one could then foresee that in 1940 the library would again be destroyed by the Germans.[2]

In France, once noble ecclesiastical and civic structures and countless villages stood in ruins. The Carnegie Endowment for International Peace reconstructed the civic center of Faginers. At Rheims it built a new library in the shadow of the crumbled cathedral. Nor was the Carnegie Endowment France's only benefactor in the restoration of the architectural monuments in which she had taken such pride. In 1924 John D. Rockefeller, Jr., gave a million dollars for rebuilding the cathedral itself and for repairing Versailles and Fontainebleau. This he did because of his admiration for "the marvellous French masterpieces, the influence of which must remain intact and perpetuate itself through centuries for the great benefit of successive generations," and also as a token of his admiration of the courage and patriotism of the French people. Three years later the American philanthropist gave $1,600,000 for continuing the restoration of French national monuments, which in a depressed economy public and private sources in France found too burdensome to carry through. "The whole of France," declared J. J. Jusserand, former

[2] Nicholas Murray Butler, *Across the Busy Years: Recollections and Reflections* (2 vols.; New York: Scribner's Sons, 1939-40), I, 111 ff.; Herbert Hoover, *Memoirs, vol. I: Years of Adventure, 1874-1920* (New York: Macmillan, 1951), 230. The funds remaining after the completion of the library, chiefly from the Belgian Relief Commission, were used to endow the Belgian-American Educational Foundation, an agency for exchange of students.

French ambassador in Washington, "now and later will bless the name of one who, unasked and simply for having seen the danger, came to the rescue at the hour when it was most needed and when we could do the least for ourselves." [3]

Beyond the need for help in restoring institutions and monuments was the far more pressing one of caring for refugees, orphans, and those stricken with tuberculosis. Such needs made it natural for American agencies which had been on hand at the armistice to continue their help. And the agencies did help: the Rockefeller Foundation, the American Committee for Devastated France, the YMCA and the YWCA, the Fatherless Children of France, the French Heroes Lafayette Fund, the Permanent Blind Relief Fund, the French Tubercular Children's Fund (also known as the Edith Wharton Memorial), the American Friends Service Committee and, of course, the Red Cross. (The last, to the disappointment of many, soon tapered off its services.) In due course these agencies, working in community reconstruction projects or for certain classes of the handicapped and the needy, cooperated with the emerging European Relief Council. Most of them tried to build permanent welfare agencies after American models.[4]

The Italian War Relief Fund of America with other organizations aided a variety of charitable projects, both those concerned with emergency relief and, in lesser part, those involving health and other long-range needs. Of these the most important was the aid and stimulus given to local Italian organizations in initiating and carrying forward an anti-tuberculosis campaign. The American Red Cross unit which arrived in Rome shortly before victory, organized, in cooperation with Italians, a nation-wide survey of factors affecting the incidence of the disease, such as child labor, school hygiene, housing conditions, and existing public health programs. Once the preliminary investigation had been carried through, provincial organizations were set up to work with local committees in providing dispensaries and visiting nurses and in carrying through an educational campaign. In the beginning the Red Cross gave financial help, but its chief contribution was to put at the disposal of the Italian committees the experience gained in similar campaigns in America. Thus the aid to Italy formed "a natural transition from emergency war work to the persistent problems of sickness and suffering that every nation . . . must solve for itself. . . ." [5]

As in Italy so in Greece and the Balkans the American committees that had been formed or were now formed, together with the American Red Cross, carried on emergency relief and health work. The head of the Red Cross Unit in Montenegro, Henry Ruston Fairclough, a professor of classics at Stanford, surmounted tough transportation problems and avoided entanglement with local politics as he and his coworkers set up soup kitchens, hospitals and orphanages, and carried out child care and health programs. On returning to this area in 1931 he was happy to find excellent public programs in operation.

Many Americans working in Serbia were, however, disappointed in what they accomplished. The hope had been to establish a model child welfare service for the whole country; but ignorance of the language and the desire to do things as they were done in America sometimes irritated the Serbs who, bursting with national pride, did not want anything imposed from without. Yet the emergency relief in such remote areas as the Sandjak of Novibazar and Bosnia was invaluable. Clearing houses for destitute children and orphanages helped thousands through a crisis that seemed hopeless. In the Petch area a Friends' Unit under Drew Pearson built houses for stranded Montenegrins, showed them how to break, plow, and sow the waste land, and provided food until harvest. The work of pulling thorn bushes and dynamiting tree stumps, sinking wells, and making thousands of bricks and wooden frames, taxed the strength of the young Quakers and Mennonites. Although lonely and homesick, they stuck at the job until it was done. [6]

Of the existing war agencies, none faced more overwhelming problems than the Committee for Armenian and Syrian Relief which, in June, 1918, had taken the name of the Committee for Relief in the Near East. Despite the fact that in the three years of its war

[5] Charles M. Bakewell, *The Story of the American Red Cross in Italy* (New York: Macmillan, 1920), 207; Joseph Bykofsky, "History of the American National Red Cross," vol. XXIX: "Foreign Relief in the Post Armistice Period, 1918-1923," (mimeographed monograph in the Library of the American National Red Cross, Washington, D. C.), *passim*.

[6] Lasker, *Survey XLIII*, 513-23, 553, 558; Henry Ruston Fairclough, *Warming Both Hands* (Stanford: Stanford University Press, 1941), 341 ff., 390, 406 ff.; Francesca M. Wilson, *In the Margins of Chaos: Recollections of Relief Work in and Between Three Wars* (New York: Macmillan, 1945), 95-97, 112.

operations it had spent over $11,000,000, conditions were now even more appalling than during the conflict itself. Civil war raged between the disintegrating Ottoman Empire and the Greeks, Syrians, Arabs, and Armenians. The Greeks wanted to be united with their homeland, the Arabs demanded an independent state centering in Damascus, and the Syrians, though accepting French protection, also desired independence. The Armenians, long eager to have their own land free, struggled hopelessly to federate independent republics in the Caucasus and the neighboring areas in the old Ottoman Empire. Persia, disrupted by a huge flood of refugees and by other conflicts, presented additional problems. To complicate matters further, the Turkish leaders insisted that the interests of Britain and France would best be served by insuring an independent Ottoman regime as a bulwark against Russian Soviet expansion. A commission of the Committee for Relief in the Near East, headed by William Barton, reported that the Levant was in desperate plight. At least 4,000,000 were homeless, hungry, disease-ridden refugees and 400,-000 orphans languished in danger of immediate starvation.

America responded to the need through several volunteer agencies, including the Committee for Relief in the Near East, the Red Cross, the YMCA, the American Women's Hospital, and the Commonwealth Fund (recently established by the Harknesses). Such non-American groups as the Canada Fund, the Lord Mayor's Fund, and the Friends of Armenia also contributed. But the financial resources of private philanthropy were too meager to cope with the situation. Nor was existing personnel, partly the old missionary hands, partly civilian recruits, adequate. The United States army lent a hand, and its services, while useful, in the eyes of the Committee for Relief in the Near East left much to be desired.

Discouraged by the lagging interest of the 20,000,000 Americans who had given support during the war, the Committee decided that a political approach was the only feasible one. It proposed that the United States assume a mandate for all or for a part of Turkey, particularly for the Armenian republics. Still blaming Turkey for all that had happened and was happening, the Committee went to work as a pressure group in Washington. The administration sympathized with the idea of an American mandate, but Congress, sensitive to the costs and headaches involved and to public opinion, in 1920 refused to jump into the task of trying to bring and keep order in this chaos.

There was nothing to do for Armenia but to continue the over-all Near East program—to keep on with soup kitchens and breadlines, establishing workshops for those who could help support themselves, and offering elementary medical aid. This was only patchwork, the Committee realized, but it gave some comfort and some hope to millions of refugees.

The problem of temporary relief and of the first steps toward rehabilitation in the Near East was aggravated in September, 1922, when the entire non-Moslem section of Smyrna, recently occupied by the Turks, burned to the ground. The devastation sent thousands of naked, scorched, and hungry refugees into a wasted countryside. The American Red Cross, which had been in this area, went to work. In the next two years it appropriated over $2,700,000 to aid some 800,-000 people.[7]

The Near East Relief Committee set itself the special job of helping refugees and children. It gathered as many boys and girls as it could into temporary asylums, teaching them skills which in time might enable them to make their own way, and embarking on the formidable task of placing as many as possible in foster homes. Supplementing emergency aid with rehabilitation, the Committee distributed seeds and farm tools and increasingly emphasized agricultural training which, as the years passed, was to become a distinctive self-help feature of this path-breaking agency.

But the program was inadequately supported even with the help of the Red Cross, the Commonwealth Fund, the American Women's Hospital (which raised $100,000 for medical work), and the American Relief Administration, an official agency headed by the seasoned philanthropic administrator, Herbert Hoover. The Near East Committee redoubled its fund-raising efforts in America to meet staggering costs. It made widespread use of "Golden Rule Sunday," a device for fund raising through special sermons, reports of poignant suffering, and dinners in some 2,000,000 American homes, costing four cents per person, and identical with the fare of a relief orphanage. The Near East Committee also entered into a cooperative agreement with the Canadian Armenian Relief Fund and publicized itself increasingly as an international organization.

In 1923 the Near East Relief spent almost $9,500,000, an outlay enabling it to provide care for 500,000 refugees and to furnish at least 200,000 with food and clothing. The next year, 1924, the organi-

[7] *New York Times*, April 9, 1924.

zation, in addition to paying off an obligation of $1,000,000 incurred for relief after the Smyrna disaster, disbursed almost $4,000,000. This budget supported during the year 47 orphanages, 65 hospitals, and 23 other institutions. Altogether, the program helped over 500,-000 human beings in 1924. Well might Henry Morgenthau, in appealing for continued support, declare with pride that since he first appealed in 1914 for a relief organization in the Near East field almost $100,000,000 had been given for food, clothing, and medical supplies to the peoples living in a part of the earth to be cherished among other reasons for having cradled the human race in the dim past. But the officers of the Near East Relief were disappointed at the shrinkage of funds after 1925. Still the support that had been given was significant in view of the fact that there were few ethnically related immigrants to give, that no obvious or pressing national interests were at stake, and that areas nearer home were also in desperate need.[8]

Both in appeals for further funds and in general discussion of the Levant the point was sometimes made that American generosity had staved off the triumph of Bolshevism. President Calvin Coolidge, for instance, emphatically made such a claim in an address given at a Golden Rule dinner of the International Near East Association in October, 1924.[9] It is true that most of the area did not go Communist. After a brief bid for independence, a good part of Armenia was, however, incorporated in the Soviet Union. But a key figure in the Near East Relief, H. C. Jaquith, argued that the relief program in Armenia played an essential part in preventing violent upheavals by curbing the radical tendencies of the inexperienced Communist revolutionaries who headed the Armenian government. The aid given, Jaquith believed, was probably a sufficiently stabilizing influence to explain the restoration of "normal" conditions "without the upheavals, abortive counter-revolutions, famines and consequent agonies of the helpless population which have been endured elsewhere in Russia. . . ."[10]

[8] New York Times, Feb. 3, 29, 1924; July 1, 12, 1924; Dec. 6, 1924, Dec. 8, 1925. This summary is also based on the American Committee for Armenian and Syrian Relief's News Bulletin and on its sequel, Near East; on James L. Barton's Story of Near East Relief, 1915-1930 (New York: Macmillan, 1930) and on Robert L. Daniel, "From Relief to Technical Assistance in the Near East, A Case Study: Near East Relief and The Near East Foundation" (unpublished Ph.D. dissertation, University of Wisconsin, 1953).

[9] New York Times, Oct. 25, 1924.

[10] H. C. Jaquith, "Armenian Reds Curbed by American Philanthropy," Current History XXI (Feb., 1925), 719.

One cannot determine the extent to which the Near East program in Armenia actually achieved these results. But it is true that the Soviet authorities not only tolerated but expressed appreciation for the work of the Near East Relief in Armenia. Thus in 1925 the premier of the Transcaucasus Federation declared that the relief work deserved gratitude, not only by reason of the suffering it had reduced, but because it promoted genuine good will between nations.[11] In similar vein a special commission of the Transcaucasian Government a year later termed the care of Armenian orphans by the Near East Relief both efficient and satisfactory. It expressed the hope that the agency would keep on with its humanitarian efforts until the Armenian government was able to take care of the children.[12] Visiting an orphanage housing 8,000 boys and girls, Commissar Rykoff of the Central Government in Moscow similarly expressed satisfaction with the achievements of the Near East Relief. This dignitary could not forbear telling the children that they were victims of imperialistic war and of nationalistic strife and assuring them that they need never again fear atrocities now that they were under the protection of the Free Soviet Federation. Kissing several children, Rykoff bade them a fond farewell.[13]

Relations between Soviet authorities in Armenia and Near East Relief, however, were not always smooth. Two years after the Communist praise of the organization twenty-eight Armenian employees of Near East Relief were arrested. The American director announced that there would be no protest against these arrests, partly because the agency never interfered in political matters and partly because it was not unlikely that out of a thousand native employees some might have spread anti-Soviet propaganda.[14] Such incidents bolstered the Communist claim, of which the world was to hear much, that philanthropic humanitarianism was only a cloak for counter-revolutionary activities.

If the efforts of the Near East Relief did have some effect in the larger political world of the Levant, such influence was not a main aim. To American supporters the chief purpose was to provide emergency relief to refugees, especially to orphans. In Ida M. Tarbell's words, "It is a work which gets down to bedrock, lessening the amount of the threat to the future which must lie in rearing these

11 *New York Times,* March 11, 1925.
12 *New York Times,* Nov. 1, 1925.
13 *Ibid.,* March 12, 1925.
14 *Ibid.,* Sept. 29, 1927.

great masses of children to know nothing but bitterness and misery, starting counteracting forces of goodness and sympathy." [15]

By 1925 the end of the immediately pressing problems of relief was in sight and the question of the future of Near East Relief was duly canvassed. A competent fact-finding committee was named to conduct field surveys in the eight Near East countries to assess the strength and weaknesses of American philanthropic programs and to determine whether further American aid was needed in the rehabilitation and modernization already under way in these countries, and if so how this might most effectively be given. The lengthy report expressed appreciation of the work accomplished by American and foreign philanthropic agencies and analyzed the nature of existing problems in education, health, welfare, agriculture and industry. It recommended the federation of American agencies in the interest of preventing overlapping and promoting efficient action. It also made a great point of the need of reaching masses of rural peoples in the interior hitherto little affected by the Near East Relief, the YMCA, the YWCA, and the missionary schools and colleges. Above all the report stressed the importance of working with and through governments and through religious and other indigenous local organizations in programs designed to promote self-help. This truly impressive survey paved the way for the establishment of the Near East Foundation and gave direction to a new emphasis in overseas programs to become known in time as technical assistance.[16]

Meantime, the crisis in Europe itself demanded the attention of Washington and of those responsible for overseas relief work. Most pressing was the food shortage which in central and eastern Europe was reaching starvation proportions.[17] Tuberculosis, scurvy, and worst of all, typhus, were taking hundreds of thousands of lives each month. Of the late enemy powers, only Germany, despite her depressed economy, had enough goods to export and sufficient gold and liquid assets to pay for food. But the Allies insisted on maintaining

---

[15] *Ibid.*, Dec. 12, 1924.

[16] Frank A. Ross, C. Luther Fry and Elbridge Sibley, *The Near East and American Philanthropy: A Survey Conducted under the Guidance of the Near East Survey* (New York: Columbia University Press, 1929), especially vii-xii, 289-98.

[17] Public Information Committee, *Official United States Bulletin*, Jan. 3, Jan. 8, 1919; Hoover, *Memoirs*, I, 276 ff. Herbert Hoover's *An American Epic*, vol. II: *Famine in Forty-Five Nations; Organization Behind the Front* (Chicago: Regnery, 1960), especially 189 ff., treats overseas American relief activities in this period.

the blockade, partly to be sure that German power of resistance was really crushed and partly because they saw in the blockade a way of enforcing a punitive "peace" and of advancing their national interests. The Allies were also unwilling to lift the blockade until the United States, with large farm surpluses, reduced food prices. This was something which no administration in Washington could do without bringing disaster to the farmers who had expanded their operations during the war under assurance of government-maintained prices.

As for the newly liberated states—Albania, Hungary, Czechoslovakia, Poland, Finland, and the other Baltic countries—none had more than a small amount of goods or other assets to exchange for desperately needed necessities. Even with American loans, it seemed obvious that charity was also required. People in Great Britain and the Dominions and in the more prosperous neutral countries able and willing to give could be counted on for some help, but the Americans alone were in a position to shoulder the major responsibility for large-scale giving.

Two conditions, however, made further American charity uncertain. In the first place, it was not clear to many Americans, despite continued appeals for the relief of Europe's plight, that things were as desperate as they were reported. Thus in Columbus, Ohio, those in charge of the War Chest, which had a provision for overseas giving, returned to donors a fourth of the funds in hand. In the second place, many Americans just did not want to give. They were eager to forget the war and to resume their accustomed and comfortable ways of living, or they were weary of what were called "sob-story appeals." Some felt that further giving would confirm Europe in thinking that America was a great Santa Claus, thus discouraging people from helping themselves.[18] One woman who had visited Europe wrote to the *New York Times* that the Europeans "are perfectly willing to take all the help from America which we will give, in the meantime hating us because we have it, money made by our commercialism which pains them so." In her opinion they had reached the place where they practically say: " 'Oh well, the Americans will do that for us—why worry?' "[19] Responsive to this mood, the Red Cross curtailed its work in France. It remained important in the relief of the Near East and between July 1, 1919, and June 30, 1920,

---

[18] Lasker, *Survey* XLIII, 515-16.
[19] *New York Times*, Sept. 22, 1924.

contributed over eight million dollars for relief in Poland. But it was not prepared to undertake major responsibilities.

During the armistice period the Wilson administration decided that conditions abroad required what Hoover was to call "the second American intervention." The American Relief Administration, established by executive order on February 24, 1919, and approved the next day by Congress, commenced operations with Hoover acting as Director General. The new agency was given broad powers to get food and other needed material to Europe through the cooperation of the Food Administration and the Grain Corporation, which Hoover also headed, and the United States Navy. At Hoover's request President Wilson secured a special Congressional appropriation of a hundred million dollars to be used for loans, for the purchase of American food, and for charity abroad, if it proved necessary, as it was certain to be in the newly liberated countries unable to borrow from the United States by reason of having had no governments in exile when Congress passed the authorizing legislation.

This federal help was not given hit and miss. Senator Henry Cabot Lodge's amendment, which Congress approved, stipulated that no part of the appropriation was to feed any "enemy" child or adult. Hoover was sure that no effective peacemaking could result until Central Europe was reasonably certain of some stability and recovery. He believed that such recovery was necessary if Germany was to buy food and to meet the reparations the Allies were demanding. Moreover, some arrangement must be made with the Allies for advancing loans to Austria to enable that country to receive an emergency advance from the United States. Hoover was also of the decided opinion that it would be well to require the newly liberated states to borrow for the needed food, rather than have it given them outright. Even if in the end the loans might have to be cancelled, the immediate advantages over outright giving seemed clear: loans could be made on conditions that would permit the American Relief Administration to secure a greater measure of economy and efficiency in distribution than would be possible on a gift basis. Also, loans promised to provide a face-saving device, since no one liked to be the recipient of charity.

Hoover's real power rested on the fact that he was still United States Food Administrator and that American resources and the will to use them for a second intervention to save Europe gave him tangible material with which to operate. To be sure, the Allies also named him their Director of Relief and Rehabilitation. But they threw many obstacles in his path. They refused to lift the blockade; only after great pressure did they agree to do this in April, 1919. They held out for American reduction of prices for its surplus food. Aware of the availability of cheaper foods in the Southern Hemisphere, they implied that United States policy was designed to provide a profitable disposal of American surpluses. And although the Allies were in a position to contribute only four per cent of needed tonnage and five per cent of the necessary credits, they insisted that all economic resources—American and Allied—be pooled and jointly administered over an indefinite future.

The Americans, however, refused to give up control of their own resources. In the words of T. C. C. Gregory, an American Relief Administration official, rivalry existed among Allies as to who should "be found carrying the basket containing the loaves and the fishes." [20] Hoover was determined that Great Britain should not run off with the credit. There was, in addition, some difference over policy toward Russia. France demanded the continuation of Allied military intervention in Russia and Siberia. While the United States had gone along with this policy, to some it seemed open to question. Not that there was any sympathy for Bolshevism. On the contrary, Hoover, like most Americans, saw it as a tremendous threat not only to American social, political, economic, and ethical values, but to freedom and hope for Europe. Indeed, Hoover was insisting that one basic reason for breaking through all snags of power politics in Allied circles and getting food and medical supplies into Central Europe at once was to strengthen the weak parliamentary regimes that they might escape the Communist wave that had already engulfed Hungary. Although some food was sent into Hungary for children, supplies were halted when Bela Kun set up his government based on the Russian model, and they were not resumed until November, 1919, some months after a new, non-Bolshevik group had taken control.

Some evidence lends support to the contention that the overthrow of the Pilsudski government in Poland, and the accession of Paderewski, was due in part to Hoover's activities. An abortive coup d'état against Pilsudski had moved the representatives of the Polish

[20] T. C. C. Gregory, "Stemming the Red Tide," *World's Work* XLI (April, 1921), 610.

section of the Hoover mission to inform Warsaw that "food relief—imperatively needed to keep Poland alive and free from that push of misery that meant revolution and Bolshevism—could only be hoped for in the presence of a government so truly representative and so universally accepted by the people that it could be relied on by America and the Allies to keep order and maintain a safe control of the imported foodstuffs." [21] In the face of these conditions, Pilsudski decided to bring the Conservatives into his government and make Paderewski prime minister. The government remained as thus constituted until the Hoover mission left late in 1919. At that time Paderewski lost out and exiled himself from Poland.[22] "Food and politics," Vernon Kellogg wrote, "have had an inevitable and inseparable connection ever since the beginning of the war; and they have it still." [23]

Getting the blockade broken, finding ships, repairing harbor facilities, building up internal transport, procuring and moving food, securing credit—all these things had to be done under unfavorable conditions. The price level of American agricultural produce had to be maintained. In Allied power politics, feeding Central Europe was subordinated to Allied national interests. The worst source of difficulty was that all regimes were unstable and that east and southeast of the Rhine nothing less than political chaos threatened. Yet during the period of coordination 27,000,000 tons of food were moved overseas into Europe, over 18,000,000 of which came from the United States. In addition, 840,000,000 pounds of clothing, medical, and miscellaneous supplies were sent to those in direst need. Most of the cost of this relief was borne by direct charity or by loans which ultimately proved to be charity since it was impossible to collect them.[24]

---

[21] Vernon Kellogg, "Paderewski, Pilsudski, and Poland," *World's Work* XXXVIII (May, 1919), 112.

[22] Louis L. Gerson, *Woodrow Wilson and the Rebirth of Poland, 1914-1920* . . . (New Haven: Yale University Press, 1953).

[23] Kellogg, *World's Work* XXXVIII, 112.

[24] Suda Lorena Bane and Ralph Haswell Lutz, eds., *Organization of American Relief in Europe, 1918-1919, Including Negotiations Leading up to the Establishment of the Office of Director General of Relief at Paris by the Allied and Associated Powers* (Stanford: Stanford University Press, 1943); 604 ff., 698 ff., 721; Frank M. Surface and Raymond L. Bland, *American Food in the World War and Reconstruction Period: Operations of the Organizations under the Direction of Herbert Hoover, 1914-1924* (Stanford: Stanford University Press, 1931), *passim*; Hoover, *Memoirs*, I, 425-27; Hoover, *American Epic*, II, 241 ff.; U. S., Congress, House, *Receipts and Expenditures under the Act Approved February 25, 1919 . . . Appropriating $100,000,000 for Relief in Europe*, 66th Cong., 2d Sess., 1919, House Doc. 449.

The American Relief Administration also organized a food draft system through which Americans with relatives and friends abroad could send gift packages or certificates good for food at the Administration's warehouses. This combination of private giving with businesslike administration through a government agency proved to be a useful innovation. It enabled needy Germans, for instance, to receive gifts from America valued at $2,000,000 when official giving was impossible and when a great many in the United States were disinclined to help Germans.

The alarming spread of typhus from the Baltic to the Black Sea led Hoover to suggest to the Red Cross that it undertake a delousing program. That organization was ready to help and did, but it felt unable to assume entire responsibility for so big a job. And so with the cooperation of several voluntary agencies and the United States Army, which allocated discarded but clean clothing, soap, portable baths and medical equipment, the American Relief Administration saw through a life-saving program of impressive magnitude.[25]

Undernourished, diseased, and stunted children—anywhere from twelve to sixteen million in varying degrees of need and danger—presented special problems. For one thing, there was no assurance that general supplies, provided for cash or credit and sold by the governments receiving the food, actually reached the children most in need. When the Red Cross decided that it could not take responsibility for a special child feeding program in the enemy and liberated countries, the American Relief Administration set up the Children's Feeding Section. The new subagency proceeded in liberated countries to use some $12,000,000 from the Congressional appropriation of $100,000,000. Since the Lodge amendment forbade the use of these funds for feeding the "enemy," supplementary funds supplied by charity were necessary to get food, clothing, and medical supplies to needy German and Austrian children. Hoover decided that whatever was given should be a gift. The Administration turned over the job of actual distribution to local committees of leading citizens who, thanks to the support of the national governments, established orphanages and provided transportation and the service necessary to

---

[25] Hoover, *Memoirs*, I, 324-27; Mary Hoxie Jones, *Swords into Ploughshares: An Account of the American Friends Service Committee, 1917-1937* (New York: Macmillan, 1937), *passim*.

feed one supplementary meal a day to every child in school. Thus these local committees in effect became partners in the program.[26]

Relief of German children was baffling since the Lodge amendment to the Congressional appropriation stipulated that government funds were not to be used for food for either adults or children in the enemy countries. Hoover was not blind to the needs of Germany's future generation. But in view of the anti-German feeling in the United States and the pressing needs in the recently liberated countries, he seems to have assumed that German-Americans would provide relief for the needy in the old country. To some extent they did, both through gift packages and prepaid drafts on the American Relief Administration warehouses as well as through German-American religious and secular organizations. However, a quick survey of conditions, which Jane Addams and other social workers made in the summer of 1919 at the suggestion of the American Friends Service Committee, revealed that at least a third, possibly two-thirds of German children were suffering from malnutrition. When the AFSC asked Hoover for a useful assignment, he invited it to be responsible for the child-feeding program in Germany. It was, in other words, to be the representative in that country of the Children's Feeding Program of the American Relief Administration, which provided the food. In the end the ARA's direct contribution of $5,000,000, constituted two per cent of the total American deliveries to Germany, the German government itself purchasing $205,000,000 worth of American relief supplies.[27] The Friends contributed some funds in addition to their services. They also received contributions from those German-American organizations which did not insist on turning their

[26] Hoover, *Memoirs*, I, 321 ff.; Thomas J. Orbison, *Children, Inc.: The Post-War "Administration" of the Whole Child Life of One Baltic State in Its Critical Period: A Factual Narrative* (Boston: Stratford, 1933); *Three Years of the American Relief Administration in Austria* (Vienna, 1922); American Relief Administration's European Children's Fund, *Final Report of the Work in Hungary* (Budapest, 1920); American Relief Administration, *The American Relief Administration in Czecho-Slovakia: A Sketch of the Child Feeding Operations of the A.R.A. to Czecho-Slovakia, 1919-1921* (New York: American Relief Administration, ca. 1922); Harold H. Fisher, *America and the New Poland* (New York: Macmillan, 1928), 214-237.

[27] *New York Times*, Nov. 27, Dec. 7, Dec. 18, 1919, Jan. 21, March 23, 1920; Sidney Brooks, *America and Germany, 1918-1925* (New York: Macmillan, 1925), 142-81; Charles Strickland, "American Aid for the Relief of Germany, 1919-1921," (unpublished Master's essay, University of Wisconsin, 1959). Mr. Strickland estimates that American institutional relief to Germany from May, 1919, to August, 1921, amounted to $7,788,000.

donations over directly to German religious institutions or to the German Red Cross.[28]

When it became clear in the winter of 1919-1920 that available funds in the American Relief Administration were inadequate to meet the needs of the child feeding program in Europe, including German needs, Hoover suggested an appeal to the American public. The European Relief Council was organized to manage the campaign. Its constituents included the American Relief Administration, the American Friends Service Committee, the Joint Distribution Committee, the American Red Cross, the Federal Council of Churches and other organizations. The Council estimated that $33,-000,000 was needed for food, clothing, medical supplies, and services for Europe's needy, especially for children.

The campaign ran into trouble. To begin with, a depression had struck the country. People were weary of appeals for overseas relief. The initial response of certain groups did not meet expectations. Many German-Americans, for example, resented the widespread talk about German war guilt and like some other Americans had no enthusiasm for a program to be administered in Germany by American Quakers. The $861,000 which Americans of German and Austrian nativity or parentage, approximately 10 per cent of the total population in 1920, gave to the campaign was less proportionately than the contributions of Americans of other national backgrounds. (In a later campaign, conducted by the Quakers, Americans of German and Austrian background did, however, give $1,500,000, which was 14 per cent of America's contribution to German and Austrian relief.) The resentment among liberals, progressives, and socialists of Hoover's use of charity to influence European politics also discouraged giving in these circles.

Although in certain quarters there was less than whole-hearted enthusiasm, the American people on the whole responded generously. Church organizations, business leaders, and the press, especially the *Literary Digest*, did yeoman's service. All these spokesmen emphasized the humanitarian obligation to save life. The religious groups stressed the doctrine of stewardship. Business leaders appealed to pity too, but echoed Hoover's argument that charity was the best way of checking Bolshevism. There were large givers—a few gifts of

[28] Wilbur K. Thomas, "The American Friends Service Committee in Europe," *American Relief Administration Bulletin*, Series 2, V (Dec., 1920), 42-45; Hoover, *Memoirs*, I, 390; Jones, *Swords into Ploughshares*, 75 ff.

$1,000,000—and the Rockefeller Foundation contributed $2,000,000. Farmers, unable to sell corn at deflated prices, offered 15,000,000 bushels (13,000,000 of which were to be sent to China, which was in the throes of a famine). Small givers came through—some seven million names were listed. By February, 1921, $29,000,000 had been raised, the largest sum thus far contributed in a campaign for overseas relief.[29] There is no reason to doubt that the seven million donors acted mainly out of sympathy and compassion.

The American Friends Service Committee, adopting the general pattern of reliance on local committees worked out by the Children's Feeding Program in other countries, put to good use the resources at hand. The German government made substantial contributions in transport, supplies, and services, as did German voluntary associations. By the end of the first half year the program was feeding 700,000 children in eighty-eight cities: the high point was reached in 1921, when the feeding lists numbered over a million children. Hoover insisted that the feeding everywhere be nonpartisan, but he allowed the Quakers to print a message on each food card: "To those who suffer in Germany, with a message of good will from the American Society of Friends (Quakers) who for 250 years, and also all through this great war, have believed that those who were called enemies were really friends separated by a great wall of misunderstanding."[30]

With conditions improving, the Friends withdrew from the child feeding program in Germany in the summer of 1922. But the next year reports of recurring need among German children reached the United States and moved General Henry T. Allen, who had been Commander of the occupation in Germany, to launch an American Committee for the Relief of German Children. The Committee announced a plan of providing daily to 625,000 children one supplementary meal of five hundred calories, a plan to which the German government would contribute half of the cost of the food, and trans-

---

[29] *New York Times*, Jan. 15, 22, 23, Feb. 8, 11, 1921; Strickland, "American Aid for the Relief of Germany, 1919-1921," *passim*; Hoover, *American Epic*, II, 228 ff.

[30] Brooks, *America and Germany*, 151 ff.; Rufus M. Jones, *A Service of Love in War Time: American Friends Relief Work in Europe, 1917-1919* (New York: Macmillan, 1920), 252 ff.; Surface and Bland, *American Food in the World War and Reconstruction Period*, 77-78, 117-19; J. V. Forbes, "Quaker Relief and Government" (unpublished Ph.D. dissertation, University of Pennsylvania, 1951), *passim*; R. I. Cary, "Child-Feeding Work in Germany under the American Friends Service Committee," *Annals of the American Academy of Political and Social Science* XCII (Nov., 1920), 157-62; Jones, *Swords into Ploughshares*, 117 ff.

portation on the German railways.[31] To this campaign German-Americans made generous contributions. Outstanding among the large donors was Julius Rosenwald, whose total gifts to war and post-war relief exceeded two million dollars. He now gave $100,000 and persuaded others to give. Despite urgings on the part of some Jews that, in view of anti-Semitism in Germany the gift be accompanied by the condition that allocations of food should not be limited to "Aryan" children, Rosenwald replied: "The fact that the Jews 'are giving more than their share toward helping all the different creeds in Germany' is known and, to my mind, it is more helpful to give without protest which would make it appear that the money was given for the purpose of having the Jew-baiting stopped." [32]

One minor incident threatened the campaign. When Woodrow Wilson died the German Embassy in Washington refused to lower its flag or to observe any of the customary amenities. The Federal Council of Churches urged that the understandable public criticism of Germany should not interfere with support of the campaign. "Certainly," wrote Bernard Baruch, a close friend of the late President, "there can be no reprisal among civilized people against the starving children of any blood or breed. I am mailing my check for $5,000." And Wilson's widow asked the American people not to let the flag incident interfere with relief efforts.[33]

In all, the campaign to feed German children raised $4,300,000. At its height the program fed over 1,000,000 German children. Meals costing sixty cents a month were also provided for pregnant and nursing mothers. The program was continued until the summer of 1924.[34]

In Austria the American Friends joined their British brethren too late to be pioneers. But, in the words of an English relief worker, "they accepted a somewhat subordinate role with self-discipline and generosity." They also brought a high degree of professionalism into the distribution of relief, for nearly all of them had had training either in social work or organization. "We learnt to know an America," concluded this witness, "that was very different from the usual

---

[31] *New York Times*, Jan. 29, 1924.

[32] W. C. Graves to J. W. Cansey, Feb. 18, 1924, and Sherwood Eddy to Rosenwald, Oct. 11, 1927, in the Rosenwald Papers, University of Chicago Library, vol. 66; Morris R. Werner, *Julius Rosenwald: The Life of a Practical Humanitarian* (New York, London: Harper, 1939), 255-56. Paul M. Warburg and Felix M. Warburg each contributed $25,000, *New York Times*, Jan. 22, 1924.

[33] *New York Times*, Feb. 8, 11, 13, 1924.

[34] *Ibid.*, March 31, June 22, 1924.

Big Business or globe-trotting America, the only one familiar to many Europeans at that time." [35] The Quakers, British and American, supplemented the food provided by the American Relief Administration which, in terms of calories, was about half that required for normal growth. Faced with a shortage of milk, the Quaker mission imported cows from Switzerland and Holland and provided shoes for children who had been kept from getting American Relief Administration rations by their inability to walk to school in winter weather.

The Friends were not alone in carrying out relief programs for Germany and Austria. Of the cash and food ($1,500,000) and clothing ($2,500,000) which the National Lutheran Council for World Service had distributed in seventeen countries by August, 1922, a substantial part went to Germans and Austrians. This continued to be true in the following years. Between 1919 and 1930 the Council's contributions of almost $8,000,000 to the countries in which it operated brought incalculable relief to America's late enemies.[36] Of the secular agencies that lent a hand to the vanquished, the Commonwealth Fund, established in 1918 by Mrs. Edward Harkness with major emphasis on social welfare in the United States, provided through an existing Austrian organization means for maintaining eighty-four kitchens.[37]

Testimony to the appreciation of American aid was not lacking. General Allen reported a radio message from German welfare workers: "Teachers, physicians, directors of child feeding and representatives of national welfare organizations in joint conference express deep gratitude for the efforts of you and your associates, which will result in renewed health for over one million children." [38] The Quakers were singled out for warm praise. As one German said: "It will not be easy for you to realize what all this means to us. For years we were cut off from everything; for years we heard nothing but strife and hatred. Now, suddenly, you come to us and show us that behind the world of political strife, the real world still exists, the world of brotherhood and love." [39] In reporting to President Wilson on child

---

[35] Wilson, *In the Margins of Chaos*, 149-50; Norah Curtis and Cyril Gibley, *Malnutrition* (New York: Oxford, 1944), 44 ff.; Jones, *Swords into Ploughshares*, 146 ff.

[36] *Lutheran World Almanac, 1922* (New York: National Lutheran Council, 1922), 107; *Lutheran World Almanac, 1923*, 38-39; *Lutheran World Almanac, 1933*, 67.

[37] Commonwealth Fund, *Annual Report, 1923-24* (New York, 1925), 41-42.

[38] *New York Times*, April 19, 1924.

[39] Anna Ruth Fry, *A Quaker Adventure: The Story of Nine Years' Relief and Reconstruction* (London: Nisbet, 1926), 345; Henry J. Cadbury, "A Nationwide Adventure in Friendship," *Survey* XLV (Nov. 27, 1920), 309-13.

feeding in the many countries in which it operated officially until the demise of the American Relief Administration, Hoover wrote: "The reaction which I receive from all over Europe indicates that we have touched the heart of the populations at large as much by this child feeding department as in any form of American intervention in Europe." [40] That American aid did not eliminate anti-American prejudice on the part of Europeans during the 1920's is obvious. Without the aid that was given, these prejudices might, however, have been even more pronounced.

Europeans also did a good deal for each other. The Swiss contributed to soup kitchens in Germany which at one time fed 1,500,-000 a day. German and Austrian children were taken for recuperative vacations into Swiss, Dutch, and Scandinavian homes. Between 1919 and 1924, Norway alone gave almost $2,000,000 to help German children.

It is impossible to distinguish beyond a certain point between the effects of American aid and that of Europeans in a position to help. But American relief did have some impact—how much no one can say—on European social attitudes and behavior. It was, for instance, felt that the example of American women in relief work contributed to the growing freedom of Continental women and to their search for new careers of service. Nor is there any way to test the claim that the example of self-help, so conspicuous in American relief, actually did provide, as some believed, effective training in initiative and leadership on the part of the nonofficial classes. [41] It is, however, certain that American aid, together with that of the British and of the European neutral powers saved millions of lives and made existence bearable for millions more.

Of all American overseas relief programs in the aftermath of the war, the largest and the most complex in character was that inaugurated for Soviet Russia in the summer of 1921. An obvious difficulty was the absence of diplomatic channels between the two countries. So was the desire of the Soviets for recognition and trade and for using relief aid to strengthen Soviet policy and power as well as to help the starving. There was also the insistence of France that Moscow assume responsibility for the debts of the Czarist regime. The desire of England, Germany, and the United States to protect their interests in

---

[40] Hoover, *Memoirs*, I, 323.
[41] See the article by Herbert C. Thompson in the *New York Times*, April 22, 1928.

Russia also figured in the complex situation. In the United States itself depressed prices of the vast grain surplus was an important factor in prevailing hard times, which in turn tended to discourage giving. Moreover, fear of Communism was strong and growing.

In the years between 1917 and 1921 those in charge of the program also had to deal with the Kremlin's suspicion that any foreign relief was designed to undermine the regime. Nor was this suspicion entirely without foundation. Raymond Robins, for example, had, as a representative of the American Red Cross in Moscow, held out to Lenin the promise of American aid on condition that the war against Germany be continued in the autumn of 1917, which Soviet authorities held to be incompatible with furthering the Revolution.[42] One of Robins's associates, William Boyce Thompson, mine operator and broker of great fortune, spent over a million dollars for a propaganda campaign to keep the Russian army fighting.[43] All this strengthened Soviet suspicion that aid was merely a bribe to force the new Russian regime to fight when it was unable to do so and when it had no faith in the Allied cause. Soviet suspicion of American philanthropic aid was further confirmed when the Red Cross provided relief to White Russian refugees in Constantinople and to the counterrevolutionary White Russian forces cooperating with the Allies in the Archangel region and in Siberia.

Nor were the Soviets alone in feeling that such aid reflected American antagonism to the new regime. General William S. Graves, commander of American forces in Siberia, declared that it was "most unfortunate" that the American Red Cross operated hospitals and relief exclusively for the White Russian commander, General Kolchak, in effect becoming his supply agent.[44] In America the liberal press maintained that the Red Cross was violating its professed neutrality by acting as an arm of the State Department. Thus it is not hard to understand that the Bolsheviks, having before them the example of the use of food as a political weapon in Hungary and

[42] Foster Rhea Dulles, *The American Red Cross: A History* (New York: Harper, 1950), 190; George F. Kennan, *Soviet-American Relations, 1917-1920*, vol. I: *Russia Leaves the War* (2 vols.; Princeton: Princeton University Press, 1958), *passim* and vol. II: *The Decision to Intervene* (Princeton, Princeton University Press, 1958), *passim*; and the Raymond Robins manuscripts, Wisconsin State Historical Society, Madison, Wisconsin, *passim*, are the sources for this interpretation.

[43] *Dictionary of American Biography* XVIII; Kennan, *Soviet-American Relations*, I, 52-66, II, *passim*.

[44] William S. Graves, *America's Siberian Adventure, 1918-1920* (New York: Cape, Smith, 1931), 330-31.

Poland, and, further, having no faith in the possibility of disinterested humanitarianism on the part of capitalist nations, regarded American proffers of aid as a thin coating to conceal capitalistic intervention on the counterrevolutionary side. This impression was deepened when, during the Paris peace negotiations, and later, in the Polish-Russian war, Hoover proposed an international neutral relief organization for saving Russian lives endangered by food shortage, on condition that the Russians cease fighting for what they regarded as their legitimate boundaries and that they also stop fighting counterrevolutionary forces.[45]

By the spring of 1921 the food shortage in Soviet Russia reached famine proportions. During the war itself, the area under tillage had been reduced by 25 per cent and by 1921, thanks to the blockade, civil war, and the policies of the Soviet government itself, the area given to crop production was, by some estimates, little more than half of what it had been in 1914. A severe drought laid waste the great grain-producing Volga valley and southern Ukraine. In 1921 the total crop was short by seven million tons of the minimum amount necessary to feed the population. There were no reserves, but even had there been, transportation was so crippled that these could have been got to the starving areas only with great difficulty. By the mid-summer of 1921 anywhere from fifteen to twenty-five million people were threatened by starvation and the diseases that follow in its wake.

No doubt the Bolsheviks feared that mass starvation would incite further resistance to their authority. The West, however, had little knowledge of the actual attitude of Moscow toward the famine, little information in fact regarding the extent of hunger for, thanks to diplomatic isolation and Russian censorship, Russia was largely a sealed book. An American Friends unit of six women social workers who reached Russia in September, 1917, to join a British Quaker relief group, was virtually unheard from until after it had left Siberia in July, 1919.[46] One of the first American reports on conditions resulted from the twenty-seven-day investigation in August, 1921, of Paxton Hibben and two associates representing Near East Relief.[47]

On July 13, 1921, Maxim Gorky, Russia's best-known writer, is-

---

[45] Hoover, *Memoirs*, I, 411 ff.

[46] Jones, *Swords into Ploughshares*, 42-44.

[47] Paxton Hibben, *An American Report on the Russian Famine* (New York: The Nation, ca. 1922).

sued an appeal to "all honest European and American" people for food and medicine. This was followed shortly by one from Lenin to the international proletariat. The American Relief Administration was about to wind up its affairs in Europe, but it still had some resources. Hoover, nominally its head but primarily concerned with his work as Secretary of Commerce in the Harding cabinet, replied to Gorky that the American Relief Administration would help provided Russia at once released all United States prisoners, that Americans would be free to administer relief, organize local committees, and distribute food and medicine on a non-political basis, and on the further condition that Russian authorities provide free storage, transportation, and offices for the administrators. On August 20, 1921, Walter L. Brown, representing the American Relief Administration, and Maxim Litvinov, signed at Riga an agreement which met the American conditions.

On a broiling day in that same August Hoover summoned representatives of the American Red Cross, the YMCA, YWCA, Quakers, Knights of Columbus, and other voluntary agencies to his office in the Department of Commerce, and announced the terms of the Riga agreement. As James N. Rosenberg recalls the meeting, each organization had its own ideas and something like a quarrel resulted. Turning to Rosenberg who, with Felix M. Warburg, was representing the Joint Distribution Committee, Hoover said, with some impatience, "Rosenberg, work this out" and left the meeting. Rosenberg proposed that each contributing organization have autonomy in particular regions in Russia.[48] Hoover agreed but later insisted that there be one central organization with Americans exclusively in charge of the distribution of American donations.

Under these terms the program was launched. The participating agencies included the American Joint Jewish Distribution Committee, the Mennonite Central Committee, the American Friends Service Committee, the American Red Cross, the Southern Baptist Convention for Russian Relief, the Federal Council of Churches of Christ, the National Lutheran Council, the National Catholic Welfare Council, the Student Friendship Fund of the YMCA and YWCA, the Volga Relief Society (German groups in the United States and Canada interested in the Volga Germans), and the American Committee to Aid Russian Scientists. In addition, several independent agen-

[48] James N. Rosenberg to Rockwell Kent, Sept. 20, 1960, Rosenberg Papers.

cies collected funds for one or another of the affiliates. The several affiliated voluntary organizations gave perhaps as much as $6,000,-000.[49]

Since Hoover's survey indicated that millions of Russian children would die unless at least $50,000,000 could be raised, it was necessary to provide additional funds. It was possible to make available $10,000,000 from American Relief Administration assets. In good help-yourself tradition Hoover insisted that the Soviets use some of their gold reserves to finance part of the program: between $12,000,-000 and $18,000,000 came from this source, according to who did the calculating. In addition the Soviets spent possibly as much as $14,000,000 in local currency.

Even with this it was necessary to turn to Congress, to follow what was by now the established pattern of combining private, voluntary contributions with public funds. Congress was therefore asked to appropriate $20,000,000 from the United States Grain Corporation's funds. Opponents of the proposal argued, as predecessors had so often done on earlier and comparable occasions, that it was unconstitutional, that charity begins at home, that the money ought to be used to help America's own needy unemployed, that relief on such a scale would invite other beggars to demand help, and that public, tax-supported relief would discourage private philanthropy. Others contended that the proposal savored of an international charity racket and that Hoover and his men did not deserve their reputation for efficiency and disinterestedness. Some also held that any food sent would be diverted to feed commissars and the Red Army, and that relief was bound to strengthen a regime which might already be tottering. But in view of the fact that the debate took place in the midst of the Red Scare, less emphasis than might be expected was put on the point that aid ought not be given to a communist country with values so diametrically opposed to those of the United States.

In support of the proposal it was argued that since the funds were

---

[49] For breakdowns see the statistical tables in Appendix A, Document XVI and XVII and Appendix B in Harold H. Fisher's authoritative *The Famine in Soviet Russia, 1919-1923: The Operations of the American Relief Administration* (New York: Macmillan, 1927); Xenia J. Eudin and Harold H. Fisher, *Soviet Russia and the West, 1920-1927: A Documentary Survey* (Stanford: Stanford University Press, 1957), 28-36; Hoover, *Memoirs*, vol. II: *The Cabinet and the Presidency*, 23 ff. The Mennonite Central Committee, founded in 1920 specifically to aid brethren in Russia and Siberia, alone dispatched $1,292,625 in funds and goods to Russia between 1921 and 1926: John D. Unruh, *In the Name of Christ: A History of the Mennonite Central Committee and Its Service, 1920-1951* (Scottsdale, Pa.: Herald, 1952), 18-23.

to be used to purchase American surplus crops the measure, by raising domestic prices, would prove a boon for all American farmers.
Although the debates do not reflect the interest that some business
men felt in famine relief as a means of opening opportunities in
Russia, this may have been in the minds of some who supported the
measure. Some maintained that government aid would be of propaganda value in letting the Russian people know that America was not
an enemy. Still others held that it was a duty to feed the starving,
whether or not the famine resulted from communist experiments.

On December 17, 1921, the House, by an 181-71 vote, approved
the appropriation. The Senate concurred without a roll call. Thanks
in part to the effective work of Christian Herter, a Hoover aide, Congress also authorized the allocation of $4,000,000 surplus Army med-
ical supplies to the American Red Cross for Russian relief.[50]

Great credit must be given Hoover, not only for his part in persuading Congress to act and in effecting the cooperation of voluntary agencies with government, but for his efficiency in getting relief speedily
to Soviet Russia. Under the Hoover program a steady procession of
ships carried 740,571 tons of publicly and privately contributed gifts
of food, medicine, and clothing to Soviet Russia, representing a total
value of over $80,000,000.[51]

Convinced that there could be no assurance of honest expenditures
of the funds raised by liberal, radical, and pro-Communist agencies
in the field, Hoover urged the public to contribute to the American
Relief Administration or to one of the groups affiliated with it. This
confirmed the conviction of his critics in liberal and radical circles
that despite Hoover's profession to the contrary he envisaged relief
as a counterrevolutionary instrument. Support for this contention
came from the publication in the *World's Work* of articles by a former
ARA official who claimed that relief had stemmed the "red tide,"
especially in Hungary where the Communist regime of Bela Kun fell
when food reached the starving.[52]

It is probably fair to say that Hoover's policies rested on several

---

[50] *Congressional Record*, 67th Cong., 2d Sess., 1921, LXII, Pt. 1, 44-51, 428-31,
452-89; 586-88, 608-10; U. S., Congress, House, Committee on Foreign Affairs, Hearings, *Russian Relief*, 67th Cong., 2d Sess., 1921. See also George F. Kennan, *Soviet-
American Relations, 1917-1920*, vol. II: *The Decision to Intervene* (Princeton:
Princeton University Press, 1958), 8-9.

[51] Hoover, *Memoirs*, I, 420. The food, clothing, and medical supplies sent under
Hoover auspices to White Russia totaled 27,588 tons.

[52] T. T. C. Gregory, "Stemming the Red Tide," *World's Work* XLI (April, 1921),
608-13; XLII (May, 1921), 95-100; (June, 1921), 153-64.

presuppositions and reflected several motives, the precise influence of any one being impossible to determine: disapproval of agencies designed to strengthen Russian communist economy;[53] disapproval of agencies which in effect were arms of the Soviet government; approval of efficiency, economy, and fairness in the administration of relief; the compatibility of his program with the American national interest of absorbing surplus agricultural produce and, possibly, of paving the way (should the Soviets fall) for a favorable reception in Russia of American exports and enterprise; and, underlying all the others, the desire and the obligation to help suffering humanity.

Convinced that Hoover and the American Relief Administration were, despite denials, political in the sense of being in intention and effect counterrevolutionary, a number of agencies began to raise funds and, in the course of their campaigns, spared no words in denouncing Hoover. The number of such organizations is uncertain. In a letter to President Harding written on February 9, 1922, Hoover mentioned three and added that there were "some 200 affiliated organizations,"[54] which, however, were never identified. Many were not Communist, even though their leaders sometimes addressed meetings of agencies that definitely were; and sometimes confusion resulted from mistakes of the press in mixing the names of organizations—even the *New York Times* was guilty of this on at least one occasion. It is impossible to give reliable estimates for many of these agencies, but Hoover estimated that the American Federated Russian Famine Relief Committee had apparently received from its affiliates $350,000 in cash and $200,000 in kind by February, 1922. Years later the Dies Committee reported that the "Communist drive" accumulated more than a million dollars.[55]

The Friends of Soviet Russia, which was openly Communist, reported through its organ, *Soviet Russia*, that by November, 1922, it had spent over $800,000 for relief purposes.[56] At the time Abraham

[53] *Nation* CXIII (Dec. 7, 1921), 648-52.

[54] Fisher, *The Famine in Soviet Russia*, 548.

[55] U. S. Congress, House, Special Committee on un-American Activities [Dies Committee], *Hearings, Investigation of un-American Propaganda Activities in the United States*, 76th Cong., 1st Sess., 1939, VII, 4541; Benjamin Gitlow, *The Whole of Their Lives: Communism in America: A Personal History and Intimate Portrayal of Its Leaders* (New York: C. Scribner's Sons, 1948), 85-87, 221; *Congressional Record*, 81st Cong., 1st Sess., 1949, XCV, Pt. 1, 1959 ff.

[56] *Soviet Russia* VII (Dec., 1922), 307. The magazine, in addition to attacking Hoover and the ARA as politically inspired, campaigned for trade treaties and for the permanent economic reconstruction of the Soviet economy.

Cahan's *Jewish Daily Forward* accused the Friends of Soviet Russia of diverting its collections to the support of Communist activities in the United States. While the charge was denied, the Friends of Soviet Russia did not present a complete financial statement.[57] What funds and provisions went to Russia were sent to the Russian Red Cross, an arm of the Soviet Union not unequivocally recognized by the International Red Cross Society, or to the International Trade Union Help Committee.

In addition to the Friends of Soviet Russia and its allied organizations (such as the Technical Aid Society for Soviet Russia, the Famine Scout Club, the American Labor Alliance, and the Soviet Russian Medical Relief Society), several agencies, composed of socialists, ex-socialists, and liberals, and also distributing through the Russian Red Cross, appeared on the scene. One of the leading ones was the American Committee for Russian Famine Relief, in which the chief movers were Walter Liggett, an archcritic of Hoover, David Dubrowsky, head of the Russian Red Cross in the United States, and Paxton Hibben. It enlisted, at least for a time, the support of many governors and mayors as well as of leading educators, editors, and religious figures. Eventually the Committee, after Hoover's criticism based on its connection with the Russian Red Cross, asked the American Friends Service Committee to administer its funds, which was done. The *New York Times* estimated that by February, 1922, this committee had collected $500,000.[58]

Lying somewhere on the political spectrum between the American Relief Administration and the Communist groups were a number of liberal-progressive fund-raising committees. The most influential of these was the Russian Famine Fund, organized in September, 1921. Its national leadership represented a wide variety of political views, including Alfred E. Smith and Ogden Mills, Bull Moose Progressives such as Raymond Robins and Gifford Pinchot, and socialists such as Norman Thomas and Ernest Poole. Some members of the national committee favored recognition of the Soviet government and

[57] *New York Times*, July 28, August 1, 23, 1922.
[58] *Ibid.*, Feb. 9, 10, 16, 1922; Fisher, *The Famine In Soviet Russia*, 242-43; Paxton Hibben, "The Famine and the Foreign Powers," *Soviet Russia* VI (March 1, 1922), 108-112; U. S., Congress, House, Special Committee on un-American Activities [Dies Committee], *Hearings, Investigation of un-American Propaganda Activities in the United States*, 76th Cong., 1st Sess., 1939, VIII, 5138-55.

economic aid to Russia; others adamantly held that the United States should not resume diplomatic relations. On one thing most of the Famine Fund personnel agreed: the ARA was as much inspired by political as by humanitarian motives. In particular they resented Hoover's refusal to issue a general public appeal for funds and his "high-handed efforts" to force all independent agencies to distribute through the American Relief Administration. Assuming that many people were dissatisfied with the ARA, the Russian Famine Fund appealed to liberal and labor groups, political independents, religious, fraternal, and social organizations, women's clubs, and the general public.

While distrusting the ARA, the Famine Fund had no greater confidence in the Russian distribution agencies. All relief raised by the fund was administered by the American Friends Service Committee, the most thoroughly nonpolitical and independent of the agencies receiving ARA sanction. At first Hoover made no effort to discourage the work of the Russian Famine Fund. In fact until the Congressional appropriation for the ARA was made in December, 1921, the Famine Fund received his endorsement. Thereafter Hoover was less than cordial to all independent agencies for relief, and some of the Fund's leaders were greatly angered by his attempts to discourage further appeals. There is no available estimate of the total amount raised by the Russian Famine Fund. Probably it was less important as a fund raiser than as a protest against the ARA.[59]

Factual information, especially in the early stages of the famine, left much to be desired. In the spring of 1922, the National Information Bureau which, since its establishment in 1918, had helped protect the contributing public from fraudulent relief projects and provided information for member agencies, appointed a three-man commission which went to Russia as an impartial fact-finding agency. It engaged the cooperation of Soviet authorities. Its summary report, issued in February, 1923, discussed the two major famines of 1921-1922 and 1922-1923, the factors contributing to these catastrophes, the resources available in Russia and among foreign relief agencies, and

[59] Fisher, *The Famine in Soviet Russia*, 164-66; *New York Times*, Oct. 14, Nov. 8, 1921; "Memorandum Plan for Russian Famine Fund," Sept. 19, 1921; Harry Powers Story to Raymond Robins, Sept. 22, 1921; Alexander Gumberg to Robins, Sept. 22, 1921; Robins to Dr. Sidney Gulick, Sept. 30, 1921; Allen Wardwell to Robins, Oct. 22, 1921; Judah Magnes to Allen Wardwell, March 29, 1922 (copy), in the Raymond Robins manuscripts, Wisconsin State Historical Society, Madison, Wisconsin.

the steps being taken by the Soviet government to augment agricultural production and ease the obstacles to distribution of food, work animals, and medical relief in the worst-stricken districts.[59a]

Independent agencies included the American Committee for the Relief of Russian Children, in which Paxton Hibben took an active part. It raised funds through public meetings, and seems to have achieved the modest record of dispensing almost $24,000 for clothing, medical supplies, and milk. Hibben reported that these supplies went "right where they are intended to go," to feeding stations and to hospitals.[60]

Labor unions also contributed to Russian famine relief. The most important was the Amalgamated Clothing Workers of America, a union with more than a casual interest in Soviet Russia. By the end of 1921 it had collected from its membership $250,000, which it used to outfit a ship with 65,000 bushels of wheat and hundreds of tons of condensed milk, clothing, and drugs.[61] At the annual convention of the Amalgamated in 1922, a committee reported that not even the prolonged unemployment nor the raising of the two-million-dollar lockout fund had kept the membership from making donations.[62] Other unions which contributed included the United Cloth Hat and Cap Makers of North America and the International Ladies' Garment Workers' Union. The nonpartisan, nonpolitical Trade Union National Committee for Russian Relief, organized in mid-1922, represented nearly all the large and international unions. Generally speaking, the trade unions distributed through the American Friends Service Committee or through Nansen's international committee.[63]

Probably the American Relief Administration handled 85 per cent of American contributions, the independent organizations the rest.[64] The publicity of the fund-collecting agencies, especially the ARA

[59a] National Information Bureau, *Report*, 1918-1919 (New York, 1919); National Information Bureau, *The Russian Famines 1921-1922, 1922-1923* (New York, 1923), 3.

[60] Paxton Hibben, *Report on the Russian Famine, 1922* (New York: American Committee for the Relief of Russian Children, 1922), 17 ff.; *New York Times*, April 15, May 22, Nov. 13, 1922.

[61] Matthew Josephson, *Sidney Hillman: Statesman of American Labor* (Garden City: Doubleday, Page, 1952), 257.

[62] Amalgamated Clothing Workers of America, *Proceedings*, 1922, 272.

[63] *New York Times*, August 12, 1921, June 4, 1922; International Ladies' Garment Workers' Union, *Proceedings*, 1922, 94-95, 101.

[64] Frank A. Southard, Jr., "Famine," *Encyclopedia of the Social Sciences*, ed. Edwin R. A. Seligman, VI (1931), 89.

bulletins, the releases of the American Friends Service Committee and the Joint Distribution Committee, all helped to convey to Americans the horrors of famine and pestilence in Russia. Especially effective were the addresses of Fridtiof Nansen. He not only described what he had seen, but also showed photographs he had taken: pictures of peasants fighting in village streets for the carcases of dogs, cats, and other animals, often dug from the ground; of other peasants desperately tearing out thatched roofs and mixing the thatch with grass, moss, leaves, and bark; of the dead and dying in streets and railway stations; of bearers so weak that two could carry a sack of corn only with the greatest difficulty. The evidence indicated that necrophagia was common, and that there were well-authenticated cases of cannibalism, including the sale in the bazaars of human flesh of victims of murderers. Hearers wept and fainted. Some, unable to take any more, left the hall.

The horror of the facts presented pierced the very marrow of the bones of those who heard and saw. "I say now and I shall continue to say," declared Fridtjof Nansen, "never shall I forget the death agony in the eyes of those Russian children. Save Russia!" Nansen did not confine his appeals to Americans. He spoke in Europe, and the International Relief Committee he headed collected approximately $4,000,000, the expenditure of which he supervised in Russia. But Nansen's hope of arousing official Europe and the League of Nations to advance loans to Russia for large-scale relief met with indifference and opposition.[65]

Meantime the American Relief Administration was losing no time in moving food and medical supplies into Russia, in setting up kitchens, in bringing nourishment and medicine to the incredibly wretched shelters in which children, sick, starving, dying and dead, lay huddled in tattered rags, without blankets, in the midst of indescribable filth. At the height of the operations in 1922, the ARA fed 10,500,000 people at 18,000 feeding stations. To accomplish a task of such magnitude with limited means involved reducing the diet to the lowest common denominator. In addition to flour and milk, corn was the chief item despite the fact that peasants were unfamiliar with it. But the nutritive value of a dollar's worth of corn was higher

[65] Jon Sorensen, *The Saga of Fridtjof Nansen*, trans. J. B. C. Watkins (New York: American Scandinavian Foundation, 1932), 297-99; Fisher, *The Famine in Soviet Russia*, 547.

than that of any other food which the same sum could buy and, besides, Congress in its appropriation had specified corn. The starving, as Hoover observed, quickly accommodate themselves to any food.

It was believed that a Russian could be kept alive at a cost of a dollar a month. Between August 27, 1921, when the first work was begun, through June, 1923, the ARA expended over $61,500,000 and distributed over 700,000 tons of food, flour, milk, corn, seeds, and miscellaneous foodstuffs, in addition to medical supplies and clothing. More than three-fourths of these commodities were from American sources. In addition, ARA administered the food remittance program by which the buyer in America paid ten dollars to ARA, naming the beneficiary in Russia. The total value of the program was $13,680,193. Finally, the ARA engaged in cleanup campaigns with the help of recipients able to work. These campaigns helped control and prevent cholera and typhus.[66]

The head of the American Relief Administration mission to Russia was Colonel William Haskell, a former ARA administrator in southeast Europe and Armenia. The problems he and his staff of two hundred-odd Americans faced have been soberly described in Professor Fisher's account of the famine in Soviet Russia. Some of the difficulties were inherent in the situation, such as the incapacity of the transportation system, pilfering by brigands, and most of all, the sheer magnitude of the job. But many of the difficulties sprang from the workings of the Soviet bureaucracy and from the suspicion of the most doctrinaire Communists that the program was designed to overthrow the regime. The insecurity which most officials felt for its future was reflected in the determination of some to seize the ARA supplies and to use them to strengthen their control over the population. On many occasions Haskell and his associates, reminding those with whom they dealt in Moscow that such procedures violated the Riga agreement, threatened to cut off further imports.

Often obstacles were deliberately thrown in the way of the ARA staff: fewer trains were provided for transport than had been promised, with the result that food and supplies stayed in the harbors while people died. The mail of the staff was censored, the secret police, with whom the Americans had to deal, sometimes arrested Russian helpers or forced them to obey their commands while they were nominally taking orders from ARA. The interminable waiting

[66] Hoover, *Memoirs, vol. II: The Cabinet and the Presidency,* 25; Fisher, *The Famine in Soviet Russia,* 553-54.

for decisions, the mounting tension, the occasional showdowns, the reiterated public attacks on the ARA, required tact, patience, toughness. The Americans, according to *The Times* of London, proved to be both ingenious and brilliant in meeting these obstacles.[67] Thanks to the notebooks of Frank A. Golder and Lincoln Hutchinson and to Professor Fisher's research, abundant evidence testifies to the appreciation of those who received American relief. Even more graphic are the photographs of pitiful children and their parents when food was being distributed.[68] With the end of the program approaching in mid-1922, Maxim Gorky, by this time an exile from Russia, wrote to Hoover: "In all the history of human suffering I know of nothing more trying to the souls of men than the events through which the Russian people are passing, and in the history of practical humanitarianism I know of no accomplishment which in terms of magnitude and generosity can be compared to the relief that you have actually accomplished. . . . The generosity of the American people resuscitates the dream of fraternity among people at a time when humanity greatly needs charity and compassion." [69]

On the eve of their departure, Hoover's associates were given an official banquet in Moscow. High Soviet officials spoke warmly in appreciation of what had been done. Hoover himself received an elaborate scroll of thanks signed by the President of the Council of People's Commissars, Lev B. Kamenev, bearing the words: ". . . in the name of the millions of people who have been saved, as well as in the name of the whole working people of Soviet Russia and of the Confederated Republics, and before the whole world, to this organization, to its leader, Mr. Herbert Hoover, . . . and to all the workers of the organization, to express the most deeply felt sentiments of gratitude, and to state, that all the people inhabiting the Union of Soviet Socialist Republics never will forget the aid rendered to them by the American people, through the agency of the American Relief Administration, holding it to be a pledge of the future friendship of the two nations." [70]

But memories are not always long, and the historical record can be rewritten. In 1959 George F. Kennan called attention to the ex-

[67] Fisher, *The Famine in Soviet Russia*, 195 ff.; Review of *The Famine in Soviet Russia* by H. H. Fisher, *Times* [London] *Literary Supplement*, August 25, 1927.
[68] Frank A. Golder and Lincoln Hutchinson, *On the Trail of the Russian Famine* (Stanford: Stanford University Press, 1927).
[69] *American Relief Administration Bulletin*, series 2, XXVIII (Sept., 1922), 6.
[70] Hoover, *Memoirs—The Cabinet and the Presidency*, 25-26.

change of words between Deputy Premier Kozlov and Secretary of State Herter over the question of who paid for the famine relief of 1921-1922. Historical accounts written in the Soviet Union in our time ignore Gorky's appeal, maintain that the ARA itself took the initiative in proposing American aid, make light of what the ARA actually did in Russia, and play up unrealistically the contributions of the Soviet government and the foreign proletariat.[71]

In spite of these contentions, the ten to eleven million children and adults in Russia kept alive by the American Relief Administration, by allied religious American groups, and by liberal-radical organizations in the postwar years testify to the vitality and to the broad gauge of American philanthropy. The partnership of the official ARA and its affiliated voluntary agencies, comprising the bulk of relief, accomplished more than such past partnerships had ever done. The criticisms in Russia and among radicals in the United States that the program was inspired by considerations of national interest and policy were not without some truth. But the relief, whatever its intent, also helped to stabilize conditions in the Soviet Union, including the existing government.[72] The campaigns in America, with all the bitterness involved, nevertheless stimulated a growing good will toward Russia. And the total achievement, notwithstanding mistakes, shortcomings, and criticisms in the Soviet Union, was a remarkable testimony to the leadership and efficiency of Herbert Hoover. What was done by all the agencies constituted the most constructive phase of American-Russian relations in the 1920's.[73]

Also important were the contributions of American Jewish groups to their coreligionists in Russia. During 1922, for example, the American office of Idgezkom had a total of over 700 children's institutions with 91,000 children under its control in Soviet Russia, in addition to medical, sanitary, and other institutions. The chief contributor was, of course, the American Jewish Joint Distribution Committee which had begun its work before the American Relief Administration was established and which in March, 1922, entered into an arrangement with the ARA by which it financed a program for feeding 800,000 children and 400,000 adults under the ARA and on a

[71] George F. Kennan, "Our Aid to Russia: A Forgotten Chapter," New York Times Magazine, July 19, 1959. See also E. M. Halliday, "Bread Upon the Waters," American Heritage XI (August, 1960), 69, 104-05.
[72] New York Times, August 4, 1921.
[73] William A. Williams, American Russian Relations, 1781-1947 (New York: Rinehart, 1952), 91 ff., 177 ff.

strictly nonsectarian basis. In 1922-23 the Joint Distribution Committee contributed to Russian relief over $3,650,000 and, in addition, sent large quantities of woolen and flannel cloth, sheeting, and underwear. The ARA permitted the Joint Distribution Committee to send representatives and helpers into Russia, the most notable of whom were Dr. Boris Bogen and Dr. Joseph Rosen. The latter, a Russianborn but naturalized American agronomist, began a cooperative project resulting in the planting of 2,700,000 acres with American corn. This was in 1923 when hunger was still great. Later, as we shall see, Rosen played a major role in one of the most dramatic and significant American philanthropies of the 1920's and 1930's—the settlement of thousands of Russian Jews on hitherto unused land in the Crimea.[74]

Meantime attention was focused on the fortunes of the Jews of Poland and its borderlands which, with Russia, contained the greatest number of the world's Jews. The plight of the Jews in this area resulted from the liquidation of the Austro-Hungarian Empire, the rise of the new succession states, the nationalistic upsurge in Poland, including its war with Russia in 1920, and the brief communist regime in Hungary, together with the Russian revolution and counterrevolution, especially as they affected White Russia and the Ukraine. The war and postwar movements destroyed Jewish charity organizations, as well as Jewish homes and businesses, and sent hundreds of thousands into exile, to become the prey of marauding bands, revolutionary and counterrevolutionary forces, famine and pestilence. Jewbaiters in the borderlands made matters worse. In Ukraine alone, for example, during the war and postwar years pogroms liquidated some 200,000 Jews.

All sectors of American Jewry were deeply concerned over this situation and all gave through one channel or another and frequently through several. In 1922 the People's Relief Committee, one of the constituent donors to the Joint Distribution Committee, transmitted to Europe $475,000, representing the gifts of 41,000 persons.[75] But

---

[74] *American Jewish Yearbook*, Sept., 1923–Sept., 1924 XXV (Philadelphia: Jewish Publication Society of America, 1923), 80-81; *New York Times*, Feb. 10, 1924; Surface and Bland, *American Food in the World War and Reconstruction Period*, 57-58, 105-06; Moses A. Leavitt, *The JDC Story: Highlights of JDC Activities, 1914-1952* (New York: American Jewish Joint Distribution Committee, 1953), 6; David A. Brown, *Report to the Special Commission of the American Jews Relief Committee* (n.p.: n.d.), *passim*; Hoover, *American Epic*, II, 214-23.

[75] *American Jewish Yearbook*, Sept., 1923–Sept., 1924, XXV, 80.

the JDC was the largest agency in the field. Its leaders, like other American Jews in the months after the armistice, felt that in view of the vast need of their coreligionists and of the prevailing anti-Semitism in Poland and other parts of Europe, Jewish contributions ought to go directly to these desperate men, women and children.

Hoover took a different position. In view of the cooperative nature of the pre-Armistice war relief drives and with the conviction that only concentrated authority could work effectively in the stricken areas, Hoover held that Jewish funds ought to be thrown in with general relief, handled by the American Food and Grain Administration and, later, the American Relief Administration. Rising above partisan considerations, Felix Warburg persuaded his associates to give $3,300,000 to the Hoover organization.[76] In addition, the Joint Distribution Committee contributed to the programs of the YMCA, the American Red Cross, and the Polish Relief Committee of America.

But the Joint Distribution Committee did not rest content in cooperating with other agencies. In January, 1919, it dispatched the steamship *Westward Ho*, laden with a cargo of food, clothing, and medicines valued at $2,000,000, to Danzig. The journey was repeated eight weeks later.[77] Two teams, including experts in sanitation, child care, and economic reconstruction, braved formidable risks in their conduct of direct relief work—dispensing food and medicines, warding off pogroms, and finding transport and shelter for the wounded and terrified during the brutalities of the Polish-Russian war. Two of the JDC's agents were killed by marauding guerillas.[78] With the help of the enfeebled Jewish community agencies and of other international organizations, Jewish and non-Jewish, the JDC units helped finance nearly 500 medical and sanitary institutions, rescued starving scholars in the Orthodox Yeshivoth, and saved countless lives.

Under direction from headquarters in New York the JDC teams scrupulously avoided all tendency to dictate, confining themselves to suggestions and to financial and technical aid. Also in line with

[76] Boris D. Bogen, *Born a Jew* (New York: Macmillan, 1930), 125-29. "In Warburg," Bogen wrote, "was the spiritual elevation becoming to the Jew. The small Jewish politics of the period raged about him, but he walked with his head high above it. For angry and envious men he set an example of sweetness;" Herbert Agar, *The Saving Remnant: An Account of Jewish Survival* (New York: Viking, 1960), 31.

[77] *New York Times*, Jan. 27, March 16, May 11, 1919.

[78] Joseph C. Hyman, *Twenty-Five Years of American Aid to Jews Overseas: A Record of the Joint Distribution Committee* (New York: American Jewish Joint Distribution Committee, 1939), 9 ff.; Agar, *The Saving Remnant*, 31 ff.

JDC policy, every effort was made to encourage self-help lest recipients become pauperized and lest aid be looked on as a necessary and permanent crutch. Thus for example in 1921, when the American Relief Administration withdrew from Poland, the Joint Distribution Committee launched a campaign to raise funds through the matching device. This only partly succeeded, since Jews who could help their worse-off fellows feared to do so lest any public knowledge of their ability to give prove ruinous in the highly charged anti-Semitic atmosphere.[79] The self-help emphasis, however, worked increasingly well as the years passed. Between 1919 and 1923, JDC spent over $3,700,000 in its Polish program.

Although the JDC had tried to meet immediate needs resulting from highly abnormal circumstances, it became more and more clear that the refugee problem, the plight of the Jews in Russia and Siberia, and the situation in Palestine were to be more than temporary emergencies. With this in mind, the Committee in 1920 reorganized its structure and program. It set up a European Executive Council. Felix Warburg persuaded the gifted lawyer and artist, James N. Rosenberg, to head the Council, an assignment which was to have notable results.[80] In New York itself committees were organized to supervise relief and rehabilitation—committees on refugees, medicine and sanitation, child care, and cultural affairs. Drawing on the $20,000,000 raised between 1920 and 1923, these committees gave emergency relief through indigenous agencies which were encouraged to take financial and managerial responsibility for the program as soon as possible, for JDC had a horror of pauperizing the recipients of its aid or seeming to dictate policy. And besides, even after the reorganization of 1920, it still thought of itself as presently to go out of business.

The committee on child care provided milk stations, clothing, fuel for schools, summer camps, and almost everything else that was needed. In 1920 Louis Marshall reported that in Poland alone Joint Distribution Committee was feeding 300,000 children. It also took responsibility for almost that many orphans elsewhere in Europe and the Near East, though lack of funds and personnel curtailed what could be done. By 1923 the Federation of Orphan Care in Poland took over the program that the JDC committee on child care had

[79] Bogen, *Born a Jew*, 246 ff.
[80] James N. Rosenberg, *On the Steppes: A Russian Diary* (New York: Knopf, 1927), viii ff. and *Painters Self Portrait* (New York: Crown, 1958), 51 ff.

begun. Similar orphans' committees were organized in other countries.[81]

Of long term importance was the work of the American ORT Federation, established in 1922. This was a branch of an organization founded in Russia in 1880—the Society for the Promotion of Trade and Industry Among Jews (the Russian letters were ORT). The American ORT Federation, which in 1923 raised $1,000,000, drew additional resources from the Joint Distribution Committee. It carried on the established program of providing technical and vocational training for young Jews all over Europe, in North Africa, and in Palestine. It also made available through ORT raw materials and mechanical equipment for vocational schools. In Poland alone JDC subsidized 670 trade schools which trained over 30,000 craftsmen before the outbreak of the Second World War.[82]

In some ways the work of the Committee on Reconstruction, headed by Herbert Lehman, dovetailed with that of ORT. This committee created, revived, and fostered consumers' and producers' cooperatives and substantially aided the credit banking cooperatives or Loan Kassas. These made loans to small Jewish business men and artisans to enable them to get on their feet, and, in so doing, proved useful in restoring Jewish economic life.[83] In 1924 the American Joint Reconstruction Foundation was established by the collaboration of JDC and the Jewish Colonization Society, the organization founded and munificently supported by Baron de Hirsch in the later nineteenth century, which in addition to helping Jewish emigrants become farmers in North and South America gave some aid to those who preferred not to migrate. The American Joint Reconstruction Foundation extended credit cooperatives, not only in Poland but in Lithuania and in other countries. The money the Foundation supplied on a strictly business basis became a revolving fund constantly increasing in value. The stimulus to self-help was evident in the fact that whereas at first the Foundation supplied as much as 80 per cent of the funds, its subsequent contribution was only from 10 per cent to 18 per cent of the credit cooperative's budget. The 323 credit co-

[81] *New York Times*, March 8, Nov. 15, 1920. These figures may be misleading. Agar reports that 400,000 children were being helped soon after the establishment of the committee in 1920, including 75,000 orphans: Agar, *The Saving Remnant, passim.*
[82] *New York Times*, March 19, 1923, Nov. 10, 1924, June 3, 1928; *American Jewish Yearbook*, Sept., 1926–Sept., 1927, XXVIII, 44 and Sept., 1929–Sept., 1930, XXXI, 34 ff. See also American ORT Federation, *ORT: A Record of Ten Years Rebuilding Jewish Economic Life* (New York, 1956).
[83] Leavitt, *The JDC Story*, 8; *New York Times*, March 30, 1924.

operatives at the start of the program with a membership of 115,000 seemed modest indeed in contrast with the 767 associations of 1930 which were making loans totaling $65,000,000 to 50,000 of the 320,000 members. Thus did pump-priming of a self-help variety on the part of the Foundation rebuild Jewish economy.[84]

The medical and sanitary aid JDC rushed to Poland after the Armistice and during the conflict with Russia saved countless lives. Though JDC helped rebuild hospitals, bathhouses, and homes for the infirm,[85] health conditions among Polish Jews continued to be deplorable: tuberculosis, trachoma, and favus took heavy tolls. To help build a long range health program the committee on medicine and sanitation stimulated the organization of a Jewish Health Society known by its alphabetical identification as TOZ. This was modeled on the famous Russian OSE (also meaning Jewish Health Society) which after a long and distinguished record had been abolished by the Bolsheviks in 1919.

Polish Jews fairly soon took over complete management of TOZ which by 1939, when its program had increased twenty-fold, was largely self-supporting. Its record in decreasing the incidence of epidemic diseases and lengthening the life span among Jews was a notable one. From Poland, the idea of Jewish health societies—under the original Russian designation OSE—spread to the Baltic states, to Roumania and at length to western Europe, North Africa, and Palestine. JDC contributed, especially in the early stages, to the support of these health organizations.[86]

The Cultural Committee of the Joint Distribution Committee, chaired by Cyrus Adler and representing Orthodox, Reformed, and labor groups, had one of the hardest jobs. Despite its composition, it was subject to much criticism both in the United States and across the seas. The more traditional communities in the Old World felt that too little was done for the all-important Yeshivoth and other religious agencies. On the other hand, many secularly-oriented Jews

[84] Agar, *The Saving Remnant*, 43-44; Hyman, *Twenty-Five Years of American Aid to Jews Overseas*, 22 ff.; *American Jewish Yearbook*, Sept., 1926–Sept., 1927, XXVIII, 85; *New York Times*, July 31, 1921, Sept. 4, Nov. 7, 1922, March 19, August 26, 1923, Feb. 10, March 30, 1924, March 28, 1926, Jan. 30, 1927.

[85] When JDC began to liquidate its medical work in Poland it transferred to the Jewish Health Society (TOZ) three nurses' training schools, 12 sanatoria, 43 hospitals, and 213 bathhouses: *American Jewish Yearbook*, Sept., 1924–Sept., 1925, XXVI, 83; *New York Times*, May 29, 1926.

[86] Agar, *The Saving Remnant*, 41-42; *New York Times*, April 10, 1925; Israel Cohen, *Contemporary Jewry* (London: Methuen, 1950), 39-40.

frowned on the use of JDC funds for reviving and sustaining Orthodox religious and cultural institutions at the expense of health, refugee
work, and economic reconstruction. These critics disapproved the aid
given to the more conservative of the 1,900 schools on all levels.
Yet this aid, and the direct contributions to needy scholars, writers,
rabbis, and spiritual leaders did much to keep alive not only dedicated human beings but the hard core of Jewishness itself.[87]

The displacement during the war and the related revolutionary
upheavals of hundreds of thousands of Jews who could not or did not
want to return to what had been their homes was by no means all of
the postwar refugee problem. This problem concerned the newly
established League of Nations and occasioned the organization of a
nonofficial agency, International Social Service. This stemmed from
a committee formed in 1920 at the World's YWCA convention in
London. With relatively small contributions from several countries,
including that of the Laura Spellman Rockefeller Foundation, International Social Service developed what was to be a continuous
program of safeguarding refugees against unscrupulous steamship lines
that promised a haven, and gave other help, regardless of the politics,
religion, race, or nationality of those in need.[88] There were also, of
course, many other refugee organizations, an example being the Russian Refugee Relief Society of America. This met arrivals at Ellis
Island and at San Francisco, provided temporary homes, and aided in
language and employment problems. It received commendation from
the High Commissioner of the League of Nations refugee organization for its "fine humanitarian work." [89]

The Joint Distribution Committee also concerned itself with those
who could not migrate to Palestine because of the restrictions placed
on immigration by the British mandate, or to the United States which
in 1931 and following years limited the number of immigrants from
eastern European countries to a tiny fraction of the prewar inflow.
The JDC's special committee on refugees, established in 1920, fed

[87] It is estimated that 2,000 educational and religious institutions enrolling 250,000
students received grants at one time or another in the 1920's and early 1930's. For
this story, and the subsidies given an American committee formed to aid an isolated
Jewish community—the Falasha—see Cyrus Adler, *I Have Considered the Days* (Philadelphia: Jewish Publication Society of America, 1941), 391; Miriam Eisenstein, *Jewish
Schools in Poland*, 1919-39 (New York: Kings Crown, 1950), 38, 49-50, and Agar,
The Saving Remnant, 32, 69-70.

[88] International Social Service, *In a World They Never Made: The Story of International Social Service* (New York, ca. 1958), 7.

[89] *New York Times*, Oct. 16, 1924.

stranded newcomers in various ports and provided other types of re-lief. One of the most difficult jobs was that of helping the 10,000 Jewish prisoners and the some 10,000 refugees in Siberia, some of whom were pushing toward Vladivostok and some toward Europe. The Committee spent large sums in helping some 300,000 persons before in 1923 it turned over its tasks to a new agency.[90] In these years JDC was careful to steer clear of any semblance of "assisted immigration," which American law forbade. With much circumspec-tion it avoided association with the League of Nations programs since the United States was not a member of the new organization.[91]

In the early years of its concern for refugees, JDC conflicted in some respects with the Hebrew Sheltering and Immigrant Aid Society (HIAS). This agency in 1919 could boast of having interceded in the ten years of its existence in almost 29,000 cases of Jewish immi-grants held for special inquiry and of having helped in all almost 83,000 men, women, and children reach their American destination. In September, 1921, HIAS opened a drive for $1,000,000 to help Jews stranded in Europe and, if possible, to divert some of the stream to Latin America. By the end of 1921 HIAS had helped some 800,000 men, women, and children in the United States and abroad at a cost of over $1,000,000. The aid had taken various forms: temporary re-lief, dealing with officials in matters of passports and visas, maintain-ing classes in English and Spanish, providing training in agriculture preparatory to a new life in strange lands, and transmitting cash from American relatives to kinfolk in various countries who needed it in preparing to migrate.[92]

In 1924 the overlapping of functions was largely surmounted when the American Jewish Committee, representing the JDC, the National Council of Jewish Women, and HIAS agreed to organize and support the Emergency Committee on Jewish Refugees headed by Louis Marshall. Further cooperation resulted in 1927 when HIAS joined with two European agencies to establish an agency com-

[90] *American Jewish Yearbook*, Sept., 1923–Sept., 1924, XXV, 80; Leavitt, *The JDC Story*, 8.

[91] Charles Reznikoff, ed., *Louis Marshall: Champion of Liberty; Selected Papers and Addresses* (2 vols.; Philadelphia: The Jewish Publication Society of America, 1957), I, 196-97, 202-03.

[92] Harry S. Linfield, *Jewish Migration* (New York: Jewish Statistical Bureau, 1933), *passim*; Mark Wischnitzer, *Visas to Freedom: The History of HIAS* (Cleveland: World, 1956), 91 ff.; *American Jewish Yearbook*, Sept., 1925–Sept., 1926, XXVII, 68 ff.; *New York Times*, March 16, 1919, June 7, 1920, Feb. 14, Sept. 11, 1921, Sept. 24, 1924.

monly referred to as HICEM. Chiefly supported by HIAS, which was giving $500,000 in 1927, the new agency settled Jewish refugees in cooperation with welfare agencies throughout the world.[93]

The refugee problem that grew out of the First World War and the revolutionary upsurges tapered off, but new conditions, economic and political, brought to the fore the whole issue of peoples uprooted against their wishes. The problem was to become acute in the 1930's when Hitlerism made all previous Jewish troubles seem small and when, partly in consequence, the American Jewish community sharply divided in its philanthropic activities over the long simmering issue of Zionism.

In 1925, just as the Joint Distribution Committee planned to close shop, an economic crisis developed in Poland which convinced Felix Warburg, on seeing conditions, that the work which was to have been temporary must go on. During that very year JDC appropriated for its various programs over $1,300,000. This brought its total outlay since its formation in 1914 to almost $50,000,000. It estimated that its contributions had saved at least three million lives at a cost of about $20 a life.[94] This record, though only a small part of American overseas philanthropy during the First World War and its aftermath, was outstanding. It was also a preparation for a new holocaust.

[93] *American Jewish Yearbook*, Sept., 1928–Sept., 1929, XXX, 33; Mark Wischnitzer, *To Dwell in Safety: The Story of Jewish Migration Since 1800* (Philadelphia: Jewish Publication Society of America, 1948), 55; *New York Times*, April 17, Oct. 17, 1927.
[94] *New York Times*, March 20, 1924, May 17, 1925.

XI

Searches for International
Peace and Progress

No very sharp break marked the established patterns of American overseas philanthropy in the years between the two World Wars. American generosity, both on the part of men and women of wealth and of a considerable segment of the population, found many overseas expressions despite the cynical caveats of such antisentimentalists as Hergesheimer, Nathan, and Mencken. The last went so far as to declare that giving money to starving children in Europe was one of "the least engaging ways in which money can be spent" and that "doing good is in bad taste."

During the prosperous twenties and even in the rough thirties Americans continued to give, as they had in the past, for the relief of sufferers in such natural disasters as the earthquakes in Japan in 1923 and the chronic famine in China. Giving to such causes was not confined merely to members of churches. Most giving was in some degree influenced by the ideal of brotherhood which was, theoretically, basic in our Judeo-Christian culture. Welfare activities of Christian missionaries continued to expand in every quarter of the globe. During these years Jewish philanthropy found particular expression in the colonization of coreligionists in the Soviet Union, for which giving during the years of famine and pogroms had provided the background. At the same time the thorny issue of Zionism, which had become acute during the First World War and in the early 1920's, divided American Jewry in its attitude toward philanthropy in the Old World. And, in a manner long familiar, individuals interested in a country by reason of birth or affiliation bestowed gifts and left legacies as testimonials of sentimental affection in France, Italy, Czechoslovakia, and other countries.[1]

Of special note in this last category was the response of Irish-Americans to the need of the homeland in the years of intense civil strife during and following World War I. Organized in December, 1920, under the auspices of well-known figures, including Cardinal Gibbons, the American Committee for the Relief of Ireland raised over $5,000,000 through its state and local committees. While endorsed by President Harding and Vice-President Coolidge, and humanitarian rather than religious or political in its appeal, the Committee emphasized the responsibility of Americans of Irish background in the fund-raising campaign. Distribution of relief was largely channeled through the Irish White Cross.[2]

Although the establishment in the prewar period of the World Peace Foundation and the Carnegie Endowment for International Peace had shown the way,[3] there was notable development of philanthropic support for international understanding during the 1920's and 1930's. In a sense, this unofficial movement was an American counterpart of the official approach to the problem that other countries were making through the League of Nations and the World

[1] Typical of such gifts in this period were those of the Tucks to France, already mentioned; those of William Nelson Cromwell, a wealthy New York lawyer, to worthy causes in the same country: *New York Times*, Jan. 13, 1928, and Arthur Hobson Dean, *William Nelson Cromwell, 1854-1948: An American Pioneer in Corporation, Comparative, and International Law* (New York, 1957), 157, 160; the bequest of Mrs. Leonard Cohen of Wilkes-Barre to Posen, her birthplace, of $100,000 to help "poor Jews": *New York Times*, Sept. 10, 1924, Feb. 6, 1929; a gift of the same amount from Carl Landsee, a Milwaukee tanner, to Rotenburg, Germany: *New York Times*, June 19, 1934; the $600,000 gift of Joseph Deutsch, a wealthy New York furniture manufacturer, to a synagogue: *New York Times*, Sept. 25, 1924; and that of Robert Douglas, founder and former president of Certo Corporation in Rochester, New York, who gave $1,000,000 to his birthplace, the town of Scone, Scotland, to be used for "public, charitable, and educational work;" *New York Times*, April 12, 1930. In the case of the Cohen bequest, litigation arose on the ground that there were no "poor Jews" in the town to accept it. Some years later it was accepted for the repair of an old folk's home and for the support in Jewish institutions of the sick and needy. For a general discussion of the position of American courts on similar bequests see Neill H. Alford, Jr., "Voluntary Foreign Aid: The Element of State Control," *Virginia Law Review* XLVI (April, 1960), 477-511.

[2] *Report of the American Committee for Relief in Ireland* (New York, 1922), 7-49. Edward L. Doheny, a member of the executive committee of the American Association for the Recognition of the Irish Republic, was reported at the time of his death as having contributed $4,000,000 for the relief and aid of the Irish in the last phases of their struggle for independence, but this was probably greatly exaggerated: *New York Times*, Sept. 9, 1935. See also Charles C. Tansill, *America and the Fight for Irish Freedom, 1866-1922* (New York: Devin-Adair, 1957), 415.

[3] See above, Chapter VII, 34-35.

Court, which Congress rejected in its reaction against Wilsonian internationalism. In the period between the two world conflicts the World Peace Foundation and the Carnegie Endowment sought through the promotion and dissemination of knowledge and understanding to strengthen the forces making for peace.

The Carnegie Endowment, more amply supported than the World Peace Foundation, may be taken as representative of philanthropy in this sphere. One of its principal officers, Nicholas Murray Butler, was convinced that a true international mind might be developed by doing rather than talking, by practice rather than by preaching, and that the multiplication of international contacts was the best means by which "the men and women of one land might come to know more intimately the life, the language, and the customs of another." [4] To this end aid was extended for the rebuilding of devastated libraries and other institutions in Belgium, France, Serbia and Russia. On the assumption that knowledge is indispensable to international understanding, Butler's Division of Intercourse and Education distributed books on American history, literature, and institutions to selected libraries in Europe, South America, and Asia.

The Division also distributed its own publications on international understanding both to American and foreign libraries. It supported collegiate international relations clubs, first in the United States, and then abroad. By 1936, the number had reached 805. Besides providing for the entertainment of well-known foreign visitors, the Endowment, building on a 1917 precedent, developed the interchange of foreign and American professors. And despite increasing emphasis on its own operating program, it also subsidized such agencies for international education and understanding as the Institute of Pacific Relations, the Foreign Affairs Forum, the League of Nations Association, and the Foreign Policy Association. [5]

Under the direction of Professor James T. Shotwell of Columbia University, the Division of Economics and History carried through a multi-volume study by foreign scholars of the economic and social history of the World War. The project was intended to aid needy

[4] Carnegie Endowment for International Peace, *Year Book*, 1925 (Washington: The Endowment, 1926), 52.
[5] *Ibid.*, 1919, 65 ff., 1921, 36 ff., 1928, 35-36, and other *Year Books*. Although the Endowment continued on a reduced scale to subsidize European peace organizations for a time, the development of its own operating program resulted in the virtual abandonment of this policy.

European scholars and also to help shape attitudes toward war to the end that histories in the future might dwell, not on the glory of battle, but on the social and economic effects of war. "We have erected, almost without knowing it," wrote Shotwell, "a sort of international academy intent upon the realization of a great enterprise, studying the phenomena of war in a new spirit and with a growing sense of the moral, as well as the scientific implication of the economic and social displacement which it has caused." The study, published in 152 volumes, cost $750,000. It was received favorably at home and abroad. In the eyes of the Endowment, it was a unique contribution to the scholarly understanding of war.[6]

The Division of International Law of the Carnegie Endowment edited and published classics in the field. In the United States and elsewhere it supported research, including the compilation and publication of the records of international arbitration. It also offered student and teaching fellowships. It planned and largely maintained The Hague Academy of International Law which brought together scholars from all over the world. The division also made its resources available to the State Department during the naval disarmament conference of 1921 and, through the American Institute of International Law, prepared thirty projects which were accepted by the Pan American Commission of Jurists at the Rio meeting in 1925.[7] In the words of a leading authority, the Endowment exerted a considerable influence on the Latin-American policy of the United States, "particularly in supporting, materially, morally, and intellectually, a movement for treaties for conciliation and arbitration, until they finally became a reality in government policy and action." [8]

All these programs involved considerable expenditure and led to varying evaluations. Up to June, 1940, the income of the Carnegie Endowment from its capital fund amounted to over $15,500,000 and in addition to this it had received almost $3,000,000 from the Carnegie Corporation.[9] Eight years earlier, in 1932, Dr. James Brown Scott, the learned head of the Division of International Law, in summing up twenty-one years of the Endowment's activities, noted that it had established for itself "such a position of world-wide confidence, respect and usefulness as would lead to the conclusion that its plans

[6] *Ibid.*, 1919, 89; 1920, 73; 1922, 82.
[7] *Ibid.*, 1919, 128-32, and other *Year Books.*
[8] Samuel Flagg Bemis, *The Latin American Policy of the United States: An Historical Interpretation* (New York: Harcourt, Brace, 1943), 232 ff., 321.
[9] Carnegie Endowment for International Peace, *Year Book,* 1941, 22-24.

and methods for promoting international peace have been sufficiently tried and not found wanting." Had Mr. Carnegie lived, he added, he would not have been disappointed in what had been achieved.[10] On the other hand, such a favorable verdict was not always given outside the organization. To some it seemed that the Endowment had spent a vast sum on a kind of scholarship and on a concern for an intellectual elite which left both governments and public opinion in a broad sense virtually unaffected.[11]

The historian has no method for assessing with any great confidence such conflicting opinion. But he can suppose that the Endowment must have contributed in some unmeasurable degree to the understanding that developed between the United States and her allies in the second world conflict. Many factors, material as well as cultural, helped pave the way for the United Nations, but the Carnegie Endowment played an important part in this period of preparation. The same thing may also be said of the contributions, some not too impressive, others appreciable, of other agencies in this field.

Apart from the Carnegie agencies, the only major prewar foundation was the Rockefeller Foundation. It too included in its program work for international understanding. To this end it contributed indirectly through the promotion in many countries of research in the field of health, and directly by subsidizing agencies committed to the advancement of international understanding. These included the Foreign Policy Association, the Council of Foreign Relations in New York City and abroad, the Canadian Institute of International Affairs, the Geneva Research Center, the International Studies Conference at Paris, the Institute of Economics and History in Copenhagen, and the Royal Institute of International Affairs in London. All these institutions operated, as did the Rockefeller Foundation, on the assumption that the increase and diffusion of knowledge is an essential factor in promoting international understanding.

With the growing tensions in the 1930's the interest of the Rockefeller Foundation in promoting international understanding through knowledge increased markedly. "To speak of research in the field of international relations in such an anxious and disillusioned hour as

[10] *Ibid.*, 1932, 20.
[11] For example, Horace Coon, *Money to Burn; What the Great American Philanthropic Foundations Do With Their Money* (New York: Longmans, Green, 1938), 109-30.

this," the annual report for 1938 declared, "may seem almost like a jest. Everywhere reason is on the defensive and we live in danger that mass hysteria will completely overwhelm it at a time when it is most needed as a safeguard. . . . Friendly relations between nations must be based on an intelligent understanding of the contribution which each is in a position to make to the other. Too often cultural values have been conceived as something that one nation offers to another, and the other, if enlightened, thankfully accepts. But this one-sided arrangement," continued the report, "if it works at all, is apt to produce unhappy results. Moreover, it sacrifices at the start half the advantages that could accrue." The report cited the failure of the missionary movement to appreciate the value of cross-fertilization as an example of the wrong sort of approach to the problem of mutual understanding.[12]

The Rockefeller Foundation tried to spell out this position in two areas, Latin America and the Far East. In the one case it made grants to several colleges and universities in the United States to develop Latin-American studies and to two institutions in Mexico and Argentina "directed toward the development of personnel for special tasks of international usefulness." [13] In the other instance, the Foundation increased its support for enterprises dedicated to the promotion of mutual understanding with China and Japan through knowledge and cultural interchange. One of these enterprises was the Institute of Pacific Relations to which its contributions were larger than those of any other donor save Jerome D. Greene, who, though not a very wealthy man, gave both his time and some $20,000 to $30,000 a year. The Institute sponsored researches and conferences in Honolulu, Kyoto, and other key centers designed to help forestall crises in international relations.[14]

The League of Nations and its associated activities for which there was considerable enthusiasm in limited circles benefitted from

[12] Rockefeller Foundation, *Annual Report*, 1938 (New York: Rockefeller Foundation, 1939), 47, 56.

[13] *Ibid.*, 1940, 284.

[14] In 1929-1930 the Laura Spellman Rockefeller Foundation also contributed to the Institute, giving $60,000 and promising an additional $70,000 contingent on a like gift from other sources. Rockefeller also made contributions to the Institute apart from those of the Foundation. Other substantial contributors were Secretary of the Interior, Ray Lyman Wilbur, and Julius Rosenwald: Edwin Embree to Julius Rosenwald, Sept. 11, 1931, Jerome D. Greene to Edwin Embree, May 19, 1930; J. Merle Davis to Rosenwald, June 5, 1929, Rosenwald Papers, University of Chicago Library, box 42. See also Chester Rowell, *The Kyoto Conference of the Institute of Pacific Relations* (New York: Carnegie Endowment for International Peace, 1930).

private American giving. The Rockefellers donated $500,000 for the League Library, and Edward Filene put up $25,000 for an inquiry by the International Labor Office into real wages. In the summer of 1929 American gifts to the League and its programs totaled $965,000.[15] In the interest of creating favorable attitudes toward the new organization, many Americans contributed in large and small amounts to the League of Nations Non-Partisan Association. Other unofficial agencies dedicated to the promotion of international understanding and peace also enlisted financial support. These included Count Coudenhove-Kalerge's Pan-European Union and the American Arbitration Association.[16]

A number of agencies geared their program to the promotion of better understanding between the United States and a particular country. The American Scandinavian Foundation, a pre-World War I agency, led the way. Its program in the 1920's and 1930's, supported by limited resources, did not essentially differ from that worked out in the pioneering period.[17] Inspired perhaps by this organization, or perhaps by that of the English-speaking Union, Edward Bok [18] founded the Netherlands American Foundation. With a counterpart organization in Holland the new agency's program included translations of books in both languages and exchange of students and professors.[19]

Other countries came within the purview of those wanting to better relations with the United States. In 1928 Ralph Strassburger, former diplomat, and currently publisher and gentleman farmer in Pennsylvania, set up a prize award to authors and journalists of

---

[15] *New York World*, July 5, 1929. The American Foundation for International School, in which Thomas W. Lamont, John D. Rockefeller, Jr., Julius Rosenwald, Mrs. Emmons Blaine and others were interested, was organized to develop an international school in Geneva for the children of members of the League Secretariat. By 1929 the Foundation had raised $220,000 to buy a villa for the school. American Foundation for International School Folder, in the Foundation Library Center, New York City.

[16] Felix Warburg to Henry Wisansky, Sept. 21, 1927, Rosenwald Papers, 52, and Edwin R. Embree to Clark Eichelberger, Dec. 20, 1928, Rosenwald Papers, box 46.

[17] See above, Chapter VII, p. 20. The Foundation's financial difficulties are discussed in an interesting letter from Colonel Oscar Solbert in which Rosenwald was asked for help in the fellowship program: Col. Oscar Solbert to S. C. Graves, Jan. 22, 1927, Rosenwald Papers, box 3.

[18] Bok established a $100,000 prize for the most practicable plan by which the United States might develop cooperation with other countries. Twenty plans were submitted and published as *Ways to Peace*. Since half of the offered prize was conditional on an adequate degree of public support for the plan, the winner, Charles H. Levermore, received only $50,000 from Bok.

[19] *New York Times*, Dec. 18, July 21, 1921, Jan. 4, 1922.

France, Hungary, Austria, and Germany for the best contribution through books and other publications to friendship between their native countries and the United States.[20] To counteract lingering prejudice against Germany, a heritage of the war, and to improve cultural understanding between the Fatherland and America, seven men in 1930 incorporated in New York the Carl Schurz Memorial Foundation. Three of these men led the way in the fund-raising campaign with contributions of $50,000 each.

Although the depression was a blow to the high expectations of the founders and the rising Nazi movement in Germany an even more serious one, professors and students were exchanged, American books, music and musicians were sent to Germany, and exhibits of the German arts were brought to the United States. The temptation to indulge in cultural chauvinism was resisted and the record of the Foundation was commendable. One of its founders, G. A. Oberlaender, gave $1,000,000 to an agency bearing his name. The Oberlaender Trust, in effect an endowed section of the Carl Schurz Memorial Fund, carried on its program until 1953, when its assets and projects were turned over to the Foundation.[21]

Still another approach to the improvement of understanding in the United States of particular countries and areas was developed in the early 1930's by the wealthy and cosmopolitan Chicagoan, Charles R. Crane. The Institute of Current World Affairs maintained promising young men for a period of two or more years in a foreign land in order that they might acquire a sufficiently broad knowledge of its problems and culture to interpret these to fellow Americans. The Institute, with modest support, has continued its program in an experimental way.[22]

It might seem that the one country about which American friends of international peace and understanding needed to have little concern was Great Britain. Yet in the 1920's, in both that country and in the United States, there was a good deal of suspicion and misunderstanding of the institutions and national purposes of the other.

[20] *Ibid.*, May 7, 1930; *Publisher's Weekly* CXIX (Feb. 14, 1931), 832.
[21] Carl Schurz Memorial Foundation, Inc., *Annual Reports*, 1930-   (Philadelphia: Carl Schurz Memorial Foundation, 1931-   ); Eugene E. Doll, *Twenty-five Years of Service*, 1930-1955 (Philadelphia, Carl Schurz Memorial Foundation, 1955), 3 ff. The Foundation's activities, which included the publication of the *American German Review*, were similar to those of the English-Speaking Union, the Alliance Française, the Kosciuzko Foundation and the American-Scandinavian Foundation.
[22] Walter S. Rogers to Merle Curti, May 19, 1958.

And, because of the common language and the cultural indebtedness of the United States to the mother country, men and women of means naturally wanted to help reduce tensions and strengthen existing ties. The contributions of the Carnegie agencies and the Rockefeller Foundation led the way. But in the period between the two wars one name looms especially large in the story of efforts to improve the cultural relations between the United States and Great Britain. The name, of course, is Harkness.

The Commonwealth Fund, established by the widow of Stephen Harkness in 1918, initiated its program of promoting child welfare, health and education by contributing $2,000,000 to relief and rehabilitation in Central Europe.[23] In 1924 the Fund took a significant step in its educational program, a step intended to promote in a practical way international understanding and unity of thought and purpose on the part of the two great English-speaking nations. Its directors knew that British acquaintance with American subjects was more limited and superficial than American acquaintance with British literature and thought. The Rhodes scholarships had enabled many young Americans to acquire a firsthand acquaintance with England; there was no similar provision for young Britishers to come to America. Hence the Commonwealth Fund established twenty, and presently thirty, two-year fellowships for graduates of British universities to continue their studies in the United States. The fellows were chosen in Great Britain by British authorities, and the program, in the interest of flexibility, gave an unusual amount of freedom to the fellows in study and travel experience in the United States. The scheme was broadened to include the graduates of Dominion universities studying in Britain and public administrators of British descent in any part of the Empire who might profit from specialized work in the United States.[24] The personal reports of some of the fellows showed that, while it was too soon to evaluate the success of the program in terms of its larger objectives, the plan had met with much favor in both countries. A similar assessment

[23] Commonwealth Fund, *Annual Report*, 1924 (New York: Commonwealth Fund, 1925), 41-44; 1925, 49-53. On the death of Mrs. Harkness in 1926, the original endowment had increased to over $40,000,000.

[24] Commonwealth Fund, *Annual Reports, passim.* By 1936, 13 per cent of the total appropriations went to Commonwealth Fund Fellowship program.

after the Second World War strengthened the impression that the plan had indeed met with a high degree of success.[25]

Mrs. Harkness's benefaction, including as it did encouragement of child care, health, and education both overseas and in America, was paralleled by the generosity of her son, Edward Stephen. This self-effacing philanthropist once said that he spent almost as much time dodging publicity as he did in studying philanthropy.[26] His initial gifts in the 1920's to the Shakespeare Memorial Theater, to Oxford, and to St. Andrews (which received £100,000) were made anonymously.[27] In 1930 the press announced a new benefaction, the Pilgrim Trust. The terms of the deed of gift bear quoting:

> Whereas it is acknowledged by all that Great Britain in the War spent her resources freely in the common cause, and, in the years that have elapsed since Peace, has sustained honorably and without complaint, a burden which has gravely increased the difficulties of life for her people And Whereas by the bounty of Providence America has of late enjoyed an ample measure of prosperity and the donor himself has been blessed with worldly means And Whereas the donor feels himself bound by many ties of affection to the land from which he draws his descent And Whereas it seems to him that it is right for a Private American citizen to show his admiration of what Britain has done by a gift to be used for some of her more urgent needs And Whereas he is in hopes that such a gift, widely applied, may assist not only in tiding over the present time of difficulty, but in promoting her future well-being. . . .[28]

The capital fund, unannounced at the time, was £2,000,000. It enabled the British trustees to spend annual sums varying from £130,-000 to £80,000, on whatever way they might decide: by 1953 the grants totaled £1,190,606. Under the chairmanship of Stanley Baldwin, leader of the Conservative Party, and, after 1934, of Lord Macmillan, the Trust was carefully and thoughtfully administered with a minimum of public criticism.[29]

In both Great Britain and the United States the reactions to the

---

[25] Edward Bliss Reed, ed., *The Commonwealth Fund Fellows and Their Impressions of America* (New York: The Commonwealth Fund, 1932), 12; Samuel G. Putt, ed., *Cousins and Strangers: Comments on America by Commonwealth Fund Fellows from Britain, 1946-1952* (Cambridge: Harvard University Press, 1956). The Commonwealth Fund also established a lectureship on American history at the University of London.

[26] *Nature* CXLV (Feb. 17, 1940), 254.

[27] *The Times* [London], Sept. 29, 1930.

[28] *Ibid.*, Sept. 29, 1930.

[29] *Ibid.*, June 24, 1943; *The Illustrated London News*, July 23, 1955.

announcement of the gift were highly appreciative. "In the nature of things," declared the *Times* of London, "it cannot be easy to find a collective voice to express authentically the spontaneity and warmth of a myriad individual responses to today's announcement. . . ." [30] In noting that Mr. Harkness was utterly unlike the popular image of the American millionaire, *The Spectator* spoke of the perfect manner in which the gift had been made. He could have slipped into his offering words "which might have seemed oppressive or have suggested the superiority of the rich man who in helping a distressed friend implies the culpability of his needs. . . . Never has a donor displayed more thorough confidence in the wisdom of the recipient and never has a donor by sincere compliment suggested more gracefully that the recipient is the better partner in a friendship." [31] At a dinner honoring Mr. Harkness the Archbishop of Canterbury echoed these sentiments.[32] In America the *New York Times* was sure that there must be millions of Americans who wished that they had been able to do what Mr. Harkness had done. Other papers commended the indefiniteness of the limitations imposed on the trustees of the Fund.[33]

Harkness did not try to channel grants into favored charities. Yet the American source of the gift influenced what the trustees did, whether in the field of education and learning, or the preservation of historic buildings, or social welfare. Mindful of the fact that an early donor to the Royal Society, Count Rumford, was of American birth, the first grant was to that organization for lectures in alternate years in London and Washington by an American and a British man of science, respectively.[34] The augmenting of student loan funds and the building of a student union at Belfast followed American precedents. Aware of the American interest in historic buildings, ecclesiastical and civil, the trustees made substantial grants for the repair or reconstruction of cathedrals, including St. David's, St. Giles, Lincoln, and Gloucester, of parish churches, and of Parliament Square. Generally speaking, the grants were small in size, and often conditional on self-help.

In the early years an amount almost equal to the contributions for these purposes was channeled into social welfare projects, in-

[30] *The Times* [London], Sept. 29, 1930.
[31] *The Spectator*, no. 5336 (Oct. 4, 1930), 433.
[32] *The Times* [London], June 25, 1931.
[33] Quoted in *Ibid.*, Oct. 1, 1930.
[34] *Ibid.*, Dec. 12, 1930.

cluding boys' clubs, social settlements, the giving of tools and other instruments to the unemployed, and similar aids to those out of work. As economic conditions worsened, a shift in favor of such projects was made, so that in 1936, for example, £58,875 went to these, and only £4,650 for the preservation of ancient buildings.[35] With the war, the program shifted again, with special emphasis on welfare work for the wounded and prisoners of war, and on adult education in the armed forces and among civilians. Finally, with the advance of the postwar welfare state, the trustees allocated larger sums to art, education, and learning.[36] In 1956, in summing up the use made of the £2,750,000 in grants of all kinds since the establishment of the Trust, *The Times* seemed to express a consensus in stating that the Harkness gift, wisely administered, had enriched British life in many phases "immeasurably more" in the indirect effects than in monetary value.[37]

American aid to overseas education, broadly defined, was of course not always inspired solely or even chiefly by a conscious desire to promote international understanding although in a vague sense it was often implied. Individuals and foundations supported specific or general educational aims out of an interest in a particular city or country or because of a concern with research or learning as such. Moreover, the schools and colleges founded and largely maintained by missionary boards reflected the Christian concept of stewardship.

Contributions to research institutes abroad founded by Americans to assist American researchers were chiefly concentrated on the American School of Classical Studies at Athens, the American Academy in Rome, and the American School of Oriental Research in Jerusalem. In 1920 the American School of Classical Studies at Athens initiated a campaign for a large endowment. By 1925 it had raised the $150,000 the Carnegie Corporation asked for to match its offer of $100,000. The Corporation in addition provided over $200,000 for constructing the library to house the rich collection given to the School by Johannes Gennadius, a Greek scholar and diplomat. The School also

---

[35] *Ibid.*, March 20, 1936. These figures need, however, to be related to the analysis of all grants made between 1930 and 1939: £287,063 toward the preservation of the national heritage of historic buildings and landscape, and £494,122 toward social service: *Ibid.*, May 11, 1938.

[36] *Ibid.*, Sept. 15, 1941, August 26, 1942, August 14, 1946.

[37] *Ibid.*, July 6, 1956.

received $100,000 from Mr. Rockefeller. But its most generous donor was James Loeb who, before his death in 1933, contributed a million dollars to increase salaries of instructors and to support the program in Greek literature. Thanks to these and other gifts, the American School of Classical Studies at Athens took its place in the 1920's in the first rank of the learned bodies of Europe.[38]

The American Academy in Rome also enlarged its plant, staff, and collections with a grant of $1,000,000 from the International Education Board, made contingent on the raising of an additional $500,000 by the Academy itself.[39] Although the national character of the American Academy was clear, in many ways it served international culture in its relations to the heritage of Rome. By the time the Second World War closed the Academy for the duration, its assets had reached $3,000,000.[40] It took pride in its achievements, one of which demonstrated the advantages of the collaboration of classical scholars, architects, sculptors, and artists, a collaboration exemplified in the contributions of some twenty of its former fellows to the artistic achievements of the world's fairs at New York and San Francisco in 1939.[41] At Jerusalem the excavations and publications of the American School of Oriental Research rested largely on contributions from almost fifty American colleges and universities and on the gifts of several private donors, including J. B. Nies and Julius Rosenwald.[42]

[38] The Carnegie Corporation of New York, *Report of the President and of the Treasurer*, 1922 (New York: Carnegie Corporation, 1922), 59, 62; *American Jewish Yearbook*, Sept., 1937–Sept., 1938, XXXIX (Philadelphia, Jewish Publication Society of America, 1937), 179-201; Louis E. Lord, *A History of the American School of Classical Studies at Athens*, 1882-1946 (Cambridge: Harvard University Press, 1947), 114 ff.

[39] William Graves to William A. Boring, May 14, 1927, and Roscoe Guernsy to Julius Rosenwald, Jan. 24, 1928, Rosenwald Papers, box 1. Rosenwald did not contribute to the campaign on the ground that his activities were largely restricted to the United States.

[40] *American Academy in Rome, Twenty-fifth Anniversary* (n.p., n.d.), and American Academy in Rome folder in the Foundation Library Center.

[41] *The American Academy in Rome at the World's Fair and the Golden Gate Exposition*, 1939 (New York: Offices of the American Academy, 1939).

[42] Julius Rosenwald to Morris Jastrow, Feb. 11, 1919, and Jastrow to Rosenwald, Jan. 28 and Feb. 24, 1921, Rosenwald Papers, box 3. Jastrow reported that the work done through the generosity of Jacob Schiff, the chief donor, had not been spectacular, but that the publications of the excavators showed increasingly important results. In this connection note should be taken also of the work in Near East archaeological scholarship by other institutions in the United States, especially the University of Chicago, which had special Rockefeller grants, the University of Michigan with help from the Rackham fund, and the University of Pennsylvania with various philanthropic gifts.

From individual Americans many old and well-established universities received substantial gifts. Carnegie, it will be recalled, broke the path long before the First World War in what he did for the Scottish universities. His compatriot, John Stewart Kennedy, who gave $100,000 to Glasgow before his death in 1909, would no doubt have been pleased by the fact that, allowed to accumulate, it had increased to £100,000 by 1922, when it was used to enlarge the crowded main building of the faculty of arts of this ancient seat of learning.[43] In addition to the gifts of Harkness to Oxford and St. Andrews, British universities received other American contributions, including the $200,000 of George Eastman to the American Trust Fund of the University of Oxford, recently established by former Rhodes fellows, to be used for the support of the George Eastman Visiting Professorship of American Studies.[44]

On the Continent, James Loeb gave the University of Munich a student home.[45] Ambassador Jacob Gould Schurman, a graduate of Heidelberg University, initiated a movement to collect $400,000 for his alma mater in gratitude for its training of American scholars. The sum, to which among others John D. Rockefeller, Jr., George F. Parker, James Speyer, Julius Rosenwald and Paul Warburg contributed, was used to repair the sadly dilapidated and "lamentably old-fashioned" buildings.[46] Before his death the Jewish philanthropist, Jacob Schiff, was one of the chief American donors to the endowment of Frankfort University: when Hitler came to power, his name, engraven, with those of other contributors in the stone of one of the main structures, was removed.[47] Across the Rhine in France the University of Paris, which was undertaking to build student residences, received gifts from Mr. and Mrs. Murray Guggenheim ($400,-000), Albert Kahn, and Georges Blumenthal. To the same project

[43] Sir Hector Hethrington to Merle Curti, April 27, 1959.

[44] George Eastman to Dr. Frank Aydelotte, Eastman Personal Letter Book, 24, Letter No. 25, Eastman Papers, Eastman Kodak Company, Rochester, New York. The movement to supplement the British contribution with American gifts for a chair of American history at London succeeded in its aim. See Nicholas Murray Butler, *Across the Busy Years* (2 vols.; New York: C. Scribner's Sons, 1940), II, 141.

[45] *New York Times*, May 29, 1933. Despite eloquent urging, Rosenwald did not contribute to the building of a woman's dormitory at Munich. Rosenwald to Henrietta von Klenze, Rosenwald Papers, 50.

[46] Paul Warburg to Julius Rosenwald, Jan. 10, 1928, Rosenwald Papers, 50.

[47] Frieda Schiff Warburg, *Reminiscences of a Long Life* (New York: privately printed, 1950), 69.

the senior John D. Rockefeller contributed $2,000,000 in the interest of developing a common bond between students of all nations.[48]

Perhaps the most unusual gift to a foreign university was that of Louis Gedemin, a kitchen steward at the Detroit Club who, living alone in miserly fashion, was persuaded by his broker to make a will lest his fortune revert to the state. He surprised everyone who had known him for more than a quarter of a century at the Club by leaving an estate of $200,000, two-thirds of which was earmarked for the University of Krakow "to further science in all its branches." [49]

Gifts of individuals to secular institutions of higher learning abroad were overshadowed in magnitude by the contributions of American foundations. No new major foundations with primary emphasis on aiding education in other countries were established in the years between the two wars. But at least three smaller ones, in fulfilling special functions, testified to the initiative and originality of their promoters. In memory of their son, who had, after his military service in France during the First World War, developed a marked interest in youth, and who had also wished to do something for the natives of his beloved Samoa, Mr. and Mrs. William S. Barstow of Great Neck, New York, established in 1931 a $200,000 foundation for the education of the natives of Samoa. The foundation built in Pago Pago a senior boarding school to equip the sons of chiefs both with the language and arts of the West and a respect for native customs and competence in ancient skills. The dual program was in part a response to the impression of a Congressional commission sent to investigate unrest in Samoa that a too rapid introduction of Western ways was not without danger.[50]

Two other new foundations concerned themselves with higher education in Europe. In 1922 a group of Americans of Hungarian background established the American-Hungarian Fund Library. For several years it supported an exchange of professors and students

---

[48] *School and Society* XXVII (Feb. 25, 1928), 224; XXVIII (Sept. 15, 1928), 322-23. Kahn's gift of 500,000 francs was accompanied by a promise to give an additional 9,500,000 francs conditional on success in the solicitation of funds from others. *American Jewish Year Book*, Sept., 1926–Sept., 1927, XXVIII, 145; Sept., 1929–Sept., 1930, XXXI, 88; Sept., 1930–Sept., 1931, XXXII, 150-51. For the Rockefeller gift, see *New York Times*, Jan. 5, 1931, and *School and Society* XXXIV (August 15, 1931), 220.

[49] *New York Times*, Oct. 21, 1930.

[50] *Ibid.*, Sept. 17, 1931, May 16, 1937; "Education in Samoa: The Barstow Foundation," *Pacific Affairs* V (Dec., 1932), 1063; "A New School for Chiefs in Samoa," *Political Quarterly* V (April, 1934), 229.

between the two countries and developed in Budapest a library of American scientific periodicals. By 1945 the foundation was, however, practically unknown in Hungary.[51]

In contrast, the story of American relations to higher education in Belgium has been sustained and successful. Thanks to the foresight, wisdom, and practical efficiency of Herbert Hoover and of Emile Francqui, his associate in the administration of relief in Belgium in the First World War, the considerable funds remaining at the time of the Armistice in the treasury of the Commission for Relief in Belgium were channeled into two leading agencies. One, the Foundation Universitaire, has an enviable record in advancing the interests of higher education in Belgium. The other, the Belgian-American Educational Foundation, has since its inception in 1920 assisted higher education and scientific research in Belgium, partly through support to summer university courses in the history of Belgian art and the sending of 150 American scholarly journals to Belgium, but chiefly through the system of postgraduate fellowships which has brought many Belgians to America and many Americans to Belgium.[52]

One of the two major prewar agencies. the Rockefeller Foundation, in addition to its emphasis on medical research and health programs abroad, directly and indirectly did much for international scholarship in other fields, thus materially enriching several foreign institutions of higher learning. Between the end of the First World War and 1934 it spent $15,000,000 on the exchange of scholars.[53] It also aided several institutions by direct grants. In 1936 it enabled Dalhousie University to establish the first Canadian course in public administration.[54] It gave Oxford $2,000,000, three-fifths of the cost of a much needed expansion of the great but overcrowded and beetle-

[51] Ernest A. Bessey, "American-Hungarian Fund Library," *Science* LXII n.s. (Dec. 11, 1925), 536-37; American Hungarian Foundation folder, Foundation Library Center, New York. As late as 1931-32 the agency sponsored exchange of Hungarian and American art exhibits.

[52] Perrin C. Galpin, *Belgian Higher Education and Belgian American Exchanges between the Two Wars* (New York: Belgian American Educational Foundation, ca. 1948), *passim*. In 1956 the total assets of the Foundation were over $4,000,000: Belgian American Educational Foundation, Inc. folder in the Foundation Library Center.

[53] Carnegie Corporation, *Report of the President*, 1934, 22-23.

[54] Rockefeller Foundation, *Annual Report*, 1936, 377; *New York Times*, June 14, 1936.

infested Bodleian Library.[55] The Rockefeller Foundation also provided the University of London with means to acquire a ten-acre
site in Bloomsbury for its new quarters.[56]

To the Universities of Oslo and Copenhagen the Rockefeller
Foundation made grants for theoretical astrophysics and atomic physics, the latter grant to have momentous consequences.[57] After the
earthquake of 1923 destroyed the library of Tokyo Imperial University, the Rockefeller Foundation built a new home, at the cost of
$1,000,000, for collections donated by institutions all over the world
to replace in part those destroyed.[58] And in keeping with the Rockefeller interest in the development of medicine in China, $250,000
was given to match an equal amount for the endowment of Yenching University, the income of which was used for strengthening the
premedical sciences.[59]

In line with its founder's interest in the advancement and diffusion
of knowledge in the British Empire the Carnegie Corporation made
several grants to Canadian universities which resulted in educational
innovations. Thus chairs of geology and of chemistry were established at Dalhousie and at Mount Allison.[60] A junior college, which
also served as a center for adult education, broke a new educational
path in Newfoundland.[61] In 1923 a conditional promise of $3,000,-
000 toward a project for the development of a federation of denominational colleges in the Maritime Provinces, with a central university
at Halifax, resulted in richer educational opportunities.[62] Thanks to
a gift of $100,000, a Roman Catholic college developed at Edmonton,
affiliated, as a condition of the gift, with the University of Al-
berta.[63] And academic Canada watched with interest the establishment of a dormitory with a $100,000 grant to the same institution.[64]
The assistance given to St. Francis Xavier's College in Nova Scotia
for developing a unique program in adult education and rural econ-

[55] *New York Times*, May 20, 25, 1932. In an editorial in the issue for May 21,
the *Times* called the gift a recognition of "an inextinguishable debt to Britain for the
heritage of letters which we share with her children."
[56] *Ibid.*, July 17, 1932.
[57] *Ibid.*, August 17, 1924, May 10, 1931.
[58] *Ibid.*, July 15, 1924.
[59] *Ibid.*, July 23, 1932.
[60] Carnegie Corporation, *Report of the President*, 1933, 37.
[61] *Ibid.*, 1926, 26.
[62] *Ibid.*, 1923, 45.
[63] *Ibid.*, 1923, 45.
[64] *Ibid.*, 1926, 26-27.

omy was so successful that by 1938 some 1,500 Americans crossed the boundary to learn of the experiment at firsthand.[65]

Higher education in New Zealand, Australia, and South Africa profited from substantial grants by the Carnegie Corporation to institutes of educational research. It also profited during 1929 to 1934 from participating in the program which enabled 790 scholars from all parts of the world to spend a year in an American university,[66] and from what was done to stimulate the development of libraries.

In addition to personal gifts for public library buildings in the British dominions and colonies, Carnegie, with foresighted generosity, set aside $10,000,000 to be used in these areas for the advancement and diffusion of knowledge. In general, the Corporation paralleled its American library program, so far as possible, by improving services and standards in Canada. Regional demonstrations kept Canadian libraries abreast with developments across the border, and the British Columbia Library Commission, using a $100,000 grant given in 1929, pushed the library extension services into sparsely settled and barely accessible parts of the province.[67] Academic libraries received collections for instruction in music and art, as did those in the United States.

Both in Canada and elsewhere the Carnegie Corporation tried to encourage initiative and responsibility. This was easier to do in the dominions than in the Crown colonies: in the British West Indies and neighboring British possessions on the mainland, grants were made for library buildings and surveys of libraries, museums, and educational enterprises. This, in the words of the President, was merely to scratch the surface. But until the British government itself took a more vigorous interest in this part of the empire, or until local leaders did, little could be done. The situation in the southern dominions was, of course, quite different, for here there was some awareness of prevailing inadequacy and backwardness of library facilities among at least a few spokesmen, together with a desire to improve matters.

Although the public library movement in Australia anticipated that in other dominions, the situation in 1930 was in some ways

[65] Ibid., 1939, 19-24.
[66] Ibid., 1934, 30.
[67] Ibid., 1929, 14. The Corporation also helped to place European refugee scholars on Canadian university faculties.

worse than it had been fifty years earlier. Overdependent on inadequate federal subsidies, the libraries suffered not only from this fact but from a related woefully deficient local support. The lending library was virtually unknown. No facilities existed for training librarians, and library services were generally backward. At the invitation of interested leaders the Corporation sent Ralph Mun of the Carnegie Institute of Technology to survey the situation and to make recommendations. The mission proved to be stimulating and, though progress was slow, it was real. Moreover, the inquiry in New Zealand resulted in an important movement to develop rural library services.[68]

In response to a similar request, the Corporation in 1928 sent to South Africa Milton J. Ferguson, state librarian of California, who initiated a conference of those interested in libraries and conducted a survey. The survey showed how much was to be done: many collections in colleges and universities compared badly with those in the better American high schools; there were few trained librarians, and no library school; cataloguing and services were highly inadequate. Worst of all, the dominant view was that the library was a symbol of the white man's superiority. Hence little or nothing had been done to make books in the vernacular available to native populations. The conference and the survey, bringing to the fore all these things, developed a plan for a true public library system. To get this under way, the Corporation agreed to match government funds over a period of years. The movement spread to Southern Rhodesia and the Kenya Colony. Progress was slow, but tangible results clearly owed much to the Ferguson survey and to the material aid and encouragement which the Corporation gave.[69]

The Carnegie Corporation claimed only modest credit for the improvement in public support, professional standards, and more widespread library services. But by 1939 it admitted, on the basis of appreciative statements by the Secretary of State for the Colonies, and the prime ministers of Australia, New Zealand and South Africa, that if only half of what these men said were true, "the Corporation

[68] Ralph Mun and Ernest R. Pitt, *Australian Libraries* (Melbourne: Australian Council for Educational Research, 1935), 11 ff.

[69] Milton J. Ferguson, *Memorandum. Libraries in the Union of South Africa, Rhodesia, and Kenya Colony* (New York: Carnegie Corporation of New York, 1929), *passim*. In the five-year period 1929-1933, the Corporation contributed $614,250 to the South African program: Carnegie Corporation, *Report of the President*, 1932, 17.

has during these years rendered an important and in some ways a unique service to the British Empire." [70]

Supplementing by grants the initiative taken by other groups, the Carnegie Corporation supported related enterprises in Africa more far-reaching than the public library movement. The step which American missionaries had taken from interest in the Southern Negro to interest in the African Negro was broadened in the early 1920's when Dr. James Hardy Dillard, director of the Jeanes Fund and an officer of the Phelps-Stokes Fund, was chiefly responsible for sending a commission to West Africa to inquire into both the educational situation and the whole problem of white contacts with primitive peoples.[71] During its survey the commission established fruitful cooperation both with government officials and with missionaries. A short time later a similar inquiry led to an equally significant report on East Africa.

Dr. Thomas Jesse Jones and Dr. J. E. K. Aggrey were largely responsible for the wise, statesmanlike, and forward-looking character of these reports. At its best the education offered the natives had much to commend it, for virtually all of the rising leaders received their training at such admirable South African institutions as Adams College, maintained by the American Board. But much of what the some 2,000 mission schools of many denominations and many countries did failed to come to grips with the needs and potentialities of the native peoples.[72] The reports not only indicated the shortcomings of what was being done and made positive suggestions for more useful programs, but in focusing public attention on the pressing problems of the African peoples and on the whole issue of interracial friction they proved to be landmarks.

As to concrete accomplishments, the reports had much to do with the introduction of the Jeanes Visiting Teacher Plan which had done so much in the American South to improve the welfare of Negroes. In the fall of 1925 with the aid of a grant from the Carnegie Corporation, a training school of the Jeanes type for rural teacher-welfare

---

[70] Carnegie Corporation, *Report of the President*, 1939, 49.

[71] Benjamin Brawley, *Doctor Dillard of the Jeanes Fund* (Chicago and New York: Revell, 1930), 83-86.

[72] African Education Commission, *Education in Africa: A Study of West, South and Equatorial Africa* (New York: Phelps-Stokes Fund, 1922), xii ff.; *Education in East Africa. A Study of East, Central and South Africa by the Second African Commission under the Auspices of the Phelps-Stokes Fund, in Cooperation with the International Education Board* (New York: Phelps-Stokes Fund, ca. 1925).

workers was opened in Kenya under the direction of the government department of education, with students drawn from the missionary societies. Five additional schools were set up and given support conditional on aid from African sources. In addition, twenty-two men and women were chosen to visit the United States to study rural education and social welfare.[73]

These programs were broadening and imaginative, but many educational enterprises in Africa remained traditionally backward. Bronislaw Malinowski, a leading anthropologist, concluded in 1945 that, with notable exceptions, Western education in Africa had too often laid the basis for roles which many Africans could not play, thus raising hopes that could not be fulfilled. Insofar as this was true and insofar as Western education weakened or destroyed tribal bonds, Malinowski argued that it was a blight rather than an asset. At the same time he emphasized the point that the missionary educational enterprise faced a formidable obstacle in preaching a gospel of universal brotherhood in areas where the color bar officially or nonofficially stood in marked contrast to such preaching.[74]

Realizing the complexity of the racial problem, the Carnegie Corporation enabled Dr. Kenyon Butterfield and Professor Charles Coulter to make a study of the poor whites in South Africa. This led to the publication in 1933 of a five-volume study which attracted "an extraordinary amount of attention, not only in South Africa, where for the first time the citizens have become generally conscious of the serious situation which faces the Union, but among students of similar social situations in other parts of the world."[75] Meantime the Royal Institute of International Affairs, acting on a suggestion of General Smuts, initiated and carried through, with a generous grant from the Carnegie Corporation, a comprehensive survey of Africa. Directed by William M. H. Hailey and first published in 1938, this survey included lengthy sections on the geography, peoples, languages, population records, systems of government, law and justice, non-European immigrant communities, native administration, problems of labor, systems of taxation, land relationships, water supply, agriculture, forests, health, transport, and education. A store-

[73] Carnegie Corporation, *Report of the President*, 1928, 17-19; 1929, 21; 1939, 25; Brawley, *Doctor Dillard of the Jeanes Fund*, 85.
[74] Bronislaw Malinowski, *The Dynamics of Cultural Change: An Inquiry into Race Relations in Africa* (New Haven: Yale University Press, 1945), 68-69.
[75] Carnegie Corporation, *Report of the President*, 1933, 29; *Kenyon Leech Butterfield: A Tribute to the Memory of a Man of Vision* (Amherst, 1937).

house of factual knowledge, it has remained a standard contribution to African studies.[76]

Limited though all these efforts were in relation to the magnitude of the problems, the importance of such fact-finding surveys can hardly be overemphasized. British and other colonial authorities in Africa became more sensitive to the obligations of preparing native populations for continued and expanding contacts with white populations and, though this was not generally sensed at the time, ultimately for self-rule. What was done immediately in terms of pioneering with a new and more practical type of education geared to welfare, was, of course, a mere drop in the bucket; but as a more realistic approach it opened the way for larger efforts.

The reconsideration of traditional Western approaches to the education and acculturation of native colonial peoples represented by these American and British experiments in Africa was not limited to that continent. At the suggestion of the Institute of Pacific Relations and with the cooperation of the Dutch government, the Rosenwald Fund with contributing support by the Carnegie Corporation undertook a study of education in the Dutch East Indies. The survey was conducted by the Fund's president, Edwin Embree, reared in the South and long interested in education as a means of racial adjustment and cultural growth. Embree had traveled widely in the Pacific in connection with the Rockefeller Foundation programs in public health and human biology. He had the help of Margaret Sargent Simon, a native of New Orleans and a teacher and administrative officer, and of W. Bryant Mumford, superintendent of education in the British colonial service in Tanganyika and organizer of the Malangali School based on native culture.

The report may have been too generous in its praise of Dutch colonial policy. But it was on unquestionably sound ground in emphasizing the mounting conflict between the values and techniques of the industrial West and the changing and diverse cultures of the East, and the imperative need for readjustment, a need accentuated by the rapid communications which were making the whole world increasingly interdependent. Careful study and wise action were, the

[76] William M. H. Hailey, *An African Survey* (rev. ed.; London: Oxford University Press, 1957). The Rhodes Trust also contributed to the undertaking. Carnegie Corporation, *Report of the President*, 1933, 34-35; 1943, 33.

report insisted, needed in what had come to be a common world problem.[77]

These new approaches toward education in Africa and the South Pacific were important for the future. But philanthropic interests in overseas areas during the 1920's and 1930's concentrated on two areas of long-standing concern to American missionary educators: the Near East and China.

The American colleges in Turkey and neighboring lands showed remarkable power to recuperate from the damages and deprivations of the First World War. But the path continued to be rough. The fanatical nationalism of Mustapha Kemal's regime was expressed in the closing of one school and in demanding that the institutions employ no native teachers other than Turks.[78] In appealing for funds, the American College of Teheran stressed the Red danger though, admittedly, this was sometimes exaggerated in the desire to open the pocketbooks of potential American donors.[79] As in the past, contributions did not come with the mere asking.

Of special significance in fund raising was the gradual development under the leadership of Cleveland Dodge of the Near East College Association. This at first consisted of Robert College and the American University at Beirut, but it was later joined by the Istanbul Woman's College, the International College at Smyrna, Athens College, and the American College at Sofia. None of the institutions lost independence to the board of trustees of the Near East College Association.[80]

A goal of $2,500,000 was set to be reached by the summer of 1925. Shortly after the deadline, a thousand small givers had, with the $25,000 grant of the Rockefeller Foundation for the medical school at Beirut, contributed $1,630,000. John D. Rockefeller, Jr., who had over the years shown his interest by giving for building to Beirut and to the Woman's College at Istanbul, offered $625,000 to the

[77] Edwin R. Embree, Margaret Sargent Simon, and W. Bryant Mumford, *Island India Goes to School* (Chicago: University of Chicago Press, 1934), 113 ff.

[78] *New York Times*, June 7, 1925.

[79] R. C. Hutchinson to Rosenwald, Nov. 5, 1929, April 5, 1930, S. M. Jordan to Raymond Rubinow, April 25, 1930, Rubinow to Hutchinson, Nov. 26, 1929, Rubinow to Embree, April 19, 1930, Rubinow to Hutchinson, April 21, 1930, Rosenwald Papers, box 2. Rosenwald was not impressed by the anti-communist arguments, emphasizing, instead, the need of positive arguments and achievements.

[80] Mary Mills Patrick, *A Bosphorus Adventure* (Stanford University, Calif.: Stanford University Press, 1934), 221-22.

fund.[81] The campaign succeeded, to be followed by another for $15,000,000. To this the Rockefeller Foundation gave $1,000,000 for medical work at the American University of Beirut.[82] A $3,000,000 windfall came from the estate of Charles M. Hall, who, when a student of chemistry at Oberlin, had discovered a highly profitable process for making aluminum.[83] By early January, 1929, the endowment fund of the American University at Beirut alone had reached $10,250,000, with contributions from many countries in America, Europe, and the Near East.[84] As a personal tribute to Cleveland Dodge, who died before the campaign was over, Edward S. Harkness added $1,000,000 to the fund.[85]

This large measure of success in fund raising enabled the constituent colleges to expand and improve plant and instruction and to make their influence still further felt. In evaluating what had been done, pride was not always expressed without qualification. Thus Bayard Dodge, president of Beirut, confessed in 1925 that in the past too much emphasis had been put on proselytizing and propagandizing in "a spirit of racial and religious superiority." The work was at its best, he went on, when "we forget to preach, forget to think of our creeds, or our territories or our trade, and grow absorbed in conferring benefits—equal benefits upon those who are and those who are not 'of the household of faith.'" [86] On another occasion President Dodge made it clear that "our policy is not to Americanize the Levantine peoples but to teach them to love their native cultures and to serve their own communities. It is for us to share our responsibility with the Near East, so as to help it to help itself." [87]

A fair statement of aims was that of George P. Hayes, who emphasized the significance of giving instruction in both English and the native languages, and the inclusion of subjects to prepare students for better citizenship (sociology, civics, business ethics). He also stressed the value of physical education and athletics, and the attempt

[81] *New York Times*, May 11, 1925. Dodge reported that in the last campaign for funds the Laura Spellman Rockefeller Foundation had given one-third of the amount asked for.

[82] *Ibid.*, Dec. 3, 10, 1927.

[83] *Ibid.*, Dec. 3, 1927; Junius David Edwards, *The Immortal Woodshed: The Story of the Inventor Who Brought Aluminum to America* (New York: Dodd, Mead, 1955).

[84] *New York Times*, Jan. 5, April 25, 1928.

[85] *Ibid.*, March 27, 1929.

[86] Bayard Dodge, "The Genius of America in Eastern Education," *Asia* XV (April, 1925), 345.

[87] Bayard Dodge, "An Eastern Challenge," *Asia* XXVIII (Dec., 1928), 1019.

to develop Christian character, together with initiative, independence, responsibility, and a spirit of cosmopolitanism and internationalism.[88] The assumption was that formal instruction and a Christian atmosphere could overcome the pull of native child-rearing practices and cultural tradition. In some cases and in some degree, such results were realized.

In these years the contributions of Jewish Americans played a major part in the development of the greatest university in the Near East. The roots of the Hebrew University of Palestine were nourished by Old World Zionism.[89] But in 1912 a leading American rabbi, Judah Magnes of New York, became deeply interested in what seemed to almost everybody an impossible dream, and dedicated himself to its realization.[90] Fund raising began in several countries and in 1918 enough money was on hand to buy a site on Mt. Scopus and to lay the first foundation stones.

American interest owed a great deal to the eloquence of Albert Einstein and Chaim Weizmann, who visited the United States in 1921. The first notable response was the organization in that year of the American Jewish Physicians Committee in which, among others, Dr. Nathan Ratnoff, Dr. Israel Wechsler, and Dr. David Kaliski took active parts. Money was raised to buy the land on which the Hadassah-Rothschild University Hospital and the Ratnoff Medical Building were in time built. The Committee also established the Institute of Microbiology and contributed annually to the Institute of Chemistry. Together with Hadassah, the Zionist Woman's Organization, the American Jewish Physicians Committee was the major factor in the evolution of the medical center which was completed in 1939.[91]

Meantime, in 1925, the Hebrew University had been opened with Dr. Magnes as chancellor. In that very year, under the leadership of

[88] George P. Hayes, "American Contributions to Near East Education," *School and Society* XXIII (May 1, 1926), 544-48.

[89] Rabbi Stephen Wise recalled having heard the idea of the Hebrew University discussed at the Zionist Congress in Basle in 1898: *The Challenging Years: The Autobiography of Stephen Wise* (New York: Putnam's, 1949), 54-55.

[90] For an appreciative but not uncritical portrait of Magnes see Louis Lipsky, *A Gallery of Zionist Profiles* (New York: Farrar, Straus and Cudahy, 1956), 175 ff.

[91] Lotta Levensohn, *Vision and Fulfillment: The First Twenty-five Years of the Hebrew University, 1925-1950* (New York: Greystone, 1950), 91 ff.; *American Jewish Year Book*, Sept., 1934–Sept., 1935, XXXVI; Sept., 1937–Sept., 1938, XXXIX, 195-97; Dr. I. S. Wechsler to Merle Curti, March 22, 1960 and Dr. David J. Kaliski to Merle Curti, March 14, 1960; *New York Times*, Feb. 22, 1925.

Felix M. Warburg, the Advisory Committee was organized to help with the support and growth of the University. It presently developed into the American Friends of the Hebrew University. This organization raised from the start approximately 60 per cent of the annual budget of the University, stimulated interest and broadened the base of support. The example it set was followed by the organization of similar societies in other countries—England, Belgium, France, Holland, Italy, Poland, Spain, Sweden, Switzerland, and Argentina. Support for the Hebrew University rested on contributions from local welfare funds, special campaigns, individual gifts, trust funds, bequests, legacies, and the activity of lawyers, scientists, and educators, organized in independent agencies affiliated with the American Friends of the Hebrew University.[92]

Many American gifts, some of considerable size, were anonymous, and many contributions came, of course, from persons all over the country known only in their own localities. But well-to-do Jews were also notable contributors. The first large contribution to endowment, to be used for the Institute of Jewish Studies, was the $500,000 gift of Mr. and Mrs. Felix Warburg.[93] Sol Rosenbloom of Pittsburgh was the second largest contributor to the Institute. His widow gave the Rosenbloom Memorial Building (to house the Institute of Jewish Studies) and $500,000 for an auditorium.

The list of large givers to the Hebrew University, even in the period before the Second World War, is too large to give in its entirety, but some idea of what was done can be suggested by a few examples. Montagu S. Lamport gave botanical gardens; Mrs. Dora Schapiro and Philip Wattenberg provided funds for the Schapiro Building, which housed the Einstein Institute of Physics, and Wattenberg in addition gave the building bearing his name for the use of the Einstein Institute of Mathematics. Samuel Untermyer built the Minnie Untermyer Memorial Open Air Theater. The endowment of chairs was made possible by Louis Bamberger and Mrs. Felix Fuld (Oriental Studies), Jacob Epstein (hygiene and bacteriology), Israel Unterberg (Talmudic philology), Leon Miller (higher Jewish learning), David Shapiro (Yiddish language and literature) and the Schul-

---

[92] Levensohn, *Vision and Fulfillment*, 146 ff.; *American Jewish Year Book*, Sept., 1937–Sept., 1938, XXXIX, 191 ff.; Miss Rita Blume to Merle Curti, March 18, 1960.
[93] *New York Times*, Sept. 30, 1925. The gift supplemented an earlier one of $100,000.

man Brothers of New York (philosophy). Special gifts included several for scholarships and a number of collections for the libraries.[94] Such philanthropies were forerunners of many similar gifts for other endowed chairs in the years after the Second World War.

Thus in the first fifteen years that followed the opening of the Hebrew University in 1925 an institution developed with a general arts and science program, a medical school, work in agriculture, law, and education, and a group of research institutes in mathematics, the natural sciences, and the humanities. The reputation of the Hebrew University was well established. (In 1937 a Royal Commission, reporting on Palestine, expressed a general view in declaring that its standards of scholarship, caliber of faculty members, and success in research compared favorably with many older institutions.[95]) Tributes from Henry Woodburn Chase, John Haynes Holmes, Harry Emerson Fosdick, and John Dewey indicated that in the United States too the new institution was genuinely appreciated.

Though in 1947 the University was deprived of its campus and a new start had to be made, the foundations were firmly laid, the standards had been set, the spirit had been nourished, the cause had found generous and widespread support. And the University had not only harbored scholars unwelcome in their own lands. It had begun to make notable contributions to the development of the economy and culture of Palestine and to the world's treasury of knowledge.

Halfway around the world lay China, scene of a long-established interest on the part of Americans who hoped through mission schools and colleges to improve the quality of life for at least some part of the vast, teeming population. The situation was now, in the 1920's and 1930's, far more complex than it had ever been. This was not only or even chiefly because a famine of unprecedented severity invited American benevolence to allay hunger and to help with effective preventive measures. It was mainly because China's nationalistic

[94] *American Jewish Year Book*, Sept., 1926–Sept., 1927, XXVIII, 147-48; Sept., 1928–Sept., 1929, XXX, 35; Sept., 1929–Sept., 1930, XXXI, 36-37, 76; Sept., 1934–Sept., 1935, XXXVI, 275; Sept., 1935–Sept., 1936, XXXVIII, 245; Sept., 1936–Sept., 1937, XXXVIII, 419; Sept., 1937–Sept., 1938, XXXIX, 197; Rita Blume to Merle Curti, March 18, 1960.

[95] Quoted in Noah Nardi, *Education in Palestine, 1920-1945* (Washington: Zionist Organization of America, 1945), 149-52.

revolution, now well under way, was already, in the years after the armistice of 1918, profoundly affecting the American effort to promote progress and welfare through Christian education. On the one hand, the revolution promoted a lively interest in Western secular, as opposed to religious education. John Dewey was only one among American educators to take a serious look at China's educational problems and to offer constructive suggestions.[96] On the other hand, the revolution put the missionary agencies on the defensive.

In Europe the argument was heard that American missionaries were chiefly responsible for the current upheaval in China: they had held up to the Chinese the wonderful benefits of self-determination and had encouraged the masses to seek a political millennium.[97] On their part, the Nationalists, even some whose training had been in missionary schools and who, as European critics insisted, owed many of their ideas to them, took these institutions to task for inadequate instruction in Western subjects, for neglect or even belittling of Chinese classics and culture and, in some cases, for curtailing freedom of thought in imposing Christian dogmas. Numerous Chinese felt that the paternalism of the Christian schools and colleges had failed to produce graduates that could become leaders in developing the industries of China on an independent Chinese basis. At the most, it was felt, they were fitted merely for subordinate positions in foreign managed industries because of their reasonable competence in the English language.

Criticism was not confined to the alleged "slavish mentality" of the Chinese trained in these Christian colleges. Many also resented the fact that Chinese members of the faculty received smaller salaries than westerners and enjoyed less administrative responsibility and social dignity. As the Nationalist tide gained force in the middle 1920's the government insisted that American presidents and board members be replaced by Chinese, and that much more attention be given to Chinese studies. In the turmoil violent outbreaks occurred,

---

[96] John Dewey, *Character and Events* (2 vols.; New York: Holt, 1929), I, 285 ff., 309 ff.; John and Alice Dewey, *Letters from China and Japan* (New York: Dutton, 1920), 182 ff.; Thomas Berry, "Dewey's Influence in China," in John Blewett, *John Dewey: His Thought and Influence* (New York: Fordham University Press, 1960), 199-231.

[97] *New York Times*, June 8, 1925, Jan. 27, 1927. The *Echo de Paris*, to cite an example, warned the French government against permitting the YMCA and other agencies to work in Indo-China lest their picture of the glories of American independence lead the inhabitants to revolt against French rule.

mission property was looted, and at least some missionaries lost their lives. Local authorities closed schools and colleges or forced the American staffs to turn them over to the Chinese.[98]

All these criticisms and pressures provided the background for a reassessment of missionary education. Under the sponsorship of several boards the Burton Commission surveyed the situation and in 1921 reported that while much of the work was valuable, shortcomings were all too real. These included, in the Commission's verdict, wasteful use of funds, duplication of work, and lack of coordination and cooperation. Partly as a result of the recommendations and partly in realization of the long-felt need for leaders in the missionary field, a considerable measure of cooperation was achieved in 1922 with the organization of the forerunner of the United Board for Christian Colleges in China. Further steps toward consolidation and cooperation were more easily taken as a result. Competition in fund raising was also reduced.[99]

Despite the upheavals in China and the hostile policies of the government, American contributions in the 1920's and even in the depression years enabled the colleges and universities to expand and improve their plants, to raise academic standards, and to enlarge their staffs with specialists equipped to teach particular subjects, including Chinese studies.[100] New sources of support supplemented the traditional ones. The Rockefeller China Medical Board helped several institutions develop premedical work and the Laura Spellman Rockefeller Foundation contributed one-third of a special $3,000,000

[98] *New York Times*, August 10, 1925, Feb. 2, August 14, Sept. 1, October 3, 1927; Edward H. Hume, "Christian Schools in China," *The Nation* CXXIV (March 30, 1927), 341-43; John Dewey, *Character and Events*, I, 307; Foster Rhea Dulles, *China and America: The Story of Their Relations since 1784* (Princeton: Princeton University Press, 1946), 182-83; Alice H. Gregg, *China and Educational Autonomy; the Changing Role of the Protestant Educational Missionary in China, 1807-1937* (Syracuse: University of Syracuse Press, 1946), 101 ff.

[99] Mary Lamberton, *St. John's University, Shanghai, 1879-1951* (New York: United Board for Christian Colleges in China, 1955), 110-11.

[100] For details, see the histories of several of the colleges sponsored by the United Board for Christian Colleges in China: Lamberton, *St. John's University, Shanghai, 1879-1951*; Charles Hodge Corbett, *Shantung Christian University* (New York: United Board for Christian Colleges in China, 1955); Roderick Scott, *Fukien University: A Historical Sketch* (New York: United Board for Christian Colleges in China, 1954); W. B. Nance, *Soochow University* (New York: United Board for Christian Colleges in China, 1956); and Clarence Burton Day, *Hangchow University* (New York: United Board for Christian Colleges in China, 1955).

fund for the women's colleges of China, India, and Japan.[101] Veterans like Henry Luce continued to journey over the United States raising money when they would have preferred to be taking part in the new developments in the institutions which the money made possible: between 1918 and 1923 Luce was chiefly responsible for collecting nearly $2,000,000 for the endowment and plant of Yenching.[102] Several American colleges and universities, including Yale and Princeton, each adopted a Chinese institution and through annual student and alumni gifts gave the needed help. Thus Smith, which sponsored Ginling as its sister institution, contributed, through undergraduates and alumnae, an average of $10,000 a year, while the Alumnae Association gave $50,000 for a new recreation building.[103] Also, some institutions benefitted from bequests to a missionary board: the largest one was the $2,500,000 bequest of Mrs. Stephen Harkness in 1926 to the Presbyterian Board of Foreign Missions.[104]

Several institutions in China benefitted from the estate of Charles M. Hall, who left approximately a third of a very large fortune to education in the Near East, in Japan, and in Continental Asia.[105] The Trustees assigned the Oberlin Shansi Memorial Association three quarters of a million dollars to be used as endowment funds in support of the school the Association was operating in Shansi Province. Up to the time the money was received, the Association had been having a hard time to make ends meet. The new income enabled the Association to construct badly needed buildings, to expand the agricultural and industrial work of the school and to send faculty members to America for advanced study. It was, in the judgment of a former staff member, and also of a trustee and President of the United Board for Christian Colleges in China, of decisive influence in assuring the enterprise permanence and significant development.[106] In the case of other Chinese institutions the Hall

[101] Nance, *Soochow University*, 55; Matilda S. Thurston and Ruth M. Chester, *Ginling College* (New York: United Board for Christian Colleges in China, 1955), 26-29. Edward Harkness, Mrs. Willard Straight and others made substantial gifts to the joint fund.

[102] B. A. Garside, *One Increasing Purpose: The Life of Henry Winters Luce* (New York: Revell, 1948), 173 ff.

[103] Thurston and Chester, *Ginling College*, 18.

[104] *New York Times*, April 4, 1926.

[105] *School and Society* I (Jan. 23, 1915), 127; John M. Oskison, "The American Creator of the Aluminum Age," *World's Work* XXVIII (August, 1914), 438-45; *New York Times*, Dec. 28, 1914.

[106] Margaret H. Leonard of the Oberlin Shansi Memorial Association, to Merle Curti, Feb. 26, 1960, and Wynn C. Fairfield to Merle Curti, March 8, 1960.

money was less decisive since endowment and missionary board contributions represented a larger proportion of the budget. But in an important respect, it benefitted all seven of the institutions receiving it by enabling them to develop Chinese studies, without which it would have been impossible to maintain reputation and influence.[107]

One aspect of the advancement and dissemination of knowledge, that of the promotion of medical research and public health, enlisted a good deal of interest on the part of contributors to and directors of missionary enterprises, individual philanthropists, and foundations. All these made striking contributions in this area in the period between the two wars.

Medical missionaries, it will be recalled, had become an important part of the work of spreading the gospel in non-Christian lands in the later nineteenth century and in the first two decades of the twentieth. The re-evaluation of missionary activities in the 1920's and 1930's emphasized this approach not merely as religious propaganda in the older and narrower sense but as testimony of the character and value of the Christian life.[108] Hospitals, clinics, and the training of doctors and nurses received increasing support in the budgets of missionary boards. In terms of need the work was infinitesimal. Yet its importance cannot be questioned. In 1915 Dr. Herbert Welch of the Johns Hopkins Medical School declared that "the work that these men have done is beyond all praise. I would like to pay the highest tribute to those who felt the impulse to treat men's bodies as well as their souls. . . . Considering the insufficient staffs and meager equipment it is a wonder what they have done." [109]

It may seem unwarrantable to select for comment any one of the large number of overseas medical programs which owed their existence primarily to Christian inspiration. Yet an example may be appropriately chosen in an area close at hand which, as in many other cases represented the international character of the missionary endeavor. During the first decade of the twentieth century more and more Americans became interested in the medical missions among

---

107 These funds, administered through the Harvard-Yenching Institute, were responsible for a considerable measure of success in the development of Chinese studies in the recipient institutions: Edwin O. Reischauer to Merle Curti, March 8, 1960.

108 See The Commission of Appraisal, William Ernest Hocking, Chairman, *Re-Thinking Missions: A Laymen's Inquiry after One Hundred Years* (New York: Harper, 1932).

109 Corbett, *Shantung Christian University*, 46.

the Labrador fishing folk of Dr. Wilfred Grenfell, a British subject. Although initially supported by British and Canadian missionary agencies, by 1909 contributions from the United States reached $71,000. In 1912 American admirers led by Eugene Delano of the banking firm of Brown Brothers organized the International Grenfell Association, which was largely directed from New York and to which Americans were the chief contributors. The mobile clinics into which small boats were converted took aid to remote and isolated groups during the long summers. Many college youths volunteered their services during vacation to this rough and risky but exciting adventure.[110]

Fairly early Dr. Grenfell realized that his medical work failed to touch the basic cause of the prevailing diseases. In other words, personal ministrations to sufferers was in medical missionary work overemphasized at the expense of attacking the causes of suffering. Leaving the operating room he often wondered what the point really was in patching up a few lives to exist a little longer under conditions which offered too little for living. Not that he failed to appreciate the value of every act of unselfishness designed to help individual victims of circumstances to regain health and to thus stand a better chance of responding to the message through which alone eternal life could be realized. But, Grenfell felt, "love is dangerously near to sentimentality when we actually prefer remedial to prophylactic charity." Far from regarding as "side-lines" his efforts in the latter kind of charity—orphanages, vocational schools, and cooperative industrial enterprises—Grenfell felt them to be central. But his view was not generally shared by boards and donors entrapped by the imperatives of traditional missionary ethic and bureaucracy.[111]

Grenfell shared the deep-seated prejudice many had against organized professional fund raising. He resented the idea that God Himself is a supplicant even for our help. But immediately after the First World War he was persuaded to throw himself into an energetic campaign which involved even more speaking and traveling than he had long been doing. The postwar depression and the demands for relief in Europe and China made it a bad time to beg for money. Yet the endowment campaign proved a great success. In addition to

110 Lennox Kerr, *Wilfred T. Grenfell: His Life and Work* (New York: Dodd, Mead, 1959), 189 ff.
111 Wilfred T. Grenfell, *A Labrador Doctor* (Boston and New York: Houghton Mifflin, 1919), 235.

such substantial donors as Mrs. Willard Straight, Nettie Fowler McCormick, and Julius Rosenwald, small contributors responded in an encouraging way. A benefit at the Metropolitan Opera raised $8,000 (this became an annual event). The Garden Clubs of America provided a greenhouse. John Hays Hammond supported a biological survey of Labrador and helped with an experimental fur farm. In the first three months of the campaign half a million dollars had been raised, and by the end of the year, thanks to Grenfell's eloquent, vivid description of the tragic lives of his people, the sum had reached $790,000.

Although Grenfell met with opposition from local interests and even from admirers, he did not waver in his conviction that only if the Labrador people were able to develop a more varied economy would efforts to remedy the effects of malnutrition amount to very much. Grenfell not only succeeded in many of his aims but also in making a great part of the world aware of a very small population and its needs, in changing this program of overseas philanthropy from alleviation to prevention, and in enlisting the services of hundreds of young men and women in the field.[112]

The role of philanthropists in overseas medical enterprises was sometimes, as in the case of the Presbyterian industrialist Louis Henry Severance of Cleveland, associated with missionary motivation. In addition to gifts for hospitals in China and India, Severance made possible, through contributions beginning in 1902 and continued by members of his family after his death, the building of the first modern Western type of hospital in Korea. It not only saved the lives and restored to health thousands of Koreans but, in training doctors, made its influence so widespread that the hospital became central to the entire medical life of the country.[113]

In some cases individual gifts for medical research and therapy abroad reflected the interest of the donor in a particular disease. In 1927 William John Matheson, a leader in the scientific and practical aspects of the dye industry, established a fund for an interna-

[112] Wilfred T. Grenfell, *Forty Years for Labrador* (Boston and New York: Houghton Mifflin, 1932), 250 ff.; Dorothy Sterling to Julius Rosenwald, Jan. 22, 1921, Dorothy Sterling to W. Graves, March 18, 1925, and other letters in the Rosenwald Papers, box 32.

[113] Gregory Henderson, Cultural Attache, American Embassy, Seoul, to Merle Curti, Jan. 4, 1960; Dr. Y. S. Lee to Gregory Henderson, Dec. 30, 1959; L. George Paik, *Facts about Yonsei University* (Seoul: Yonsei University, 1960). The total Severance contributions amounted to $165,000. A new plant was built with contributions from various sources after the Second World War.

tional study of epidemic encephalitis. By the terms of his will, announced two years later, the $2,000,000 foundation he directed to be established was to make research in this field its first project.[114] Before his death from a heart disease William D. Kerckhoff of Los Angeles decided to give a large sum for the creation of a research institute in the cardiac field. In keeping with this decision his widow in 1929 gave to the Bad Nauheim in Germany a sum reported to be over $1,000,000 but, probably, considerably less. The Institute, bearing the donor's name, developed an extensive library and comprehensive medical museum and made stipends available for research. When Hitler came to power, there was much confusion over the funds and in 1939 the director of the Institute, being part Jewish, was forced to flee to America.[115]

Still another example of benefactions to a medical cause reflecting a personal interest is the story of what James Loeb, classical scholar, art connoisseur, and scion of a famous Jewish banking family, did for the Institute for Experimentation in Psychiatry in Munich. Founded as a result of the suggestions of Emil Kraepelin and other German psychiatrists in 1918, the Institute faced ruin in the inflationary period after the First World War. Loeb not only saved it—for without his help it could not have survived the period of inflation—but in 1924 established in New York the Solomon Loeb Memorial Fund to be used to secure the salaries of departmental chairmen. In 1929 Loeb made still another grant of $150,000 and on his death bequeathed his residuary estate of over $1,000,000 to the Institute. The program of research in organic mental illness, neurobiochemistry, experimental psychology, serology, and microbiology was sustained, although during the Nazi period two prominent scientists were discharged. It was ironical in view of Loeb's contributions that the Institute was compelled to accept ideologically oriented staff members in its department of racial heredity. Subsequently the Institute was able to convince American authorities that it had not worked directly on behalf of the National Socialist regime.[116]

---

[114] Matheson Commission, *Epidemic Encephalitis* (New York: Columbia University Press, 1929), v; *New York Times*, June 5, 1927, Nov. 17, 1929, May 16, 27, 28, 1930.

[115] *New York Times*, Sept. 19, 1929; *Los Angeles Times*, Sept. 19, 1929; report of conversation of George Mowry with Mrs. Webster Holmes, Mrs. William D. Kerckhoff's daughter; *Bad Nauheim, Das Internationale Hertzheilbad* (n.p., n.d.); Dr. Kleinert to Merle Curti, March 17, 1960.

[116] *American Jewish Year Book*, Sept., 1934–Sept., 1935, XXXVI, 274; Dr. W. Scholz to Merle Curti, March 26, 1960.

It was not unnatural for a donor whose benefaction to a cause in the United States had been appreciated as an original and significant one to want to extend the idea to other countries. In 1927, when his philanthropies had reached the sum of $30,000,000, George Eastman decided to make available to the needy children of London the kind of free dental care that the clinic he had founded and supported in Rochester had been doing for the young of his home town. Lord Riddell, together with wealthy British friends, agreed to provide for the maintenance of such a clinic, to be built by Eastman on the grounds of the Royal Free Hospital and to be administered by the London Dispensary. At the opening the speeches emphasized the relation of teeth to diet, health, efficiency, well-being and happiness and, of course, the implications of the benefaction for Anglo-American relations.[117]

Within the next four years Eastman's offers of a million dollars to each of several other cities for similar dental clinics, to be subsequently maintained along the line of the parent institution in Rochester, were accepted. Thus the Eastman idea of free dental clinics for needy children resulted in the establishment of such institutions in Rome, Paris, and Brussels.[118] The one in Stockholm, in particular, illustrates the point that even in a highly developed welfare state philanthropy may have a useful role, for dental care is not included in public medical services.

In answer to an American protest against such giving to peoples abroad Eastman replied: "What I have contributed for dental dispensaries abroad is but a very small percentage of what I have given in our own country; whereas my money has been made in the Kodak business which is carried on all over the world." [119] The Eastman example was followed by Rosenwald who, in the year before Hitler

---

[117] *New York Times*, April 23, 1927; Eastman to Dr. H. J. Burkhart, March 1, 1927, Personal Letter Book, 23; Eastman to George B. Dryden, March 31, 1927, Personal Letter Book, 23; Eastman to Dr. Abraham Flexner, April 18, 1927, Personal Letter Book, 23; Eastman to Lord Riddell, June 18, 1927, in the Eastman Papers; Carl W. Ackerman, *George Eastman* (London: Constable, 1930), 476.

[118] Eastman to his Excellency, Giacomo De Martino, and Prof. Amedeo Perna, August 22, 1929, Personal Letter Book, 26; Eastman to Vicomte De Lantscheere, April 2, 1931, Personal Letter Book, 28; Eastman to Hon. Nils Hellstrom and Hon. Victor Karlsson, Oct. 6, 1930, Eastman Personal Letter Book, 27; Eastman to Hon. Le Prefet de la Seine, Paris, Oct. 13, 1930, Personal Letter Book, 27, all in the Eastman Papers.

[119] Eastman to Mrs. Lyman Donaldson, Feb. 22, 1932, Personal Letter Book, 28, Eastman Papers.

took power, gave $1,000,000 to Berlin for the establishment of a similar dental clinic.[120]

In the field of overseas philanthropy the 1920's and 1930's saw the continuance of programs for improving health which the Near East Foundation had developed during the postwar turmoil in what had been the Turkish empire. Until 1929 the Commonwealth Fund continued its work in child care and preventive medicine in Austria.[121] A newcomer, the Kellogg Foundation, organized in 1930, concentrated on public health programs in Michigan but gradually extended its work to Canada, Great Britain, and South America. In 1937 it gave its first fellowships to two Montreal physicians to finance a year's study in public health experiences in the United States and at about the same time subsidized courses in postgraduate medicine for physicians in McGill University. This was only the beginning of a program which came to include sixty Canadian projects involving grants of more than $2,000,000.[122]

The most extensive and intensive work in medical research, training, and public health was done by the Rockefeller Foundation and its affiliated agencies, the China Medical Board and the Rockefeller Institute for Medical Research.[123] In supporting research, grants were made to centers in several countries for work on basic problems. Thus, for example, before Hitler took power the Kaiser Wilhelm Institute was given $655,000, a part of which was used to establish a research laboratory in the field of cellular physiology (and some of which went for research in "pure physics").[124] In 1932 the newly created neurological institute at McGill received $1,232,-652—one of several grants for research abroad and at home in psychiatry. Research grants also contributed to the discovery and development of methods for making clinically useful sulfanilamide by Dr. Leonard Colebrook of Queen Charlotte's Hospital in London.[125] The Rockefeller Institute itself attracted a staff of distin-

[120] *American Jewish Year Book*, Sept., 1932–Sept., 1933, XXXIV, 107.

[121] Commonwealth Fund, *Annual Report*, 1926, 67 ff.; 1927, 61 ff.; 1939, 50 ff.

[122] Horace B. Powell, *The Original Has This Signature—W. K. Kellogg* (New York: Prentice Hall, 1956), 327 ff.

[123] Raymond B. Fosdick, *Story of the Rockefeller Foundation* (New York: Harper, 1952), chap. 9.

[124] In 1936 Fosdick was quoted as saying that the Foundation would probably not have made the grant could it have foreseen conditions existing in that year in Germany: *New York Times*, Nov. 24, 1936.

[125] Rockefeller Foundation, *Annual Report*, 1932, 212; Raymond B. Fosdick, *Chronicle of a Generation: An Autobiography* (New York: Harper, 1958), 262.

guished research men whose contributions to medical knowledge made it one of the greatest research centers in the world.[126]

In a related field—medical education—it was necessary to exercise great tact both in relations with professional men and with governments. Out of the interest of the senior Rockefeller in China, an interest encouraged by Frederick Gates, Abraham Flexner, Herbert Welch, Wallace Buttrick and others, the China Medical Board was developed. It did a good deal for medical education in several Chinese centers but its great achievement was the establishment in 1921 of the Peking Union Medical School. This compared favorably with the best Western institutions and occasioned many expressions of appreciation from the Chinese. The Foundation's ultimate outlay for medical education in China was almost $45,000,000, the largest expenditure for any single objective. When the Communists took over, the research program relaxed, but what had meantime been contributed to the health of China had not been lost.[127] In addition to building up or improving medical training institutions in Canada, Great Britain, France, Belgium, Brazil, in Beirut, Singapore, Bangkok, and in the South Pacific area, the Rockefeller Foundation through its division of medical education enabled thousands of men to increase their knowledge of medicine through fellowship study in other countries.

The Foundation's greatest contribution abroad was in the field of preventive medicine. Wicklyffe Rose, who had been chiefly responsible for the Rockefeller Sanitary Commission's triumph over hookworm in the Southern states, projected onto the international scene what had been done at home, a pattern familiar in so much of American philanthropy abroad. The program, begun under the International Health Board, was carried forward by its successor, the International Health Division, organized in 1927. The international approach was evident in the contributions made to the public health work of the League of Nations and in the determination of Rose and his great coadjutor, Dr. Victor Heiser, to let no national prejudices on any side stand in the way of opening the doors of health to the masses of people in the whole world.

[126] Rockefeller Institute for Medical Research, *History, Organization and Present Scope of the Scientific Work* (New York, 1921, 1923-29, 1931-32, 1934, 1936-37).
[127] Rockefeller Foundation, *Annual Report*, 1921, 280-81; Fosdick, *Story of the Rockefeller Foundation*, 90; interview with Raymond Fosdick, March, 1958.

In the interest of immediate and certain results, known methods of attacking diseases were followed in the medical surveys and pump-priming demonstration projects. Yet the International Health Board and the International Health Division also encouraged new types of demonstration qualitatively different from established practice. Working, as it was so clearly necessary to do, through governments and insisting that these bear a part of the initial costs and assume complete responsibility for subsequent support, Rose and his associates in their campaigns against hookworm, yellow fever, and malaria demonstrated the necessity of tax-supported public health institutions at both the local and the national level.

Thus in the course of successful campaigns against malaria in Albania and other countries and against yellow fever in South America and in parts of Asia and Africa, the Foundation developed in the minds of authorities and the public at large an awareness of the fact that diseases long regarded as inevitable and ineradicable could be controlled.[128] It also developed the idea of self-help and community responsibility in the field of public health.

The officers and field workers of the Foundation did not find the job an easy one. In many places there was prejudice against America and American ideas and a special prejudice against anything bearing the Rockefeller name. The Foundation deserved great credit for its modesty, tact, and leadership in developing wise programs and in showing how money, knowledge, and skill could be efficiently and fruitfully used. In the course of his work, Dr. Heiser made sixteen trips around the world. His surveys and proposals of programs in preventive medicine in forty different countries yielded results which in his words literally staggered the imagination. The work involved both the promotion of field research and the development of methods for bringing about the more general use of scientific methods and discoveries, all to the potential benefit and well-being of the human race.[129]

---

[128] Fosdick, *Story of the Rockefeller Foundation*, 37.
[129] Victor George Heiser, *An American Doctor's Odyssey* (New York: Norton, 1936), 326, 345 ff., 532-33.

XII

Responses to Natural Disasters

In the years between the two World Wars man's ineptness in human relations and cruelty to his fellows put demands on American compassion far greater than those resulting from natural disaster. Yet, in addition to minor hurricanes and earthquakes in various quarters of the globe that invited aid, three major catastrophes in greater or lesser degree of nature's making also tested American responsiveness to suffering. The responses to these catastrophes affected the national reputation as no earlier disasters had done.

During the Washington Disarmament Conference of 1921 when tension between the United States and Japan reached a high-water mark Prince Tokugawa spoke of the continuing need of humanitarianism in the postwar world. "May the Red Cross, the emblem of the true heart," he admonished, "combine together the people of America and Japan." [1] Two years later a frightful catastrophe in his homeland resulted in the most considerable American response to human need that any foreign natural disaster had ever occasioned.

On September 1, 1923, the press informed the public of a horrible earthquake and fire which laid Tokyo and Yokohama in ruins. Later dispatches indicated that 2,000,000 people were homeless, that at least 100,000 were seriously injured, that upwards of 200,000 had been killed, and that a far larger number were in imminent danger of death from starvation and epidemic. In Japan itself, Christian leaders well known in America, including Toyohiko Kagawa, declared that the catastrophe should arouse the Japanese to see their need for repentance and righteous living and should further unite the na-

[1] Foster Rhea Dulles, *The American Red Cross: A History* (New York: Harper, 1950), 263.

tions in prayer and in speedy aid for desperately needed help.[2] The help came. The governments of twenty-eight nations (counting the British Commonwealth as one) contributed over 21,000,000 yen, the yen being valued at about fifty cents. These gifts were chiefly made through the Red Cross organizations of the several governments.[3]

The greater part of this contribution—over 15,000,000 yen—came from voluntary American gifts. In addition, the executive branch of the government, without waiting for Congress to convene, ordered the Asiatic Fleet and the Philippine Department of the Army to speed emergency relief to the stricken cities. Directed by Governor General Wood, Admiral Anderson, and General McCoy, the Philippine relief expedition rushed food, medicines, doctors, nurses, and other supplies and services to Japan.[4] When Congress met it passed without protest legislation covering the costs. These added up to over $6,000,000.[5]

President Coolidge asked his fellow citizens to contribute through the American Red Cross. After allocating $100,000 for emergency relief, the Red Cross started a campaign for $5,000,000. It seemed, as the *San Francisco Chronicle* had foretold, hardly necessary to do more than ask; but the local Red Cross organizations, each with a quota to meet, no doubt welcomed the publicity given by the press, the movies, the church, and business organizations.

Although humanitarian sympathy was most often reflected in the campaign for funds, self-interest and prejudice sometimes were in evidence. The National Association of Credit Men, representing 30,000 manufacturing and banking establishments, declared in its meeting at Atlantic City that Japan was just as good a credit risk as before the disaster and that for the sake of future trade, business should extend all possible consideration.[6] A writer in *American Industries* was more blunt. Reviewing the need in reconstruction for

---

[2] "Christian Suffering and Relief in Japan," *Missionary Review of the World* XLVIII (Jan., 1924), 12-13. Gratitude was expressed that no Christian evangelists or pastors were killed with the exception of two Salvation Army volunteers.

[3] *Japan Year Book*, 1924-1925 (Tokyo: Foreign Affairs Association of Japan), 55-56. Miss Chizuko Ibuka at Tokyo University provided the author with similar figures from the Japanese language history of the Japanese Red Cross.

[4] *New York Times*, Sept. 3, 4, 1923.

[5] U. S., Congress, House, *Relief of Earthquake Sufferers in Japan*, 68th Cong., 1st Sess., 1924, House Doc. 195, 1-2; U. S., Congress, House, Committee on Military Affairs, *For the Relief of Sufferers from Earthquake in Japan*, 68th Cong., 1st Sess., 1924, House Rept. 893, 1.

[6] *New York Times*, Sept. 20, 1923.

railroad equipment, building materials, and consumers' goods, this spokesman for business declared that the potential market should not be overlooked either by those that had been trading with Japan or by those that had never entered its market.[7]

This writer was not the only one to sense opportunities for exports: lumber, engineering, and electrical concerns saw that the disaster had important market implications and thought that bread cast on the waters was sure to be returned.[8] The *Omaha Bee*, self-appointed spokesman for the midwest farmers, telegraphed President Coolidge that his appeal had touched the heart of the country and that it was expressing this sentiment in associating "the dire need of Japan with the emergency of the farmers of the grain belt" by urging "that an immediate purchase of flour on a large scale be made by the United States for the relief of Japan." [9]

Some went further. In the camp of labor a writer in the *Paper Makers' Journal* declared that the Supreme Ruler of the Universe had brought about the destruction as a means of reducing a surplus population which in accepting competitively low wages reduced the living standards of American workers.[10] In the midst of the fund-raising campaign other spokesmen for labor revealed prejudices against the rapidly increasing Japanese population. Gompers himself in promising cooperation of labor declared: "Every man who has a dollar should give a quarter to save the life of one Japanese. Something must be done to help these people, even if they are of a different race than we." [11] Something was also said about improving friendly relations with Japan. Many suggested that generosity might soften the resentment in that country over the concessions her government had recently reluctantly made at the Washington Disarmament Conference.[12] Who can say whether such expressions, together with an awareness of California's discrimination against

[7] Manuel Gonzales, "Rebuilding Industrial Japan," *American Industries* XXIV (Oct., 1923), 36; J. S. Ruble, "Yankee Builders Aiding Japan," *American Industries* XXIV (April, 1924), 39.

[8] *Red Cross Courier* II (Sept. 22, 1923), 8; "Japan's Disaster to Boom American Industries," *Nation's Business* XI (Nov., 1923), 96-98, quoting *Lumber World Review* and *Engineering News-Record*.

[9] Quoted in the *Boston Evening Transcript*, Sept. 7, 1923.

[10] *Paper Makers' Journal* XXII (Sept., 1923), 19-23.

[11] *New York Times*, Sept. 4, 1923; *American Federationist* XXX (Nov., 1923), 917-18.

[12] See the *New York Times*, Oct. 22, 1923; *Boston Evening Transcript*, Sept. 11, 1923; and *Current Opinion* LXXV (Oct., 1923), 400-02.

Japanese-Americans, stimulated many Americans to give out of an uneasy conscience?

But overshadowing all else was the reminder that after the San Francisco earthquake and fire Japan had given in relief more than half as much as all other nations together.[13] Expressions of gratitude constituted only one evidence that the primary motive in giving was sheer humanitarianism.

To some, this generalization may be questioned in view of the fact that while many contributions came in small sums, large donors gave most of the money. In New York City (which gave between one-fourth and one-fifth of the nation's total to the Red Cross campaign) more than half of the contributions to earthquake relief came from business organizations in sums of $5,000 or more. Among the $25,000 donors were Bethlehem Steel, the Guggenheim Brothers, Kuhn, Loeb and Company, the J. Pierpont Morgan Company, and the Allied Chemical and Dye Corporation. Standard Oil of New Jersey and the Japan Society, whose members included many men with overseas business interests, gave $40,000 each. General Motors and National City Bank each gave $50,000, Bell Telephone $100,000, United States Steel $150,000, the Stock Exchange $171,000, and the American Silk Association $400,000.[14] John D. Rockefeller's gift of $100,000 was one of the largest individual contributions.[15] In Massachusetts the entire state quota of $225,000 was subscribed by twelve men.[16]

Even when allowance is made for the small contributors who sent in the $100,000 raised by the *Christian Herald* and the many thousands of little gifts from Japanese Americans (the total from this source was $1,380,000),[17] it is still true that in this campaign the Red Cross chest was filled in impressive proportions by large gifts from the business community. Within little less than two weeks after the news of the disaster reached America the $5,000,000 asked for was oversubscribed. The $11,600,000 ultimately collected was the more impressive when it is remembered that on the seventy-fifth

---

13 *New York Times*, Sept. 6, 1923.

14 *Ibid.*, Sept. 5-9, 13, 16, 21-23, 26, 1923.

15 *Ibid.*, Sept. 6, 1923. The Laura Spellman Rockefeller Memorial Fund also gave $100,000.

16 *Red Cross Courier* II (Sept. 12, 1923), 11.

17 *New York Times*, Sept. 9, 1923, Sept. 13, 1923. In giving $10,000 the Japanese colony in Los Angeles requested that at least $1,000 be used to relieve Americans in the disaster area.

anniversary in 1935 the Red Cross had spent only $35,000,000 in overseas relief.[18] The Red Cross's fund-raising methods were, moreover, virtually beyond reproach, for it used funds from its own regular budget to pay costs of collection.

The Red Cross donation did not represent all that Americans gave. Some sent their contributions directly to Japan: this was true, for example, of Rodman Wanamaker's $25,000 gift. The Salvation Army initially sent $5,000 and though its sale of cherry blossoms in the streets and its drive for second-hand clothing failed to add up to the $5,000,000 that Commander Evangeline Booth asked for, its record was praiseworthy. To the replacement of ruined buildings Americans also contributed. S. P. Fenn of the Sherwin-Williams Company gave $500,000 for the rebuilding of the Tokyo YMCA and the Laura Spellman Rockefeller Fund offered $75,000 toward the $250,000 needed for a new YWCA. A group of well-known women led a campaign to rebuild Tsuda College for Girls. Churches with missions in Japan gathered funds for putting up new places of worship.[19]

The Red Cross decided to turn over all shipments and purchases of goods in Japan to the Japanese Red Cross and to the Japanese government for distribution. Although some missionaries and some Americans at home criticized this procedure, the *Red Cross Courier* often spoke of the competence and good organization of the Japanese Red Cross. Certainly the policy was appreciated in Japan, testifying as it did to American faith in the efficiency and fairness of the Japanese agency.

Altogether the Red Cross shipped to or bought in Japan 8,000 tons of rice, 1,850 tons of flour, 14,500 cases of milk, 43,000 cases and 300 barrels of fish, and 65 tons of hardtack. Some Americans in Japan, in criticizing the Red Cross for what it sent, claimed that these items were simply not usable in the Orient.[20] But actually the Red Cross showed more consideration for Japanese dietary habits than for American agricultural surpluses. In addition to food, it sent five tons of drugs, five portable hospitals, 11,000,000 feet of lumber, 5,000,000 bundles of shingles, 728 tons of galvanized iron, 100,000

---

[18] American National Red Cross, *The Red Cross Activities of the American People during 75 Years: 1881 through 1935* (Washington: The American National Red Cross, 1955), 7, 22; *New York Times*, Sept. 11, 1923.

[19] *New York Times*, Sept. 4, 12, 16, 1923, Feb. 27, 1924.

[20] "The Japanese Red Cross and the Earthquake," *Missionary Review of the World* XLVII (June, 1924), 418-19.

pairs of shoes, 15,000 kimonos, and 1,540,000 items of other clothing.[21]

Criticisms of the food items sent were not the only ones that Americans directed at the Red Cross. Missionary voices regretted the decision forbidding Red Cross contributions from being used to restore churches and felt that the quick and generous response of church members to the appeals of the Red Cross depleted purses that would otherwise have been opened to missionary rehabilitation.[22] A Jesuit priest in Japan, in complimenting the Red Cross, nevertheless added that the total contribution would at best succor not more than five per cent of the afflicted Japanese.[23]

On the whole, however, Americans took satisfaction not only in what was done but in its presumable effects on Japanese-American relations. "The help which America has given, and which she will continue to give as long as there is need for it, should go far toward disarming the hostile feelings which some Japanese, as individuals, have cherished toward the United States," commented the *Boston Evening Transcript*. "Under the shadow of a great national catastrophe," continued the editorial, "the Japanese people have seen that our professions of good will are genuine, that we wear no mask of feigned friendship." [24] That the feeling of Americans toward Japan was also at last a friendly one was the opinion of many who expressed themselves on the subject. "Whatever coolness may have sprung up between us and Japan during recent years," wrote another observer, "is completely swept away, and in this country there remains only a sorrowful and anxious feeling of neighborliness and a widespread desire to repair the damage." [25] The decision of the Red Cross to use what was left of its relief fund, some $3,000,000, for a hospital in Japan, met with general approval and suggested that this enduring testimony of good will might make it harder for the Japanese to forget the American response to the great disaster.

In thanking Rodman Wanamaker for the $25,000 check that he sent directly to Japan, Viscount Shibusawa asked that Americans "give up sympathy and . . . exercise a powerful influence to bring

[21] *Red Cross Courier* III (March 15, 1924), 2.

[22] *Red Cross Courier* III (March 15, 1924), 1-2.

[23] Mark J. McNeal, "The Destruction of Tokyo: Impressions of an Eyewitness," *Catholic World* CXVIII (Dec., 1923), 316.

[24] *Boston Evening Transcript*, Sept. 11, 1923.

[25] "America Rushes First Aid to Stricken Japan," *Current Opinion* LXXV (Oct., 1923), 402.

success when the necessity of floating a foreign loan in America arises because the amount required for restoration work will be so enormous as to make it difficult for the domestic market alone to finance it." [26]

But over against this somewhat dour reaction there were countless Japanese expressions of unqualified appreciation. Ambassador Cyrus Woods reported that "three things have impressed the Japanese—the size and spontaneity of America's gift, the promptness with which it was made available, and, last and greatest of all, the fact that it was absolutely unconditional." [27] Japanese Ambassador Hanihara, in his remarks at a meeting of the American Red Cross in Washington, declared that in remembering the genuine and generous sympathy the Japanese would lose all thought of American aggressiveness in the Far East. "It will henceforth be difficult indeed for professional jingoes to terrorize an ignorant public opinion to a point where it will countenance policies of military aggrandizement . . . against fancied American threats. The natural reaction of a Japanese to the mention of America will be a thrill of gratitude and warm friendliness." [28] Baron Nikokichi Ijuin, the new foreign minister, announced that it was the most ardent desire of his government and people to repay the kindness shown by foreign friends, especially during the earthquake, and to act with a firmer determination than ever for cooperation with the powers in the promotion of world peace and international welfare.[29] And Baron Kanda, an Amherst graduate who had taken a leading role in promoting Japanese-American understanding, declared that the prompt and generous American relief would go far toward assuring the Japanese of the depth of human kindness across the seas.[30]

Such sentiments on the part of public leaders were echoed in the principal newspapers. "What is most remarkable," the Tokyo *Nichinichi* wrote editorially, "is the attitude shown by the Americans. They have come out and behave consistently like the Americans of old—stupendous in scale and enterprise and marvelously to the point of laying plans for rescue work. They have been efficient, sentimental

[26] Telegram to Rodman Wanamaker from Viscount Shibusawa, *New York Times,* Sept. 18, 1923.
[27] *Red Cross Courier* II (Dec. 1, 1923), 12.
[28] *New York Times,* Sept. 25, 1923.
[29] *Ibid.,* Sept. 21, 1923.
[30] Kanda Memorial Committee, ed., *Memorials of Naibu Kanda* (Tokyo: Toko-Shoin, 1927), 61.

and generous in giving and forgetful of everything else in their zeal to help helpless sufferers." [31] To be sure, the geographical proximity of the United States and the higher level of wealth were taken into account in expressions of gratitude in the Japanese press. But by and large it hailed American contributions as proof of good will and of a more sympathetic attitude toward Japan.[32]

Yet even while Americans were trying to cement friendly relations by offering aid without strings during a great disaster, at the same time, ironically, opinion and policy moved rapidly toward the complete exclusion in 1924 of Japanese immigrants, a decision having unfortunate effects on Japanese attitudes toward America. The deterioration of Japanese-American relations in the 1920's and 1930's was, of course, the result of other factors as well. But together the forces which sharpened tension overshadowed the impact of what Americans had done during the earthquake catastrophe.[33]

In 1930 a major hurricane in the Dominican Republic, virtually an American protectorate, resulted in the destruction of the capital, in damage to property estimated at $20,000,000, in the injury of many thousands, and in the death of possibly 3,000 men, women and children.[34] Marine planes flew in emergency relief and Governor Theodore Roosevelt, Jr., of Puerto Rico lost no time in sending government vessels with food, serums, doctors, and nurses. Canteens and hospitals were set up in the stricken areas. The Red Cross contributed over $200,000 for relief and sent a special mission to help with reconstruction.[35] President Trujillo, who assumed dictatorial powers during the emergency, warmly thanked President Hoover for the aid which in some part softened the resentment many Dominicans had felt toward the American occupation.[36] Hardly was the news of this disaster missing from the front pages when new ones struck. Hurricanes in Cuba and San Salvador and an earthquake in New Zealand brought help from the American Red Cross.[37]

[31] Quoted in the *Red Cross Courier* II (Nov. 17, 1923), 7. See in addition the Tokyo *Nichinichi*, Sept. 15, 21, 1923, and the Miyagi *Kahoku Shimpo*, Sept. 9, 10, 22, 25, Oct. 5, 6, 1923.
[32] Miss Chizuko Ibuka of Tokyo University made a survey of comments in Japanese newspapers, both national and local, for the author.
[33] Eleanor Tupper and George McReynolds, *Japan in American Public Opinion* (New York: Macmillan, 1937), 170-98.
[34] *New York Times*, Sept. 5, 6, 1-12, 1930.
[35] *Ibid.*, Sept. 6, 9, Nov. 16, 1930.
[36] *Ibid.*, Sept. 18, 24, Nov. 16, 1930.
[37] *Ibid.*, Feb. 10. 1931, Sept. 15, 20, 1933, June 12, 16, 1934.

Far worse than these was the horrible earthquake in southern Chile during the night of January 24, 1939. The worst catastrophe in the nation's history, the earthquake laid Chillán and Concepcíon in ruins, killed over 20,000 people, injured at least 50,000, and forced some 100,000 to become refugees. Torrents of rain heightened the danger from contaminated water reservoirs: the peril of epidemics was frightening.[38] Within six days United States army planes based in the Canal Zone arrived with Red Cross serums and vaccines. A B-2 bomber sped additional supplies. The Army sent 500 tents.[39] President Roosevelt called on the public to open its purse. The Red Cross appealed to its 3,700 chapters for help, and within three weeks the central organization had sent $25,000 in cash and kind together with service personnel.[40] Panagra Air Service flew supplies into the devastated areas and moved hundreds of injured to hospitals in Santiago. Pan-American Grace also used its planes to move supplies and gave free postal service. The American community in Chile quickly raised 25,000 pesos for relief.[41] Other foreign communities also responded generously. The British, for example, took on the feeding of an entire town of 16,000 people. And Argentina, Brazil, Peru and other countries sent medical supplies and food by plane, train, and ship. Pan-American solidarity appeared to be a reality.[42]

It was clear, however, that voluntary aid, even on the prevailing generous scale, was not enough. Representative Hamilton Fish of New York proposed that Congress give a million dollars to finance shipments of grain, meat, and milk to the earthquake area. Such help, he urged, would do more to offset anti-American propaganda in Latin America than had the recent Lima conference.[43] The Salt Lake City Chamber of Commerce telegraphed Senator King suggesting that some of the surplus agricultural commodities in government hands be given to the Red Cross as a means of cementing the good neighbor policy. But some representatives objected to the Chilean relief bill, sponsored by Sol Bloom of New York, on the ground that such a "handout" was unjustified in view of a bankrupt treasury. Bloom replied that other countries had given official aid, that

[38] *Ibid.*, Jan. 25-29, 31, 1939.
[39] *Ibid.*, Jan. 28, 31, Feb. 3, 1939.
[40] *Ibid.*, Feb. 2, 1939.
[41] *Ibid.*, Jan. 26, 27, 1939. Air France and German Condor joined in similar service.
[42] "Earthquake in Chile," *Bulletin of the Pan American Union* LXXIII (March, 1939), 172-75.
[43] *Congressional Record*, 76th Cong., 1st Sess., 1939, vol. LXXXIV, Pt. 1, 967.

the money was to be spent in this country for commodities for which there was no demand, that no cash was to go abroad. Other members of Congress, however, contended that charity should begin at home and that domestic claims came first. Fish, who had initially favored aid, now opposed it on the ground that the popular front Chilean government, headed by a socialist, intended to develop public housing and had repudiated $200,000,000 worth of bonds owned by American investors. Bloom withdrew the bill from consideration.[44]

Chilean appreciations of the aid given by the Army, the Red Cross, and the local American community were warm and apparently genuine. But these must have been somewhat dulled by the prolonged negotiations over a desired loan for reconstruction. The State Department made it clear that any radical Chilean legislation unfavorably affecting legitimate investments would jeopardize a loan through the Export-Import Bank.[45]

For American overseas philanthropy in the period between the two wars China posed problems far greater and much more complex than those in any other part of the world. Famine, of course, had long been endemic in that country, but in 1920 and 1921, and again in 1929, conditions became so acute and so intertangled with internal political issues, so appalling, that American benevolence was challenged as in no other situation in the 1920's and 1930's. The magnitude and novelty of the challenge resulted in sharp conflicts of opinion in American philanthropic circles, in innovations in fund raising, and in experiments in relief, rehabilitation, and prevention.

The traditional American interest in maintaining the Open Door in China, the actualities of commercial ties, the relations of banking firms with the prewar Consortium, and the continued awareness that the vast Chinese population might provide American markets, suggest that the philanthropic concern with China was related to economic considerations. But this was hardly the case. During his visit to China immediately after the First World War, Thomas Lamont concluded that it would be inadvisable under the prevailing political conditions for American finance to reconsider floating loans for economic rehabilitation and development.[46] No doubt having this in mind, an American business man in China remarked to John Dewey that whereas their countrymen were willing to invest millions in famine relief and in an effort to duplicate American educational institutions, they were unwilling to risk capital in expectation of profit-making. This, Dewey observed, really symbolized American attitudes toward China, which he saw as essentially parental: one might hope that one's children would be of help later on, but uppermost was a sense of obligation to implant parental ideas and ideals through advice, instruction and precept, for which, in return, gratitude was expected.[47] And this was a sound observation. For while the argument was sometimes heard that relief and rehabilitation promised to increase Chinese purchasing power and to expand American markets, these considerations appear to have been minor. The context in which American benevolence operated was, in short, essentially psychological rather than economic.

By the early autumn of 1920 the famine which Lamont saw in the offing during his stay in China became a hideous reality. Disastrous crop failures in north central China threatened death to 45,000,000 people and reduced at least 15,000,000 men, women, and children to the starvation level. Reports indicated that desperate families were eating pumice stone, sawdust, elm bark, corn cobs, and thistles.[48] Foreign and Chinese relief societies tried, not very effectively, to do what they could. The American Minister in Peking, Charles Crane, and John Earl Baker, a fiduciary railway expert in the Chinese government service, reactivated the local chapter of the Red Cross, raised funds in the American community, and, after much conferring, brought together the relief societies of six foreign and fourteen Chinese groups in the International Famine Relief Committee. Funds to support this cooperative federation came from several sources. Of a total, figured in "Mexican dollars" (currently used in China), of over $17,358,000 some $6,549,000 came from the American Advisory Committee, the clearing house of several American contributing agencies. Various religious groups made special contributions. The Protestant

---

[46] Thomas W. Lamont, *Across World Frontiers* (New York: Harcourt Brace, 1951), 250-51.

[47] John Dewey, *Characters and Events: Popular Essays in Social and Political Philosophy* (2 vols.; New York: Holt, 1929), I, 309-11.

[48] Peking United International Famine Relief Committee, *The North China Famine of 1920-1921, A Report* (Peking, 1922), 13.

Episcopal Church gave $262,899 (Mex.). The YMCA and the Salvation Army also gave generous support.[49]

The Committee and the subordinate bodies to which it allocated funds for relief in special areas opposed direct money relief and the establishment of soup kitchens and refugee camps, though in some cases it relied on these methods. It distributed large amounts of free grain, which the Chinese government transported at special rates to famine areas. Some two million people were thus helped. The Committee also established 672 special schools which cared for 45,787 pupils, each of whom was given every month food valued at approximately $1.40, which was also to feed the parents of the children. As the selling of children was common during Chinese famines, this program made the children economic assets rather than liabilities and, at the same time, gave some impetus to the idea of education for the young. The schools also encouraged industry by teaching girls how to make hairnets and straw-braid commodities. In the later stages of its work the Committee followed the example of the American Red Cross in establishing work-relief projects.[50]

Support of the International Committee was only a part of the aid provided by the people of the United States. In the autumn of 1921 the Red Cross, on the advice of the State Department, responded to the appeals of Crane and Baker by appropriating $500,000. This was supplemented three months later by a similar amount. The Red Cross stipulated that its representatives should administer its funds, and the International Committee assigned western Shantung as the area for which it was to have special responsibility.[51]

Even before the Red Cross made its first allocation the *Christian Herald* was publicizing the famine conditions and appealing for funds—in the end it contributed more than $500,000 to relief.[52] But it was clear, as each report from China revealed the gravity of the situation, that the need was far greater than the *Christian Herald* and the Red Cross could meet. On December 9, 1920, President Wilson appealed to American compassion for generous aid and ap-

[49] *Ibid.,* 17. $500,000 gold equalled $750,000 "Mexican dollars."
[50] *Ibid.,* 59, 61, 63, 123.
[51] American National Red Cross, *The Report of the China Famine Relief* (Washington: American National Red Cross, 1922), 6.
[52] *New York Times,* Oct. 7, Nov. 17, Dec. 8, 1920, April 5, 1921; *Christian Herald* XLIII (Nov. 6, 1920), 1138, (Dec. 18, 1920), 1303; XLIV (April 16, 1921), 292; XLIV (June 25, 1921), *passim.*

pointed a committee headed by Thomas Lamont.[53] The prestige of the committee members, President Wilson confided to one of them, would, he hoped, lend weight to the plan for wide-scale popular subscriptions.[54] Lamont threw himself into the job at hand. In the course of the campaign he made innumerable speeches in many parts of the country in which he assured his audiences of his faith in the future of a people he had found to be industrious, sober, intelligent, peace-loving and on the road to becoming a strong, united nation.[55]

In view of the Hoover appeals for feeding Europe and the presumed weariness of the American people with "drives," the new American Committee for the China Famine Fund decided against a large-scale, high-pressure campaign.[56] But the decision was in effect set aside when the John Price Jones Corporation was engaged to plan and direct activities. State and local organizations, all headed by prominent men and women, were set up. Speaking tours were arranged and material was provided for the speakers. Newspapers and periodicals were enlisted to publish feature articles and to give free advertising. Theaters arranged benefit performances, movie stars staged luncheons. Fashion shows and Chinese costume balls helped swell the fund. Posters in street cars and public places made their appeals through graphic photographs of starving Chinese children and through a battery of slogans.

The campaign was carried into the service clubs, the Exchange, the Chambers of Commerce, the schools. The Committee gave widespread publicity to the *New York Times* editorial, "Where Death is Welcomed," reported the daily mortality rate, and sent workers special pep messages to buck up flagging spirits. It brought to the reading public the endorsement of the campaign by three presidents—Taft, Wilson, and Harding.[57] Considerable stress was put on giving the equivalent of what one might save by eating no more than he

[53] Governor Harding of the Federal Reserve Board, William Howard Taft, Charles W. Eliot, Dr. Livingston Farrand, Cleveland H. Dodge, George M. Cohan, Cardinal Gibbons, Adolph S. Ochs, Norman H. Davis (Acting Secretary of State), and others served: *New York Times*, Dec. 10, 1920.

[54] Woodrow Wilson telegram to Julius Rosenwald, Dec. 9, 1920, Rosenwald Papers, University of Chicago Library, box 19.

[55] Lamont, *Across World Frontiers*, 260-61.

[56] Lamont to Rosenwald, Dec. 28, 1920, Rosenwald Papers, box 19.

[57] The preceding account is based on the report of the campaign in the archives of the John Price Jones Corporation, deposited in the Baker Library, Harvard University, Cambridge, Massachusetts.

needed. To catch those who ate out, restaurants and hotels put China bowls on their tables for free-will offerings. Either at the suggestion of the Committee or on their own initiative women's clubs urged housewives to bring the message of sacrifice into the home by cutting out one course from each meal or by giving up one meal a week. After exchanges between Mrs. Carrie Chapman Catt and the First Lady, who was accused of not doing her part, Mrs. Harding announced that one course would be dropped from White House repasts.[58]

By the end of April, 1922, the Committee for China Relief had sent $3,600,000 across the Pacific. In the words of Thomas Lamont, its contributions had cut 10,000,000 people from the 15,000,000 who were estimated to be doomed to death by starvation. A second phase of campaigning promised to save the other 5,000,000.[59] In the end the Committee, despite competition from the Hoover campaigns for feeding Europe, raised over $4,600,000. Most of this came in small contributions: the only two big gifts were those of John D. Rockefeller and the Laura Spellman Rockefeller Memorial Fund ($250,000 each). Cooperating Chinese organizations in the United States raised $250,000. The Red Cross raised $1,112,000. Churches sent directly to their missionary agencies for relief purposes $1,700,000. The grand total was $7,750,000. At the end of the campaign the control of the situation in China was well enough in hand for the Committee to announce a residue of $1,250,000. This was to be treasured until a new emergency arose or to be used by two Chinese universities for research in and programing of measures to prevent future famines.[60]

Gifts of food were made in this campaign, as in earlier ones. Through the Farm Bureau Federation, mid-west corn growers, having a surplus on hand and hoping to popularize taste for the product, offered to give several million bushels. The Chicago, Burlington and Quincy Railroad offered free freight, and the Railway Brotherhoods were willing to give their services on all roads running to the West Coast. The Shipping Board felt that there would be no difficulty in getting naval reserves to volunteer for the ocean trip without pay. In response to a bill introduced by Senator William S. Kenyon of Iowa, the Senate voted an appropriation of $500,000 to cover the

[58] *New York Times*, March 14, 1921.
[59] *Ibid.*, May 1, 1921.
[60] John Price Jones Corporation Report; *New York Times*, Jan. 6, 1924; *Christian Herald* XLIV (June 25, 1921), *passim*.

cost of moving the corn to China. But the House refused to go along partly because it would take $5,000,000 to transport 10,000,000 bushels of corn across the Pacific and partly because of the testimony that commercial trade on that ocean would be ruined if the transport ships brought back any return cargo.[61]

Although these and other considerations kept the starving Chinese from having this kind of American bounty, contributions in cash were distributed in various ways. Some were used by the International Committee for direct relief and for the maintenance of its schools and other projects. Those which missionaries received from church collections bought food in Manchuria for distribution; and those of the Red Cross were used for a significant experiment in work relief which anticipated the New Deal WPA.

After rejecting the proposal for rehabilitating part of the Grand Canal, the Red Cross adopted a road-building program under the supervision of John E. Baker, an American statistician long associated with philanthropic movements, and business enterprises in China. Headmen in the Chinese villages chose the labor crews: it was felt they knew where the need was greatest. The Red Cross provided housing for the crews and twice as much food for the laborer's family as he himself received. At the end of the first day twenty died from overeating, but the labor force did not relish the grain (which was often dirty) or the beancakes (which in better times were mixed with manure and used for fertilizers). A minor problem was the failure of the Chinese to develop a taste for chewing gum: Wrigley Brothers had contributed 49 cases! More serious was the matter of labor turnover. This resulted in part from the desire of the headmen to have the work shared as widely as possible, in part from the success of the Japanese in persuading workers to quit, in part from the refusal to stay on the job when missionaries handed out food without asking anything in return.

There were other problems. Thieves stole supplies. Transportation sometimes failed. And the Chinese who owned property on the right of way did not want to give it up even when compensated. Despite all these thorny problems and some outright failures, the project on the whole came out well. Over 3,600 wells were dug, 40,000

[61] *New York Times*, Jan. 23, Feb. 13, 26, 1921; U. S., Congress, House of Representatives, Committee on Appropriations, Subcommittee in charge of Deficiency Appropriations, *Hearings, Famine Relief in China*, 66th Cong., 3d Sess., 1921, 4; *Congressional Record*, 66th Cong., 3d Sess., 1921, vol. LX, Pt. 3, 3293, Pt. 4, 3724, 3832-33, 3964.

trees were set out, and 840 miles of good roads were built. John Baker hoped that the work-relief project strengthened the morale of communities and that the Chinese would see the advantage of this way of meeting famine over handouts with their pauperizing aspects.[62]

In 1926 the American Geographical Society published under the title *China: Land of Famine* the report of Walter Mallory, secretary of the China International Famine Relief Commission. This body acted as a caretaker of funds left in the treasury of the International Committee at the end of the crisis, studied the causes of famine, and outlined preventive measures. After discussing the natural, economic, political, and social factors in the famines which periodically befell a fourth of the human race, Mallory took note of the varied proposals for attacking the problem. Missionaries of the traditional type argued that if the Chinese masses would only become Christians, God would provide. Conservation engineers, mindful of the prewar efforts of the Red Cross and the Chinese government to launch flood control projects, insisted that the most urgent need was the control of China's rivers, the development of irrigation, and the reclamation of the land by reforestation and other means. Economists proposed more efficient banking, particularly methods for lower interest rates to make possible the application of urban capital to rural needs. Some recommended recolonization in Manchuria and Mongolia, better transport, and industrialization. Others felt that the most promising approach was through education in better farming methods with the use of agricultural machinery. Still others argued that nothing could be accomplished until banditry and the internecine strife of war lords were suppressed and China became a unified, stable, efficient country.

All these diagnoses and specifics figured in what was done and not done in the great famine of 1927.[68] In the context of such conflicting views about preventing chronic floods and crop failures in China, the difficulties encountered in that great disaster and the years following are the more understandable. By December, 1927, reports indicated that 9,000,000 people on the Shantung peninsula were starving. The China International Famine Relief Commission meeting in Peking appealed to the American Red Cross and to other foreign

[62] John Earl Baker, "Fighting China's Famines" (unpublished typescript, Rare Book Department, Memorial Library, University of Wisconsin, 1943), 22 ff.; American National Red Cross, *Report of the China Famine Relief*, 14, 22, 185-86, 211, 218.

[68] Walter H. Mallory, *China: Land of Famine* (New York: American Geographical Society, 1926), xii ff.

agencies for emergency relief.[64] Eleven months later, in November, 1928, the Commission at its meeting in Tientsin asked the same groups for $12,000,000, reported that 12,000,000 people were starving and that the figure was expected to reach 20,000,000 by spring. One delegate to the Commission testified that he had seen some twenty women and girls sold in a single day; others declared that conditions were so bad that there were no buyers. Eyewitnesses sent gruelling accounts of the mass suicide of children and of outright cannibalism.[65]

John Baker, who was in New York in behalf of Yenching University's endowment campaign, turned to the seemingly hopeless job of raising money for relief. The greater part of the remaining funds from the Lamont committee's efforts had been spent, presumably in the relief work during a 1924 flood in Kwantung in which over 13,000 had lost their lives. It was apparent that most supporters of China had turned sour on the matter of relief because of repeated outbreaks of antiforeign sentiment and the seeming hopelessness of effective relief and preventive measures. Such was the position of the Red Cross. Many missionary groups were reluctant to take part in a fund-raising campaign lest it hamper their own cause. Even members of the China Famine Relief, which had kept a skeleton organization, backed out of the plans for fund raising. No one was willing to head it. At last Dr. S. Parks Cadman, president of the Federal Council of Churches, let himself be drafted. And David A. Brown, the experienced chairman of the United Jewish Campaign, agreed to chair the board of the China Famine Relief and to help raise money. Under Baker's prodding an appeal was made for $10,000,000 for relief and work projects and for far-reaching measures for famine prevention. But there was little interest. Of the 8,500 men and women invited to a meeting to open the campaign, only 150 turned out. It was clear to Brown that the public failed to grasp the situation: let anyone, he said, fast for three days, and that person might begin to understand what starvation means.[66]

Funds came in very slowly; the highest figure reported for a ten-day period was $50,000.[67] Newspapers continued to report that bandits and war lords seized a large part of what relief there was and that

[64] *New York Times*, Dec. 24, 28, 1927.
[65] *Ibid.*, Nov. 16, 1928, May 1, 1929.
[66] Baker, "Fighting China's Famines," 188-96.
[67] *New York Times*, Nov. 27, 1928, May 1, 12, 1929.

political chaos and inefficiency had led to a breakdown of transportation. The problem was made the harder when the National Information Bureau, whose approval was so necessary in any fund-raising campaign, refused support to the China Famine Relief which it declared to be an agent of the war lords and a bunch of "horse thieves." [68]

In midsummer of 1929 the Red Cross, under some pressure to modify its hands-off policy, sent an investigating commission to China to find out whether a truly "abnormal" emergency existed and whether it could do anything effectively to relieve the situation. In announcing the departure of the commission the *New York Times* noted that it was normal in China for some 20,000,000 people to exist in a state of undernourishment and for thousands to die of hunger every year. "The remedy for these conditions must be achieved by economic, political, and social reconstruction and rehabilitation, upon which," the *Times* added, "the Red Cross cannot embark." [69]

The Red Cross commission, led by Colonel E. P. Bicknell, reported that distress was the result of chaotic political and military conditions, that the greatest need was for political reform, and that, in any case, normal conditions were returning.[70] The *New York Times* described the report as "one of the most depressing documents that has ever been issued by this organization, which has done so much to alleviate human suffering. Friends of China will join with the Red Cross in hoping that the unfortunate country will soon have a government not only willing but strong enough to bring about the necessary reforms and to provide the periodic relief by which alone the evils of famine may be lessened." [71] In discussing the report, a writer in *Commonweal* stressed the point that the Chinese government had used the proceeds of a bond issue floated for relief to increase the army. "So long as the United States sends abroad something like fifty millions of dollars each year for missionary and charitable enterprises, there is little to indicate that the American heart beats any less warmly in sympathy with other nations in distress than heretofore. It had been evident for several years," the

[68] Baker, "Fighting China's Famines," 194.

[69] *New York Times*, July 21, 1929.

[70] *Ibid.*, Sept. 28, 1929; Catherine Finnely, "History of the American National Red Cross," vol. XXI: "American National Red Cross Disaster Services, 1918-1939" (mimeographed monograph in the Library of the American National Red Cross, Washington, D. C.), 162 ff.

[71] *New York Times*, Sept. 30, 1929.

author of the *Commonweal* article continued, "that there has been a change in the nature and direction of this sympathy, particularly in a feeling that more discrimination should be shown by charitable people in the distribution of . . . funds." Why should Americans continue their gifts to other countries, he asked, "so long as the conditions which give rise to the need of them are allowed to continue. One can 'pauperize' a nation as well as an individual." [72]

To such criticisms the spokesmen for The China International Famine Relief Committee replied that conditions in China were much worse than the Red Cross report indicated, that this organization had helped Russia and the Near East when these areas also lacked a stable government, that losses from banditry and official interference had totaled only $400 out of the million dollars spent thus far during the famine and that, further, the Chinese themselves had contributed proportionately to relief funds far more than they had in 1921.[73]

Returning to China in 1930 to oversee the relief program of both the China Famine Relief and the China International Famine Relief Commission, John Baker found a good deal of discouragement in many Chinese circles and criticism on the part of American businessmen and missionaries of any further efforts at foreign relief. It was clear to him that these critics were right in holding that political disorder had contributed substantially to the prevailing famine. Yet there was immediate work to be done and, fortunately, some reason for encouragement. The Nationalist government expressed appreciation of foreign aid and readiness to cooperate in work relief projects. From the Chinese in Honolulu came $135,000 for building irrigation dams in Shensi. The largest Buddhist society in Peking allocated $100,000 for another irrigation project. And by the spring and early summer of 1930 grain and seed beans were arriving in the famine section of Shensi. These were distributed, together with funds from the $500,000 that had by this time been received from America, by agencies named by the All-American Advisory Committee, which was made up of mission board executives and the heads of American firms in China.[74]

Under Baker's direction, work relief projects got under way: well-

---

[72] George E. Anderson, "Common-sense Charity Abroad," *The Commonweal* XI (Nov. 13, 1929), 44-45.

[73] *New York Times*, Sept. 30, Dec. 22, 1929, Feb. 6, 1930.

[74] Baker, "Fighting China's Famines," 219 ff.; *New York Times*, Feb. 27, May 18, 21, June 24, 1930.

digging, irrigation devices, and dams. The projects took two years to finish and, with the direct relief which saved countless lives, absorbed the million dollars available. On returning several years later to Shensi, Baker was pleased at the evidences of the lasting and beneficial effects of the irrigation projects.[75]

But no sooner had the crisis of 1930 been passed than another catastrophe struck. This time the Yangtze flooded, affecting about as many people as had the great famine of 1921 and destroying even more property. The river reached a crest three feet higher than the previous 1870 record. All Hankow was reported to be under water. In August word came that the Yangtze was claiming at least a thousand bodies daily and that disease was now rampant. At Nanking the government announced that 50,000,000 people were on the verge of starvation.[76] Some indication of what conditions were like is suggested by the experiences of the Lindberghs who flew to China to report on the disaster. Thinking the plane had brought food, starving Chinese mobbed it as it alighted in Northern Kiangsu Province. When the occupants of the plane sought refuge in a nearby sampan, it was sunk by the sheer weight of the numerous Chinese who jumped aboard in a desperate effort to get food.[77]

Obviously neither private charity nor government action could alone cope with such a situation. The Chinese government appropriated large sums for emergency relief and bought on credit the 15,000,000 bushels of wheat (half of it was flour) which the United States Grain Commission released. Retracting somewhat from its earlier stand, the Red Cross gave $100,000 for relief. Flood Relief in China, a cooperative agency under David Brown's direction, got into action and, thanks to the support of church and missionary groups, succeeded despite the depression in raising respectable sums.

Meantime in China a new relief organization was launched. At Baker's suggestion the League of Nations appointed as its director Sir John Hope Simpson of Great Britain who had had much experience in relief work in India. Thus the appearance of any one nation's taking leadership was avoided. Transportation problems, Communist disturbances, and hostile engagements with the Japanese made it hard to carry out the program. Nevertheless it fed between ten and

---

[75] Baker, "Fighting China's Famines," 317.

[76] *New York Times*, May 31, Aug. 8, 15, 20, 24, Sept. 3, 1931.

[77] *Ibid.*, Sept. 20, 27, 1931. Mrs. Lindbergh made a radio appeal for contributions for China's stricken millions, *New York Times*, Feb. 22, 1932.

fifteen million people and rebuilt 5,000 miles of dikes, all for less than $15,000,000.[78] David Brown, accompanied by Sir John, visited the area and reported in 1932 that the reclamation and irrigation projects had been well executed, that with the new roads that had been built the likelihood of so serious a catastrophe in the future was improbable, and that the Chinese were not only deeply appreciative but greatly impressed by the value of long-range preventive measures in comparison with mere palliative relief.[79] Another firsthand observer, G. Findley Andrew, a China-born missionary who had in 1930 supervised the expenditure of $250,000 for the China Famine Relief, declared that what had been done had enhanced the American reputation, given a lead to the new government in self-help programs, and warded off a Communist seizure of power.[80]

John Baker's verdict was probably nearer the truth. He was pleased that the 5,000 miles of dikes built in 1932 had saved the city of Hankow in 1935.[81] But in looking backward he was sure that the widely held idea that famine in China was inevitable had indeed led to an arrogant attitude toward relief on the part of some, and heightened misunderstanding and resentment on the part of the Chinese people. The American press and other agencies were only partly right in dismissing floods and famines as the result of political corruption and inefficiency. Only in economic unity, in political stability, in flood control, in the development of rural credit cooperatives, and in similar measures could there be any real hope of preventing such disasters.[82] For these measures the Chinese themselves must in the end be responsible. American philanthropy had not yet succeeded in implementing in any large and substantial way what its most thoughtful and realistic exponents had recommended and on a small scale helped to initiate.

Natural disasters, of course, did not end with the catastrophes in Japan, Chile and China. A typhoon in Japan (1959), an earthquake in Chile (1960), floods in Viet Nam (1961), and a severe earthquake in Iran (1962) testified to the helplessness of man before elemental forces. Because they are both unpredictable and divorced from human

[78] Baker, "Fighting China's Famines," 328 ff.; *New York Times*, Aug. 8, 15, 20, 26, 29, Sept. 1, 3, 11, 1931.
[79] *New York Times*, Nov. 20, Dec. 25, 1932.
[80] *Ibid.*, Dec. 25, 1932.
[81] *Ibid.*, July 26, 1936.
[82] Baker, "Fighting China's Famines," 447-76.

causation, natural disasters have usually resulted in generous gifts to the stricken district on the part of Americans. But man's inability to live in peace with his fellow man has added vast new fields to the scope of American overseas giving. Philanthropy in response to man-made catastrophes has formed an important part of American giving in the 20th century.

XIII

The Plight of the Jews

No catastrophe of the 1920's or 1930's for which man was responsible had more far-reaching implications for American philanthropy than the plight of the European Jews. The presence in the Jewish problem of deeply rooted economic and social difficulties, often tangled by political issues, taxed the will and capacity of American giving. Moreover, the threatened annihilation of Europe's Jews came at a time when the great depression narrowed the means to give and heightened the need for charity at home. Nevertheless, a host of American philanthropic agencies mobilized their forces to mitigate the mass suffering. Some were already well established with considerable experience and a well-defined constituency. Others arose as events, ideologies, and cross purposes seemed to require.

No group was so closely involved with overseas needs as the five million American Jews.[1] Non-Jews often failed to recognize the variations in values in the so-called Jewish community. Many American Jews were only slightly interested in Judaism, which they thought of less as a way of life than as a religion or body of ethical teachings. Some were only slightly involved with Judaism while others were deeply committed. Nor were the cleavages between the old, well-established and often well-to-do and the poorer newcomers from Eastern Europe the only ones. Some synagogues adhered to Orthodoxy, some to the Conservative position, others to Reformed Judaism. Sharp differences also existed over Zionism, the growth of which in the United States was slow and halting. All these differences, together with the general decline of the religious foundation of Judaism, favored the development of a small and active leadership, largely

---

[1] Eli Ginzberg, *Agenda for American Jews* (New York: King's Crown, 1950), 1-83, illuminates the role of American Jewry in overseas relief and rehabilitation.

of the well-to-do elite, of a bureaucracy of activists, and of professional fund raisers.

The most important result of all this for the relations of American Jewry to overseas needs and crises was the accentuated development of philanthropy as the chief bond holding the various sectors together. Although as late as 1930, and even after that, many who gave had little understanding of the problems of their overseas brethren, the rise of Hitlerism and the growth of the Jewish community in Palestine proved to be educational and at the same time to offer new cement for the otherwise slightly coherent character of American Judaism. This, together with the development of a high level of efficiency in fund raising, which, for a voluntary group involved a good deal of pressure, is the large context for what was done. What was done, though not without inner conflicts and even bitterness, is the most significant story in American overseas philanthropy between 1925 and 1939. It is, to be sure, only part of a still larger story—that of the generous response of Jews in Great Britain and the Commonwealth, the countries of Western Europe and of Latin America.[2]

The major conflict in overseas philanthropy involved the relative merit of two broad positions. One emphasized the primary importance of meeting emergencies as they arose in as nonpolitical and nonpartisan a way as possible. Relief and rehabilitation seemed in this frame to be the best way of helping European Jews find a tolerable life in "their own countries." The Joint Distribution Committee had been the chief exponent of this view. Between its founding in 1914 and 1925 it spent $58,866,000 in its overseas programs. It was led by well-educated, well-to-do and well-established Jews with American roots. So was the older and closely allied American Jewish Committee organized in 1905 and dedicated, under the leadership of Dr. Cyrus Adler, to working for the security and the rights of Jews and to opposing anti-Semitism everywhere. It expressed itself, in times of grave emergency, in representations at the White House and at the State Department.

The other major position stressed the primary importance of establishing a national homeland in Palestine. This was regarded by its exponents both as the only realistic way of helping the persecuted Jews in Europe and as the most effective way of integrating religious,

[2] Of special importance is Norman De Mattos Bentwich's *They Found Refuge: An Account of British Jewry's Work for Victims of Nazi Oppression* (London: Cresset, 1956). Bentwich's *The Refugees from Germany April 1933 to December 1935* (London: Allen & Unwin, 1936) is also useful.

national, and cultural values in a regenerated world Judaism. Increasingly the American Zionist Organization, which by the mid-1920's numbered some 75,000 adherents, and its affiliates, had come to enjoy the support of the American Jewish Congress. This agency, it will be recalled, represented the more recent Jewish immigration. It resented as antidemocratic and even as un-American the patrician leadership of the Joint Distribution Committee and the American Jewish Committee which, in its eyes, seemed presumptuously to speak for all American Jews without taking mass Jewish opinion into account. The conflict between these two principal groupings in American Jewry was dramatic and at times acrimonious. To complicate things still further, the Zionists had to meet not only the opposition of many Orthodox Jews but of virtually all Jewish Marxists. They also had to face the opposition of prominent gentiles. Dr. Henry Pritchett of the Carnegie Endowment for International Peace, for example, reported after a visit to Palestine in 1926 that Zionism was a visionary program led by fanatics who stressed the antiquated idea of a Chosen People. He further maintained with a good deal of truth that Palestine was an incredibly poor land in which the legitimate possessors, the Arabs, deeply resented Jewish immigration.[3]

Within each of the broadly defined Jewish groups, sharp differences further complicated the story of Jewish overseas philanthropy. Louis Marshall, Felix M. Warburg, James N. Rosenberg, Paul Baerwald, who succeeded Warburg as chairman of JDC in 1932, and other leaders in the non-Zionist JDC and American Jewish Committee, came increasingly to recognize constructive achievements of colonists in Palestine and the educational value of Zionism. Without becoming Zionists this group favored cooperation with the builders of the homeland and, in 1929, effected a measure of cooperation in broadening the Jewish Agency of Palestine, which was thenceforward to include non-Zionists in its executive committee. But many in the older and more traditional groups, of whom Rabbi Jonah B. Wise was an effective representative, found it hard to make this transition and were often denounced by the *New Palestine*, the organ of American Zionism, and by Dr. Stephen S. Wise, prominent Zionist.[4]

[3] *New York Times*, Nov. 29, 30, 1926.
[4] Alpheus Mason, *Brandeis: A Free Man's Life* (New York: Viking, 1946), 441 ff., 593 ff.; Stephen S. Wise, *Challenging Years: The Autobiography of Stephen Wise* (New York: Putnam's, 1949), 182 ff.; Louis Lipsky, *A Gallery of Zionist Profiles* (New York: Farrar, Straus and Cudahy, 1956), 143-65; *The New Palestine* XXVII, May 14, 1937; "Julian W. Mack," *Survey Graphic* XXXII (Oct., 1943), 372.

Nor did the Zionists themselves see eye to eye. One group, led by Mr. Justice Brandeis and Judge Julian W. Mack, bent their efforts toward "Americanizing" Zionism through separating the philanthropically supported institutions of education, health, and other social services from colonization and economic development. This, they felt, should be promoted by corporate investments managed on sound business principles. Defeated in 1921, when the Keren Hayesod or Palestine Foundation Fund was adopted as a means of colonization and development through the voluntary contributions of world Jewry, the Brandeis-Mack group withdrew from active leadership in American Zionism. The helm was taken by the group led by Morris Rothenberg. In time, however, both courses, the philanthropic and the business-oriented, contributed substantially to the colonization and economic growth of Palestine, for the work of the Palestine Foundation Fund was supplemented by the development of corporate enterprises largely financed by wealthy American Jews. By 1946 Americans had invested over $45,000,000 in Palestine and loaned $22,000,000 through the Palestine Economic Corporation.[5] This money greatly furthered the advancing economy.

Still another cleavage, more important in Palestine itself and in Zionist world circles than in America, was the so-called revisionism. This subordinated the interests of rank-and-file workers in Palestine to national development and institutionalized a militant nationalism which such Zionists as Dr. Stephen Wise regarded as a Jewish fascism.[6] Other differences also divided American Jewry in its attitude toward overseas emergencies and needs. All these cleavages represented honest differences in personal loyalties to rival leaders and ideologies. The existence of these cleavages was bound to affect fund raising and to create friction. Yet even before Hitler seized power, wise and statesmanlike leaders, including Felix Warburg and others associated with him, sought to bring about as much cooperation and mutual understanding as possible.[7]

---

[5] Israel Cohen, *The Zionist Movement*, rev. Bernard G. Richards (New York: Zionist Organization of America, 1948), *passim;* Elihu Katz, *Source Book on Zionism and Israel* (New York: Zionist Organization of America, 1948), 36; *The New Palestine* XXVI, Jan. 3, 1936, XXVII, Feb. 3, 1937, Feb. 26, 1937; Palestine Economic Corporation, Incorporated, *Annual Reports*, 1926- (New York: Palestine Economic Corporation, 1927-).

[6] *The New Palestine* XXV, March 15, 1935.

[7] Cyrus Adler, "Felix M. Warburg," *American Jewish Year Book*, Sept., 1938–Sept., 1939, XL (Philadelphia: Jewish Publication Society of America, 1938), 29-30; Justine Wise Polier and James Waterman Wise, eds., *Personal Letters of Stephen Wise* (Boston: Beacon, 1956), 244; Frieda Schiff Warburg, *Reminiscences of a Long Life* (New York: privately printed, 1956), 114 ff.

The story of American Jewish philanthropy in foreign lands between the programs of relief and rehabilitation following the First World War and the outbreak of the second global conflict in 1939 may be appropriately begun with a decision of the Joint Distribution Committee in 1924. Several months before this Felix Warburg took satisfaction in the fact that a good part of the $12,000,000 collected by this organization for Russian relief was spent on non-Jews and in the prospect that a return to normal times might make it possible for the Committee greatly to curtail its program or even to disband.[8] But the officers of the Committee could not close their eyes to the reports of its representative abroad, Dr. Joseph Rosen, an American citizen of Russian birth who had, it will be recalled, helped the Hoover famine relief program in his native land by distributing JDC funds and in promoting drought-resisting seeds, crop diversification, and improved farm methods.

As Rosen pointed out, the Soviet government's official banning of anti-Semitism had neither ended this blight nor solved the problems of the 3,000,000 Russian Jews. In fact, the Revolution had aggravated the plight of these people. Save for a small number that had become farmers (thanks to minor concessions of the Czarist regime and the help of Baron de Hirsch's Jewish Colonization Society), the great majority could no longer carry on the petty trading and small crafts by which they had been forced to make a living before the Revolution. Small trading was now outlawed and new government cooperatives made the individual crafts obsolete. As an ostracized group the Jews had no means of livelihood and no access to the medical and other social services established for workers and peasants.

It is not altogether clear how the idea originated of colonizing the Jews in the arid parts of the Crimea and Ukraine and on the confiscated estates of nobles. In 1923 the Association for the Promotion of Trade and Agriculture or ORT (now Organization for Rehabilitation through Training) proposed land settlement, a proposal publicized by Abraham Bragin, organizer of the All Russian Agricultural Exhibition of 1924.[9] Much credit for the idea must, however, be given to Joseph Rosen, who, during the years of famine relief, had used a small part of the JDC funds at his disposal to help needy

[8] *New York Times*, Feb. 10, 1924.

[9] Dr. Solomon W. Schwarz, an authority on the matter, credits ORT with making this suggestion: Schwarz, *The Jews in the Soviet Union* (Syracuse: Syracuse University Press, 1951), 163; *New York Times*, Feb. 18, 1924.

farmers in the old but now disrupted Jewish agricultural colonies established before the Revolution. Eager to increase food production and to solve the Jewish problem, Soviet officials looked with favor on the colonization of this minority in agricultural communities.

As a result of Rosen's persuasive arguments, the JDC on July 21. 1924, established the American Jewish Joint Agricultural Corporation (Agro-Joint) to cooperate with the Soviets in settling Jews on the land and to provide means for rebuilding broken lives under new conditions. Somewhat hesitantly the JDC embarked on the experiment, making an initial grant of $400,000 for getting under way through loans and services the establishment of the colonies.[10] Agro-Joint's Russian workers, under Dr. Rosen's lead, set up loan societies, dug wells with American driller machines, built villages, imported agricultural machinery, and opened farm schools and dispensaries. By terms of the agreement Dr. Rosen made with Komzet, the Kremlin's agent in the project, the government was to provide the land, including standing timber for building purposes, transportation at reduced rates, and the admission of agricultural machinery free of duty. On its part, Agro-Joint was to provide the tools and machinery, oversee the laying out of fields and the construction of buildings, and give the agricultural training which people who had never seen a tractor so much needed. In this and in the development of medical facilities, Agro-Joint was over the years aided by other Jewish Agencies, including the long-established Jewish Colonization Society (JCS) in London and Paris, ORT (Society for the Encouragement of Hand-craft), and OSE (an international agency for protecting the health of East European Jews). But Agro-Joint did the lion's share, especially in the early years, when its contributions were 89 per cent of the total funds as against the 11 per cent given by Komzet. By 1934 Komzet had taken over 76 per cent of the program's support.[11]

---

[10] A dispatch from Riga took JDC to task for its appropriation, charging that "millions collected from Jews throughout the United States have been used by Jewish communists to crush Jewish life." The Committee was especially criticized for giving funds to Jewish communist social workers in Russia without obtaining "concessions" from them. Louis Marshall, chairman of the American Jewish Relief Committee, denied the charges and made it clear that the new grant for colonization would not be turned over to Idgeskom (Communist Jewish organization) but administered solely under the auspices of the JDC: *New York Times*, August 25, 27, 1924.

[11] Evelyn Morrissey, *Jewish Workers and Farmers in the Crimea and Ukraine* (New York: privately printed, 1937), 120 ff., 125; Avrahm Yarmolinsky, *The Jews and Other Minor Nationalities under the Soviets* (New York: Vanguard, 1928), 88 ff.; *New York Times*, July 21, 1925; *American Jewish Year Book*, Sept., 1925–Sept., 1926, XXVII, 58-62. Tool Campaign for Jews in Russia, supported by the United

Under the skillful and creative leadership of Dr. Rosen, who got along well with Komzet, the experiment made a fine start. Jews wanting to take part in it formed voluntary settlers' associations, at least 10 per cent of whose members were experienced farmers. The associations were largely self-governing and, under Soviet encouragement of self-expression among cultural minorities, used Yiddish and developed a Jewish communal life. The Soviet government further encouraged cultural self-determination by declaring some of the contiguous colonies to be "autonomous Jewish areas." Only two years after the incorporation of Agro-Joint, it had settled 50,000 Jews on 500,000 acres of land in the Crimea and Ukraine—on an expenditure of over $2,000,000. By the spring of 1928 JDC had made available to Agro-Joint $5,800,000 in loans for land settlement and had given outright an additional $1,800,000 for agricultural training, medical supplies and other services. At this time 100,000 Jews had been settled on a million acres of land in 49 colonies.[12]

James N. Rosenberg, prominent New York lawyer and artist, was one of the most ardent backers of the project. The vivid diary kept on his visit to the colonies in 1926 glows with appreciation and enthusiasm. What he saw was indeed inspiring: a people, only a few years ago in the depths of despair, hard at work building a new life. Thanks to the scientific methods of farming that Dr. Rosen and his staff had been teaching and to American tractors and other modern equipment, bumper crops were being harvested, livestock was flourishing, vineyards and orchards were thriving. The settlers were managing their own local affairs. Dispensaries and nursing-training programs were bringing better health. Schools had been started with an emphasis on vocational programs. But cultural life was also well rooted: even plays in Hebrew were being produced. No one feared pogroms, for the colonists were on good terms with their non-Jewish neighbors. No one questioned would even consider returning to the city ghettos. And the movement for expanding the program was in progress with the cordial cooperation of the Soviet authorities.[13]

Hebrew Trades, The People's Workmen's Circle, and the *Jewish Daily Forward* helped in supplying tools for small industrial enterprises: *New York Times*, Feb. 3, 4, 1929.

[12] Morrissey, *Jewish Workers and Farmers*, 144; *New York Times*, May 26, Nov. 18, 1926; *American Jewish Year Book*, Sept., 1926–Sept., 1927, XXIX, 77, 81; Sept., 1928–Sept., 1929, XXX, 32-33.

[13] James N. Rosenberg, *On the Steppes: A Russian Diary* (New York: Knopf, 1927), *passim*. See also David A. Brown, *The New Exodus: The Story of the Historic Movement of Russian Jewry Back to the Soil* (New York: American Jewish Joint Distribution Committee, 1925).

Not that the road was easy. Dr. Rosen, who compared the experiment to pioneering on America's frontiers, reported that much suffering had been involved in planning villages, building houses, schools, dispensaries, digging wells, granting loans for livestock, seeds, and farm machinery. "We have had our full share of troubles, disappointments, heartbreaks, and heartaches, from without and within." [14] In the United States the experiment met with bitter criticisms from the Zionists, who insisted that it was "fraught with dangerous consequences both for the Jews of Russia and for the Jews of America." [15] In Zionist eyes, the JDC and its agent, Agro-Joint, were diverting monies from the far more important and realistic job of helping emigrants get a start in Palestine. At a meeting of the Zionist Convention in June, 1926, a large vote condemned the Russian colonization scheme as "tending to counteract the efforts of the Zionists . . . to mobilize the public sentiment of Jewry in favor of a Jewish homeland in Palestine." [16] This criticism continued to be made and was in part responsible for cleavages and hard feelings among American Jews and for serious troubles in fund-raising campaigns.

Encouraged by what had been accomplished, the principal backers of the experiment in colonizing Russian Jews on the land organized in 1928 the American Society for Jewish Farm Settlements in Russia. Led by Felix M. Warburg, Paul Baerwald, Herbert H. Lehman, and James N. Rosenberg, the Society undertook to raise in private subscriptions $10,000,000 to match a like sum offered by Komzet. The Soviet government, by contractual agreement, issued bonds for the capital investment of the Society which were ultimately redeemed in cash. American contributors to the fund included Louis Marshall ($100,000), Herbert H. Lehman ($100,000), Paul Baerwald ($200,-000), and Felix Warburg, whose million dollar subscription testified to the deep impression made by what he saw of the colonies during his visit the year before.[17]

Julius Rosenwald, feeling that the Soviet government's provision of the land made the movement more practical than the efforts to transplant a large population to a small and crowded Palestine,

[14] Quoted in Morrissey, *Jewish Workers and Farmers*, 130-31.
[15] *New York Times*, Sept. 13, 1925.
[16] *Ibid.*, June 30, 1926.
[17] Moses A. Leavitt, *The JDC Story: Highlights of JDC Activities, 1914-1952* (New York: American Jewish Joint Distribution Committee, 1953), 10; *American Jewish Year Book*, Sept., 1928–Sept., 1929, XXX, 75, 77, 78.

where the land had to be bought, contributed $5,000,000.[18] "That," wrote Herbert Hoover to Rosenwald, "is indeed a princely bene-faction and I believe I know something of the great heart and the willing hand with which it is given. The dedication of that wealth to make it possible for a people who have been starving as petty trades-men, to return to their ancient calling and become producers of the necessities of life from the soil, is a great experiment in human en-gineering, and you and I, who have watched together the fruition of so many enterprises born of a realization that the welfare of other human beings is the concern of all of us, can entertain no misgiv-ings for its ultimate success."[19] Rosenwald, deeply touched, kept Hoover's letter as a treasured document to be passed on to his chil-dren. "It is a high honor indeed," the Chicago philanthropist wrote to the former director of the American Relief Commission, "to have my name coupled with yours as you have been kind enough to do."[20] Although the project lay outside the scope of the philanthropies of John D. Rockefeller, he expressed pleasure in following the example of his friends, Warburg and Rosenwald, giving $500,000 to what he regarded as a notable and creative example of "social engineer-ing."[21]

Thanks to the funds thus brought together, the American Society for Jewish Farm Settlements in Russia expanded the project. By 1936 there were 215 Agro-Joint colonies with 20,000 families in the Ukraine and the Crimea: 100,000 Jews had been moved into areas entirely operated by Agro-Joint. Much equipment had been brought from the United States: 1,000 tractors, 700 tractor plows, 100 deep-well pumps, 36 combine harvesters. Ten thousand houses had been built. In addition, Agro-Joint had helped 3,500 families outside the districts allotted to it, aided 10,000 families in the old Jewish colonies, and given a hand to 15,000 non-Jewish peasant neighbors of the set-tlers. By 1937 JDC, Agro-Joint, and the Society for Jewish Farm Settlements in Russia had spent $16,000,000.[22]

[18] *American Jewish Year Book*, Sept., 1928–Sept., 1929, XXX, 32-33; Sept., 1932–Sept., 1933, XXXIV, 166.
[19] Herbert Hoover to Julius Rosenwald, Feb. 13, 1928, Rosenwald Papers, Univer-sity of Chicago Library, box 36.
[20] Rosenwald to Hoover, Feb. 16, 1928, Rosenwald Papers, box 37. Hoover later gave to Rosenberg an eloquent testimonial regarding "the practical idealism of the Jewish people": Morrissey, *Jewish Workers and Farmers*, 141.
[21] Morrissey, *Jewish Workers and Farmers*, 141.
[22] *American Jewish Year Book*, Sept., 1938–Sept., 1939, XL, 305-06; Leavitt, *The JDC Story*, 10.

In view of the limited amount of unoccupied land in European Russia and concern over the encroachment of Chinese and Japanese in Siberia, the Soviet government decided to encourage Jewish settlement for agricultural and industrial development in an area on the Amur River in Siberia known as Biro Bidjan. This thinly settled territory was both swampy and heavily forested, and the preparations for establishing a colony were grossly inadequate, both in terms of the little that was done in the area itself and the failure to train the colonists for the hardships they had to face. The first attempt to encourage voluntary emigration led to unsatisfactory results, after which Komzet tried to recruit settlers. In 1934 the area was declared a Jewish Autonomous Region. But the first ten years—1928-1938—saw the permanent settlement of only 18,000 or at the most 20,000 Jews instead of the 100,000 for which the plan called.[23] Agro-Joint did not take part in the movement, but a pro-Soviet American agency, the Jewish Colonization Organization for Russia (ICOR), contributed $250,000 in farm equipment. A related group, the American Committee for the Settlement of German Refugees in the USSR, held mass meetings and dinners, graced by Ambassador Troyanovsky, Earl Browder, and other figures prominent in the Communist movement.[24] A meeting in New York in the spring of 1936, attended by 500 delegates, expressed satisfaction with the Soviet program which allegedly had enabled 5,000 Jewish families from Poland and Roumania to settle in the area.[25] The meeting also met head on the Zionist claim that the scheme was a fantastic effort to divert the flow of philanthropic funds and victimized Jews from Palestine, by denying that there was any conflict between the two colonization movements.[26] Little headway was made, however, in the campaign for $350,000 to help finance the Biro-Bidjan project. Despite the attempt of the Soviet government and the American Communist press to make out that things were in good shape in a truly autonomous

[23] Walter Zander, *Soviet Jewry, Palestine and the West* (London: Gollancz, 1947), 29 ff.; Schwarz, *The Jews in the Soviet Union*, 174 ff.; Gregor Aronson, *Soviet Russia and the Jews*, trans. Benjamin Schultz (New York: Jewish League Against Communism, 1949), 5 ff.; *New York Times*, Feb. 28, June 3, August 26, 1934; *American Jewish Year Book*, Sept., 1930–Sept., 1931, XXXII, 123-24; Sept., 1934–Sept., 1935, XXXVI, 235; Sept., 1937–Sept., 1938, XXXIX, 246-47.

[24] *New York Times*, Dec. 18, 26, 1935.

[25] *Ibid.*, March 12, 1936. Former Representative William W. Cohen headed the committee which was in working relations with the World Committee for the Relief of German Fascism. See also *American Jewish Year Book*, Sept., 1936–Sept., 1937, XXXVIII, 199-200; Sept., 1937–Sept., 1938, XXXIX, 246-47.

[26] See, for example, the *New Palestine* XXV, Oct. 18, 1935.

Jewish republic, it proved hard to induce either Russian or Polish Jews to cast their lot with Biro-Bidjan. The experiment was little more than a fiasco.[27]

In 1938 the Soviet government announced that aid from abroad was no longer needed in colonizing Jews. Komzet was liquidated and Agro-Joint, the American Society for Jewish Farm Settlements in Russia, and ORT, were asked to leave. The government's about-face resulted from several considerations, including the rapid industrialization of the economy and the drive toward large-scale collectivization of agriculture, administrative snarls, the alleged fear of a counter-revolutionary movement in Biro-Bidjan, the Crimea, and the Ukraine, plus, perhaps, the anti-Semitism revealed in the 1938 purge trials.[28]

It is not easy to evaluate the colonization of the Jews in Crimea and the Ukraine and the part of American philanthropy in it. Critical scholars have noted that only a small fraction of Russian Jews were colonized. The decision in 1938 to give up the project confirmed those who had said all along that it was impossible to depend on continued cooperation from the Kremlin, without which nothing could have been done. The Zionists were of course strengthened in their conviction that it was fantastic to suppose that Jewish cultural autonomy could be safely built on a few little islands in a vast atheistic communist sea. Even so ardent a participant in the Agro-Joint and American Society for Jewish Farm Settlements as James N. Rosenberg in the end felt that a glorious and potentially successful program had failed and was to be regarded as one of the great tragedies of modern times. For when Hitler's hordes reached the Crimea in the Second World War, wholesale murder of the Jewish settlers followed. When Rosenberg finally succeeded in finding one of the colonists in Israel in 1950, that one knew of no other survivor. "Our Crimean effort," Rosenberg concluded, "ended in dust, ashes and death." [29]

But there was another side to the story. The Soviets reimbursed the private organizations for their investments—Agro-Joint alone had put $10,000,000 into the colonies, including workshops, apparatus

[27] Schwarz, *The Jews in the Soviet Union,* 174-88; Walter Bedell Smith, *My Three Years in Moscow* (New York: Lippincott, 1950), 276.

[28] *American Jewish Year Book,* Sept., 1938–Sept., 1939, XL, 304-06.

[29] Rosenberg to Merle Curti, April 27, 1960; Rosenberg to Rockwell Kent, Sept. 20, 1960, carbon in the possession of Merle Curti.

and equipment.[30] Moreover, the experiment involving 250,000 persons was one of the largest Jewish colonization enterprises in the world. As Joseph Rosen said "a fundamental problem in human ecology" had been tackled and solved: "the mass adaptation of a whole stratum of the population to new environments created by a volcanic upheaval." [31]

Instrumental in this adaptation were the forty-two trade and farm schools, the sixty-three medical societies, and the three hundred loan societies (in the organization of which the Jewish Colonization Association cooperated with Agro-Joint). Looking back over the project and comparing the position of his coreligionists in Russia with those in certain other countries, Rosen summed up his evaluation: "We cannot help feeling keenly what a tremendous change for the better has taken place for the Jews in the USSR and what a potent part in the improvement of the Jewish situation the work of our organization has played." [32] Evelyn Morrissey agreed. This devoted and able JDC worker wrote, after a visit to the colonies in 1936 under Rosenwald's sponsorship, that instead of "declassed pariahs," the Jewish colonists had become "full fledged citizens of the country, enjoying for themselves and their children equal rights with all other Russian workmen and peasants." [33]

It is true, as Rosen, Morrissey, Rosenberg, Warburg and others again and again noted, that what had been done could not have been done without the help of the Soviet government which gave its blessing to the movement and, not counting the land, contributed more than half of the total $40,000,000 involved. But neither could this success have been achieved without the help, financial, technical, supervisory, and psychological, of the American backers. Nor is it to be forgotten that this project seemed to prove the feasibility, under certain conditions, of using philanthropic funds and services not merely for relief but for the rebuilding of social life through helping the needy to help themselves. Such a demonstration was, as we have seen, being worked out during these very years by the Near East Relief in another theater. Taken together, the two programs emphasized the value of large-scale efforts at rehabilitation, efforts that have become of great significance in our own day.

[30] *American Jewish Year Book*, Sept., 1938–Sept., 1939, XL, 306.
[31] Quoted in Morrissey, *Jewish Workers and Farmers*, 132.
[32] Morrissey, *Jewish Workers and Farmers*, 131-32.
[33] *Ibid.*, 125.

The JDC also supported self-help programs for economic reconstruction of Jewish communities in Poland and neighboring countries. When the Committee was on the verge of closing down many of its activities in 1925, economic crisis in Poland and other parts of eastern Europe dealt especially hard blows to the Jews who, in the midst of a new anti-Semitic surge, were in effect second-class citizens at the best.[34] Of 210,000 Jewish workingmen in Poland, half were without work: in Warsaw the unemployment figure stood at 83 per cent. Crop failures in Bessarabia and elsewhere sharpened the problems of economic depression. Fortunately the instruments for giving aid still existed in Poland and southeast Europe, and JDC between 1925 and 1932 poured into these areas almost $19,000,000.[35] The program begun in the early 1920's was in part continued. This included soup kitchens, child feeding, orphan care, and health provisions. Of special importance was the organization of interest-free credit cooperatives under the auspices of the American Joint Reconstruction Foundation. This, it may be recalled, had been formed by JDC and the Jewish Colonization Association, a European agency. Able to work with assets of $5,000,000, the Foundation by 1938 had established or strengthened 687 such cooperatives numbering 191,000 members.[36]

The program operated in thirteen eastern countries. These cooperatives were virtually the only source of credit to Jewish businessmen, artisans, farmers, and refugees. In the 1930's the program was curtailed in part because the depression depleted available funds, in part because of the needs of Jews in Hitler's Germany dwarfed those of everyone elsewhere.[37]

The help given in Eastern Europe to Jews in rebuilding their economic life did not blind leaders in philanthropy to the fact that emigration could also play a part in the solution or relaxation of economic problems. The matter of refugee resettlement and emigration had become acute ever since the United States established

[34] *New York Times*, May 17, 1925, reporting the comments of Felix Warburg, chairman of JDC, on his return from Europe.
[35] Leavitt, *The JDC Story*, 11; *New York Times*, Dec. 18, 1925, Jan. 13, 1926; *American Jewish Year Book*, Sept., 1927–Sept., 1928, XXIX, 72-74.
[36] Joseph C. Hyman, *Twenty-five Years of American Aid to Jews Overseas, A Record of the Joint Distribution Committee* (New York: Jewish Publication Society of America, 1939), 34-35; *New York Times*, Jan. 15, 1928.
[37] *American Jewish Year Book*, Sept., 1928–Sept., 1929, XXX, 41 ff.

its postwar restrictive policy, an example followed by Canada, South Africa, Argentina, and other Latin countries. The problem had its short-term as well as its long-term aspects. To meet a situation involving 15,000 would-be immigrants who had been stranded in European ports and in Cuba, and who, though they had passports, could not enter America by reason of the new restrictive legislation, an Emergency Committee headed by Louis Marshall and Rabbi Stephen Wise was formed in the autumn of 1924. By spring it had raised $250,000 for relief purposes—half of the goal.[38] In the interest of greater efficiency in meeting the continuing problem, the Jewish Colonization Society, with headquarters in Berlin, and the Hebrew Sheltering and Immigrant Aid Society (HIAS) joined forces to form a new agency, HICEM.

Among other things, HICEM publicized researches on opportunities for immigrants in Latin America and worked closely with welfare agencies throughout the world in helping refugees make a new start in life. In 1927 a campaign was launched for $500,000. HIAS was the main support. In the whole business of emigration-immigration, the part that Palestine could or should try to play was to become the most controversial issue.[39]

The problem of cooperation in fund raising to avoid duplication of effort and to increase assets proved to be a thorny one. At least as early as 1925 such Zionist leaders as Rabbi Stephen S. Wise took the Joint Distribution Committee to task for concentrating its efforts on the 9,000,000 Jews in Galicia and the Pale in an effort to help them build a decent life. Wise felt that in the actualities of anti-Semitism such an effort could not succeed and insisted that migration to Palestine was the only realistic course.[40] Unwilling to accept as final the British policy of admitting only a trickle of Jews into the Palestine mandate and the resistance of the Arabs to the presence of Jews in the Holy Land, Zionists complained that the most wealthy Jews refused to give of their means to the agencies working for the establishment of a Jewish state and the upbuilding of the homeland,[41] and, worse, undermined Zionist fund-raising campaigns.[42] The efforts of Dr. Chaim Weizmann, president of the World Zionist

---

[38] *New York Times*, Oct. 19, 1924, April 6, 1925.
[39] *Ibid.*, April 17, Oct. 17, 1927; *American Jewish Year Book*, Sept., 1928–Sept., 1929, XXX, 33-34.
[40] *New York Times*, Oct. 26, 1925; Wise, *Challenging Years, passim.*
[41] *New York Times*, Feb. 22, 1926.
[42] *Ibid.*, July 17, 1927.

Organization in Europe, to soften antagonisms between the two American groups led to little for the time being.[43]

In such a situation it was natural for the first efforts at fund raising to be made within each of the two large divisions of American Jewry. By 1925 the record of giving to Zionist agencies was an impressive one: American Jews had given, in the four years since the Palestine Foundation Fund (Keren Hayesod) had been established by the World Zionist Congress, more than 60 per cent of the total of over $7,200,000 that had been raised. But what the Palestine Foundation Fund had done in developing colonies, reforesting land, and promoting education and religious life, though notable, was obviously only a start.[44] Hadassah, the women's Zionist organization founded by the Baltimore teacher and social worker Henrietta Szold, also had no reason to be ashamed of its record: in the three years preceding 1925, it had raised and spent upwards of $1,000,000 for hospitals, infant welfare work, and orphan care in Palestine.[45] The Jewish National Fund (Keren Kayemeth), which celebrated its twenty-fifth anniversary in 1926, received the previous year more than $490,000, of which 21 per cent was donated by Americans.[46] Yet all of these achievements might, it was felt, be upgraded through greater cooperative efforts.

Thus in 1925 the United Palestine Appeal, which included the Jewish National Fund and Hadassah, launched a joint fund-raising campaign with Dr. Stephen Wise as chairman. Nathan Straus gave $650,000 as a token of his confidence in Dr. Wise, under heavy Orthodox attack for having declared that Jews should accept Jesus as a great ethical leader of whom all Jewry could be proud. At the end of the second year $6,200,000 had been collected.[47] A national conference at Cleveland in the fall of 1927 set as a goal for the next year the impressive sum of $7,500,000 to support not only Hadassah and the Jewish National Fund, but the Palestine Foundation Fund

[43] *Ibid.*, Jan. 23, 1927.

[44] *Ibid.*, Feb. 15, 1925; *American Jewish Year Book*, Sept., 1925–Sept., 1926, XXVII, 142; Sept., 1927–Sept., 1928, XXVIII, 128.

[45] Alexandra Lee Levin, *The Szolds of Lombard Street: A Baltimore Family, 1859-1909* (Philadelphia: Jewish Publication Society of America, 1960), *passim; New York Times*, July 2, 5, 1925.

[46] *New York Times*, Oct. 18, 1926; *American Jewish Year Book*, Sept., 1926–Sept., 1927, XXVIII, 128. By this time the Jewish National Fund had bought 50,000 of the 250,000 acres of land in Palestine owned by Jews on which thirty-four agricultural communities had been established.

[47] *New York Times*, Dec. 26, 1925, Jan. 3, 1926, July 13, 1927.

and other Zionist organizations as well.[48] Despite tumult, occasioned in part by the charge that Louis Lipsky, president of the Zionist Organization of America, mismanaged finances,[49] the joint campaign by October, 1928, had raised over $4,500,000.

Between 1925 and 1927 the United Palestine Appeal collected over $9,000,000. This was the more impressive since the Zionist organizations enjoyed few large contributions. The chief donors included Nathan Straus of New York ($650,000), Isadore Morison of Baltimore ($100,000), Mrs. Sol Rosenbloom of Pittsburgh ($500,-000), Mrs. Max Guggenheimer of Lynchburg, Virginia ($100,000), and Felix Warburg who, besides giving $50,000 almost every year, contributed in the later drive of 1929 $150,000 and $500,000 to put the new Jewish Agency of Palestine on its feet.[50] The Jewish National Fund in particular depended on small gifts at times of births, weddings, and national holidays.[51] What was garnered was the more striking since, as Ludwig Lewisohn noted, the money given to the Palestine funds brought the givers neither credit nor conventional praise nor any expectation that they might one day visit the land in which their gifts were used: they gave with a sense of some inner urgency as for a still shadowy dream.[52]

Parallel to this cooperative program in the Zionist groups was the United Jewish Campaign to which the Joint Distribution Committee was a party. In the spring of 1925 the JDC decided to launch a drive for $15,000,000 under the name of United Jewish Campaign for aiding Jews in foreign lands over a three-year period. A national conference, meeting in Chicago in October, 1925, after much jockeying among the several groups, approved the work of the JDC and urged it and its cooperating agencies to continue their heroic efforts in Russia, Poland, Palestine, and other places where Jews needed help.[53] Between September, 1925, when the campaign got under way, and December, 1926, pledges totaled over $18,600,000. Organized labor, particularly in the New York garment trades, took an active part in the

[48] *Ibid.*, Oct. 31, 1927.

[49] *American Jewish Year Book*, Sept., 1928–Sept., 1929, XXX, 36-37.

[50] *American Jewish Year Book*, Sept., 1926–Sept., 1927, XXVIII, 147-48; Sept., 1927–Sept., 1928, XXIX, 115; *New York Times*, Dec. 26, 1925. Mr. Justice Brandeis was to bequeath at his death in 1941 half of an estate of over $3,000,000 to Hadassah and the Palestine Endowment Fund "For the upbuilding of Palestine as a national home for the Jewish people": Mason, *Brandeis*, 638.

[51] *New York Times*, Oct. 15, 1927.

[52] Ludwig Lewisohn, *Israel* (New York: Boni and Liveright, 1925), 210-11.

[53] Polier and Wise, eds., *Personal Letters of Stephen Wise*, 206.

whole movement, which David A. Brown directed with much skill. Moreover, Christian groups lent a hand. In the autumn of 1926 the Christian Fund for Jewish Relief, sponsored by the Congregational minister, Dr. S. Parkes Cadman, and by John F. O'Ryan and other Catholic laymen, was organized. At a Catholic-Protestant-Jewish rally at the Cathedral of St. John the Divine, 1,500 men and women braved a blizzard to listen to appeals from O'Ryan, John J. Pershing, and Louis Marshall. In making this gesture, Cadman declared some-what later, the primary object was not financial but rather unmis-takably to register opposition to enmity based on race, creed, or color, a timely manifestation indeed in view of the strength of the Ku Klux Klan. At the same luncheon at which Dr. Cadman made his statement, Cardinal Patrick J. Hayes urged the obligation of all Americans to support the needy overseas Jews not only because the Jews had done much for Christians in time of distress but also be-cause of common allegiance to the American ideal of justice.[54] The campaign of the Christian Fund for Jewish Relief mustered $500,000 and, in David Brown's opinion, testified to the closer feeling of the two religious groups as they witnessed from afar the sufferings of Jews in foreign lands.[55]

The first promising effort at cooperative fund raising between Zionists and non-Zionists was occasioned by the riots which broke out in Jerusalem in August, 1929, when Arabs disturbed Jews in prayer at the traditional wailing wall. At once the Zionist Organiza-tion of America sought funds for the sufferers, and David A. Brown, the skillful fund raiser of the United Jewish Campaign, led the Palestine Emergency Fund which collected more than $2,000,000 in just a little over two months.[56] Partly as a result of this cooperation, partly because of the enlargement of the Jewish Agency in 1929 to include non-Zionists, and partly because Felix Warburg and others in the JDC and the American Jewish Committee had come to be increasingly impressed by the achievements and the needs of Pales-tine, an agreement was reached. On January 17, 1930, at a con-ference of JDC leaders and American members of the Jewish Agency, it was decided to launch a joint campaign for $6,000,000. Of this, $3,500,000 was to go to the work of the JDC and $2,500,000 was to be the American contribution to the 1930 budget of the Jewish

[54] *New York Times*, Dec. 9, 1927.
[55] *Ibid.*, Sept. 18, 1927.
[56] *Ibid.*, Aug. 27, Nov. 3, 1929.

Agency for Palestine. The new effort, known as the Allied Jewish Campaign, got off the ground at a national conference in Washington on March 8, 1930. Local campaigns in many communities throughout the country were pushed forward, though some postponed action because of the economic depression.[57] The American Palestine Campaign, however, which was at first a part of the Allied Jewish Campaign, decided in 1931 to make an independent effort. Despite the depression, it sought $2,500,000 for its constituent agencies, Hadassah and the Palestine Foundation Fund. In November it announced that little over $1,000,000 had been raised, but since separate campaigns had also been made by the Palestine Foundation Fund, the Jewish National Fund, and Hadassah, this did not represent the total contribution of American Jewry for Palestine.[58] In the following year the American Palestine Campaign raised over $600,000 more toward its objective of $2,500,000.

None of these experiments went very far and none lasted. The deepening depression made more demands for domestic charities. Under economic stress and unfavorable government action the plight of the Polish Jews worsened. In Palestine the progress of the colonists inspired hope but their conflict with the Arabs, the forbidding terrain, and the British Labor government's restriction of immigration, invited more American aid. Finally as the fury of Hitler's anti-Semitism took jobs from Jews and sent many to prison, the new demands for overseas contributions argued more cogently than ever against the inefficiency and competition of fund raising. But the situation was complicated by the variety of demands on American Jewish communities: the general municipal campaigns, the appeals in some places for the support of local federations of Jewish charities and in others for contributions to the competing campaigns of HIAS, JDC, and the Zionist organizations. Fortunately, the outlook for cooperation was brighter in view of the growing interest of leaders in the JDC and American Jewish Congress in Palestine.

After long negotiations an agreement was at last reached in March, 1934, between the Joint Distribution Committee and the American Palestine Appeal. The new United Jewish Appeal aimed at $3,200,-000 to be allocated according to an agreement in part worked out and in part left to later decision. Felix Warburg and almost every other

57 *American Jewish Year Book*, Sept., 1930–Sept., 1931, XXXII, 69-70.
58 *New York Times*, Jan. 14, Feb. 1, Nov. 10, 1931; *American Jewish Year Book*, Sept., 1932–Sept., 1933, XXXIV, 23.

leading Jew helped get the campaign off to a lively start. Jews were urged to bury their differences and to support the United Jewish Appeal in meeting the crying needs of relief and rehabilitation in both Europe and Palestine. Eloquent speakers, including well-known European visitors, told of the broken lives, the unimaginable fears, the incalculable suffering, the high tragedy of Old World Jewry. "No sane being," declared Dr. Stephen Wise, "pretends that the United Jewish Appeal can solve the Jewish question in Nazi Germany today; no honest man can claim that the Jewish problem that has arisen in Nazi Germany can be faced without ensuring the results of the United Jewish Appeal to American Jewry." The goal was not reached, but despite hard times, the effort yielded over $2,000,000. In the next nation-wide campaign a dazzling performance in New York of musical and theatrical talent in the "Night of Stars" brought to Madison Square Garden 21,000 people and netted $45,000.[59] But it was nevertheless felt that large cities, Cleveland alone excepted, did not meet quotas and that even in many of the 700 odd smaller communities which did better, the return to the scale of pre-Depression giving had not been realized. Only $1,600,000 was on hand by autumn.[60]

In October, 1935, the executive committee of the United Jewish Appeal discontinued the joint campaign. The official reason was that the experiment had not yielded the results that might have been expected from separate campaigns. *New Palestine* spoke for the Zionist groups in regretting that the decision had been made without public debate. It held that in many localities the paramount needs of Palestine had not been presented to the welfare fund leaders, and criticized one group within the JDC, identified with Rabbi Jonah Wise, for playing down the potentialities of Palestine as a solution for the crisis.[61] Felix Warburg met the criticism that JDC had little interest in Palestine by pointing to the substantial sums it had given for preparing German immigrants to Palestine for new occupations they would have to follow and for transportation.[62]

In 1936 the United Palestine Appeal, which supported the Palestine Foundation Fund and the Jewish National Fund, with its allied

---

[59] *New York Times*, March 12, 23, 1934; *The New Palestine* XXV, Oct. 4, 1935. This show, which became an annual event in fund-raising campaigns, enlisted among others Eddie Cantor, Irving Berlin and Al Jolson.

[60] *The New Palestine* XXV, May 31, July 12, 1935.

[61] *Ibid.*, Nov. 1, 8, 29, Dec. 13, 1935; XXVI, April 3, 1936.

[62] *American Jewish Year Book*, Sept., 1936–Sept., 1937, XXXVIII, 211-12, 313.

Zionist groups, raised over $2,100,000, the largest comparative total since 1928. On its side the JDC announced that 1,000 cities and towns in the United States and Canada had contributed over $2,800,-000 to the 1936 campaign. The funds for both groups were to be even larger in the years of mounting crisis. Yet what was allocated for overseas work represented, according to a 1936 report of the National Council of Federations and Welfare Funds, only 7 per cent of the $48,000,000 contributed to Jewish welfare needs at home and abroad. Palestine activities got the largest share—$1,675,000.[63]

The uses made of these contributions can best be evaluated in the context of the crisis in international Jewry created by the Nazi seizure of power in March, 1933. At first some Jewish leaders in both Germany and England insisted that the Nazi attack on their coreligionists was a local matter of no pressing concern to international Jewry. When in January, 1934, Felix Warburg and James N. Rosenberg met seventy-five prominent Jewish business men in a crucial gathering at New Court, the Rothschild bank in London, these leaders doubted that a grave menace required sustained and comprehensive action. Nor were these English Jews impressed by the supporting testimony of another American, James G. McDonald, who after a career in teaching and in the Foreign Policy Association, had become League of Nations High Commissioner for Refugees. They refused to be swept into action by "American alarmists" despite Rosenberg's vigorous protest against their cavalier indifference to facts which could not be denied. For a time this position was shared by important American Jews, some of whom waited on President Roosevelt to insist that emotional self-appointed spokesmen were exaggerating the situation in the representations made at the White House.[64]

Dr. Stephen Wise of the American Jewish Congress on the other hand felt that the initial acts of anti-Semitism in Germany were not only ominous but required vigorous action. When the American Jewish Congress announced a protest mass meeting in Madison Square Garden for March 27, 1933, the German Foreign Office indicated through the State Department that if the meeting were cancelled and if there was no more talk about atrocity stories Berlin would

    63 *Ibid.*, Sept., 1937–Sept., 1938, XXXIX, 244-45.
    64 Wise, *The Challenging Years*, 233 ff.; Polier and Wise, eds., *Personal Letters of Stephen Wise*, 219; James G. McDonald, *My Mission in Israel*, 1948-1951 (New York: Simon and Schuster, 1951), 252-253.

moderate the treatment of German Jews. Wise and his associates were shaken. Could they rely on such assurances and, even if they could, ought they to do so? Brandeis forthrightly said, "Go ahead and make the protest as good as you can." [65] The meeting, the first of a series, called for an emergency relief fund and for vigorous protests, official and unofficial. It took steps to initiate a boycott of all German goods. Through the Merchandising Council and with the support of organized labor, the boycott became a reality notwithstanding the opposition of leading Jews in Germany, England, and America. [66] The opposing position was publicized by Judge Joseph M. Proskauer of the American Jewish Committee who regarded the boycott as excessively emotional and the product of a "noisy minority." Let the American Jews, he argued, protest in a reasonable way and do what they could to alleviate hardships; but let them in all other ways follow a nonpartisan and nonpolitical course proper to their status and role as Americans. [67] Dr. Wise, on the other hand, quoting Lincoln's words that slavery is local and freedom national, insisted that although the boycott was by no means a complete solution, it promised to have some effect on Germany. Moreover, he argued, it symbolized the unity of Jews all over the world and testified to the conviction that action speaks louder than words. [68] The boycott, under the leadership of Samuel Untermyer, became a world movement. [69]

The support given to the boycott by organized labor was only one evidence of the growing concern of working people with the mounting wave of Nazi and fascist fanaticism. Besides supporting the boycott and contributing to Jewish and non-Jewish refugee funds, Jews and gentiles in the labor movement followed two additional courses.

The National Labor Committee for Jewish Workers and Pioneers of Palestine stepped up its contribution for the promotion of welfare work and for the purchase of tools and materials that newly arrived

[65] Wise, *The Challenging Years*, 245.

[66] In addition to the support given to the boycott by the American Jewish Congress and organized labor, prominent leaders of opinion, including John Haynes Holmes, Dr. S. Parkes Cadman, Harry Emerson Fosdick, Bishop Manning and Bishop M. Connell, supported the movement.

[67] *The New Palestine* XXV, Feb. 8, 1935; *New York World-Telegram*, Feb. 5, 1935; Joseph M. Proskauer, *A Segment of My Times* (New York: Farrar and Straus, 1950), 196 ff., 237 ff.

[68] *New York World-Telegram*, Feb. 6, 1935.

[69] *New York Times*, June 4, 1933; *The New Palestine* XXVI, Feb. 7, 1936; Samuel Untermyer, *The Boycott Is Our Only Weapon Against Nazi Germany* (New York: American League for the Defense of Jewish Rights, 1933).

refugees in Palestine needed: on the occasion of the tenth anniversary, it announced that it had sent $1,000,000 to Palestine.[70] In the autumn of 1934 Sir Walter Citrine, general secretary of the British Trades Union Congress and president of the International Federation of the British Trades Union Congress addressed the San Francisco convention of the AF of L. The British leader's visit led to the organization of the Labor War Chest for the Aid of Oppressed Peoples of Europe. In the next several years the Labor Chest collected substantial sums for labor victims of Hitler's persecutions. The movement owed much to William English Walling, who had played a leading role in American socialism. Despite grave illness, Walling gave the last years of his life unstintingly to this cause. In 1936 he enlisted the cooperation of British, French, and Dutch labor groups, as well as that of the International Labor Office in Geneva. He died in Amsterdam where he was working with German labor leaders in an effort to help a larger number of workers flee from Nazi persecution.[71]

Besides arousing organized labor, the crisis led others to act. An American Committee Appeal for the Relief of Jews of Poland, formed in 1936 and convinced of the need of a separate campaign, announced a drive for $1,000,000. Its program included emergency relief, credit to small businessmen and artisans, schools for apprentices, the strengthening of farm cooperatives, and aid for migration to Palestine. The interest of La Guardia and certain non-Polish Jews gave the movement a wider base although the funds collected seem to have fallen considerably short of the goal.[72]

At the time of the mass meeting at Madison Square Garden organized by the American Jewish Congress in the early spring of 1933, international committees sponsored protest meetings in sixty-five cities in twenty-five states. The most important force in arousing non-Jewish groups, however, was James G. McDonald. In his capacity as League of Nations High Commissioner for Refugees from Germany, he helped some 65,000 refugees before his resignation two years later in protest against the apathy of the League and its member

[70] *American Jewish Year Book*, Sept., 1935–Sept., 1936, XXXVII, 148.

[71] Anna Strunsky Walling, *et al.*, eds., *William English Walling: A Symposium* (New York: Stackpole Sons, 1938), 18-33, 94.

[72] *New York Times*, Jan. 7, 1935, Jan. 10, 25, May 18, 1936; *American Jewish Year Book*, Sept., 1933–Sept., 1934, XXXV, 60; Sept., 1936–Sept., 1937, XXXVIII, 198. The United Roumanian Jews of America, at their twenty-fifth annual convention held on Feb. 18, 1934, also sought funds to defend the interests of Jews in the country of their origin and to work for their economic reconstruction and rehabilitation: *American Jewish Year Book*, Sept., 1934–Sept., 1935, XXXVII, 193-98.

states.[73] McDonald realized that nonofficial efforts, while in themselves insufficient, were desperately needed. "I am fed up," he told a group in New York in June, 1934, "on Christian protestations of interest, academic expressions of concern and the empty holding out of the hand of fellowship. It is high time that Christian leadership took its obligation seriously." Noting that Jews often generously helped needy Christians, he called on the public to rescue the victims of Nazi degradation and pauperization. McDonald's appeals had much to do with the forming of two organizations.[74]

One of these was the American Christian Committee for German Refugees, headed until his death by Dr. S. Parkes Cadman of the Federal Council of Churches of Christ in America. In December, 1937, the Committee appealed to 100,000 clergymen throughout the nation for a Christian fund of $400,000 to relieve victims of oppression in Germany.[75] Dr. Harry Emerson Fosdick made a fundraising appeal movie. It was shown, among other places, at his church on Riverside Drive, at which occasion Erika Mann, daughter of the famous refugee novelist, spoke on "Women and Children as Hitler's victims." A Berlin newspaper called Miss Mann a "notorious cabaret performer," accused her of inciting Jewish agitation against her own country, and professed disgust that a church should be used for political agitation.[76] The funds collected by the American Christian Committee for German Refugees were largely used in Germany by the American Friends Service Committee, the personnel of which, Clarence Pickett said in 1936, had to regard as standard equipment for German work "the ability to stand confinement in jail and the pain of the third degree." [77]

The other organization was the Emergency Committee for Aid of Political Refugees from Nazism. Its Chairman, Dr. Frank Bohn, stressed the persecution not only of Jews but of trade unionists, Protestants, and Catholics. The Emergency Committee publicized the meager response of non-Jews to the violence and wholesale ter-

[73] *New York Times*, July 18, Oct. 12, Dec. 6, 30, 1935. See also Bentwich, *The Refugees from Germany*.

[74] *New York Times*, June 13, 1934, Oct. 22, 1935. In response to McDonald's indictment of Christians an unnamed Christian in London gave $10,000 to help Jewish refugees from Germany, *New York Times*, May 4, 1934.

[75] *New York Times*, Sept. 30, Nov. 29, Dec. 26, 29, 1935, May 22, June 26, Oct. 7, 1936; *American Jewish Year Book*, Sept., 1937–Sept., 1938, XXXIX, 219-20. The *New York Times*, July 13, 1936, has an obituary and an editorial on Cadman.

[76] *New York Times*, April 14, 1937.

[77] *Ibid.*, April 5, 1936; Clarence Pickett, *For More Than Bread: An Autobiographical Account of Twenty-Two Years' Work with the American Friends Service Committee* (Boston: Little, Brown, 1953), 296-98 and *passim*.

rorism of the Nazi onslaught against nonconformists. In 1935 the Committee campaigned for $250,000 from non-Jewish liberals, the proceeds to be divided between the Labor Chest and socialist and communist groups aiding refugees.[78] Another welcome hand was the half million dollars given by the Rockefeller Foundation to tide refugee intellectuals over until they might find at least a temporary place in American cultural life.[79]

But James McDonald and others concluded that however important voluntary efforts were they were nevertheless inadequate. Jewish and non-Jewish groups knocked at the doors of the White House, the State Department, and Congress to ask more vigorous protests against Nazi terrorism and for a wider opening in American restrictive policies. Words of sympathy and good will were forthcoming. Secretary of State Cordell Hull went further: he proposed an international committee, financed by private contributions, to explore ways of persuading Berlin to ease the restrictions that made it all but impossible for Jews to leave Germany and, without upsetting the limitations on immigration that most countries followed, to find havens for the victims of Nazi racism and political persecution. A committee was formed, with an American, George Rublee, as director, and with Lord Winterton as chairman. The committee helped some thousands of Jews find homes but obstacles kept it from meeting more than a tiny part of the need.[80] President Roosevelt made it clear that in extending the helping hand to the oppressed of other lands, the government would not enlarge its immigration quotas.[81] Had the United States and other governments been more resolute in helping Jews find sanctuary before war sealed the doom of 6,000,000 in "the final solution" of extermination, hundreds of thousands might well have been saved from Hitler's crematoria.[82]

---

[78] *New York Times*, Sept. 30, Nov. 24, 1935, Oct. 7, 1936, Feb. 28, 1936.

[79] *American Jewish Year Book*, Sept., 1937–Sept., 1938, XXXIX, 220.

[80] U. S. Department of State, *Press Releases*, March 24, 1938 (Washington: Govt. Printing Office, 1938), XVIII, 411. *New York Times*, July 16, 31, Aug. 5, 8, 18, 1938; Cordell Hull, *The Memoirs of Cordell Hull* (2 vols.; New York: Macmillan, 1948), I, 578. General Trujillo, the recently established dictator of the Dominican Republic, was the exception in offering to receive 100,000 refugees and to provide generous help in making a new start. Some refugees accepted the offer but colonization on a large scale did not seem practical in view of the unaccustomed climate and the precariousness of accepting another dictatorial regime.

[81] Elliott Roosevelt, ed., *F.D.R.: His Personal Letters, 1928-1945* (4 vols., New York: Duell, Sloan and Pearce, 1950), II, 1004-05; *New York Times*, March 26, 27, 1938.

[82] Herbert Agar, *The Saving Remnant: An Account of Jewish Survival* (New York: Viking Press, 1960), 90 ff.; *New York Times*, July 18, 1935.

In view of the meager response of non-Jewish agencies and the ineffective role of governments, the burden of saving as many victims as possible from actual and impending disaster fell on the Jews themselves. Here American Jews did not of course stand alone. Through the Central British Fund for German Jewry and the broader-based Council for German Jewry, British Jews set a high record of generosity. Of the $10,000,000 raised in all countries between 1933 and 1935 for the relief and rehabilitation of refugees, British Jews contributed $2,500,000 as against the $3,000,000 given by twelve times as many American Jews.[83] In 1936 the American effort lagged behind the British, to be intensified, however, in the year ahead. Between 1933 and 1939 the personnel of the Central British Fund spent £3,000,000 for refugees, exclusive of what individuals did to support persons they had brought from Germany and helped after their arrival. In addition, the British Children's Movement helped find homes abroad, chiefly in Great Britain, for almost 10,000 German boys and girls.[84] Nor should one overlook the contributions of British Jewry to the $47,000,000 which had, by 1935, been raised by world Jewry for Palestine (Stephen Wise put the American contribution at $18,000,000).[85] What British Jews did was often paralleled by those in other parts of the Commonwealth. Jewish communities in the Latin-speaking world also responded to the needs of Central Europe.

Impressed by the need of cooperation, leading British Jews promoted the World Council for German Jewry with headquarters at London. In 1935 Sir Herbert Samuel, Viscount Bearsted, and Simon Marks came to the United States to enlist American support for the agency, which included Zionists as well as non-Zionists. Spokesmen for American Zionism hesitated to identify their efforts at fund raising, relief, and assisted immigration to Palestine with an international agency in which they might not be adequately represented. Other American Jewish groups, notably the JDC, worked with the British in the international agency.[86]

---

[83] Bentwich, *They Found Refuge*, chap. 3; Agar, *The Saving Remnant*, 91, 92, 96.

[84] Bentwich, *They Found Refuge*, 41-42.

[85] *New York Times*, Feb. 16, 1936. The American figure does not include investments which according to Consul George Wadsworth, approximated $33,000,000 of the total $300,000,000 foreign investments: *The New Palestine* XXVI, Oct. 7, 1936. The same journal in its issue of Feb. 3, 1937, estimated that American investments equalled $40,000,000.

[86] *American Jewish Year Book*, Sept., 1936–Sept., 1937, XXXVIII, 216; Sept., 1937–Sept., 1938, XXXIX, 242-43; *The New Palestine* XXVI, Jan. 10, Feb. 7, March 6, 13, 20, 1936.

In the big job of helping Jews flee from Germany to Palestine and to American countries, several agencies helped shoulder the burden, some in close cooperation with others. The German Jewish Children's Aid, beginning in 1934, placed several hundred children in private homes and helped with their training and education.[87] In association with Recha Freier in Germany, Henrietta Szold of Hadassah developed the Youth Aliyah. This movement, dating from 1933, received thousands of German children from parents willing to see them take their chances for survival in Palestine and, after preliminary training, transported them to the homeland and established them in farm settlements.[88]

Other groups performed special tasks. In 1939 ORT, deeply concerned with the overseas situation and not included in the United Jewish Appeal, opened a nation-wide campaign for $1,257,000 to promote vocational and agricultural training of Jews in Europe, to prepare those able to migrate, and to adjust themselves to new occupations in new lands.[89] Of special interest was the work of HIAS-HICEM. This group, it will be recalled, worked with the Jewish Colonization Society in Europe and with the JDC in a far-reaching immigrant-aid program. It intervened with Nazi authorities in behalf of Jews trying to leave the country; it appealed orders for deportation issuing from Washington; it met steamers, provided temporary sustenance, and found jobs and shelter.[90] In 1937 it helped over 27,000 refugees from central and eastern Europe find new homes overseas;[91] and the following year it staged a million dollar drive.[92]

The JDC was faced with tasks no one had foreseen in 1932 when it had looked as if the program of relief and reconstruction in Central and Eastern Europe had succeeded well enough to allow withdrawal and when such withdrawal seemed imperative in view of the depletion of funds for overseas work by the demands for charity for American Jews caught in the depression. But by 1935 the Polish govern-

[87] *New York Times*, June 10, Sept. 7, 1934; *American Jewish Year Book*, Sept., 1934–Sept., 1935, XXXVI, 315.

[88] *The New Palestine* XXVI, Jan. 24, 1936; Paul Goodman, ed., *The Jewish National Home: The Second November, 1917-1942* (London: Dent, 1943), 216 ff.

[89] *American Jewish Year Book*, Sept., 1939–Sept., 1940, XXXIX, 208.

[90] *Ibid.*, Sept., 1936–Sept., 1937, XXXVIII, 131; Sept., 1937–Sept., 1938, XXXIX, 248.

[91] *Ibid.*, Sept., 1938–Sept., 1939, XL, 115; *New York Times*, March 21, 1938.

[92] *American Jewish Year Book*, Sept., 1939–Sept., 1940, XLI, 208.

ment's discriminations against Jews had thrown 60 per cent on charity.[93] The JDC took up its suspended relief work, reopened soup kitchens and resumed child feeding. But the rising tide of Nazi persecutions demanded attention as well. Jewish schools cried for support when children were driven out of the public schools. It was also necessary to step up contributions for the vocational training which alone promised to keep alive the million Jews deprived of their ordinary occupations and which was sure to prove a godsend for those who could escape and face a new life in foreign lands. In doing all these things JDC was still following its traditional course of helping Jews find a tolerable place in the land of their fathers. But it did more than this: by the end of 1935 it had borne 60 per cent of the cost of the immigration of the 100,000 Jews who had fled since Hitler came to power.[94]

Meantime, concentration camps were claiming terrified victims and insults and acts of violence against Jews multiplied. Jews everywhere, as well as many gentiles, were horrified at the report of the wanton brutality all over Germany on the night of the broken glass, November 9 and 10, 1938. Synagogues, shops, and houses were looted and burned; children and women as well as men were beaten; cemeteries were desecrated. Jewish adult males were arrested and sent to concentration camps, and over 35,000 were never heard from again. As a penalty for the murder in Paris of a German official by a crazed Jewish lad, German Jews were ordered to pay an indemnity of a billion marks. The shock of this terror led those in the executive committee of the JDC who had insisted on putting major emphasis on helping Jews in Central and Eastern Europe adapt themselves to conditions, to concede that "the saving remnant" must find haven wherever they could go and that everything possible must be done to push open further the closing doors of Palestine.[95]

Working through German Jewish relief societies the JDC had, by 1939, helped 85,000 men, women, and children escape, at least for a time, from the Fuehrer's mad grasp. The help was given in such a way as to give no comfort to the Nazi economy. Jews that could be

[93] *Ibid.*, Sept., 1938–Sept., 1939, XXXIX, 244-45.
[94] *Ibid.*, Sept., 1935–Sept., 1936, XXXVI, 142-43; Sept., 1936–Sept., 1937, XXXVIII, 313.
[95] *American Jewish Year Book*, Sept., 1939–Sept., 1940, XXXIX, 190 ff.; Agar, *The Saving Remnant*, 52 ff. During 1938 the JDC expended $4,111,979, nearly a million and a quarter dollars more than in the previous year. The newly organized United Jewish Appeal asked for $20,000,000 for 1939: *American Jewish Year Book*, Sept., 1939–Sept., 1940, XXXIX, 206.

got out left with approved welfare agencies a stated proportion of whatever money or goods that had not been squeezed out of them: the average was thirty marks for each dollar that went into prepaid transportation tickets. Wherever possible, especially in countries still willing to admit Jews, JDC arranged to have local Jews and welfare groups advance funds for transportation and for initial help on the arrival of refugees, with the promise that when possible JDC would repay whatever was given.[96] Thus in applying where possible the principle of self-help and in using in new situations an experienced field personnel, JDC shifted its emphasis without breaking sharply with its past.

But the achievements of JDC before the curtain fell in the all-out war cannot be appreciated by any figures or by general discussion. One specific episode may represent scores of similar ones, for only concrete details of what was done for victims of crushing brutality have much human meaning. On the night of October 28, 1939, some 15,000 Jews of Polish origin living in Germany were rounded up without notice or explanation, permitted to take only the clothing they wore, sealed in trains or buses and deported to the border village of Zbaszyn. These luckless victims of Nazi madness were forced to sleep in the streets, in open fields, in empty stables. Not even the bare necessities of life could be had. But within twenty-four hours JDC officials in Warsaw organized a relief corps and rushed truckloads of food, clothing, medical supplies, doctors, and nurses to Zbaszyn and the few other receiving villages. First-aid stations and kitchens appeared in a matter of hours. Stables were turned into barracks. For the time at least lives were saved and hope reborn.[97] Herbert Agar has given graphic and moving accounts of other rescues involving even greater effort, stamina, and resourcefulness on the part of the rescuers.

In 1938 in the interest of greater efficiency in meeting in some part the rising refugee problem the National Coordinating Committee was set up as the operating agency to care for the most pressing needs of those who had been able to flee. Between 1935 and the organization of the new committee three years later, some $2,000,000 had been raised for refugee needs by the several Jewish voluntary agencies in America. In 1939 the National Refugee Service spent

[96] Leavitt, *The JDC Story*, 11; Eli Ginzberg, *Report to the American Jews on Overseas Relief* (New York: Harper, 1942), 10.

[97] *American Jewish Year Book*, Sept., 1939–Sept., 1940, XXXIX, 377-78.

over $2,000,000, in 1940 almost $3,500,000, for the monthly support of refugees—in numbers varying between 5,000 and 9,000—for help in finding jobs for those able to work, providing legal aid, and for fighting the efforts of power groups determined to cut off all immigration.[98]

The National Refugee Service was not the only example of cooperation in the sustained emergency. In 1939 a new effort in joining forces in fund raising was made. The result was the United Jewish Appeal for Refugees and Overseas Needs. It was supported by the JDC, the United Palestine Appeal, and the National Coordinating Committee and the National Refugee Service.[99] What had been done in the 1930's was now, with the whole world at war, to be overshadowed by new needs and efforts.

The main burden of the relief of Jews in Central Europe was naturally shouldered by Jewish organizations. But gentiles also lent a hand. In addition to the help given by the Christian Fund for Jewish Relief, the Quakers took an increasingly important part in the crisis. It may be recalled that as an aftermath of the Quakers' relief activities in Europe following the First World War, the American Friends Service Committee (with the help of British Friends) continued to operate four Centers in Europe—in Geneva, Berlin, Paris, and Vienna. Staffed by American and local Friends, the Centers carried on youth programs and organized conferences to help reconcile the peoples of Europe in peaceful cooperation. In 1933 the Centers began to expand their programs. The one in Paris supported Entr'aide, a mutual self-help organization initiated in 1932 by French Friends. A kindergarten and club room were opened to help German refugees; fuel and food were provided for refugees from Hitler's Germany who had been herded into cold, unfurnished barracks made available by the French government. By 1934 the Paris Center was sharing responsibility for the care of some 4,000 German refugee families. The Vienna Center took up the task of succoring victims of the February (1934) civil uprising and the July disturbances. Funds provided by the International Federation of Trade Unions and the

[98] Ginzberg, *Report to American Jews*, 26-59.
[99] In 1951 an agreement was made by which, after the deduction of expenses, the United Israel Appeal, as the United Palestine Appeal was renamed when Israel became a recognized independent state, was to receive 67 per cent and the JDC 33 per cent of the first $55,000 collected. Of collections in excess of this amount, United Israel Appeal received approximately 66 per cent and JDC 33 per cent.

Quakers helped over 8,000 families until their plight became hopeless in the general holocaust beginning in 1939.[100]

Three Friends, of whom Rufus M. Jones was the best known, decided to brave all odds by going to Berlin to seek permission for investigating the suffering of the Jews and arranging for all possible relief. As foreseen, all doors in the German capital were closed, and the mission seemed doomed to fail. After much persistence, the group at last managed to break the barriers sufficiently to talk with two chief officers at Gestapo headquarters. The hard-faced, iron-natured men were sufficiently touched by the recital of what Friends had done for Germany after the First World War to secure from the high chief, nicknamed "the hangman," a verbal promise to permit the desired investigation and relief efforts. Of course the promise was not kept. But for a time the Berlin Center enjoyed more freedom in getting relief to Jewish families and in facilitating emigration arrangements.[101]

To the refugees who flooded into the Centers in Berlin, Vienna, and Paris and to similar ones set up in Amsterdam, Copenhagen, and Frankfurt, advice and such help as resources permitted were given by augmented staffs that included social workers and migration experts. The AFSC Centers cooperated with Jewish agencies, but took special responsibility for those refugees who did not fall logically within the scope of other agencies, Jewish, Catholic, and Protestant. In the United States, the AFSC located the necessary individuals to provide affidavits and passage for refugees, welcomed newcomers at hostels in Nyak, Bryn Mawr, West Branch, Iowa, and Havana. These offered instruction in English or Spanish and training in crafts and agriculture in preparation for re-migration.[102]

Before the world plunged into war in 1939, a dress rehearsal had been taking place in Spain. In that tragic civil war the Friends were to play an even larger part than, up to that time, they had taken in the first act of Hitler's war against the Jewish community. What was done in Spain and in the expanding refugee problem provides a significant case history in the story of American philanthropy overseas.

[100] American Friends Service Committee, *Annual Report*, 1933 (Philadelphia: American Friends Service Committee, 1934), 5; *Annual Report*, 1934, 2; *Annual Report*, 1935, 16-17; *Annual Report*, 1936, 13-15; *Annual Report*, 1937, 13-18; *Annual Report*, 1938, 8-12; Pickett, *For More Than Bread*, 138 ff.
[101] Pickett, *For More Than Bread*, 134-37.
[102] American Friends Service Committee, *Annual Report*, 1939, 9-14.

XIV

Spain

While tension was rising and refugee problems in Central Europe were becoming more acute, Spain burst into flames. The Civil War, begun in the summer of 1936 and dragging out for three bitter years, proved to be a testing ground for new techniques of war, this time of total war, with the forces of Italy and Germany intervening on one side and the Soviet Union on the other.[1] It also tested world philanthropy both in traditional and in new ways, for the situation in the Iberian Peninsula projected ideological conflict into Western Europe and America in an even sharper way than Hitlerism had yet done. American overseas philanthropy reached into the turmoil in vast proportions, and this despite the demands of a continuing depression. In bringing aid to Spain, American relief efforts were torn in acrimonious conflict beyond precedent.

Moreover, as never before, what was done to relieve distress meshed with national policy and in so doing anticipated the character of overseas relief in the decades ahead. The story further involved a resumption of the use of public agricultural surpluses, initiated in the First World War, and in so doing rebuilt a policy which was to become a major characteristic of relief efforts in the years that followed the second global conflict.

The problem of carrying through relief in Spain itself was complicated by the fact that even before the Civil War no country in Western Europe lived on so low a nutritional standard. In no country were the obstacles to transportation so difficult, obstacles complicated during the Civil War by the constantly shifting lines of battle, the

---

[1] The most recent account is Hugh Thomas, *The Spanish Civil War* (New York: Harper, 1961).

censorship on both sides, and the effectiveness of the blockade of Loyalist ports by Franco's fleet and air force, augmented by Mussolini and Hitler. Nor were social services in Spain organized as well as elsewhere. Despite all these handicaps, the Spaniards themselves were by no means indifferent to the hunger and misery which civil conflict bred. In Franco Spain the Red Cross and the Auxilio Social, organized by Germans on the pattern of the Winter Relief, enlisted devoted men and women; and Republican Spain consolidated voluntary agencies into an official relief agency. But Spanish resources were inadequate to meet in more than small part the suffering, hunger, homelessness, and sickness of civilians and combatants. If suffering was to be relieved in any appreciable way, outside aid was imperative.

When Sylvester Jones, a former missionary in Cuba and a Chicago businessman, went to Spain early in 1937 to report to the American Friends Service Committee the actualities of the situation, he found the country stretched upon a cross, torn by the passions of civil war and class hatred. At least 150,000 refugee children in Loyalist territory and some 30,000 war orphans within the Nationalist lines were desperately in need of food, clothing, and medical help. "Shall we send food to these undernourished orphans and refugee children and mothers who stretch out their hands in hunger to us?" he wrote in his journal. "Shall we mediate a love that will reach those who suffer in the dark shadows of this modern crucifixion?" [2]

A year later some 3,000,000 refugees posed insuperable problems for the Loyalists. The number in Franco Spain remained approximately 90,000.[3] Toward the end of the struggle, in the spring of 1939, the Loyalists were faced with the desperate needs of some

[2] Sylvester Jones, "Through Loyalist and Insurgent Spain, December 1936–January 1937," in Mary Hoxie Jones, *Swords into Ploughshares: An Account of the American Friends Service Committee, 1917-1937* (New York: Macmillan, 1937), 296-98; Clarence E. Pickett, *For More Than Bread: An Autobiographical Account of Twenty-Two Years' Work with the American Friends Service Committee* (Boston: Little, Brown, 1953), 107.

[3] Claude Bowers to Cordell Hull, July 8, 1938, in *Papers Relating to the Foreign Relations of the United States* (Washington: Govt. Printing Office, 1938), I:364-65; Alfred Winslow Jones, "Behind the Battle Lines in Spain," *New York Times*, April 3, 1938. I am indebted throughout this chapter to Charles Wetzel, "American Relief to Spain during the Spanish Civil War, 1936-1939" (unpublished Master's thesis, University of Wisconsin, 1959), and to John Van Gelder Forbes, "A Short Account of the Collection, Administration, and Distribution of Relief for Spanish Civilians by the American Friends Service Committee During the Spanish Civil War (unpublished manuscript, 1942), and hereafter cited as "Relief for Spanish Civilians."

7,000,000 civilians, refugees, and those still living on near-starvation rations in their own homes.[4] By 1939 the government-provided ration in Barcelona had been reduced to seven ounces of beans, rice, or lentils. The refugees were existing, when they existed at all, on 800 calories a day, barely enough to sustain an inert near-life for no longer than eight weeks. Little wonder that infant mortality in Valencia multiplied twelvefold by the spring of 1939.[5] The need for clothing and shelter and for medical care for old and young alike can hardly be exaggerated. In all, the struggle took a million lives.

It was natural for Spain's neighbors to respond first to the cry for aid. The International Red Cross offered medical services and help in the exchange of prisoners and search for lost persons. Swiss Aid and Service Civil International were on the ground in the early stages of the conflict to do yeoman's service. In England the Medical Aid Committee, a pro-Loyalist agency, and the pro-National Committee of Cardinal Hinsley, got under way in the early months of the struggle. In cooperation with Save the Children Fund (the British branch of the Save the Children International Union) the Friends Service Council of London launched a small child-feeding program in Barcelona on Christmas Day, 1936. In the following year the initiative of British Quakers resulted in the organization of the International Commission for the Assistance of Spanish Child Refugees, one-third of whose officials and relief workers were Friends. Ably led by its president, Judge Michael Hansson, a distinguished Norwegian jurist, the Commission played a major part in its special field of relief. Twenty-four governments and a great number of voluntary organizations and individuals in many countries, including the United States, supported its efficiently managed and greatly needed program.[6]

The American response to Spain's holocaust must, in the first place, be understood in the context of the help given by all these national and international agencies. But it must also be understood in relation to the American commitment to the maintenance of a

[4] John Van Gelder Forbes, *Recent Relief Programs of the American Friends in Spain and France* (Russell Sage Foundation, 1943), 14-15.

[5] *Ibid.*, 3-4.

[6] Pickett, *For More Than Bread*, 106; Howard E. Kershner, *Quaker Service in Modern War* (New York: Prentice-Hall, 1950), xv-xviii.

strict neutrality lest the country become involved in war.[7] The so-called neutrality legislation, first enacted at the time of Mussolini's attack on Ethiopia, was extended in 1937 by the Pittman-Mc-Reynolds resolution. This forbade loans and the export of war material to a country engaged in civil war and authorized the President to control relief to such a nation.[8] Most left-wing and many liberal groups opposed the embargo. In their eyes it discriminated against the Loyalists, whose ports were blockaded by the Nationalists, and, in effect, thus aided the Nationalists, whom Mussolini and Hitler were supporting with arms and military personnel in death grip with democracy.[9] But the State Department, determined to maintain American neutrality, instructed its officers abroad not to contribute to the Spanish Red Cross and further rejected requests for the allocation of American Red Cross funds to counterpart agencies in Spain.[10] Secretary of State Hull, rightly convinced that some of the voluntary medical units were essentially partisan rather than humanitarian in purpose, refused to have passports issued to the American personnel of such units.[11]

Under pressure from liberal groups and at the suggestion of President Roosevelt himself [12] this restriction was relaxed for doctors, nurses, and necessary attendants engaged in "bona fide medical and

[7] Assistant Secretary of State Sumner Welles reported a "stampede" of "peace-at-any-price" groups to Washington right after the 1936 election; Welles, *The Time For Decision* (New York: Harper, 1944), 60. Secretary of the Interior Harold L. Ickes, a Loyalist supporter, also ruefully contended that the opinion of the nation generally opposed intervention in the Spanish conflict: Ickes, *The Secret Diary of Harold L. Ickes* (3 vols.; New York: Simon and Schuster, 1953-1954), I, 655-56.

[8] U. S. Department of State, *Press Releases*, May 1, 8, 1937 (Washington: Govt. Printing Office, 1937), XVI, 290-92, 309-10.

[9] See for instance the activities of the Lawyers Committee on American Relations with Spain which included among its members Arthur Garfield Hays, former Senator Smith W. Brookhart, and Nathan R. Margold, solicitor for the Department of the Interior: *New York Times*, March 13, Oct. 3, 1938; also a petition sent to President Roosevelt by 21 leading liberals: *New York Times*, July 5, 1937. When Dr. John Van Schraick of the Associated Church Press commented to Roosevelt that the embargo seemed to favor Franco, the President replied that to lift the embargo would help Franco more than the Loyalists because of Franco's effective blockade. As a consequence of the embargo, Roosevelt hinted, both sides had to obtain U. S. manufactured war materials through friendly intermediate countries, so that we maintained our neutrality in the strictest sense, "not to help one fellow more than the other": *The Public Papers and Addresses of Franklin D. Roosevelt*, Samuel I. Rosenman, ed. (13 vols.; New York: Macmillan, 1941), VII, 251-53.

[10] *Foreign Relations*, 1936, II, 685-86, 721-22.

[11] Department of State, *Press Releases*, March 13, 1937, XVI, 139-41; *Foreign Relations*, 1937, I, 488-91.

[12] Cordell Hull, *The Memoirs of Cordell Hull* (2 vols.; New York: Macmillan, 1948), I, 504 ff.; Ickes, *Secret Diary*, II, 93.

relief missions." [13] Executive orders designed to implement neutrality legislation did, however, require voluntary overseas relief agencies, except for the Red Cross, to register with the State Department and each month to report receipts and expenditures.[14] Under this provision twenty-six agencies did register despite Hull's hope that all aid might be channeled through the Red Cross and the American Friends Service Committee, in whose nonpartisanship he had confidence. The agencies represented almost every shade of political opinion from right to left. Thus was begun an official supervision of voluntary giving for overseas relief which was to become a continuing aspect of American policy. Later, when conflicts between the agencies became unusually bitter, when it seemed as if contributions might fall off, and when there was some fear that neutrality might be endangered, the President encouraged the organization of a Committee for Impartial Relief in Spain. This tried to raise funds for an impartial grain distribution program under the auspices of the Red Cross and Quakers.[15]

The Loyalists, representing Spanish democratic and left-wing groups, aroused the strongly antifascist sympathies of American labor unions, liberals, socialists, and communists. Organized into seven main groups, some with numerous affiliates, and into an even larger number of smaller agencies, American liberal and radical aid to Loyalist Spain represented over 80 per cent of all partisan-oriented American contributions in cash, kind, and medical equipment sent to Spain.[16]

The first group to respond to Loyalist needs was organized labor which made its contributions through the International Federation of Trade Unions.[17] Two weeks after the outbreak of the conflict, the International Ladies Garment Workers Union raised $5,000 and the Amalgamated Clothing Workers of America a like amount. Within a month after David Dubinsky of the ILGWU opened a campaign to raise among trade unions a $100,000 fund for Spain, half

---

[13] Department of State, *Press Releases*, March 13, 1937, XVI, 154.

[14] *Ibid.*; F. Jay Taylor, *The United States and the Spanish Civil War, 1936-1939* (New York: Bookman Associates, 1956), 87.

[15] Taylor, *The United States and the Spanish Civil War*, 132; *New York Times*, Dec. 22, 1938; *Nation* CXLVII (Sept. 24, 1938), 282; *America: A Catholic Review of the Week* LX (Jan. 14, 1939), 338.

[16] Wetzel, "American Relief to Spain," 20.

[17] *New York Times*, July 31, Aug. 4, 5, 9, 1936; *Daily Worker* [New York], Aug. 1, 6, 1936.

the amount was in hand. Labor's Red Cross, as the Dubinsky movement became, sent $130,000 to the needy workers in Loyalist Spain.[18]

Overshadowing Labor's Red Cross and its successor, the Trade Union Relief for Spain, was the North American Committee to Aid Spanish Democracy. This was by far the most important of the pro-Loyalist fund-raising agencies. Headed by Bishop Francis J. McConnell, a prominent Methodist liberal, the North American Committee enjoyed the support of some sixty local chapters and of at least fifteen affiliated groups. These included the League for Industrial Democracy and the Socialist Party, the American Student Union, the American League Against War and Fascism, a common front organization in which the Communists played an important if not a leading role, and the Communist party and its organ, *The Daily Worker*.[19] Early in 1938 the North American Committee joined in a union with the Medical Bureau to Aid Spanish Democracy.[20] The latter organization had been formed shortly after the outbreak of the Civil War with the support of Dr. Walter B. Cannon of the Harvard Medical School and other nationally known medical leaders. It was a pioneer in getting a medical unit off to Spain early in 1937 and it sent three additional ones before summer.[21] By midsummer the Bureau had sent eighteen ambulances and ninety-nine surgeons, nurses, and drivers, and had established six hospitals at a cost of $118,000. Together, the North American Committee and the Medical Bureau to Aid Spanish Democracy contributed, in cash and kind, aid totaling over $800,000.[22]

Many other organizations also contributed to the Loyalist cause. Among them were the committees to aid Americans wounded in fighting for the Loyalists, whose sponsorship included such prominent figures as Edgar Mowrer, Ernest Hemingway, and Louis Bromfield.[23] The American Society for Technical Aid to Spain, sponsored by Van Wyck Brooks, Lewis Mumford, Malcolm Cowley and other well-known writers added its bit.[24] Of special interest was the Foster

[18] *New York Times*, March 14, 19, 1937.

[19] Taylor, *The United States and the Spanish Civil War*, 129; *New York Times*, Oct. 27, Nov. 21, 23, 27, 29, Dec. 6, 1936, Jan. 23, Feb. 9, 20, 1937.

[20] *New York Times*, Feb. 4, 1938; *Daily Worker* [New York], Feb. 12, 1938.

[21] *New York Times*, Jan. 5, 11, 12, 15, 16, 31, April 12, May 9, 1937,

[22] Department of State, *Press Releases*, April 29, 1939, XX, 372-73.

[23] Taylor, *The United States and the Spanish Civil War*, 130-31.

[24] *Daily Worker* [New York], Jan. 9, April 20, 1937; *New York Times*, May 25, 26, 1937.

Parents Plan for Children in Spain, a branch of an organization formed in England in 1937. The American agency enlisted the support of President Roosevelt's wife and mother, of Helen Keller, Louis Untermeyer, Helen Hayes, Paul Douglas, Rockwell Kent, Katherine Lewis, the daughter of the CIO leader, and Herbert Hoover. By the end of 1939 the Plan was caring for 1,200 children in France and England. It was the only agency born of sympathy for distressed Spaniards that survived the Civil War. As the Foster Parents Plan it has, in our own time, maintained a home for children in Belgium and cared for some 15,000 children in many parts of the world.[25] In terms of actual contributions none of these organizations could, however, be compared with the larger American agencies like the North American Committee and the Spanish Societies Confederated to Aid Spain. This latter organization, composed of fraternal groups of Spanish Americans, contributed $289,000. A similar group, the Comité Popular Democrático de Socorro a Espagna, raised $133,-000.[26]

In virtually all pro-Loyalist groups the dedication and emotional commitment exceeded the public response to earlier crises abroad. This was evident in the contributions in kind that filled thousands of receptacles placed at strategic street corners not only in New York but in many other cities. It was also evident in the endless collection of nickels and dimes in tin cups held out at theaters and at factory gates. Documentary films featuring Nationalist atrocities and Loyalist heroism, fiestas given both by Hollywood stars and society leaders, the auctioning of works of art and of manuscripts of well-publicized books by well-known authors, musical benefits, and special theatricals, all helped swell the funds for the needy of Loyalist Spain. Enthusiastic supporters arranged public dinners at which distinguished figures who had observed the struggle at firsthand reported on the situation. On one occasion *The Nation*, which launched its own fund, took in $9,000 from the 700 people at a dinner in honor of André Malraux, who had just come to America from the front.[27] Now and then enthusiasm for the cause expressed itself in ways only

[25] *New York Times*, April 5, June 29, Oct. 18, 1938, April 16, June 24, July 16, 30, August 13, Sept. 10, 18, 1939; Foster Parents Plan, *Foster Parents Plan, Inc.* (ca. 1958).
[26] *New York Times*, Jan. 5, 1937; *Daily Worker* [New York], Aug. 6, 1936, Jan. 12, 1937; Department of State, *Press Releases*, April 29, 1939, XX, 372-73.
[27] Wetzel, "American Relief to Spain," chapter 3. While the Loyalist cause received a few sizable gifts, the bulk of the money and contributions in kind came in small amounts.

indirectly connected with fund raising: a woman, walking a New York Loyalist picket line, attacked the pro-Franco editor of the Jesuit weekly, *America*, with an iron cane as he entered a hotel! [28]

Pro-Franco groups commonly charged supporters of the Loyalist cause with being Communists, fellow travelers, or, at best, dupes of Moscow.[29] It is true that Communists were active in many pro-Loyalist agencies, particularly in the North American Committee and its affiliates. It is also true that leading Communists openly gloried in the contributions the Party made to the Loyalist cause. Nor can it be denied that such prominent figures in the pro-Loyalist agencies as Dr. Harry Ward and, to a lesser degree, Bishop Francis McConnell and Bishop Robert Paddock, had worked for causes also supported by Communists. But the witnesses at the hearings of the Dies Committee on Un-American Activities who indicted these leaders and often accused the whole pro-Loyalist movement of being Communist-dominated hardly proved their case.[30] In view of the well-known opposition to Communism of such pro-Loyalist supporters as Albert Einstein, Eleanor Roosevelt, and John Dewey, to name but three, the effort to smear everyone associated with Loyalist relief work as Communists or fellow travelers reflected the emotional tension and bitterness of the competing ideologies and an inability to make distinctions.[31]

The champions of Nationalist or Insurgent Spain were less numerous, in general less prominent, and less successful in fund raising, though not less articulate, than Loyalist sympathizers. Those committed to Franco's cause included the small group of American Fascists. Also included were Americans who saw in Franco the best means of checking the spread of Socialism and Communism. But the most influential component was the Catholic hierarchy. It followed the Pope in deploring the anticlericalism of the Loyalists and

[28] *America* LIX (June 18, 1938), 252-53.
[29] Richard Steele, "American Catholic Reaction to the Spanish Civil War, 1936-1939" (unpublished Master's thesis, University of Wisconsin, 1958), *passim*.
[30] U. S., Congress, House, Special Committee on Un-American Activities, *Hearings, Investigation of Un-American Propaganda Activities in the United States*, 75th Cong., 3rd Sess., 1938, I:445-6, 870, 909, 78th Cong., 2nd Sess., 1944, XVII:10344; Wetzel, "American Relief to Spain," 31-39.
[31] The roster of Loyalist sympathizers who supported fund-raising campaigns included Franz Boas, Max Ascoli, Olin Downes, Serge Koussevitsky, Rabbi Stephen S. Wise, Tallulah Bankhead, Edna St. Vincent Millay, Norman Thomas, Henry Pratt Fairchild, and Paul H. Douglas.

in holding that only a Franco victory could restore the Church in Spain to its traditional influence and power.[32]

The fund-raising agencies for relief of Franco Spain included that initiated by the *Brooklyn Tablet,* which the *Commonweal* supported; the American Spanish Relief Fund, sponsored by the Jesuit organ, *America,* and, in terms of funds raised, the most successful of the pro-Nationalist committees; the Spanish Nationalist Relief Committee, which enjoyed the blessing of Cardinal O'Connell and Cardinal Dougherty; and the National Spanish Relief Association, identified with the New York exporter, Emilio Gonzalez. The most spectacular event in the pro-Franco fund-raising campaigns was launched by a fifth group, the American Committee for Spanish Relief, which organized a pageant held at Madison Square Garden in May, 1937. The Committee professed to include all creeds and to distribute relief without reference to political affiliations: but the fact that it planned to channel its contributions through the Bishop of Toledo, in Franco territory, meant that it was actually partisan in character. On this score, a prominent figure in the theatrical world, Walter Hampden, who had agreed to take part in the pageant, withdrew. Fifteen thousand people attended the show, but $25,793 of the $30,753 collected was used for administration and publicity. No money ever reached Spain! [33]

The total of cash and kind collected by the pro-Franco relief agencies added up to only $200,000, in contrast with the $1,600,000 contributed to the Loyalist groups. The poor showing can be attributed in part to the fact that the Nationalist agencies relied chiefly on the Church's established mechanisms for collecting money, agencies already burdened with commitments to Catholic charities. It also appears, however, that there was truth in the frequent complaints of the hierarchy and of the Catholic press that the laity was not responding in sufficient numbers or with "proper generosity" to the Nationalist relief agencies. It is impossible to say how many Catholic laymen were merely indifferent, or how many shared the neutral position of Dorothy Day's *Catholic Worker* and, after the summer of 1937, of the *Commonweal.* What is significant is that a few well-known Catholic laymen, including Westbrook Pegler and

[32] *New York Times,* Jan. 21, 23, 1937; Steele, "American Catholic Reaction to the Spanish Civil War," *passim.*
[33] *New York Times,* April 11, May 5, 13, 15, 20, 21, 1937; *Commonweal* XXVI (May 14, 1937), 57-58; (June 4, 1937), 141-42; Department of State, *Press Releases,* Sept. 4, 1937, XVII, 193.

Kathleen Norris, expressed pro-Loyalist sympathies, as did some trade union leaders.[34] Also relevant was the poll of Catholics taken in December, 1938, well toward the end of the Civil War. According to the report, 42 per cent of the Catholics sampled professed Loyalist sympathies.[35]

Opportunities for giving through nonpartisan agencies to both Loyalist and Nationalist sufferers included, of course, those provided by the American Red Cross. Deeply concerned over the failure to raise its million-dollar goal for the needs of China, convinced that public apathy for overseas needs argued against a special drive for Spain, and fearful of jeopardizing its neutral status, the Red Cross decided against making a special drive. It did, however, accept somewhat less than $5,000 in voluntary contributions earmarked for Spain and it sent $200,000 from its own assets to the International Red Cross to be allocated equally to Red Cross organizations in the two parts of Spain. And the American Red Cross gave substantial help to a child-feeding program which it encouraged the Friends to undertake.[36] In addition to the American Red Cross, several other neutral agencies solicited funds or gave support. The Spanish Child Welfare Association raised $46,000 of which $28,000 was spent for relief in Spain, and the Committee for Impartial Civilian Relief for Spain, organized late in 1938 at the request of President Roosevelt, collected $48,-000.[37] The Mennonite Relief Committee and Brethren Board of Christian Education pitched in with volunteer workers. Other nonpartisan organizations donated funds for relief work in Spain.

None of the nonpolitical groups, however, approached the relief record of the Quakers. When the first call for help came, the Ameri-

[34] George N. Shuster, "Some Further Reflections," *Commonweal* XXV (April 23, 1937), 716-17; Taylor, *The United States and the Spanish Civil War*, 152-53.

[35] Hadley Cantril, *Public Opinion*, 1935-1946 (Princeton: Princeton University Press, 1951), 808; Steele, "American Catholic Reaction to the Spanish Civil War," *passim*.

[36] American National Red Cross, *Annual Report*, 1936-37 (Washington: American National Red Cross, 1937), 130, 156; 1937-1938, 130, 157; 1938-1939, 78-79, 90-91; 1939-1940, 100-02; *The Red Cross Courier* XVI (Nov., 1936), 6; XVI (Feb., 1937), 19; XVII (July, 1937), 7-8; XVIII (March, 1939), 5. Foster Rhea Dulles, *The American Red Cross: A History* (New York: Harper, 1950), 340-45. In 1938, when the American Red Cross received less than $3,500 for Spain, it received as voluntary contributions $22,500 for Czechoslovakia, $26,500 for Chile, and $184,189 for China. During the same year the Red Cross organizations of Mexico and Argentina contributed jointly $150,000.

[37] *New York Times*, April 11, Nov. 29, Dec. 30, 1938; Department of State, *Press Releases*, April 29, 1939, XX, 372-73.

can Friends Service Committee hesitated to embark on a venture that might well overtax its resources, already strained by the demands of refugees from the Nazis and by commitments to see through reconstruction projects in distressed areas of the United States. Besides, a bitter civil war posed complex and difficult problems for an agency dedicated to complete nonpartisanship and to giving food and medical aid as a religious expression of faith in nonviolence and of the transcending power of the love of mankind. The report of a representative sent late in 1936 to find out how great the need was, and whether both parties would welcome the Quakers and work without partisanship, convinced the American Friends Service Committee that it must send a mission to Spain to help the British Friends Service Council.[38]

To that end the AFSC invited the cooperation of the Mennonites and the Brethren, both of whom responded. It seemed best, in view of the participation of these traditional peace churches and of other religious groups, including the Federal Council of Churches and the American Unitarian Association, to set up within the frame of the AFSC the Spain Committee. Through personal solicitations and the use of many mailing lists the Committee collected $140,000. Had it been willing to accept contributions from the Young Communists, the sum would have been much larger. But it was clear that a good part of the money the Communists raised for Spain went for purposes other than the relief of the Spanish needy. With limited resources, the Spain Committee of the AFSC restricted its operations to providing supplementary feeding for children and, when possible, for mothers, and to medical services. It sent to Spain twenty-seven workers, Friends, Brethren, Mennonites and others. These men and women risked their lives in the voluntary service they rendered. Sympathizing personally as many of them did with the Loyalists, they found themselves put to it to maintain the self-discipline required in carrying through a strictly nonpartisan mission of love.[39] Criticism of the AFSC at home did not make the task any easier. "We would be attacked at one time," wrote Clarence Pickett, "because our relief was going entirely to children on the Republican side of the line; a few weeks later, however, liberals would be attacking us because we insisted on feeding children in what had come

[38] Pickett, *For More Than Bread*, 105-107.
[39] *Ibid.*, 106-109.

to be Franco territory. We might be feeding the very same children." [40]

The AFSC worked in Spain very closely with the British Friends, with Swiss Aid, the Service Civil International and, especially, with the International Commission for the Assistance of Child Refugees in Spain. Established in late 1937 through the initiative of British Quakers, this agency received cash and kind from individuals and voluntary organizations in many countries and from twenty-four governments. The AFSC took food, clothing, and medical supplies from this agency, as did the British Friends, for distribution in both Loyalist and Nationalist Spain (the larger share of the work was done in the former because its shifting boundaries contained at any one time the greater number of refugees). Before the war was over, the AFSC took responsibility for maintaining three children's hospitals—in Murcia, Alicante, and Almeria—originally established by British Friends. It also supported milk clinics, children's colonies, public dining rooms for refugee children, and distribution of clothing and supplementary rations for mothers and old people. At the height of the program, the AFSC fed some 350,000 persons, chiefly children, with one meal a day. [41]

This record was made possible by a policy announced by the State Department on September 17, 1938. [42] The Federal Surplus Commodities Corporation was authorized to sell government-owned wheat at a token figure to the AFSC and to give it to the American Red Cross which in turn was to mill the wheat into flour and transport it to American seaports. Ocean freight to French harbors was provided by the United States Maritime Commission. In some instances the Loyalist and Nationalist governments provided transportation from the French ports to their respective territories, in other cases, the Quakers trucked the wheat and flour overland. American and British Friends chiefly supervised the distribution. The American government's contribution was valued at approximately $500,000,

[40] *Ibid.*, 108.

[41] *Ibid.*, 109 ff.; Francesca M. Wilson, *In the Margins of Chaos: Recollections of Relief Work in and Between Three Wars* (New York: Macmillan, 1945), *passim;* American Friends Service Committee, *Annual Report*, 1937 (Philadelphia: American Friends Service Committee, 1938), 21-22; 1938, 20; 1939, 22-23; John Van Gelder Forbes, "The American Friends in Spain, 1937-1939," *Administration of Relief Abroad: Recent Relief Programs of the American Friends in Spain and France,* ed. Donald S. Howard (New York: Russell Sage Foundation, 1943), 3 ff.

[42] Department of State, *Press Releases*, Sept. 17, 1938, XIX, 190; *The Red Cross Courier* XVIII (Oct., 1938), 4.

a sum roughly equalled by the cash grants of the British government to the International Commission. Brazil, at the suggestion of the State Department, donated 1,320,000 pounds of coffee; Belgium gave £10,000 worth of food; the Swedish and Norwegian governments gave £80,000 and £20,000 respectively; and twenty other governments gave smaller amounts. Thus the feeding of Spain's hungry and starving children became an international partnership of governments and of voluntary associations, among which the Friends played a leading role.[43]

The government's subsidy of surplus wheat did not escape criticism. *America*, the Jesuit weekly, declared that the operation was not truly neutral since the bulk of the wheat went to Loyalist Spain and since, in any case, Franco Spain did not need wheat. The truth of the matter was that Loyalist Spain contained by far the greater concentration of needy refugees. After the fall of Madrid and the collapse of the Loyalist regime in March, 1939, American Catholics raised $32,000 to load 250,000 bushels of wheat on a ship which sailed from Baltimore for Spain.[44]

Tangled problems arose again and again in connection with getting American contributions to Spain, whether in the form of government wheat and flour, or condensed milk, chocolate, and other food, or clothing and medical supplies, and whether these supplies were sent in the three ships Loyalist agencies chartered or as cargo on regular freighters. The background of the problems was in part the bitter ideological and emotional conflicts between the several American competing charities concerned with Spanish relief. But the trouble also stemmed from the charges and countercharges of each side that the other was guilty of violating or condoning the violation of American neutrality regulations. Pro-Nationalists bitterly resented the presence in Loyalist Spain of some 4,000 young American volunteers enlisted in the Abraham Lincoln Brigade.

Notwithstanding the neutrality legislation, military equipment and munitions from America reached both sides through Germany, Holland, Belgium, England, and France.[45] At least one relief ship

[43] Pickett, *For More Than Bread*, 109-110; Kershner, *Quaker Service in Modern War*, 3 ff., 49; Forbes, "Relief for Spanish Civilians," *passim*.

[44] *America* LIX (Oct. 1, 1938), 602, LX (Dec. 31, 1938), 290, LX (Jan. 7, 1939), 315, LX (Jan. 14, 1939), 338, LX (Feb. 18, 1939), 458, LXI (April 22, 1939), 27, LXI (May 20, 1939), 123.

[45] Rosenman, ed., *The Public Papers and Addresses of Franklin D. Roosevelt*, VII, 252-53.

chartered by the American Loyalists carried, in addition to food, clothing and shoes, airplanes and airplane parts loaded in Mexico. It never reached Loyalist Spain: in one account it was sunk by a Franco cruiser, in another, captured and taken to a Nationalist port. American pro-Franco organs charged that the Medical Bureau and North American Committee deliberately tried to goad the Nationalists into attacking a third relief ship in order to involve the United States in the Civil War on the Loyalist side and, if the plan failed, to sink the ship and charge the act to Nationalist fury. The charge was quickly denied as a pro-Franco lie, and the ship arrived safely.[46]

In such a context it is somewhat easier to understand the charges launched against the Nationalist attitudes toward American relief as the pro-Loyalist United States Ambassador, Claude Bowers, reported them. Franco officials, according to Bowers, denied at the very time that American relief was saving the lives of children and mothers in Nationalist as well as in Loyalist Spain, that America had sent any food or clothing into Franco territory. A Quaker agent informed Bowers that flour sent to the Rebel Nationalists was left unloaded for a month while children starved and that, finally, Franco officials announced that the great part of it was to be used for the armed forces. According to the report, these officials backtracked only when the Quakers threatened to refuse to have any of the food unloaded unless all of it went for civilian relief.[47] Whether this particular incident happened or not, it is certainly true that difficulties of working with the Nationalists confirmed some Friends in their pro-Loyalist feeling. On the other hand, there is evidence that many officials in the Nationalist Auxilio Social and the Spanish Red Cross often proved cooperative in working with the Friends and the International Commission.

The fall of Barcelona to Franco late in January, 1939, heralded the end of the Spanish Republic. Two months later Madrid and Valencia surrendered. The Loyalist cause collapsed despite unparalleled courage and heroism. The International Commission and the AFSC had large supplies in what was now Nationalist Spain. To insure that these be used only for the relief of suffering and administered in a nonpartisan way, the AFSC representative, Howard Kershner, needed in his negotiations with the Franco government all the hard-headed and

---

[46] Wetzel, "American Relief to Spain," 99-104.
[47] Claude G. Bowers, *My Mission to Spain: Watching the Rehearsal for World War II* (New York: Simon and Schuster, 1954), 336-37.

determined Quaker business spirit he had in such abundance. Given Spanish red tape, procrastination, and the heady sense of victory along with the chaos and confusion inevitable after so long and destructive a civil war, the wonder was that he succeeded in inducing the Franco government to promise to observe the stipulations he made.

But as had so often proved true, it was one thing to effect an agreement with Spaniards, another thing to hold them to its implementation. Local authorities sometimes moved without authorization from the central government. This happened when the military in Barcelona confiscated supplies of the AFSC and International Commission. Under pressure, restitution was made. And Nationalist authorities, despite the necessity of reversing an early insistence that Spain did not need outside aid, accepted, however reluctantly, the help that the AFSC and the International Commission were still able and willing to give on condition that inspection of the Spanish agencies of administration be guaranteed.[48]

A good many of the thirty-one relief workers under Kershner's direction left Spain, some because of other commitments, some because, having a deep though concealed commitment to the Loyalist cause, they doubted the possibility of continuing nonpartisan relief in Nationalist Spain. On his return from Spain, Alfred Cope, in an interview with a New York *Herald Tribune* representative, related the incident of the Nationalist seizure of relief supplies and, though cautious, expressed doubts of the possibility of continuing a fair distribution in the new regime.[49] The interview was given international publicity. American donors expressed an unwillingness to continue giving; European donors were incensed at the implication that the supplies had been American gifts when for the most part they represented European contributions; and the Franco government was so bitterly indignant at what it regarded as misrepresentation, that it looked as if all foreign relief work was at an end. Kershner, deeply embarrassed, issued a counterstatement. The AFSC, equally embarrassed at the adverse publicity, instructed its overseas staff henceforth to make no statements for the press without first clearing with the Philadelphia office.[50]

---

[48] Kershner, *Quaker Service in Modern War*, 37-46; Pickett, *For More Than Bread*, 113.
[49] *New York Herald Tribune*, June 9, 1939; *New York Times*, June 9, 10, 1939.
[50] The most complete account of American Quaker relief in Spain is the unpublished Forbes manuscript, "Relief for Spanish Civilians," previously cited.

Relief work, including the use of mobile ambulances supplied from America and staffed with Spanish doctors and nurses, continued until the last months of 1939. In view of the fact that there were often no precedents for meeting completely new situations, and in consideration of the innumerable difficulties, the record was a remarkable one. At least 350,000 children were kept alive and thousands of adults were enabled to exist. In the course of carrying through the program, the difficult problem of deciding who was to receive the never sufficient food was met by systematically weighing children, keeping records and giving to those in the greatest need. In all future relief work, this procedure became standard practice. It is, of course, impossible to say to what extent the Friends succeeded in getting through to survivors—and to those who did not survive—the message that relief was given, not merely to keep human beings alive, but as an evidence of the even greater gift of love.[51]

Before considering what the Friends and the International Commission did in aiding refugees once the Civil War was over, the total American relief effort may well be summed up. American voluntary and government contributions together amounted to approximately $3,000,000. This was used in large part to keep alive the hungry, the sick, the ill-clad, the homeless—well over 7,000,000 people. Of this sum, $1,600,000 represented pro-Loyalist contributions, $200,000 those of pro-Nationalists. The rest came to nonpartisan agencies from individual gifts and from government allocation of surplus wheat, as well as from the Red Cross. Inadequate information makes it impossible to offer meaningful comparisons between American and non-American contributions. When differences in population and wealth are taken into account it is clear that the aid, official and nonofficial, given by Great Britain, Sweden, Norway, Switzerland and other countries compared favorably with that from the United States. In relation to what Americans were giving for all overseas philanthropy in the years 1936-1939—a total of $141,800,000—the $3,000,000 channeled to Spain represented a tiny fraction.[52]

The fall of Madrid and Valencia at the end of March, 1939, did not end the suffering born of the struggle. The example of the *Stanhope*,

[51] Pickett, *For More Than Bread*, 116-17.

[52] Paul De Witt Dickens and August Maffry, *Balance of International Payments of United States in 1939*, U. S. Department of Commerce, Foreign and Domestic Commerce Bureau, Economic Series 8 (Washington: Govt. Printing Office, 1940).

a British registered vessel, is only a tragic symbol of the prolonged pain of the defeated. Two days before Franco's troops marched into Valencia, 2,300 desperate Loyalists crowded into the small ship and demanded that the captain head for Oran in French Africa. There was no room on the *Stanhope* for any one of the 2,300 to lie down, and barely enough for a few to sit down at a given time. Sanitary conditions quickly became unspeakable. In the torrid heat of Oran harbor the men, hungry, thirsty, exhausted, waited aboard ship for six days: the French authorities refused permission to land, British authorities refused permission to take the wretched human cargo to a British port. Howard Kershner promised on behalf of the International Commission that if the French would give temporary right to stay in Oran, the Commission would fumigate and re-clothe the men and care for them until a haven could be found in Latin America and the survivors transported at British expense to the new world. The French reluctantly agreed. But before arrange-ments could be made for the new venture the approaching Second World War put so great a premium on ships that nothing could be done. For the men who could not somehow make a place for them-selves in the big world, there was no future.[53]

Before this tragic episode, hundreds of thousands of Loyalists sought refuge in France itself for it was clear that the Republic must fall and that Franco's vengeance might know no bounds. Some went by boat. Most braved the formidable Pyrenees in the chill of a late winter and early spring. The American Friends Service Committee hastily set up canteens on the routes the refugees must take and thereby provided some sustenance to the weary, hungry, numbed, and hopeless travelers. With a generosity unprecedented in the his-tory of modern governments, France accepted the uninvited guests—a half-million of them. It went further and provided, in some 2,000 camps, shelter, blankets, and minimum rations. For the time, none dared return to Spain in view of the reports of wholesale executions, of torture and imprisonment, of fellow Loyalists still in Spain. The Friends and the International Commission supplied supplementary nourishment for 8,000 of the neediest adults and for 8,000 children. Under the direction of Kershner and his wife, the Friends and the Commission established or took responsibility for a score of children's camps, the best known of which was named Pax. In these camps

[53] Kershner, *Quaker Service in Modern War*, 77-81.

the children received not only physical care, but encouragement to become self-reliant, and, most important of all, love and understanding. The response exceeded all hope: soon the children were expressing themselves in painting, in singing, in dancing, and in performing needed tasks in the colonies. Some finally went back to Spain. Others fitted into the French agricultural economy. A few received scholarships from French universities and took places of importance in the life of their adopted land.

When the Second World War broke out in September, 1939, some 200,000 adult refugees were still in French camps. With a million of her own people evacuated from their homes, France found it difficult to care for the Spanish refugees as well. The Quakers, through the International Commission, then headed by the director of the AFSC, Howard Kershner, took over the major burden of caring for the refugees in the camps of southern France. At first the Commission supplied milk, blankets, medication, and orthopedic materials for needy refugees and wounded soldiers. It took over more and more of the children's colonies. Materials were supplied for sewing, tailoring, cobbling, and carpentry. At the camp in Montauban, amputees taught themselves to make artificial legs and arms. The Commission supplied them with material for making additional ones to be used, ironically, for the new legless and armless victims of the Second World War. In June, 1940, when France concluded a separate armistice with the victorious Germans, British Friends remained until the United States and Vichy France broke off diplomatic relations. The job was then turned over to Secours Quaker, a French group of Friends. In 1943 it was learned that nine American Quaker representatives in southern France had been interned in Baden-Baden, Germany.

The failure of the western democracies, including the United States, to prevent the intervention of Hitler and Mussolini in the Spanish Civil War, and the fascist triumph in Spain, encouraged the dictators to launch further aggression. But it was not only in this respect, nor in the fact that the Civil War provided opportunities for the totalitarian powers to test new implements and methods of destruction, that the tragedy in Spain proved to be the curtain raiser to a global conflict exceeding man's imagination. The Spanish struggle showed that if many men are insufficiently civilized to prevent mass murder and destruction, some are civilized enough to join forces in giving token relief to the victims of man's inhumanity. In some cases that relief, as we have seen, stemmed from ideological motives. In other instances, the impelling force was pity and compassion. In some, it was based on the faith that man can even in the most bitter conflict of ideas and emotions transcend inhumanity through the lesson of love. The relief operations during the Spanish Civil War bore evidence of the yet existing richness in the human spirit which was able to give not only means for sustaining life but the hope that makes life so sustained endurable.

XV

The Years of Neutrality

The World War feared for so long at last burst out in Europe with the German invasion and conquest of Poland in September, 1939, followed by the Soviet attack on Finland in November. On the other side of the earth the Japanese war on China moved relentlessly forward. Whatever their personal sympathies, all but a small part of the American people strongly supported national neutrality. But a great many, particularly those with ties of kinship and sentiment to one or another of the belligerents, felt the impulse to aid the suffering and the destitute. Never before had aid been given under such complex conditions as the ones now existing, and never before had it been so deeply enmeshed with the official policy of the nation.

Between 1919 and 1939 Americans had given evidence of concern for the needs and plight of their fellows beyond the seas by contributing through voluntary agencies a total of $1,270,100,000. In general, overseas gifts had declined between 1919 and 1935 and had then, in the next three years, sharply risen with the mounting crises in Central Europe and in the Far East.[1] Of the total $1,270,100,000, nonsectarian organizations gave $431,400,000 for educational, scientific and philanthropic purposes, largely to countries bordering the eastern Mediterranean and to China. The Protestant contribution, chiefly channeled to India, China, and Japan, with substantial gifts to Latin America and Africa, added up to $599,800,000. Catholic organiza-

[1] Paul De Witt Dickens and August Maffry, *Balance of International Payments of the United States in 1939*, U. S. Department of Commerce, Foreign and Domestic Commerce Bureau, Economic Series 8 (Washington: Govt. Printing Office, 1940), 70-71. The Department of Commerce has kept records beginning with 1919 on the annual overseas expenditures of religious and philanthropic groups, believing that the amounts expended are great enough to affect the balance of international payments. Recorded in the totals of the religious organizations are funds spent to maintain missionary activities.

tions sent, mainly to Europe and China, $89,600,000. American Jews, by far the smallest but for philanthropic purposes the best organized of the religious groups, were recorded as having contributed $149,- 300,000, a large part of which had gone to Poland, Germany, and Palestine.

Considering capacity to give and the needs in other lands, the record might have been more generous, but it gave assurance that in the new global conflict Americans would not turn a deaf ear. This was the more certain in view of the considerable numbers of the population who were tied to belligerents by origin and sympathy and in view, further, of the receding depression as America moved from the New Deal to relative prosperity, a prosperity not without irony by reason of the stimulation which military expenditures provided. Moreover, within a year after the outbreak of the war in Europe, Protestants and Catholics took steps to coordinate fund raising within each of their camps. In 1939 the Catholics organized the Bishops' War Emergency and Relief Committee. In the summer of 1940 the Federal Council of Churches organized a Committee on Foreign Relief Appeals and urged Christian citizens to contribute generously not only through the Red Cross but, especially to church affiliated overseas agencies. Organized labor likewise encouraged greater giving for overseas purposes.[2]

In many ways, the Russo-Finnish war of 1939-1940 was a separate chapter in the larger story. When Poland fell before Nazi violence, the Soviet Union demanded that Finland cede the Karelian Isthmus, twenty-five miles from Leningrad, as a means of strengthening Russian borders against attack. The Finns refused to yield. Despite a non-aggression pact, Soviet forces struck at Finland on November 30, 1939, by air, land, and sea. In the following spring the Finnish government had to accept harsh terms involving the loss of a tenth of its territory. American sympathy throughout was largely pro-Finnish. In part this sympathy rested on the remembrance that of all the nations indebted to the United States in the years after the First World War, Finland alone had made regular repayments. In part American sympathy reflected anti-Communist feeling which Soviet aggression against a small neighbor deepened.

In response to Finland's plight, Herbert Hoover sought to organize

2 *New York Times,* March 15, 1941; *Christian Century* LVIII (March 5, 1941), 310.

Americans behind a full-scale relief effort. In Washington there was a rumor to the effect that Hoover, after declining to accept a Red Cross post in Finnish relief, had organized the Finnish Relief Fund for political reasons, but this was vigorously denied by the former President as "malicious." According to Hoover, Finnish authorities inquired whether he and his colleagues might be willing to aid the stricken country as they had done through the American Relief Administration in 1918 and 1919. He turned to the Red Cross, which had sent a representative to Helsinki on the outbreak of the war and had furnished medical supplies and clothing, to find that the burden of general relief was beyond it.[3] Thereupon Hoover appealed to the American press for support, with the result that 1,400 newspapers opened their columns for subscriptions. The Finnish Relief Fund, with local committees representing ethnic, religious, industrial, and labor groups organized on a state basis, kept overhead at a minimum by depending largely on volunteers and by accepting special donations for transport costs. (The administrative expenses of the whole operation added up to only 3.7 per cent.)[4] The Fund, making it clear that gifts would be used only for civilian relief, kept aloof from a group headed by General John F. O'Ryan which was raising money for munitions.

The donor base was broad. As on earlier occasions, the theater world responded with enthusiasm. One anonymous philanthropist bought out Washington's Palace Theatre which was showing *Gone with the Wind*, resold the 2,357 seats at $3 to $10 each and turned over the resulting $13,000 to Herbert Hoover's Finnish Relief Fund.[5] New York theaters put on special benefit performances. At a Hollywood fete at the Hotel Roosevelt celebrities auctioned personal gifts from the great stars: a sarong belonging to Dorothy Lamour, a pair of evening gloves contributed by Carmen Miranda, an evening bag donated by Joan Crawford, a lock of hair from Lana Turner. Artists and cartoonists of national fame gave their handiwork for the cause. Hendrick Van Loon, Dr. Lin Yutang, Stephen Vincent Benet, Fannie Hurst, and others autographed books which Lowell Thomas sold to

[3] *Newsweek* XIV (Dec. 25, 1939), 12-13; S. J. Woolf, "Mr. Hoover Tackles Another Relief Job," *New York Times Magazine*, Jan. 21, 1940. Secretary of the Interior Harold L. Ickes noted in his diary on December 14, 1939, that Hoover was "making a play of marshalling relief for Finland": *The Secret Diary of Harold L. Ickes* (3 vols.; New York: Simon and Schuster, 1953-1954), III, 95.

[4] Finnish Relief Fund, Inc., *Report to American Donors, December 1939–July 1940* (New York: Finnish Relief Fund, 1940), 9.

[5] *Time* XXXV (Feb. 5, 1940), 20.

collectors.[6] In the fund-raising drive Hoover was photographed with Tallulah Bankhead, Babe Ruth, and such labor leaders as Matthew Woll and David Dubinsky.[7]

In one reckoning, labor's contributions added up to $200,000, those of industry, $600,000.[8] Americans of Finnish background, divided among themselves on religious and political issues, joined in making very substantial donations. Not counting the $336,000 the American Red Cross spent for surgical dressings, anesthetics and refugee garments,[9] the Finnish Relief Fund sent, in supplies and cash, a total of $3,500,000. This was more than half of the total amount contributed by all other countries.[10] Since the great need of Finland could not be met by voluntary gifts, Congress appropriated a loan of $30,000,000 for nonmilitary relief, most of which was used to buy and ship lard, grain, dried fruit, peas, and soybeans, as well as trucks, tractors, factory machinery and parts, cotton, chemicals, and medical supplies.[11]

To administer the fund raised by the Hoover organization, the Finnish government created an official relief committee which worked with American representatives in helping 600,000 civilians through gifts of shoes, clothing, blankets, food, and medical supplies, through establishing children's hospitals and clinics, and through family rehabilitation. Finnish appreciation was generous and widespread. Prime Minister Rusto Ryti wrote that "the American people, whom we have always admired as a nation of active realists, wished to show their sympathy in deeds. The collection, started under the leadership of President Hoover, serves as a magnificent example of this desire to help us in a practical way." [12] Nor did appreciation come only from

[6] *New York Times*, Feb. 25, 1940.

[7] *Life* VIII (Feb. 19, 1940), 28-29.

[8] *Time* XXXV (March 11, 1940), 17.

[9] Foster Rhea Dulles, *The American Red Cross: A History* (New York: Harper, 1950), 349.

[10] Contributions broke down into personal and miscellaneous, $1,914,892, newspapers, $652,869, corporation employees, $174,758, sports events, $89,494, entertainments, $58,337, theaters, $50,789, motion pictures, $24,568, American Scandinavian organizations, $78,872, foundations, $45,107, civic organizations, $41,674, labor organizations, $27,294, colleges and schools, $17,725, women's clubs, $10,842, etc.: Finnish Relief Fund, *Report to American Donors*, 10. In Finnish marks, Sweden contributed 73,415,051, Denmark, 14,885,258, Switzerland, 12,479,000, England, 5,208,179, Holland, 3,281,919, South Africa, 1,421,641, and other countries in smaller amounts: *Ibid.*, 12.

[11] *Congressional Record*, 76th Cong., 3d Sess., 1940, LXXXVIII, Pt. 3, 2336; *Commonweal* XXXIII (Oct. 25, 1940), 6; *Time* XXXV (March 11, 1940), 20-21.

[12] Finnish Relief Fund, *Report to American Donors*, 17.

the Finnish side. An American supervisor declared that "for those of us to whom the great privilege was given to work in Finland for the Hoover Finnish Relief Fund, a very wonderful memory will ever remain of a people endowed with the finest human traits." [13] Hoover noted that "by helping a small country which had been attacked by a nation whose entire system is hateful to us, we are supplying an outlet for feelings which might well otherwise lead us into war." [14] In the same vein, *Commonweal* urged the canalization of emotional tensions, built up by reports of Europe's ordeal, into such an effort of charity as the world had never yet seen, in order that emotions might be put to constructive use.[15] There was to be ample opportunity for such canalization—including contributions to the Finns in a second war with Soviet Russia waged in 1941 and lasting until 1944.

In the years between 1939 and 1941, a period of neutrality at times jeopardized by American support for the underdog, government supervision of nonofficial aid to the needy in belligerent countries became established policy. In a sense, the policy began with the requirement in the Spanish Civil War that relief agencies register with the State Department. Now, on November 4, 1939, two months after the Nazi violation of Poland and three weeks before the Russian invasion of Finland, Congress passed a Neutrality Act designed to insure the neutral position of the country by prohibiting specified kinds of economic aid to nations the President might declare to be in a belligerent state.[16] The Act permitted private measures to relieve suffering in these countries, but only under government regulation. At first, the regulation was nominal: the State Department in effect gave to every applicant the benefit of any doubt, waiting for trouble to start after the licensing. To a writer in *Survey* this seemed like locking the barn door after the horse was out.[17] By early February, 1940, no less than 362 agencies had registered under the terms of the Neutrality Act. This number did not include various unlisted organizations collecting funds for China and Finland—countries the President had not declared to be at war. Nor did it include the American Red Cross. Only after nine months of experience was official control increased over voluntary agencies concerned with foreign relief.

[13] *Ibid.*, 53.
[14] *New York Times*, Jan. 21, 1940.
[15] *Commonweal* XXXII (June 14, 1940), 157-58.
[16] *Congressional Record*, 76th Cong., 2d Sess., 1939, LXXXV, Pt. 2, 1397.
[17] *Survey* XVII (Nov., 1939), 334.

Of 128 organizations licensed shortly after the passage of the Neutrality Act a hundred—more or less—were committed to Polish relief and included all sorts of clubs, "circles" and even newspapers and radio stations. The main instrument for money raising was, however, the Paderewski Fund, which transmitted its cash to the Commission for Polish Relief, the food purchasing and transport agency formed in September, 1939, and headed by Henry Noble MacCracken and Chauncey McCormick.[18] The problems of getting food to occupied Poland were brought home to the public at a mass meeting in the spring of 1940 which some 15,000 people attended. In a special message to the meeting, President Roosevelt urged that it be borne in mind that welfare, although it be economic and not military, might become "the pawn in the diplomatic and military chess game." Aid, he continued, had flowed freely from America to foreign countries in need and had never been "colored or distorted" by political motives. Hoover, who spoke in person, was more specific in indicating what had to be done to get food to Poland: an agreement must be secured from the British, French, and German governments that shipments might pass through the blockade; that neutral supervision of distribution be assured; and that a single unified agency for the shipment and distribution be put in charge.[19] Hoover had already testified at a hearing before the House Committee on Foreign Affairs that between $400,000,000 and $500,000,000 would be needed to feed the 7,000,000 destitute men, women, and children in Poland and that one-fourth to one-half of this ought to come from the United States. "Such humanitarian assistance embraces no threat of involvement in European wars," Hoover insisted.[20]

Meantime the Commission for Polish Relief was hard at work. By good fortune it secured the services of Maurice Pate and Colonel J. W. Krueger, old hands in the American Relief Administration at the end of the First World War. Dr. E. V. McCollum and Dr. Hazel Stiebeling, outstanding authorities on nutrition, gave advice as to what foods were desirable and practicable. By early summer, 1940, three shipments of evaporated milk, rye flour, vegetable fats, sugar, and hominy grits had left America for Genoa. The Italian railroads agreed to carry the supplies at half the normal rate, the German

18 John F. Rich, "Aftermath in Poland," *Survey Graphic* XXVIII (Dec., 1939), 740-41.
19 *New York Times*, March 13, 1940.
20 *Ibid.*, March 1, 1940.

railroads, free of charge. On their side the Allies agreed to lift the blockade of food providing shipments were accompanied by American inspectors. Berlin agreed to permit Americans to accompany the shipments through Germany to Poland, where the German Red Cross was to act as a liaison agent with local distributing groups. After Italy entered the war, supplies had to be shipped through Vilna and thence to Warsaw.[21]

As soon as the *blitzkrieg* crushed Poland the Commission for Polish Relief in cooperation with the American Friends Service Committee sent representatives to Poland to report on the situation. Warsaw, a city of 1,300,000 presented an appalling picture: a rubble of broken glass and masonry, blood-stained streets, the stench of corpses, shrouded silence. It was estimated that 250,000 Jews had been killed or had died and that 80 per cent of the living were reduced to beggary. And the survivors were excluded from the relief that the *National-sozialistische Volkswohlfahrt*, the counterpart of the U. S. Army's Civilian Affairs Division, was dispensing. The Russian area of Poland contained an estimated 600,000 Jewish refugees, Roumania 30,000, Lithuania 100,000. In Warsaw itself the Joint Distribution Committee undertook to feed once a day between 50,000 and 75,000 Jews. The American Red Cross, which attempted to make sure that American food did not reach the German military occupation, spent, by midsummer, 1940, $606,427 in Polish relief. The Commission for Polish Relief and the other American agencies also provided food, clothing, and medical supplies for Polish refugees in neighboring states.[22] To meet special needs Dr. Frank Kingdon raised funds for the Polish children's camps which Save the Children International Union was establishing in Hungary.[23]

In some cases circumstances limited what could be done for a beleaguered people. Between the Munich pact and Hitler's occupation of Czechoslovakia, the newly established group out of which was to develop the American Unitarian Service Committee helped 1,200 Czechs escape the country and, when it was impossible to work any longer in Prague, provided help to refugees in France and

21 Bertha Anne Peet, "How Polish Relief Works," *Commonweal* XXXII (July 12, 1940), 242-44; Victor Weybright, "Altruism at Armageddon," *Survey Graphic* XXIX (June, 1940), 373-77; Benjamin Anuskewicz, "Relief for Poland," *Current History* LI (June, 1940), 40-41.
22 Rich, *Survey Graphic* XXVIII, 740-41; Victor Weybright, "Sympathy Is Not Enough," *Survey Graphic* XXIX (April, 1940), 213-16; *New York Times*, July 17, 1940.
23 *New York Times*, Feb. 11, 1940.

Portugal.[24] The Friends of Czechoslovakia also helped refugees who managed to get to France, England, and other countries.[25] The Belgium Relief Society, under Hoover's direction, could not develop a program similar to the one that had proved so successful after the First World War. Its eighteen chapters became branches of Bundles for Britain, a leading relief organization, and earmarked its contributions for Belgian refugees in England.[26] Similarly the Queen Wilhelmina Fund, headed by Hendrik Van Loon, used the $400,000 it collected largely from the half-million Americans of Dutch background, for helping Netherlanders in England, France, Portugal, and the Pacific Ocean countries.[27]

When the Nazis invaded France, Americans sent ambulances with trained volunteer drivers to give emergency aid to military and civilian casualties. The American Field Service in France, initiated by the American Legion and by men who had driven ambulances in the First World War and by their sons, raised $363,741. It kept its operating costs at the remarkably low figure of 3.5 per cent.[28] The American Volunteer Ambulance Corps also took part in the rescue work. In all, Americans sent 110 ambulances and 120 volunteer drivers to France before it crumbled under the Nazi armored tanks and air raids. Many of these drivers were college men who paid their own expenses. The best known was Robert Montgomery, a Hollywood star. French newspapers of all viewpoints, including *Populaire*, *L'Action Française*, *Le Matin*, *Figaro*, and *Le Petit Journal*, were warm in their appreciation. So was Prime Minister Reynaud, who, in a letter to James Wood Johnson, founder and president of the American Volunteer Ambulance Association, testified that the Americans accomplished their mission "with a disregard of fatigue and danger beyond all praise." [29]

But ambulances were not the only token of American sympathy. The American Friends of France Committee, headed by the veteran Francophile, Miss Anne Morgan, lent aid in many quarters, including the invaded areas. (On one occasion, Miss Morgan, in her sixty-seventh year, barely escaped injury or death when a German bomb

---

[24] *Newsweek* XIX (April 6, 1942), 60-61.
[25] *Independent Woman* XIX (Jan., 1940), 16.
[26] *New York Times*, May 16, 1940, Feb. 7, 1941.
[27] *Ibid.*, May 24, 1940, Jan. 13, May 6, 1941; *Survey* LXXVIII (Sept., 1942), 231-36.
[28] *New York Times*, May 6, 1941.
[29] *Ibid.*, Jan. 5, 27, March 22, April 5, July 20, 1940; *Life* VIII (June 24, 1940), 74-79. The American Scandinavian Ambulance unit arrived in Bergen early in April, 1940, to work chiefly in Finland: *New York Times*, April 6, 1940.

exploded where she was at work.) [30] The French War Relief sent clothing, cloth, food, and other donations to be distributed by any relief organization specified by the donor.[31]

With the collapse of France, Howard Kershner of the American Friends Service Committee and the International Commission for the Assistance of Child Refugees in Spain, took charge of the unified administration of the funds raised for the several relief organizations in France. A major problem, as Kershner pointed out, was the inadequacy of the funds.[32] A Red Cross ship, with a million-dollar cargo of hospital equipment and food, reached Marseille in the summer of 1940, to be followed by others.[33] The AFSC and other groups supervised distribution both of Red Cross contributions and of those of their own constituencies. The AFSC and the International Commission, for example, established hostels and canteens in Paris, Toulouse, Bordeaux, Angoulême, Potiers, Montauban, and other cities, fed and cared for refugees from occupied countries, provided rations for 30,000 school children and Swiss milk for 10,000 babies in unoccupied France. In 1941, in cooperation with the Unitarian Service Committee, the AFSC tried resettling refugees in abandoned French villages, a project which involved the establishment of cooperative factories.[34] During the first year of the German occupation of France, the Joint Distribution Committee spent $600,000 in giving emergency relief and in helping some of the 100,000 alien Jewish refugees in southern France escape to other countries before the Nazis deported them to unknown horrors.[35]

Meanwhile, ten hours after Mussolini's first troops crossed the Albanian frontier on their way to Athens, some 2,000 Americans of Greek background, sponge divers in Tarpon Springs, Florida, collected upwards of $3,000 for the relief of the homeland and voted

---

[30] *New York Times*, May 17, 1940. Miss Morgan was the sister of J. Pierpont Morgan.

[31] *Ibid.*, March 5, 1940.

[32] *Ibid.*, June 9, 1940.

[33] Dulles, *The American Red Cross*, 350.

[34] American Friends Service Committee, *Annual Report*, 1941 (Philadelphia: American Friends Service Committee, 1942), 7-10; Pickett, *For More Than Bread: An Autobiographical Account of Twenty-Two Years Work with the American Friends Service Committee* (Boston: Little, Brown, 1953), 107-55; Howard E. Kershner, *Quaker Service in Modern War* (New York: Prentice-Hall, 1950), 141 ff.; Kate Vernon, "Quaker Relief in France," *Commonweal* XXXV (Dec. 5, 1941), 163-65.

[35] *American Jewish Year Book*, Sept., 1941–Sept., 1942, XLIII (Philadelphia: Jewish Publication Society of America, 1942), 91-92; *New York Times*, Oct. 12, 1941; *New Republic* CIV (Jan. 13, 1941), 43-44.

to augment the fund by setting aside the best of the sponge harvest and the choicest embroideries made by the women of the community for sale in New York.[36] Hard on this initiative, business men of Greek extraction organized in New York and other cities the Greek War Relief Association with supporting branches. Throughout the country hundreds of Greek Americans raised money to buy ambulances, medical supplies, clothes, and food for Greece.[37] Within six months the Association had raised $1,000,000 and reportedly was unsurpassed by any similar relief organization in its intelligent direction.[38] This auspicious beginning was sustained after the United States entered the war.

Russian relief, to become a major program after Pearl Harbor, was launched while the United States was still nominally a neutral. In this case it was not so much ethnic groups that took the initiative. It was rather prominent native-born leaders in banking and professional circles. The American Committee for Medical Aid to Russia, acting on the assumption that any people who opposed Nazi Germany deserved support, was early sending, under convoy, shipments of drugs, bandages, surgical instruments, and X-ray machines over the long, risky northern route to Murmansk and Archangel.[39] Russian War Relief, organized a bit later, got off to a dramatic start at a rally at Madison Square Garden at which Joseph Davies, former ambassador to Moscow, spoke with considerable eloquence. The new organization enlisted in thirty-five major cities the support of Russian Orthodox, Roman Catholic, Protestant, and Jewish religious bodies. Commercial and business groups also took a leading part: Pierre Jay, chairman of the Fiduciary Trust Company, accepted the office of national treasurer. Labor organizations also responded, some with zest. But in the autumn of 1941 David Dubinsky announced that the International Ladies' Garment Workers Union had refused to contribute to the Russian War Relief because it believed that some of its top officials followed the Communist party line.[40]

In the years of neutrality the chief focus of attention was, however, neither Poland, France, Greece nor the Soviet Union, but, rather, Great Britain. This was natural in view of the cultural and

[36] Howard Hartley, "The Greek Way," *Collier's* CVII (May 17, 1941), 18-19.
[37] *New York Times*, Nov. 14, 1940.
[38] *Life* X (Jan. 6, 1941), 15-19.
[39] *Reader's Digest* XL (May, 1942), 122-24.
[40] *Ibid.*; *New York Times*, Nov. 9, 1941.

political ties between England and the United States, and also because of the widespread feeling that Britain, in fighting Nazism at
the risk of her own national extinction, was upholding interests and
values identical with those of the United States. The Lend-Lease program also gave British war relief an aura of government sanction.
Out-and-out interventionists saw in voluntary as well as official aid
a partial American commitment to the side of their choice, just as
the partisans of the two contendants in the Spanish Civil War had
done. Those sympathetic with Britain, but reluctant to become involved in the war, could feel that aid was some sort of solution of
conflicting sympathies and desires. Such considerations explained the
fact that by early 1941 at least 70 organizations were raising funds
for British relief.[41] On the other hand, Americans having no sympathy with Great Britain and those who put neutrality above all
other values, disapproved of both voluntary and official aid. Whenever a leading British relief organization rented headquarters it often
found that America First immediately opened an office next door,
sometimes without any rental charge at all.[42]

Several organizations provided medical aid to civilian and military
casualties. The British American Ambulance Corps raised, by the
end of 1940, over $856,000 from individuals, organizations, and
towns. This sum provided 219 desperately needed ambulances, with
blankets and medical supplies.[43] The Harvard Medical School and
the American Red Cross equipped and staffed, with a crew of seventy-
five doctors, nurses, and technicians, a pre-fabricated hospital of
twenty-two buildings with mobile units to study and check communi-
cable diseases.[44] Less successful was the appeal of the American
Medical Association and President Roosevelt for 1,000 young doctors

[41] *New York Times*, Oct. 27, 1941.

[42] Minutes of the Conference with leading British war relief agencies, May 2, 1941,
at the office of Joseph E. Davies, chairman, in "Compilation of Documents of the
President's Committee on War Relief Agencies and the President's War Relief Control Board," mimeographed copy in the National Archives, Washington, D. C. [here-
after cited as "Compilation of Documents"]. In January, 1941, the American Institute
of Public Opinion reported that two out of every three voters questioned indicated a
willingness to aid Britain even at the risk of the country's becoming involved in the war.
Only a small minority, however, advocated American entrance into the conflict: *New
York Times*, Jan. 24, 1941.

[43] *New York Times*, Jan. 1, 1941.

[44] *Ibid.*, Jan. 13, 1940; *The Times* [London] as quoted in "The American Health
Unit in Great Britain," *Science* XCIII (March 14, 1941), 251-52; *Hygeia* XIX (July,
1941), 532-35.

to care for civilians and military injured in air raids: by midsummer, 1941, only sixty-five had volunteered their services.[45]

One of the most successful of the organizations, Bundles for Britain, was started in January, 1940, when Mrs. Natalie Wales Latham, a New York society matron who had earlier originated the fad of mother-daughter matching outfits, bought a small supply of wool and opened a shop in New York in which women could knit sweaters and socks for soldiers and refugees. The place was besieged with eager volunteers. Within sixteen months the movement had expanded from a single shop in Manhattan to 975 branches scattered over the country enlisting almost a million helpers. Following the specifications of the British Admiralty, Army and Air Force, Bundles by the spring of 1941 equipped the armed forces with some 40,000 sleeveless sweaters, 10,000 sweaters with sleeves, 30,000 scarves, 20,000 pairs of wristlets and mittens, 18,000 pairs of sea-boot stockings, 50,000 pairs of socks, 2,000 jerseys, 8,000 caps, and 300 afghans. In addition it had sent abroad more than 40,000 civilian garments, twenty-four ambulances, 186 hospital beds, 2,500 children's cots, 500 sleeping bags, sixty-four blood transfusion sets, twenty-one X-ray machines, twenty-four portable surgical kits, 200 cases of surgical instruments, and other needed materials, totaling in value $1,500,000.

The Bundles for Britain were paid for by Americans of many ethnic strains, by the rich and the poor, by the obscure and by the famous. In Welch, West Virginia, representatives at the outlet of the mines collected $600 on one payday. Negro students and Indian squaws, Oregon sheepmen, blind women and children, and an Alaskan trapper made their contributions. Over $1,000,000 was raised through donations, parties, and sales of bridge sets, earrings, beach bags and like items. Mrs. Latham enlisted Mrs. Winston Churchill as an honorary member. She successfully solicited, for sale, poems and songs by well-known writers, including Christopher Morley, and paintings by British artists (25 per cent of the sale price went to the relief fund). She persuaded Lynn Fontanne and Alfred Lunt to pose for their pictures while packing bundles at the warehouse. Mrs. Latham's critics felt that her overhead was needlessly high because of her use of paid workers, and questioned her emphasis on publicity.

[45] *New York Times*, April 21, 1941, July 4, 1941.

But she was convinced that this was necessary, that, indeed, the chief value of the whole movement was to awaken Americans to British needs and to strengthen the morale of the British who found sewn in every garment the label "From your American Friends." [46]

Bundles for Britain was often on less than cordial terms with its chief rival, the British War Relief Society. Organized three months after the war broke out, the latter was ably led by Winthrop Aldrich, prominent in corporate finance. The Society's remarkable organization included committees in the New York Stock Exchange, the textile, metal, and hotel industries, in shipping, insurance, and the big retail stores, to name only a few.[47] But the giving base was even broader. Several local units of the American Labor Party collected clothing and gifts, while the administrative committee of the Party engaged in an active campaign for the British War Relief Society on the ground that a Nazi victory might easily endanger the gains labor had made in this country in the last few years.[48] Under the stimulus of the American Labor Committee to aid British Labor thirteen governors proclaimed the week of July 14 to 20, 1941, "Aid to British Labor Week." [49] The International Ladies' Garment Workers Union announced that British War Relief was the second largest recipient among the eleven relief agencies to receive the $305,000 it had allocated for overseas aid.[50] To increase the number of small contributors the British War Relief Society launched in one of its drives "My Bit for Britain" with emphasis on the exact amount and kind of relief a single dollar would buy. Social leaders, too, took a part in raising funds. New York's "cafe Anglophiles" staged a Star Spangled Ball at which Gypsy Rose Lee "dispensed her pentacled costume, star by star, for England's sake." In Seattle, socialites gambled at bingo and roulette for the Spitfire Fund and in Richmond the

[46] *New York Times*, March 1, 1940, Jan. 10, 1941; Dorothie Bobbe, "Bundles for Britain," *New York Times Magazine*, Dec. 1, 1940; "Life Calls on Mrs. Natalie Wales Latham," *Life* X (May 19, 1941), 132-34; (Jan. 6, 1941), 15-19; Geoffrey T. Hellman, "Profiles: Mrs. Wales Latham," *New Yorker* XVII (April 19, 1941), 21-26.

[47] *New York Times*, Feb. 1, 1941.

[48] *Ibid.*, Jan. 28, 1941. Irving Abrahamson, president of the New Jersey State CIO Council, in reporting the aid given to the British American Ambulance Corps for the maintenance of a group of houses to shelter British workers' children, declared in the same vein: "We consider the struggle of the British workers in resisting the forces of dictators to be the struggle of American Workers": *New York Times*, Sept. 2, 1941.

[49] *Ibid.*, June 21, 1941.

[50] *Ibid.*, Sept. 19, 1941. The largest amount was given to the JDC. Other donations went to ORT, the Jewish Labor Committee, Hebrew Sheltering Society, Russian Medical Aid, Italian Refugee and War Prisoners Relief, and the Red Cross.

first families, including that of Governor Price, graced an English relief ball.[51]

Thanks to all these and many other activities, the British War Relief Society during its first year shipped in freight-free British vessels commodities valued at $3,116,000 and sent cash gifts of $1,201,-000. By the summer of 1941 the Society had purchased 136 of the 144 vehicles comprising the so-called "Queen's Messengers." These food convoys brought speedy relief to bombed areas. When a series of air raids hit Plymouth, Bristol, Manchester, and Hull, each received help administered by the American Committee for Air Raid Relief, a subsidiary of British War Relief Society. By the summer of 1941 the Society had collected more than $10,000,000 for these and other relief programs.[52]

Overwhelming though the needs of Great Britain and the occupied countries in Europe were, China's plight could hardly be ignored. When the Japanese struck at Pearl Harbor, the Chinese had for almost a decade been resisting the war lords of Tokyo whose forces held a large part of Chiang Kai-shek's Republic. The bombing of civilian population centers and the disruption of transportation and services had reduced millions to a state of homelessness, malnutrition, and medical need that neither the Chinese government nor the national Red Cross could meet. To make matters worse, the Japanese deliberately destroyed dikes already weakened by the disrepair into which they had fallen as a result of the labor shortage incidental to the war. As a result, a flooded area of 30,000 square miles ruined harvests and homes and thrust more than 20,000,000 men, women, and children to the point of starvation. In the opinion of John Baker, an old China hand with two decades of experience in famine relief, so great a loss by a people always near the margin of subsistence is tragic beyond Western comprehension.[53]

Apart from the appeal to compassion of such mass suffering, several things assured the Chinese of a helping hand from the United States. One was the age-old tradition of American friendship which

[51] *Life* X (Jan. 6, 1941), 15-19.

[52] *Ibid.*; *Survey* LXXVIII (Sept., 1942), 231-36; *New York Times*, Jan. 5, 1941; *Christian Science Monitor Weekly Magazine*, August 2, 1941. The Christian Science Board of Directors presented BWRS with two mobile canteens.

[53] Charles H. Corbett, "How Relief Works in China," *Christian Century* LVIII (March 5, 1941), 319-20; John Earl Baker, "Fighting China's Famines" (unpublished typescript, Rare Book Department, Memorial Library, University of Wisconsin, 1943).

several thousands of missionaries refused to let their fellow countrymen forget. Another was the feeling that China was the first line of American defense in the Pacific. As the *New York Times* put it, "The Japanese have been working to instigate civil war in China. Desperate need might accentuate this tendency. Democracy, with its lesson of moderation and patience, will have a far better chance of winning, not only over foreign aggression, but over traditionalism and dissension, if America is sympathetic, understanding, and helpful." [54] Still another factor was the uneasy conscience of those who knew that many Americans were making handsome profits by selling war material to the Japanese aggressors while blockaded China, cut off from similar aid, struggled for her national life.

The first to respond were the Chinese-Americans. Merchants, laundrymen, and restaurantkeepers raised $30,000,000 (in a five-year period), a sum made possible only by real sacrifice on the part of many of the givers. Of the organized American groups the United Council for Civilian Relief of China was one of the first to get under way. It planned "bowl of rice parties" at which the price of the food went into a fund for supporting the American Bureau for Medical Aid to China.[55] The Bureau, with some seventy chapters, sent during 1938 medical supplies valued at $500,000, and built and kept up several first aid stations.[56]

In the summer of 1939 the Federal Council of Churches of Christ in America, the Foreign Missions Conference of North America, and China Famine Relief, Inc., organized the Church Committee for China Relief. In less than two years the Committee sent to the American Advisory Committee in Shanghai (composed of businessmen and missionaries) $720,000 to be distributed by missionary organizations, the International Red Cross Committee for Central China, the International Relief Committee, and other agencies. By April, 1942, the Church Committee reported that the bulk of what it had collected, $1,463,000, had been given mainly by small fractions of the denominations of some of the churches, and that the total equaled only the take of one good Joe Louis fight or less than one cent annually from each Protestant Christian.[57]

[54] *New York Times*, March 9, 1941.

[55] *Independent Woman* XVIII (Sept., 1939), 296; *New York Times*, Jan. 18, Oct. 13, Dec. 17, 1940; *Life* X (June 23, 1941), 63.

[56] "First Aid in China," *Time* XXXVII (Feb. 17, 1941), 64-66.

[57] Corbett, *Christian Century* LVIII, 319-20 and M. S. Bates, "The Church Must Still Help China," *Christian Century* LIX (April 8, 1942), 463-65.

In the spring of 1941 seven agencies committed to Chinese relief joined forces in the United China Relief, Inc.[58] James G. Blaine, grandson of the Republican leader and president of the Marine Midland Trust Company, headed the new organization. Its officers included Pearl Buck, Paul G. Hoffman, Robert Sproul of the University of California, David O. Selznick, Thomas W. Lamont, John D. Rockefeller III, Henry Luce, and Wendell Willkie.[59] Eleanor Roosevelt served as honorary chairman and, presently, a list of advisors of well-known national figures was announced.[60]

That United China Relief was not without political overtones was clear despite the declaration that the organization was "concerned only with the human needs of a people making a magnificent fight, in the face of overwhelming odds, to establish themselves as the first great independent nation in Asia with democratic objectives." [61] In proclaiming a China Week, Governor Herbert H. Lehman appealed for support regardless of race, creed or political beliefs and declared that "China must be recognized as the frontier of democracy in the far Pacific." [62] Another supporter, William Allen White, wrote that "if America is to be free, Americans must help wherever freedom is threatened." [63] Henry Luce, speaking through *Life*, admitted that there were many practical reasons "why a democracy like the United States should try to help a democracy like China," an obvious one being that China was fighting a potential enemy of America. Luce added, however, that "somehow the political reasons seem pale beside the need for saving China some of the epic pain she is suffering." [64]

Writing from the left, Kate Mitchell regretted that the board of the new organization listed no representative of labor, and expressed concern lest its financial and industrial members shape policy in such a way as not to embarrass the State Department in its dealings

[58] The organizations were the American Bureau for Medical Aid to China, the China Emergency Relief Committee, the American Committee for Chinese War Orphans, Church Committee for China Relief, American Committee for Industrial Cooperatives, China Aid Council, and the Associated Boards for Christian Colleges in China.

[59] *New York Times*, March 3, 1941.

[60] This included Cleveland H. Dodge, Milton G. Ochs, Gifford Pinchot, Eugene O'Neill, Katharine Cornell, Booth Tarkington, James Truslow Adams, and Fiorello LaGuardia.

[61] *New York Times*, March 3, 1941.

[62] *Ibid.*, May 7, 1941.

[63] *Ibid.*, April 24, 1941.

[64] *Life* X (June 23, 1941), 59.

with foreign powers and with little reference to the encouragement in China of the truly democratic forces which were struggling against a native bureaucracy that could hardly be thought of as democratic.[65]

United China Relief at once launched a campaign for $5,000,000 to enlarge the work of the cooperating agencies.[66] By autumn the national chairman could announce to a cheering rally that $2,000,000 had been collected toward the much-publicized goal. Now as earlier, stage and radio stars provided entertainment. Hollywood also did its part. On a nation-wide radio hookup Shirley Temple asked children to send nickels and dimes to her, or to their favorite star. In many communities to which such messages came citizens arranged luncheons, dinners, and teas. Sometimes parades marched in which Chinese-Americans took part. In South Bend, the tiny Chinese-American community donated and prepared a meal of watermelon seeds, chow mein, and ice cream which 750 citizens consumed with chopsticks as they heard the speakers (Paul Hoffman, Louis Bromfield, and Consul General Chang-lik Chen) describe conditions in China and appeal for cash. On this occasion $15,000 was raised. In other places college rallies augmented the fund. Speakers furnished by United China Relief publicized the plight of China at meetings of women's clubs and service organizations. In New York, Thomas J. Watson, president of IBM, Vincent Astor, John D. Rockefeller III, and Thomas Lamont, among others, attended a Chinese costume party at which guests played Chinese games and even braved a rainstorm to ride on a Chinese junk which conveniently put in at the dock of the New York City River Club.[67]

The funds thus collected were used not only for relief but for other needs, including support of the crippled Christian colleges in China. Some participants looked beyond mere relief and keeping existing agencies alive. Thus the American Committee in Aid of Chinese Industrial Cooperatives, an affiliated agency, supported 3,000 small-scale industrial units which employed 100,000 refugees and produced needed medicines, consumer goods, and capital goods and, however dubious from the point of view of American neutrality, military supplies as well. In one month the materials made in these cooperatives were valued at approximately $500,000.[68]

[65] Kate Mitchell, "United China Relief Inc.," *Amerasia* V (April, 1941), 63-65.
[66] *New York Times*, March 3, 1941.
[67] "China Relief, U. S. Opens Purse," *Life* X (June 23, 1941), 59-67.
[68] *New York Times*, May 28, 1941.

Before considering the relations of the relief agencies to the federal government during the years of neutrality (September, 1939, to December, 1941), it may be useful to summarize contributions by voluntary agencies and to indicate general trends. This is not easy to do since many of the available reports are by calendar year, rather than by month. Moreover, the American Red Cross used not only voluntary contributions but government allocations and its own capital funds; additionally, Red Cross expenditures for overseas relief were not included in the figures kept by the State Department on the work of voluntary agencies since, under existing laws, the Red Cross did not have to register with the Department. Similarly contributions to all agencies for Finland and China did not appear in the State Department's reports since the President had not declared these countries at war and therefore subject to legal regulations. The following table is suggestive. It should be kept in mind, of course, that the figures for 1939 include the nine months prior to the outbreak of the war in Europe in September, as well as contributions made between that time and the end of the calendar year: [69]

Table I. Totals of Contributions Collected and Disbursed by Registered Voluntary Agencies for Foreign War Relief

	1939	1940	1941
Funds Received:	$2,546,341	$17,969,032	$28,541,644
Funds Spent for Relief Overseas:	1,608,886	12,399,467	23,614,026
Funds Spent for Administration, Publicity, Promotion:	146,138	1,733,636	3,741,995
Unexpended Balance, Including Cost of Goods Still on Hand:	791,317	4,542,418	5,735,523
Percentage of Total Administration Expenses to Cash Receipts:	5.7%	9.6%	13.1%

In other words, during the period of neutrality, the registered voluntary agencies received $49,000,000 in cash contributions, plus substantial donations of gifts in kind. The value of exports sent abroad by the agencies registered with the State Department reached $50,000,000 for the three years of neutrality. In the same period, 1939-1941, the Department of Commerce reports for total expenditures of private American institutions abroad, Protestant, Catholic, Jewish, and nonsectarian (including the Red Cross), reveal that

[69] U. S. Department of State, President's War Relief Control Board, *Voluntary War Relief During World War II*, Department of State Publication 2566 (Washington: Govt. Printing Office, 1946), 49; Press Release, Sept. 30, 1942, in "Compilation of Documents."

$174,400,000 was sent, in cash and supplies, to all foreign nations whether involved in the war or not.[70] This would include the work of the Finnish and Chinese agencies as well as relief ventures in Latin America, Africa, and other areas outside the scope of conflict.

By one estimate the amount given for overseas purposes between the outbreak of the European war and Pearl Harbor was 30 per cent of the total American contribution to all private and welfare agencies, foreign and domestic. By an official estimate 80 per cent of the funds reported by the registered agencies engaged in overseas relief came from those having a special interest through ties of sentiment or ethnic relationship to the countries aided.[71]

In view of the great needs abroad and of what Americans spent on luxuries for themselves, many felt that the giving was much too small. This was particularly true among a growing number who believed that Great Britain, the Soviet Union, and China were making great sacrifices in fighting for the freedom to which America gave such eloquent lip service.

A not uncommon criticism was that the overseas relief organizations were given to racketeering. A "Prince Alexis" announced in New York a fashion show and "war relief" party. His mistake was to solicit Fifth Avenue business men for advertising, one of whom called the police who picked up the bogus prince. Salesmen marketed tickets for boat passage from Oslo, Norway, to Portland, Oregon, in an intriguing way. Norwegian-Americans were approached by furtive agents who gave them letters from a mysterious Captain Johnson. A "mercy ship" equipped to bring 3,000 refugees was ready to sail except for needed food and supplies estimated to cost a few hundred dollars. Secrecy was important lest "foreign agents" discover the plan

---

[70] Dickens and Maffry, *Balance of International Payments of the United States in 1939*, U. S. Department of Commerce, Foreign and Domestic Commerce Bureau, Economic Series 8 (Washington: Govt. Printing Office, 1940), 70; U. S. Department of Commerce, Foreign and Domestic Commerce Bureau, *International Transactions of the United States During the War, 1940-45*, Economic Series 65 (Washington: Govt. Printing Office, 1948), 208. Part of the $174,400,000 reported by the Commerce Department was used for missionary maintenance which normally might not be considered in terms of voluntary relief. However, during the chaotic years just preceding America's entry into the war, American missionaries, especially those heavily concentrated in China, carried a major share of the relief burden of foreign peoples affected by hostile bombing and invasion.

[71] *New York Times*, Oct. 5, 1941; Arthur C. Ringland, "The Organization of Voluntary Foreign Aid, 1939-1953," *U. S. Department of State Bulletin* XXX (March 15, 1954), 384.

and sink the ship. Scores of Norwegian-Americans were taken in, and Captain Johnson was never caught.[72]

Jonathan Daniels, while suspecting that racketeers often befuddled the issue, was probably right in holding that such rascals as Captain Johnson were in some ways less dangerous than men of good will among whom the growth of competing organizations led to inefficiency and duplication of effort. "If the good organizations will get together," Daniels wrote, "we people in the country will have less trouble in spotting the racketeers. Today the confusion of good works is a rank-growing jungle in which racketeers with only a cash interest in our hearts get beyond them into our pocketbooks. Honest directors of war charity," Daniels concluded, "must thin this forest, if they hope to get rid of the weeds." [73]

Many well-wishers felt uneasy at reports that some overseas relief organizations opened their doors too generously to publicity-seekers and lavished money needlessly in fund-raising spectacles. In describing Chicago's March of Freedom for Greek Relief, one observer declared that this serious effort was in marked contrast to many other drives characterized by "a welter of extravagance, saloon socialites, and press agentry in which original humanitarian motives seemed hopelessly subordinated." This writer felt that relief was being harmed more than helped by the dilettantes who noisily appeared and reappeared at its big city shows. "Many begin to wonder," he concluded, "how many dollars were left when all the bills for ballrooms and champagne had been paid." [74] At least in one large city the answer was at hand, for after the promoter and commissary had been paid, and after the cost of "incidentals" had been met, only $20 was left to send to Great Britain from the $2,300 collected from the sale of tickets for a help England dinner.[75]

Bad management or allocation of collections to purposes other than overseas relief also existed. The War Association of American Youth, Inc., which cited the President's mother and other notables as honorary committee members, reported such high operating costs as to have failed to send anything at all in the stated area of relief at the time of registration. In one case administration and publicity

[72] Frank W. Brock, "Fake, Hoax, and Charity," *Survey Graphic* XXXI (March, 1942), 158-59.
[73] Jonathan Daniels, "A Native at Large," *Nation* CLII (April 12, 1941), 436.
[74] "U. S. Balls, Brawls, Pagents and Parades Turn War Relief into Show Business," *Life* X (Jan. 6, 1941), 15-19.
[75] *Survey Graphic* XXXI (March, 1942), 158-59.

costs ran to 98 per cent, in two others, to over 90 per cent, in still another to 80 per cent, and in several, to more than 40 per cent. On the other hand, the Greek War Relief Association, singled out for its efficiency and dedication, spent only four per cent and the British War Relief Society only 8 per cent for overhead. The average seems to have been around 10 per cent.[76]

Another problem arose in relation to the provision in the Neutrality Act forbidding aid to belligerent countries by voluntary organizations in effect acting on behalf of the belligerent countries. In the spring of 1941 Secretary of State Hull revoked the licenses of the Federation of the Italian World War Veterans in the United States of America and its Providence ladies auxiliary branch on the ground that its distributors in Italy were so closely tied to the government that they must be regarded as acting in its behalf. Shortly after this the State Department revoked the licenses of five other relief agencies for "failing to comply with rules and regulations." [77]

In the context of such considerations Secretary Hull wrote to the President on March 3, 1941, noting that the natural concern of the American people to provide in every way possible for the young men who had been called for military service was likely to increase. In view of this and of the growing danger that unless the volunteer agencies for foreign relief were better coordinated the fine human instincts calling them into existence were likely to be frustrated, Hull felt that a more effective regulation of all agencies ought to be instituted. He called attention to the fact that many agencies in foreign relief were raising funds without full knowledge of the relief sources already at hand, of the needs actually requiring relief, and of the limitations on shipping, particularly in the case of the British. It also was advisable, Hull went on, for all overseas relief efforts to be considered in their relation to the program of the American Red Cross which held an official status under American law and international agreements, and had special responsibilities both to foreign relief and to the welfare of our own armed forces. Hull suggested the President appoint a committee "to examine the entire problem and to make recommendations as to what steps might be taken to preserve local and essential welfare services, and to maintain a balance between the facilities and resources available for foreign relief with particular regard to the financing of our new welfare activities

[76] *New York Times*, May 2, Oct. 5, 1941.
[77] *Ibid.*, May 11, 1941.

in connection with national defence measures." [78] In other words, charity abroad was not to militate against charity at home.

President Roosevelt named a committee of three. The chairman, Joseph E. Davies, a wealthy lawyer, had served in various capacities both in the Wilson and Roosevelt administrations, including diplomatic posts in Belgium and Soviet Russia. Frederick P. Keppel, formerly Dean of Columbia College, had given up the presidency of the Carnegie Corporation for war work in Washington. The third member, Charles Phelps Taft, a son of the former President, was a leading figure in legal and philanthropic circles in Cincinnati. Appropriately, the committee began its work by inviting communications from the voluntary agencies, many of which in replying expressed pleasure at the proposal of the Secretary of State for a centralized agency to gather information in the whole field and make it available to the voluntary agencies. [79]

On May 2, 1941, the committee met for exploratory talks with representatives of the leading agencies concerned with relief for Britain. Winthrop Aldrich of the British War Relief Society was asked whether the cash contributions of his organization did not merely supply the London government with additional dollar exchange with which to purchase military supplies. The New York banker admitted that such contributions did relieve "a half day's pressure on the sterling market"; but in view of the "inconsequential" relationship of this to total British government expenditures, the committee was not inclined to press the point that such an operation might bring American technical neutrality into question.

The discussion explored the extent to which the several agencies concerned with British relief competed against each other and militated against the fund-raising activities of other agencies, particularly the new United Service Organization, an agency for the American military. Chairman Davies felt that the British-oriented agencies ought to soft-pedal their own programs, at least for the time, to avoid enmity and to give such newcomers as the USO a chance to raise their quotas. Members of the Committee also felt that the British relief agencies ought to avoid the numerous and irksome fund-raising campaigns, especially tag days and "can rattling," of which the public

[78] Cordell Hull to Franklin D. Roosevelt, March 3, 1941, in "Compilation of Documents."

[79] U. S. Department of State, Press Release, March 20, 1941, in "Compilation of Documents."

had become critical. In reply, representatives of the agencies insisted that Americans were spontaneously eager to support the British in their tragic plight and would do so even if the agencies soft-pedaled their work, and that, moreover, the fund-raising campaigns, regardless of the amounts raised, had proved to be important morale builders. Spokesmen for the agencies did admit that when one supported a certain kind of program, another was apt to follow its example lest it lose some of its own constituency. On the other hand, the fierce competition had sometimes led to useful new ways of getting money. There seemed to be general unwillingness to accept any suggestion that the larger British relief agencies merge. Yet, after Davies remarked that unless the agencies themselves cooperated to avoid duplication of effort, the local community chests or the federal government might intervene, the group agreed to try to work out some of the problems that had been raised.[80]

After studying the Canadian National Advisory Board, which allocated a specific time in which nation-wide fund-collecting agencies might conduct their campaigns, the President's Committee on War Relief Agencies recommended a similar practice. The proposal that the State Department extend its supervision over the hitherto unlicensed agencies operating in the so-called nonbelligerent countries, similarly reflected the tendency of the Committee to think in terms of a larger measure of government control over the private agencies. In some degree the same thinking was reflected in the recommendation that the functions of the Red Cross, a quasi-official body, be more fully recognized, especially in cases where these functions were operative in the voluntary agencies. An even more marked indication of the trend toward closer government oversight was the proposal that the State Department revoke at some future date the licenses of agencies operating in the belligerent states and, before issuing new ones, require the submission of satisfactory proof that these agencies were in a position to transmit efficiently and economically the relief for which they planned to solicit funds, and without duplicating the work of the Red Cross and other existing agencies.[81]

The Committee, through its general influence and its policy of making recommendations to the State Department in matters of

[80] Minutes of the conference with leading British war relief agencies, May 2, 1941, at the office of Joseph E. Davies, chairman, the President's Committee on War Relief Agencies, in "Compilation of Documents."

[81] President's Committee on War Relief Agencies, *Interim Report*, October 4, 1941 (mimeographed copy released for the press), 13-16.

licensing, was in part responsible for the elimination of competing and overlapping agencies and splinter groups, and for the merging of local and national agencies into larger organizations. The table indicates the trend: [82]

Table II. Number of Foreign War-Relief Registrations Approved and Withdrawn Annually from September, 1939, Through December, 1945

Year	Number of Agencies Approved During the Year	Number of Licenses Withdrawn	Number of Agencies in Operation at Year's End
(Department of State Registrations of Voluntary Foreign Relief Agencies Operating in Belligerent Countries)			
1939	235	22	213
1940	173	90	296
1941	126	122	300
1942	11	88	—
(The President's War Relief Control Board—All Foreign War Relief)			
1942	9	41	191
1943	15	104	102
1944	10	25	87
1945	12	9	90
Total	591	501	—

The growing emphasis on government regulation of the voluntary associations engaged in overseas relief was not the only indication that philanthropy was associated with national policy. When Hitler watched the British retreat from Dunkirk the government at Washington, unable to act quickly for legal reasons, approached United States Steel which, with other corporate contributors, shipped a collection of vital guns and ammunition to England in time to rearm the British troops.[83]

Providing food to the hungry in Nazi-occupied lands on the other hand conflicted with national policy as President Roosevelt interpreted it. By the end of June, 1940, Belgium and Holland, under Nazi occupation, faced starvation. When Secretary of the Interior Harold L. Ickes asked President Roosevelt if the American Red Cross planned to go into Nazi-occupied countries to supply those in need, the President's reply was in the negative. In the summer the Minister of Norway asked Roosevelt whether Red Cross relief for his country

[82] President's War Relief Control Board, *Voluntary War Relief During World War II*, 8-9.
[83] Roger M. Blough, *Free Man and the Corporation* (New York: McGraw-Hill, 1959), 118.

was possible. The President asked what he thought should be done. Minister Morgenstern replied that, speaking officially, relief should be given; but unofficially admitted that everything sent would be taken by the Germans.[84]

Having taken the initiative in the relief of Poland and Finland in the early stages of the conflict and remembering both the horror of starvation during and after the First World War and the success of the American Relief Administration in fighting it, Herbert Hoover again stepped into the picture. As the English and Scots fought for their countries in the Battle for Britain, the former American President asked the British to relax their blockade of Europe and to permit food to enter the occupied lands. His representative in Berlin had asked the Germans to promise not to confiscate such food. The needy countries could and would pay for the food.[85] Prime Minister Churchill, in announcing Hoover's proposal in the House of Commons, maintained that the relief of occupied Europe would directly or indirectly help the Germans: for even if airtight controls could be established, the Germans would be then freed from the obligation of providing for the occupied nations and could thus prolong their capacity to resist the British blockade.[86] The British government in informing Washington of its opposition to relaxing the blockade urged that to do so would prolong the war with all its suffering and lengthen the enslavement of the German people and those in conquered countries.[87] Secretary of State Hull agreed with the President and Ickes that the British position was the correct one.[88]

What followed was a hotly contested struggle of the conflicting positions for public support. In October, 1940, fifteen leading Americans, including the presidents of the American Federation of Labor, of Harvard, Princeton, and the Union Theological Seminary, issued

---

[84] Ickes, *Secret Diary*, III, 223-25, 274.

[85] *New York Times*, August 11, 1940.

[86] *The Times* [London], August 21, 1940. Churchill did, in this speech in the House of Commons on August 20, 1940, promise to arrange in advance for the speedy entry of food into any part of the enslaved area when it had been wholly cleared of German forces and had genuinely regained freedom. "We shall," he continued, "do our best to encourage the building up of reserves of food all over the world so that there will always be held up before the eyes of the peoples of Europe, including—I say it deliberately—the German and Austrian peoples, the certainty that the shattering of the Nazi power will bring them all immediate food, freedom, and peace." *Foreign Policy Reports* XVIII (October 15, 1942), 204.

[87] *Papers Relating to the Foreign Relations of the United States* (Washington, Govt. Printing Office, 1940), II, 537-38.

[88] Cordell Hull, *The Memoirs of Cordell Hull* (2 vols.; New York: Macmillan, 1948), I, 805.

a statement opposing the feeding of occupied Europe on the ground that the British blockade was an indispensable means of defending all democratic nations. "Between the agony of empty stomachs for a time in one part of the world and the agony of stricken souls in every part of the world there can be but one choice," the statement contended. "By the declared intention of the totalitarian powers, this is a total war, imperilling the life of every citizen in the nations within its orbit. No one can hope to evade a share in the common suffering." [89]

As soon as the presidential election was over, Hoover resumed his campaign for an alternative policy. He was aided by the Committee on Food for the Small Democracies—Belgium, Holland, Norway, Finland, and Poland. The Committee included 600 prominent men and women and organizations in 1,500 cities and towns. Hoover himself spoke and wrote continuously.

The question, the former President insisted, was a practical one. At least 15,000,000 human beings were in peril of starvation and pestilence. The experience of the Belgian Relief Commission in the First World War proved that it had been possible to provide food, without military benefit or loss to either side, and that this relief had saved 10,000,000 lives. The plan involved no charity on the part of Americans: the governments-in-exile of the small nations that had fought for democracy until German arms crushed their resistance were eager to pay, with funds in hand, for food from our supluses and from those of other neutrals. Nor was this food to be sent through hazardous seas in American vessels. If the Nazis agreed to provide some food and accept neutral supervision of that imported from neutral countries, there could be no military advantage for them. Moreover, the plan had still other practical aspects. It would actually help the British: food permitted to reach the suffering peoples in the occupied countries would keep their good will, a valuable asset. If, on the other hand, food were not permitted to reach them, they would have to seek work in German munition plants and thus strengthen the Nazi war economy. Finally, if on experiment the Nazis violated their guarantees, the whole thing could be ended at once. [90]

Hoover did not explicitly answer Churchill's charge that American food would relieve the Germans of having to feed people in the oc-

[89] *New York Times*, Oct. 6, 1940.
[90] *New York Times*, Nov. 16, 1940; Herbert Hoover, *Addresses Upon the American Road, 1940-1941* (New York: Scribner's, 1941), 144 ff.

cupied countries and that this imported food would thus help the Nazi war effort regardless of any controls that might be effected. Nor did he consider the possibilities that the Nazis might force men and women in the occupied countries to labor in war plants or that starvation itself might provoke internal revolt against the Nazis.

Hoover's moral argument was nevertheless a powerful one. The United States, he insisted, had a responsibility toward the nations that had fought to maintain freedom and democratic ideals. Above all else was the obligation of Christian compassion which had inspired the vast fabric of benevolent institutions dedicated to help the weak and unfortunate and which could not turn its back when the lives of more than ten million people were at stake. With aid being given to preserve free nations still in combat, was it not right to suggest that other free peoples, friends of America through her whole existence, also ought to be allowed to live? "I sometimes think," Hoover lamented, "the world is to be saved from everything but starvation."[91]

It is hard to assess the reactions of the public to Hoover's eloquent appeals, presented with strong emphasis on the practicableness of his proposal. Roosevelt feared that the publicity would increase anti-British feeling since the British would be put in the position of refusing to accept a plan designed to save millions of lives without, presumably, disadvantaging their own interests. Thus the White House welcomed the promise of Thomas Lamont to do what he could to "keep Hoover in control."[92] More significant was the presentation of 6,000 petitions to Congress, allegedly representing 20,000,-000 citizens. These urged the State Department to initiate negotiations for international action for the relief of Belgium, Norway, Holland, Finland, Poland, and other similarly afflicted areas.[93] That the resolution which Congress passed asking for such action was ignored or, at least that those chiefly concerned had no knowledge of any action, seemed to Hugh Gibson, an associate of Hoover, "a strange spectacle in a democracy."[94]

On the other hand, a Gallup Poll left considerable doubt about the public's position. Asked whether the United States should try

---

[91] Herbert Hoover, "When Winter Comes to Europe," *Collier's Magazine* CVI (Nov. 23, 1940), 72; Hoover, *Addresses Upon the American Road*, 154.

[92] Ickes, *Secret Diary*, III, 385.

[93] *Congressional Record*, 76th Cong., 3d Sess., 1940, LXXXVI, Pt. 6, 6768.

[94] Hugh Gibson, *The Road to Foreign Policy* (Garden City: Doubleday, Doran, 1944), 222.

to send food in American ships to France, Holland and Belgium if these countries faced starvation, 62 per cent of those who replied opposed any such action. Questioned whether they favored sending food if some of it went to Hitler, 78 per cent of the sample replied in the negative. Hoover, though, insisted that the poll was invalid. It failed to include his stipulations for the protection of food from seizure by the German military. The questions asked also implied that the food was to be paid for by American money and sent through the war zone in American ships.[95]

Although Hoover continued to urge an experimental action in Belgium, with the additional safeguard of having all food distributed only at soup kitchens, the project never got off the ground. One reason was that while Berlin did promise to meet some of Hoover's conditions, its response was not regarded as adequate in either London or Washington. Another reason for the outcome of the campaign was that many doubted, even in the face of impressive evidence, that the conditions were as bad as Hoover represented. But the chief reason was that both the British and the Roosevelt administration remained convinced that the relaxation of the blockade, even for a trial feeding of three million Belgians, could only strengthen Germany.[96]

In view of this outcome it seemed clear, especially with the collapse of France and the imminent danger that Britain too might be crushed, that the government had some obligation to supplement voluntary contributions for war relief. It is true that the disadvantages of such action were noted by the *Commonweal:* relief through government appropriations lacked "that personal element which imparts to charity its true nature and its characteristic graces" and, moreover, left the taxpayer generally unaware of the connection between what he paid and what his money did.[97] But for the most part, such objections were not pressed. Indeed, they were not even mentioned during the discussion in Congress of the proposal for government support of overseas need. Jerry Voorhis, a New Deal Democrat, for once found himself agreeing with Hamilton Fish, a conservative Republican and an isolationist, that the government ought to purchase surplus farm commodities for overseas relief. Fish added that $50,000,000 was a mere drop in the bucket, that within the next few years America would have to spend millions to keep Europe alive. But it was, he continued, a moral obligation to do so. And, he concluded, let what was given be given not as a loan, but outright with no expectation of anything in return, not even thanks.[98] The act appropriating the $50,000,000 specified that it be used by such government agency or agencies as the President designated for the purchase, exclusively within the United States, of agricultural, medical, and any other relief supplies for sick and destitute people as a result of hostilities or invasion, the actual allocation to be made by the American Red Cross or such agencies as the President indicated.[99] The appropriation was used by the secretaries of agriculture and the treasury for purchases and for transporting and distributing supplies.[100] Ten days after Pearl Harbor Congress appropriated an additional $35,000,000 to be used in the same way to relieve victims of hostilities and invasions.[101]

Before the allocation of these government funds the role of the Red Cross in the Second World War had been a cautious one. In part this was the result of the fact that the medical units in the foreign national Red Cross organizations were much better prepared for the conflict than had been the case in 1914, when emergency units from America had been welcomed. More important, operations were far more difficult in the Second World War than in the first by reason of the free bombing of hospitals, the disruption of transportation systems, and the restrictions that the belligerents imposed on Red Cross activities.[102] But the most important reason for the limited role of the American Red Cross in overseas relief was its dependence on the public for funds, a public which, as the earlier lukewarm response to the million-dollar campaign for the relief of the victims of war and famine in China showed, was either indifferent to such pleas or fearful that even a humanitarian involvement might lead to outright participation in the world struggle. On the other hand, the Red Cross, as a quasi-official organ, was closely tied to the White House, the State Department, and the War and Navy Departments.

[98] *Congressional Record*, 76th Cong., 3d Sess., 1940, LXXXVI, Pt. 8, 8163, 8865.

[99] U. S., *Statutes at Large*, LIV, Pt. 1, 627.

[100] U. S., Congress, House, *Draft of a Proposed Provision Pertaining to the Appropriation for Refugee Relief*, 1941, 77th Cong., 1st Sess., 1941, House Doc. 169, 1-2.

[101] U. S., Congress, Senate, *Appropriations, Budget Estimates, Etc.*, 77th Cong., 1st Sess., 1941, Senate Doc. 114, 515.

[102] *New York Times*, May 5, 1940.

Its officers did not regard the organization as truly independent, and, indeed, it was not.[103]

Thus between the outbreak of the war in September, 1939, and the decision of Congress in June, 1940, to make the Red Cross the dispensing agent of the government appropriation, the aggregate figure for war relief in Europe, including the supplies donated by the chapters, was only $2,662,000. This had been used for medical and other supplies to Finland, Poland, and the refugees in France. The supplies had been distributed through national organizations in the receiving countries.[104]

With the Nazi invasion of the Low Countries and the fall of France in the early summer of 1940, the American Red Cross launched its first wartime drive for funds. The goal was set at $10,000,000, to be presently doubled. The President urged Americans "to respond quickly and generously to this appeal" and Eleanor Roosevelt reminded Americans "if we turn away from the need of others, we align ourselves with those forces which are bringing about the suffering and which we must eventually try to defeat." [105] The public, now awakened to the seriousness of the situation, responded well: within eight weeks more than $20,000,000 had been raised.[106]

By December, 1941, the Red Cross had sent abroad in supplies and provisions for civilian war sufferers more than $50,000,000. It had spent more than two-thirds of the $20,000,000 it had raised in its special war drive. The rest represented contributions of local chapters and of goods made available through government appropriation.[107]

None of this relief went, after June, 1940, to countries controlled or occupied by the Nazis. In July a million-dollar cargo of hospital equipment and foodstuffs reached Marseilles, to be followed by several other cargoes, for use among the millions of refugees of unoccupied France. In November, 1940, the Red Cross decided to curtail its relief program in France because of difficulties of getting shipments through the British blockade. By January, 1941, however, London, at the request of President Roosevelt, agreed to permit the American Red Cross to deliver food and medicine to unoccupied France through the British blockade.[108]

[103] Dulles, *The American Red Cross*, 340 ff.
[104] *Ibid.*, 349.
[105] *New York Times*, May 27, 1940.
[106] *Ibid.*, July 27, 1940.
[107] Dulles, *The American Red Cross*, 350.
[108] *New York Times*, Nov. 9, 1940, Jan. 9, 1941.

Great Britain, which was bearing the burden of resisting Germany, received the greater part of what the Red Cross had to give, the actual distribution being made by the British Red Cross and the Women's Voluntary Services for Civilian Defense. Thanks to the grants given, nursery schools for bombed-out children were kept open, canteens were provided in air-raid shelters, and medical supplies and clothing were distributed. Between June, 1940, and Pearl Harbor, the Red Cross also distributed aid in the British Middle East, Spain, Greece, China, and the USSR.

In accounting for its expenditures between the Congressional grant of $50,000,000 in June, 1940, and April 30, 1942, the Red Cross reported that it had helped over 15,000,000 persons in Asia, Africa, and Europe. Apart from the government appropriation, it gave substantial relief from its own funds. To the overall program, volunteers gave their services: some 1,500,000 women sewed, without pay, garments for refugees from textiles for which the Red Cross paid $17,000,000 from its total working fund.[109] The countries receiving major allotments of garments, food, medical and other supplies are indicated in the following table.[110]

Table III. Relief Distributed Between July, 1940, and April 30, 1942

Country	Total Relief Supplied by American Red Cross	Amount of the Total Purchased with U. S. Government Funds
British Middle East	$ 2,295,651	$ 1,457,650
China (since summer, 1940)	3,842,365	3,113,940
Finland	2,396,608	1,480,995
France	6,136,526	3,597,840
Fr. Equatorial Africa	140,500	132,980
Great Britain	32,861,145	14,910,872
Greece	462,937	38,209
Iceland	45,161	40,577
Spain	1,687,748	1,613,787
USSR	3,766,631	3,177,540
Yugoslavia	60,923	—
Total all countries	$60,732,195	$31,909,401

Spokesmen for the voluntary agencies felt that the $50,000,000 appropriation for overseas relief did not make up for the restrictions on the admission into the United States of victims of Nazi and fascist

[109] U. S., Congress, House, *Refugee and Foreign War Relief Programs*, 77th Cong., 2d Sess., 1942, House Document 807, viii.

[110] *Ibid.*, 1-13.

persecution. In 1939, at a hearing on a bill to admit beyond the quota limits 20,000 German refugee children, Congressmen asked whether there were not already enough orphans in the United States, and why other countries did not shoulder their own responsibilities. The bill never even left the committee.[111] Such a position seemed startling and shameful when contrasted with the British acceptance of any refugees reaching England's shores, and with the hospitality of the Dominican Republic in opening its doors to those with no place to go.

Not that Washington did nothing at all. President Roosevelt, it will be recalled, initiated in 1938 a conference of diplomats at Evian to consider the refugee problem and continued to express sympathy for the increasing thousands of these helpless and hopeless human beings. The President's Advisory Committee on Political Refugees, created in July, 1940, to unblock quotas and give preference to those in special danger, eased the entrance of 2,000 political refugees in the twelve-month period in which it functioned.[112] Also, in the summer of 1940, the Department of State and the Department of Justice simplified the reception of refugee children from Great Britain. Under the new program children under sixteen, on proof of an intention to return home after the war, could enter on a visitor's visa.[113] A month later, in August, 1940, Congress authorized American vessels to help evacuate children to the United States if all belligerents agreed to their safe passage. The Germans, however, rejected such a stipulation, making the refusal the more pointed by torpedoing the *City of Benares*, a British vessel carrying many refugee children.[114] It was not until 1944 that the American government created a "free port" near Oswego, New York, to promote the objectives of the recently established War Refugee Board and to relieve overtaxed supply resources in Italy. A thousand refugees of various national origins were given sanctuary in an abandoned army camp enclosed with wire and guarded by soldiers. To one critic they seemed to be like so much "stored merchandise" allowed to stay on the chance that they might some day find something besides a temporary haven. Voluntary agencies and local citizens provided for education, recrea-

111 U. S., Congress, House, Immigration and Naturalization Committee, Hearings, *Hearings, Admission of German Refugee Children*, 76th Cong., 1st Sess., 1939; Pickett, *For More Than Bread*, 15.
112 Maurice R. Davie, *Refugees in America* (New York: Harper, 1947), 31-32.
113 *New York Times*, July 13, 1940.
114 *Ibid.*, Sept. 23, 1940.

tion, and worship. At the end of the war the great majority received permanent visas and resettled in 65 cities in 19 states.[115]

More might have been done, even under the immigration quotas. The law authorized the admission of 153,774 persons a year, exclusive of those entering the country from the Western Hemisphere. The quota, as the figures show, was never filled.[116]

Table IV. Foreign Immigration and Emigration to the U. S., 1939–1942

Fiscal Year	Number of Immigrants	Emigrant Aliens Leaving U. S.
1939	82,998	26,651
1940	70,756	21,461
1941	51,776	17,115
1942	28,781 *	7,363

* 10,000 from Canada, 5,000 from Latin America.

What was the trouble? Many felt that government regulations rather than any lack of transportation or opposition on the part of the public was the key.[117] The mere mechanical business of getting a visa for a would-be immigrant was so involved that, as one in a position to know put it, only sponsors "plentifully endowed with time and money can afford to undertake the task of vouching for an immigrant." After the affidavit of support had been obtained, every visa applicant had to be approved by an interdepartmental committee representing War, Navy, and State. To add to the difficulties, no visa could be granted to anyone with a close relative in an Axis-

[115] *Commonweal* XL (May 12, 1944), 76-77; *Life* XVIII (August 21, 1944), 25; Edward B. Marks, Jr., *Token Shipment: The Story of America's War Refugee Shelter*, U. S. Interior Department, War Relocation Authority (Washington: Govt. Printing Office, 1946); Harold L. Ickes, Secretary of the Interior to the President, June 14, 1945, Truman Papers, OF 127 (1945), Truman Library; William Rosenwald, National Refugee Service, to Harry S. Truman, Feb. 2, 1946, Truman Papers OF 127 (Jan.-Aug.,1946), Truman Library. In the summer of 1945 79 per cent of the 523 persons responding to a questionnaire favored giving the Oswego refugees freedom and a chance to remain in the country, 17 per cent were opposed, and 4 per cent were uncertain, Joseph H. Smart, Friends of Fort Ontario Guest-Refugees to Dillon S. Myer, Director, War Relocation Authority, Sept. 10, 1945, Truman Papers, OF 127 (1945), Truman Library.

[116] U. S. Bureau of the Census, *Historical Statistics of the United States* (Washington: Govt. Printing Office, 1960), 63-64; "Asylum in Britain and America," *New Republic* CIX (August 30, 1943), 311-13.

[117] According to a survey conducted by the American Institute of Public Opinion in June, 1940, more than 5,000,000 American families expressed a willingness to take child refugees from Britain and France and to care for them until the end of the war. Of those polled, 58 per cent said that they believed English and French women as well as children should be admitted to the country for the duration of the war: *New York Times*, June 26, 1940.

dominated country. Thus interminable delays doomed an unknown number of human beings who, when the longed-for visa at last came through, were in a territory that meantime had fallen into Nazi hands, or in a concentration camp, or in a grave.[118]

The problem of helping refugees was accentuated not only by government regulations but by the attitude of officials. One experienced hand wrote that those immediately concerned with the issue struggled against great odds "in an atmosphere of opposition and suspicion with minimum support from the official makers of our foreign policies." The refugee effort, it seemed, was "at best a stepchild in Washington, to be beaten and buffeted, and at worst a football for anti-Semitism and for petty bureaucrats, including those who take delight in sabotaging the President's program just because it is his." The word "refugee," continued this observer, meant "alien" to the bureaucrat; "secret agent" to the military.[119] The reaction of one official to the circumspect proposal of Clarence Pickett of the American Friends Service Committee may have been exceptional, but it is part of the record. Knowing that American consulates abroad were hopelessly understaffed as the personnel tried to cope with long lines of waiting refugees, Pickett offered to provide from private sources helpers with proper language equipment and training. But he met with a cold rebuff from the official who replied that if more staff were wanted the State Department would ask Congress for supplementary appropriations.[120]

That many officials sympathized with the unfortunate refugees who sought asylum in America is also part of the record. But many individuals with firsthand experience would no doubt have agreed with the indictment of a writer in *Commonweal*. Someday, he wrote, when United States consuls and vice-consuls write books about their work they will say: "we carried out the law; we made sure that every line of the questionnaire was properly filled, we counted the photographs, we demanded the birth certificates; and then if everything was all right we affixed the Consular Seal and then, although there was always the line of applicants stinking up the office, there would be at least the applicant with only eleven photographs instead of twelve, the applicant who could not answer Question 73 C, who

[118] *New Republic* CIX (August 30, 1943), 311-13.
[119] Alfred Wagg III, "Washington's Stepchild: The Refugee," *New Republic* CIV (April 28, 1941), 592-94.
[120] Pickett, *For More Than Bread*, 140-41.

would not be in any line anymore, and he might be back in the concentration camp from which he came, or he might be back on his way to Germany, to Poland, or he might be only in a hotel garret with his face to the wall waiting to die." Thus like the Germans, the Americans too, this writer added, refused these human beings the right to live.[121]

Within the limits of government restrictions something could be and was done by the voluntary agencies. Broadly speaking, assistance took the form of emergency relief to victims who could not flee, or who could not get beyond Nazi-dominated lands; to the smaller number who luckily got to England or to far-off Shanghai; and, finally, to the most fortunate of all, those who, thanks to help from an American or other voluntary agency, found permanent homes in Latin America and in the United States, but who nevertheless needed help in coming to terms with a new life.

First: the most unfortunate of all were those who were trapped in Germany or Nazi-dominated Central and southeast Europe. The Commission for Polish Relief spent nearly a million dollars in feeding some 50,000 children in the homeland, in Roumania, and in Vilna (as well as 20,000 Poles in unoccupied France). The American Red Cross, through its affiliates, managed, before the end of 1942, to send over two million dollars worth of supplies to Cairo for the relief of Greek and Middle East refugees, to get medical supplies, clothing, and foodstuffs to refugees in Roumania, Hungary, Yugoslavia, Latvia, and Lithuania, and to transport supplies valued at over a million dollars for Poles and Polish refugees in Europe, with half that amount for Polish refugees stranded in Iran and southern Russia. But it was the American Jewish Joint Distribution Committee that shouldered the greatest burden. To be sure, the relief provided to the Warsaw ghetto and the food packages sent to concentration camps (as long as the Nazis permitted this to be done) often only delayed death from starvation and epidemic or from extermination in gas chambers. With the help of the War Refugee Board and the Swedish government the JDC prevented, at least for the time, the deportation of 20,000 Budapest Jews. Even after all the doors were closed, the JDC and its heroic European representative refused

121 C. G. Pauling, "The Grafton Plan," *Commonweal* XL (May 12, 1944), 76-77.

to give up the effort to save any life that might conceivably be saved.[122]

Help was also given refugees in occupied and in Vichy France. The Joint Distribution Committee kept alive, at least for a time, 55,000 alien Jews who managed to get to southern France. For a time it kept a countless number of human beings from the clutches of the Gestapo. Refugees in France also had help from the Red Cross, which supplied almost $3,000,000 worth of food and medicine to other agencies, chiefly the American Friends Service Committee, until the break of diplomatic relations between Vichy and Washington put an end to emergency programs. Also on the scene, but with a very limited budget, was the American Unitarian Service Committee, which kept dispensaries in a few French cities as well as in refugee-crowded Lisbon.[123] In response to the pathetic plight of refugee children, Foster Parents Plan for War Children, the American branch of an agency organized in England during the Civil War in Spain, set up in France ten colonies that cared for a thousand homeless boys and girls.[124]

Second: the refugees, children and adults who had escaped to Great Britain. The Foster Parents Plan was operating eight social service projects in the spring of 1941 that looked out for 4,000 refugee children. These youngsters were supported by "foster parents" in the United States who paid ten dollars monthly for the keep of each child.[125] Save the Children Federation, by the end of 1940, had given $100,000 in aid of child refugees in England.[126] As Britain's cities were bombed, English children also in effect became refugees. The United States Committee for the Care of European Children, with which Marshall Field was identified, helped evacuate children,

---

[122] American National Red Cross, *Foreign War Relief, September 1, 1939–December 31, 1942* (Washington: American National Red Cross, 1943), 16-18; *American Jewish Year Book*, Sept., 1941–Sept., 1942, XLIII, 89-92.

[123] Herbert Agar, *The Saving Remnant: An Account of Jewish Survival* (New York: Viking, 1960), 132 ff.; Moses A. Leavitt, *The JDC Story, 1914-1952* (New York: American Jewish Joint Distribution Committee, 1953), 13; Pickett, *For More Than Bread*, 153-55; The Unitarian Service Committee, *Fact Sheet*, July 14, 1958 (Boston: Unitarian Service Committee, 1958), 2.

[124] The American branch was organized in 1937 as a result of the mission of the British founders, John Langdon-Davies and Eric Muggeridge, with Edna Blue as the chief promoter. Foster Parents Plan, Inc., *Foster Parents Plan, Inc.* (New York: Foster Parents Plan, Inc., ca. 1958), 4 ff.; *New York Times*, March 13, 1940.

[125] *New York Times*, April 20, 1940.

[126] *Ibid.*, March 16, Dec. 6, 1940.

including those of foreign as well as British origin, from bombarded areas.[127] Two organizations gave American children a chance to begin an experience in good will and to appreciate their own good fortune. One was the Children's Crusade for Children, with Mrs. Franklin D. Roosevelt, William Allen White, Monsignor John Ryan, and Dorothy Canfield Fisher as leading sponsors. The 13,500,000 pennies it collected were handed over to agencies, chiefly in Britain, that served uprooted children.[128] Another organization was somewhat picturesquely named Young America Wants to Help. Its national chairman, Mrs. Kermit Roosevelt, reported in October, 1941, that in its first year it had sent $125,000 to England for refugee children.[129] What all this help meant can be imagined from the report that some of the children had been born and brought up from their first years in underground shelters, that many bore Nazi tattoo numbers on their arms, and that others had suffered so intensely from fear that it was necessary to tie them to their nurses with strings made longer and longer each day until they could be removed.[130]

In addition to the agencies set up to care for refugee children in England, others, including those supported in America by national-origin groups, aided adult refugees who had suffered too much to earn a living in the land that now sheltered them. And across the oceans in Shanghai, the JDC kept alive some 20,000 refugees in a country that did not require visas but that was now dominated by Japan, a Nazi ally.[131]

Third: refugees who had found an asylum in Latin America and the United States that promised to be permanent. Thus the Jewish Joint Agricultural Corporation contributed $50,000 to a planned resettlement in the Yungas district of Bolivia.[132] Working on a larger scale the Refugee Economic Corporation, with a capital of $1,500,000, promoted refugee settlement in Bolivia, the Dominican Republic, and the Philippines.[133] In all, the JDC spent $52,285,300 between

[127] *Ibid.*, August 12, Oct. 3, Nov. 3, 1940; *Survey* LXXVII (Oct., 1941), 297; *Commonweal* XXXII (July 12, 1940), 237-38.

[128] *New York Times*, April 16, June 30, 1940.

[129] *Ibid.*, Oct. 30, 1941. Young America Wants to Help worked in conjunction with the British War Relief Society.

[130] Foster Parents Plan, Inc., *Foster Parents Plan, Inc.*, 10-12.

[131] *American Jewish Year Book*, Sept., 1940–Sept., 1941, XLIII, 90-92; Laura L. Margolis, "Race Against Time in Shanghai," *Survey Graphic* XXXIII (March, 1944), 168-71.

[132] *Christian Science Monitor Weekly Magazine*, July 26, 1941.

[133] Refugee Economic Corporation, *Quest for Settlement: Summaries of Selected Economic and Geographic Reports on Settlement Possibilities for European Immi-*

1939 and 1944 in helping more than 81,000 refugees escape from Nazi Europe and begin life elsewhere.[134] Although it was the most important agency in this work, the JDC was not alone. Supported by left-wing contributors, the New World Resettlement Fund and the American Rescue Ship Mission aided some thousands of Spanish refugees in France in finding new homes in Latin America.[135]

In the United States itself, several established organizations helped refugees meet the countless problems associated with finding a place in American life. It will be recalled that the American Friends Service Committee established centers in Iowa, Indiana, Pennsylvania, and New York to smooth the path, which at best was rough, and that the Hebrew Immigrant Aid Society provided initial shelter and meals, and aided in job-getting. In 1939 some thirty agencies federated in the National Refugee Service. Although mainly supported by Jewish relief funds and concerned chiefly with Jewish refugees (110,000 by 1941), the organization was nonsectarian: the American Committee for Christian Refugees, a Protestant group, and the Committee for Catholic Refugees from Germany worked with it.

Ably led by Professor Joseph Chamberlain of the Columbia University Law School and employing some 450 social workers and other personnel in addition to volunteers, the National Refugee Service helped its clients become self-supporting as quickly as possible with care to avoid any charge that the refugees were a drag on the labor market or, when able to have businesses of their own, employed only refugees. The Service enlisted the help of the New York Adult Education Council, which offered English language instruction and encouraged Manfred George, a German refugee, in a self-help program which included an employment agency, a physicians' training and a sports program, all duly publicized in the refugee newspaper *Aufbau*. The National Refugee Service enlisted over four hundred communities in sponsoring refugees while they struck roots in their new home.[136]

grants (New York: Refugee Economic Corporation, 1948), 9-12; Alfred Wagg, III, "An American Program for Refugees," *Christian Science Monitor Weekly Magazine*, July 26, 1941; Albert Horlings, "Who Aids the Refugees?", *New Republic* CIV (Jan. 13, 1941), 43-46.

[134] Leavitt, *The JDC Story*, 13.

[135] *New Republic* CIV (Jan. 13, 1941), 44-45; *Newsweek* XVII (Feb. 17, 1941), 21.

[136] Albert Horlings, *New Republic* CIV, 43-46; "Refugees Build U. S. Industries," *Business Week*, April 27, 1940, 18, 20; Frank Kingdon, "All Learning One Tongue," *Survey* LXXVI (Sept., 1940), 254-55; Kathryn Close, "In a Strange Land," *Survey* LXXV (Dec., 1939), 367-69.

All these agencies, in addition to those aiding political and labor leaders, professionals, scholars and students, some organized earlier, some later, formed part of a world-wide effort to help victims of fascist and Nazi persecution. Some of the larger agencies, bogged down in overwhelming tasks, may have sometimes failed to give the personal understanding that many of the smaller groups offered and that was needed almost as much as shelter, food, and jobs. But at least no refugee was deported on the ground of being a public charge. On the whole the voluntary agencies in helping well over 125,000 men and women and 4,000 homeless children get to America and in giving a hand in finding a spot in city and small community, wrote a new and honorable chapter in the history of American immigration.

Of the $91,000,000 contributed in 1940-1941 for overseas war relief, somewhat more than $2,000,000 was given by German-Americans to help German war prisoners and those who survived in Hitler's Reich.[137] It is not known how much of this was given at the demonstrations arranged to celebrate Nazi victories over France and England and to express enduring devotion to the fatherland. But those in charge of a celebration on May 19, 1940, as the Battle of France was ending and the Battle for Britain beginning, expressed pleasure at the generous response of the 11,000 who paid their respect at a shrine displaying two bronze plaques. One was of the late President von Hindenberg, the other of Chancellor Adolph Hitler. Each plaque was flanked by candles, swastikas, and American flags.[138]

[137] *New York Times*, Feb. 3, June 5, 1941.
[138] *Ibid.*, May 20, 1940.

XVI

In War Again

The need for helping homeless children, older refugees, prisoners of war, persecuted minorities, and the sick and starving in belligerent and conquered lands did not end when Pearl Harbor thrust the United States into the world conflict. On the contrary, these needs mounted as the war dragged on. The attempt to meet them even in part meant new problems and determined effort.

In the first place, higher taxes put a strain on voluntary giving. So did the demands of both established charities and of the agencies organized to help families divided and often harassed by the war effort as well as the men and women in the armed forces. The YMCA, YWCA, Navy Relief Society, Army Relief Society, Aid to American Prisoners, Red Cross, and the United Service Organization all had important functions and all needed support. In response to the State Department's recommendation that the first concern of Americans should be the war effort of their own country, several organizations announced that henceforth their emphasis would either be on American needs or that, as in the case of the relief committee of the CIO, aid would in the future be given to needy laboring families at home as well as abroad.[1]

The *New York Times* did not doubt that charity begins at home but a few weeks after Pearl Harbor commented on the need to continue relief aid to other countries despite domestic demands. "This," wrote the *Times*, "is a civilian as well as a military war. . . . Dollars given for relief work among the allied peoples are not mere expressions of sentiment. They contribute to victory by stimulating civilian morale and strengthening the ties of friendship among democratic

[1] *New York Times*, Dec. 18, 1941.

peoples. In spite of our coming burden of taxation," the editorial admonished, "we should continue to give out of what is still a relative abundance." [2]

And give the American people did. In 1940 contributions to overseas relief totaled $20,000,000. By 1944, the last full year of the war, this figure had increased by more than 500 per cent and in 1945 more than twice the 1944 amount was given. The following table indicates the annual volume of giving for overseas relief.[3]

Table I. Annual Contributions Received by Voluntary Agencies for Overseas Relief, 1939-1945

1939	$ 2,900,000
1940	20,600,000
1941	39,000,000
1942	37,100,000
1943	62,100,000
1944	109,100,000
1945	233,900,000
Total	$504,700,000

The increase after 1942 resulted from the opening of areas hitherto closed to relief, as allied victories were wrenched from the foe in Africa, Italy, and France; from the improvement of fund-raising organization; and from the publicity given to overseas needs.

Among the reasons for the rising volume of giving for overseas relief special note must also be taken of what one observer described as a revolution in American philanthropy: "the almost unnoticed emergence of the labor movement as the largest single source of revenue for philanthropy in this country or in the world." [4] Labor of course had long done its share in community fund raising but what had been given for domestic charities had generally been lumped together with the contributions of management and the clerical force as the gift of "the XYZ Corporation." In part the increasing role of labor in organized giving stemmed from the high wages it received in wartime prosperity and from the development of payroll deductions for charitable contributions. Other factors were, however, also at work.

[2] *Ibid.*, Feb. 3, 1942.
[3] U. S. Department of State, President's War Relief Control Board, *Voluntary War Relief During World War II*, Department of State Publication 2566 (Washington: Govt. Printing Office, 1946), 8.
[4] Kermit Eby, "Organized Labor and Philanthropy," *Christian Century* LX (Sept. 8, 1943), 1011-12.

Organized labor was in many ways identifying itself in larger measure with community activities. Labor leaders recognized the public relations value of large union contributions and in turn those in charge of local fund raising belatedly asked labor's representatives to serve on committees and to take bows at the end of successful campaigns. Also important was the fact that organized labor was learning the techniques of cooperation common in fund-raising operations. Thus in March, 1943, the AF of L and the CIO agreed to launch a joint drive, with a quota of $4,000,000, for the New York Labor War Chest. The next year the two major labor organizations reached agreements with the Red Cross and the National War Fund which avoided undue competition, overlapping, and duplication.[5]

A breakdown of labor's contributions in 1943 is illuminating. It gave $30,000,000 to over-all war relief, some 20 per cent of which went overseas. In addition contributions in excess of $200,000 were made to the British War Relief Society. At the same time the American Labor Committee to Aid British Labor, an AF of L agency, collected, with the help of several CIO unions, $208,000.[6] This supported nursing and rest homes for shell-shocked workers, schools, nurseries, and rehabilitation centers in Great Britain.[7] In 1943 a large part of the $1,500,000 that the International Ladies' Garment Workers Union gave to philanthropic purposes went to favored overseas projects. Allocations from special war funds collected by other unions were also directed to foreign relief.[8] Thus American labor, in addition to the British workers' causes, supported special projects, including provision of clothes and food for women and children in Soviet Russia and assistance to antifascist underground movements in China and other countries.[9] It is likely that the larger role of labor in overseas relief during American participation in the war helps explain the fact that while in the years before Pearl Harbor 80 per cent

[5] Bent Taylor, "Labor Becomes a Big Giver," *Survey Graphic* XXXII (Feb., 1943), 49, 61-62; American Federation of Labor, *Report of Proceedings* (Boston, 1943), LXIII, 574-75 (New Orleans, 1944), LXIV, 277-78; *New York Times*, Jan. 25, Dec. 15, 1942, March 3, 4, 1943, March 2, July 15, 1944; Harold J. Seymour, *Design for Giving: The Story of the National War Fund Inc.*, 1943-1947 (New York: Harper, 1947), 68-70.

[6] *New York Times*, June 11, 1942.

[7] *Ibid.*, Dec. 15, 1942; *Survey Graphic* XXXII, 49.

[8] *New York Times*, Jan. 18, 1943; Arthur C. Ringland, "The Organization of Voluntary Foreign Aid, 1939-1953," *Department of State Bulletin* XXX (March 15, 1954), 383-93.

[9] *Survey Graphic* XXXII, 49; *New York Times*, Dec. 15, 1942.

of the giving was related to national origin or sympathy, this was true of only 20 per cent of what was given between 1942 and 1945.

Religious organizations had of course long been major contributors to overseas charities. During the years of American fighting the growing church collections reflected several factors in the total picture of giving but particularly the development of coordination and efficiency in fund raising.[10] The Church Committee for Overseas Relief, an organization of cooperating Protestant churches, increased its budget in 1944-1945 by 50 per cent of that of the year before. In Catholic circles the Bishops' War Emergency and Relief Committee, organized in 1939, carried on the major assistance to victims of the war abroad. In addition, other Catholic agencies engaged in foreign relief, including refugee programs. In 1943 the War Relief Services (an agency sponsored by the National Catholic Welfare Conference and later called Catholic Relief Services) was organized to integrate foreign relief efforts by Catholic agencies and groups.[11]

A significant aspect of voluntary overseas relief during the war years was the increasing government control over the private agencies. Philanthropy, like other aspects of national life, was mobilized in the interest of efficiency and speedy victory. Deeming it unwise to leave to the voluntary agencies the entire responsibility for coordinating programs, and wishing to reduce confusion in the public mind regarding competing organizations and to scale down overhead costs, the President's Committee on War Relief Agencies in July, 1942, recom-

---

[10] The figures below come from U. S. Department of Commerce, Foreign and Domestic Commerce Bureau, *International Transactions of the United States During the War, 1940-1945*, Economic Series 65 (Washington: Govt. Printing Office, 1948), 208.

INSTITUTIONAL CONTRIBUTIONS TO FOREIGN COUNTRIES BY MILLIONS OF DOLLARS, 1940-1945

	Protestant	Catholic	Jewish	Nonsectarian	Total
1940	16.5	3.0	10.1	19.2	48.8
1941	17.8	3.3	12.1	49.4	82.6
1942	15.9	2.3	11.6	35.0	64.8
1943	19.6	3.5	14.7	76.8	114.6
1944	23.2	7.1	27.2	123.5	181.0
1945	32.3	7.9	37.2	156.4	233.8

[11] *New York Times*, March 12, 1943, June 23, 1944; U. S., Congress, House, Special Subcommittee of the Committee on Foreign Affairs, *Voluntary Foreign Aid: The Nature and Scope of Postwar Private American Assistance Abroad with Special Reference to Europe*, 80th Cong., 1st Sess., 1947, committee print [hereafter cited as the *Fulton Report*]. Portions of this report are printed in U. S., Congress, House, Select Committee on Foreign Aid, *Final Report on Foreign Aid*, 80th Cong., 2d Sess., 1948, H. Rept. 1845, 785-827.

mended that the executive reconstitute the committee by enlarging its functions.[12]

The revamped agency, known as the President's War Relief Control Board, was given authority over "all solicitations, sales or offers to sell merchandise or services, collections and distribution or disposal of funds and contributions in kind for the direct or implied purpose" of charities for foreign and domestic relief, rehabilitation, reconstruction and welfare arising from war-created needs at home and abroad, refugee relief, and related activities. It was also to register and coordinate fund-raising agencies, to define ethical standards of solicitation and collection, to require accurate accounting, and to eliminate or merge some agencies in the interest of efficiency or economy, as well as to protect local charities. Thus the role of the government in voluntary philanthropy was given wider scope than ever before. Joseph E. Davies remained chairman, Charles P. Taft continued to serve, and Charles Warren was to replace Frederick P. Keppel, whose death left a vacancy.[13]

The Board did not hesitate to use its regulatory powers. It asked agencies to rename themselves whenever existing names failed to reflect clearly the fact that the aid given was American in origin. "In the creation of good will between the United States and countries which are being helped by the generosity of our people it is important," the directive ran, "that they know that it is Americans who are sympathetic with their position and are endeavoring to help in the alleviation of distressing conditions." In the latter stages of World War II a number of agencies took the request to heart: the French Relief Fund became the American Relief for France; the Queen Wilhelmina Fund was renamed American Relief for Holland; and Russian War Relief took the new title of the American Society for Russian Relief. Thus the inclusion of "American" in the title of the agencies identified them with the people of the United States and with national policy.[14]

[12] Press Release, July 27, 1942, in "Compilation of Documents of the President's Committee on War Relief Agencies and the President's War Relief Control Board," mimeographed copy in the National Archives, Washington, D. C. [hereafter cited as "Compilation of Documents"]; Franklin Delano Roosevelt Papers, Hyde Park, N. Y., Official File 4356.

[13] U. S., Congress, House, Select Committee on Foreign Aid, *Final Report on Foreign Aid*, 80th Cong., 2d Sess., 1948, H. Rept. 1845, 796; Executive Order No. 9205 in "Compilation of Documents"; Roosevelt Papers; *New York Times*, July 28, 1942.

[14] Melvin D. Hildreth, general counsel, to the constituent agencies, Oct. 23, 1943, in "Compilation of Documents"; President's War Relief Control Board, *Voluntary War Relief During World War II*, 19.

Chairman Davies also used the Board's licensing power to reduce still further the number of agencies: whereas at the end of 1941, 300 were in operation, only sixty-seven were listed at the end of the year 1943. The number of fund-raising campaigns was further reduced by forbidding agencies to solicit when the American Red Cross was conducting its drives and when the United States War Bond sales were under way. Thanks to the elimination of agencies unable to operate efficiently and to the consolidation of competing ones, administrative costs were cut from an average of 10.6 per cent in 1942 to 4.8 per cent in 1944. More important, the War Relief Control Board reported that in 1942 about 200 agencies competed for the collection of less than $10,000,000, while three years later only half as many agencies raised and distributed more than five times as much money and supplies.[15]

Some of the Board's actions led to criticism. This happened when it licensed one of the several ethnic-oriented agencies the politics of which sharply differed from those of competing Italian relief agencies. Representations, counter-representations, and misrepresentations led to the reversal of decisions and to much explanation.[16] Others took the Board to task for restricting free private action and for the effects of its controls on discouraging new organizations from forming to meet unprecedented charitable needs. Restrictions forbidding organizations to make specific appeals were also held to lessen American interest in relief work.[17] But on the whole the voluntary agencies appreciated what the Board did to lift the whole matter of war relief above the level of tangling competition and bitter partisanship.

Even so, the Board, operating as it did at the national level, could not entirely eliminate the mounting confusion among the hundreds of agencies issuing appeals to relieve the suffering of America's allies. Thus the Board suggested a united national war fund. This was approved by the United Service Organization (a popular new agency designed to aid military personnel), the various community chests

[15] *New York Times*, May 17, 1945; President's War Relief Control Board, *Voluntary War Relief During World War II*, 8-9; circular dated Feb. 10, 1943, in "Compilation of Documents."

[16] *New York Times*, May 3, 5, Sept. 1, 1944.

[17] James Wood Johnson, "What Private Relief Can Do After the War," *Commonweal* XL (April 21, 1944), 13.

and councils, war chest organizations representing local federated fund-raising efforts for various war relief causes, and the major foreign relief organizations. It was obviously necessary to have the drive sponsored by an over-all national agency with prominent leaders at the helm. Early in 1943, six well-known men under the chairmanship of Winthrop W. Aldrich of the Chase National Bank and British War Relief, responded to the request of the War Relief Control Board to organize a National War Fund. In making the announcement, Aldrich declared that the plan would preserve local autonomy in fund raising and afford an opportunity for support of our men in uniform, our allies, and the home front.[18] The new National War Fund was a private organization with the task of reducing the number of competing agencies, cutting down overhead, and minimizing the irritation and confusion resulting from constant requests for funds. Its story has been well told by its general manager, Howard J. Seymour.[19]

The story of the National War Fund is important in American philanthropy. It united the well-organized local and community chests with the popular appeal of the United Service Organization, already serving military personnel, and the national agencies with overseas relief programs. The work demanded an ever larger amount of cooperation between these agencies and the grass-roots donors on the one hand and the War Relief Control Board and other relevant government agencies on the other. Much of the success of the National War Fund stemmed from the decision to admit no agency unless the Board had already certified it; to admit among these, only one agency for a given country or a given function (as refugee aid); to forbid participating agencies to conduct independent drives at any time; and to permit the Fund to serve no special interest, to insist, that is, that monies collected in the many hundreds of local communities and allocated to the selected national relief agencies working overseas, be disbursed without reference to color, creed, race, or political affiliation.

If this decision solved many problems, it created others, for it seemed important to include the National Catholic Welfare Conference's agency, War Relief Services, and the AF of L and CIO,

---

[18] Seymour, *Design for Giving*, 3.
[19] *Ibid.*

whose committees already had carefully thought-out programs to help needy workers in foreign lands. The labor leaders laid aside their plans for special campaigns among their membership and accepted a special status as "cooperating organizations" which did not involve giving up sponsorship of projects in which there was a well-defined interest. A similar solution was worked out for War Relief Services.[20]

Since there was never enough money and since each participating agency set much store on its own program, the job of fixing budgets was a hard one. On the whole, the decisions of National War Fund were accepted as evidencing a spirit of fair play. Although Joseph E. Davies, in addressing a Florida meeting, assured potential donors that not more than 20 per cent of contributions went to foreign aid, the figures in Seymour's account indicate that approximately one half of the total of $750,000,000 contributed in 1943, 1944, and 1945 was allocated to overseas relief agencies.[21]

Important though this sum was, it was clear that the growing needs during the war and the overwhelming shortages and disruption in sight when the fighting stopped, required governmental action both at the national and international levels. In the nature of things, such action was bound to have not only humanitarian motives but also to be closely associated with national policy. Since government aid was to affect voluntary giving, the broad outlines of what was done needs to be summarized.

In September, 1942, at an inter-Allied meeting in London, an agreement was made by Great Britain, Canada, Australia, Argentina and the United States for cooperative buying and storing of wheat reserves. The special responsibility of the United States by reason of its great agricultural output was dramatized late in 1942 by the establishment of the Office of Foreign Relief and Rehabilitation Operations (OFFRO). The coincidence of this action with the vigorous pleas of Hoover in *Collier's* magazine for feeding captive peoples and planning for vast relief programs in the postwar period led some to think that Roosevelt's action was a political move to steal his rival's thunder. Actually, OFFRO not only emphasized the points Hoover

[20] *Ibid.*, 7 ff.
[21] Press Release, Nov. 18, 1943, in "Compilation of Documents"; Ona K. D. Ringwood and H. P. Whidden, Jr., "European Relief as Seen from Britain," *Foreign Policy Reports* XVIII (Oct. 15, 1942), 204; Seymour, *Design for Giving*, 70-71.

made but went further in identifying these with national interest and policy: food was to be used as a means of winning the war by impressing Axis peoples with the abundance that was accessible to them on surrender and, further, long-range postwar rehabilitation was to set the world's economy in order since America and American ideals could not be safe when millions were dying of hunger, want, and disease. At Roosevelt's request Herbert H. Lehman resigned the governorship of New York to head OFFRO—an appointment applauded by the *Christian Century:* ". . . the fact that a Jew is to direct this work of international brotherhood should help to exorcise the devils of race hatred which the malignant nazis have loosed on Europe." [22]

During the Allies' North African campaign about 150,000 children received daily feedings of milk from American supplies under OFFRO auspices. General Eisenhower built up a 10,000-ton relief stockpile before the Tunisian advance and requisitioned some 30,000 tons of supplies monthly for feeding Moroccans and Algerians. OFFRO was soon absorbed into the United Nations Relief and Rehabilitation Administration (UNRRA), which the Allies established in the fall of 1943 to coordinate relief distribution after the war was won. The United States, because of its great wealth, played the dominant role in UNRRA. Lehman held the post of UNRRA director-general. Congress authorized the first appropriation of $1,-350,000,000 in March, 1944. Ultimately the United States was to supply over $2,600,000,000—about 70 per cent of UNRRA's expenditures.[23]

At the time, spokesmen for voluntary agencies expressed concern lest the American people cut down on private giving for overseas relief in the impression that a few millions thus given would be as nothing in relation to the vast sums OFFRO and UNRRA had

[22] *Christian Century* LXIX (Dec. 9, 1942), 1552-53; Herbert H. Lehman, *Vital Speeches* IX (August 1, 1943), 621-24. For interesting reactions from the business community see "On Order—Goods from Europe," *Business Week* (July 17, 1953), 38-42, and "Foreign Relief Job Expands," *Ibid.* (July 24, 1943), 42, 44, 46.

[23] George Creel, "Food for a Ravaged World," *Collier's* CXII (July 17, 1943), 21; "Agreement for United Nations Relief and Rehabilitation Administration, November 9, 1943," and "Participation in UNRRA, March 28, 1944," in U. S., Congress, Senate, *A Decade of American Foreign Policy: Basic Documents, 1941-1949,* 81st Cong., 1st Sess., 1950, Senate Doc. 123, 14, 21; George Soloveytchick, "After the Armies—UNRRA," *Survey Graphic* XXXIII (June, 1944), 312; U. S., Congress, House, *U. S. Foreign Aid: Its Purpose, Scope, Administration, and Related Information,* 86th Cong., 1st Sess., 1959, House Doc. 116, 26.

at their disposal. The impression was the more likely to stick because it was clear to almost everyone that the United States would be the major contributor to UNRRA's budget and that what the government did would in the end come out of the taxpayers' pockets.[24]

Such was the background of the joint statement issued by Herbert H. Lehman, Norman H. Davis of the Red Cross, and Joseph E. Davies of the War Relief Control Board:

"The united resources and services of Government, supplemented by those of the American Red Cross and the International Red Cross organization, and by the voluntary efforts of all people will be required for the relief of distressed civilians in countries associated with America in this war. While the resources and services of Government will be drawn upon to furnish the primary supplies for mass emergency relief of civilian populations, voluntary organizations rendering essential services will also need to be maintained. . . . Continuation of such voluntary relief work is essential not only as an expression of the generous sympathies of the American people but also as a distinctive service that quasi-public and voluntary agencies can render to complement public resources and services." [25]

With the surrender of Germany in May, 1945, the War Relief Control Board urged Americans to continue support of the National War Fund because the end of the fighting increased rather than decreased the need for overseas aid in the recently liberated areas hitherto inaccessible to relief.[26]

Some months before the Nazi surrender, in anticipation of the continuing problem of overseas voluntary aid and its administration, Charles P. Taft, acting for the War Relief Control Board, made an interesting proposal to UNRRA and to the War Department, both of whom, presumably, would exercise jurisdiction over American relief agencies in occupied foreign countries. It was necessary, Taft indicated, to know, from the authority abroad, its wishes and its judgment of the situation in order that the Board in turn might carry out its function "to determine the propriety of appeals to the

[24] Seymour, *Design for Giving*, 15.
[25] "Continuation of Relief Work by Private Organizations," *Department of State Bulletin* VIII (Jan. 16, 1943), 37-38.
[26] *New York Times*, May 14, 17, 1945.

American public for funds." If, as Taft understood, the Army had decided not to admit private relief agencies during its administration, it might still find it convenient to deal with one agency representing all of the American organizations for foreign relief. Thus Taft proposed the organization of a council of voluntary agencies to which the Board could transmit specific information on needs in occupied countries and which it might help in the task of laying before constituent members precise program requirements.[27] The need of such a council must have been strengthened by the reply Taft received from General J. J. McCloy to the effect that although the Army would oppose the admission of private agencies in relief work in areas under its control it would certainly prefer, if such agencies were admitted into the field, to deal with one body representing the others than with each individually.[28] This reply stimulated the development of two major relief agencies, each representing its members, during the occupations in Europe and Asia.[29]

Even before Taft had sent his inquiry to the War Department Professor Joseph Chamberlain of Columbia University and the International Migration Service, Clarence Pickett of the American Friends Service Committee, and C. E. Miller of the Near East Foundation, together with representatives of a dozen other agencies, organized the American Council of Voluntary Agencies for Foreign Service. Designed to work out plans for relief in the liberated areas of Europe, the Council at first could do little more than exchange views and facilitate communication between member organizations and the War Relief Control Board.[30]

Among the charter members of the American Council of Voluntary Agencies for Foreign Service were a number of agencies which appealed to the American people for aid to individual countries. As the end of the war approached, however, the National War Fund's

[27] Charles P. Taft to J. J. McCloy, Assistant Secretary of War, Jan. 8, 1944, in the files of the Advisory Committee on Voluntary Foreign Aid, International Cooperation Administration, Department of State, Washington, D. C. [hereafter cited as Advisory Committee Files].

[28] J. J. McCloy to Charles P. Taft, Jan. 13, 1944, Advisory Committee Files.

[29] See below, pp. 488 ff.

[30] Allen T. Burns, "Leadership with World Horizons," *Survey* LXXXIII (April, 1947), 120-23; James Wood Johnson, "What Private Relief Can Do After the War," *Commonweal* XL (April 21, 1944), 12-13.

decision to admit only one agency for each country forced these organizations to federate into single national units. So, for example, the various French relief groups, torn by differences over the support of Petain at Vichy versus the support of the Free French under De Gaulle, finally merged in the early part of 1944 into American Relief for France. By early 1945 the new organization had nearly 300 centers in more than forty states, the majority being sewing groups. The people of Dunkirk, New York, contributed $75,000 for the people of Dunkirk, France. Ultimately American Relief for France shipped 12,000,000 pounds of clothing, medical supplies and food, operated disaster units and mobile canteens for those without homes, and helped restore the health of some 300,000 children by special feeding programs. A value of $400,000 was set on the gifts in kind that some 11,000 American volunteers gave or prepared each year, while the total budget approved by the National War Fund was $7,-325,000.[31] By 1950 American Relief for France had turned much of its equipment and facilities over to French groups and was in the process of liquidating its overseas programs.

Another ethnically oriented agency that flourished during and after the war, the British War Relief Society, maintained over 300 ambulances, surgical units and first-aid vehicles while keeping up 200 hostels for the injured and infirm. After the organization of the National War Fund, Bundles for Britain merged with the British War Relief Society but kept on with its own work which included aid for children. In 1944 the British War Relief Society disbursed $4,679,-000 and shipped donated goods, chiefly clothing, valued at over $2,000,000. "We shall not forget this work," wrote Winston Churchill, "and we all send our grateful thanks to the two million voluntary workers and the hundreds of thousands of other citizens of the United States whose efforts and generosity have made it possible." [32] When the countries on the Continent were liberated, the British War Relief Society withdrew from the National War Fund to permit it to concentrate on those more needy than the British.

Russian relief activities had been consolidated into Russian War Relief in September, 1941, later to be renamed the American Society

[31] *American Relief for France* (New York: American Relief for France, 1945); *New York Times*, May 8, 1942, Jan. 2, 1943, July 15, 1944; Seymour, *Design for Giving*, 82-83.
[32] *New York Times*, March 15, 1945.

for Russian Relief. Contributions amounted to $32,000,000 in 1945 and to $80,000,000 over the existence of the agency from 1941 to 1946. Bennett Cerf served as chairman of a "Books-for-Russia" campaign which dispatched more than a quarter-million English-language classics to Russian readers. In April, 1944, the numerous Italian organizations merged into American Relief for Italy. Ultimately this agency helped over 4,000,000 Italians with $40,000,-000 worth of aid distributed through the Italian government, the Vatican, the Italian Red Cross, and the General Confederation of Labor. Active organizations serving Norway, Holland, Poland, and Czechoslovakia were also established.

The war-time activities of these organizations were similar. Most were based in New York, where they filled warehouses with goods collected from all over the country. Clothing, food, blankets, household equipment and medical supplies were stockpiled against the day of liberation, transported to the closer ports of Britain or Sweden, or sent on to aid nationals caught in neutral countries. American Relief for Holland shipped on an average 3,000 pounds daily; $830,-000 in funds and goods were dispatched in the single year ending October 31, 1947. The New York offices frequently supplied publicity material as well as cloth and yarn to sewing circles and other local groups throughout the country. American Relief for Poland worked chiefly through Roman Catholic parishes. It sent $7,500,000 in food, clothing, and hospital and school supplies in the period from January, 1946, until all "foreign" relief organizations were invited to leave Poland by its government in 1949. A New York-based agency could also render effective aid to servicemen and merchant seamen fighting the war through their governments in exile. American Relief for France, for example, established recreation centers for the Free French forces and adopted six ships of the French navy to which were sent books, phonographs, games and personal comforts.[33] The

[33] *American Relief for France* (New York: American Relief for France, 1945); American Relief for Italy, Inc., *Second Anniversary Report* (New York: American Relief for Italy, 1946); C. F. Horsley, comp., "Foreign Voluntary Aid to Poland, 1945-1949," manuscript in the files of the American Council of Voluntary Agencies for Foreign Service, New York [hereafter cited as American Council Files]; Edward C. Carter, "Russian War Relief," *Slavonic and East European Review* XXII (August, 1944), 61-74; American Relief for Holland, Inc., *Final Report* (New York: American Relief for Holland, 1947); "Basic Information About National War Fund Agency: American Relief for Norway, Inc.," undated mimeographed copy in the American Council Files; C. G. Michalis (former president of the Queen Wilhelmina Fund—later, American Relief for Holland), to Merle Curti, Feb. 23, 1961; *New York Times*, May 24, 1940.

table in footnote 34 indicates the value of relief provided by these national agencies.[34]

Greece deserves special comment. In the years of neutrality the Greek War Relief Association, headed by Dr. Homer Davis, former president of Athens College, was often singled out for its low overhead and efficient management. Even during the German occupation, the Association managed, with the help of the International Red Cross of Geneva, to arrange with the Axis and UN powers for a trans-blockade feeding program much like that which Hoover continued to advocate for the small occupied democracies of northern

[34] The total by year of funds and gifts in kind actually *sent abroad* by all U. S. agencies between September 6, 1939, and December 31, 1945, according to President's War Relief Control Board, *Voluntary War Relief During World War II*, 26-39, 49.

Year	Funds	Value of Gifts in Kind
1939	$ 1,608,886	$ 191,717
1940	12,399,467	2,476,093
1941	23,614,026	10,180,019
1942	23,297,540	5,860,071
1943	44,893,933	11,250,027
1944	72,072,934	26,933,033
1945	87,416,654	141,997,374
	$265,303,540	$198,888,334

Apart from agencies whose work extended into many countries, the agencies which specialized in relief to one particular country sent the following:

Country	Funds	Value of Gifts in Kind
Albania	$ 100,020	$ —
Armenia	545,064	22,531
Austria	—	—
Belgium	1,472,438	884,238
Britain	24,775,437	13,149,358
China	35,202,508	87,832
Czechoslovakia	1,342,766	510,993
Denmark	302,197	280,650
Estonia	6,800	2,000
France	5,914,420	96,579
Greece	25,127,938	4,905,145
Hungary	101,345	7,181
Italy	3,499,217	10,537,335
Latvia	4,253	11,201
Lithuania	442,676	392,900
Luxembourg	227,140	—
Netherlands	3,103,114	603,883
Norway	2,603,032	1,595,360
Palestine	35,439,944	581,661
Poland	7,156,907	3,715,548
Russia	22,104,713	32,027,390
Switzerland	61,526	—
Yugoslavia	2,895,716	778,151

and central Europe.[35] Fourteen Swedish ships, carrying 700,000 tons of food and supplies, furnished by the Canadian government, the Lend-Lease Administration, the American Red Cross, and the Greek War Relief Association made over a hundred Atlantic crossings from Canadian ports to the Piraeus in a period of three years. The food and relief, distributed under the strict supervision of the International Red Cross, saved perhaps a third of the Greek people. After the country was freed in October, 1944, the Greek War Relief Association helped refugees in the Near East, opened almost five hundred clinics and sent forty mobile medical units to give desperately needed help in remote and devastated villages. Disabled veterans were retrained, while feeding centers provided for 1,200,000 children and 29,000 expectant and nursing mothers. Besides all this, 8,000,000 garments and pairs of shoes were distributed and 12,000 animals given to farmers so that the country could again feed itself.[36]

The story of Russian relief takes on special interest in view of the controversies over America's role in the famine of 1918-1923 and later the cold war. In September, 1941, an American commission toured Russia and reported on the country's needs. Russian War Relief, formed at once, enlisted the support of William Green of the AF of L, Philip Murray of the CIO, Thomas J. Watson of the IBM Corporation, and Major General William H. Haskell, who directed relief in the Caucasus in 1921-1923.[37] Russian War Relief's president, Edward C. Carter, had considerable experience in YMCA work.[38] Despite the support of leaders whose American loyalty was above suspicion, Russian War Relief felt it well to assure the public that it need not feel squeamish lest in giving aid it advance the cause of communism, since the supplies were not directed to any political purpose.[39] At a dinner opening the 1942 campaign our former am-

---

[35] Herbert Hoover, "We'll Have to Feed the World Again," *Collier's* CX (Nov. 28, 1942), 11-12, 59, 61, and (Dec. 5, 1942), 32-34, 36; Herbert Hoover and Hugh Gibson, "Feed the Starving Now," *Collier's* CXI (Feb. 20, 1943), 11; *Nation* CLVI (March 27, 1943), 437; *New Republic* CVIII (March 15, 1943), 332; *Christian Century* LX (March 3, 1943), 277-78.

[36] *New York Times*, April 27, Dec. 2, 1942, March 25, 1945; "Food Ships Sail for Greece," *Christian Century* LIX (August 12, 1942), 971; Carlton K. Matson, "How War Relief Gets Through," *Survey* LXXVIII (Sept., 1942), 231-36; Gerard Swope, "Along the Firing Line," *Survey* LXXIX (Sept., 1943), 234; *Fulton Report*; Seymour, *Design for Giving*, 83.

[37] *New York Times*, June 4, 1942.

[38] Edward C. Carter, "Our War Relief Gets Through," *Survey Graphic* XXXIII (Feb., 1944), 52-55.

[39] Matson, *Survey* LXXVIII, 231-33.

bassador to Russia, Joseph E. Davies, contended that Nazi stooges were trying to frighten people into believing that American democracy would be endangered if the Soviets, with American help, were to defeat the Axis. Davies insisted that the Soviet government ought to be trusted, that it was fighting on the American side, and that it was "neither good Christianity, good sense nor even good sportsmanship to challenge or impugn the good faith, honor or integrity of the promises of the Soviet Government." He pointedly added that the $1,400,000 contributed was in sharp contrast with the $100,000,000 given to other countries.[40] Two days later Lord Marley claimed that the British people were sending ten times as much assistance to Russia as the Americans, in other words, $1,200,000 a month as against $164,000 per month from the United States.[41]

In the end the American contribution was nevertheless considerable. In 1943 Russian War Relief, an agency of the National War Fund, sent $16,781,333 worth of relief supplies to the Soviet Union.[42] In March, 1943, the Jewish Council for Russian Relief pledged a minimum of $1,000,000 to Russian War Relief.[43] During the years 1943 and 1944 when Russian War Relief was a member of the National War Fund, it shipped millions of pounds of clothing, seeds for replanting "the scorched earth," needed household goods, medical supplies, and foodstuffs, valued at close to $46,000,000.[44] Administrative expenses amounted to only 4.3 per cent of the total contribution.[45] In addition to what the Russian War Relief and other agencies did, the American Red Cross poured into the Soviet Union medical and other supplies, bought largely with Lend-Lease funds, valued at nearly $6,000,000.[46]

The Soviets through Amtorg, their trade agency, provided free shipping of Russian War Relief goods in Russian bottoms. Distribution was made through Voks, the Russian Red Cross Society, and the Red Crescent Society. Great quantities of the supplies went to homes set up by the government for war orphans and to each article a card was attached giving the name of the donor with a second card

---

[40] *New York Times*, May 8, 1942.
[41] *Ibid.*, May 10, 1942.
[42] *Ibid.*, Jan. 4, 1944.
[43] *Ibid.*, March 1, 1943.
[44] Seymour, *Design for Giving*, 87.
[45] *New York Times*, Feb. 15, 1944.
[46] Matson, *Survey LXXVIII*, 231-36; American National Red Cross, *Foreign War Relief Operations* (Washington: American National Red Cross, 1947), 15.

on which the recipient could reply if he so wished. Thousands did thank donors for their gifts. Maxim Litvinov and Andrei Vyschinski drank toasts to the Russian War Relief, spoke appreciatively of what had been done, and hoped that American donors would be stimulated "to still greater achievements in the future."[47] The total program of relief for Russia contributed, for the time, to a better understanding between the two peoples and to the Allied victory.

No country needing help presented so many problems as China. Forced to move into the remote interior and to set up a capital at Chungking, the Nationalist government was cut off from the supplies it had been receiving over the perilous Burma road when the Japanese seized it early in 1942. The American Red Cross had already sent supplies exceeding $3,000,000 in value, but many of these lay in India.[48] Some were flown "over the hump," but for the most part new ways of helping the beleaguered Chinese had to be found. United China Relief deposited its receipts in the Bank of China in New York and cabled them to Chungking. In 1941 some $3,000,000 was available, in 1942, over $5,000,000. In 1943, when the agency became a constituent of the National War Fund, it received $8,621,-155 and a somewhat larger sum the next year. The allocation to the several causes in China did not greatly vary from the formula worked out in 1942 when medical and health work received 35 per cent, education 20 per cent, child welfare 15 per cent, and social and economic rehabilitation and disaster relief smaller proportions.[49] In this way food, shelter, and clothing were given to 4,000,000 refugees. Over 3,000,000 civilians received medical service, over 13,000,000 soldiers, similar medical and surgical help. Emergency subsidies kept over 300,000 students and professors alive, while 100,000 professional men and women received training for work in health and welfare programs.[50]

The story of the Friends Ambulance Unit in China has been told more than once and may well be told many more times. Its begin-

[47] Matson, *Survey* LXXVIII, 231-36; W. H. Lawrence, "Thanks from Russia's Homeless Millions," *New York Times Magazine*, August 13, 1944, 22-23; *New York Times*, Jan. 12, 1943, March 1, 1943; *Survey Graphic* XXXIII (Feb., 1944), 35; Seymour, *Design for Giving*, 88.
[48] American National Red Cross, *Foreign War Relief Operations*, 15.
[49] *New York Times*, Feb. 16, 22, March 8, Sept. 2, 1942, Jan. 5, March 2, 1943, April 30, 1944; Matson, *Survey* LXXVIII, 231.
[50] Seymour, *Design for Giving*, 81.

nings in 1941 represented an important decision for the American Friends Service Committee. Except for the help given to British Quakers in the refugee-aid program in Shanghai, the AFSC had no experience in the Far East. It did, to be sure, join the United China Relief on assurance that no "hate Japan" campaign was to be sanctioned. This was the situation when Christopher Sharman, a young British member of the Friends Ambulance Unit, visited the Philadelphia headquarters in February, 1941, to ask for help in the work undertaken in China. The Unit could not keep up its program in the Nazi-dominated countries of Europe. Its personnel, courageous young British and Canadian conscientious objectors, wanted to undertake the perilous job of aiding the wounded and sick millions in China. The officers of the AFSC hesitated: some felt that relief activities involving military as well as civilian populations came dangerously near jeopardizing the Quaker peace testimony. But in view of the intense need and the idealism of the young Britishers in the Ambulance Unit, the AFSC decided to join in the effort.[51]

With financial help from the British Foreign Office, English Quakers, the American United China Relief and the American Red Cross, the Friends Ambulance Unit organized a convoy of ten ambulances, fifty trucks, and two mobile hospitals to transport medical supplies from Rangoon to the besieged cities of western China. The new Burma road itself was rough and so steep that driving had to be in low gear. Already, so it was said, 1,500 trucks had slid off the road into the abyss. Thousands lay stranded on the road because it was impossible to find needed repair parts. Yet the Unit's personnel, which included at first only a few Americans, faced with fortitude not only these conditions but brigands and typhus. When the Burma road was closed by the Japanese, the Unit reassembled in China and began the work of medical transport from Kutsing to the far corners of the besieged country. The program had grown: besides seventy young Englishmen, some Canadians, and a good number of Chinese, the Unit included seventeen Americans. The contingent from the United States would have been much larger had Congress not stipulated in an Army appropriation bill that no conscientious objectors were to leave the country. Incredible conditions, including cholera, typhoid, and dysentery, took a heavy toll, but the young Friends

[51] Clarence E. Pickett, *For More Than Bread: An Autobiographical Account of Twenty-Two Years' Work With the American Friends Service Committee* (Boston: Little, Brown, 1953), 211 ff.; *New York Times*, June 22, 1941.

succeeded in transporting 90 per cent of all the medicines to reach western China in the later years of the war.[52] Major William Hadsell, commanding the Chinese Expeditionary Force, expressed his admiration of what the Ambulance Unit did: "These people have," he reported, "served courageously and unselfishly the officers and men of the division, in medical aid, throughout the whole campaign west of the Salween River. During combat they were at forward medical installations performing operations and rendering first aid and assistance to the wounded. The zeal and energy which they put into their work under extremely dangerous conditions, never complaining of their own hardship with practically no rations and very little equipment and clothing, won the whole-hearted respect of the Chinese and American personnel serving with them." [53] After the war the Ambulance Unit joined its activities with those carried on in China by UNRRA.

Meantime the Unit provided in India a tiny but significant spearhead of emergency relief in a calamitous famine, the result of cyclones, rainstorms, tidal waves, and the war, which cut off India's food imports from Burma, Indo-China, and Thailand, strained the transportation system, and led to runaway inflation. By October, 1943, some 100,000 persons were reported as dying weekly in Bengal alone. By February, 1944, the University of Calcutta announced a toll of three and a half million above the normal death rate. The Mennonite missionaries in India had established in 1942 an ongoing relief group, the Mennonite Relief Committee of India. This agency increased its normal flow of aid during the famine crisis so that between November, 1943, and February, 1944, it distributed more than 140 tons of rice to over 6,200 persons. But a new agency, the India Famine Relief Committee, organized in the United States by Pearl Buck and Richard J. Walsh, was able to raise only small sums, and the American Red Cross did not plan to send more than the $57,000 worth of milk and medicine for which it had arranged. An agreement was made between these agencies, the National War Fund, and the AF of L and CIO to channel relief through the American Friends Service Committee, the Friends Ambulance Unit, and the Indian Red Cross. By 1943, $100,000 was available; in 1944, $700,000; and

---

[52] Pickett, *For More Than Bread*, 214 ff., 223; A. Tegla Davies, *Friends Ambulance Unit: The Story of the F.A.V. in the Second World War, 1939-1946* (London: Allen and Unwin, 1947), 273 ff.

[53] *Afserco News* V (April, 1945), n.p.

in 1945, nearly $600,000. It was all too plain that such funds were utterly inadequate and that in such a disaster only government and intergovernment aid could cope with the situation.[54] When the National War Fund discontinued its support, a new agency, American Relief for India, with Friends taking a leading part, kept at the job.

American contributions included milk for children's canteens, 40,000,000 multi-vitamin tablets, sulfa, atabrine and other drugs, and support for orphanages. Hoping to encourage self-help and to point the way to prevention of such disasters in the future, the program supported agricultural and industrial cooperatives. The little that could be done was indeed little in view of the need. But at least an example was given of the feasibility of bringing together peoples of different castes, religions, and politics to work on common human objectives. It was also hoped that the Anglo-American-Indian cooperation in one of the world's greatest tension areas might make a small bridge across cultural differences.[55]

While the fight against famine went on in India, events in Europe moved rapidly. The year 1944 proved to be a watershed, for the magic word "liberation" began at last to take on reality as one country after another was freed from the Axis noose.

On December 1, 1944, representatives of several American agencies met in Allied-occupied Paris to discuss ways of cooperation with each other and with UNRRA. Present, among others, were members of the Church Committee on Overseas Relief, the National Catholic Welfare Conference, the Jewish Joint Distribution Committee, the American Friends Service Committee, and the American Council of Voluntary Agencies for Foreign Service. Their task was a staggering one. In Normandy, which had paid a heavy toll during the invasion, there was food, but bridges and roads were in ruins. In every town from 20 per cent to 80 per cent of the houses were completely destroyed: the rest were badly damaged. At Le Havre,

[54] *Afserco News* IV (Jan., 1944), n.p., IV (March, 1944), n.p., IV (May-June, 1944), n.p.; American Friends Service Committee, *Annual Report*, 1943 (Philadelphia: AFSC, 1944), 8; 1944, 10; 1945, 8; Pickett, *For More Than Bread*, 246 ff.; John D. Unruh, *In the Name of Christ: a History of the Mennonite Central Committee and Its Service, 1920-1951* (Scottsdale, Pa.: Herald, 1952), 73-75.

[55] American Friends Service Committee, *A Report on Friends Famine Relief in India, 1945, together with a Report of American Relief for India, Inc. supporting the Work of AFSC* (Philadelphia: AFSC, 1946), 21; Eric Johnson, "Aftermath of Famine," *Survey* LXXXI (June, 1945), 173.

8,000 had been killed in the bombing, 40,000 were homeless, and 20,000 were sleeping without blankets on tables and on floors. Shortage of food in southern France was acute; children were sick and tubercular. Of the 30,000 Jewish children living in France when the war struck, half had been killed or deported during the German occupation, while of those left at least half had lost their parents through death or deportation.[56]

It is impossible in the present account to picture what each of the agencies did, or to describe the precious help of the Council of British Societies for Relief Abroad, the British Friends, and organizations in neutral countries. But the work of two or three American groups can suggest the story.

For the Friends, relief had never been the only or the main object. It was more important to demonstrate an unshaken faith in the power of love to heal the broken dignity of the human soul, to reconcile and restore, and to find paths to peace and understanding.[57] But material aid as the outward expression of such a purpose best lends itself to description. Even before the Allied invasion of France, the AFSC had put $200,000 on deposit in Switzerland and Portugal for quick aid once it was possible to pick up the threads in France that had been broken in 1942. Joining hands with the British Friends and their French counterpart, *Secours Quaker*, the AFSC during the bitter winter of 1944-1945 supplied $700,000 worth of food, clothing and workshop materials.[58] "We hope," one young French girl wrote, "little American children will never be as hungry as we are, but if they are, we will save our centimes for them." [59] For Italy, many tons of clothing were collected by Friends and handed to the American Relief for Italy. But the big task was reconstruction: the AFSC and the Ambulance Unit took hold by helping the people of Chieti Province rebuild their homes before winter set in.[60] Refugees and

[56] Pickett, *For More Than Bread*, 184-89; American Friends Service Committee, *Annual Reports*, 1944, 5-6; *Afserco News* IV (Sept., 1944), n.p., V (Jan., 1945), n.p.
[57] Henry J. Cadbury, *After Thirty Years, 1917-1947* (Philadelphia: American Friends Service Committee, 1947); American Friends Service Committee, *Annual Report*, 1944, 5.
[58] Roger C. Wilson, *Quaker Relief. An Account of the Relief Work of the Society of Friends, 1940-1948* (London: Allen and Unwin, 1942), 114 ff.; American Friends Service Committee, *Annual Report*, 1944, 5-6; *Annual Report*, 1945, 6-7; *Afserco News* IV (Sept., 1944), n.p., IV (Dec., 1944), n.p.
[59] Howard E. Kershner, "We Starve Our Friends," *Collier's* CXII (July 31, 1943), 22.
[60] American Friends Service Committee, *Annual Report*, 1944, 8; 1945, 7; *Afserco News* IV (Feb., 1944), n.p.; V (April, 1945), n.p.

displaced persons in Sweden, North Africa, and the Near East received help from the Quakers in 1944, while ten medical personnel worked with UNRRA's Balkan mission and in a camp near Cairo that offered sanctuary to 30,000 Yugoslavs.[61] What was done in Central Europe and other countries belongs to the postwar story.

Although less well known to the public than the Quakers, the Mennonites and the Brethren were also demonstrating a kindred faith in the religious obligation to resist war and to serve men in need as evidence of brotherhood. Having established the Mennonite Central Committee to coordinate the work of relief agencies already formed by constituent Mennonite sects, the Committee in 1943 began to work with Polish and Balkan refugees in the Middle East, first in cooperation with MERRA (Middle East Relief and Refugee Administration), a British organization, and after 1944 with UNRRA which assumed MERRA's responsibilities. The Mennonite Central Committee became active in Ethiopia (at the time of Italian withdrawal) and in Europe and Asia without giving up the pioneer rehabilitation program it had launched in Paraguay in the 1930's.[62] The Brethren, who had worked with the Mennonites and Quakers in the Spanish Civil War, formalized overseas relief work by setting up the Brethren Service Committee in 1939. Two years later this committee began its work in India, and when Allied victories opened the doors in Europe, joined with other religious agencies in providing emergency relief.[63]

On many occasions the Friends, Mennonites, and Brethren worked with the Joint Distribution Committee and other Jewish agencies concerned with overseas relief, especially with refugee escape, resettlement, and rehabilitation. Nor was the help that Jews received from gentiles limited to the so-called peace sects. In many lands Protestant and Catholic clergymen and laymen took great risks and made big sacrifices to aid Jews who were hiding from the Gestapo or trying desperately and almost hopelessly to escape the crematories. The penalty for helping wanted Jews was death. But this did not stop numberless men and women from taking part in the underground

[61] American Friends Service Committee, *Annual Report*, 1943, 8; 1944, 10; *Afserco News* IV (Dec., 1944), n.p.

[62] Unruh, *In the Name of Christ*, 13-16; Irvin B. Horst, *A Ministry of Goodwill* (Akron, Pa., 1950), 17-18, 20, 22, 30-31, 38, 43, 52, 58-59.

[63] Lorell Weiss, *Ten Years of Brethren Service, 1941-1951* (Elgin, Ill.: General Brotherhood Board, 1952), 3-11, 33-44.

operations that enabled thousands to escape to Lisbon and, if lucky, to Latin America or Shanghai or Palestine. Nor did penalties stop the underground work for thousands of others that the Swiss government, relaxing its early rigid neutrality, now sheltered, nor for additional thousands who found sanctuary in Sweden. Far greater numbers—perhaps 350,000 people—reached the Persian border of the Soviet Union.

Skeptical for too long a time about the bloodcurdling crimes of Auschwitz, Belsen, Dachau, and Buchenwald, neutral and Allied peoples and governments were at last forced to admit the realities that were speeding six million Jews to death, some by starvation and preventable disease, but most by the gas chamber after unspeakable anxieties, agonies, indignities, and tortures. To be sure, Britain did not go very far in yielding to pressure to open wider the doors of Palestine. For various reasons, including fear lest enemy agents or political undesirables filter through, Congress did not change the immigration restrictions. In fact, Congress did not relax restrictions sufficiently to fill the quotas set by law. The State Department did, to be sure, sometimes give a liberal interpretation to regulations. The Treasury, too, in general took a position somewhat more generous than that of its counterpart in London in permitting the use of frozen assets and the changing of dollars into needed Swiss francs when specified lives clearly hung in the balance.[64] In January, 1944, President Roosevelt also created the War Refugee Board to aid in the relief work of the voluntary organizations by speeding up their work through averting unnecessary delays and facilitating the movement of refugees out of the work and concentration camps of occupied countries.[65]

In its main overseas operations between Pearl Harbor and V-J Day, the JDC, one of the chief agencies cooperating with the War Refugee Board, worked closely with many Jewish agencies and often allocated funds to them. Its achievements owed much to the cooperation between JDC and local Jewish welfare agencies still in existence in France, Switzerland, and other countries as well as international Hebrew organizations and the Palestine institutions concerned with immigration and resettlement.[66] JDC moved its head-

[64] Agar, *The Saving Remnant*, 138, 141, 148.
[65] Roosevelt Papers: *American Jewish Yearbook*, Sept., 1945–Sept., 1946, XLVII (Philadelphia: Jewish Publication Society of America, 1946), 211, 296-97.
[66] *American Jewish Yearbook*, Sept., 1944–Sept., 1945, XLVI (Philadelphia: Jewish Publication Society of America, 1945), 164-68. See pp. 387-88.

quarters to Lisbon but kept in close touch with overground and underground operations in Switzerland and Sweden. It made a point of working within the law, but its European representatives managed to find ways of stretching and of bypassing legal regulations.

One job, of course, was to keep alive the Jews in hiding such as the 40,000 in France who were provided with food. Another task was to smuggle concentrated food and medicines into camps in Vichy France and in Poland. This smuggling continued until the hundreds of thousands of Jews in Warsaw's loathsome ghetto had died or been put to death in gas chambers.[67] On the Persian border of Soviet Russia some 150,000 of the 350,000 refugees from Central and Eastern Europe who could get no further toward Palestine, were kept alive by a highly ingenious system. Packages of much desired consumers goods (razor blades, soap, needles, tobacco, tea) were bought and sent in through Teheran, to be bartered for food which the Russians would not sell but were glad to exchange for scarce goods. Thus at a cost of $5,000,000 the 150,000 survivors of the trek were kept alive for two and a half years until at the end of the war many reached Palestine.[68]

But to keep people alive, especially in France and certainly in Poland, was only too often merely to save them for the crematories. Thus, despite overwhelming odds the effort was never given up to get people to safety. The risks and difficulties involved in the initial and early stages of escape to a neutral country or to the Black Sea ports can hardly be exaggerated. Operations had to be largely underground. Anyone caught trying to escape, or helping someone else in the attempt, was almost certain to be hanged. That others might take warning, bodies were often dangled publicly for days. What such European representatives of JDC as Dr. Joseph Schwartz and Morris Trooper undertook, in the all but hopeless effort to save at least a few lives through escape, has been dramatically related by Herbert Agar. Special tribute must be paid to Saly Mayer, a retired lace manufacturer of St. Gall. With his own funds and the help of his wife, he saved hundreds of lives partly by delaying Gestapo action against Hungarian Jews through negotiations for possible Nazi release of Jewish prisoners in exchange for needed commodities. Nevertheless 400,000 or more Hungarian Jews went to death at Auschwitz.[69]

Through determined effort, some 6,000 children were smuggled

[67] Agar, *The Saving Remnant*, 142 ff.
[68] *American Jewish Yearbook*, Sept., 1945–Sept., 1946, XLVII, 309.
[69] Agar, *The Saving Remnant*, 147 ff.

from France into Switzerland and thousands of adults were helped to reach that country and Sweden. The JDC and allied groups chartered freighters at Lisbon and the Black Sea ports in an effort to move refugees who succeeded in reaching these beacons of hope to the Americas or to Palestine. One little ship, the *Struma*, crowded beyond the limits of imagination and incredibly unseaworthy, was held up for three months in the harbor of Istanbul while every effort was made to get permission to land the pitiful cargo of 769 human beings in Palestine. But the British served notice that they would arrest the passengers. At last the ship, driven to sea by the Turks, headed for Roumania where the inevitable death train for Auschwitz would be waiting. Luckily perhaps, Agar comments, the *Struma* struck a mine and sank. One person survived. But other ships fared better, and thousands did reach points of safety.

The cost in human effort and sacrifice involved in thus salvaging some hundreds of thousands who reached safety or who survived through help received can never of course be calculated. It is possible to indicate the money cost of what the JDC and its affiliates did or tried to do. During 1942 the United Jewish Appeal raised $14,428,252 which was divided between JDC, United Palestine, and the National Refugee Service. In 1943 the total rose to $18,000,000 ($8,360,000 to JDC, $5,640,000 to United Palestine, and $2,760,000 to National Refugee Service). The next year, 1944, over $25,000,000 was collected, while in 1945 the figure reached $32,875,535. In this, the last year of the war, the JDC appropriated $28,307,772 for its work, which included sending relief in kind to Europe, particularly to central Europe, with substantial sums for technical retraining and for other types of refugee work in the Middle East, northern Africa, and Latin America.[70] JDC also had to pay back the $6,000,000 lent by Frenchmen during the war for the aid and hiding of Jews and the $5,000,000 similarly lent to keep alive the 20,000 refugees in Shanghai. In addition, Jewish overseas agencies set themselves the task of rebuilding communities wherever there was anything left on which to build. At the most, only fragments of Jewish populations had survived. But the spirit of the remnant lived: Edward Warburg found that the survivors sought not philanthropy but participation in the rebuilding.[71]

[70] *American Jewish Yearbook*, Sept., 1943–Sept., 1944, XLV, 174, and Sept., 1945–Sept., 1946, XLVI, 304-10.
[71] American Jewish Joint Distribution Committee, *Annual Report*, 1946 (New York: American Jewish JDC, 1947), 1.

During the actual war years the United States continued to be the main source of funds for Palestine. In addition to the allocations from the United Palestine Appeal, the Keren Kayemeth (Jewish National Fund) and the Keren Hayesod (Palestine Foundation Fund) received special gifts and bequests from Americans. In the year ending in June, 1942, Hadassah contributed a million and a half dollars to various immigration and welfare projects, particularly those involving health and youth adjustment in Palestine.[72] In the same year the National Labor Committee for Palestine contributed $500,000 for economic institutions, a labor organization, and other social, religious, and cultural agencies. Girls' training and residence centers and the Haifa Technical Institute received substantial sums.[73] During the crucial year 1943-1944 the American Friends of the Hebrew University contributed approximately three-fourths of the $892,000 budget of the University.[74]

Thus, even in the midst of war determined and constructive philanthropy continued in Palestine. Land was purchased, agricultural colonies were settled, commercial and industrial institutions were developed, and health, welfare, and cultural agencies were strengthened. All this could be accomplished, thanks to what the people of Palestine themselves contributed and what continued to come from the overseas Jewish agencies interested in the homeland. In 1945 the American Fund for Palestinian Institutions, which coordinated the fund-raising activities of fifty-two educational, cultural, and welfare agencies, contributed 30 per cent of their normal budget of $1,200,000, the rest being raised in Palestine.[75]

Both before Pearl Harbor and in the years following the American Red Cross contributed directly and indirectly to relief in Spain, France, Britain, China, Russia, and Greece. It aided refugees from Germany, Poland, and Yugoslavia. It took special responsibility for getting food parcels to American and United Nations prisoners: in all, over $5,000,000 was spent on this project. During the years in which the United States was involved in the conflict, the Red Cross's direct overseas relief contributions approximated $13,000,000. In addition to this it distributed large quantities of bandages and other

---

[72] *American Jewish Yearbook*, Sept., 1941–Sept., 1942, XLIII, 98.
[73] *Ibid.*, 101.
[74] *American Jewish Yearbook*, Sept., 1945–Sept., 1946, XLVII, 334.
[75] *Ibid.*, Sept., 1944–Sept., 1945, XLVI, 184.

medical supplies furnished by local chapters, as well as clothing, blankets, sanitary supplies, and food provided by Congressional appropriation. In all, the aid that passed through Red Cross channels for the years of American participation totaled some $148,000,000. Yet this aid, which went chiefly to Great Britain, Soviet Russia, France, Italy, and China, was overshadowed by a vastly greater sum spent on the American armed forces at home and abroad and on families of the military in need of help.[76]

In relation to what the Red Cross and other secular and religious agencies did the role of the foundations was a minor one. The Kellogg Foundation continued its projects to improve rural life in selected areas in Canada and Latin America, and the Near East Foundation did a good deal for refugees. The larger and older foundations bearing the Carnegie and Rockefeller names were compelled to curtail many of their overseas projects under way at several scientific centers in the occupied countries, nor could the exchange of scholars continue along established lines.[77] On the other hand, these foundations did a good deal which bore on immediate problems and which contributed to planning for the resumption of cultural interchange, for political and economic reconstruction, and for building a durable peace once the Axis surrendered.

In the first category, the Rockefeller Foundation's Division of Public Health continued its cooperation with the Brazilian government in the fight against malaria and instituted on request a similar program in Nigeria and in Egypt.[78] When Allied armies took over Algiers and southern Italy the Rockefeller Foundation took responsibility for delousing millions of military and civilian population to prevent epidemics, ingeniously devising a technique enabling the process to be effectively done without disrobing—an achievement appreciated by the sensitive Moslems. Less spectacular but important both for the time being and the long run were the researches supported at Marseilles on the nutritional problems of children and the advances made in brain surgery in British medical centers.[79]

In wartime, culture was less important than food and health. But

[76] American National Red Cross, *Foreign War Relief Operations,* 4-18; Foster Rhea Dulles, *The American Red Cross: A History* (New York: Harper, 1950), 373.
[77] Rockefeller Foundation, *Annual Report,* 1940 (New York: Rockefeller Foundation, 1941), 7, 16, 176-77; *Annual Report,* 1941, 7; *Annual Report,* 1942, 44; *Annual Report,* 1943, 36.
[78] *Ibid., Annual Report,* 1945, 18-20.
[79] Rockefeller Foundation, *Annual Report,* 1944, 29-39.

at a cost of a million and a half dollars, the Rockefeller Foundation brought over to the United States 300 refugee scholars, providing support until they could find places in American academic life.[80] The Foundation also initiated and later worked with the government in mapping the great cultural monuments in Europe in order that these might be spared by American bombers.[81] Looking forward to the difficult years after military victory, the Rockefeller Foundation supported researches designed to facilitate political, social, and economic reconstruction,[82] and also took steps to make available to overseas libraries back issues of American learned periodicals the transmission of which had been cut off by the war.[83] Meanwhile, the Carnegie Endowment for International Peace put its resources at the service of the State Department in the plans that were being made for a lasting international organization.[84]

Raymond Fosdick, president of the Rockefeller Foundation, sadly observed that in so complete an international cultural blackout, the little that foundations could do was painfully inadequate: but that little at least kept alive the established, but overlooked, fact that civilization had come to depend on cultural internationalism.[85] "The war," Fosdick wrote, "has re-erected many of these old partitions and has sealed the doors and windows of the nations. The great constructive task immediately ahead of us is to level these unnatural barriers against ideas and knowledge and experience—to open the doors and windows of the world and 'let the winds of freedom blow.' " [86]

[80] *Ibid., Annual Report,* 1945, 31.
[81] *Ibid., Annual Report,* 1943, 33-34; Janet Flanner, "Annals of Crime: The Beautiful Spoils," *New Yorker* XXIII (March 8, 1947), 38-42.
[82] Rockefeller Foundation, *Annual Report,* 1942, 34, 173-75.
[83] *Ibid., Annual Report,* 1941, 27-28.
[84] Carnegie Endowment for International Peace, *Year Book,* 1942 (New York: Carnegie Endowment for International Peace, 1943), and subsequent *Year Books.*
[85] Raymond B. Fosdick, *Chronicle of a Generation* (New York: Harper, 1958), 264 ff.
[86] Rockefeller Foundation, *Annual Report,* 1944, 11-12.

XVII

Helping the Victims Survive

The Second World War, involving Asia and Africa as well as Europe, left in its wake destruction far exceeding that which had stunned the world in 1918. In Europe much of the cultural life that had nourished the New World for centuries was either badly damaged or destroyed. The physical damage was even more dramatic. In great areas of Europe it seemed as if the broken pieces could never be put together again. For America's friends and foes alike, wrecked industrial plants and broken transportation and communication added to the confusion accompanying the collapse of governments. Rubble cluttered up great sections of half a hundred cities. At least 25 per cent of the housing in the areas fought over had been destroyed. In Warsaw, for example, 90 per cent of prewar housing was in ruins. One Polish province, Kielce, reported 146,000 persons living in hollows dug out of the rubble of their ravaged homes. Reports from the wartorn countries of Asia were even more disheartening. In Japan it was estimated that 80 per cent of the larger cities had been destroyed and that 21,000,000 people had lost their homes. In China the destruction resulting from the Japanese occupation and resistance to it was intensified by the continuing civil war that raged between Nationalist and Communist forces. Added to this, the perennially underdeveloped economies of other Asian countries were experiencing new depths of dislocation.[1]

Millions of people in these and other places were not only home-

[1] Herbert Hoover, *Addresses Upon the American Road, 1945-1948* (New York: Van Nostrand, 1949), 183, 271; Clarence E. Pickett, *For More Than Bread: An Autobiographical Account of Twenty-Two Years' Work with the American Friends Service Committee* (Boston: Little, Brown, 1953), 239. Arthur C. Ringland, "The Organization of Voluntary Foreign Aid: 1939-1953," *Department of State Bulletin* XXX (March 15, 1954), 383-93, is a pathbreaking study of relief in this period.

less but without adequate clothing. To cite only one example, in the winter of 1946 over 400,000 Polish children, with rags tied around their feet as their only protection against bitter snow, daily left unheated dugouts for unheated schools.

People without food found it hard to think of anything else. One can imagine the preoccupation with it in Germany where the ration was only 1,000 calories a day. In Vienna someone overheard the bewildered chatter of waifs in an underground dugout: they could not understand the mysteries of the calories that everyone was talking about. How was it you died in a concentration camp on 800 calories, that you died in Vienna on 1,100, but that the Americans ate as many as 6,000 a day and still lived? [2]

A year after V-E Day the situation had grown worse rather than better. The world was facing the most severe and widespread famine in history. Conditions resulted in part from wartime depletion of agricultural manpower, livestock, and fertilizer plants, and from the looting of food piles. Severe droughts in the Mediterranean countries and especially in South Africa and India, together with floods and continuing civil war in China, imperiled millions of lives. In Liuchow, in China's Kwangsi Province, ragged beggars, young and old, gathered to pick up grains of rice as they fell from the weekly rations of soldiers. [3]

Herbert Hoover, who had been urging in vain a program similar to the one he headed after the First World War, accepted President Truman's invitation to serve on the Food Emergency Committee. The seventy-three-year-old veteran, likening himself to the retired family doctor who was asked in to help in a crisis, in the spring of 1946 journeyed 35,000 miles to find out needs, discover sources of surplus, and coordinate efforts to control the alarming situation. Hoover estimated that 500,000,000 people, almost a third of the world's population, were suffering from food shortages. [4] While the governments of Western Europe had assets for buying food if it could be made available, this was not the case in Central and southeastern Europe. And, over all, orphaned children and displaced persons were dependent on charity. The immediate question was one of survival.

[2] Robert Neuman, *Children of Vienna* (New York: Dutton, 1947), 77.
[3] Douglas Charlwood, "Breadbasket in China," *Christian Science Monitor Magazine*, Feb. 8, 1947, 2.
[4] Hoover, *Addresses Upon the American Road, 1945-1948*, 172, 221.

To meet in some part these vast needs not only of former allies but of vanquished foes, people in many countries helped—Canadians, Australians, and Latin Americans, as well as European neutrals. Even in badly wartorn countries such as Britain the response was generous. Yet with American industry in high gear, with potatoes and other agricultural surpluses being dumped and plans afoot for actually curtailing farm production, it was obvious that Americans, now as in 1919, were better able than anyone else to shoulder the main burden.

In the crisis period of 1919-1923 Americans had given generously, but not a few subsequently turned their backs with the self-righteous slogan "let Europe stew in its own juice." Some still felt that way. Many were preoccupied with other things or were just indifferent. Governor Thomas Dewey of New York believed that the administration's voluntary food conservation program in the spring of 1946 was, despite Hoover's blessing, "a failure and a farce." [5] It was by no means clear that the great majority of Americans appreciated the extent of foreign need nor the national responsibility of meeting it.

Yet it seemed to many men and women in the United States that the future of civilization might depend on how well their country accepted its responsibility for giving material aid and for providing leadership. Far-reaching changes in attitude had indeed taken place since the 1920's. Poverty and want at home were no longer generally regarded as badges of failure and guilt, and in many circles this view had been extended to unfortunate peoples beyond the national domain. In addition to this shift other factors indicated that Americans would not shut their eyes to Europe's needs. Many agreed with Hoover's position, which he made clear in a personal report to Truman: "We can," the ex-President said, "carry on the Military Government of Germany by the tenets of the Old Testament of 'a tooth for a tooth, and an eye for an eye,' or we can inaugurate the precepts of the New Testament. The difference in result will be the loss of millions of lives, the damage of all Europe, and the destruction of any hope of peace in the world. I recommend the New Testament method." [6]

Other considerations also figured in men's thoughts and feelings. Letters written or turned over to the House Committee on Foreign

[5] Walter Millis, ed., *The Forrestal Diaries* (New York: Viking, 1951), 326.
[6] Louis P. Lochner, *Herbert Hoover and Germany* (New York: Macmillan, 1960), 186.

Affairs in the postarmistice years generally took the position that the economic and political interests of the United States required the restoration of the European economy and living standards. Testimony from many parts of the country indicated considerable support for the view that America had a responsibility to assume and a tradition to continue. Letters also expressed the view that the recovery of Europe would stave off further Communist victories.[7] To let people starve in areas controlled by American military forces seemed, in Hoover's words, unthinkable, since no one wanted to see American boys machine-gunning famished rioters. Moreover, to let people starve in the occupation zones was sure to bring total destruction of morals and to expose American soldiers to the infectious diseases that go hand in hand with famine. Indifference, Hoover further emphasized, was also unthinkable by reason of the compassion in the American character.[8] If there was evidence of American generosity, as there indeed was, the response of government circles and a considerable segment of public opinion was also affected by practical considerations.

Amid such discussions of responsibility and concern American relief agencies, some already in existence, others newly formed, made ready to carry out as best they could the tasks which they had never doubted it was their duty to meet. In the immediate postwar period two problems in American overseas philanthropy transcended all others. The first was the necessity of adjusting to the greater governmental and intergovernmental activity. The second was the continuing pressure for organization and coordination of private voluntary agencies. The accommodation and the resistance of voluntary agencies to these main trends is a key to much that took place in the efforts to help victims of the war survive through general relief.

Many voluntary agencies were anxious to begin overseas ministrations as quickly as possible. But the chaos which might have resulted from eager but poorly coordinated relief ventures was checked by two national organizations established to prevent such confusion. Founded in 1943 and incorporated the next year, the American Council of Voluntary Agencies for Foreign Service was essentially

---

[7] House Committee on Foreign Affairs, HR 80A-F, 18794, 18816 (March-May, 1947), National Archives, Washington, D. C.

[8] Hoover, *Addresses Upon the American Road, 1945-1948*, 226.

a coordinating clearing house for the seventeen initial members and the fifty-five organizations to which the membership had increased by 1947. (In that year the combined budget of the member agencies was $200,000,000.) During the last year of the war the Council facilitated discussion among its members of ways of meeting emergency needs once the fighting stopped. It also established criteria for membership—stability in financial record, acceptance of approved standards in fund raising, and demonstration of reasonable overhead for administration, publicity, and promotion. Criteria also included proof that objectives were humanitarian rather than propagandistic and political, and that these purposes were clearly defined, realistic in terms of assets or expected assets, and broad enough to render the program of genuine significance in foreign relief and administration.

The structure and functions of the Council took form fairly quickly. It was not an operating agency. It made no decisions without the approval of its constituents' officers. It did recommend procedures to its members, and it tried to influence agencies to emphasize humanitarianism in the few cases in which objectives included political or propagandistic considerations. But its suggestions had no binding force. Its small but competent and dedicated staff was headed during the first year by Clarence King of the New York School of Social Work. Charlotte Owen, whose training was also in social work, then began a long service as executive director. The cost of maintaining staff and other activities was met by prorata contributions from members. Much of the work was done by committees composed of staff and representatives of member agencies who worked on matters related to geographical and functional areas of concern.

In addition to facilitating exchange of experience and information among members, the Council built channels through which voluntary efforts could be effectively correlated with official agencies and programs. The staff and committee members also spoke for constituent agencies at Congressional hearings: the files of the Council testify to the appreciation for such services of key men in Congress.

Nor were the contributions of the Council of Voluntary Agencies limited to the United States. A good deal was done to keep members in touch with international organizations in the field of relief and rehabilitation. In the latter days of the war, representatives of member agencies in foreign countries found it hard to coordinate their work. The Council then fostered the organization, in countries in which two or more of its members operated, of counterpart national or regional coordinating councils, the functions of which were much like its own. The Polish council, for example, did a splendid job in developing cooperation between American, foreign, and Polish relief agencies, both in the relations among themselves and between the agencies and the Polish government.[9]

As the years passed, some felt that the American Council was not aggressive enough in dealing with matters of common concern, in presenting the claims of voluntary relief to the public, and in sponsoring basic research on pertinent problems.[10] But the continued support it enjoyed together with its record testified to its usefulness.

In a sense the counterpart of the Council in governmental circles was the Advisory Committee on Voluntary Foreign Aid, which was organized on May 14, 1946, when President Truman dissolved the old War Relief Control Board. Attached to the State Department, it was headed by Charles P. Taft, whose accumulated experience in the former War Relief Control Board was appreciated and much needed. Arthur C. Ringland, an old Hoover lieutenant in overseas work after the First World War, played an important role as executive officer. The new Advisory Committee did not have, as its predecessor did, power to grant licenses or to limit and control fund-raising campaigns. But it could investigate the legitimacy and practicality of cooperating agencies, maintain records that such agencies might voluntarily file, and serve as the responsible official body for recommending policies affecting the relations of the voluntary agencies with government. It was, in other words, empowered to "invite" cooperation and to "advise" private agencies. A nonpolitical body representing the public interest in facilitating communication between government agencies and voluntary societies concerned with overseas relief, the Advisory Committee naturally assumed more

[9] Working Group on Contracts, typescript; Working Group on Health, typescript; Working Group on Fundamental Education, typescript; Foreign Voluntary Aid to Poland, 1945-1949, bound typescript; Memorandum on the "Fulton Report," Jan. 26, 1948, all in the files of the American Council of Voluntary Agencies for Foreign Service, New York [hereafter cited as American Council Files]; interviews with Charlotte Owen, Elizabeth Clark Reiss, Dr. Wayland Zwayer, and other members of the ACVAFS staff, June, 1960.

[10] Program and Management Study of the ACVAFS, prepared by Walter W. Pettit, Shelby Harrison, and Eduard C. Lindeman, dated April 7, 1952, American Council Files.

than merely advisory functions when government subsidies to voluntary agencies became national policy.[11]

Some years before the policy of government subsidy to voluntary relief agencies developed, while, in fact, the war still raged, the foresighted had realized that the task of relief and rehabilitation of whole continents was too vast for voluntary agencies alone. Having frankly expressed this view, American Red Cross executives made no effort to repeat the large scale civilian relief undertaken after the First World War. They did, to be sure, spend $10,000,000 in the immediate postwar period for milk-feeding programs, medical supplies, hospital units, and other relief in several European countries and in China. But its main emphasis was in helping the Red Cross societies of war-torn countries rebuild themselves, in bringing them up to date in new medical techniques, especially the uses of blood, and in sharing American experience in organization and procedure.[12] Other agencies, without showing any disposition to turn the whole job over to the government, shared in greater or less degree the feeling of the Red Cross that needs were too massive for private philanthropy alone.

In planning for the postwar emergency the American Council of Voluntary Agencies for Foreign Service urged Americans to help win the peace by supporting UNRRA, the international agency of the allied nations designed to channel relief contributed mainly by governments with such supplementary private donations as might be collected. It will be remembered that the first official response was the appropriation by Congress in March, 1944, of $1,350,000,000 for UNRRA. Between that date and the death of UNRRA in 1947, the United States government provided over $2,600,000,000 or about

[11] Allen T. Burns, "Leadership with World Horizons," *Survey* LXXIII (April, 1947), 120-23; U. S., Congress, House, Select Committee on Foreign Aid, *Final Report on Foreign Aid*, 80th Cong., 2d Sess., 1948, H. Rept. 1845, 797 [hereafter cited as *Final Report on Foreign Aid*]; Charles P. Taft, "Résumé of Remarks . . . in A Speech Delivered at the Opening Session of the Food for Peace Conference, Sept. 1, 1960," mimeographed sheet distributed by the Advisory Committee on Voluntary Foreign Aid; Ringland, *Department of State Bulletin* XXX, 384-86.

[12] Between V-E Day and June, 1946, the Red Cross also contributed 13,000,000 surplus war prisoner packages and aided substantially in the exchange of war prisoners. It also, of course, maintained its disaster relief program, taking the field in seventy-five major disasters in the decade following the end of World War II: Foster Rhea Dulles, *The American Red Cross: A History* (New York: Harper, 1950), 516-17; *New York Times*, June 21, 1946; *For the Common Weal: A Ten-Year Report on the International Activities of the American Red Cross* (Washington: The American National Red Cross, 1955).

70 per cent of the total budget of the international agency.[13] A growing partnership of government and private effort in meeting overseas needs was evident in the voluntary cash contributions of $1,347,832 which Americans made directly to UNRRA, along with the proceeds of the United States Emergency Food Collection. This latter drive yielded canned goods valued at over $1,000,000, and clothing and other commodities estimated as worth $145,481,955.[14] The cooperation of private philanthropy with government was also reflected in the large number of trained personnel that the voluntary organizations lent to UNRRA and in that agency's remuneration of many relief workers who were operating overseas programs for their own agencies.

Despite an impressive record of feeding and clothing needy Europeans and Asians and in giving temporary help to millions of displaced persons, in the spring of 1946 UNRRA was, according to Hoover's estimate, helping not more than 30 per cent of those in need of food in the area between the English Channel and the Russian border.[15] Nor did it provide the large-scale and effective international mechanism necessary for meeting other emergency needs and for speeding European recovery.[16] Reports reached America that of the $132,250,000 worth of food, machinery, fishing boats, water buffalos and other produce sent to China for relief and rehabilitation, only a trickle had found its way to those needing them most. The bulk of supplies lay piled up in warehouses, filtered down into the depths of the black market, or enriched the morass of government corruption.[17] Moreover, many Americans complained that the United States could not prevent its very large contributions from being channeled to the relief of peoples that did not seem to have

---

[13] George Soloveytchik, "After the Armies—UNRRA," *Survey Graphic* XXXIII (July, 1944), 311-12, 334-36; Frances Bowes Sayre, *Glad Adventure* (New York: Macmillan, 1957), 253-61; Herbert H. Lehman, "UNRRA on the March," *Survey Graphic* XXXIII (Nov., 1944), 437-40, 470-71; George Woodbridge, *UNRRA: The History of the United Nations Relief and Rehabilitation Administration* (3 vols.; New York: Columbia University Press, 1950), II, 70 ff.; Samuel I. Rosenman, comp., *The Public Papers and Addresses of Franklin D. Roosevelt* (13 vols.; New York: Harper, 1950), XIII, 416-18.

[14] *New York Times*, Sept. 4, 1946.

[15] Hoover, *Addresses Upon the American Road, 1945-1948*, 191.

[16] UNRRA worked chiefly as a supervisory agency, allocating supplies on a cash-purchase basis, and giving relief outright only to governments that were unable to afford purchases.

[17] *Time* XLVIII (July 22, 1946), 27; "Report from China," *Nation* CLXII (June 29, 1946), 794.

adopted all reasonable measures for self-help and, above all, to Communist-dominated countries. This criticism reached its peak when UNRRA supplies were being loaded in New York for Yugoslavia at the very time that Tito's forces were firing on American aircraft. After due notice, the United States withdrew from UNRRA on December 31, 1946. Most of its major programs had to be closed out in the early months of 1947.[18]

When it was clear that the United States would pull out of UNRRA, the voluntary agencies at once planned to enlarge their own programs. JDC announced that the end of UNRRA's work, without any provision for replacement, would require drastic expansion on its own part: it was already feeding 500,000 Jews in Europe and thousands in the Far East. At least $25,000,000 would be needed to continue this work in the next six months in view of the responsibilities in the offing. Another well-established agency, the American Friends Service Committee, reported an increase in its budget for Austria from $400,000 to $600,000 in the year ahead.[19] On its part the Red Cross responded by putting aside an additonal fund of $2,000,000 for Austrian relief, while John D. Rockefeller III offered such help as the foundation bearing the family name could give.[20]

Notwithstanding such plans and promises, the need was too great for voluntary philanthropy alone to meet. The Reverend Edward Swanstrom of Catholic Relief Services-National Catholic Welfare Conference voiced a common view in declaring that some form of governmental or intergovernmental activity would be necessary even if private groups were able and willing to try to fill the gap left by America's withdrawal from the relief and rehabilitation efforts of UNRRA.[21] Such, indeed, was the view of the government itself and it was still providing substantial help for civilians in the occupied zone in Germany (some of which was repaid), in Austria, and in

[18] Brookings Institution, International Studies Group, "Problem Paper 'B': American Assistance to Europe," *Major Problems of United States Foreign Policy, 1947* (Washington: Brookings Institution, 1947), 153-206; the files of the House of Representatives Select Committee on Foreign Aid deposited in the National Archives; Charles P. Taft, "Relief Organizations," *Vital Speeches* XI (March 2, 1945), 371-74; "Get a Horse," *Life* XXI (Dec. 30, 1946), 18; "Failure of UNRRA," *Commonweal* XLI (March 2, 1945), 484; *New Republic* CXIV (March 25, 1946), 398.

[19] *New York Times*, Aug. 8, 9, 1946.

[20] *Ibid.*, Aug. 18, 1946.

[21] *Ibid.*, Aug. 19, 1946.

Japan.[22] By midsummer of 1947 the government was enabling over 6,000,000 malnourished children of Germany and Austria to have supplementary feeding—a program for which Hoover has been given credit.[23] In February, 1947, President Truman, having these relief programs in mind, told a delegation from the American Council of Voluntary Agencies for Foreign Service that while voluntary help was as necessary as ever before, the provisioning of whole populations and the settlement of refugees had to be primarily a public task in view of the magnitude of the need.[24]

Within a few months the government indicated that the words of Truman were to be followed by additional deeds. While continuing its feeding programs in the American zone in Germany and its contributions to the United Nations International Refugee Organization and the International Children's Emergency Fund, the federal government initiated and sustained the European Recovery Program or Marshall Plan, which embodied many of the points for which Hoover had been contending.[25] After almost a year of study and debate, Congress approved a four-year program and authorized expenditures of $5,000,000,000 during the first year. From 1948 to 1952 the United States government continued to underwrite European recovery through the Marshall Plan. During these years over $13,000,-000,000 was spent, nearly 80 per cent of which went for raw materials, food, fuel, farm supplies, and finished goods.[26] In promoting the economic recovery of Western Europe, the Marshall aid program took an impossible burden of large-scale relief from the shoulders of voluntary agencies.

Another less publicized government decision affected even more directly the overseas relief agencies. During the debates in March,

[22] The announcement was made in Washington on January 20, 1961, that the West German government had repaid one-third of the $3,000,000,000 postwar foreign aid debt, which included underwriting of relief and rehabilitation in the immediate postwar years, but that no similar move had been made in Japan, where the Tokyo governments had not been at pains to disabuse the Japanese people of the misconception that the immediate postwar government aid had been a "gift": *New York Times*, Jan. 21, 1961.

[23] Hoover, *Addresses Upon the American Road, 1945-1948*, 269-85.

[24] *New York Times*, Feb. 28, 1947.

[25] U. S., Congress, Senate, *A Decade of American Foreign Policy: Basic Documents, 1941-49*, 81st Cong., 1st Sess., 1950, Senate Doc. 123, 1268-70.

[26] Harry B. Price, *The Marshall Plan and Its Meaning* (Ithaca: Cornell University Press, 1955), *passim*; U. S., Congress, House, *U. S. Foreign Aid: Its Purpose, Scope, Administration, and Related Information*, 86th Cong., 1st Sess., 1959, House Doc. 116, 41.

1947, on a joint resolution providing for unilateral agreements between the United States and countries deemed to be in need and worthy of American aid, Senator H. Alexander Smith of New Jersey, acting on a suggestion from the American Council of Voluntary Agencies for Foreign Service and the Advisory Committee on Voluntary Foreign Aid, offered an amendment to the resolution. This provided for $5,000,000 to pay necessary expenses incurred in the ocean transportation of supplies donated by voluntary agencies for foreign relief. The resolution, as amended, became Public Law 84. Relief supplies distributed under the authority of this law were to be given without regard to race, creed, or political belief; representatives of the press and government of the United States were to be allowed to observe distribution freely; and goods were to be marked conspicuously in order that their ultimate recipient might know their American origin.[27]

Other legislation provided that under certain conditions easily perishable agricultural surpluses might be given to voluntary agencies registered with the Advisory Committee.[28] Five years later this policy was extended and enlarged by the Agricultural Trade Development and Assistance Act of 1954 (Public Law 480). Under the leadership of Senator Hubert Humphrey increasing emphasis was put on the idea that the program ought to promote in a positive way the economic development of underdeveloped areas and world peace—an emphasis President Eisenhower helped to publicize and which President Kennedy was to stress even more emphatically. Under the basic legislation of 1954 and subsequent laws including one sponsored by Humphrey and passed in the spring of 1961, nine and a half billion dollars worth of surplus agricultural products were channeled to over a hundred countries by the summer of that year; this was approximately a fourth of American agricultural exports.[29] The program, which came to be known as Food for Peace, rested on the assumption that the private agencies had a significant role to play in overseas relief and rehabilitation, a role to be furthered by government in the interest of the agencies and their objectives as well as in that of national policy. Thus great opportunities were opened to the volun-

27 *Final Report on Foreign Aid*, 801-803; *Congressional Record*, 80th Cong., 1st Sess., 1947, XCIII, Pt. 4, 5122 ff.

28 *Final Report on Foreign Aid*, 801-803.

29 *Congressional Record*, 87th Cong., 1st Sess., 1961, CVIII, no. 15, 12293, 13354: *New York Times*, March 17, 24, 1961; "Food for Peace: A Success Story," *Foreign Policy Bulletin* XXXIX (July 15, 1960), 21, 163, 166.

tary agencies for expanded programs. These opportunities also carried concomitant problems.

Before what was to be called the "remarkable partnership" of government and the voluntary agencies got under way, however, the agencies had already thrown themselves into the overwhelming, almost hopeless task of getting immediate emergency relief to peoples—friends and former foes alike—in the greatest need. With the cooperation of the President's War Relief Control Board and the American Council of Voluntary Agencies for Foreign Service the participating members, pooling interests and experience, took an important part in founding three coordinating agencies which played a major role in immediate postwar emergency relief, in the long-range problems growing out of the war, and in self-help projects in underdeveloped areas.

Wishing to rush immediate relief into the occupied nations, the voluntary agencies faced a tangled knot of problems. These included transportation difficulties and the necessity of making arrangements with the military authorities governing Germany and Japan. Several American Council members carried on a joint study program with the War Relief Control Board and, late in 1945, the State Department and War Department permitted a mission of relief representatives to be sent to Germany to investigate the need and opportunities for private charity. The occupation authorities expressed a strong preference for dealing with a single representative of the American agencies interested in the relief of needy Germans in order to avoid confusion and duplication of effort. Finally, with President Truman's approval, several voluntary agencies formed the Council of Relief Agencies Licensed to Operate in Germany (CRALOG).[30]

CRALOG worked out a single agreement with the military government similar to ones earlier made by the International Red Cross and the Swedish, Danish, and Swiss agencies that had been first to reach Germany after the armistice.[31] Operations were begun in March, 1946, with the shipment of 2,000 tons of relief supplies. In the following summer, CRALOG negotiated an agreement through which private relief could also be sent into the French and British zones. By the end of January, 1947, CRALOG, as an agent for its

[30] Irvin B. Horst, *A Ministry of Goodwill* (Akron, Pa., 1950), 41; Burns, *Survey* LXXXIII (April, 1947), 122; *Final Report on Foreign Aid*, 808-809.
[31] Interview with Pastor Hans Diehl, Sept. 11, 1960.

member agencies in the United States, transmitted 24,000,000 pounds of food, clothing, and medicine. By the autumn of the next year the contributions totaled 110,000,000 pounds valued at $40,000,000. Nor did the stream stop: in 1950 CRALOG shipped 39,950,000 pounds of relief material.[32]

The German Central Committee for the Distribution of Gift Parcels, approved by the occupation authorities, allocated supplies to German voluntary agencies. These included labor groups and the non-sectarian social agency, *Arbeiterwohlsfahrt*. Also important was the Catholic organization, CARITAS, which, like other church-related agencies, had been greatly restricted during the war years. CARITAS displayed an amazing resilience in proliferating such works of mercy as *Bahnhofs Missions* (for the wandering homeless), reception centers (for the *Heimkehrer*), tracing services (for missing children and parents) and new institutions, all of which made fruitful use of supplies received from the German Central Committee. The Protestant counterpart of CARITAS, *Hilfswerk*, was to play a far-reaching role in postwar Germany. The relief thus supplied to these secular and church-related agencies went first to the young, the old, the sick, and the poor. But some of it also supplemented the meager rations of workers, thus contributing to the comeback in the productive capacity of the German labor force.[33]

In addition to helping the needy and strengthening workers, American voluntary aid affected German life and outlook in other ways. Evidence at hand supports the testimony of General Lucius Clay and other military administrators in the American zone that voluntary aid contributed to the emerging German democracy and to the orientation of the new republican state toward America and the West.[34] The German distributing agencies provided training in leadership for many on their administrative staffs, some of whom were thus in an advantageous position to take prominent parts in later national constitution-drafting and in the launching of the Fed-

[32] Horst, *A Ministry of Goodwill*, 43; Edward McSweeney, *American Voluntary Aid for Germany, 1945-1950* (Freiburg im Breisgau: Caritas-Verlag, 1950), *passim;* Albert Kohler and Eugen Rendt, *Wir Danken Euch* (Mindelheim: Selbsthilfe-Verlag, 1949).

[33] *Hilfswerk* requested and obtained pulp for paper, leather for shoes, metal for lamp filaments and other materials to enable German factories and workers to manufacture finished products as well as materials for the construction of churches, thus contributing further to German economic recovery. Interview with Dr. Georg Federer, German Consul General in New York, June 20, 1960, and Pastor Hans Diehl, September 11, 1961.

[34] *Final Report on Foreign Aid*, 791.

eral Republic. This was notably true of *Hilfswerk*. The administration of voluntary relief by this agency also stimulated German Protestantism to develop greater social consciousness.[35] The voluntary approach, with a greater flexibility than was common in the official bureaucracy, conveyed a sense of individual aiding individual, people helping people. A concrete example was the support given by some American agencies, notably those of the Friends and Unitarians, to neighborhood or community centers that were new to Germany. These took root and helped Germans to cope with their own welfare needs, such as planning for housing facilities, working out methods for securing jobs, and developing discussions of international affairs.[36] Informed Germans testified that American aid, especially voluntary aid, was an indication that the Germans were not to be regarded as guilty participants in an evil plot and isolated from the outside world to work out their problems alone; but rather that the hand that was lent on terms of Christian brotherhood and equal participation did much to help the German people again take a place in the larger Western community.[37] Testimonials of appreciation for what was done came from Catholic and Protestant German dignitaries, from mayors, from the man in the street, the child in the school.[38] Most eloquent of all testimonies, however, has been the growing readiness of many Germans to share some part of their new prosperity with those in other countries experiencing the hunger that they themselves once knew.[39]

In conquered Japan, problems similar to those in Germany were met by the formation in April, 1946, of Licensed Agencies for Relief in Asia (LARA). The eleven participating organizations were, with few exceptions, the same agencies that formed CRALOG: all were members of the American Council of Voluntary Agencies for Foreign Service. LARA was the sole private relief organization recognized by the Supreme Commander of the Allied Powers (SCAP), the governing authority for Japan. Allied authorities left the actual distribution of relief to the Japanese government, which set up a committee composed of representatives of SCAP, LARA, and Japanese welfare

[35] Interviews with Federer, June 20, 1960, and Diehl, Sept. 11, 1961.
[36] Florence Black, Chief, Welfare, Office of U. S. High Commissioner for Germany, to Miss Helen Fogg, Unitarian Service Committee, Jan. 5, 1952, Advisory Committee Files.
[37] Interviews with Federer, June 20, 1960, and Diehl, Sept. 11, 1961.
[38] McSweeny, *American Voluntary Aid to Germany*, 92-94.
[39] Interview with John Abbott, Church World Service, June 17, 1960.

agencies. In the first ten months of its operation, LARA sent to Japan well over half a million dollars in relief.[40] The regard General Douglas MacArthur had for LARA was reflected in a message he sent early in 1948 urging its continuation.[41]

The tendency to attack the vast postwar needs through the federation and cooperation of voluntary organizations under a government umbrella was reflected in a third agency, CARE (Cooperative American Remittances to Europe, in time, Cooperative for American Relief Everywhere). This agency differed qualitatively and existentially from all other voluntary agencies that had developed. It was a revealing symbol of our time: it was organized to meet a special, temporary need; it had no well-defined constituency in the sense that religious and other secular relief agencies had; it succeeded in capitalizing on a skillful use of mass media and in meeting certain needs to such an extent that in many minds it was identified with all American overseas relief.

The origins of CARE are complex. Its establishment resulted from the initiative of several men and agencies, private and governmental.[42] As in many other postwar relief programs, experience after the First World War provided precedents. Before the fighting in the Second World War was over, various New York gift package firms, department stores, and shipping agencies announced plans through which Americans could, as they had in 1918 and 1919, again send food parcels to friends and kinfolk in the devastated areas.[43] But transportation and customs fees in Europe often made the cost of such packages exorbitant.[44] Moreover, voluntary agencies working

---

[40] Burns, *Survey* LXXXIII (April, 1947), 122; U. S. Department of State, *Occupation of Japan, Policy and Progress,* Far Eastern Series 17 (Washington: Govt. Printing Office, 1946), *passim; Final Report on Foreign Aid,* 809-10.

[41] *New York Times,* Jan. 5, 1948.

[42] Charles Bloomstein's manuscript dealing with the early history of CARE, dated June, 1952, is in the CARE Archives, New York. Stanford Cazier is working on a full-length study.

[43] E. A. Jasper, President of the Paramount Shipping Board to War Shipping Administration, May 31, 1944; Liberty Shipping and Traveling Company to War Shipping Administration, July 20, 1944; Mrs. J. Hampden Dougherty, chairman of French-American Wives, to Arthur C. Ringland, April 3, 1945; Carl G. Grossman to Colonel Laughton Gambrell, Oct. 17, 1945: all in the files of the Advisory Committee on Voluntary Foreign Aid, International Cooperation Administration, Department of State, Washington, D. C. [hereafter cited as Advisory Committee Files]: interview with Mr. William McCahon, Advisory Committee, June 29, 1960.

[44] Margaret Frawley, American Friends Service Committee, to Mrs. Lois Kellogg Jessup, quoted in letter from Mrs. Jessup to Arthur Ringland, June 12, 1945, Advisory Committee Files.

in the liberated areas, when asked to deliver these packages to designated persons, found themselves unequipped for such a time-taking service. Broadly speaking, therefore, CARE took shape as a means of unsnarling the chaos surrounding private package-sending to Europe and of taking the burden of direct personal package relief from the shoulders of several voluntary agencies.

Yet the organization of CARE was not an easy or simple response to these problems. As early as 1943 inquiries from the American Friends Service Committee and a number of Italian-Americans led Arthur C. Ringland, a consultant of the President's War Relief Control Board, to give a good deal of thought to a package program similar to that of the American Relief Administration, with which he had firsthand experience.[45] The State Department's Special War Problems Division developed Ringland's memorandum into a concrete proposal for a nonprofit organization authorized to buy large quantities of food at advantageous prices, to make agreements with recipient countries for free entry, local transport and storage, and the guaranty that packages consigned to individuals and groups would be unmolested and that distribution would operate without discrimination within existing ration regulations. Ringland enthusiastically backed the plan, in the making of which E. G. Burland, who had been in charge of Hoover's ARA food parcel project in Austria and the USSR, took a leading part. But neither UNRRA nor the American Red Cross felt able to sponsor it.[46] To continued inquiries from voluntary organizations and the American Council of Voluntary Agencies for Foreign Service, Ringland replied that the plan for the time was "in a pigeonhole" where, he feared, it might stay.[47]

Fortunately, this was not to be the case. In the late summer or early fall of 1945 Ringland learned that the Army was ready to declare surplus 7,600,000 Ten-in-One rations, each of which might take care of the average family's calorie deficiency for about two weeks. A plan was envisaged by which a certain number of these rations might be earmarked for distribution through the various na-

[45] Ringland to Clarence Pickett, Feb. 12, 1944; Ringland to Margaret Frawley, Feb. 26, 1944, Advisory Committee Files.

[46] E. G. Burland to Dr. Louise W. Holborn, April 9, 1957, Advisory Committee Files; Eldred D. Kuppinger, "War Problems," Sept. 26, 1945, typescript, Advisory Committee Files.

[47] Charlotte E. Owen, American Council of Voluntary Agencies, to Arthur C. Ringland, Feb. 27, 1945; Ringland to Miss Owen, March 8, 1945; Ringland to Mrs. Jessup, June 12, 1945, Advisory Committee Files.

tional relief agencies, which in turn would handle the sales to would-be donors for relatives and friends abroad, arrange for shipments, and work out details for free entry and distribution.[48]

Before the possibility of the purchase of Army surplus had come into the picture, Ringland had tossed the basic idea to Dr. Lincoln Clark, a cooperatives specialist in UNRRA. Clark got in touch with Wallace Campbell of the Cooperative League's international committee which was raising a freedom fund to help European cooperatives. Both men were much taken by Ringland's suggestion. The plan was canvassed by leading executives of religious, labor, and other overseas relief agencies. Interest was considerable, but there was no consensus as to just what shape the new agency should take or what its relations with member organizations ought to be.

At last representatives of the Cooperative League, the American Friends Service Committee, and the Catholic Relief Services-National Catholic Welfare Conference, working together for three weeks in the office of the American Council, came up with an acceptable organization plan.[49] Twenty-two agencies, religious and secular, agreed to become members of the new organization, which was for a brief time headed by Donald Nelson. In November, 1945, Alexander B. Hawes, of a Washington law firm, secured a broadly written District of Columbia charter, thus beginning a long term of indispensable service as legal counsel. A capital fund of $800,000 was borrowed from cooperating agencies. General William N. Haskell, then head of the Save the Children Federation, became the executive director, with E. G. Burland as his deputy.[50]

The next steps were both slow and difficult. Despite the fact that Ringland and State Department officials had encouraged the organization of the new cooperative of voluntary agencies, some in government circles doubted the ability of any private agency effectively to carry through large-scale purchases, the sale of these to a donating constituency, and the transport and delivery of packages in Eu-

[48] Eldred D. Kuppinger, "War Problems," Sept. 26, 1945, typescript, Advisory Committee Files; "Arthur C. Ringland," *New York Times*, May 14, 1958.

[49] Murray D. Lincoln, *Vice President in Charge of Revolution* (New York: McGraw-Hill, 1960), 204 ff.; "CARE, a Report to the People," Special Advertising Supplement, *New York Times*, Feb. 10, 1957; E. B. Burland to Dr. Louise W. Holborn, April 9, 1957, Advisory Committee Files.

[50] Harold S. Miner, Address to Field Staff Conference, March 31, 1960, New York University Club, typescript, American Council Files; Arthur C. Ringland to Miss Hazel Firth, Corresponding Secretary, the Christian Science Board of Directors, Oct. 4, 1945, Advisory Committee Files.

rope.[51] The President's War Relief Control Board at first refused to register CARE on the ground of the need of assurances of enough material to enable the program to move successfully, competent executive management, and adequate financing (in the first months of operation the initial capital fund was largely exhausted). Without such registration, CARE had no chance of negotiating purchase of Ten-in-One Army rations from the War Department.[52] Controversies also arose within CARE's Board of Directors, made up of a representative from each of the twenty-two member agencies, which were without food package experience, and which represented varying and often conflicting views on the proper scope of CARE's program. To make matters even more complicated, friction developed between members of the staff. Finally, sales of the packages acquired from the Army lagged and there was a good deal of unfavorable newspaper publicity.[53]

Yet headway was made. Burland succeeded in talking the War Assets Administration into reducing the price of Ten-in-One packages which enabled CARE's executive committee to cut the sales price to the public from $15 to $10. Sales soon mounted. The first CARE packages were delivered in Le Havre in May, 1946, and before the end of the year relief valued at $500,000 had been distributed under the terms of contracts negotiated with the occupation authority in Germany. The contracts guaranteed that relief packages would enter the country free of duty and taxation; that there would be no political interference with distribution; that individuals receiving packages would not be "docked" on their ration cards; and that CARE supplies would enjoy police protection. The Army gave logistical support to CARE, as it did to other voluntary agencies, and extended billeting, post exchange, commissary, and other privileges to the personnel.[54] Further, in order to increase the quantity of relief, the Army specified that each addressed package be accompanied by an

[51] Lincoln, *Vice President in Charge of Revolution*, 207.

[52] Alexander B. Hawes to War Relief Control Board, Dec. 6, 1945, Jan. 2, 1946; James Brunot, executive director, for the Chairman, War Relief Control Board, to Hawes, Jan. 10, 1946; General William Haskell to War Relief Control Board (telegram), Jan. 16, 1946; Joseph E. Davies to Lt. Gen. E. B. Gregory, War Assets Corporation, Jan. 18, 1946, Advisory Committee Files. See also the files in CARE Archives.

[53] E. G. Burland to Dr. Louise W. Holborn, April 9, 1957, Advisory Committee Files; Newton Randolph to HBS, incoming cable, Oct. 10, 1947, CARE Archives.

[54] Agreement between the Deputy Military Governor of the United States Zone of Occupation in Germany and Cooperative for American Remittances to Europe, Inc., June 5, 1946; memorandum of Bertram D. Smucker to E. Gordon Alderfer, both of CARE staff, August 1, 1961, Advisory Committee Files.

identical one to be distributed by German relief agencies. This was unacceptable to the New York office, which did, however, agree to publicize the idea that Americans ought to make contributions for general distribution and to plow back into the occupied zone for charitable purposes a share of the balance of funds remaining to it after costs were paid.[55] This was not the only time that American officials encouraged CARE to broaden its program.[56]

The decision to encourage nondesignated giving, the publicity that accompanied it, and the growing reputation of CARE's efficiency, resulted in the increasing tendency of donors to send funds with the request that the food packages purchased with them be distributed where the need was greatest. When food packages were increasingly sent for general relief and supplemented by shipments of blankets, clothing, and coal, several of CARE's religiously oriented members felt that it was being transformed from a temporary agency for sending food packages given by Americans to relatives and friends abroad into a general relief organization. These voluntary agencies regarded comprehensive overseas relief as a function of organizations already established for that purpose. It seemed to them that CARE was duplicating and competing with their own work, even though less well-equipped to supervise such programs.[57]

On the other hand, several secular member agencies, especially the Cooperative League and the CIO, having no operating programs of their own, but increasingly interested in overseas relief and rehabilitation, thought of CARE as an agency organized to meet not only the postwar emergency relief needs but to promote reconstruc-

[55] Office of Military Government for Germany, Berlin, to the War Department, No. CC 2903, April 12, 1946; CARE teletype to OMGUS, No. WARX 86540, from the Civil Affairs Division, April 29, 1946, Advisory Committee Files.

[56] *New York Times*, Feb. 10, 1957; Ringland to Nathaniel Evans, May 27, 1946; Evans to Ringland, May 29, 1946; Edward M. O'Connor, Chairman, CRALOG, to General William N. Haskell, June 17, 1946; Haskell to O'Connor, June 25, 1946, Advisory Committee Files.

[57] Although the American Friends Service Committee as early as 1946 expressed the view that CARE should not become just another relief organization and should not expand its operations beyond the capacities of its staff for effective administration, it remained a constituent member longer than many of the religiously oriented agencies: mimeographed minutes of the Foreign Service Executive Committee of AFSC, May 6, 1946; Nathaniel H. Evans to Arthur C. Ringland, May 29, 1946, Advisory Committee Files; and Lewis H. Hoskins to Merle Curti, June 20, 1961. The criticisms of the religious agencies are reflected in a letter from Wynn C. Fairfield (Church World Service) to Murray D. Lincoln, June 2, 1952, CARE Archives; CARE's point of view was expressed in a statement of Paul C. French, dated June 3, 1952, and in a letter to Dr. Lincoln Clark (Unitarian Service Committee), Jan. 3, 1955, CARE Archives.

tion in a creative and flexible manner.[58] This fundamental difference in the conception of the organization led to many crises. One
took place in 1946 when CRALOG, speaking for member agencies
operating in Germany, protested against CARE's appeal to German-
American organizations for funds for undesignated packages as in-
imical to the programs of the voluntary agencies. General Haskell
and E. G. Burland resigned, in the main because it seemed to them
that the future of CARE was in so much doubt it had best end its
operations.[59]

The basic problem of policy, inherent in the varying purposes of
the constituent agencies, continued to be reflected in internal controversies and crises. The Advisory Committee in Washington tried,
as was proper under its mandate, to iron out differences in CARE's
executive committee. But this was a hard task. For one thing, in
urging CARE to accept undesignated packages in order to insure the
continued support of the American occupation, the Advisory Committee seemed to some of CARE's religiously oriented members to
threaten the principle of separation of church and state. For another,
the new executive director, Paul Comley French, felt that the Advisory Committee's admonition to refrain from competing with member agencies in fund raising was beside the point in view of all that
had been done to avoid such competition. The influence of the Advisory Committee and, more important, the increase of member
representatives in the CARE board who took a broader view of its
role, led to the decision, by a very narrow vote, to include undesignated packages up to 22 per cent of the total number sent.[60]

The path thus opened to an expanded program was widened in
1949 when government agricultural surpluses became accessible to
CARE. The agencies that had always looked on CARE as a limited
service organization, designed to meet a temporary need, felt more
strongly than ever that the organization had outlived its original
purpose and that, moreover, it was not equipped to administer a
new and expanded program. In addition, some were critical of the

[58] Lincoln, *Vice President in Charge of Revolution*, 207; Richard Reuter, CARE
Member Agency Relations, Jan. 19, 1955, mimeograph report; interview with Mr.
Reuter, August 19, 1960.
[59] Edward M. O'Connor, chairman, CRALOG, to General William N. Haskell,
June 17, 1946; Haskell to O'Connor, June 25, 1945, Haskell to Burland, Oct. 21,
1946, Advisory Committee Files.
[60] Correspondence between the Advisory Committee and the officers of CARE,
Dec. 1947–July 1948, Advisory Committee Files; minutes of the Board of Directors
of CARE, Nov. 26, 1947, to July 25, 1948, CARE Archives.

new executive director on other grounds: he seemed to them an empire builder. Church World Service and Catholic Relief Services-National Catholic Welfare Conference withdrew from CARE in 1952, and the American Friends Service Committee in 1954, the Unitarian Service Committee in 1957. Other agencies withdrew for reasons of their own: the Christian Scientists when medicines were included in CARE packages, the Joint Distribution Committee when its own program developed in a different direction.[61]

Although the personality and policies of the new executive director, Paul Comley French, figured in CARE's internal problems to some extent,[62] no one could question his vigorous talents. CARE soon developed its own packages, offering a variety of items including seeds, tools, and technical books. Agreements were made with British and French occupation authorities in Germany to operate in these areas. Programs in 1946 included not only West Germany but Italy, Greece, Norway, Benelux, France, Austria, Czechoslovakia, and Poland; they were extended in 1947 to the British Isles, Bulgaria, and Rumania, and in subsequent years embraced non-European countries. Before long French pushed a new policy of self-help as part of the growing general concern with improving living standards. He also enlisted the support of the Advertising Council which enabled CARE to enjoy a vast amount of free publicity. This in turn led to a "business boom." As some of the larger church agencies withdrew, new agencies, including some of the large women's and national service organizations augmented CARE's strength. With a marked genius for promotion, French, during the nine years he served as executive director, stood CARE on its feet and made a major contribution in developing an important segment of postwar overseas philanthropy.[63]

These troubles within the organization affected only slightly, if

[61] Wynn C. Fairfield (Church World Service) to Murray D. Lincoln, June 2, 1952; Monsignor Edward Swanstrom to Murray Lincoln, June 2, 1952; Paul Comley French to Dr. Lincoln Clark (Unitarian Service Committee), Jan. 3, 1955, CARE Archives.

[62] The European Director and Assistant Director blamed French for failing to insure the specified quality of package contents and for giving directives that led to confusing embarrassments in overseas operations. In some of the member agencies French was criticized for encouraging European authorities to bestow medals and honors on CARE which he then wrote and spoke about as if they were solely personal recognitions. Some also felt that his management of advertising conveyed to the public the impression that CARE was the major or even the only voluntary agency engaged in overseas relief.

[63] Harold S. Miner, Address, March 31, 1960, CARE Archives; Lincoln, *Vice-President in Charge of Revolution*, 209.

at all, relations with the American public. CARE did not seriously suffer from a rival organization, SAFE (Save a Friend in Europe), which two former officials organized in 1947 with a liberal borrowing of ideas, techniques, and list of members.[64] Before long millions of Americans came to identify all overseas relief with CARE. This resulted not only from skillful and free advertising, but from the fact that CARE gave a world-wide base to the old American custom of neighbor-helping-neighbor. It enabled every donor to keep his individuality in indicating to what person or country he wanted his gift directed, and he received a notice that this had been done. Thus CARE provided the small donor with a way of identifying his gift with a specific recipient or project that had formerly been available only to the large philanthropist. CARE, in other words, was applying the concept of person-to-person and people-to-people giving, before it had become a cliché in American political vocabulary.[65]

The overseas achievement of CARE also makes its story worth a case study. The inclusion of tobacco and coffee in packages in the early years invited some black market operations and instances of malfeasance occurred,[66] but the record of honest and efficient handling of large-scale operations was commendable. Many things were responsible for this: the cautious, precisely worded contracts negotiated with occupation authorities and foreign governments, and the patient and diplomatic approach to both as subsequent problems arose; clear and securely labeled packages; and finally scrupulous accounting, including insistence that no single package miscarry, less for the intrinsic value of the package than because such miscarriage indicated some fault in the organization. Yet this emphasis on accounting did not tie CARE into bureaucratic knots: it was singularly flexible and able to act quickly when quick action was needed. It is also obvious that CARE's overseas success owed a great deal to the experienced, efficient, practical and dedicated mission chiefs in countries where the program operated.[67]

Also important was the *ad hoc* limited approach to the job at hand. Harold S. Miner, who succeeded Murray Lincoln as president

[64] *New York Times*, Jan. 30, 1948; Arthur Ringland to Charles P. Taft, Jan. 30, 1948, Advisory Committee Files; Wallace J. Campbell to Arthur Ringland, Dec. 2, 1947; Harold Miner to Ringland, Dec. 2, 1947, Advisory Committee Files.

[65] Interview with Richard Reuter, August 19, 1960.

[66] Interview with Pastor Hans Diehl, Sept. 11, 1960.

[67] Interviews with Richard Reuter, E. Gordon Alderfer, and several heads of CARE missions, September, 1958, and on other occasions.

of CARE, has emphasized this single-minded philosophy as a key to CARE's achievements. "We are not engaged in political venture to entice people away from Communist leanings (however worthy such an effort may be). We are not trying to buy friends for America (even though we succeed, as a byproduct, in making many friends for our country). We are not attempting," Miner continued, "to convert the recipients of our help to Christianity or to any other religious belief (even though we are sure that the work of the agencies so engaged is more effective with people whose stomachs are no longer empty, whose bodies are clothed, and who have regained hope and dignity). We are not attempting to argue the American people into the support of CARE on the grounds of enlightened self-interest (a more palatable expression than 'selfishness'). We ask the people of America to give of their plenty that these under-privileged peoples may be fed, healed, and helped to become self-supporting, self-respecting members of the world society." [68]

What did CARE accomplish in helping victims of the war to survive? Part of the accomplishment must be summed up later in discussing what the voluntary agencies did for refugees. The $500,000 value of CARE's overseas relief in 1946 expanded to $21,500,000 in 1947 and to $25,600,000 in 1948 when the program in Japan was begun. At the end of the first five years individual packages had reached one out of five families in Germany and one out of five persons in Austria. In the spring of 1948, thanks to a promotion project of the Texsun Company, CARE enabled Save the Children Federation to take part in the distribution of 800,000 cans of citrus juices. In the fall of the same year, 1,350,000 cakes of soap (so important in preventing typhus) were made available through a joint distribution project with Lever Brothers. In 1949 CARE worked out a project with Greek War Relief which substantially supported Queen Frederika's Children's Fund Committee. These are only a few examples of the specific programs of the member agencies that supplemented CARE's general relief operations. With the improvement of conditions in Central Europe, CARE concentrated on relief

[68] Harold S. Miner, Address, March 31, 1960, CARE Archives. Emphasis on relief as an instrument in checking the spread of Communism was, however, expressed in a letter of Richard Reuter to Allan Wilson, May 10, 1954, as cited in E. Gordon Alderfer, Notebook on CARE History, notes, 1954-1955, CARE Archives, and in the testimony of Paul C. French, U. S., Congress, Senate, Agricultural and Forestry Committee, *Hearings, Emergency Famine Assistance Authority*, 83d Cong., 1st Sess., 1953, 42-44.

of the never-ending stream of displaced persons and refugees in Germany and Austria.[69]

Relief was also carried on in Poland and other Communist countries until 1948 and 1949, when restrictions made it clear that CARE's missions in the satellite countries were not wanted. As a result of a great food shortage, CARE did engage in a program in Yugoslavia in 1950-1951 which turned out to be one of the largest country-wide programs of voluntary relief since Hoover's work after the First World War. The Yugoslav program was also the first significant use of agricultural surpluses by a voluntary agency in a national effort. It set a pattern by which some five billion pounds of such surplus were being moved in 1961 by voluntary agencies. The undertaking succeeded, in part because of a preliminary stipulation that the Yugoslav government provide effective guarantees against loss, and in part because of the sustained cooperation of Belgrade.[70] Package distribution was also extended to victims of the war in the Middle East, in Japan, and in Korea. In India, southeast Asia, and Latin America the child-feeding programs were related less to postwar relief than to an effort to meet endemic needs in a small way. What was done in these countries in emergency relief can best be indicated in a later discussion of CARE's role in self-help and technical assistance efforts to improve living standards.[71]

What was the impact of CARE's package relief in the postwar years? The Communist press now and again attacked the American agency for allegedly filling its packages with inferior, cast-off food,

[69] See p. 560.

[70] CARE administered the International Cooperation Administration's contribution of $30,000,000 worth of surplus food. Although probably embarrassed at having the world know that a Communist country needed help in feeding its people, the government did not try to conceal the American origin of the help. Arthur Ringland to Paul Comley French, August 31, 1951, Monsignor Edward E. Swanstrom to Murray Lincoln, June 2, 1952, CARE Archives; interview with C. Mathius, CARE mission chief in Yugoslavia, Sept. 2, 1958.

[71] The following figures taken from U. S. Department of State, International Cooperation Administration, Advisory Committee on Voluntary Foreign Aid, *Summary Statement of Income and Expenditures of Voluntary Relief Agencies* . . . (Washington: Govt. Printing Office, 1946-1960) [hereafter cited as Advisory Committee, *Reports*] give the spread of CARE's overseas relief contribution:

1946	$ 500,000	1954	$15,118,173
1947	21,536,262	1955	53,900,807
1948	25,592,578	1956	32,220,715
1949	17,337,989	1957	34,614,963
1950	8,691,564	1958	42,113,131
1951	10,647,567	1959	36,029,801
1952	7,938,501	1960	48,229,171
1953	10,880,897		

clothing, and useless items, and for serving the interests of American imperialism.[72] But the overwhelming testimony at hand supports the conclusion that recipients of packages, local welfare agencies, Protestant and Catholic clergy, and highly placed government officials in Germany and Austria, greatly appreciated what CARE did. "Had it not been for the help of CARE," wrote Dr. Heinrich Luebke, president of the German Federal Republic, "I feel that in postwar Germany the struggle for survival would have hardly been won." [73] Chancellor Adenauer in 1951 testified that not only the Federal Government but the German people appreciated the extensive aid CARE provided to the largest possible groups of his countrymen. Nor, he continued, was the significance of what was done to be reckoned merely in sustaining life: coming as it did from a recent enemy people, the help created in Germany "the first basis for a renewal of understanding and human solidarity." [74] Similar expressions of appreciation and of the effectiveness of CARE's work on the material, psychological, and spiritual level from the officers of *Hilfswerk*, CARITAS, the German Red Cross, and *Arbeiterwohlfahrt* have the ring of sincerity.[75]

Evidence from humble people was certainly more than ceremonial: a cartoon in a comic paper [76] or the judgment of a young priest that the people in Germany and Austria gained greater love and respect for Americans through CARE than through the Marshall Plan are only illustrations of the abundant record at hand.[77] Most eloquent of all was the growing tendency of Germans, when conditions permitted, to give, both to CARE and to other agencies with programs of relief and rehabilitation in lands where the level of existence had always been precarious.[78]

[72] Radio Moscow German language broadcast, Jan. 8, 1949, Advisory Committee Files.

[73] Dr. Heinrich Luebke to Richard Reuter, Bonn, May 18, 1960, CARE Archives.

[74] Adenauer to Neff (chief of CARE mission to Germany), Jan. 29, 1951, quoted with permission of Dr. Adenauer, in CARE (Jan.-June, 1951), Advisory Committee Files.

[75] Pastor H. J. Diehl to Richard Reuter, Bremen, April 25, 1960; Dr. Eugen Gerstenmaier (President of the Bundestag) to Reuter, Bonn, May 5, 1960; Dr. Weitz, President of the German Red Cross, to Reuter, May 2, 1960; Martin Vorgrimler, German CARITAS, to Reuter, Freiburg, April 21, 1960; Fritz Ripf, Chief of Organization, *Arbeiterwohlfahrt*, Bonn, to Reuter, April 27, 1960, in CARE Archives.

[76] See the *Wespennest* (Stuttgart), Dec. 9, 1948, in the Advisory Committee Files.

[77] Harold S. Miner to Reuter, March 2, 1959, CARE Archives.

[78] Non-American contributions to CARE came to 13 per cent of the total in 1954: Reuter to Allan Wilson, Advertising Council, May 1, 1954, Alderfer, Notebook, CARE Archives. For contributions of the Canadian government and Canadian groups see Fact Sheet: The Tely Milk Ship, Sponsored by *The Telegram* (Toronto) and CARE of Canada, August 6, 1959, and minutes of the executive committee, June 27, 1956, in Alderfer, Notebook, CARE Archives.

Expressions of appreciation were not confined to recipients of help in Germany and Austria. Madame Benes declared in 1947 that the arrival of even twenty-five packages in Prague had "tremendous moral significance" in the crisis her country was experiencing.[79] Mrs. Pandit, president of the General Assembly of the UN, in speaking of CARE, declared that "this is the kind of warm-hearted and spontaneous gesture that spread honor and love to the American people throughout the free world." [80] Members of the United States foreign service often reported instances of appreciation from humble people as well as from officials. So did chiefs of CARE missions. As prominent Americans—Chester Bowles, William O. Douglas, Adlai Stevenson, and Richard Nixon, to name only a few—traveled about the world, many examples came to their attention which made them feel the importance of supplementing government aid programs by such voluntary contributions as those of CARE. For in what it did these Americans saw concrete evidence that friendship and understanding were being built by one individual reaching out to another in need.[81]

CARE packages, however significant, represented only a small part of American giving to overseas victims of war and the dislocations which followed. Between 1946 and 1956, Americans sent overseas six billions of dollars in gifts of cash and kind. Not all of this, to be sure, was channelled to those whose need was for sheer physical survival: a good deal went to strengthen religious and cultural agencies and to train medical and other technical personnel. Of the total sum of six billion dollars some 60 per cent was remitted in cash or kind by individuals to kinsmen or to friends directly, while two and a half billion (exclusive of the value of government contributions) was given through religious and secular agencies. The flow of both private remittances and philanthropic contributions was the highest in the immediate postwar years, reaching a peak in 1948,

[79] Paul Comley French to Arthur Ringland, Dec. 1, 1947, Advisory Committee Files.
[80] CARE Archives.
[81] George V. Allen, American Ambassador to Greece, to George B. Mathues, Chief of CARE mission, Athens, May 25, 1957; Chester Bowles to Paul Comley French, Sept. 11, 1952; William O. Douglas to Paul Comley French, Feb. 11, 1952; Adlai Stevenson to CARE, August 25, 1954; Richard Nixon to Reuter, Feb. 21, 1957, CARE Archives. An extensive questionnaire transmitted to Americans in countries receiving official and unofficial aid, at the direction of a Special Senate Committee to Study Foreign Aid (1956), evoked the opinion that CARE was strongly approved by indigenous populations among whom it operated: U. S., Congress, Senate, *Foreign Aid Program*, 85th Cong., 1st Sess., 1957, Senate Doc. 52, 1570.

when $715,000,000 went overseas. But even in the later years of the postwar decade, when the immediate emergency was largely over and when allocation of government surpluses to voluntary agencies tended to discourage giving, the annual average was approximately $500,000,000.[82]

What explained such giving on the part of individuals through private remittances and, more particularly, through philanthropic agencies? All the complex motives that had long led men and women to contribute of their bounty and their services during times of trouble also inspired action in this great emergency. Just as pride, national interest, and a sense of mission figured in earlier instances of giving, so these motives also now operated. Officials and opinion makers during the war again and again told Americans that they were fighting for, and against, an ideology. So in the postwar years the public was week after week, month after month, reminded of the relationship between relief, rehabilitation, and democracy.

The point can best be made by citing a few examples from almost innumerable ones at hand. "Before we can hope for a permanent mechanism to secure enduring peace and stable world economy," UNRRA's director, Herbert H. Lehman, declared, "we must first make certain that the nations, and the men, women and children who make up the nations, are not driven by starvation and desperation to embrace ideas as horrible as those of the Axis which we are seeking to exterminate." [83] The head of Truman's Famine Emergency Committee, Newbold Morris, phrased the same idea succinctly in 1946 when he appealed for contributions to an emergency food collection. "Democracy on an empty stomach is a luxury," he warned. "Totalitarianism . . . is a political philosophy and a political system which thrives on despair, and despair begins with hunger and ends in war." [84] General Lucius D. Clay believed that the voluntary giving of individuals that reached the defeated foe made him

[82] Jessie L. C. Adams, "Postwar Private Gifts to Foreign Countries Total $6 Billion," *Foreign Commerce Weekly* LVII (June 17, 1957), 13-15. Personal remittances to Western Europe made up 60 per cent of the total of this category. Remittances to China in 1946 were substantial, when it became possible for Chinese-Americans to transmit accumulated savings. Institutional remittances to China in 1946 were larger than to any other Far East country, but were discontinued, save in exceptional circumstances, after the Communist domination of the mainland.
[83] Quoted in George Creel, "Food for a Ravaged World," *Colliers* CXII (July 17, 1943), 21.
[84] *New York Times*, June 23, 1946.

feel "that he has not been completely forgotten in this world and it has, I think, more effect in molding him to our way of thinking and to a belief in democratic processes than almost anything we can do. The more of it that can happen, the better." [85] While preparing to ship clothing to Germany in 1945 the Protestant Church Committee on Overseas Relief and Reconstruction echoed this same idea in explaining that it hoped to "help win German Christians' support for democratic ideas." [86]

The related belief that overseas aid was an effective means of combatting the spread of communism was expressed again and again. One of the early explicit statements was that made in 1946 by the National Catholic Welfare Conference, the parent organization of the Catholic Relief Services.[87]

The identification of national values and interests with universal values and interests, the sense of an American mission to promote worldwide welfare were not, of course, the only reasons for giving to help victims of the war to survive. The habit of sharing, by this time fairly well established, was certainly a factor. So was the sense of social pressure to give.

Among the many and complex considerations that led Americans to contribute to the voluntary agencies, humanitarianism and religion were, as had long been the case, of major importance. Sometimes the religious desire to do good arose out of the simple concepts of brotherhood and charity. Pope Pius XII, in a nationwide radio appeal in 1947, dwelt on "the spirit that unites all men as children of their Father, Who is in Heaven, and makes their hearts beat fast with sympathy for their brothers in suffering and distress." [88] At other times, however, sectarian and proselyting expectations were involved in religious overseas activities. Thus a fact book on foreign aid prepared for the Federal Council of Churches in 1946 called attention to "the far-reaching ministry" of the Roman Catholic Church, and asked Protestants to contribute to overseas relief to avoid leaving foreign Protestant churches in a "difficult position." [89] In similar vein the National Lutheran Council in 1947 heard a minister appeal for foreign relief contributions on the grounds that "Catholicism has failed in France." It was up to the Protestants, the

[85] *Final Report on Foreign Aid*, 791.
[86] *New York Times*, Dec. 20, 30, 1945.
[87] *Ibid.*, Nov. 17, 1946.
[88] *Ibid.*, Nov. 24, 1947.
[89] *Ibid.*, March 5, 1946.

minister argued, to present "the pure and more Christ-centered Christianity." [90] Many Protestants in every denomination were, of course, unaffected by such sectarianism. By common agreement, this seems to have been notably true of the Friends.

Whatever the nature of the religious appeal, church groups raised substantial sums in the postwar years. While nonsectarian giving during wartime, including contributions to the American Red Cross, overshadowed sectarian contributions, by 1947 sectarian charity outstripped the nonsectarian, and sectarian giving has continued to dominate private overseas charity in terms of dollar volume ever since, as the chart on pages 506-7 clearly shows. [91] Also, although record peaks of giving were registered in the years immediately after World War II, there has been no subsequent drastic falling off of overseas charitable effort such as occurred in the 1920's when Americans, satisfied that the immediate crisis after World War I had been met, accordingly reduced their contributions. In fact, the 1950's saw total contributions again approximating those of the peak post-World War II years: $253,000,000 in 1959, for instance, compared with the record $309,000,000 in 1948.

Figures for 1960 and 1961, which became available after the chart had been prepared, are as follows: 1960 (revised), in millions of dollars, Protestant, 124.4; Catholic, 39.7; Jewish, 75.8; nonsectarian and international, 54.8 for a total of 294.7. The preliminary figures for 1961 are Protestant, 131.0; Catholic, 40.2; Jewish, 71.8; nonsectarian and international, 57.0, totaling 300.00. These figures were supplied by the U. S. Department of Commerce, Office of Business Economics.

Several factors must be considered when viewing trends in overseas philanthropy as they seem to be revealed on the chart. Ob-

[90] *Ibid.*, Nov. 24, 1947.

[91] Sources for the information used to prepare the chart are: for the period 1919 through 1939: Paul Dewitt Dickens and August Maffry, *Balance of International Payments of the United States in 1939*, U. S. Department of Commerce, Foreign and Domestic Commerce Bureau, Economic Series 8 (Washington: Govt. Printing Office, 1940), 70; for the period 1940 through 1945: U. S. Department of Commerce, Foreign and Domestic Commerce Bureau, *International Transactions of the United States During the War, 1940-45*, Economic Series 65 (Washington: Govt. Printing Office, 1948), 208: through 1956: Adams, *Foreign Commerce Weekly* LVII, 13-16; for 1957-1959, typescript charts furnished by Mrs. Jessie L. C. Adams, International Balance of Payments Division, U. S. Department of Commerce. Additional clarification of types of donations included or excluded from the gross figures was obtained by letter from Walther Lederer, Chief, Balance of Payments Division, U. S. Department of Commerce and Jessie L. C. Adams of the same division. Commerce Department figures are based primarily upon annual circularization of voluntary agencies.

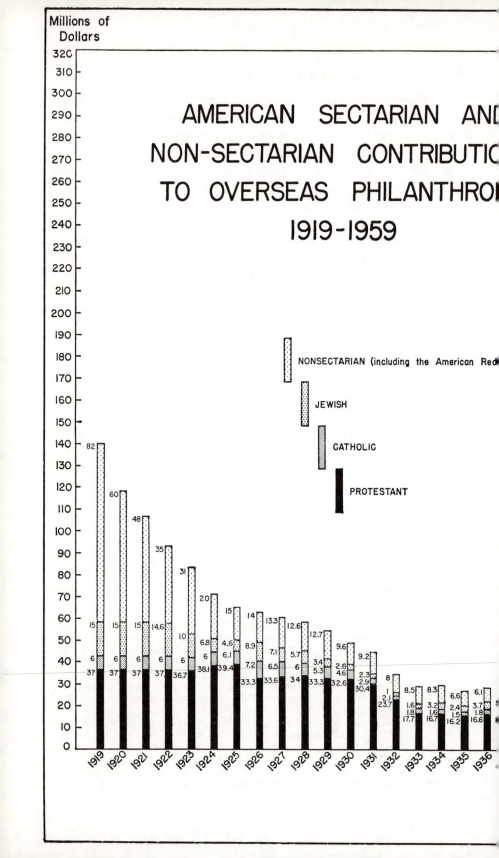

AMERICAN SECTARIAN AND NON-SECTARIAN CONTRIBUTIONS TO OVERSEAS PHILANTHROPY 1919-1959

Millions of Dollars

NONSECTARIAN (including the American Red Cross)

JEWISH

CATHOLIC

PROTESTANT

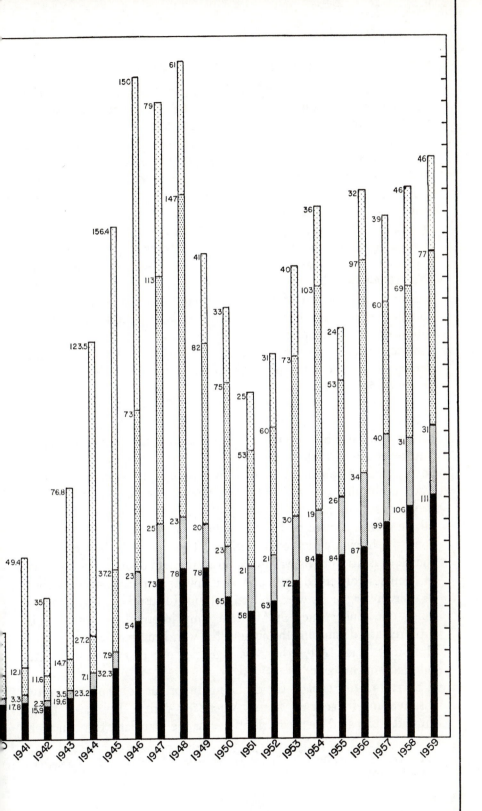

meo

viously, periods of currency inflation or deflation have affected the buying power of dollars given; hence, the annual amounts shown on the chart cannot be compared absolutely. Also, some of the sectarian contributions have been used for proselytizing and not for material relief as such. But since support of missionary work has continued throughout the period, the much-increased volume of sectarian giving during and after World War II must be related primarily to relief and rehabilitation activities. Third, the figures given on the chart refer to private contributions and do not include the value of government surpluses distributed through private agencies, a program which has further expanded the scope of post-World War II voluntary assistance abroad. Finally, the nonsectarian totals include only so much of Red Cross work as has been financed by voluntary donations. The chart, therefore, largely omits government subsidization of voluntary charity ventures in any form and retains the focus on the beneficence of private citizens and their agencies, among which the religious organizations currently hold an almost pre-eminent position.

Ethnic and national loyalties, factors that had loomed large in earlier overseas efforts, played a somewhat diminished role in organized relief after World War II. In the prewar years, 1939-1941, over 80 per cent of contributions to voluntary agencies working overseas were ethnically oriented. During the war years, the percentage dropped by half, and in the period of 1946-1953, contributions from ethnic groups accounted for only a little over 10 per cent of the income of foreign relief organizations. This marked change in the source of contributions was mirrored in the reduction in the number of agencies concerned with only one country. In 1940, almost four of every five agencies were collecting funds for use in a single foreign land: only one agency in five had truly international aims. This ratio remained constant throughout the war. But about 1945 a major shift took place. After that, two agencies out of every three were international in scope.[92]

Several factors explain the declining importance of the nationality-inspired relief agencies. Many Americans with a European background designated their contributions for the homeland through such

[92] U. S. Department of State, President's War Relief Control Board, *Voluntary War Relief During World War II*, Department of State Publication 2566 (Washington: Govt. Printing Office, 1946), 23.

secular agencies as CARE and such nonnational organizations as Lutheran World Relief, both of which, because of their size and much-advertised efficiency of operation, had a wide appeal. The postwar decline in contributions through ethnic agencies also resulted from an increased use of parcel post for shipments overseas to friends and relatives. In 1947 privately mailed "gift packages" to foreign countries reached a total value of $205,000,000.[93] The volume of parcel post shipments overseas in that year was almost thirty times as great as it had been in 1939, and post office officials estimated that 95 per cent of the packages were gifts.[94]

Again, the continuing zeal of organized labor in promoting its own overseas programs no doubt drained off potential contributors to the ethnic agencies. The Free Trade Union Committee of the AF of L, which had been organized in 1944, helped rebuild the shattered trade union movement in Europe and Japan. It sent food packages to labor leaders who had suffered unusual privations. Early in 1947, the International Ladies' Garment Workers Union allocated $470,000 for relief activities, an additional $100,000 to the JDC, and $175,000 for the support of a trade school in Palermo. The CIO, in the autumn of 1947, announced a $1,000,000 emergency relief project for twelve countries. And the AF of L's Free Trade Union Committee spent liberal sums for the relief of workers in France, a contribution more largely inspired, however, by trade union fraternalism than by ethnic kinship and sympathy.[95]

Also to be taken into account in any effort to explain the declining importance of agencies with specific national-aid objectives was the confusion and competition which must have discouraged many potential donors from trusting contributions to them. Thus in 1946 seven Polish relief agencies were competing for funds. Many of these merely confused the picture. Even the names were bewildering: there was a Paderewski Fund for Polish Relief and a Paderewski Testimonial Fund, the Polish American National Alliance of the United States, the Polish National Fund, the Polish National Committee of the United States, and the Polish Women's Committee. Similarly competing organizations tried to get funds and supplies for Yugoslavia, Czechoslovakia, Russia, and Norway. This congestion

---

[93] *New York Times*, March 20, 1948.

[94] *Final Report on Foreign Aid*, 822, 824.

[95] *New York Times*, Jan. 30, 1947; Nov. 26, 1947; "The AF of L Aids Labor Abroad," *Fortune* XL (July, 1949), 154; Max D. Danish, *The World of David Dubinsky* (Cleveland: World, 1957), 163-64.

of relief agencies was, to be sure, somewhat relieved by 1948, partly because the expansion of USSR influence in the satellite countries and Cold War tensions made relief to some areas impossible, but also because many of the small agencies simply stopped functioning. Thus fewer than half of the fifty national agencies registered in 1946 with the Advisory Committee on Voluntary Foreign Aid continued operations through 1947. Only twelve of the national agencies remained active in 1948.

The relative place of all the contributions of ethnic or national-interest agencies compared with those of a religious and general character is indicated in the following table, the figures representing millions of dollars.[96]

Table I. Sources of Contributions of Funds and Goods

	Ethnic Agencies	Religious Agencies	General Agencies	Total
1939-1941	$ 50.4	$ 9.6	$ 1.9	$ 61.9
1942-1945	179.5	116.7	140.8	437.0
1946-1953	125.0	710.0	168.9	1,003.9

The table shows that despite the declining importance of the agencies of ethnic interest and national predilection, residual loyalties by no means ceased to play a part in American postwar relief efforts. Greek War Relief, for example, responding to a truly desperate situation in the homeland, collected and distributed over $9,000,000 in 1946, 1947, and 1948.[97] Equally concerned and active were such organizations as American Relief for Italy, American Relief for Norway, American Relief for Holland, and American Relief for France. The French, Norwegian, and Dutch groups had been in existence throughout the war, previously under different names. The Queen Wilhelmina Fund, for example, became American Relief for Holland and, after 1947, United Service to Holland. American Relief for Italy, however, was newly organized under the auspices of President Roosevelt and the War Relief Control Board. Myron C. Taylor directed its outpouring of relief which in 1945 and 1946 reached over 4,000,000 Italians through the Italian government, Italian Red Cross,

[96] Ringland, *Department of State Bulletin* XXX, 391.
[97] Advisory Committee, *Reports*, 1946, 1947, 1948 (see full citation in note 71). In the period after the Second World War these reports are the best source of figures for the philanthropic activities of voluntary relief agencies. For whatever reasons there are occasional minor differences between these figures and those in the reports of the various organizations.

the Vatican, and the General Confederation of Labor.[98] The Dutch group, meanwhile, shipped an average of 3,000 pounds daily to Netherlanders and encouraged Americans to adopt Dutch communities and help rebuild schools and hospitals. The French agency dispatched over $3,000,000 in relief to France from 1944 to 1946. And Norwegian Relief carried to the homeland supplies which it had already in large measure stockpiled in Great Britain before Norway's liberation.[99]

Meantime, Cold War politics had not yet lowered the Iron Curtain between the Soviet Union and the West and in 1945 alone donors sent $32,000,000 in goods and cash to their war-ravaged Russian ally. By May, 1946, communities and nationality groups had adopted fifty-two Russian hospitals and children's institutions; over 250,000 English-language books had been shipped to Russian readers through the American Society for Russian Relief's "Books-for-Russia" campaign, headed by publisher Bennett Cerf. Leading Americans like W. Averell Harriman, Henry Wallace, and Senator Claude Pepper of Florida urged action on behalf of the Russian people.[100] But the Russian government soon declared that it could handle its own needs, and by 1949 the other nations within the Soviet sphere asked "foreign" organizations to cease relief work. It was this interdiction in Poland in 1949 which ended the activities there of American Relief for Poland, not, however, before the agency had sent nearly $7,500,000 in food, clothing, hospital, and school supplies for needy Polish nationals.[101]

Most Chinese-Americans probably contributed to their overseas families through private remittances, but American contributions to China through agencies and institutions in 1946 were larger than to any other part of the Far East. In addition to the work of the American Friends Service Committee, which continued after 1945, other

[98] American Relief for Italy, *Second Anniversary Report* (March, 1946), 2-9.

[99] "Operational Report of United Service to Holland, Inc., for First Half of 1947" (1947), "Condensed Annual Report of American Aid to France, Inc., for Year Ended Dec. 31, 1946" (1947), "Basic Information about National War Fund Agency: American Relief for Norway, Inc.," in the American Council Files; A. N. Rygg, *American Relief for Norway: A Survey of American Relief Work for Norway During and After the Second World War* (Chicago, 1947), 3, American Council Files.

[100] "Inter-Committee Memo" (May, 1946); Edward C. Carter, "Russian War Relief," *Slavonic and East European Review* XXII (August, 1944), 61-74.

[101] C. F. Horsley, "Foreign Voluntary Aid to Poland, 1945-1949" (1949), American Council Files; Dr. Francis X. Swietlik, "Report of the President to the Plenary Session of the Board of Directors of American Relief for Poland, February 21st and 22d, 1948, at Chicago, Illinois," American Council Files.

voluntary agencies directed attention to China's vast needs. Of these United Service to China appealed to Americans in a special campaign in 1946 and 1947. William Sloane, the publisher of *Thunder out of China* (1946), a widely read book by Theodore H. White and Annalee Jacoby, expressed regret that many readers cited the book as a reason for refusing to contribute to the campaign. Sloane made it clear that such had not been the intention of the authors. He himself, during the months he spent in wartime China, had concluded that United Service to China was one of the few ways in which Americans might help the Chinese people since its funds, spent on education, child welfare, health, and agricultural improvements, were designed to undercut the causes of misery and were controlled, not by corrupt Chinese politicians, but by responsible Americans.[102] Whatever truth there was in the alleged effect of *Thunder out of China* on fund raising, United Service to China raised $6,411,270 in 1946, $2,159,713 the following year, $919,449 in 1948, and $406,252 in 1949. With the Communist takeover, it became, after 1950, almost impossible for any voluntary agency to work in mainland China.[103]

The foreign relief agencies for the most part conducted their own fund-raising operations, but in 1948 twenty-five organizations tried to recapture the pattern of cooperative money raising of the National War Fund, which had been more or less imposed by the President's War Relief Control Board during the second world conflict and which had in many ways proved satisfactory. The new campaign, known as American Overseas Aid-United Nations Appeal for Children, was conducted in partnership with the UN's attempt to stimulate private contributions to the United Nation's International Children Emergency Fund (UNICEF). UNICEF was to get about $21,000,000 of the $60,000,000 goal, and the participating agencies agreed not to conduct competing drives and to content themselves with a prearranged share of the proceeds.[104]

American Overseas Aid included such well-known and successful agencies as Church World Service, the American Friends Service Com-

---

[102] William Sloane to the Editor, *Wilson Library Bulletin* XXI (March, 1947), 580.
[103] Advisory Committee, *Reports*, 1947, 1948, 1949.
[104] *New York Times*, Sept. 25, Nov. 3, 21, 1947; " 'American Overseas Aid,' Global Community Fund," *Saturday Evening Post* CCXX (May 15, 1948), 196; Helen Walker Homan, "The Crusade for Children," *Catholic World* CLXVII (May, 1948), 166-67; *Final Report on Foreign Aid*, 812-17.

mittee, and the War Relief Services of the National Catholic Welfare Conference. It also had the support of the major public figures —President Truman, General Eisenhower, Secretary of State Marshall, and Governor Thomas E. Dewey, at the time a presidential candidate.[105] But the campaign failed. At midyear, only $12,000,000 of the $60,000,000 was at hand, and the members taking part lost confidence in the drive. Officials of the American Overseas Aid cited public apathy as the main reason for failure, but over-all contributions to overseas relief decreased only slightly in 1948. A more likely cause of the campaign's failure was faulty organization. The United Nations Appeal for Children, which was a worldwide affair, planned to ask people in all nations for one day's pay on February 29, playing on the notion that in a leap year workers got one more day's wages than in a normal year. The United States drive was officially opened in early February of 1948, but the organization faltered and active solicitation did not begin until late April. By July, the agencies cooperating in the appeal began to carry on independent campaigns for funds.[106]

The impulse to organize and coordinate relief activities nevertheless expressed itself in ways other than in this fiasco and in the successful federation which in effect CARE was. Protestant relief efforts, for example, had for some time showed only a small degree of cohesion. It may be recalled that in 1920, to meet the crisis of severe drought and famine in China, the Foreign Missions Conference and the Federal Council of Churches cooperated to form China Relief, U.S.A., Inc. Following Japan's attack on China in 1937, China Famine Relief became the Church Committee for China Relief. In 1944 the organization's title was again changed, this time to the Church Committee for Relief in Asia. In the meantime, the World Council of Churches, working for European refugee resettlement and emergency relief set up a Commission for Church World Service. The Commission was designated to coordinate the activities of several religious groups, including the older Church Committee for Relief in Asia, the International Committee of the YMCA, and the YMCA's World Emergency Fund. Twenty-six Protestant denominations also took part toward the end of World War II in the so-called Church Committee for Overseas Relief and Reconstruction. This jungle of religious philanthropy was finally cleared up in 1946 when

[105] *New York Times*, Feb. 25, March 19, May 18, 19, June 3, 1948.
[106] *New York Times*, July 9, 1948.

the Church Committee for Overseas Relief and Rehabilitation, the Commission for the World Church Service, and the Committee for Relief in Asia amalgamated to form Church World Service. The new organization was the creature of the founding agencies, designated to carry out relief and recovery programs for them.[107] Thus Church World Service became the first fully unifying and coordinating instrument for overseas relief and reconstruction in the history of American Protestant and Orthodox Churches.[108]

While cooperating in many ways with Church World Service, several denominations maintained their own autonomy and fund-raising pattern. Thus in 1948 the Baptist World Alliance, the Congregational Christian Service Commission, Lutheran World Relief and the Unitarian Service Committee collected over $1,500,000 for overseas relief.[109] While it seems likely that much of this might otherwise have gone to Church World Service, it is also true that, in combining sectarian appeals for funds for purely sectarian purposes with the larger appeal, churches reached both the narrowly parochial and the broader giver who preferred to go beyond sectarian channels.[110] It is noteworthy that the new agency developed a coordinated fund-raising effort in "One Great Hour of Giving," an annual nationwide observance, and that, gradually, Sunday Schools emphasized through concrete lessons the Christian obligation of giving.

Church World Service took care to avoid any suggestion of using relief for proselytizing. At the same time, however, funds were collected and distributed in the belief that food prepared the way for Christian grace, and that churches had to feed the hungry as well as care for souls. Consequently, while much of the money spent in Europe was budgeted for food, clothing, and other immediate relief needs, a substantial amount of Church World Service's budget was allocated for "religious rehabilitation"—church repairs, aid to pastors, Bibles, and youth programs. "Governments will be struggling

[107] *New York Times*, March 5, May 10, 1946; Russell Stevenson, *A More Excellent Way* (New York: Church World Service, n.d.), 5; "Protestant World Relief," *Christian Century* LXIV (May 14, 1947), 614.

[108] U. S., Congress, House, Foreign Affairs Committee, *Voluntary Foreign Aid: Nature and Scope of Postwar Private American Assistance Abroad with Special Reference to Europe*, 80th Cong., 2d Sess., 1948 (subcommittee print); Church World Service, *Together We Serve: The Story of the Cooperative Overseas Ministry of the Protestant and Orthodox Churches of America in 1947* (New York: Church World Service, 1947).

[109] Advisory Committee, *Reports*, 1948.

[110] Interviews with Dr. Wayland Zwayer, June 14, 1960, and John Abbott, June 17, 1960.

to provide food and shelter and agricultural and industrial recovery for their peoples," a Church World Service spokesman announced in 1946. "But to arouse them from spiritual apathy, to give churches of these lands the means with which to heal their own people and reach a helping hand to the distressed beyond their own community, the fellowship and giving of the ecumenical church is necessary." [111]

Occasionally misunderstandings arose between the Advisory Committee and some of the voluntary agencies that were especially sensitive on matters affecting the relation of church and state. An example was the friction in the Friendship Train movement of 1947, sponsored by various communities and organizations, including Junior Chambers of Commerce and other civic as well as church groups, to collect thousands of tons of food and clothing for distribution in France, Italy and other countries, on which the United States government paid ocean freight. The Advisory Committee felt that in delivering the Friendship Train supplies to Europe, Church World Service was exacting in its demand to have its share regardless of its ability to distribute supplies provided by the whole American public. Moreover, the federal agency held that Church World Service did not always seek its advice or provide required information in negotiating shipping agreements with the Department of Commerce during the Korean war, when, because of conditions in Korea, the military command set up specific regulations for relief operations. [112]

On the other hand, some officers in Church World Service interpreted the necessary procedures of the Advisory Committee as an effort to "control" its operations. "It is fair to say," wrote one Church World Service executive, "that a number of influential leaders in the Protestant churches are becoming uneasy about increasing control by the state over relief, rehabilitation, and technical assistance programs carried on as a voluntary service. . . . Some of our people are fearful that voluntary relief agencies are coming to be looked on as semiofficial adjuncts to governmental foreign aid programs and therefore suspect as agents of national policy. That would be a most unfortunate point of view. Governmental and official aid does not necessarily make friends of the recipients for the United States, but few of the needy can fail to respond to the voluntary generosity

[111] *New York Times,* Dec. 15, 1946.
[112] Memorandum of Arthur Ringland, August 17, 1951; Agency Letter No. 15, August 31, 1950; Ringland to Joseph Lehman (American Relief for Korea), August 31, 1951; Ringland to Arnold Vaught (Church World Service), June 22, 1951; Vaught to Ringland, July 26, 1951, Advisory Committee Files.

of the American people as individuals, given outside of all official aid programs. . . . We yield to none in our concern for the welfare of the people of the United States while we remain strong in our Christian conviction that the welfare of all God's children everywhere is also our responsibility." [113] The immediate issue was resolved, but the larger conflict of ideas was to reappear in other connections during the 1950's.

Since World War II, Church World Service has assumed an ever-growing importance in American overseas philanthropy. The agency began shipments of food to Austria, Hungary, and India a short month after it got under way in May, 1946. Collections and distributions were stepped up for the rest of the year, and in 1947 the organization was able to spend over $14,000,000 for relief in Europe and Asia.[114] By the spring of 1950 Church World Service had channeled approximately $20,000,000 in cash for relief and rehabilitation (two thirds went to Europe, one third to Asia—the highest proportion which any voluntary agency during this period sent to that Continent). In addition Church World Service shipped $30,000,000 worth of supplies, chiefly clothing, vitamins, and medicines.[115]

In the late spring of 1962 Church World Service, which during the preceding year had distributed to 1,200,000 people in Taiwan 49,437,000 pounds of government surplus food valued at $3,000,000, announced that it would discontinue the program. At issue was dissatisfaction with the Taiwan government's ration card system, which had, according to Church World Service, given rise to favoritism and to black marketing. Moreover, Church World Service was committed to emphasizing self-help projects rather than mass family feeding. Officials in AID (Agency of International Distribution, the new arm of the State Department for handling surplus distribu-

---

[113] Vaught to Ringland, July 11, 1951, Advisory Committee Files.

[114] Advisory Committee, *Reports*, 1947.

[115] "Protestant Honor," *Christian Century* LXVII (March 29, 1950), 389-91. The following figures taken from Advisory Committee, *Reports* indicate Church World Service's overseas contributions in the postwar years:

1946	$ 8,791,166 *	1954	$12,175,426
1947	14,342,160	1955	25,120,272
1948	15,336,070	1956	38,403,444
1949	9,247,542	1957	44,964,294
1950	6,370,717	1958	41,493,612
1951	7,250,597	1959	33,813,262
1952	4,539,539	1960	35,065,244
1953	10,089,763		

* Includes earlier 1946 expenditures of forming groups.

tions) noted that the cessation of the program would work hardship to many of Taiwan's needy and that abuses had been corrected. The discussion indicated that problems of distribution had not been entirely solved and that differences between voluntary religious agencies as to whether these should be involved with government surpluses, still existed.[116]

Among its many overseas programs, Church World Service introduced CROP (Christian Rural Overseas Program). CROP committees, working through state councils in twenty-two states, received donated farm commodities or funds to buy needed relief foods.[117] Under the related Share the Surplus program, termed by Church World Service "the greatest food bargain in the history of our overseas relief ministries," each dollar given enabled the church organization to ship and distribute more than 300 pounds of food from government surpluses. In many cases transportation to a foreign country was paid by the American government or by that of the receiving country.[118] The continuing programs of Church World Service not only in emergency relief but in rehabilitation and refugee aid were to be, as we shall see, impressive.

The Unitarian Service Committee was in the field when Church World Service took form. While cooperating in many ways with the newer and much larger agency, it maintained its own overseas relief programs. The Unitarian committee did some emergency relief work but its main emphasis was on promoting self-help in such fields as specialized medical training of foreign doctors through short courses by American medical experts, and through social work and education.[119]

The Quakers, whose overseas service had long been established, took a leading part in post-World War II relief. Much that was done can best be summed up in a later discussion of refugee aid and technical assistance, which in the case of the Friends developed naturally from a traditional emphasis on rehabilitation, self-help, and joint participation in community projects. But temporary relief was not

[116] *New York Times*, May 9, 10, 11, 1962.
[117] Church World Service, *For the Love of Christ . . . We Share* (New York: CWS, ca. 1958), n.p.
[118] Church World Service, *Share Our Surplus* (New York: CWS, ca. 1958), n.p.
[119] See pp. 549, 584. The Universalist Service Committee and the contributions of the Christian Science Church, channeled through CRALOG and CARE until the latter organization included medicines in its packages, testified to the interest of these denominations in the needs of people abroad.

slighted. The work projects begun by the American Friends Service Committee in Italy were, two years later, providing as many as 7,000 *reconditioned rooms a month for homeless families. By the fall of 1946 the American Friends Service Committee had shipped 2,000,-000 pounds of food and clothing to Germany. A year later a supplementary feeding program was in operation in Austria. Five Quaker clinics offered medical aid in Poland. In Finland, the Friends administered a program of child-feeding and managed day nurseries, orphanages, and work camps. The award in 1947 of the Nobel Peace Prize to AFSC and its British counterpart was a significant recognition of tested and constructive service to people in distress.[120]

Nor was the need of Asia's teeming millions overlooked. The AFSC, it will be recalled, remained in China to give nonpartisan relief during the civil war, and to conduct campaigns against malaria and blackwater fever. It continued to work even after the Communist takeover, withdrawing its organized effort only when it became impossible to secure new visas to replace personnel returning home. In the words of an officer of AFSC, whatever residue of good will toward Americans remained in China was certain to be the result, not of official policy, but of the endeavor of the several voluntary agencies that conducted programs in that turbulent land. The livestock sent to Japan as well as to China contributed to relief and rehabilitation. Famine relief was administered in India and help given to victims of religious fanaticism. After the Korean war, the Friends contributed more than $3,000,000 in material aid, including 1,274,000 pounds of clothing, cloth, yarn, bedding, medicines and other supplies. It also distributed 10,605,000 pounds of government surplus food. One program provided aid in housing projects while still another employed needy widows or established them in small businesses through loans.[121]

Other so-called "peace churches" also made important contribu-

---

[120] *New York Times*, Nov. 1, 1947.
[121] "Friends of the Helpless," *Newsweek* XXXIX (April 28, 1947), 84; Pickett, *For More Than Bread*, 211 ff., 403 ff.; Lewis M. Hoskins, to Merle Curti, June 21, 1961; American Friends Service Committee, *Annual Report*, 1956 (Philadelphia: American Friends Service Committee, 1956), 6 ff. The following figures from Advisory Committee, *Reports* indicate AFSC's overseas expenditures in this period:

1946	$7,510,369	1951	$2,836,745	1956	$4,558,691
1947	4,548,923	1952	2,801,604	1957	3,785,408
1948	4,586,123	1953	3,982,247	1958	2,931,649
1949	3,392,487	1954	3,976,366	1959	2,593,654
1950	2,552,996	1955	5,824,572	1960	2,312,061

tions to post-World War II relief. The Mennonite Central Committee, which fed many of India's starving villagers during the dreadful famine in Bengal, remained to give succor during the rioting that accompanied independence and partition. In addition, the Committee worked in several Western European countries. In Hungary it helped distribute food to needy Budapest families, set up two child-feeding programs, helped feed 5,000 university students (in conjunction with AFSC and Swedish and Swiss relief organizations), and cooperated in relief for 5,000 victims of the Tisza River flood in 1948. During the peak of the postwar crisis in Germany, 141,000 persons in the British and French Zones received supplemental feeding at Mennonite hands. By the end of 1946, 84 per cent of all food supplies received by *Evangelisches Hilfswerk* through CRALOG had come, it was reported, from the Mennonite Central Committee. The Mennonites supplied nearly a third of all relief materials which reached Germany through CRALOG in 1947, and in 1948 the Central Committee ranked fourth among agencies participating in German relief.[122]

The Brethren Service Commission was equally active. Based on the conviction that Christians should practice brotherhood toward all men, the Brethren supported relief programs in many Asian nations after their liberation from the Japanese, and continued the work begun in India in 1941. They also provided help in Belgium, Holland, France, Greece and other European nations.[123]

In addition to these pre-World War II agencies, new ones were organized. Baptist World Alliance Relief Committee also tackled the job of postwar emergency relief. Launched in 1947, the Relief Committee worked in Germany with an American agency calling itself American Baptist Relief and a German organization known as *Brüderhilfe*. By December 31, 1949, through *Brüderhilfe* and *Evangelische Hilfswerk*, American Baptists had sent needy Germans about 2,500,000 pounds of food valued at $540,000, plus 3,710,985 pounds of clothing and shoes valued at some $3,450,884. At twenty-nine feeding stations in Germany, 2,743 persons received daily meals; about 80 per cent of the recipients were non-Baptists. The Relief Committee also bought and sent abroad Bibles and song books—

[122] John D. Unruh, *In the Name of Christ: a History of the Mennonite Central Committee and Its Service 1920-1951* (Scottsdale, Pa.: Herald, 1952), 132-33, 147-53; Horst, *A Ministry of Goodwill*, 45-46, 64-65, 74-75.
[123] Lorell Weiss, *Ten Years of Brethren Service, 1941-1951* (Elgin, Ill.: General Brotherhood Board, 1952), 3-11, 33-44.

13,603 Bibles alone went to Christians in the Russian zone of Germany.[124] Of total relief, money, and goods administered by Baptist World Alliance in 1950, Americans gave $8,457,980, Canadians, $308,922, Swedes, $98,794, and the British, $21,018.[125]

The Congregational Christian Service Committee, organized in the summer of 1943, made no independent shipments abroad but maintained some representatives in the foreign field and worked mainly through Church World Service. It did maintain supplementary feeding programs in its long-established missionary and educational centers in Turkey and Lebanon, and it made its own special appeals for relief work in Greece, Italy, Germany and other countries. One of its truly original programs, the Homeless European Land Program (HELP), enlisted the support of several other agencies and illustrated the growing emphasis on self-help, rehabilitation, and technical assistance.[126]

Of the newer agencies that predated the establishment of Church World Service and that maintained fund raising and overseas operations independent of it, the largest was Lutheran World Relief. This developed in 1945 in response both to the natural interest of American Lutherans in German need and to a specific situation, namely, the volume of letters written by European blackmarketeers to American families begging for food parcels (which were promptly sold to their fellow countrymen at excessive prices). Many non-Lutherans as well as church members resorted to Lutheran World Relief to provide food and clothing for the needy. In 1947 LWR cooperated with Church World Service and the National Catholic Rural Life Conference in establishing CROP (Christian Rural Overseas Program) which shipped great quantities of donated farm commodities abroad. The Lutherans, who in the first three years had sent from their farms $1,500,000 worth of produce, gave up their participation in CROP in 1953, when interest had fallen off.[127]

In the same year that CROP was established, the American sec-

[124] Baptist World Alliance Relief Committee, *The Romance of Relief* (Washington: Baptist World Alliance, 1950), n.p.

[125] *The Baptist World* V (May, 1958), 6.

[126] Congregational Christian Service Committee, "The Service Committee: Relief and Reconstruction 1958" (mimeographed); *Ministering in His Name* (New York: CCSC, ca. 1957), n.p.; Congregational Christian Service Committee, *Report*, 1958 (New York: CCSC, 1958), 1-5; W. H. Williams to Charlotte Owen, Jan. 11, 1950, American Council Files. Additional material was consulted in the Advisory Committee Files. Earl H. Ballou to Merle Curti, Feb. 9, 1959.

[127] Lutheran World Relief, *Report* (mimeographed, n.d.), 1-2.

tion of the Lutheran World Federation voted more than $200,000 for Lutheran World Service's operations in Europe and Asia.[128] In 1950, five years after the war, Lutheran World Service gave 13,764,-436 pounds of relief supplies to CRALOG's donation of 39,950,908 pounds to Germany.[129] Also important were the fall and spring clothing collections, the Dorcas Project (kits of homemade new clothing for children in the Holy Land), and the Medical and Surgical Relief Committee, which worked through other relief agencies. We shall see that no denomination rivaled the Lutherans in aid to refugees and displaced persons. And long after the postwar emergency was over, Lutheran World Relief was carrying on child feeding and similar programs in Austria, Yugoslavia, India, and Korea. By 1958 the Lutheran agency had spent $70,000,000 in aid to Europe and $21,000,-000 in Asia.[130] Its record was clearly one of the largest church-directed humanitarian efforts in Protestant history.

The record is the more significant in view of the traditional separateness of the several Synods (the cooperation of the various branches of American Lutheranism in common relief ventures, however, promoted closer understanding and cooperation). The achievement was also notable in that no denomination put more stress than the Lutherans on a strict separation between church and state, a stress which led some leaders to question the wisdom of receiving large government surpluses and freight reimbursements for distribution as evidence of Christian love. The whole accomplishment was accompanied further by a new emphasis which regarded the traditional conception of the Good Samaritan as inadequate unless it was supplemented by the conviction that the church must also be the conscience of society.[131]

Protestant concern for the relief of the warshattered world was matched by similar concern among Catholics. Catholic Relief Services (an agency sponsored by the National Catholic Welfare Conference and formerly called War Relief Services) assumed much of the postwar burden of helping needy European and Asiatic Catholics. But relief was also distributed without reference to creed. Like Protes-

---

[128] Lutheran World Relief, Inc., *Annual Report*, 1958, 167; *Christian Century* LXIV (Feb. 12, 1947), 214.

[129] *Christian Century* LXVII (April 25, 1951), 517.

[130] Lutheran World Relief, Inc., *Annual Report*, 1958, 168-73.

[131] *Look* XXII (April 1, 1958), 88; interview with Pastor Ove Nielsen, Lutheran World Relief, June 24, 1960.

tant organizations, it put primary emphasis on stewardship and the religious obligation to help those in need, but it was also one of the most vociferously anticommunist of the relief agencies.[132] Until ordered by Communist authorities to leave, it operated extensive programs in Hungary and Poland. Italy, too, was a focus of attention. In Asia, Japan, Korea, and Taiwan received a good deal of help, and gradually Latin America and Africa were included.[133]

In many ways, Catholic Relief Services resembled other religiously oriented groups. It cooperated with Protestant, Jewish, and international secular agencies in distributing through CRALOG and LARA,[134] in supporting the "Crusade for Children" drive organized to raise $60,000,000 from private individuals in the United States, of which $21,000,000 was to be distributed for child relief through the United Nations Appeal for Children (UNAC). At the time, Catholic Relief Services was one of nine of the twenty-four cooperating groups to earmark money for German children (many groups limited their work to victims of Nazi aggression).[135] In countries in which it was only one of several foreign agencies, an effort was made to see that government-provided supplies were equitably distributed by the several organizations in the field. Despite its cooperative policy, Catholic Relief Services encountered some criticism on the score that it made use of religious in garb for actual distribution and thus, when government surpluses were involved, jeopardized the American policy of separation of church and state.[136]

Catholic Relief Services' record was an outstanding one. In 1946, $18,206,309 was spent. Annual contributions fell somewhat below

[132] *New York Times*, Nov. 17, 1946; Catholic Bishops' Relief Fund, 1959 *Appeal Handbook* (New York: CBRF, 1959), 10. It is, to be sure, also true that other agencies, secular as well as religious, associated giving for overseas relief with the anti-Soviet goals of government and the general public. See, for example, the testimony of Paul C. French, CARE's executive officer, in U. S., Congress, Senate, Agriculture and Forestry Committee, *Hearings, Emergency Famine Assistance Authority*, 83d Cong., 1st Sess., 1953, 42-44, and Richard W. Reuter's letter to Allan Wilson of the Advertising Council, May 10, 1954, cited in Alderfer, notebook, CARE Archives.

[133] Edward E. Swanstrom to Arthur Ringland, Jan. 16, 1952, Advisory Committee Files; Catholic Bishops' Relief Fund, 1959 *Appeal Handbook*, 6 ff.; Aloysius J. Wycislo, "Escape to America," *Catholic World* CLXXXIV (Feb., 1957), 326-32; interview with James Norris, June 17, 1960.

[134] In 1950, as one of the sponsoring agencies of CRALOG, Catholic Relief Services provided 10,540,829 pounds of relief supplies for Germany of the total 39,950,908 pounds CRALOG program for the year: *Christian Century* LXVIII (April 25, 1951), 517.

[135] Homan, *Catholic World* CLXVII, 167; *Saturday Evening Post* CCXX (May 15, 1948), 196.

[136] Interviews with James Norris and Eileen Egan, June 17, 1960.

this until 1950, when almost $25,000,000 was channeled overseas. Thus between the end of the war and 1950, over $85,000,000 allocated to overseas relief and related programs testified to the concern of American Catholics for the hungry, the ill, and the homeless in other lands. In 1957 some 30,000,000 Catholics were contributing $146,939,128 in cash and goods for overseas relief.[137] In 1958, Catholic Relief Services was, in terms of budget, the largest of the American voluntary overseas agencies. Thanks to the sustained program of teaching in parochial schools the Christian obligation of charity, the rising generation of Catholics promised to be well grounded in the sense of responsibility for the unfortunate wherever they might be.

After the end of World War II, American Jews shouldered even larger responsibilities for helping coreligionists overseas than had been the case during the conflict itself. In contrast with the Protestant philanthropies in the postwar period, which went largely to domestic causes, the larger share of Jewish contributions was designated for overseas relief.[138] In the postwar emergency, attention was focused on saving the lives of the remnant: in 1947, for example, the Joint Distribution Committee provided 224,000 rations daily in the Displaced Persons areas alone.[139] Yet the cultural and religious goals of rebuilding the shattered communities were not forgotten. Expenditures of the JDC during the single year 1946 were over $48,000,000—a sum almost equal to the combined budgets of the years 1939-1945. In that same year JDC spent more than any other

[137] Advisory Committee, *Reports*, 1946-1950. The following figures from Advisory Committee, *Reports* indicate the expenditures of Catholic Relief Services sponsored by the National Catholic Welfare Conference for overseas relief:

1946	$18,206,349 *	1954	$ 58,619,941
1947	12,994,182	1955	127,508,418 †
1948	15,503,706	1956	137,819,353
1949	12,215,505	1957	146,939,128
1950	24,994,030	1958	124,866,381
1951	23,942,212	1959	91,721,008
1952	16,380,132	1960	115,890,326
1953	40,273,432		

* War Relief Services.
† Catholic Relief Services.

[138] F. Emerson Andrews, *Philanthropic Giving* (New York: Russell Sage Foundation, 1950), 176.
[139] Moses A. Leavitt, *The JDC Story: Highlights of JDC Activities 1941-1952* (New York: American Jewish Joint Distribution Committee, 1953), 13-14.

American relief agency, and in 1947 its expenditures again increased sharply to more than $70,000,000. The next year, 1948, Jewish contributions in money and kind almost equalled all Protestant, Catholic, and nonsectarian contributions combined: a Jewish population of approximately 5,000,000 contributed $147,000,000 for peoples overseas, an average of thirty dollars a person.[140] In the many programs of rehabilitation and technical assistance, JDC, ORT, and the Palestine agencies concentrated on the problem of refugees, on retraining and on strengthening the welfare and cultural agencies of Israel, which was established as an independent state in 1948. But, as Charles J. Jordan, the executive director-general of JDC declared, "our job is to help Jews in need wherever they are and wherever we may be able to help them."[141] Nor was Edward M. Warburg, Joint's chairman in 1952, overstating the matter in writing that "there is no Jewish community anywhere in the world in which there are not hundreds and thousands of Jews who speak with love and admiration of JDC and its efforts on their behalf."[142] In the summer of 1961 JDC reported having helped, in the year that had just ended, 232,500 persons in twenty-five countries through the expenditure of $28,225,-740 obtained chiefly from the campaigns of the United Jewish Appeal.[143]

These agencies, religious and secular, were supplemented by several others that operated on a much more limited scale for specific

[140] American Jewish Joint Distribution Committee, *Annual Report, 1957* (New York: American Jewish JDC, 1957), 15; *American Jewish Year Book*, Sept., 1946–Sept., 1947, XLVIII (Philadelphia: Jewish Publication Society of America, 1947), 202 ff., Sept., 1947–Sept., 1948, XLIX, 223 ff.; Leo Schwartz, "Summary Analysis of AJDC Program in the United States Zone of Occupation, Germany," *Menorah Journal* XXXV (Spring, 1947), 217 ff.; Hal Lehrman, "The 'Joint' Takes a Human Inventory," *Commentary* VII (January, 1949), 19-27.

The following figures of JDC expenditures for overseas relief taken from Advisory Committee, *Reports* do not include contributions of ORT and other agencies, a good part of which benefitted Jewish sufferers from war and post-war conditions:

1946	$48,491,945	1954	$26,289,604
1947	70,400,537	1955	25,946,401
1948	68,962,627	1956	30,845,455
1949	57,377,457	1957	28,460,577
1950	36,361,961	1958	28,765,580
1951	21,930,576	1959	27,838,540
1952	20,786,588	1960	28,628,270
1953	22,437,463		

[141] Quoted in *A Guide to Overseas Operations of the American Joint Distribution Committee* (New York: JDC, 1958), 1.

[142] Leavitt, *The JDC Story*, 3.

[143] *New York Times*, Aug. 27, 1961.

purposes. Children, refugees, and universities and their students claimed the attention of such functional relief agencies as the Foster Parents Plan, the International Refugee and Relief Committee (later International Refugee Committee), and World University Service. While emergency relief sometimes figured in their operations, the primary objectives were rehabilitation, and this story may best be told in a later discussion.

Note should also be taken of the fact that religious contributions for missionary enterprises continued to play a role in relief during the postwar emergency. Although much of the work of missionary groups was strictly religious, a number of boards included programs of direct relief in the form of food and clothing. The mission boards also performed important services in areas that were relatively neglected during the postwar period. South Africa, India, Ceylon and other countries received but little of the aid of agencies registered with the Advisory Committee on Voluntary Foreign Aid, but were key areas of missionary efforts.[144]

Leaving out such contributions, the agencies registered with the Advisory Committee collected more than $205,000,000 in cash and gifts in kind in 1946, $173,000,000 in 1947, and $167,000,000 in 1948. Thus in the four years 1945-1948 Americans contributed over three quarters of a billion dollars to foreign relief programs.[145]

However impressive such figures seem, they are relatively small when compared with the contributions of Americans to charities and other organized philanthropies at home. Even during World War II and its aftermath, domestic causes claimed almost all the attention of donors. In no year between 1945 and 1948 did contributions to foreign relief agencies account for more than seven per cent of all philanthropic gifts, including charitable bequests and the gifts of corporations.[146] Only among American Jews, whose people abroad had undergone the most extreme suffering, did concern for foreign relief generally outweigh the urge to give to charities at home.

This is not, however, to say that overseas relief efforts were negligible adjuncts to the more important government programs. Between 1945 and 1948, the receipts of the voluntary agencies varied from

[144] Andrews, *Philanthropic Giving*, 87-88. The American denominations included in the Foreign Missions Conference of North America spent in 1948 $10,800,000 for "relief and special projects" in addition to their regular budgets of $34,300,000.

[145] Advisory Committee, *Reports*, 1946, 1947, 1948. These figures did not include the value of parcel post food packages sent privately by American individuals to friends and relatives abroad.

[146] Andrews, *Philanthropic Giving*, 73, 75 ff.

about 7 to as much as 10 per cent of government appropriations for programs involving foreign relief and rehabilitation.[147] The government programs provided relief only indirectly—such as the provision of semi-finished goods for industry through the Marshall Plan, and were often motivated more by considerations of national security than by humanitarianism. If relief agencies were sometimes guided in part by aims other than humanitarian, in general their main goal was to get food and clothing to the needy as quickly as possible. In doing so, they played an important role in the recovery of Europe and the rest of the world from the devastation of war. This, however, was only part of their contribution, for the needs of refugees and displaced persons proved to be a continuing one. The problem of raising living standards in many parts of the world through self-help projects and technical and educational assistance came to overshadow the immediate task of saving the surviving victims of the war.

[147] *Ibid.*, 81, 86. In making this estimate Lend-Lease aid, aid to China, Greek-Turkish assistance, and Inter-American aid have been excluded.

XVIII

Migration to Hope

Part of the task of helping victims of the war survive involved the refugee problem, at once harsh, dramatic, and poignant. The disheartening plight of uprooted persons had, of course, been continuous ever since the First World War. That plight had been intensified in the 1930's and during the Second World War. The persisting needs of the Spanish exiles in France were a reminder that the problem facing Europe was not new. But its magnitude and complexity in the years following the collapse of the Axis Powers was unprecedented. In the decade and a half after 1945 the migration in various parts of the world of 40,000,000 human beings led many to speak of their time as "the century of the uprooted" or "the age of the homeless man." Of this number, many moved in planned migrations to reduce surplus population in one place and to supply needed labor in another. But the great majority were displaced persons—DP's, that is to say, refugees, expellees, and escapees.

The devastating effects of the Second World War diminished with the years but did not disappear. Movements and events, such as the upsurge of colonial peoples demanding freedom, created new refugee problems. Often the birth of nations in Asia and Africa with unstable regimes and ill-defined boundaries bred conflicts with neighbors which in turn led to refugee problems. By 1961, for example, some 300,000 Baluba tribespeople had fled from their Congo home. In the same year the exodus of 75,000 Angolans from Portugal's restless colony indicated the continuing nature of the problem. Another mass movement, related to anticolonialism and nationalism, was the revolutionary demand for better conditions of life. The chaos and repression associated with revolution sent thousands who could not accept the new order into exile. Thus by mid-1961 over 100,000 refugees from Castro's Cuba had sought sanctuary in the United States and other countries. Meshed with such anticolonial and revolutionary movements was the Cold War with its conflicting ideologies, suspicions, and hatreds. Korea and Hungary were vivid symbols, while the stream of escapees from Communist countries to West Germany and to Hong Kong was an arresting reality. In a sense the refugee drama was an aspect of the overarching political and economic problem of the age—the search for freedom, peace, and order in a world of change and conflict.[1]

In the immediate postarmistice months in Europe hundreds of thousands of war prisoners and victims of political and religious persecution survived in Nazi concentration and slave labor camps. During the last stages of the war countless numbers of other people fled with the approach of hostile armies: these wretched people were often the victims of rape, hunger, disease, and sheer terror. Under the dogma of mass guilt, which held all of the German national background responsible for what the Nazis had done, Czechoslovakia, Poland, Rumania, and Yugoslavia expelled more than 12,000,-000 German-speaking peoples, some 8,000,000 of whom poured into West Germany. Mass transfers of peoples in Bulgaria and Turkey and in Yugoslavia and Italy swelled the appalling number of the uprooted.

Nor was it only Europe that was involved in this seemingly hopeless problem. In Asia, the displaced Chinese, Indians, Japanese, Javanese, Malayans, and Koreans stranded in one or another country other than their own, totaled, according to the Far Eastern mission of UNRRA, between three and four million men, women, and chil-

[1] The literature, primary and secondary, is vast, some of which will be cited in the following discussion. Among the personal narratives of refugees, especially noteworthy is K. O. Kurth, comp., *Documents of Humanity During the Mass Expulsions* (Goettingen: Goettingen Research Committee, 1952). U. S., Congress, House, Special Subcommittee of the Committee on the Judiciary, *The Displaced Persons Analytical Bibliography*, 81st Cong., 2d Sess., 1950, H. Rept. 1687 and U. S., Congress, House, Special Subcommittee of the Committee on the Judiciary, *Displaced Persons in Europe and Their Resettlement in the United States*, 81st Cong., 2d Sess., 1950, H. Rept. 1507 are useful. Any student of the subject must be especially indebted to the work of three experts, Jacques Vernant, *The Refugee in the Post-War World* (London: Allen & Unwin, 1953), undertaken at the request of the United Nations High Commissioner for Refugees at the time the office was set up in 1951 and subsidized by a $100,000 grant from the Rockefeller Foundation; Louise W. Holborn, *The International Refugee Organization; a Specialized Agency of the United Nations: Its History and Work 1946-1952* (London, New York: Oxford University Press, 1956), and her shorter work, *The World's Refugees: Everyone's Concern* (Washington: American Association of University Women, 1960); and Elfan Rees, *Century of the Homeless Man* (New York: Carnegie Endowment for International Peace, 1957).

dren. The victory of Communism in China led to a further migration over the years of more than four million from the mainland—to Hong Kong, Taiwan, and many other countries. In French Indo-China independence and Communist triumph in the northern area were followed by the flight of almost a million to South Vietnam. The partition of India in 1947 uprooted 17,000,000 people, the majority of whom lived a wretchedly precarious existence in one of the two countries into which the subcontinent was divided. And the partition of Palestine with ensuing conflict between Israeli and Arabs led more than 800,000 of the latter to leave their homes.[2]

Millions died in the tumult of the two hemispheres, others just disappeared. Officially, as the YMCA International Committee so well put it, those who survived were statistical facts. Despite files, dossiers, and case histories, only the holding of a ration card identified hundreds of thousands as human beings. Once they had lived in homes of their own, with roots in a community. Now, often broken in mind and spirit as well as in body, they were unwanted, drearily marking time in enforced idleness in camps or improvised shack settlements, or existing in the squalor of lofts and the grim hallways of strange cities.[3] Yet there was courage and stamina and hope in great numbers of these men and women. Nor did brutal frontier guards, explosive mines, and tangled barbed wire keep scores of thousands from braving everything in the desperate effort to flee from new terror and tyranny during the decade and a half that followed the collapse of Hitler.

Although the occupying Allied armies provided temporary relief, rations, and improvised shelter, the main job was to repatriate displaced persons as quickly as possible. Within a year after the war ended, 7,000,000 prisoners of war and DP's were repatriated from German and Austrian camps to their home countries. But it was impossible to repatriate some 1,250,000 DP's. Of these, many had

[2] *New York Times*, May 20, 1946; "The Problem of Displaced Persons," Report of the Survey Committee on Displaced Persons of the American Council of Voluntary Agencies for Foreign Service, June, 1946 (mimeographed), in the files of the American Council of Voluntary Agencies for Foreign Service, New York [hereafter cited as American Council Files]; Don Peretz, *Israel and the Palestine Arabs* (Washington: Middle East Institute, 1958), *passim*; Emile Samaan, *The Arab Refugee after Five Years; an Eye-Witness Report* (New York: American Friends of the Middle East, 1953), 14; Edvard Hambro, *The Problem of Chinese Refugees in Hong Kong* (Leyden: Sijthoff, 1955), *passim*.

[3] Material may be found in the files of the Advisory Committee on Voluntary Foreign Aid, International Cooperation Administration, Department of State, Washington, D. C. [hereafter cited as Advisory Committee Files].

no countries to which to go because of the shifting of boundaries; some were unacceptable to the governments of the countries to which they might logically be sent; others refused to consider returning to what had been their homes even in those cases in which they might have been permitted to do so and consequently remained stateless persons. Some, because of age, mental or bodily sickness, or other incapacity, could neither return, nor care for themselves where they were, nor find permanent asylum. These men and women, the "difficult cases," were often, somewhat inhumanely, spoken of as "the hard core."

National governments, let alone voluntary agencies, could not cope with problems of such magnitude and complexity. During the Second World War the Intergovernmental Committee on Refugees marked out the broad paths to be followed during the aftermath and the troubled 1950's. From the time it was launched, UNRRA supplied emergency relief to those in work camps and assembly centers. When the end of UNRRA was in sight, the International Refugee Organization was created to house, clothe, feed, and help reestablish refugees and displaced persons who either could not or would not return to places they had once called home. The United States government provided approximately $100,000,000 or 60 per cent of the International Refugee Organization's budget. Its mandate carefully defined the categories of refugees eligible for aid, 1,619,000 of whom received some kind of help. IRO continued to operate until 1952, before which time it had resettled over a million refugees by individual migration and mass resettlement at a cost of $430,000,000.[4]

Upon the demise of the International Refugee Organization its functions were taken over by several agencies. One, the Provisional Intergovernmental Committee for Movement of Migrants from Europe (PICMME), resulted from a conference initiated by the United States and Belgium and attended by representatives of twenty-seven governments. Under its first director, Hugh Gibson, former ambassador to Belgium and associate of Hoover in relief operations after the First World War, PICMME or, as it came to be called, the Migration Committee, took over part of the International Refugee Organization's chartered fleet and remaining funds, with which it transported 12,000 refugees still covered by IRO's mandate. In 1952

[4] Holborn, *International Refugee Organization*, 433 ff.; International Refugee Organization, *Migration from Europe* (Geneva: IRO, 1951), 12, 46, 71-78.

PICMME was replaced by the Intergovernmental Committee for European Migration, or ICEM, an agency working outside the UN and designed to help transport migrants from countries with surplus population to those in need of workers. ICEM was also in part a response to the fear that unemployed masses were easy prey to Communist propaganda. Each year between 100,000 and 125,000 refugees found new homes under ICEM auspices: by 1961 ICEM had transported and settled more than a million.[5]

In addition to ICEM, other intergovernmental agencies were involved in the refugee problem. Of these the most important was the Office of the United Nations High Commissioner for Refugees, the successor to the International Refugee Organization. Its initial task was to provide international protection for refugees within its mandate and to seek permanent solutions for the problems of these refugees through voluntary repatriation or assimilation within new national communities. Starting in 1952 as a nonoperating agency with a limited mandate and almost no financial support, the office was fortunate in having vigorous and imaginative leadership from its High Commissioners.

At the time, government interest in the refugee problem was at a low ebb. In Germany, where most refugees did not come within the High Commissioner's mandate, unemployment, inadequate housing, and other deprivations fed the discontent that broke out into rioting and threatened extremist political actions. Determined not to become a useless institution for useless people, the High Commissioner, with voluntary agencies deeply involved in the refugee tragedy, applied to the Ford Foundation for a large grant to attack the over-all problem. The Office of the High Commissioner ultimately received grants totaling $3,100,000, to be allocated to voluntary agencies and to be used "without discrimination among refugee groups" for pilot projects to integrate refugees into the country of residence. The grants brought supporting contributions from governments and private sources which, with skillful administration, added up to over $9,000,000. The High Commissioner, acting as a

[5] Malcolm J. Proudfoot, *European Refugees, 1939-1952: A Study in Forced Population Movement* (London: Faber and Faber, 1957), 433-35; John George Stoessinger, *The Refugee and the World Community* (Minneapolis: University of Minnesota Press, 1956), 60 ff.; Marcus Daly, "Assistance to a Million Migrants," *ICEM Migration News* III (1960), 1-4; Intergovernmental Committee for European Migration, *Handbook*, 1960, 5-22; interviews with Sydney Shore and Raymond Kissam, Lutheran Immigration Services, July 28, 1960; Louise W. Holborn to Merle Curti, June 6, 1961; John G. Stoessinger to Merle Curti, Oct. 4, 1961.

coordinating agency for the participating voluntary agencies which received allocations and which operated the program, developed both in Germany and elsewhere projects for low rent housing, agricultural settlement, loan funds, counselling and community centers, youth homes, and student aid.[6] James M. Read, Deputy High Commissioner for several years and historian of the agency, has pointed out that the program undertaken with the Ford funds led to a greatly increased awareness of the importance of the German refugee problem. It proved to be a psychological stimulus to increased concern and active support of the refugee programs, both on the part of trade unions and employers and friends of the UN in several countries as well as of governments and the UN itself, and it enabled voluntary agencies to expand their efforts. The program also focused attention on the problems of youth among the refugees. It stressed integration in communities, thus marking a turning point from the older emphasis on mass migration, an emphasis which has remained basic to the activities of the Office of High Commissioner for Refugees. Its significant achievements, which also included emergency aid at the time of the Berlin crisis, were recognized in 1955 by the award of the Nobel Peace Prize.[7]

In response to special situations, the United Nations Relief and Works Agency for Palestine Refugees and the United Nations Korean Reconstruction Agency performed important services for refugees.

The operations of all these intergovernmental agencies dovetailed with those of the voluntary organizations, European, American, and international. By the end of 1945, seven agencies, with personnel already in the field, had signed agreements with UNRRA. During the existence of the International Refugee Organization, agreements were entered into with some sixty American voluntary agencies and with more than that number in other countries. To enable voluntary agencies to perform needed services difficult or impossible for official agencies to carry out between 1946 and 1953, the International Refugee Organization, Intergovernmental Committee for European Migration, the UN High Commissioner for Refugees, and other UN

[6] Communication from the United Nations High Commissioner for Refugees, March 20, 1959, in the American Council Files. The UNHCR, *Final Report on the Ford Foundation Program for Refugees, Primarily in Europe* (Geneva: UNHCR, 1958), describes how the money was spent.
[7] James M. Read, "Ten Years of the Office of the United Nations High Commissioner for Refugees," 1961 (mimeographed), *passim*; James M. Read to Merle Curti, August 8, 1961; UNHCR, *Final Report on the Ford Foundation Program for Refugees, passim.*

agencies supported voluntary agencies with the sum of $39,200,000 in allocations and reimbursements. Between 1950 and 1960 voluntary agencies helped over 600,000 displaced persons find homes, chiefly in the United States, to which they brought talent and purchasing power.[8] A much larger number received food, clothing, medicine, and special training.

Of the many contributions of the voluntary agencies, one of the most important was the pressure exerted on governments for continuing and expanding the support for the refugee, including the liberalization of immigration policy. America's official record in dealing with refugees before World War II had not been particularly laudable. Rigid adherence to national origins quotas, together with overcautious and tedious processing of visas because of fears of subversiveness within the country and without, had closed the gates to all but a mere trickle of fleeing peoples, often those with money or influence rather than those who most needed to escape. But in the postwar era the record was considerably better. In addition to the subsidies to UNRRA and other international agencies, the United States adopted a more generous immigration policy. President Truman's Directive of December 22, 1945, operating within the confines of existing immigration policy, specified that quota immigration from the areas in which the refugee and DP problems were most pressing be resumed at once, gave preference to orphaned children, directed that visas be distributed fairly among persons of all faiths and nationalities, and introduced the "corporate affidavit" or "assurance." This was a guarantee of financial support, given by voluntary agencies on behalf of refugee immigrants to insure that these would not become public charges. Under the Truman Directive about 40,000 persons were admitted to the United States.[9] To the voluntary agencies this seemed, in view of the need, a small number.

In 1946 the Committee on Displaced Persons of the American

[8] Arthur C. Ringland, "The Organization of Voluntary Foreign Aid, 1939-1953," *Department of State Bulletin* XXX (March 15, 1954), 390; Lewis M. Hoskins, "Voluntary Agencies and Foundations in International Aid," *Annals of the American Academy of Political and Social Science* CCCXXIX (May, 1960), 62; interview with Miss Charlotte Owen, Miss Etta Deutsch, and Mrs. Margaret Littke of the American Council, June 15, 1960.

[9] Vernant, *The Refugee in the Post-War World*, 482; United States Displaced Persons Commission, *The DP Story: The Final Report of the United States Displaced Persons Commission*, August 15, 1952 (Washington: Govt. Printing Office, 1952), 7 [hereafter cited as *The DP Story*]; Stoessinger, *The Refugee and the World Community*, 133.

Council of Voluntary Agencies for Foreign Service undertook to co-ordinate and give direction to the work of many voluntary agencies serving DP's. It faced a chaotic situation in which intergovernmental, governmental, and voluntary agencies were working without clear lines of responsibility. There was no general plan nor was there even any clear realization of just how well the operations of all agencies put together were meeting the problem. In conjunction with the President's War Relief Control Board the ACVAFS set up a Survey Committee on Displaced Persons with voluntary, governmental, and intergovernmental agencies represented. The survey was headed by Dean Earl G. Harrison of the University of Pennsylvania Law School, a former United States Commissioner on Immigration and Naturalization. Various members of the Council financed the survey. It sought reliable sources of information on the DP problem, including resettlement, and examined the long-term issues in the light of governmental and intergovernmental agency functions.

In making its study, the Survey Committee circularized fifty-two voluntary agencies, thirty-two of which had substantial programs for DP's. It discovered that ten agencies were in some way connected with DP programs, but had no provision for direct aid or else provided relatively small services, that thirteen included all nationality groups, that nine served but one such group, and that ten helped only Jewish DP's. The Committee's report stated that the work of the voluntary agencies should supplement that of official organizations, which, in view of the magnitude of the problem, must take primary responsibility. It further recommended that the supplementary services of the voluntary groups might best concentrate on meeting the health needs of individuals on a case basis (special diets for the sick, appliances for the handicapped, psychiatric therapy), on placement, including the finding and reestablishment of contact with relatives, on vocational guidance and training, legal aid, and religious, recreational, and morale services. The need for an office to coordinate the activities of official and voluntary agencies was emphasized, a need highlighted by the President's recent Directive, which, with no general prior consultation, had asked the voluntary agencies to insure the financial independence for large numbers of persons brought into the country under the Directive.[10]

The emphasis in the report on the primary responsibility of government was followed by carefully planned public discussion and

10 "The Problem of Displaced Persons," 3.

pressure designed to persuade Washington to broaden still further the admission policy of the Truman Directive. In December, 1946, religious and nonsectarian agencies joined forces in organizing the Citizens Committee on Displaced Persons. This Committee won the active support of over 150 national organizations of veterans, welfare agencies, women's clubs, professional groups, and labor federations. A report of the Committee which reached the White House declared that "among themselves the Jews split into unfriendly factions on the question of Zionism. Catholic-Jewish and Catholic-Protestant cooperation on other questions is slight. And the nationalities groups are frequently in disagreement with the Jews on various questions. Yet on the question of displaced persons they have combined in one organization for one common objective." [11]

Between December, 1946, and July, 1948, the Committee published more than a hundred brochures, pamphlets, leaflets and documents running to millions of copies. It wrote, directed, and produced radio and TV programs on 1,800 stations which reached between 30,000,000 and 40,000,000 persons. All the reasons for admitting more DP's were thus publicized; all those against doing so rejected with concrete arguments.[12] A favorable climate of opinion was created.

Many individuals and organizations had vigorously opposed these efforts to help displaced persons. The American Legion, the Veterans of Foreign Wars, and kindred groups, held that the United States had already done its fair share for refugees. It was argued that neither the employment nor the housing situation warranted letting larger numbers into the country, and that in any case the American population could not assimilate the DP's, who were pictured as degenerates, criminals, and subversives. Subsequently these organizations somewhat softened their opposition, but their animosity helped defeat the bill introduced by Congressman William Grant Stratton of Illinois on April 1, 1947, which would have authorized the admission of 100,000 refugees annually for a period of four years.[13]

In 1948, thanks to the desire in Congress to reduce American costs

[11] *Ibid.*

[12] Vernant, *The Refugee in the Post-War World*, 523 ff.; Stoessinger, *The Refugee and the World Community*, 134-35. For the comment on the Committee's report that reached the White House see "Comments on the Revercomb Report," Feb. 14, 1947, Truman Papers, Official File 127 (Sept., 1946–Aug., 1947), Truman Library, Independence, Missouri.

[13] *The DP Story*, 11-16; Stoessinger, *The Refugee and the World Community*, 136-37; *New York Times*, April 2, Sept. 1, 10, 11, 1947.

of maintaining refugee camps in Europe, to President Truman's prodding, and to the continued pressure of the voluntary agencies, Congress passed a compromise measure—the Displaced Persons Act. This permitted the admission by June 30, 1950, of 205,000 refugees. It provided that each entrant was to have a sponsor, either a relative, friend, employer, or voluntary agency. The sponsor was to secure employment without displacing an American, to find housing without infringing on any citizen's prior claims and rights, and to secure transportation by relatives or agencies to the final destination in the United States.

In several ways the act was discriminatory. In specifying certain preferences and priorities which favored the DP's of northern and western Europe it militated against Catholics and Jews. It also required that at least 30 per cent of those admitted be engaged, prior to emigration, in agricultural pursuits and be guaranteed similar employment on reaching the United States. In addition to the categories of persons excluded by basic American immigration legislation, the Act barred all who had taken part in any movement deemed hostile to the United States in its form of government. (An amendment, passed in 1950, excluded those who advocated or adhered to any economic system which was directed toward the destruction of "free enterprise.") No wonder that the *New York Times* regarded the bill as a "sorry job." It expressed deep regret that "every liberalizing amendment which would have treated DP's equally as members of the human race was voted down." [14]

President Truman, reacting even more vehemently, characterized the bill as the worst sort of compromise. He gave it his signature only because it had been sent to him on the last day of the congressional session: its rejection would mean an intolerable delay in helping DP's. "The bad points of the bill are numerous," he declared. "Together they form a pattern of discrimination and intolerance wholly inconsistent with the American sense of justice . . . I know," the President concluded, "what a bitter disappointment this bill is to the many displaced victims of persecution who looked to the United States for hope; to the millions of our citizens who wanted to help them in the finest American spirit; to the many members of the Congress who fought hard but unsuccessfully for a decent displaced persons bill." An amendment in 1950 removed some but not all of the objectionable clauses and provided for the further admission over

[14] *The DP Story*, 26.

the next two years of an additional 200,000 DP's. The President finally concluded that all in all the administration had succeeded in getting the DP legislation it wanted.[15]

This legislation directly affected the voluntary agencies. One section permitted the "mortgaging" of quotas; that is, half of the visas available for subsequent years could be used if those of a current year were exhausted. This provided the voluntary agencies with a source for necessary visas in case the agencies were willing, as necessity forced them to be, to "mortgage" for decades in the future. (In congressional eyes this "mortgaging" system insured that national origins discriminations of the basic immigration law quota system would be preserved.) Secondly, the law created the Displaced Persons Commission, the chief federal agency for carrying out the provisions of the act and for coordinating the work of the various public and voluntary agencies. The Displaced Persons Commission was the first formally established government agency to undertake the resettlement of other nationals in the United States. The main job of resettling the some 400,000 displaced persons admitted under the legislation was carried through by the cooperating voluntary agencies. In addition to sizable private contributions these nonofficial agencies received federal grants and loans. In the four years in which the Commission operated, it spent $19,000,000 in effecting transportation and resettlement.[16]

Later legislation modified the picture. The McCarran-Walter Immigration Act of 1952, passed over President Truman's veto, continued the quota system and excluded those to whom objections were made on grounds of health, criminality, subversiveness, and other enumerated matters. Of special importance was the 1953 Refugee Relief Act passed on the special urging of President Eisenhower. It sought to deal with major problems created by the large number of refugees escaping into the free countries of Europe from behind the Iron Curtain. As enacted, it authorized the admission of 214,-000 refugees within a three-and-a-half-year period. Unlike the DP Act of 1948, these refugees were admitted outside the normal quota

[15] U. S., *Statutes at Large*, LXII, Pt. 1, 1009. Statement by the President, June 25, 1948, Truman Papers, Official File 127 (Sept., 1947–Aug., 1948); interview with Harry S. Truman, March 31, 1961. It is worth noting that James M. Read, who was co-chairman of the group of voluntary agencies working in Washington to get the DP act passed, and who was later Deputy High Commissioner of the UN Office of High Commissioner for Refugees, feels that the achievement "was a pretty good show": Read to Merle Curti, August 7, 1961.
[16] *The DP Story*, v-vi.

limitations.[17] Other acts, including one in favor of the Hungarian refugees who fled from reprisals after the suppression of the 1956 revolt, extended the parole principle first given legal recognition in 1952 by the passage of the McCarran-Walter Immigration Act. While not granting legal residence status, the parole, extended under the discretionary authority of administrative officials, allowed temporary asylum in the United States for humane considerations or for reasons of public interest. Under this procedure, over 30,000 of the 180,000 Hungarians who fled the homeland in 1956 were admitted to the United States. An act signed in September, 1957, provided for the admission of 18,565 refugees. But it did not regularize the position of the Hungarian refugees admitted under parole. To President Eisenhower as well as to many deeply concerned with the problem it seemed a poor substitute for more liberal legislation.[18]

Two developments in the psychological aspects of the Cold War involved philanthropy and government. One was Radio Free Europe which was supported by voluntary contributions to the Crusade for Freedom. Its programs, broadcast in the languages of the peoples behind the Iron Curtain, not only provided listeners with their most reliable news of the day but influenced decisions to attempt flight to freedom. In reply to the question, "Did you listen to western broadcasts in your home country?" 90 per cent said that they had listened to Radio Free Europe. The great majority of 735 refugees from the satellite countries questioned in 1959-1960 further reported that RFE was the "most influential" of western stations.[19]

In 1954, two years after Radio Free Europe began its programs, the United States Escapee Program (USEP) was inaugurated to ensure a welcoming hand of friendship for escapees from Communist regimes and to help prevent the economy of countries bordering on the USSR and its satellites from being too heavily burdened by refugees.[20] Essentially political in its origins and activities and well sup-

[17] Charles Gordon and Harry N. Rosenfield, *Immigration Law and Procedure* (Albany: Banks, 1959), 13-16, 20. The President's Commission on Immigration and Naturalization, appointed by President Truman on September 4, 1952, conducted hearings in eleven cities and proposed major changes in the McCarran-Walter Act. The report appeared as United States, President's Commission on Immigration and Naturalization, *Whom We Shall Welcome* (Washington: Govt. Printing Office, 1953).

[18] Rees, *Century of the Homeless Man*, 219-20; U. S., *Statutes at Large*, LXXI, 639.

[19] "News from Radio Free Europe," July 4, 1960 (mimeographed release).

[20] U. S., *Statutes at Large*, LXVIII, 843; U. S., Congress, Senate, Committee on Foreign Relations, *The Mutual Security Act of 1954*, 83d Cong., 2d Sess., 1954. S. Rept. 1799, 66-67; Edgar H. S. Chandler, *The High Tower of Refuge: The Inspiring Story of Refugee Relief throughout the World* (New York: Praeger, 1959), *passim*.

ported by Congress, which recognized it as an effective instrument of psychological warfare, USEP was directed by the Office of Refugee and Migration Affairs within the State Department. It was not an operational agency. All its work was done on a contractual basis with voluntary agencies. The contracts provided a wide range of services to escapees from Communist countries, including visa documenting and processing, provision of food, clothing, and medicines, language and vocational training, legal aid, overseas and inland transportation, and reception and placement.

The positions of voluntary agencies on the question of contracts with USEP differed. A few religious groups, sensitive to the implications of strict separation of church and state and unwilling to merge religious testimony with a politically oriented and government supported program, refused to work with USEP. Others, not too happy in cooperating with a program involving psychological warfare, nonetheless did so on the ground that the funds provided enabled them to expand their refugee work in quarters where it was greatly needed. The nationality agencies, on the other hand, politically and emotionally committed as they were to opposing the Communist regimes on every level, readily went along with this aspect of United States foreign policy.

But whatever may be said adversely of such matters, a good deal was accomplished in the interest of humanitarianism by the cooperation of some twenty-five voluntary agencies with USEP. During the Hungarian refugee program, for example, USEP entered into a contract with the American Council of Voluntary Agencies for Foreign Service in support of the migration of unaccompanied minors to enable them to join relatives in the United States. Between 1952 and 1959, some 340,000 refugees in Europe and the Middle East had benefitted from USEP help, while some 222,000 escapees from Communist China were in similar debt.[21]

Achievements under the refugee and escapee programs would have been impossible without cooperation between official and voluntary

21 U. S., Department of State, International Cooperation Administration, *ICA and US Voluntary Agencies* (Washington: ICA-Federal Lithograph, 1959), 9; interviews with Sydney Shore, Raymond Kissam, James Rice, United HIAS Service, and James McCracken, Church World Service, July 28, 1960. According to Harry Grossman, Acting Chief, Operating Division, Office of Refugee and Migration Affairs, Department of State, as of Feb. 29, 1960, USEP had assisted 205,977 refugees in Europe, of whom 87,363 had been resettled, 27,071 of whom had been integrated into the local economies of the asylum countries, 68,245 had been dropped for various reasons from the caseload, and 23,025 remained on the caseload, Grossman to Miss Etta Deutsch, July 27, 1960, American Council Files.

agencies. Yet the partnership did not always work smoothly despite the helpful liaison services of both the Advisory Committee on Voluntary Foreign Aid and the American Council. Government officials and some of the voluntary agencies blamed each other for the fact that in early 1956 only 68,000 refugees of the 209,000 authorized by the Refugee Relief Act of 1953 had been admitted. Dr. Paul Empie, of the National Lutheran Council, challenged a government statement to the effect that the Refugee Relief Act program lagged because of a shortage of assurances for refugees and laid the blame squarely on the officials who admitted to a lack of sufficient personnel and "exceedingly cumbersome procedures." [22]

Both during and after the Hungarian revolt of 1956 the partnership of government and voluntary agencies in refugee relief was severely tested. The problem was not one of any lack of generosity in the free world. In England, for example, the Lord Mayor of London Fund totaled $7,280,000, and the United Nations High Commissioner for Refugees displayed great energy and effectiveness. In the United States, the Ford Foundation appropriated $1,150,000 to help Hungarian students and refugees, while constituents of eighteen voluntary agencies contributed $20,000,000. On its part, the American government spent upwards of $50,000,000 in aid of the victims of Communist repression. The President's committee, working with several voluntary agencies, operated a reception and rehabilitation center at Camp Kilmer in New Jersey. The Army maintained the basic camp facilities, and various federal agencies provided many services. Moreover, by March, 1958, the United States had admitted 38,121 Hungarian refugees. (The United Kingdom admitted 15,890, Canada, 35,164, and Switzerland, with a population of five million, 12,000.) [23]

---

[22] National Lutheran Council, News Bureau, March 9, 1957, Advisory Committee Files. According to Dr. Cordelia Cox, director of Lutheran Refugee Service, the failure of the 84th Congress to enact adequate legislation "put in jeopardy the immigration status of thousands of refugees." Lutheran Refugee Service, "Congress Hit for Failure to Amend Refugee Relief Act," Advisory Committee File. On Dec. 3, 1956, the *Department of State Bulletin* reported that American private sources (thirteen agencies) had thus far contributed $3,633,200 in cash and commodities to the Hungarian people: "Response to Relief Needs of People of Hungary," *Department of State Bulletin* XXXV (Dec. 3, 1958), 873.

[23] Martin A. Bursten, *Escape from Fear* (Syracuse: Syracuse University Press, 1958), 39 ff.; Rees, *Century of the Homeless Man*, 194; Ford Foundation, *Annual Report, 1957* (New York: Ford Foundation, 1958), 41-42; B. C. Maday, Co-ordinated Hungarian Relief, *Report of the Executive Secretary*, Oct., 1947, Oct., 1958 (mimeographed), *passim*. B. C. Maday, Co-ordinated Hungarian Relief to Merle Curti, Feb. 9, 1959; "Report of Fact-finding Committee on the Committee on Migration and Refugee Problems on the Hungarian Refugee Program," April 21, 1958 (typescript), American Council Files.

Leading spokesmen of several voluntary agencies pointed to many shortcomings. Although six or seven government agencies were dealing with Hungarian refugees, overall direction in policy was lacking. In the opinion of one voluntary agency executive, this lack partly explained conditions in the refugee camps of Austria, where as many as eighty human beings were huddled in a single room, with morale depleted through the abnormal release of inhibitions and forced inactivity. Rumors and counterrumors as to whether the United States would or would not receive them, together with uncertainty as to what alternatives were open, deepened disillusionment for many such refugees. For example, there was the issue of whether and when the United States would provide the necessary dollars for transport to Australia, which had expressed willingness to open her doors. To one experienced observer there was obvious need for an intergovernmental body in which care, maintenance, emigration, and resettlement were part and parcel of the same authority. An official in another voluntary agency similarly laid the blame for much that went wrong on a series of hasty governmental improvisations, worsened by lack of a single coordinating body. At the same time the inflexibility of the McCarran-Walter Act and of the generally constraining American immigration policy, not only prevented the adequate meeting of an emergency that involved not only thousands of human beings who had risked everything for the freedom America talked about, but also affected United States foreign policy. Still another expert within the ranks of the voluntary agencies noted the lack of coordination between the executive and legislative branches of government, including the apparent fear that each felt of what the other was doing or might do.[24]

A special fact-finding committee of the American Council of Voluntary Agencies for Foreign Service confirmed and spelled out these criticisms. Its report, together with supporting material, indicated that in the heat of political considerations of the moment the handling of the Hungarian refugee problem left much to be desired. The President, instead of summoning representatives of the voluntary agencies to plan a resettlement program, called in Tracy Voorhees, a prominent New York attorney, and asked him to set up a special committee without any consultation with the voluntary agencies on

[24] Moses Leavitt, American Jewish Joint Distribution Committee, to Tracy S. Voorhees, President's Committee for Hungarian Relief, Feb. 20, 1957; Rt. Rev. Msgr. Edward E. Swanstrom, Catholic Relief Services, to Voorhees, Feb. 16, 1957; Lewis M. Hoskins, American Friends Service Committee, to Voorhees, Feb. 28, 1957, in Advisory Committee Files.

whom the main responsibility for carrying out any program must fall. Then the government began to accept refugees for resettlement on the basis of first come, first served, while the voluntary agencies bore the load of transferring these people and getting assurances for them in the United States. Under such circumstances, the voluntary agencies could not exercise their usual careful casework approach, insuring that refugees were resettled in the proper places, with relatives when this was desirable, and with appropriate sponsors. The haste, the "crash" character of the approach, and the way in which the government itself largely chose refugees to be resettled according to its own shifting, vaguely defined, often unpublicized criteria, left the agencies more or less holding the bag and created general confusion, bewilderment, and, often, bitterness among the refugees who had risked much for freedom and suffered beyond ready description.[25]

Yet in the government's defense it must be said that after the initial over-hasty action, regular and periodic meetings were held by many official agencies with committees of the voluntary groups. Administrators responsible for immigration programs requested comments and suggestions from the voluntary agencies.[26] The original friction must be put in the context of the confusion of a crisis situation and the pressure to produce immediate evidence that the United States was doing its share to help Hungary.[27] In view of the experimental and necessary partnership of government and voluntary agencies and of the complexity of the problems involved, the positive achievements in many ways transcended the shortcomings. That so many people were resettled in so short a time was, as Elfan Rees has said, "the crowning glory of the Hungarian refugee episode." An important lesson to be learned, Rees continued, was the overwhelming need for liberalization of immigration policy and careful planning for emergencies. Such action might, in another crisis, prevent the ironical focus of attention on refugees of the moment while a much larger number of equally worthy DP's waited in vain for a chance to migrate to hope.[28]

[25] "Report of Fact-finding Committee on the Hungarian Refugee Program," April 21, 1958, American Council Files.

[26] U. S., Congress, Senate, Judiciary Committee, *Hearings, Investigation on Administration of Refugee Relief Act*, 84th Cong., 1st Sess., 1955, 27, 70 ff., contains a statement by Scott McLeod, administrator of the DP Commission; *The DP Story*, 48, 274.

[27] "Speed in Resettlement—How Has It Worked?" *Children* V (July-Aug., 1958), 123-24; Gordon and Rosenfield, *Immigration Law and Procedure*, 87.

[28] Rees, *Century of the Homeless Man*, 193-94, 236.

Notwithstanding the common concern shared by the thirty-five secular and religious agencies listed in 1957 as members of the Standing Conference of Voluntary Agencies Working for Refugees, considerable variety in motive and method marked their activities. Programs included the provision of emergency relief supplementary to official rations and shelter, whether in or outside of the camps in Europe where the so-called "hard core" of DP's continued to need help, as well as the special emergency relief in areas of armed conflict (Palestine, the Gaza strip, Vietnam, Korea, and Hungary at the time of the 1956 revolt). In addition, the agencies spent much effort in integrating into the communities in Europe and Asia those DP's who by choice or necessity were to remain in the initial receiving country. Equal effort went into retraining DP's for overseas settlement, in getting them into permanent overseas homes, and in providing means for self-help aid once they arrived.[29]

The voluntary agencies in carrying out these functions were on the whole admirably cooperative. This was partly the result of the liaison provided by the American Council of Voluntary Agencies for Foreign Service, partly the fruit of the growing ecumenical movement, and partly a common-sense response to the sheer magnitude of the need.[30] The established pattern of cooperation between religious and secular agencies was by and large sustained. Often, too, the sectarian agencies crossed lines. To be sure, the tendency was for Catholic agencies to serve Catholic refugees, for Lutherans to shoulder responsibility for Lutherans, for Jews to help Jews. But Catholic Relief Service also aided Jewish refugees and a considerable percentage of Catholic immigrants were sponsored by Quaker and other Protestant agencies.[31] The American Friends Service Committee often aided refugees without religious affiliations and took responsibility for helping refugees of mixed marriages. Church World Service, which generally looked out for Protestant DP's, also provided assurances for two hundred Moslem families. One of its many projects, undertaken with the Tolstoy Foundation under an agreement with the International Refugee Organization, was the resettlement of some six hundred Kalmuks, a Buddhist group that had been all but exterminated by Soviet aggression.[32]

[29] Gordon and Rosenfield, *Immigration Law and Procedure*, 84.
[30] Interview with Miss Charlotte Owen, Miss Etta Deutsch, and Mrs. Margaret Littke, June 15, 1960.
[31] Vernant, *The Refugee in the Post-War World*, 526.
[32] *The DP Story*, 277-78.

The achievements of American voluntary agencies cannot be fully assessed without consideration of similar and related agencies in other countries, for refugee relief and rehabilitation was in a genuine sense an international problem and undertaking. The contributions in other countries ranged over a wide scale. An outstanding example of individual initiative is the work of Father Georges Pire, a Belgian Dominican priest who, deeply concerned at the loss of hope and human dignity prevailing among the unwanted "hard core" of displaced persons existing in barns and shacks, founded and maintained through voluntary contributions the Europe of the Heart movement which established the unwanted in self-sustaining villages and decent homes.[33] The record of such organizations as *Hilfswerk*, *Aide Suisse*, CARITAS, and the Inter-Church Aid and Refugee Service of the British Council of Churches, to cite only a few examples, was generous and far-reaching.[34]

Many religious groups with an interest in refugee problems, whether based in the United States or in non-American countries, took part in the work of international church organizations. While the American participating agencies, because of numbers and means, shouldered much of the work of maintenance, the member agencies in other countries assisted as they were able. Jewish communities in many countries contributed to the JDC, ORT, and HIAS. Other examples are the Baptist World Alliance Relief Committee, which helped refugees from the Iron Curtain and the Bamboo Curtain and made arrangements for the reception of these escapees in Brazil, Paraguay, and other countries. The Lutheran Resettlement Service of the Lutheran World Federation is another example. Korean Church World Service, supported by religious groups in Canada, New Zealand, Australia, Germany, Switzerland, and the United States, provided emergency relief to refugees during and after the Korean War and established homes for widows, orphanages, and vocational training programs. The World Council of Churches Refugee Service (financed by religious groups in several countries as well as by governmental and intergovernmental funds) and the establishment in 1950 of the International Catholic Migration Commission are further examples of the application of ecumenical and interna-

---

[33] Victor Houart, *The Open Heart: The Inspiring Story of Father Pire and the Europe of the Heart*, trans. Mervyn Savill (London: Souvenir, 1959), *passim*.
[34] Proudfoot, *European Refugees*, *passim*.

tional principles to the problem of refugee relief. By the end of the 1950's the activities of over seventy nongovernmental organizations, national and international, testified to the world-wide character of the voluntary approach to the problem of relief and rehabilitation of displaced persons.

Thus the achievements of American voluntary agencies in the field of refugee relief and rehabilitation cannot be fully assessed without reference to a context larger than the American one. Nor is it feasible to relate the achievements of all the American agencies working in this field. What was done can, however, be in part understood and appreciated in terms of the records of some of the larger and smaller agencies.

Of the older religious agencies, the American Friends Service Committee shared in activities common to many voluntary organizations, such as providing food, clothing, medical aid, nurseries, orphanages, and work camps for DP's in Europe, Palestine, Egypt, India, China, and Japan. It sent, for example, more than $3,500,000 in material aid to Korea, including 1,274,000 pounds of clothing, cloth, yard bedding, medicines, and other supplies. It also distributed, largely to Korean refugees, 10,605,000 pounds of government food.[35] Realizing the magnitude of the need and the inadequacy of its resources, AFSC proposed a specific list of projects to the Ford Foundation with a request for a grant to carry these out. The Foundation was favorably impressed but deemed it inadvisable to make so large a grant to a single agency. Consequently, it allocated $2,900,000 and later an additional $200,000 to the United Nations High Commissioner for Refugees with the suggestion that this be parceled out to several agencies.[36]

With some of the funds thus received, the American Friends Service Committee pioneered, with other agencies, in developing in Germany and Austria programs for the integration into these countries of DP's who could not resettle elsewhere. Housing projects and loans

[35] American Friends Service Committee, *Annual Reports*, 1956, 1957, 1958 (Philadelphia: AFSC, 1957, 1958, 1959), 6, 6-7, 5; "Friends of the Helpless," *Newsweek* XXIX (April 28, 1957), 84, 86; Clarence E. Pickett, *For More Than Bread: An Autobiographical Account of Twenty-two Years' Work with the American Friends Service Committee* (Boston: Little, Brown, 1953), 161 ff., 261 ff.

[36] UNHCR, *Final Report on the Ford Foundation Program for Refugees* is a detailed summary of what was done with the grant.

for establishing business enterprises proved to be effective means of furthering assimilation and integration.[37] When the United Nations Relief for Palestine Refugees undertook its program for the relief of Arab DP's in 1949 it chose the AFSC as one of the three major voluntary agencies to operate its program. Working in the Gaza strip, the Committee aided some 200,000 refugees who were packed into an inhospitable space of 125 square miles in which means of transport were all but nonexistent. Convinced that prolonged direct relief contributed to the moral degeneration of the refugees and militated against a speedy political settlement of the problem, the AFSC urged the Secretary General of the United Nations to spare no efforts in pressing for a solution of the situation which had led to the sad plight of 880,000 Arab refugees.[38]

The role of the American Friends Service Committee in the Hungarian crisis of 1956 had a special significance apart from the timely emergency relief it administered along with many other agencies, American and European. The Committee played a leading part in bringing together agencies for coordination purposes and for negotiation with various government and intergovernment officials. After the uprising was crushed, the Committee together with other agencies and the United Nations High Commissioner for Refugees decided to work with Hungarians who had fled to Yugoslavia. In the light of Communist antipathy toward refugees, the cooperation between the Belgrade government on the one hand and the UN High Commissioner and AFSC on the other was noteworthy. The record seemed to give some vindication to the conclusion the Committee had come to in pondering the question of the extent to which a Christian pacifist relief organization could cooperate with a Communist regime. In facing the dangers and difficulties of working in a social order which often refused to permit recipients of gifts to receive the accompanying message of fellowship, the Committee neverthe-

[37] *Ibid.; The Integration of Refugees into German Life. A Report of the EAA Technical Assistance Commission on the Integration of the Refugees in the German Republic, March 21, 1951*, 31; Elfan Rees, *We Strangers and Afraid* (New York: Carnegie Endowment for International Peace, 1959); Lewis M. Hoskins to Merle Curti, June 20, 1961.

[38] Channing B. Richardson, "880,000 Arab Refugees," *Journal of International Affairs* VI (Winter, 1952), 20-24; Peretz, *Israel and the Palestine Arabs*, ix, 10; Deborah Kaplan, *The Arab Refugees, an Abnormal Problem* (Jerusalem: Rubin Mass, 1961), 157; Elfan Rees, "The Refugee Problem—Today and Tomorrow," address at the Conference on Refugee Problems, Geneva, May, 1957 (typescript); Martha Gellhorn, "The Arabs of Palestine," *Atlantic Monthly* CCVII (Oct., 1961), 45-65.

less felt there was justification if service in some small part made for understanding and peace.[39]

Two kindred agencies also made their impact on the refugee problem. The Mennonite Central Committee cooperated with the American Friends Service Committee and with Swedish and Swiss organizations in keeping university students alive during and after the Hungarian tragedy. It also resettled more than two hundred Mennonite families in the United States and, in cooperation with Church World Service, settled in other countries some 660 farm families, mostly of Ukrainian origin and Russian Orthodox faith. The Mennonites also fed undernourished refugees in Korea, maintained vocational schools for orphans, and provided food and clothing for refugees in Jordan and other places.[40] The Brethren Service Commission likewise continued its well-established though relatively small programs of aid which helped refugees as well as the permanently needy in several parts of the world.[41]

Of the total relief in money and goods administered by the Baptist World Alliance in 1950, much of which met temporary needs of DP's, Americans gave $8,475,980, Canadians, $308,922, Swedes, $92,794, Danes, $74,600, and the British, $21,018.[42] At the time of the uprising in Budapest, 300 Hungarians, 262 of whom were Baptists, were helped through a camp for refugees and the Baptist Church in Vienna.[43] The Baptist World Alliance Relief Committee extended aid to Baptists in the Far East and made arrangements for the public reception of 400 DP's in Brazil and Paraguay. At Pusan in Korea a free clinic, opened in 1951, treated an average of 700 patients a day. Thus deeds implemented the words of the Reverend A. Klappiks, Coordinator for Baptist World Alliance Relief: "We feel a responsibility for every Baptist who looks to us for help, and we also extend our help to as many others as we can." [44]

From the time it was registered with the Advisory Committee in 1948 the Congregational Christian Service Committee worked with-

[39] AFSC Minutes of the Foreign Service Executive Committee, Nov. 1, 1948, Advisory Committee Files; Lewis M. Hoskins to Merle Curti, June 20, 1961.

[40] Irvin B. Horst, *A Ministry of Goodwill* (Akron, Pa., 1951), 64-65, 74-75; *The DP Story*, 287.

[41] Lorell Weiss, *Ten Years of Brethren Service, 1941-1951* (Elgin, Ill.: General Brotherhood Board, 1952), 33-44.

[42] Baptist World Alliance Relief Committee, *The Romance of Relief* (Washington: BWA, 1950), n.p.

[43] *The Baptist World* V (Oct., 1958), 7.

[44] *Ibid.* (May, 1958), 6.

out stint in its effort "to meet some of the overwhelming needs of the millions of people in the world who are homeless, destitute, discouraged and bitter." Its help was given without reference to race, color, creed, or nationality.[45] Under the leadership of Edgar H. S. Chandler and Earle H. Ballou, the Congregational Christian Service Committee worked through other organizations to which it contributed. These included the United Lithuanian Relief Fund of America, the Refugee Service Program of the World Alliance YMCA, Church World Service, and the World Council of Churches Refugee Commission.[46] Thus in 1958 over 9 per cent of the budget of the Division of Inter-Church Aid and Services to Refugees of the World Council of Churches came from the Congregational Christian Service Committee.[47] The Committee carried through programs of its own in many countries—Germany, France, Italy, Greece, Turkey, Lebanon. These programs included support of work camps for refugees, vocational training, scholarships for young DP's, and, especially in Lebanon, schools for refugee children. Russian "Old Believers," long stranded in China and Hong Kong, received help in resettlement in Brazil.

The Congregational Christian Service Committee also sponsored and placed DP's in the United States.[48] In order to rehabilitate difficult cases, the Committee supported the Homeless European Land Program (HELP). This novel idea, conceived by the actor Don Murray and his friend Belden Paulson, who had served as fraternal workers for the Committee in Italy, settled in Sardinia twenty-five refugee families barred from emigration by health or other problems. The project received aid from the Italian Government, the UN High Commissioner for Refugees, CARE, the Heifer Project, the Brethren, and other agencies. It proved to be one of the creative and successful methods of helping to meet the seemingly insoluble problems of so-called "hard core" refugees.[49] Although in 1958 the Congregational Christian Service Committee had more than $800,-

[45] Congregational Christian Service Committee, *Ministering in His Name* (New York: CCSC, ca. 1957), n.p.
[46] Congregational Christian Service Committee, especially W. H. Williams to Arthur C. Ringland, March 4, 1949, and W. H. Williams to Charlotte Owen (carbon), Jan. 11, 1950, Advisory Committee File.
[47] Congregational Christian Service Committee, *In Times Like These* (New York: CCSC, ca. 1959), n.p.
[48] Congregational Christian Service Committee, "The Service Committee: Relief and Reconstruction, 1958" (mimeographed).
[49] Congregational Christian Service Committee, *Reports*, Autumn, 1958, and Spring, 1960 (New York: CCSC, 1958, 1960), *passim*.

ooo at its disposal, what it could do seemed to its thoughtful executive secretary at best "little more than a drop in the bucket." [50]

In its relations with refugees and in dispatching teams of medical experts to share new techniques and therapies with foreign colleagues the Unitarian Service Committee sought to use its limited resources for badly needed specialized services. With the passage of the Displaced Persons Act of 1948, therefore, it arranged for assurance for refugee professionals, established necessary contacts with universities and scientific institutes, provided *curricula vitae* of DP professionals, and evaluated training and educational experience by American standards. [51]

Like other agencies with overseas programs, the Unitarian Service Committee took part in relief programs designed to alleviate misery in the postwar areas of conflict and devastation, many of which, especially in France, where help continued to be given to Spaniards, and in Germany, were directed particularly toward the uprooted. [52] It also shared with other voluntary agencies in the distribution of emergency relief in the Korean War. During the Hungarian crisis of 1956 and 1957 the Committee's representatives, at considerable personal risk and without reference to religious affiliation, visited the camps in Austria, gave out clothing, made contacts with relatives in Hungary, helped to get needed documents, and established a loan fund to enable some of the refugees to establish small businesses. [53]

But the chief emphasis of the Committee, and one with special implications for displaced persons, was to help those in distress to develop their skills and resources, and thus recover a sense of human dignity and identification with mankind. This purpose was forwarded in part through supporting child welfare projects and social service seminars. Leading social workers in Germany testified to the new horizons opened as the significance of good group and individual relations was demonstrated in daily contact. [54] Similar seminars for social workers met genuine needs in Greece, which had its own refugee problems. A major achievement was the establishment at Seoul University of a permanent school for training social workers which

50 Earle H. Ballou to Merle Curti, Feb. 19, 1959.
51 *The DP Story*, 289-90.
52 Wilmer Froistad to Miss Joan Kain, March 15, 1947, Advisory Committee Files.
53 Fritz Ripp to Miss Sheridan, Feb. 28, 1957; Wilmer Froistad to Miss Joan Kain, March 29, 1947, Advisory Committee File.
54 Miss Florence Black, Office of the United States High Commission to Germany to Miss Helen Fogg, Unitarian Service Committee, Jan. 5, 1952, Advisory Committee Files.

sensibly took into account the differences between Korean and American cultures.[55]

Among Protestant denominations maintaining their own agencies for refugee aid, the Lutherans conducted a wide-ranging program. Much of the food, clothing and medicine provided by Lutheran World Relief went to refugees. In 1958, long after the postwar emergency, Lutheran World Relief was still helping 62,000 Arab refugees in the Near East, 93,000 in Hong Kong, 105,000 in Taiwan, 50,000 in Korea, and, in cooperation with Church World Service, 176,000 uprooted people in India.[56]

But the most striking achievement of the Lutherans was in helping displaced persons find homes in the United States. Up to 1949, under the Truman Directive and the DP Act of 1948, they resettled 2,700 DP's in the United States. Voldemar Beimanis, his wife, and four children, were among those the Lutherans helped. The Beimanis family, Latvians, fled their homeland in 1944 to escape Russian occupation. After wandering across Europe for many months, they ended in a Displaced Persons Camp near Ulm in Germany. Meanwhile, the Reverend Joel Njus of the Evangelical Lutheran Church in Rembrandt, Iowa, had been telling his congregation of the DP problem in Europe. One Sunday morning after service Njus was approached by Clifford L. Green, who offered a tenant house on his farm for a DP family. Njus contacted the proper authorities and shortly thereafter the Beimanises arrived in Iowa. At first there was some local resentment to "foreign" hired help, but objections were soon drowned out by the majority who enjoyed welcoming their new neighbors. The ladies' aid gave a kitchen shower at the church: two tables were laden with canned goods and pantry supplies. The Beimanises also received clothing and ten dollars in cash. Local residents donated the complete house furnishings including a washing machine.[57]

The National Lutheran Council's refugee work was reorganized in the fall of 1948 with the establishment of the Lutheran Resettlement Service. This operated in the United States, the refugee work in Eu-

---

[55] Wilmer Froistad to Austin Sullivan, Foreign Operations Administration, July 1, 1954, and United States Government Memo on social work in Korea, Oct. 7, 1954, in Advisory Committee Files; Unitarian Service Committee *Fact Sheet*, Jan., 1959.

[56] Lutheran World Relief, *Annual Report*, 1958, 168-170.

[57] "New Life for DP's," *Newsweek* XXXIII (June 27, 1949), 90. For other striking concrete examples see International Cooperation Administration, *ICA and US Voluntary Agencies*, 7-8.

rope being handled by the Service to Refugees which the Lutheran World Federation sponsored. In 1950, the Lutheran Resettlement Service of the National Lutheran Council with a budget of $1,459,-000 was operating a program which was to bring thousands of displaced persons to the United States. In the same year the Lutheran Church-Missouri Synod elected to participate in the program. In 1954 the name of the Lutheran Resettlement Service was changed to the Lutheran Refugee Service and in 1960 to the Lutheran Immigration Service.[58] The Lutheran contribution after the war of $3,-462,000 in cash and new homes enabled 38,254 refugees and DP's to be resettled in America.[59]

Church World Service was organized in 1947 to take over the program of the American Christian Committee for Refugees, an agency which had been helping refugees since 1934 through welfare, immigration counseling, and location services. On many occasions Lutherans, Friends, and other sectarian groups cooperated with this new agency. The Committee on Christian Science Wartime Activities of the Mother Church, for example, was reported in 1949 to be working with Church World Service in processing a number of assurances for DP's.[60] Much of the general relief work of CWS, including the Christian Rural Overseas Program (CROP) and Share Our Surplus (SOS) program benefitted displaced persons.[61] In July, 1950, the administration of its European operations was taken over by the World Council of Churches. The Refugee Service of the Council, supported by churches in America and in other countries as well as by the UN High Commissioner, resettled over 100,000 DP's. It was also one of the six voluntary agencies chosen by the Commissioner to develop pilot projects for the economic integration

[58] Lutheran Refugee Service, Advisory Committee Files; *The DP Story*, 286.

[59] Miss Cordelia Cox to Mrs. Florence Gonzales, April 21, 1954, Advisory Committee Files; Hartzell Spence, "The Lutherans," *Look* XXII (April 1, 1958), 86; Paul C. Empie, National Lutheran Council, to Merle Curti, Sept. 7, 1961.

[60] Russell Stevenson, *A More Excellent Way* (New York: Church World Service, ca. 1959), 5; "Protestant World Relief," *Christian Century* LXIV (May 14, 1947), 614; Church World Service, *Share Our Surplus* (New York: CWS, ca. 1958); Charles S. Sowder, Church World Service to Miss Florence Black, June 30, 1951, Advisory Committee Files; U. S., Congress, House, Special Committee on Foreign Affairs, *Voluntary Foreign Aid: The Nature and Scope of Postwar Private American Assistance Abroad with Special Reference to Europe*, 80th Cong., 1st Sess., 1947, Committee print. Portions of this report are printed in U. S., Congress, House, Select Committee on Foreign Aid, *Final Report on Foreign Aid*, 80th Cong., 2d Sess., 1948, H. Rept. 1845, 785-827.

[61] G. K. A. Bell, *The Kingship of Christ: The Story of the World Council of Churches* (Harmondsworth, Md.: Penguin, 1954), 43-49, 119.

and assimilation of refugees in Europe, the Near East, Korea and Hong Kong through the Ford Foundation grant of $2,900,000.[62]

Apart from what was done to help DP's find new homes, Church World Service provided emergency relief to refugees and helped prepare them for a new life in strange lands. At the time of the Hungarian revolt, American Protestant churches through the World Council of Churches made available food, clothing, and medicine valued at a million dollars and contributed another million for relief, rehabilitation, and resettlement.[63] Church World Service, alone or in cooperation with other church and interchurch groups, also grappled with the problems of refugees in the Near East in general and in the Arab-Israeli war in particular through providing emergency feeding, vocational training, clinics, and self-help programs, such as the making of small loans to enable uprooted artisans and tradesmen to become self-supporting. In Hong Kong, CWS distributed surplus foods to more than 60,000 DP's and took over the feeding of some 50,000 fishermen who were denied access to fishing grounds off the mainland. In India emphasis was put on distribution of surplus foods to refugees from droughts and floods, on mobile health vans, and on the establishment of small-scale industry for refugee rehabilitation.[64] In 1960 announcement was made of a project in which $1,000,000 was to be spent over a five-year period to improve the condition of more than 3,000,000 Hindu refugees in West Bengal and Calcutta who had streamed into India from East Pakistan after the 1947 partition. The project as outlined included educational, economic, and medical aid, with vocational training, for the pitiful refugees who had existed in temporary camps for over a decade in the conviction that "the gods as well as their fellow men" had turned against them.[65]

In addition to all these and other on-the-spot services to refugees, CWS resettled DP's in the United States and in other countries. Under the program which the Truman Directive established, it submitted corporate affidavits for over 2,000 DP's and extended a similar service for a smaller number of White Russians in China. By 1959 the organization had enabled 104,649 refugees and DP's,

---

[62] Chandler, *The High Tower of Refuge*, 21-22.
[63] Bursten, *Escape from Fear*, 118.
[64] Church World Service, "The Overseas Program Report," 1958 (mimeographed), 17-22.
[65] *New York Times*, Feb. 5, 1960; Church World Service, "Project Daya," Jan., 1960 (mimeographed).

many of whom were the so-called "hard core" cases—the infirm, the aged, the physically handicapped—to find new homes.[66]

Like Church World Service, the YMCA and YWCA were non-sectarian in character and supported world-wide programs which included aid to refugees. The Young Women's Christian Association Foreign Division extended help to the sister organization in Chile as the International Relief Organization representative for receiving and resettling displaced persons from Europe, aided the Lebanon YW in its work with Palestinian refugees, and the YW Service Center of Turkey in its program for Bulgarian refugees. Moreover, a considerable part of the thousands of tons of food and clothing contributed by YWCAs in all parts of the United States went to refugees in Europe and Asia.[67] While the YWCA International Committee like the YMCA World Service stressed the development of character and leadership through education and recreation and emphasized overall rural reconstruction, it also took part in many relief projects associated with the world refugee problem. In Hong Kong, for example, it developed a strong program for aiding in the assimilation of refugees.[68]

Like its Protestant counterparts, Catholic Relief Services dispensed aid to refugees wherever they were and without reference to creed or race. It is impossible to state the proportion of refugees, escapees, expellees, and DP's among the needy who received help in a given year, but it was certainly high. In 1957, for example, a billion pounds of clothing, medicine, and surplus food reached 40,000,000 "destitute and hungry" people in fifty-three countries.[69]

When the Hungarian revolt called for action, Catholic Relief Services responded at once. Father Fabian Flynn, who had administered relief in Hungary after the Second World War until driven out by Communists, returned twice to Budapest with ten truckloads of supplies donated by American Catholics. Refugees in neighboring Austria received a good part of the supplies he subsequently distributed: 8,000 tons of cheese, butter. milk and flour sent from relief supplies in Italy, and including 1,000 tons of similar goods from Spain.

---

[66] Church World Service, "Statistical Summary," Feb. 9, 1959 (mimeographed).

[67] YWCA, "At Home Abroad: A Summary History of the Foreign Program of the YWCA of the United States," August, 1954 (mimeographed).

[68] International Committee of the YWCA, Advisory Committee File.

[69] Catholic Bishops' Relief Fund, 1959 *Appeal Handbook* (New York: CBRF, 1959), 4, 8.

In December, 1956, some 500,000 pounds of used clothing collected by American Catholics on Thanksgiving Day left Hoboken for the relief of Hungarian refugees in Austria. Catholic Relief Services estimated that the aid it gave to Hungarians totaled in cost $2,500,-000.[70]

Dramatic though the response to the Hungarian crisis was, it was only a small chapter in a larger story. In 1958, 460,000 persons including many Yugoslav refugees received CRS benevolences administrated in cooperation with Austrian CARITAS, while in France the refugees from several countries were also helped. In the same year Catholic Relief Services sent 15,000 tons of relief supplies to enable German Caritasverband to help escapees, resettlers, and refugees. Shipments to the Far East in 1958, valued at $25,360,668, enabled Catholic Relief Services to carry on the largest program of any of the voluntary agencies working in the eastern hemisphere. At the same time Arab refugees in Lebanon and Jordan received more than 2,000,000 pounds of relief supplies.[71]

Generally speaking, Catholic Relief Services acted in the resettlement program as an overseas agent for a more comprehensive operation. In 1947, the Board of Bishops authorized the National Catholic Welfare Conference to establish a National Catholic Resettlement Council. This was made up of representatives of almost thirty nationality and Catholic organizations as well as the Diocesan Resettlement Committee with directors in each of the 120 dioceses in the United States. At the local level committees procured jobs and housing and assurance against public charge.[72] By 1958 the number of Catholics who had been helped to find sanctuary in the United States totaled over 200,000 and an additional 90,000 were given assistance in resettling in other Western Hemisphere countries.[73] Prominent Catholics believed that this overseas philanthropy not only brought

---

[70] Aloysius J. Wycislo, "Escape to America," *Catholic World* CLXXXIV (Feb., 1957), 326-32; "Churches Seek Funds to Aid Refugees," *Christian Century* LXXIII (Dec. 12, 1956), 1443-44; Bursten, *Escape from Fear*, 118.

[71] Catholic Bishops' Relief Fund, *1959 Appeal Handbook*, 4-8. Refugees from natural disasters also received help. Thus Catholic Relief Services in 1958 aided 70,000 victims of the Zambesi River flood in Mozambique, helped families made homeless by earthquakes and volcanic eruptions on the Island of Faial in the Azores, and relieved victims of a severe earthquake and tidal wave in Ecuador. Extensive aid was also given in 1960 to refugees from the disaster areas of Chile.

[72] *The DP Story*, 278; James L. Norris, "The International Catholic Migration Commission," *Catholic Lawyer* IV (Spring, 1958), 122.

[73] Catholic Bishops' Relief Fund, *1959 Appeal Handbook*, 21; the Catholic achievement in resettlement under the DP Act represented approximately 40 per cent of the total resettled.

happiness and freedom to numerous victims of World War II but provided tremendous advantages to the Catholic Church in America.

Cooperation between Catholic and Protestant voluntary agencies in aiding refugees was happily exemplified, among many places, at Hong Kong. In 1954 the China Refugee International Council was established to develop interagency cooperative activities, to coordinate services, and to secure action by the United Nations organizations toward a solution of the Hong Kong refugee problem. Catholic Relief Services, Church World Service, Lutheran World Relief, as well as CARE, took part in the work of the Council. The China Refugee Development Corporation, a joint Protestant-Catholic effort to set up workshops for refugees in Hong Kong, enabled many jobless men and women to make mandarin bags, Chinese dolls, and other products for which markets were found abroad.[74]

No group faced problems comparable to those of the Jews. Of the seven and a half million in prewar Europe (the USSR excepted), only a sixth survived. Nothing that could be called a Jewish community remained. The annihilation of six million Jews and the plight of the pitiful remnant demanded the mobilization of the world Jewish community and especially of the American Jews whom the war had left relatively untouched.[75]

The major part of the postwar emergency relief for Jewish refugees and escapees in Europe was handled by the experienced Joint Distribution Committee, the budget of which increased from $25,-535,295 in 1945 to $69,139,173 in 1947, tapering off to $63,505,954 in 1948 and $53,992,883 in 1949. Approximately 95 per cent of these funds came from American Jewry. The Allied military made JDC responsible for the administration of the government-supported special refugee centers.[76] Additional rations, medication, and other services were provided for the gaunt, emaciated, and mentally and spiritually benumbed survivors. Where possible, on-the-spot rehabilitation was undertaken: within three and a half years, 900 communities were restored, 140,000 children were helped, 500 medical

---

[74] American Council of Voluntary Agencies for Foreign Service, "Special Issue— Councils Abroad," *Circular Letter 1959* (April, 1959), *passim*.

[75] *American Jewish Yearbook*, Sept., 1947–Sept., 1948, XLIX (Philadelphia: Jewish Publication Society of America, 1948), 224; Proudfoot, *European Refugees*, 275, 318 ff.

[76] According to Leo Schwartz the Army and UNRRA did not at the outset have much confidence in the ability of JDC to help effectively with relief work for DPs in Germany, although both came to have genuine respect for it. Leo Schwartz, "Summary Analysis of the AJDC Program in the U. S. Zone of Occupation, Germany," *Menorah Journal* XXXV (Spring, 1947), 218.

institutions were assisted, 256 producers' cooperatives were established or strengthened, 400 synagogues were rebuilt, all in addition to the two hundred million pounds of relief goods that were sent.

In Eastern Europe the collapse following the war accompanied by political upheaval and new outbursts of anti-Semitism created tension and anxiety. With the Jewish Agency for Palestine and other organizations, JDC helped thousands of refugees move to Palestine and to the internment camps on British controlled Cyprus as well as to the Allied military zones in West Germany. In 1947, JDC thus helped 740,000 or about half of the surviving Jewish population in Europe: some of these were in their homelands (Bulgaria, 20,000, Poland, 80,000, Hungary, 90,000, Rumania, 100,000) but the majority were in the specially created Jewish camps in West Germany.[77] Nor was this all. Realizing the inadequacy of temporary relief and even rehabilitation, JDC, HIAS (Hebrew Sheltering and Immigrant Aid Society), and other agencies also exerted pressure on several governments, including that of the United States, to modify immigration restrictions. They provided transportation for emigrants and secured entrance and transit visas as well as assurances of support.[78]

In 1950 JDC announced that its major relief activities for refugees and DP's were at an end, that henceforth it would concentrate on the so-called "hard core" survivors. Two years later the new emphasis was stressed in the announcement that the time of mass solution of mass problems had passed, that more and more individualization, more concern with long-term programs was needed. But circumstances would not have it so. Among the 170,000 Hungarians who fled after the ill-fated revolt of 1956, 18,000 were Jews. Many of these were helped in getting to Israel, Canada, and the United States. JDC continued to aid the thousand refugees remaining in Austria, as well as those who were resettled in other European countries, in Australia, and in America. After the Suez crisis, some 23,000 Jews left Egypt: of these 13,000 went to Israel, 7,500 to Europe, and 2,500 to the Western Hemisphere. JDC lent a hand to a great many.[79]

[77] Hal Lehrman, "The 'Joint' Takes a Human Inventory," *Commentary* VII (Jan. 1949), 19.

[78] Proudfoot, *European Refugees*, 360.

[79] *New York Times*, Jan. 23, 1950; American Jewish Joint Distribution Committee, *Annual Report, 1952* (New York: JDC, 1953), 2; American Jewish Joint Distribution Committee, *A Guide to Overseas Operations of the American Jewish Joint Distribution Committee* (New York: JDC, 1958), 6-7.

Although JDC supported retraining programs for DP's, by far the most outstanding operations in this field were conducted by the World ORT Union. Its United States affiliate, the American ORT (Organization for Rehabilitation through Training) Federation contributed by the late 1940's almost 50 per cent of the total budget.[80] ORT has been described as "the Jewish Technical Assistance Program." Its basic assumption has been that "men and women who are equipped with effective, useful, socially necessary skills can shape their lives in dignity, assure to themselves and their families a large measure of economic security, and contribute productively to their own communities." [81]

In the immediate postwar period, when an estimated 250,000 Jews languished in DP camps, ORT stepped in with vocational training to give what one DP called "an escape from . . . negation." In the British zone of Germany, ORT classes were opened at Bergen-Belsen in December, 1945. By 1947-1948 ORT's vocational program encompassed 712 workshops throughout Europe with an annual enrollment of more than 18,000. Fifty trades were taught, including metal work, optics, construction, glass blowing, textile and garment working. With the intensifying of Communist isolation in 1949 some 260 ORT units in Rumania, Bulgaria, Czechoslovakia and Poland had to be withdrawn. In 1958, however, a program for repatriated Jews from the Soviet Union was reestablished in Poland.[82]

Much of ORT's work did not specifically benefit refugees. It is hard, in fact, to say more than that the some 40 per cent of its beneficiaries in 1949 were DP's and that this percentage tapered off appreciably in the years that followed. But refugees and DP's were never out of the picture. In 1957 ORT contracted with the United States Escapee Program for all vocational training for escapee Jews in Austria. After the Hungarian uprising ORT greatly expanded its work in Austria as it did in Egypt during the troubled years of the late 1950's. Increasingly, too, its work was expanded not only among newcomers in Israel but among the long-neglected coreligionists in other parts of North Africa who, if not refugees, bore many of the

[80] Julian Franklyn, "From ORT to UNRRA," *Contemporary Review* CLXVIII (Oct., 1945), 241-44; American ORT Federation, *ORT: A Record of Ten Years Rebuilding Jewish Economic Life* (New York: ORT, 1956), 42-43.

[81] American ORT Federation, "Facts about American ORT," Feb. 4, 1958 (mimeographed), 1.

[82] ORT, *A Record of Ten Years*, 4-7.

scars so well known to DP's.[83] The achievements of ORT were put tellingly by Herbert H. Lehman in a tribute he paid to the organization while he was still directing UNRRA. "This great work with which I am entrusted," he wrote, "is but an extension and tremendous elaboration of the work which you have already pioneered through your organization. During the last sixty-two years it [ORT] has been presenting to the world a practical demonstration of the effectiveness of the principle of helping others to help themselves." [84] ORT continued to do just this and of its beneficiaries none stood so much in need of such services as the DP's.

What was done to help Jewish DP's once they arrived in America is as remarkable a story as that of JDC and ORT in their overseas programs. In 1946 the National Council of Jewish Women, which had been concerned since 1904 with helping immigrants begin new lives of freedom and opportunity, joined forces with the National Refugee Service. The new agency, United Service for New Americans (USNA) launched a comprehensive program to help immigrants help themselves in adjusting to American life. The Hebrew Sheltering and Immigrant Aid Society, long in the field and proud of having produced the largest number of corporate affidavits, made an agreement in 1948 with United Service for New Americans by which it concentrated on individual assurances. In 1954 these agencies established a world-wide Jewish migration agency, United HIAS Service, a consolidation of USNA, HIAS, and the migration services of JDC.[85]

At the height of its activity, United Service for New Americans was aiding an average of more than 8,175 persons a month through migration services. These included temporary assistance to refugees for food, clothing, lodging, and medical attention, extending loans to enable small businessmen and professionals to get a start, providing information, helping find missing relatives, and securing affidavits. It worked through local cooperating agencies, enjoyed the support of the National Council of Jewish Women, and employed both lay and professional workers, including former DP's who knew at first hand the mentality of those pressing to find new homes. In helping in one way or another most of the 141,939 Jewish immi-

[83] ORT, A Record of Ten Years, 31-35.
[84] Franklyn, Contemporary Review CLXVIII, 242.
[85] New York Times, March 11, 1946; The DP Story, 281-82, 284; Mark Witschnitzer, To Dwell in Safety, the Story of Jewish Immigration since 1800 (Philadelphia: Jewish Publication Society of America, 1948), 276.

grants who entered the country during its separate existence (1946-1954), United Service for New Americans spent a total of $35,694,-527. Making use of the best available social service techniques and paying a good deal of attention to individual needs, it was, as its historian has rightly observed, an organization which by practical demonstration of compassion and understanding, renewed faith in mankind. Its comprehensive program of helping so many new arrivals to become happy, useful members of society succeeded because of widespread support at the local level, the imagination and understanding of its personnel, and the high administrative talents of its leadership.[86]

During the forty years between the first American fund-raising campaign for Karen Hayesod and the summer of 1961, American Jews contributed between 75 and 80 per cent of the $900,000,000 that had been raised for the migration, rehabilitation, and settlement programs of more than 1,000,000 Jews in Israel.[87]

One other distinctly religious group, world-wide in scope but with considerable American support and with headquarters in the United States, also contributed to overseas relief. Jamì at al Islam, founded in 1868 in Turkistan, had come to include members in many countries by the time of the Second World War. Among other activities it tried to get increased quotas and provide guarantees for Mohammedan refugees who were eager to get to the United States. In 1957, JAI opened an office in Amman, Jordan, to help care for Arab refugees, and it undertook similar relief, including special care of orphans, in Saudi-Arabia, North Africa, and Pakistan.[88]

Most of the emergency relief for refugees, that is, food, clothing, medicines, and other urgently needed supplies to sustain life, was handled by government agencies or religious bodies, singly or in co-operation. Private secular groups not directly connected with religious denominations more often engaged in refugee resettlement programs or self-help projects. To undertake a long-term relief program, or to gather large amounts of food, clothing and the like, required a larger, more dependable budget and a broader base of popular support than most of the non-religious groups commanded. Without the necessary

[86] Lyman Cromwell White, *300,000 New Americans: the Epic of a Modern Immigrant-Aid Service* (New York: Harper, 1957), ix, 10, 14, 105.

[87] *New York Times*, August 20, 1961.

[88] Jamì at al Islam, *Jamì at al Islam: History—Policy—Program* (Vienna: JAI, 1958), 3, 7, 32; Ahmad Kamal, JAI-International to Merle Curti, Feb. 14, 1959.

capital and wide support to undertake sizeable material relief ventures, smaller groups worked chiefly as clearing agencies for securing assurances for immigrants to the United States and for providing legal help and social counsel to overseas refugee populations. This has been largely true of the nationality-oriented agencies and of those representing functional groups in the fields of education, labor, and social work. Yet many of these agencies did maintain small refugee aid programs over a considerable period of time.

As the largest secular organization and one of the largest of all voluntary agencies, CARE was an exception to this generalization. Its packages reached refugees in Germany from the start of its program. It continued to supply refugees, in an ever-increasing number of countries in Europe, Asia, and Africa, with food, clothing, and medicine. In 1952 it developed special resettlement and apprenticeship kits for German refugees. In time such kits, directed to refugees in many parts of the world, included sewing machines, shovels, fishing nets, pumps for irrigation, and even equipment for community building projects. As CARE's emphasis on self-help and technical aid increased, it initiated many projects which helped refugees to become integrated in the community in which they found themselves. It provided, for example, pumps and a new electric system in the Gaza strip which enabled refugees to bring the desert under cultivation. At the same time, its program for improving health benefitted refugees as well as permanent residents.[89]

Occasionally, apart from the regularly established and more or less permanent relief programs which religious and nonsectarian groups supported in behalf of refugees, an unusual situation arose which called for the forming of a special committee or relief group. One such situation was the Hungarian crisis of 1956. In addition to the many religious and secular agencies involved in the relief of Hungarian refugees, Coordinated Hungarian Relief, headed by Dr. Tibor Cholmoky of Greenwich, Connecticut, was organized on an *ad hoc* basis. Early in 1957 it took over the clothing operations previously handled by First Aid for Hungary and soon had shipped 130,000 pounds of clothing to needy refugees. For the elderly and those in special need, CHR sent 2,500 food parcels overseas. Regular weekly shipments of medicines and cash totaling $10,000 were also

[89] *Executive Director, Annual Report to the Board of Directors of CARE*, August 17, 1960 (New York: CARE, 1960), 19.

sent.[90] Numerous letters testified to the appreciation of recipients. "My children had not tasted meat in 12 weeks before the package came . . . ," reported one beneficiary. "Just as important as the medicine itself," wrote another, "is the realization that there is someone in this world who cares. . . ." A third wrote: "I hope that Americans never discover what it is like to be hungry and cold, or have to ask for help. . . ." [91]

Coordinated Hungarian Relief also took part with other agencies, voluntary and official, in the operation of refugee aid and rehabilitation at Camp Kilmer. The DP's were showered with job offers, invited to parties, meetings, and family gatherings, and outfitted by department stores. Some of the cooperating agencies were distressed at the obviously commercial and selfish purposes that motivated at least a few of the gift-bearers.[92] As requests for aid increased, however, Coordinated Hungarian Relief found that its donations were decreasing. Interest shifted to other trouble spots. Clearly, one of the difficulties of an *ad hoc* committee in dealing with a particular calamity is that while its immediate impact elicits sympathy and public concern, the needs of victims persist long after public interest dwindles.

Another example of coordination in a particular emergency is American Relief for Korea (ARK). At a meeting on August 23, 1950, of representatives of the UN, the United States Mission to the UN, the Departments of Defense and State, the Economic Cooperation Administration, and the American Red Cross, an agreement was made which designated the Advisory Committee on Voluntary Foreign Aid as the channel for all offers of voluntary assistance from nongovernmental organizations and other sources in the United States other than the Red Cross. The Department of the Army took title to all supplies contributed by voluntary agencies.[93] Those associated with ARK included the American Friends Service Committee, Church World Relief, Lutheran World Service, the Brethren Service Commission, the YWCA, and Catholic Relief Services. ARK

[90] B. C. Maday, Coordinated Hungarian Relief, *Report of the Executive Secretary*, Oct., 1957 (mimeographed), 1.

[91] Coordinated Hungarian Relief, *A Torn Hungarian Flag* . . . (Washington: CHR, ca. 1958), n.p.

[92] Bursten, *Escape from Fear*, 160-63.

[93] Arthur C. Ringland to John C. Borton, Assistant Director Export Supply, Office of International Trade, Department of Commerce, June 25, 1951, Advisory Committee File.

sponsored a drive for clothing for South Korea's 4,700,000 registered refugees. Costs of collection, processing, warehousing, transportation, and distribution were paid by the United States Defense Fund, which in turn was supported by the Community Chest and the United States Army. In Korea distribution of the relief, which by 1954 exceeded $10,000,000 in value, was managed by the United Nations Command and the South Korean government.[94]

Secular agencies specifically oriented not merely to relief in a time of crisis but to the relief and resettlement of refugees and DP's of a particular nationality also played a part in the postwar upheavals.

The American National Committee to Aid Homeless Armenians (ANCHA) was organized in 1947 by George M. Mardikian, a San Francisco restaurateur, and S. M. Saroyan, also of San Francisco, "to aid those persons of Armenian descent in Europe who have been displaced from their homes during World War II, most of whom found themselves in Displaced Persons Camps upon the termination of hostilities." Brigadier-General Haig Shekerjian, retired United States Army officer, opened ANCHA offices in Stuttgart in 1948. From then through 1952, ANCHA helped 4,000 Armenians reach the United States. From 1955 to 1957, ANCHA also helped several hundred Palestinian refugees resettle in the United States, especially in the Chicago area and in California. In its work ANCHA received support from the World Council of Churches, the National Catholic Welfare Council, the Lutheran World Federation and other agencies.[95]

The American Hellenic Educational Progressive Association, founded in 1927 by Americans of Greek origin, developed into an organization of 384 chapters in forty-eight states. With the passage of the 1950 amendments to the Displaced Persons Act, it established two working committees to cooperate with the DP Commission and the State Department. One committee concerned itself with resettlement of displaced Greeks. The second committee was responsible for securing assurances of support, provisioning of reception facilities, and placing orphans.[96]

Several of the nationality-oriented agencies were stimulated to

[94] Ringland, *Department of State Bulletin* XXX, 388; "American Relief for Korea Organized," *Christian Century* LXVIII (March 14, 1951), 325.

[95] S. M. Saroyan, "A Brief Statement of Its Accomplishments, 1947-1959," March 18, 1959 (typed report sent to Merle Curti); *The DP Story*, 283-84.

[96] *The DP Story*, 283.

activity by the large number of escapees from Communist countries. The United Friends of Needy and Displaced Peoples of Yugoslavia, which was registered by the Advisory Committee in 1950 in connection with its German expellee program, submitted both blanket and individual assurances to the DP Commission.[97] The Serbian National Defense Council of America, incorporated in 1942, resettled more than 10,000 refugees under the DP Act. In every large Serbian community in the United States a committee was formed to help newcomers adjust themselves to American life.[98]

From the time of the Communist putsch in Czechoslovakia on February 25, 1948, Czechs began to flee to the West: by the first of March, 1954, the number had reached over 50,000. Dr. Jan Papanek, former Czech permanent representative to the United Nations and delegate in the United States of the Czech Red Cross, established in 1948 the American Fund for Czechoslovak Refugees. The Fund solicited material and financial contributions and sent relief shipments to DP's in Germany, Austria, and Italy, and to Czech Relief Committees in France, Belgium, Switzerland, and England. Under the DP Act and its amendments, the American Fund for Czechoslovak Refugees had by 1958 helped over 7,000 refugees resettle in the United States, while several thousand were indebted to the Fund for help in reaching Australia, New Zealand, Canada, Latin America, Africa and Asia.[99]

The American Committee for the Resettlement of Polish Displaced Persons, founded in 1947 and sponsored by American Relief for Poland and the Polish American Congress, obtained, between 1947 and 1952, assurances for 17,893 Poles from Germany, Austria, and Italy and 4,592 from Great Britain, as well as 1,065 for "out of zone" refugees. In addition to the aid given to immigrants, the Committee also sent money overseas to help "hard core" cases. Support for the American Committee came chiefly from Polish-American societies and from two annual fund-raising drives.[100]

The American Friends of Russian Freedom, founded in 1950 by Felix Cole, retired diplomat, Admiral William H. Standley, former

[97] *Ibid.*, 291.
[98] *Ibid.*, 288.
[99] American Fund for Czechoslovak Refugees, "Aide-Memoire," March 31, 1954 (typed), 1-2, and "Dear Friends," Dec., 1953, Dec., 1958 (mimeographed).
[100] Thaddeus Theodore Krysienwicz, "Polish Immigration Committee in the United States" (unpublished Ph.D. dissertation, Fordham University, 1953), 13, 15-16, 18, 29; *The DP Story*, 282-83.

Ambassador to Moscow, and General William J. Donovan, one-time chief of the Office of Strategic Services, tried to substantiate American words of friendship toward Russian escapees with much needed material help. In 1951, AFRF opened a Friendship Center in Munich, Germany, to offer a haven to fleeing Russians. In 1953, with help from the United States Escapee Program, it opened a second center in Kaiserslautern, Germany, and two years later established a project near Solingen to furnish jobs for refugees.[101] Typical of the letters of appreciation from beneficiaries was that of "N. B. and family," dated January, 1953: "You, dear American Friends, are continuing the tradition of Russian friendship and alliance which was initiated in 1880-1890 by the American Kennan. Your support and assistance to us, postwar escapees, is also a blow to Stalin's propaganda, which contrives to prove that the American people want to annihilate the Russians and make an American colony of Russia. . . ."[102]

Unlike the American Friends of Russian Freedom, which was initiated by Americans of many national origins interested in Russia, the United Ukrainian American Relief Committee, established in 1944, represented several hundred civic, religious, educational, and fraternal organizations of Americans of Ukrainian background. Its immediate problem was the plight of an estimated 138,622 DP's in Austria and Germany early in 1948. The United Ukrainian American Relief Committee encouraged their immigration to South America, Australia, New Zealand, and Canada. It made arrangements for placing 500 farm families in Maryland and Wisconsin. By June, 1952, the agency had helped 33,000 immigrants to the United States and given them a start in one of its seventy reception centers.[103]

More comprehensive in its program, the Tolstoy Foundation was organized in New York in 1939 in the apartment of former Russian Ambassador Boris Vakhmeteff. From the outset the guiding light was Alexandra Tolstoy, daughter of the Russian writer. The Foundation was especially interested in Russians of Orthodox faith, but it also aimed "to provide all aid and assistance to escapees and refugees from Soviet Russia, and from other nations, victims of communist

[101] American Friends of Russian Freedom, "Report," Nov., 1957 (mimeographed), n.p.

[102] American Council Files.

[103] United Ukrainian American Relief Committee, *Report*, Sept. 30, 1951 (Philadelphia: UUARC, 1951), 23-24; UUARC also supported vocational and language training centers in Europe: *The DP Story*, 292.

oppression, without regard to race, nationality, or religion. . . ." [104] Largely supported by private gifts supplemented with grants from the East European Fund of the Ford Foundation, the agency maintained a seventy-two-acre reception center (the gift of Mrs. Edward Harkness) in Valley Cottage, New York, where new arrivals were given hospitality until they could find jobs and homes. By 1958 the Foundation had helped 19,000 persons immigrate to America. [105] Working under a mandate from the Intergovernmental Commission for European Migration (ICEM, the successor of the International Refugee Organization), the Tolstoy Foundation also helped resettle Russian refugees in the Middle East. [106]

Nor were escapees from Communist China neglected. Although the Tolstoy Foundation did what it could for Russians marooned behind the Bamboo Curtain, the chief agency in this field was Aid Refugee Chinese Intellectuals. Led by Representative Walter Judd of Minnesota and sponsored by well-known Americans, this agency registered 20,000 professionals who escaped to Hong Kong and Kowloon, many of whom were graduates of leading American universities. At the low per-capita cost of $91, Aid Refugee Chinese Intellectuals resettled 12,500 of the group, chiefly in Formosa. The fact that the Chinese quota for America was quickly filled made it impossible to resettle any considerable number in the United States. [107]

Several agencies specialized in particular services. The American Federation of International Institutes, for example, expanded its program after the passage of the DP Act of 1948. Nonsectarian and nonnational, it supported a searching service which helped refugees in Europe locate relatives or friends in the United States. It also undertook to settle 290 "hard core" cases in some twenty American cities. [108] International Social Service, with local branches that worked across international boundaries through the central office, managed the vast paper work that enabled the United States Committee for the Care of European Children to transport 4,300 children

[104] Tolstoy Foundation, *Freedom Is Too Your Business* (New York: Tolstoy Foundation, ca. 1957), 4-5.
[105] Overseas Director of the Tolstoy Foundation, *Report to the Board of Directors, 1957* (mimeographed), 1; *The DP Story*, 289.
[106] Tolstoy Foundation, *Freedom Is Too Your Business*, 5.
[107] Geraldine Fitch, "Brains at a Bargain," *Rotarian* LXXXIX (Dec., 1956), 17-19; "Finding Jobs for Refugees from Mao's Paradise Isn't Easy," *Saturday Evening Post* CCXXX (August 24, 1957), 10.
[108] *The DP Story*, 283.

to America in the early stages of the war. Once the war was over, International Social Service undertook individual case work in refugee camps. It also organized a service for rescuing and placing orphaned and abandoned children.[109]

Another agency to play a notable role was the United States Committee for the Care of European Children, the only secular organization established exclusively to aid child refugees. This Committee submitted blanket assurances to the DP Commission on the basis of agreements with several agencies, the agreements providing that the cost and responsibility of placement planning and child care be borne by the respective voluntary agencies. Up to 1950 the DP Commission channeled all individual sponsorships through the Committee, which in turn routed them to local agencies cooperating with the national and sectarian organizations. At the Committee's reception center in New York City the children were given an orientation which included instruction in English, geography, and American history. Social workers associated with the participating voluntary agencies arranged for appropriate placement. The Committee continued its overseas operations and its reception activities until March, 1951, by which time it had received and cared for 2,798 children under the Truman Directive and the DP program.[110]

Another example of the special function agency was the National Travelers Aid Society. In 1949 it accepted responsibility for "the reception and transportation services having to do with all non-agency cases of whatever religious affiliation, including those commonly termed compassionate cases, whether sent by plane or ship." To take care of the heavy drains on its fund with the reception, handling of inland transport, and notification of sponsors of the arrival in question, the International Refugee Organization and the Ford Foundation allocated grants to the Society.[111]

In the work of voluntary agencies for refugees the International Rescue Committee also made a place for itself. This unusual organization began in 1933 when a group of Americans including John Dewey, Amos Pinchot, and Reinhold Niebuhr formed the Interna-

[109] Susan T. Pettiss, "Adoption by Proxy," *Child Welfare* XXXIV (Oct., 1955), 20-21; International Social Service, *In a World They Never Made* (New York: ISS, ca. 1958), *passim.*
[110] *The DP Story,* 290-91.
[111] *Ibid.,* 287-88; Bertha McCall, *History of the National Travelers Aid Association 1911-1948* (New York: National Travelers Aid Association, 1950), 206 ff.

tional Relief Association to aid families of Nazi and fascist concentration camp victims and to arrange for the smuggling out of Europe and the resettlement in America of anti-fascists. In 1940 another group started the Emergency Rescue Committee, an agency which helped such outstanding writers, artists and musicians as Franz Werfel, Konrad Heiden, Marc Chagall, Yllia, and Wanda Landowska. In 1942 the two agencies merged to form the International Rescue Committee.[112]

The new committee cooperated with such nationally oriented agencies as Lithuanian Relief Fund of America, the American Fund for Czechoslovak Refugees, the Hungarian National Council, and the Yugoslav National Committee in resettling refugees with whom these were concerned. The International Rescue Committee also worked with the Jewish Labor Committee and the International Ladies' Garment Workers Union in placing refugees as needle trade workers.

Making assistance to professionals a matter of special concern, the Committee launched a campaign in 1950 for the re-establishment of refugees, a program strengthened by a grant of $100,000 from the Lessing J. Rosenwald Foundation, another of $500,000 from Ford and some $300,000 from still other foundations.[113] In cooperation with a selected committee of Vietnamese intellectuals, the Committee also provided material aid to refugee students, professors, and other professionals in South Vietnam. When the Philippine Junior Chamber of Commerce launched its "Operation Brotherhood" to send volunteer teams of doctors and nurses to Vietnam to minister to refugees, the International Rescue Committee joined with the United States Junior Chamber of Commerce in support of the project.

At the time of the Hungarian revolt in 1956, the International Rescue Committee procured several thousands of beds for refugees, distributed "Freedom Packages" made up of socks, toilet articles, and cigarettes, and distributed antibiotics valued at over $200,000 (largely donated by the Charles Pfizer Company of Brooklyn). In cooperation with the Austrian Student Coordinating Committee

---

[112] International Rescue Committee, *Saving Freedom's Seed Corn* (New York: IRC, 1958), 4 ff. For the intellectual refugee in America prior to 1952 see Donald Peterson Kent, *The Refugee Intellectual: The Americanization of the Immigrants of 1933-1941* (New York: Columbia University Press, 1953), and Maurice R. Davie, *et al.*, *Refugees in America* (New York: Harper, 1947).

[113] *The DP Story*, 285-286.

and World University Service, the Committee operated two hostels in Vienna for 600 refugee students, provided weekly cash allowances for 5,000 more, and helped the entire faculty and membership of the University of Sopron, which had escaped as a body. From December, 1956, through September, 1958, IRC spent $2,180,-000 in support of Hungarian refugees besides providing material aid valued at $463,000. In addition, 4,000 refugees were resettled abroad, half of them in the United States. In many of its operations, which also included the management of a home for some fifty disturbed Hungarian refugee children and the establishment of an English Language Training Center, IRC received support from the Samuel Hird Textile Company, Dupont, the Crown Zellerbach Corporation, and the United States Escapee Program.[114]

Representative of the appreciation International Rescue Committee received from those it had helped was a letter from Ignazio Silone, the Italian author of *Bread and Wine*. "IRC has been for an ever-increasing number of men and women a refreshing center where humanitarian and democratic principles are not merely preached but practiced and where the very young and the very old receive the consideration to which their years entitle them."[115] Joseph Koevago, Mayor of Free Budapest, expressed his gratitude in simple but eloquent language. "I was one of the 200,000 Hungarians who escaped to Austria after the brutal subjugation of our country by the Soviet Army," he wrote. "There for the first time I met the International Rescue Committee. I was greatly impressed by the intelligence and devotion of the Committee's workers, by their careful attention, under the greatest pressure, to the human needs of young and old. Within recent months I had occasion to return to Austria, and while there I spent much time with the refugees and saw the IRC's projects in operation. I was impressed anew by the scope and imagination of the International Rescue Committee's work."[116] We shall meet IRC again in the record of American voluntary agencies' contributions to long-range efforts to improve conditions of living overseas.

Little evidence is at hand on the kind of adjustments made by DP's who were aided by the International Rescue Committee in finding new homes in Sweden, or by those whom the nationally

[114] International Rescue Committee, *Saving Freedom's Seed Corn*, 28-29.
[115] *Ibid.*, 15.
[116] *Ibid.*, 31.

oriented and religious agencies helped to find permanent asylum in the British Commonwealth, the Middle East, and the Latin American countries. Thanks, however, to several studies, including those of the Displaced Persons Commission, it is possible to assess the failures and successes of a great many refugees and escapees in the United States.

The unsuccessful cases of resettlement which received publicity included those in which the DP left the sponsor after a very short time, whether because of the lure of the city, or unfair treatment, or personality conflicts, or exaggerated expectations, or mishandling of placement by an agency. A particularly unhappy incident of such nature arose concerning Lithuanian DP's who had been settled on sugar plantations around New Orleans. After receiving numerous letters complaining of maltreatment sent him by these new Americans, the Reverend Joseph B. Koncius, president of the United Lithuanian Relief Fund, went himself to investigate.

The conditions Koncius found were deplorable. Families had been settled in shanties with holes in the walls so large that the rain could beat through. Their diet often consisted entirely of canned goods bought from plantation stores to which they were heavily in debt because their average pay of 32 cents an hour did not provide sufficient funds to keep them alive. One farmer said to the Reverend Mr. Koncius, "God knows who is in worse condition—my brother John and his family in Siberia or I, with my family, here under these conditions?" When one plantation owner was informed that the DP workers on his land were to be removed he exclaimed angrily that it couldn't be done because those people belonged to him. "Why the owners of these sugar plantations should take such unfair advantage of the displaced persons' ignorance of this language and conditions in this country and treat them like slaves," said Pastor Koncius, "is beyond my comprehension." Yet he had found native Americans who lived on the same plantations and who had fared no better.[117]

Aggravated instances of maltreatment of this sort obviously created some of the problems which led to failures at DP settlement. Probably many other initial failures, however, resulted as much from inadequate education and understanding on the part of the agencies, the sponsors, the DP's, and the general public.

[117] Rev. Joseph B. Koncius to Harry S. Truman, May 20, 1949, Truman Papers, Official File 127, Harry S. Truman Library, Independence, Mo.

In the opinion of those concerned the much larger number of instances of successful resettlement owed a good deal to desirable traits in the DP's and the sponsors, to a readiness or ability to give and to take and to adjust to unfamiliar conditions, to the degee to which DP's had some competency in the English language or were in touch with others of their nationality or religious group, and to the extent to which they were wisely guided and advised. In the opinion of an agency executive with a great deal of experience, Dr. Cordelia Cox, director of Lutheran Refugee Service, most of the refugees sought not charity but an opportunity to rebuild their lives. The great majority, according to Dr. Cox, proved to be resourceful, independent people who responded gratefully to neighborly friendliness, who succeeded in making effective adjustments and, in many cases, made notable contributions to American life.[118]

Despite all that was done for DP's, escapees, and refugees by governmental and intergovernmental organizations and voluntary agencies, American and non-American, a decade and a half after the end of the Second World War fifteen million homeless human beings in Europe, the Middle East, Africa, the Far East and the Caribbean, still needed help.[119] The degree of need varied from the relatively tolerable conditions for the stateless refugees still in camps in Europe to the pitiful plight of the 250,000 Algerians, half of whom were children, existing in wretched hovels in neighboring countries and to the lamentable situation of hundreds of thousands of Chinese, Tibetan, and other refugees in Asia. These fifteen million men, women, and children, sharing the universal desire to live with self-respect and self-reliance in a place they could call home, represented a vast waste of talents and skills, actual and potential, an explosive political problem in a great many areas of the world, a drain on the resources of harboring countries and the international community, and, above all, untold suffering and want.

To meet in some part the world-wide needs so painfully apparent to the informed, the United Nations on July 1, 1959, initiated the World Refugee Year. The objectives were to persuade governments to increase their financial support of refugee programs, to liberalize

[118] *The DP Story*, 211-42; National Lutheran Council, News Bureau, May 29, 1956, Advisory Committee Files.

[119] The figure, given by the United States Committee for Refugees in its 1960-61 report, is comprehensive. See also *New York Times*, July 15, 1961.

immigration criteria, to provide help for unwanted refugees, and to encourage private groups and individuals to give money and effort to finding solutions to the problem. Ninety-seven countries and territories participated, but Communist countries did not take part. The world goal for private contributions was set at $45,000,000, of which it was hoped Americans would give $20,000,000.

As the Year moved toward its close, results of the campaign varied. Private contributions in the Netherlands, New Zealand, and Britain exceeded expectations. In America the outlook for a time was less than bright. But the United States Committee for Refugees, organized to promote interest and action, reported shortly before the program officially ended that private contributions promised to reach $55,000,000. (The government appropriations for such continuing programs as the United Nations Relief for Palestine Arab Refugees and the $5,000,000 allocated by President Eisenhower from executive contingent funds brought the American total close to $100,-000,000.) [120] This did not include the largest single American gift for helping refugees, that of Miss Helen Thrunauer, whose will left $1,000,000 to the UN High Commissioner and to the American Association for the UN, earmarked for refugees cared for by the High Commissioner.[121]

The awakening of the international community to the seriousness of the refugee problem had started well before the World Refugee Year. A few governments had begun to accept a certain number of handicapped DP's. The campaign of education and action during World Refugee Year itself led to substantial gains. In the United States these included provisions in new legislation to admit five hundred "difficult to settle" refugees and to accept for two years up to 25 per cent of the total number of refugees admitted by other countries in each preceding six-month period.[122] In the fiscal year 1960-1961 the United States government spent $76,000,000 on refugee problems, about half of which was in cash and half in surplus commodities.[123]

To stimulate the greatest possible amount of aid to refugees on the

[120] *New York Times*, July 1, 1960; *World Refugee Year* (Geneva: International Catholic Migration Commission, 1960), 3-96.
[121] *Philanthropic Digest* VII (June 15, 1960), 1.
[122] U. S., *Statutes at Large*, LXXIV, 504. The refugee relief bill was described by Edward Corsi, an expert in the field, as "meager in scope;" *New York Times*, Feb. 2, 1961.
[123] United States Committee for Refugees, *Annual Audit*, July 1, 1960–June 30, 1961 (New York: USCR, 1961), 12.

part of the government and the people, the United States Committee for Refugees, an inclusive, voluntarily supported agency organized by prominent citizens during World Refugee Year, developed a continuing program to keep the issue before the public. Extensive use was made of the mass media. The Committee maintained a central information unit to guide cooperating regional, state, and local committees. It consulted with government officials on policy. It promoted fund raising and interest in improved reception services.[124]

That such continuing efforts were greatly needed was beyond doubt. Even with the gains associated with the World Refugee Year, the improvement of the economy in Europe, and the more generous support in many countries of programs to help the 15,000,000 homeless people, the problem remained formidable. In the succinct words of UN Secretary General Dag Hammarskjold, it would continue indefinitely, or at least "until the world turns more peaceful."

[124] The United States Committee for Refugees, "A Statement of Purpose and Method," April 6, 1961 (mimeographed); USCR, *The Homeless of the World Still Wait* (New York: USCR, n.d.), *passim;* Julia M. Stern, United States Committee for Refugees, to Merle Curti, August 18, 1961.

XIX

Prospects for a New World

During the trying years in which efforts to resettle DP's taxed the resources of voluntary agencies, increasing emphasis was put on helping disadvantaged peoples and attacking the causes of mass misery. The needs of the peoples in southern Asia, the Near East, Africa, and Latin America were not based on the temporary though dramatically horrible ravages of war. These needs issued rather from an inheritance of the past which condemned local populations to a life incomparably more insecure and harsh than that of the least privileged in the more fortunate nations. The heritage related in part to colonial status, in part to the lack of sound native leadership. But in even greater part the plight of these peoples was related to the lethargy imposed by ancient customs. These included gross inequality in the ownership and use of land, overworked and eroded soil, dearth of capital, and absence of the knowledge and skill to meet these and other problems. Victims of a continuous "environ mental war" against nature and, in the minds of a growing number, of outside domination as well, these peoples were ill prepared to cope with either one.

But in the later 1940's and early 1950's it was becoming apparent that in many of these less-industrialized areas of the earth a growing number of men and women were less willing than formerly to accept famine, chronic poverty, endemic disease, and insecurity as necessary facts that could not be changed. A revolution of human aspirations was stirring. India, somewhat peaceably, and China through a blood bath, set the patterns: colonialism could be expelled, native leadership could get the upper hand. The undeveloped, underdeveloped, and otherdeveloped (colonial) countries were beginning to make it plain that they would no longer be content to share so unequally in the world's knowledge and abundance. Spokesmen for populations that had long seemed backward, helpless, and inert, now more and more frequently asked the better-developed nations to show their peoples how to help themselves.

In response to the growing desire in the less-developed countries for a better life, several industrialized countries, together with the United Nations, embarked in the 1940's on various programs of technical aid. America's role, both on the official and unofficial level, owed much to a capacity to aid, thanks to economic strength and abundance. Experience at home and abroad also provided precedents for an expansion of technical assistance to less-developed countries. At home the success of social workers and county agents in helping disadvantaged Americans get on their feet provided techniques which, it was assumed, could be exported. Voluntary agencies, inspired by religious and humanitarian motives had, long before 1950, pioneered in helping less-favored peoples through educational, health, and agricultural programs. On the official level, technical aid, first proposed as a major enterprise in the Point Four Program,[1] rested on two main considerations. The first was the humanitarian and democratic desire to help nonindustrialized countries develop potential resources and improve standards of living within a framework of political freedom. The second was the effort in the Cold War to prevent the spread of communism and to win the support of the still uncommitted nations.

The growing concern with technical aid was an important factor in the shift of focus of the voluntary agencies from Europe to other parts of the world—a shift, to be sure, that was also closely related to the relative recovery of Europe by the late 1940's and to the need for emergency aid during and after the wars in Korea, South Asia, and the Near East. Thus, while Europe in the immediate postwar years received about 90 per cent of the cash and supplies sent abroad by organizations registered with the Advisory Committee on Voluntary Foreign Aid, in 1950 it was getting only about half the supplies and services offered by such agencies. In 1947, the ten nations receiving the most voluntary relief from the United States included eight European countries, plus Palestine and China. By 1958 only half of the ten major recipients of American aid were

---

[1] For the participation of the government in earlier instances of technical aid see Merle Curti and Kendall Birr, *Prelude to Point Four: American Technical Missions Overseas, 1838-1938* (Madison: University of Wisconsin Press, 1954).

European countries. And in no year after 1958 did Europe receive as much as half of what was given.[2]

On the nonofficial level the agencies engaged in technical aid included voluntary societies, religious and secular, that had dispensed emergency postwar relief and that continued to help in the refugee problem. Also included were foundations, business corporations and missionary organizations. To list even a majority of these would make a monotonous catalogue. But something needs to be said about each of the main categories.

Long before the Second World War, American and European missionaries had begun to lay the foundations, however sketchy, for constructive programs to help less fortunate peoples materially as well as spiritually. Looking back at their efforts, some recognized how poorly prepared they had been for the task, how inadequate the physical equipment was with which they worked. It had been hard for many to learn not to expect from villagers in India what might reasonably be expected from American farmers. But a growing number had come to sense in those among whom they worked conflict, often inarticulate, between the desire for better material conditions of living and a fear of change. This fear was bred of centuries of isolation and tradition: even fly control often conflicted with cherished emotions and beliefs.[3]

After the First World War and even more strikingly after the Second, missionaries from the historic churches showed greater readiness to recognize their own mistakes and to study the culture as

[2] Major recipients by rank of value of goods and funds received of American voluntary aid, 1947 and 1958 adapted from U. S. Department of State, International Cooperation Administration, Advisory Committee on Voluntary Foreign Aid, *Report of Commodities and Funds for Relief and Rehabilitation by American Agencies* (Washington: Govt. Printing Office, 1947, 1958) [hereafter cited as Advisory Committee, *Reports*].

1947		1958	
Germany	$34,766,668	Italy	$38,534,581
Hungary	12,833,570	Korea	24,309,417
Poland	11,996,244	Yugoslavia	23,334,166
Italy	10,776,214	Israel	21,694,692
France	9,920,581	Spain	14,083,958
Austria	7,685,786	Chile	14,015,281
Palestine	5,724,481	Greece	13,107,471
Greece	5,308,073	Germany	11,943,906
China	5,284,914	India	8,515,373
Rumania	4,622,851	Formosa	6,942,322

[3] William H. Wiser and Charlotte Viall Wiser, *Behind Mud Walls* (New York: Smith, 1930), vii, 174-77.

well as the language of the foreign land. Sometimes calling themselves "fraternal workers," the newer type of missionary began to shed his own cultural chauvinism and paternalism and labored, not merely for, but with, beneficiaries at the grassroots level. Even the pentecostal sects, markedly oriented to the other world, were increasingly drawn into rehabilitation as well as relief programs.[4]

The loss of China to communism, far from curbing missionary interest in overseas missions, stimulated fresh activity in the Near and Middle East, Africa, and Latin America. Whereas in 1911 Americans in the Protestant world missionary movement accounted for only 7,000 or a third of the total, the number by 1956 had reached an all-time high and an unprecedented proportion: the 23,532 Americans and Canadians constituted over two-thirds of all Protestant missionaries.[5] Donors in 1956 gave $130,000,000 for their support. In that same year American Catholics were maintaining overseas, at a cost of $50,000,000, over 5,000 missionaries.[6]

It is impossible to be sure of the proportion of the total missionary budget that was devoted to education, health, and welfare, since many missionaries, doubling in their roles, served in schools, clinics, hospitals, and village improvement projects while at the same time preaching the Gospel. With statistics admittedly incomplete, a leading authority estimated that Catholic projects in the technical assistance field in 1958 totaled over 65,000 and possibly reached 100,000. In Africa, as one example, support was being given to 1,927 middle schools, 27,727 elementary schools, 477 hospitals, 1,358 dispensaries, and 629 institutions for the aged, the disabled, and the mentally ill.[7] There were 5,300 missionaries in Latin America in 1952, and a large number of them combined technical assistance with their religious activities. Due to a lack of breakdowns in available statistics, it is difficult to compare allocations of funds and

---

[4] For a popular and useful account of missions, see Frank C. Laubach, *The World Is Learning Compassion* (Westwood, New Jersey: Revell, 1958), 42-74. See also American Council of Voluntary Agencies for Foreign Service, *The Role of Voluntary Agencies in Technical Assistance* (New York: ACUAFS, 1953), especially 5-74; R. I. McGlasson, Foreign Missions Secretary, Assemblies of God, to Merle Curti, July 1, 1960.

[5] Frank W. Price and Kenyon E. Meyer, "A Study of Protestant Foreign Missions in 1956," *Occasional Bulletin From the Missionary Research Library* VII (Nov. 16, 1956).

[6] George B. Crissey, "Missions Everywhere: the Religious Agencies," Harlan Cleveland and Gerard J. Mangone, eds., *The Art of Overseasmanship* (Syracuse: Syracuse University Press, 1957), 53-54.

[7] John J. Considine, *Technical Assistance Activities by Christian Missionary Groups; Role of the Churches*, Technical Assistance Information Clearing House Publication (New York: American Council of Voluntary Agencies for Foreign Service, 1958), 17.

services between evangelical activities and technical assistance. A sample study of 3,000 Protestant workers in Latin America showed that about a third were giving what could be called technical aid, the rest being exclusively engaged in evangelism.[8] A leading authority on Protestant missions has estimated that by the late 1950's perhaps 50 per cent of the budget for all overseas activities might be regarded as directly related to welfare and education.[9] In 1950 the major United States Protestant groups engaged in overseas technical assistance spent, by one estimate, $150,000,000. In comparison, in 1952 the United Nations Expanded Technical Assistance Program fell just short of $23,000,000 while in the fiscal year 1954 the United States Congress appropriated $122,000,000 for technical aid.[10]

Without curtailing temporary relief in such emergencies as the Korean war, the Hungarian revolt, and the typhoon and earthquakes in Japan and Chile, several religious-oriented voluntary agencies paid increasing attention to basic causes of poverty, disease, and ignorance. The main method was to help disadvantaged peoples help themselves by training qualified leaders in technical fields and by mass attacks on illiteracy, disease, and inefficient farming methods.

Secular as well as religious agencies also played important parts in the new emphasis on technical assistance as a means of creating better lives in the world's developing areas. World University Service, for example, at first distributed emergency relief to needy European students and professors but later developed a technical assistance program. It sent a mobile X-ray unit to Egyptian universities and books and educational equipment to Ghana, Nigeria, Senegal, Sudan, India, Pakistan, and Latin America. It also established scholarships to enable potential leaders to obtain training. All this was done with the conviction that, in the words of H. G. Wells, "human history becomes more and more a race between education and catastrophe."[11] The International Rescue Committee also broadened its refugee program by supporting agencies for mass literacy and vocational training.[12]

[8] James G. Maddox, *Technical Assistance by Religious Agencies in Latin America* (Chicago: University of Chicago Press, 1956), 19-22.
[9] Interview with Frank W. Price, June 22, 1960.
[10] Edwin A. Bock, *Fifty Years of Technical Assistance: Some Administrative Experiences of the U. S. Voluntary Agencies* (Chicago: Public Administration Clearing House, 1954), vii.
[11] World University Service, *World Student Relief*, 1940-1950 (Geneva: World University Service, ca. 1951), 5-6, 24, 25, 31-32, 35, 43-45, 49, 51-52.
[12] International Rescue Committee, *Saving Freedom's Seed Corn* (New York: IRC, 1958), 27, 29.

While continuing to distribute food and clothing to needy refugees and others, in 1949 CARE started a self-help program. Packages containing seeds, agricultural and craft tools, midwifery kits, and mosquito netting enabled thousands of men and women in underdeveloped countries to keep themselves and their families alive while contributing to the economy as well. From small beginnings this aspect of CARE's work so developed that by 1960 it was allocating over $3,000,000 of its total annual $40,000,000 outlay for self-help and community development programs in twenty-seven countries. The distribution of tools, fish nets, building blocks, technical books of a "do-it-yourself" character, mobile hospital equipment, and pumps for irrigation projects helped raise the level of rural living in Iran, India, the Gaza strip, Korea, Colombia, and other countries.[13]

While not regarded as partners in technical assistance as it was generally understood, the work of groups dedicated to helping the world's most needy children find a worth-while life, bore indirectly on the concept by providing thousands of boys and girls with skills needed to improve community life.[14] One of these agencies, Save the Children Federation, emphasized village self-help projects in the faith that when a country prospers, its children prosper. Thus when Save

[13] *New York Times*, Feb. 10, 1958. See also the mimeographed reports of CARE's work in Poland, Turkey and Haiti, all issued by CARE in 1959. Executive Director, *Annual Report to the Board of Directors of CARE*, August 17, 1960 (New York: CARE, 1960), 14 ff.

[14] In addition to Jewish agencies, the list included the Christian Children's Fund, founded by Dr. J. Calvitt Clarke in 1938, which raised $30,000,000 by the late 1950's, when it was supporting almost 25,000 children in 290 orphanages in 36 countries: Christian Children's Fund, *In Appreciation* (Richmond, Va.: CCF, 1958); J. Calvitt Clarke to Merle Curti, Feb. 11, 1959; John C. Caldwell, *Children of Calamity* (New York: Day, 1957), 30-35, 71, 80, 114. The Boys' Towns of Italy was run by the boys and supported largely by Italian-Americans, the International Ladies' Garment Workers Union, the Amalgamated Clothing Workers of America, and the American Food Industry Committee: Boys' Town of Italy, *Boys' Towns of Italy: The Gateway to Life* (Rome: Boys' Town of Italy, ca. 1959) and *The Story of Boys' Towns of Italy: The History of Twelve Years* (Rome: Boys' Town of Italy, 1956). Also of importance were the Refugee des Petits: A. Seymour Houghton to Merle Curti, Feb. 28, 1959, and the Pestalozzi Foundation of America: Otto Binder, *Cheerful Deeds—Happy Children: Aims of the Pestalozzi World Foundation* (Zurich: PWF, 1952). The Foster Parents Plan, which between its British founding to help child victims of the Spanish civil war and 1958 had cared for 76,000 children in many countries through its "adoption" plan: Mrs. Lenore Sorin, Associate Director, Foster Parents Plan, to Charles J. Wetzel, July 6, 1959; Foster Parents Plan, *Christmas 1958* (New York: FFP, 1958). Of note too was the establishment by Joseph and Victor Saturno of Reno, bachelor sons of an orphaned Italian immigrant, of a trust fund of $1,000,000 for Italian orphans, an act which disposed of much of the brothers' fortune remaining after they had given each resident of the impoverished village of San Marco d'Uri, where their father had been born, a bloc of shares valued at $1,200: *New York Herald Tribune*, August 28, 1960.

the Children Federation helped the inhabitants of Phokea, a Greek village, build a new dock to improve their economic well-being, the citizens dedicated part of the increased village revenue to financing a clinic and to the support of a specialist in maternal and child care.[15]

The role of corporations in overseas technical aid, while of growing importance, remained small in relation to the total American record and the scale of business operations abroad. In many cases, corporate overseas philanthropy was frankly based on self-interest: programs in education, technical training, and health were limited to employees. Expenditures less directly related to corporate interest sometimes were made on the assumption that whatever promoted a favorable image of the corporation in a given country redounded to its benefit. On the other hand, a more truly philanthropic factor also figured in overseas corporate philanthropy. This was notably true in the case of the substantial contributions that several business firms made to the self-help projects undertaken by CARE. Moreover, some of the company overseas programs, such as those for eliminating trachoma, malaria, and other endemic diseases, contributed to the general welfare. In at least a few circles the idea was also advanced that the responsibilities of a corporation as a "good citizen" to relieve the aches and pains of society at home and to advance the national goal of a good life for everyone, including the strengthening of the principle of voluntarism, did not end at the country's boundaries.[16]

Corporate experience in overseas philanthropy, as might be expected, varied. Some undertakings proved to be "headaches." At least one hospital, built at considerable cost, was turned over to the local government. On the other hand, corporation spokesmen also expressed the opinion that despite suspicion of American big business in many countries, welfare and educational programs contributed something to general good will. This seems to have been markedly the case when corporations established foundations staffed by local personnel.[17]

[15] Save the Children Federation, *Annual Report*, June 30, 1958 (Norwalk, Conn.: Save the Children Federation, 1958), 13.
[16] Roger M. Blough, *Free Man and the Corporation* (New York: McGraw-Hill, 1959), 102 ff., 110 ff.
[17] For an interesting discussion with examples see Frederick A. Harmon, "Private Aid Abroad," *Wall Street Journal*, July 14, 1958, and Jonathan B. Bingham, *Shirt-Sleeve Diplomacy: Point 4 in Action* (New York: Day, 1954), 147 ff.

If business enterprise overseas contributed relatively little to technical assistance beyond the immediate scope of its own interest, the foundations which derived their resources from American corporations played an important part in such programs.[18] It is true that in 1957 only eight cents of every dollar that foundations commanded was spent abroad, but even this represented considerable sums.[19]

Oldest in the field, the Rockefeller Foundation, during the years 1913-1960, spent $229,691,683 from its total outlay of $633,335,056 in overseas operations.[20] Convinced that the prospect of peace might be decisively influenced by events in the Middle East, Africa, and Asia, the Foundation between 1956 and 1959 dipped into capital funds to the extent of $20,000,000, which, in addition to income, was used for expanded help in these areas.[21]

In the 1950's the Rockefeller Foundation, hitherto the major institution of its kind, was overshadowed in the range and magnitude of its overseas programs by a newcomer—the Ford Foundation.[22] Convinced that the underlying causes of war are poverty, sickness, and ignorance, and that these obstacles to man's progress and well-being know no national boundaries, the Ford trustees decided in 1951 to undertake an Overseas Development Program, to be supplemented by an International Training and Research Program.[23] After much preliminary thought and study, including discussions between Paul Hoffman, president of the Foundation, and

[18] In 1960 the total assets of American foundations were estimated at $11,000,000,-000 and the yearly output at $625,000,000: *New York Times*, July 11, 1960.

[19] Ann D. Walton and F. Emerson Andrews, eds., *The Foundation Directory: Edition* 1 (published for the Foundation Library Center by Russell Sage Foundation, New York: 1960), xxxiv; F. Emerson Andrews, *Philanthropic Giving* (New York: Russell Sage Foundation, 1950), 90 ff.

[20] U. S., Congress, Senate, *Foreign Aid Program: Compilation of Studies and Surveys prepared under the direction of the Special Committee to Study the Foreign Aid Program*, 85th Cong., 1st Sess., 1957, Sen. Doc. 52, 1570; Dean Rusk, "The Rockefeller Foundation," in American Council of Voluntary Agencies for Foreign Service, Technical Assistance Clearing House's *Technical Assistance Quarterly Bulletin* III (June, 1957), 7-8; Janet Paine to Merle Curti, August 26, 1961.

[21] "Doing Good Abroad; New Models in Asia," *The Economist* CLXXXIX (Nov. 15, 1958), 504-05.

[22] In 1957 the Ford Foundation's assets—$3,316,000,000—were approximately five times as great as those of the Rockefeller Foundation: Walton and Andrews, eds., *The Foundation Directory*, xv.

[23] It is possible that the decision to expand the program of the Foundation both at home and abroad was also related to the Internal Revenue Act of 1950 which stated that "unreasonable" accumulations of funds by foundations would be considered sufficient grounds for removal of their tax-exempt status. See F. Emerson Andrews, "Foundations and Social Welfare," *Social Work Yearbook*, 1957, Russell H. Kurtz, ed. (New York: National Association of Social Workers, 1957), 274-80.

Jawaharlal Nehru, the further decision was made to concentrate on Asia and the Near East. These areas seemed particularly important in view of major tensions that threatened world peace, in view also of proximity to the Soviet Union and Communist China and the opportunity for channeling rising nationalism into constructive human purposes within a democratic framework. In 1958 programs were begun in some of the new African nations and, in 1959, in Latin America. Between 1951 and 1959 the Foundation spent more than eighty million dollars in its overseas programs.

In many ways the Ford Foundation followed on a much larger scale paths already marked out by other foundations and voluntary agencies. This was true of the emphasis on increasing food production, the first major effort of the Foundation in India and one to which, in the spring of 1960, $10,500,000 was allocated to help prevent the "stark threat" of a 28,000,000-ton food shortage by 1966. The Ford Foundation also followed precedent in attempting to improve the health and skill of villagers, in providing revolving loan funds for farmers, in rural development programs, supporting teacher training and other educational institutions, and in enabling specialists from developing countries to improve their competence in American and other research centers.

In several ways, however, the Ford Foundation broke what was essentially new ground. It went beyond anything hitherto done in supporting social and economic research, in cooperating with governments in developing and implementing over-all economic and social planning, including urban development, and in encouraging craftsmen to accept modern rationalization principles. It strengthened cooperatives and small industries. Also innovating in character was the aid given the government of India in efforts to check the rate of population growth. The programs in Asia, the Near East, and Africa designed to increase the effectiveness of government operations were rightly deemed crucial in the execution by local governments of innumerable projects for economic and social improvement.

In many of its working procedures, which were regarded as flexible and subject to periodic review, the Ford Foundation was also distinctive. It was not an operating agency in the sense of the Rockefeller Foundation and the Near East Foundation. It created no institutions to implement programs unless these did not exist, in which case it aided in their organization. The agencies through which it worked included voluntary associations and universities in the United

States and in host countries, international organizations, and government institutions in places in which it accepted invitations to give assistance. It emphasized the importance of deciding on a budget before final negotiations with a government were completed. In making decisions regarding fields of operation the Foundation gave a good deal of weight to projects which host governments had begun or decided to begin, to those that might clearly be accelerated by Ford help, to the integration of a program into the total economy and social structure, and to self-supporting potentialities. Officers of the Foundation also took into account the fact that each country differed from every other and that every program must be adapted accordingly.

Given the desirability, if not the necessity, of deepening western understanding of the developing countries and of providing American experts for overseas work, several foundations, with Rockefeller and Ford in the lead, supported area programs—Asian, Near Eastern, and African—in American universities. The millions of dollars that went into these programs brought American specialized knowledge in these studies abreast of and often ahead of that in other western nations. Such outlays in effect killed two birds with one stone: the commitment of the foundations to strengthen American educational institutions was advanced at the same time that overseas programs were enabled to move ahead.[24]

In contrast with Rockefeller and Ford, whose programs ranged over two hemispheres, several foundations concentrated on a given area. The China Medical Board of New York (supported by the Rockefeller Foundation) illustrated the flexibility on which foundations have prided themselves. When the Communists took over mainland China, the Board shifted its emphasis to Taiwan and other Asian countries. It strengthened medical training by improving plant and other facilities and by providing fellowships—174 between 1951 and 1959—for specialized study overseas.[25] The W. K. Kellogg Foundation of Battle Creek, Michigan, with assets in 1957 totaling over

[24] Rockefeller Foundation, *Annual Report*, 1946 (New York: Rockefeller Foundation, 1947), 39; 1947, 43-44; 1951, 79-80. In 1960 the Ford Foundation allocated $15,000,000 to Harvard, Columbia, and California for research and training in African, Asian, and Middle Eastern studies: *New York Times*, July 25, 1960.

[25] China Medical Board, *Annual Report*, 1959 (New York: Rockefeller Foundation, 1959), 3-8.

$215,000,000, broadened its agricultural and health programs in Latin America.[26]

In view of its importance to the United States, South Korea was understandably the focus of interest to a special bi-national agency. The American-Korean Foundation, organized in 1952 by business and civic leaders, aimed to strengthen the war-torn prowestern country through educational training in specialized fields.[27] More comprehensive in geographical range, the Asia Foundation, at first largely supported by West Coast business and civic leaders and designed to aid anti-Communists in the Far East, offered fellowships, supplied facilities for social and economic research, subsidized youth centers and organizations, and sent 650,000 textbooks and journals to schools and libraries.[28]

Of special interest among agencies concentrating on a single country was the Watumull Foundation, established in 1942 by G. J. Watumull, a Sindi-born merchant, and his American wife, to encourage greater social efficiency in India and to promote a better understanding between that country and the United States. The Watumulls pioneered in bringing students and scientists to the United States for training that would enable them on their return to promote the well-being of their country and in sending Americans to India to interpret the United States when understanding was sorely needed. The Foundation also rewarded merit in socially important but inadequately recognized fields in India and piloted planned parenthood studies in the subcontinent. It set a fine example in showing what relatively limited funds could achieve when in the hands of an imaginative, idealistic, yet highly practical family.[29]

Thus missionaries, the voluntary agencies, corporations, and foundations cut promising paths in developing overseas technical assistance. These included mass education, training in vocational skills and for leadership in economic and particularly agricultural develop-

---

[26] American Council of Voluntary Agencies for Foreign Service, *The Role of Voluntary Agencies in Technical Assistance,* 6, 65-66; Kellogg Foundation, *Report,* 1959 (Battle Creek: Kellogg Foundation, 1959), 44 ff. The Creole and the Esso Foundations also concentrated on Latin American countries, as did the Rockefeller Brother Fund.

[27] American Korean Foundation, *Annual Report,* May, 1956–May, 1957 (New York: AKF, 1957), 1-4.

[28] Asia Foundation, *The Asia Foundation: Its Purposes and Activities* (San Francisco: Asia Foundation, 1957), *passim.*

[29] See the remarks of John A. Burns, Delegate from Hawaii, in the *Congressional Record,* 86th Cong., 1st Sess., CV, Pt. 15H, August 17, 1959, A7101-03; Watumull Foundation, *Annual Reports,* 1942-   (Los Angeles: Watumull Foundation, 1943-   ).

ment, and the more efficient use of natural resources generally. When, in 1950, the United Nations and the United States began large-scale technical assistance programs, seventy-five areas in Latin America, Africa, the Near and Far East were already benefiting from some 2,500 projects in education, health, agriculture, and social welfare.[30] These were often discrete, but there was a growing tendency to coordinate projects in a given village in the interest of bettering community life as a whole.

The scope, support, and methods of the nongovernment agencies engaged in some type of technical assistance varied considerably but an interest in education, broadly defined, was the chief common denominator. Although UNESCO's program for basic education in the less-developed areas struck a responsive note in the United States as in other countries, the tradition of universal education played a major part in making many Americans want to have other nations benefit from "the little red schoolhouse" in the way it was believed the United States had profited.

Illiteracy seemed to be the prime enemy of progress in the less-industrialized areas. Mission schools of almost every kind continued to multiply and to emphasize reading. One of the most striking records was that of the Committee on World Literacy and Christian Literature sponsored by the Division of Foreign Missions of the National Council of Churches of Christ. Dr. Frank C. Laubach and his helpers developed effective methods for teaching adults as well as children to read. In twenty-three years he and his teams opened the world of books to at least 15,000,000 people in sixty-eight countries. The achievement was the more remarkable since teaching materials had to be prepared in 230 languages.[31] In Vietnam and in Lebanon the Congregational Christian Committee operated elementary schools in an effort to educate sons and daughters of refugees.[32] The Mennonite Central Committee and the Brethren Service Commission likewise supported elementary educational programs some of which served the less developed countries.[33] In Korea the Ameri-

---

[30] American Council of Voluntary Agencies for Foreign Service, *The Role of Voluntary Agencies in Technical Assistance*, 8, 17.

[31] *Ibid.*, 48.

[32] American Friends Service Committee, "Relief and Reconstruction, 1958" (mimeographed), 4, 9-11.

[33] Irvin B. Horst, *A Ministry of Goodwill* (Akron, Pa.: 1950), 81; Lorell Weiss, *Ten Years of Brethren Service, 1941-1951* (Elgin, Ill.: General Brotherhood Board, 1952), 34, 37.

can Friends Service Committee fostered courses in reading and writing and emphasized these basic skills in several rural villages in India. It also fought illiteracy in southern Italy, in many ways a depressed area, comparable to less-developed countries in its need of technical aid, both in programs of its own (subsidized by the Ford Foundation) and in cooperation with the Italian Union for the Struggle against Illiteracy.[34] Among secular agencies concerned with the problem, the International Rescue Committee in supporting the Popular Culture Association of Vietnam helped approximately 100,000 people learn how to read.[35]

What was done through all these efforts was considerable. Yet much remained to be done. Millions of adults in many lands were still denied access to the printed word. While virtually all American children went to elementary school and two out of three in 1959 finished high school, only half of the world's five hundred million children between the ages of five and fourteen in that year had access to primary schools and only one in ten could look forward to a secondary education.[36]

The battle against illiteracy was closely related to the need for improving teacher training. Of the many contributions made by voluntary agencies in this field that of the Unitarian Service Committee may serve as an example. In 1952 the Committee accepted an invitation from the Korean Ministry of Education to provide specialists in primary and secondary education in an effort to modernize and develop a socially useful school system.[37]

The Committee faced formidable problems. It knew, of course, that at least decades of effort would be necessary to change the education of a country and that any such change must be mainly effected by its own educational leaders. But Korean educators had functioned within and had been inevitably formed by the Japanese system without being given opportunity for experience in shaping policy. They were seeking a new direction, as well as a means of meeting the drastic numerical shortage of teachers resulting from the withdrawal of the Japanese and from the demands on manpower which

[34] American Friends Service Committee, *Annual Report*, 1956 (Philadelphia: AFSC, 1956), 6.
[35] International Rescue Committee, *Saving Freedom's Seed Corn*, 26-29.
[36] Ford Foundation, *Annual Report*, 1958 (New York: Ford Foundation, 1958), 12.
[37] The Unitarian Service Committee, starting in 1954, also developed a program for establishing a professionally sound department of social work at Seoul National University: Unitarian Service Committee, *Fact Sheet*, Jan., 1959 (Boston, USC, 1959), 2.

the Korean War imposed. Nor was it easy to find American educators for the assignment who were at once competent and resourceful. In attempting to influence already established teacher training institutions inertia as well as the protection of the status quo were to be expected. Those faculty members eager to cooperate were often handicapped by lack of time, inasmuch as most of them held at least two jobs in order to eke out a living: in Korea as in many countries teaching is paid for as piece work with the result that additional compensation is required to insure that time will be spent, a custom Americans have not always understood.

Despite all this, the project went well. The educational teams organized by the Unitarian Service Committee enjoyed cordial relations with Korean colleagues and came to have a good deal of prestige. The Committee believed that the project proved that a voluntary agency could work successfully on a cooperative basis with a foreign government.[38]

As underdeveloped nations faced the problem of building economic bases, a well-trained force of agricultural and industrial workers was the necessary complement to literacy. Missionary agencies had been among the pioneers in developing vocational programs in many countries. It is impossible to give in limited space an adequate impression of the useful work thus accomplished: a few examples must suggest the broad outlines. Dr. Sam Higginbottom's Agricultural Institute at Allahabad became justly famous and extended its influence on the improvement of agriculture and rural life in many parts of India. Near Calcutta the trade school developed by Bishop Louis La Ravoire Morrow of the teaching Salesian order achieved high standards in relating its program constructively to the people and government. The American Farm School in Salonica, established in 1902 by Dr. John Henry House,[39] an intrepid and independent-minded Congregational missionary, was directed for many years by his engineer-trained son. It received support from voluntary contributions, endowment income, and grants for special projects.

[38] Unitarian Service Committee correspondence in the files of the Advisory Committee on Voluntary Foreign Aid, International Cooperation Administration, Department of State, Washington, D. C. [hereafter cited as Advisory Committee Files].

[39] Susan Beers House, *A Life for the Balkans: The Story of John Henry House of the American Farm School, Thessaloniki, Greece* (New York: Revell, 1939), 8 ff.; William Webster Hall, *Puritans in the Balkans: The American Board Mission in Bulgaria, 1878-1918* (Sophia: Cultura, 1938), 187-88.

The largest part of its budget, however, was raised through the sale of the products of its farms and shops and from the work of its students and predominantly Greek staff. Among the most important factors in the extraordinary success of the School were its high degree of financial independence, its achievements in attracting official and nonofficial Greek support, and its imaginative and realistic adaptation of short courses, 4-H club activity, and demonstration centers.[40] In the 1950's, with similar objectives in mind, the Ford Foundation helped establish or strengthen vocational training in Egypt, Iran, India, Pakistan, and other countries.

In a period when large-scale, organized programs seemed to many the only practicable way of approaching the problem, a few individuals gallantly undertook projects on their own. One such man was Richard Soderberg, a young engineering professor in Afghanistan who noted that an American builder had to import all his skilled labor from the United States since there was no available native supply. Returning to the United States, Soderberg collected from individuals, churches, and schools sufficient machinery and teaching materials, together with $50,000, to establish in Kabul a much needed and successful training school. Another single-handed innovator was John Clark. During his overseas military experience Clark discovered a remote valley in Kashmir where the Hunza people lived in a true Stone Age culture. After the war Clark went back to found a school for training boys in the use of the wheel and the lathe, in leatherwork, wood-carving, and weaving. He showed the Hunza how to get adequate water, to make use of hidden minerals, and to conquer malaria.[41]

Of the organized agencies for vocational training the Organization for Rehabilitation Through Training (ORT) had the most experience, the largest support, and the most extensive programs. (In 1959 the 300,000th graduate from its training schools was proudly reported.) About 70 per cent of ORT's budget came from America. Although the International Ladies' Garment Workers Union and other labor organizations as well as the Ford Foundation contributed, the mainstay was the allocation from United Jewish Appeal and gifts of individual well-wishers.

[40] Robert Littell, "They're Helping Greeks to Help Themselves," *Reader's Digest* LXXVII (Sept., 1960), 129-34; *The Sower: The American Farm School* X (Summer, 1960), (Fall, 1960), XI (Winter, 1961), (Spring, 1961), *passim.*
[41] Laubach, *The World Is Learning Compassion*, 205-06; Charles Stevenson, "2,500 Private Foreign-Aid Programs," *Reader's Digest* LXVII (Oct., 1955), 156-59.

ORT did not give up its work in countries where young Jews still needed help in learning how to become self-sustaining, to contribute to the economy, and thus perhaps to weaken the impulse toward anti-Semitism. But it also sought new fields. With the help of the Alliance Izraelite Universelle, the Joint Distribution Committee and other groups, it maintained forty-three training schools in North Africa where it was especially important to break down the traditional antipathy to manual labor. When its trainees in Iran could not find work, ORT set up workshops to employ them. But the main emphasis after 1949 was on Israel where ORT operated the largest system of vocational high schools, embracing two-thirds of the country's appropriate age group. Training in the older skills and crafts was supplemented by new programs, particularly those that prepared the student for work in the electrical industries.[42]

ORT was not always alone in the field where it operated. Denied admission to many trade schools, Arab refugees took advantage of the vocational schools supported by the International Committee for Refugees, to which Church World Service made substantial contributions.[43]

To develop better living conditions, leadership in agriculture, industry, health, and public administration was no less necessary than mass literacy and widespread manual training. Programs for training leaders were not of course new. The International Committee of the YMCA had for many years been developing indigenous leaders infused with Christian concepts of character and service through programs in adult education, and through student conferences. In the postwar years increasing attention was given to training leaders for helping peoples develop their capacities and for meeting their own needs from their own resources. The growing attention given to training leaders for rural reconstruction was only one aspect of this emphasis.[44]

---

[42] American ORT Federation, ORT: *A Record of Ten Years Rebuilding Jewish Economic Life* (New York: ORT, 1956), 9, 17, 20, 26, 31-35; American ORT Federation, "The ORT Program in 1959," Dec. 16, 1958 (mimeographed); interview with Paul Bernick and Jack Rader, June 21, 1960.

[43] Church World Service, "The Overseas Program Report for 1958," n.d. (mimeographed), 23, 25.

[44] For early developments see *International Survey of the Young Men's and Young Women's Christian Associations: an Independent Study of the Foreign Work of the Christian Associations of the United States and Canada* (New York: The International Survey Committee, 1932), 47 ff., 199-201; Charles H. Hopkins, *History of the Y.M.C.A. in North America* (New York: Association Press, 1951), 657 ff., 720 ff.; Stanley High, "They Develop Today's Youth for Tomorrow's World," *Reader's Digest* LXIV (April, 1954), 41-45; William A. Dudde, "Geneva: On the Y Front," *Christian Century* LXXVI (Oct. 7, 1959), 1158.

On the academic level the institutions comprising the Near East Colleges Association, which built on the work begun by the missionaries, had outstanding records in training leaders of several countries. As we have seen, the Carnegie and Rockefeller Foundations had also pioneered in giving opportunities in non-European areas for training in library science, teaching, medicine, and health. But in the 1950's the rapidly widening range and the larger degree of support for such projects, together with the sharp focus on Asia and Africa, opened a virtually new era.

The most direct approach was to strengthen established institutions, American and indigenous, in the less-advantaged areas. Typical of this formula was the Rockefeller grant of $5,000,000 to the American University of Beirut, a merited recognition.[45] Recognizing the crucial importance of the troubled Congo, Rockefeller and Ford made grants totaling $500,000 to the struggling Lovanium University.[46]

The grants made by the Ford Foundation's Overseas Development Program were substantial. Almost $50,000,000 was spent between 1951 and 1956 while the figure for 1960 alone was over $30,000,000.

By 1958 the Near East was being given 23 per cent of the Ford overseas budget. In part, these grants went to existing academic institutions, which were faced by overwhelming problems in providing the specialized training on which leadership so largely depended. A million dollars went to Robert College, the American College for Girls in Turkey, and the American University in Cairo. In 1956 Beirut received over $600,000 for emergency needs and for training rural teachers, a program to which the Foundation attached much importance. Training in library science was established at the University of Ankara, which, through a grant of $285,000 to Harvard, also received means to develop a staff for its new Institute of Business Administration.[47]

In southern and southeast Asia programs were aimed at developing competent leaders in both rural and urban fields. Working in

[45] American University of Beirut, *President's Annual Report,* 1956-1957, 18.

[46] *New York Times,* Oct. 31, 1960. In 1959 the Ford Foundation gave $215,000 to the University College of Rhodesia and Nyasaland to strengthen social sciences, $124,000 to University College, Ibadan, Nigeria, $105,000 to the University of Kartoum to establish a program for training secondary school teachers, and smaller sums to other African institutions: Ford Foundation, *Annual Report,* 1959, 86.

[47] Ford Foundation, *Annual Report,* 1955, 106-07; *Annual Report,* 1956, 117-22; Ford Foundation, *Activities in the Near East Supported by the Ford Foundation* (Beirut: Ford Foundation, 1957), 32, 33; Robert W. Chandler to Merle Curti, Sept. 12, 1961.

India with the government's own plans for improving the quality of life in the country, the Ford Foundation gave assistance to six agricultural colleges and several teacher training institutions, as well as to projects for improving the skills of multi-purpose village leaders and for training much needed nurses and medical and sanitary technicians. By 1961 grants totaling $2,182,680 were made to increase the competence of six hundred engineers in the management methods worked out in the American steel industry—personnel greatly needed if the Five Year Plans were to reach their goals. In the summer of 1961 the Foundation also announced a grant of $1,400,000 to help Calcutta solve what was believed to be the world's most serious urban problem. The project was to include aid in land planning, community design, housing, transportation, engineering, sanitation, economic and social research, and fiscal planning and administration, to all of which trained leadership was indispensable.[48]

In Pakistan help went to institutions for courses in home economics, public administration, economic and social research, and for training village workers.[49] In Burma the Foundation supported the Government Agricultural Institute at Pyinmana with an American team for training extension workers and teachers in agricultural courses in the middle and high schools, strengthened the faculty at Mandalay College, and financed programs in management accounting, public administration, and related fields. Like other countries, Indonesia had its own special problems, but the difficulties were even more formidable in view of the great shortage of experienced administrators, separatism and other conflicts in public life, inflation, and the time and energy needed for even the simplest job. Through a cooperative program with the University of Wisconsin, similar to arrangements with other American institutions, an effort was made to strengthen the economics faculty at the Gadjah Mada University. Both public and private institutions at the secondary level received help in developing teachers in the technical fields.[50]

Besides strengthening and introducing new programs in existing institutions, foundations continued, on an expanding scale, the well-known policies of the Carnegie and Rockefeller agencies in offering fellowships and grants to enable technical personnel to receive train-

[48] Ford Foundation, *The Ford Foundation and Foundation Supported Activities in India* (New Delhi: Ford Foundation, 1955), 14 ff.; *New York Times,* July 30, 1961.
[49] George F. Gant, "The Ford Foundation Program in Pakistan," *Annals of the American Academy of Political and Social Science* CCCXXIII (May, 1959), 150-59.
[50] Ford Foundation, *Annual Reports, passim.*

ing in American research centers. In the course of its work for agricultural development in Latin America the Rockefeller Foundation provided an increasing number of fellowships for study in the United States—250 in 1957.[51] The Kellogg Foundation followed a similar course in broadening its agricultural and health programs in Latin America.[52] In 1956, its first year, the Creole Foundation spent over half its annual budget of $1,000,000 for the further training of Venezuelan scientists and technicians—a program which seems to have been well received.[53]

The range and volume of American contributions to educational programs designed to improve the quality of life in Israel exceeded anything done elsewhere. Many of the Jewish agencies, American, non-American, and international, had been working in Palestine, as we have seen, since the First World War. Independence in 1948 and the pressure of the Arab states and of new immigrants opened almost unlimited opportunities for Jewish philanthropy. Generous gifts continued to enrich the Hebrew University and its affiliated institutes, strengthened established programs, provided fellowships for the study of psychiatry and psychiatric social work in the United States, and contributed to the educational activities of youth centers. Young Israel, an orthodox group, the American Joint Distribution Committee, and other agencies supported various educational enterprises having utilitarian as well as cultural and religious ends.[54] Technical assistance included not only general and vocational education and training for leadership but the promotion of health through clinics, hospitals, research, and preventive measures.

UNICEF (United Nations International Children's Emergency Fund) was the outstanding example of a combined public and private effort to cope with the brutal and staggering fact that of the three children born in the world each second, one quarter died before leaving their mothers' breasts, while two-thirds of the remainder did

---

[51] Rockefeller Foundation, *Annual Report*, 1951, 50; *Annual Report*, 1954, 14; Rusk, *Technical Assistance Quarterly Bulletin*, 7.

[52] Kellogg Foundation, *Report*, 1959, 44 ff.

[53] Creole Foundation, *Creole Foundation, General Information: Scholarship Program* (n.p., n.d.); Alfredo Anzola M., executive director of Fundacion Creole in Caracas, to Merle Curti, July 30, 1958.

[54] Hadassah, *Annual Report*, 1957-58 (New York: Hadassah, 1958), n.p.; National Council of Young Israel, *President's Annual Report*, 1957-1958; American Jewish Joint Distribution Committee, *A Guide to Overseas Operations of the American Joint Distribution Committee* (Geneva: AJDC, 1958), 12-13, 24. JDC also supported child education programs in Greece, Iran, and Morocco.

not live to adolescence. The program included child feeding, nutrition education, the development of high-protein foods, disease control, and related basic health services. Participating governments made voluntary contributions to the program, which recipient nations and territories matched: by 1960, 104 countries and areas were receiving help. In addition to what governments did, voluntary agencies and individuals in many countries contributed gifts and augmented the budget by purchasing greeting cards. In 1960, over 55,000,000 children and mothers benefited directly from UNICEF undertakings.

America made generous contributions to the program. In 1960 Congress provided $11,000,000 or approximately 50 per cent of UNICEF's government-derived funds. In the same year nongovernment American contributions totaled $2,550,000—somewhat more than half of the world's private support. Of this sum $1,750,000 represented the Halloween "trick or treat" collections of some two million children. American interest in UNICEF owed a good deal to its remarkable director, Maurice Pate, who had served under Hoover in Belgian War Relief in the First World War, and to the enthusiasms of Danny Kaye, "the children's ambassador." [55]

On the purely voluntary level, the work begun earlier by the Jewish agencies in Palestine, the missionaries, and the foundations was now developed on a growing scale. It would be hard to describe in any detail the many activities of the American voluntary agencies in this field: a few examples must suggest the larger picture.

The wide-ranging programs of the YMCA encompassed in World Service, established in 1889, and the International Committee, included projects designed to improve health—education in nutrition, physical training, and over-all efforts to raise general living standards. In Taiwan, to take one example from the seventy-six countries in which the Y worked, teams of medical as well as agricultural students went to the villages to tackle, through a grass-roots self-help approach, the twin problems of poverty and disease. Games, folk danc-

[55] Robert L. Heilbroner, *Mankind's Children: The Story of UNICEF*, Public Affairs Pamphlet 279 (New York: Public Affairs Committee, 1959), *passim*; Spurgeon M. Keeny, *Half the World's Children: A Diary of UNICEF at Work in Asia* (New York: Association Press, 1957), vii ff.; UNICEF, *Some Current UNICEF Figures for Public Information*, Feb., 1961 (mimeographed); United Nations Economic and Social Council, Children's Fund, *Report of the Executive Board*, June, 1961; Mrs. Eleanor Apt Kaplan, United States Committee for UNICEF, to Merle Curti, August 15, 1961; Donald Anderson, "No Money for Guns, UNICEF Director Answers Critics on Use of Funds," *Madison [Wis.] Capital Times*, Dec. 18, 1961.

ing, hobbies, and the like were encouraged to improve mental health and reduce tensions.[56] The YWCA's Foreign Division included, among its many projects related to health, programs for training medical social workers.[57]

Best known of the individual missionary hospitals was that of the Baptist-supported institution which Dr. Gordon S. Seagrave developed at Namkham from the time he was assigned to the northern Burma field in 1922. The son, grandson, and great-grandson of Baptist missionaries in Burma, Seagrave's career, which included service in the United States Medical Corps during the Second World War, was especially notable for its emphasis on nurses' training. The books in which he graphically related his dramatic adventures as well as his far-reaching constructive work for health, became best sellers and made the name of "Burma Surgeon" almost an American as well as a Burmese household word. In commending Dr. Seagrave as he began his fortieth year of service at his "hospital in the hills," President Kennedy declared that the physician had "become a symbol to the entire world of the American tradition of humanitarian service abroad."[58]

But Dr. Seagrave was only one of a great many medical missionaries whose contributions to health in medically backward areas was notable. Among the 119 clinics and hospitals in Latin America which by the 1950's enjoyed support from the United States, that established by Dr. Frank Beck in 1928 at La Paz was an innovation. Beginning with makeshift arrangements for only three patients, the hospital developed into a well-equipped institution with fifty beds, a nurses' training school, and an enviable record of stimulating Bolivians to help themselves in the field of medicine and health. From this center, as well as from similar clinics and hospitals, church-sponsored nurses visited rural communities to give training in medication and the prevention of disease as well as in the care of the sick.[59]

---

[56] *News of YMCA World Service,* 1954-1955, *passim;* YMCA International Committee, Advisory Committee File.

[57] YWCA, "At Home and Abroad: A Summary History of the Foreign Program of the YWCA of the United States," 1954 (mimeographed), *passim.*

[58] Gordon S. Seagrave, *Burma Surgeon* (New York: Norton, 1943), *Burma Surgeon Returns* (New York: Norton, 1946) and *My Hospital in the Hills* (New York: Norton, 1955); *New York Times,* Sept. 15, 1961.

[59] Technical Assistance Information Clearing House, *Technical Assistance Seminar: Role of the Churches: The Missionary in the Field* (New York: American Council of Voluntary Agencies for Foreign Service, 1958), 113; Clarence W. Hall, "He Brought My People Back to Life," *Reader's Digest* LXIX (Sept., 1956), 195-99, 202.

The medical and health services in non-European nations conducted by Protestant and Catholic missionary bodies each year took on new responsibilities. Representative examples were the 40-bed hospital the Mennonite Central Committee built in Ethiopia, when the Italians withdrew, and the clinic established at the same time in Nazareth.[60] The rehabilitation centers for amputees and the hospitals of the Seventh Day Adventists in the two hemispheres offered superior medical services.[61] One of the most impressive projects in the medical field supported by Catholic Relief Services was that of Mother Teresa, foundress of the Missionaries of Charity. With a team of sari-dressed Sisters trained in tropical medicine and a specialist in Hansen's disease, eight anti-leprosy control stations were established in the peripheries of Calcutta. The mobile clinic contributed by Catholic Relief Services enabled Mother Teresa's group to help thousands of lepers who, untreated, would have continued to menace the community.[62]

Many of the secular agencies, like those with a religious motive, embraced several programs of which that of health and medicine was but one. Beginning in 1949 CARE included midwifery kits, mosquito nets, and other health aids in its package program to be supplemented in time with mobile medical units and equipment for clinics.[63] Between 1952 and 1957 the American Korean Foundation contributed over $862,000 toward the control of tuberculosis and leprosy and for nursing, medical schools, and public health.[64] To meet the great shortage of nurses in Turkey, the Ford Foundation supported a training program in the Admiral Bristol Hospital. When Syria refused United States government aid, a representative of the Foundation, on assurance that no strings would be attached, secured the acceptance of the much-needed equipment for four operating rooms and the services of an American surgeon for a year.[65] The contributions of secular agencies to health also included the $3,000,000 hospital that Anaconda built for employees at its mines in Chuquicamata, Chile, the tuberculosis hospital of Standard Vac-

[60] Horst, *A Ministry of Goodwill*, 22.
[61] Church World Service, "The Overseas Program Report for 1958," 22; "That the Hungry May Be Fed," *Christian Century* LXX (March 4, 1953), 247-48.
[62] Eileen Egan to Merle Curti, August 23, 1961.
[63] *New York Times*, Feb. 10, 1957, 12.
[64] American Korean Foundation, *Annual Report*, 1956-1957, 1-2. The Foundation's annual expenditures for its educational, agricultural, medical aid and other programs reached $17,000,000 by 1958, Advisory Committee, *Reports*, 1952-1958.
[65] Laubach, *The World Is Learning Compassion*, 109.

uum Oil Company in Sumatra at a cost of $400,000,[66] and Firestone support of the Samuel Grimes Maternity Center, the Baptist Hospital, and the institute of tropical medicine in Liberia.[67] In Saudi Arabia the Arabian American Oil Company combated malaria, trachoma, and other endemic diseases.[68] Several firms, including the American President Lines and the Charles Pfizer Company, awarded fellowships to Asiatics for medical study in America.[69]

Approaching a business operation in scale and efficiency although inspired by humanitarian, religious and cultural considerations, Hadassah Medical Organization was rightly the pride of the Women's Zionist Organization in America which in 1960 with its 318,000 members and budget of $9,000,000 was the largest group in the World Zionist Organization.[70] It extended much of the work it had begun in Palestine before and during the war, establishing a Department of Occupational Therapy and providing fellowships for overseas training in public health as a memorial to Dr. I. K. Kligler who pioneered Hadassah health services in Palestine over a twenty-five year period.

With the recogntion of Israeli independence in 1948, Hadassah, in cooperation with the new government, began an active diphtheria immunization program in schools and infant welfare clinics and helped combat malaria and tuberculosis with support from the Workers Sick Fund, the Anti-Tuberculosis League, and the World Health Organization.[71] In 1958 Hadassah was maintaining six hospitals in Israel. Other Hadassah-supported facilities included the Outpatient Department in Jerusalem which served a thousand patients daily, the Hansen Hospital for Leprosy, and the Lasker Mental Hygiene and Child Guidance Clinic.[72] In addition Hadassah supported in whole or in part thirty-six health welfare stations offering

[66] Harmon, *Wall Street Journal*, July 14, 1958.
[67] Harvey Firestone, "Private Enterprise and Point Four," *Building Leadership for Peace*, 21st Annual New York Herald Tribune Forum, 1952 (New York: New York Herald Tribune, 1952), 78-83; Wayne Chatfield Taylor, *United States Business Performance Abroad: The Firestone Operations in Liberia* (Washington: National Planning Association, 1956), 96, 97; Andrews, *Philanthropic Giving*, 64-68.
[68] Arabian American Oil Company, *Report on Operations to the Saudi Arabian Government*, 1957, 29-39; 1958, 25-37; 1959, 24, 32.
[69] Harmon, *Wall Street Journal*, July 14, 1958.
[70] *New York Times*, Feb. 13, 1961.
[71] Miriam C. Taub, "Hadassah's Medical Work: Origins and Development," *The Hadassah Medical Organization: An American Contribution to Medical Pioneering and Progress in Israel*, ed. Joseph Hirsh (New York: Hadassah, 1956), 16, 19, 20, 23-28.
[72] Hadassah, *Annual Report*, 1957-1958, n.p.

prenatal, mother, and child care, supplemental feeding, a school hygiene and dental service for over 25,000 children and an anti-trachoma program for almost half that number, the Nettie Lasker Social Service and Day Convalescent Home in Jerusalem, the Henrietta Szold School of Nursing, and the Hebrew University Medical School. The construction of a large medical center ten miles from Jerusalem, which brought together many medical and health services, was the most ambitious of Hadassah's projects in the later 1950's.[73]

A second health program, Malben, was supported after 1949 by the Israeli government and by the Joint Distribution Committee which in time contributed about 40 per cent of its annual budget. Malben cared for the aged, chronically ill, and physically handicapped among newcomers to Israel. It operated twenty-nine institutions with a bed capacity of over 7,000. Closely related to these services was a program, supported by the JDC, the Jewish Agency, and the Council of Local Authorities, that enabled the aged to live in their own apartments or with relatives and in many cases to open small businesses. In initiating the Parent Club Program (Golden Age Club) JDC still further contributed to the physical and mental well-being of the aged.[74]

The steady growth of American Jewish contributions to Israel in the field of technical assistance, including health and welfare, was indeed impressive. Between 1921 and 1960 American Jews contributed between 75 and 85 per cent of the $900,000 raised by the Keren Hayesod (Palestine Foundation Fund), much of which directly or indirectly contributed to the development of Israel through various types of technical assistance.[75] Another indication of the

---

[73] The United States Information Media Funds contributed $119,000 and the Wilhelm Weinberg estate $100,000 to the medical center: *Ibid.*

[74] American Jewish JDC, *A Guide to Overseas Operations of the American Joint Distribution Committee*, 20-21; *American Jewish Year Book*, 1951, LII (Philadelphia: Jewish Publication Society of America, 1951), 128; 1952, LIII, 220; American JDC, *Malben* (Tel Aviv: JDC, n.d.), n.p.

[75] The American contribution to Keren Hayesod in percentages of total contributions are indicated in the following table, for which I am indebted to Deborah I. Offenbacher of United Israel Appeal:

August 1921–September 1929	55.2%
August 1929–September 1939	36.4%
October 1939–September 1945	63.4%
July 1946–March 1948	81. %
October 1948–March 1960	78. %

(While the term United Palestine Appeal was used sporadically in the 1920's, a permanent UPA (now UIA) was established in 1936.)

scope of American aid is evident in the figures for the agencies registered with the Advisory Committee on Voluntary Foreign Aid: in 1947 these agencies contributed only $5,000,000 for Palestine, but five years later the $30,000,000 represented a six-fold increase. In the decade 1949-1958 voluntary agencies provided a grand total of approximately $200,000,000 for Israel, a good part of which went for the improvement of health.[76] One gift was especially noteworthy: on December 20, 1955, David Dubinsky made front page headlines with the announcement that the International Ladies' Garment Workers Union had pledged $1,100,000 in gifts for a hospital and other institutions in Israel. This, the largest philanthropic contribution a labor union had ever made, called attention again to the fact that Israel had become a major recipient of American overseas philanthropy.[77]

This record was not achieved without new conflicts between Zionists and non-Zionists. James P. Warburg, to cite an example, criticized the United Jewish Appeal's fund-distributing policies for diverting money to political as opposed to charitable purposes. Denying the allegation, the agency was reported in 1960 to be engaged in a review of its fund-distribution methods.[78] Such differences did not, however, reflect seriously on the motives and the achievements of one of the most remarkable of all American overseas philanthropies in the field of relief, refugee aid, and technical help.

Although not operating within the strictly medical field, the American Foundation for the Blind did much to help the world's victims of blindness. The work started in 1915 when George A. Kessler, an American businessman, who, fearing for his life in the midst of the *Titanic* disaster, had vowed that if he survived he would devote himself to some humanitarian venture. He organized committees in several countries to help the war blind. In 1919 the American group was reconstituted as the American Braille Press for War and Civilian Blind. Its officers included William Nelson Cromwell, a prominent attorney, Helen Keller, and John Foster Dulles. In 1945 the agency was again reorganized as the American Foundation for the Overseas Blind.[79]

[76] Advisory Committee, *Reports*, 1949-1958; *New York Times*, August 20, 1961.
[77] Max D. Danish, *The World of David Dubinsky* (Cleveland: World, 1957), 185, 277, 279, discusses this and other ILGWU contributions to Israeli institutions.
[78] *New York Times*, March 18, 1960.
[79] "Forty Years of Overseas Service," *New Outlook for the Blind* XLIX (Nov., 1955), 325-28.

Among its many postwar activities, AFOB provided duplicating facilities and bore about 40 per cent of the cost of reproducing talking books on magnetic tape for libraries in many countries. In Tel Aviv, the Foundation together with the American-Israeli Lighthouse, helped to integrate the education of sightless children with those able to see. American groups paid the salaries for a time of two Israeli teachers especially trained in the United States. Operating also in the Far East, the Foundation conducted in Taiwan courses for blind farmers in rice paddy construction and planting as well as in poultry management and rabbit raising. Beginning in the early 1950's, AFOB, in cooperation with the Kellogg Foundation, maintained a Braille press in Mexico and helped inaugurate the first Latin American training program for teachers of the blind at the University of Chile.[80]

Medical aid programs at once dramatic and noteworthy owed their existence to the vision and dedication of their founders. One, Norman Cousins, raised funds for bringing to America for special treatment a group of young women whose lives had been largely ruined by disfigurement in the Hiroshima bombing. Plastic surgery enabled them to live normal lives.[81]

Dr. Thomas Dooley's work was more far-reaching. Shortly after the French collapse in Indo-China Dooley, at the time a lieutenant in the Navy, helped build refugee camps which cared for hundreds of thousands of fugitives from the advancing Communist forces. He put up and operated a hospital in Laos for the International Rescue Committee. On countless occasions he risked his own life in saving others, and half a million refugees regarded the American doctor as their savior. He did much more, of course, than to fight communism with medicine. Dr. Dooley was interested, not in preventive but in curative medicine, which, he explained, was his hold on life, his salvation. If some felt that this did not get at the heart of the problem, no one could question his resourcefulness or his ability to dramatize need. "There are few if any men," President Eisenhower said of him just after his death early in 1961, "who have exhibited his courage, self-sacrifice, faith in his God and readiness to serve his

[80] American Foundation for Overseas Blind, *Region by Region Summary of Field Service Activities 1958* (New York: AFOB, 1958), appendix, 1, 2, 6; Eric T. Boulter, Field Director of AFOB, to Merle Curti, March 6, 1959.

[81] See the articles by Norman Cousins in *Saturday Review* XXXVIII (April 9, 1955), 24-25; XXXIX (Dec. 15, 1956), 40; XL (Nov. 9, 1957), 41; XLI (June 14, 1958), 26.

fellowman." In accepting honorary cochairmanship of the Dr. Tom Dooley Tribute Fund, President Kennedy declared that he and those "who are following in his steps are providing a great humanitarian service and making friends for America in many parts of the world." [82]

In 1957 Dr. Dooley joined forces with Dr. Peter Comanduras of the George Washington University Medical School to found the Medical International Cooperation (MEDICO), dedicated to bringing direct, physician-to-patient medical aid to areas of the world where the need was especially great, and to teach and train others to give such modern medical service in remote regions. Taking over the small hospital that Dr. Dooley had established in Laos, MEDICO had founded by midsummer of 1961 fifteen projects in twelve nations. The program was financed by a growing number of contributors—70,000 by 1961—most of whom gave ten dollars or less. Leading pharmaceutical, hospital and surgical supply manufacturers contributed drug and equipment valued at over $3,000,000. Physicians associated with MEDICO volunteered their services, in many cases even paying their own travel and maintenance. At the annual meeting of the American Medical Association in 1961 MEDICO was acclaimed as a major international health agency.[83]

Another novel venture was HOPE (Health Opportunity for People Everywhere). This grew out of a plan advanced by President Eisenhower in the spring of 1956 known as the People-to-People Program. Inviting leaders in many fields to the White House, the President developed the idea that a voluntary effort in people-to-people partnership would be a dynamic and fruitful corollary to "elements already effectively at work in our foreign policy." [84] The chief outcome was the establishment of the People-to-People Health Foundation, a nonprofit citizens' organization headed by Dr. William Walsh, a Washington heart specialist, designed to carry out volunteer medical aid activities as part of the President's people-to-people idea.

[82] Thomas A. Dooley, *The Night They Burned the Mountain* (New York: Farrar, Cudahy and Straus, 1960) and *Deliver Us from Evil: the Story of Viet Nam's Flight to Freedom* (New York: Farrar, Cudahy and Straus, 1960); *New York Times*, Feb. 5, 1958, Feb. 3, 1961.

[83] Between August, 1959, and the first of June, 1960, MEDICO received $800,000 from American donors: *Philanthropic Digest* VI (June 1, 1960), 2; Peter D. Comanduras, "MEDICO" in International Rescue Committee, *Saving Freedom's Seed Corn*, 36-37; *New York Times*, July 2, 1961; *This is MEDICO . . . Serving those Who "Bear the Mark of Pain"* (New York: MEDICO, March 13, 1961).

[84] *New York Times*, June 1, 1956, Feb. 5, 1957; William Harlan Hale, "Every Man an Ambassador," *The Reporter* XVI (March 21, 1957), 18-22.

As a result of considerable activity, the government "demothed" a Navy hospital ship which was renamed HOPE and equipped with a staff to teach local personnel in Indonesia and Vietnam new techniques for combating malnutrition, tuberculosis, malaria, and yaws. On this floating hospital-medical school, staff members were to treat patients and hold consultations with local doctors, sending teams inland whenever possible.[85] The project met with criticism on the part of some who felt that more effective work was already being done at much less expense in American-supported overseas hospitals and training schools, and that the continuing support of this dramatic gesture was unassured. Although the government hoped that this pilot project for "a great white fleet" would be generously sponsored by the American people many felt that, if the government favored the idea, it could pay for it, and hence seemed reluctant to give. The *New York Times*, on the other hand, characteristically wrote, as HOPE set out from San Francisco in the early autumn of 1960 to visit eight Indonesian ports, that the experiment would "bear watching." [86]

After several months of work in Indonesia and Southeast Asia, HOPE sailed for home, docking in San Francisco on September 14, 1961. The undertaking left its sponsor, the People-to-People Health Foundation, $800,000 in debt. But Dr. Walsh reported that the first year's voyage had been a great success in providing healing and medical knowledge in areas where it was greatly appreciated and in creating a "good image" of the United States. Both Indonesia and South Vietnam asked for a return visit and invitations were received from South Korea, Pakistan, and several South American countries. The Indonesian government planned to build its own HOPE for use among its islands and the British and Scandinavian countries were considering similar ventures. Dr. Walsh set a goal of $10,000,000 to finance two additional HOPE ships.[87]

In the large conception of technical aid to underdeveloped areas, attention was given not only to over-all education for the development of trained manpower and leadership and for improved health

[85] Eileen Summers, "U. S. White Fleet Idea Is Launched," *Washington Post*, March 11, 1959; *New York Times*, June 31, 1960.

[86] *New York Times*, Sept. 11, 22, 1960. A goal of $3,500,000 was set for voluntary contributions, the estimated cost of the first year's operations. American President Lines agreed to operate the ship on a nonprofit basis.

[87] *New York Times*, August 27, Sept. 15, 1961.

but also to industrial growth. Convinced that even in a quasi-socialistic economy such as that toward which India seemed headed, private enterprise had a contribution to make, the Ford Foundation during the years 1951-1957 allocated, in addition to almost $6,000,000 for economic research which bore on industrial as well as on rural problems, over $5,000,000 for the development of small industries, the training of engineers, and the enhancement of managerial skill.[88]

But the great emphasis of all the voluntary agencies was on rural problems. This was appropriate in view of the concentration of population in farming villages, the problem of land tenure, and the need of increasing the food supply. The main approach was to attack inadequate food production, a basic cause of the woes of millions of underfed people.

Having pioneered in efforts to improve agricultural methods, missionary organizations, as we have seen, expanded and organized their work in this field. While not strictly missionary in character, several new agencies owed their existence to religious motives. World Assistance and World Neighbors, for example, offered, among other types of technical aid, better breeds of milk cows and poultry, hybrid seeds, insecticides and other disease-combating materials in villages in Brazil, India, and other countries.[89] The Congregational Christian Service Committee's HELP project in Sardinia, discussed earlier in connection with the refugee problem, was a rural rehabilitation project as well as a means of providing permanent homes and useful work for "hard core" DP's. Another program was International Church Service in Greek Villages, a multinational team of young people supported by World Church Service who taught modern agricultural methods to backward villages in northern Greece. An Italian team, modeled on the Greek, began a similar project in southern Italy in 1958.[90] An early participant in agricultural improvement, the Brethren Service Commission in the postwar years cooperated

[88] Ford Foundation, *Annual Report*, 1957, 44-45; *Steelmen for India: The Indian Steel Training and Educational Program in the United States 1957-1958: An Undertaking of American Private Industry, Philanthropy, and Education* (n.p.: August 15, 1957), *passim*. It should be noted that a share of the $25,000,000 allocated in these years for education and vocational training was directed toward industrial development. For the part of the United States Steel Foundation in the program see Blough, *Free Man and the Corporation*, 119.

[89] Laubach, *The World Is Learning Compassion*, 199-201. Mention should also be made of the AWAKE program of the Koinonia Foundation of Baltimore which trained Christian technical workers for overseas service.

[90] Church World Service, "The Overseas Program for 1958," 28-30.

with UNRRA in an experimental program which sent fifty young men to teach and supervise Chinese farmers in the use of tractors. In 1947 a "goodwill mission" accompanied a shipment of cattle to Addis Ababa, staying long enough to help improve methods of animal husbandry. In 1950 the Brethren Service Committee and the Foreign Mission Commission placed a married couple on the staff of the Asaba Rural Training Center, which was maintained by several Protestant denominations in Nigeria to teach agriculture, forestry, and rural arts.[91]

A significant agricultural program was started by Dan West, who represented the Brethren in Spain during the Civil War. His common sense suggested that long-range security might be advanced if Americans sent dairy cattle abroad instead of tinned milk. Heifer Project's first load of livestock reached Puerto Rico in 1944. Supported by Protestant and Catholic agencies, the Project shipped overseas during the years 1944 to 1955 some 10,000 cattle, 390,000 chickens, 8,000 goats, and smaller numbers of sheep, pigs, ducklings, rabbits and beehives.[92] The need was publicized among members of church and nonchurch groups, who then contributed animals from their own herds or who gave funds for the purchase of livestock. Local authorities and church officials selected the recipients.

The impact was considerable. Galo Plaza, former president of Ecuador, writing in 1956 to Thurl Metzger, executive director of the Heifer Project, expressed appreciation in words similar to those used by many others who knew the program at first hand: "I am frankly amazed at the amount of good Heifer Project has done and is doing on such limited funds. More power to you and may God help you in carrying out for many, many years to come your splendid work." M. Yavuz Gor, of the Turkish Embassy in Washington, declared that "so much good will has been built up by Heifer Project that it is really hard to express in words the moral value of this simple but down to earth idea. . . ."[93]

One of the most interesting examples of technical assistance in the rural field was the work of Msgr. Joseph J. Harnett in Viet-Nam. With the support of Catholic Relief Services thousands of refugees

[91] Weiss, *Ten Years of Brethren Service*, 42, 47.

[92] *Heifer Project Inc.* (n.p., n.d.).

[93] Plaza to Metzger, Feb. 2, 1956; Gor to the *Washington Evening Post*, Jan. 23, 1955 (mimeographed copies distributed by the Heifer Project).

who crowded into Saigon were resettled in four hundred new villages carved from the jungle with bulldozers provided by an American agency and with funds from official sources and from Catholic Relief Services. The village groups founded their own cooperatives for charcoal making, mat making, mosquito net production and other commodities. In this exodus no one died of hunger or want and a new and useful life enabled the refugees to care for themselves.[94]

Business corporations as well as religious agencies contributed to the improvement of agriculture in the countries in which they operated. A few examples must illustrate what many corporations began increasingly to do. Firestone, for instance, gave to 760 Liberian farmers young and sturdy rubber trees, provided technical help in cultivating them, and transported the product to the coast. Efforts were also made to develop in Liberia a breed of disease-resistant cattle.[95] In Honduras, the American Fruit Company built the Pan American School of Agriculture, endowed it with $6,000,000, and helped many of the 3,000 students that attended it. If this was not a disinterested act and if the sums involved represented a proportionately small outgo in terms of what the company had made in Central America, the school in contributing to increased yields did greatly benefit the native population. To cite another example, Shell Company of Venezuela established in 1952 the Shell Agricultural Service which provided land and support for experimental work in agronomy, agricultural engineering, and entomology. The project was important in view of the unhealthy dependence of the Venezuelan economy on the extraction of oil from its reserves.[96] Still another example of aid to overseas agriculture was the response of commercial poultry producers in Virginia to a call for the donation of 5,000 chicks and eggs to launch the industry in Jordan and the offer of the Arabian American Oil Company to transport freight and personnel.[97]

Sensitive to the importance of getting at causes of low living

---

[94] Eileen Egan to Merle Curti, August 23, 1961; Francis J. Corley, "Viet-Nam Since Geneva," *Thought* XXXIII (Winter, 1958-59), 527.

[95] Taylor, *Firestone Operations in Liberia*, 95.

[96] Rusk, *Technical Assistance Quarterly Bulletin*, 10-11.

[97] U. S., Congress, Senate, Foreign Relations Committee, Subcommittee on Technical Assistance Programs, *Government Utilization of Private Agencies in Technical Assistance*, Jan. 9, 1956, prepared by Alwyn V. Freeman, Staff Study 5 (Washington: Govt. Printing Office, 1956), 14 [hereafter cited as *Freeman Study*].

standards, agencies that had emphasized emergency relief increasingly undertook technical aid programs in agriculture. Thus Save the
Children Federation sponsored a project in Papades, Greece, in which
apple and almond trees were first planted, after which provision was
made for the introduction of lambs and beehives. On the basis of
these, the community gained enough confidence to embark on a
2,000 man-hour land-terracing undertaking which promised to raise
income from the land thirteen-fold.[98] Or take still another example.
After CARE began in 1949 its self-help program in Europe through
the distribution of seed packages, it turned its attention to countries
in even greater need. When the modern plows it distributed in India
proved unsuited to agricultural conditions, it introduced a modified
plow, considerably superior to the traditional Indian one, which was
readily accepted. Or again: Asia Foundation's Seeds for Democracy
distributed 4,000,000 packets of seeds to farm and village organizations.[99]

These projects were overshadowed by programs of older and larger
foundations. In 1943 the Rockefeller Foundation in cooperation with
the Mexican Ministry of Agriculture initiated a program to improve
the maize yield. Controlled experiments tested the productiveness,
disease resistance, and other characteristics of the many varieties of
maize grown all over the country. Out of this developed the famous
bank of corn germ plasm. An expanding program, in which much
emphasis was put on participation of Mexican scientists, included
similar genetic and cytological investigations of beans, wheat, and
forage crops. The improved varieties of these basic staples, together
with progress in controlling pests and blights, enabled Mexican
agriculture to shift, in one category or another, from a food-import-
ing to a self-sufficient or even a food-exporting economy. Similar
programs in Colombia and Chile produced measurable results in
increased production of high quality, rust-resistant varieties of corn,
beans, wheat, and other food-crops. In 1957 the Rockefeller Foundation initiated similar programs of cooperation with the agricultural
ministries of a number of Far East countries. Of these the International Rice Institute, to the support of which the Ford Foundation
and the Philippine government also contributed, held promise for

[98] Save the Children Federation, *Annual Report*, 1958, 15, 17.
[99] Asia Foundation, *The Asia Foundation*, n.p.

meeting shortages of the great staple food of so many areas of the two hemispheres.[100]

Independent of the Rockefeller Foundation but similar in emphasizing self-help was the Rockefeller Brothers Fund established in 1940 by the five grandsons of the original "John D." Scientific research, education, and intercultural relations were supported by annual contributions from the family. Latin America was the focus of activity. The choice was no doubt related both to the traditional interest of the family and the Foundation in a part of the world that had provided a substantial part of the Rockefeller fortune and to the experience of Nelson Rockefeller in directing a government technical aid program in Latin America during the Second World War.[101] Along with private persons and business organizations, the Fund contributed to the American International Association for Economic and Social Development, founded independently by the five brothers in 1946 to encourage self-development in achieving better standards of living and in promoting cooperation and understanding among peoples throughout the world. In the decade 1946-1955 American International Association spent approximately $6,500,000 in Brazil, Venezuela and India, the host governments countering with funds of approximately the same magnitude.[102]

Accepting an invitation from the governor of Minas Gerais in Brazil, the AIA fathered the Association of Credit and Rural Assistance. This supported the supervised credit technique in an effort to help small farmers make use of fertilizers, improved seeds, livestock, insecticides, and scientific practices of soil conservation, crop rotation, and irrigation. It sponsored demonstrations and loaned farmers equipment with which to try new methods on their own land. From the start emphasis was put on moving the entire program, which included health, home improvement, and educational features, into Brazilian hands.[103] In cooperation with governmental

[100] Jacob G. Harrar, *The Agricultural Program of the Rockefeller Foundation* (New York: Rockefeller Foundation, 1956); Rockefeller Foundation, *Annual Report*, 1959, 17; *New York Times*, August 29, 1960.

[101] Rockefeller Brothers Fund, *Report*, 1959 (Garden City, N. Y.: Doubleday, 1960), 3-10. At the request of the Ghanian Social Welfare Department, the Fund helped to develop in the African republic an inexpensive method of making bricks and tiles (the block press method) for do-it-yourself inexpensive housing.

[102] American International Association for Economic and Social Development, *Annual Report*, 1956, n.p.

[103] *Ibid.*; Arthur T. Mosher, *Case Study of the Agricultural Program of ACAR in Brazil*, National Planning Association's Technical Cooperation in Latin America Series (Washington: National Planning Association, 1955), *passim*.

authorities and with the substantial support of five American oil companies, the American International Association also initiated programs for the improvement of agricultural production in Venezuela. Moving into related areas, the AIA shrewdly combined self-help and business enterprise through the International Basic Economy Corporation, an investment agency which provided Latin America with technical assistance for the invention and development of soluble coffee, the introduction of pasteurized milk, and the mass distribution of food at low prices through supermarkets.[104] Finally, the Joint India Project, developed with the Cooperative League of America, studied the problems and potentialities of agricultural cooperatives in India.

The carefully integrated community emphasis of the Rockefellers in Brazil and Venezuela was not, however, the first example of a technical assistance program in which the welfare of a specific area was advanced through coordinated services in agriculture, vocational training, home care, and health. Even before the Second World War far-sighted pathbreakers increasingly felt that no single program, whether in education, sanitation and health, or in agriculture, was in itself sufficient to improve substantially the living standards or to overcome the pull of tradition.

No agency did such effective pioneering in the improvement of community life as a whole and in developing the total personality of its inhabitants as the Near East Foundation did in 48 Macedonian villages in the 1930's and in its postwar programs in Syria, Eritrea, Iran and other countries. Under the leadership of Dr. Harold B. Allen, director of education in the Foundation, and a group of lieutenants who shared his vision and practicality, the principle was developed of bettering the community through improving the economy, health, the home, and recreational life. At every step, the objective was to help all age groups, but especially the young, to realize a larger measure of their potentialities. All this was done, not by imposing drastic changes from without, but by effecting gradual change from within. This involved the cooperation of the government—nothing was undertaken except on invitation and assurance of

---

[104] American International Association for Economic and Social Development, *Annual Report*, 1956, n.p.; "Doing Good Abroad: Latin American Laboratory," *The Economist* CLXXXIX (Dec. 6, 1958), 895-96.

support and in the expectation that the government would in time take responsibility for programs that had proved successful. It also involved the idea of self-help. In the educational programs pupils quickly took on the role of teaching others. Nothing was given as charity, nor was there any paid labor. Working with the villagers and involving them in planning as well as in executing programs, the Foundation's field staff took into account local conditions, resources, and needs. It sent carefully selected young men to America for special training. It enlisted well-chosen Americans trained in nutrition, child care, and home making who worked with native women in the delicate task of improving family life. Boys and girls were encouraged to take part in organizations resembling 4-H clubs.

When Dr. M. L. Wilson, Director of Extension in the United States Department of Agriculture, visited the Macedonian project in 1938, he felt that the Near East Foundation had skillfully and with marked success adapted many of the methods of the county agents and extension workers to a culture very different from that of America.[105] His judgment was borne out in the evidences of larger agricultural yields, improved sanitation, water supply, health, and initiative. The war, which struck Greece in 1940, liquidated most of the program. But when Dr. Allen returned to the Macedonian demonstration villages in 1948 he was glad to find that what had been learned earlier was being applied in reconstructing war-torn areas.[106]

Although the Near East Foundation in the postwar years undertook projects in several countries, including Syria and Lebanon, its work in Iran has special interest. In 1946 the Foundation accepted an invitation from the Iranian government to develop a community improvement program in five villages on the Veramin Plain thirty miles from Tehran. Lyle J. Hayden, who had been brought up on an Illinois farm, was the happy choice as director, for his technical knowledge and skill in human relations were much needed. With two peasant helpers he began farm demonstrations in the village where he was living. A school was started in which forty young men learned modern agricultural practices and public sanitation. Latrines were built, pools covered, swampy areas drained and sprayed. Farm yields

---

[105] Harold B. Allen, *Rural Reconstruction in Action: Experience in the Near and Middle East* (Ithaca: Cornell University Press, 1953), ix.
[106] *Ibid.*, 116-23.

increased; illiteracy diminished. The influence spread from village to village.[107]

Relations between voluntary organizations and the United States government in technical aid varied according to the agency and the situation. From the inception of the Technical Cooperation Administration (Point 4) in the early summer of 1950 its director, Dr. Henry Garland Bennett, sought to have his staff learn all they could from the voluntary agency people, particularly the Near East Foundation and the missionaries, whose pioneering work he admired. His precept was largely forgotten after his untimely death: government technicians and administrators in overseas assignments for the most part did not want to be associated in the minds of the people among whom they worked with "proselyting" missionaries. But the partnership initially envisioned between the Point 4 program and nonofficial agencies was nevertheless implemented in some part. The contracts stipulated that programs be nonsectarian and free from proselyting; that the services of the voluntary agencies be requested by the host government and that the agencies enjoy the good will of those among whom they worked; and that the soundness of their administrative experience be clear. Agencies also had to prove their ability to work within the frame-work of local customs, encourage self-improvement in the training of local leaders, and relate operations to the over-all Point 4 program insofar as possible.[108]

The attitudes of voluntary agencies toward the entrance of government into a field they had largely preempted varied. Many, realizing the magnitude of the work to be done and painfully aware of the limitations imposed by their own meager resources, welcomed the program. Some of these felt that their experience qualified them

[107] U. S., Congress, Senate, Committee on Foreign Relations, Subcommittee on Technical Assistance Programs, *Technical Assistance*, 85th Cong., 1st Sess., 1957, Sen. Rpt. 139, 310 [hereafter cited as *Technical Assistance Report*]; American Council of Voluntary Agencies for Foreign Service, *The Role of Voluntary Agencies in Technical Assistance*, 67-68, 106-07; U. S. Department of State, International Cooperation Administration, United States Operations Mission to Iran, *Annual Report*, June 30, 1956 (Washington: Govt. Printing Office, 1956), 13; U. S. Department of State, International Cooperation Administration, *Report of Regional Conference NEA Community Development*, Tehran, Iran, Nov. 27-30, 1954 (Washington: Govt. Printing Office, 1955), 97.

[108] U. S., *Statutes at Large*, LXIV, Pt. 1, 204; *Technical Assistance Report*, 299, 302 ff.; Lewis M. Hoskins, "Voluntary Agencies and Foundations in International Aid," *Annals of the American Academy of Political and Social Science* CCCXXIX (May, 1960), 65; *Freeman Study*, 3.

to accomplish the objectives of Point 4 if given sufficient government funds. On the other hand, some agencies feared the competition of a large, well-financed government agency. It seemed to them,
as it did to so many Americans, that any government program, being
political in nature, was bound to operate in terms of interest rather
than service. Many felt that since officials must deal with the host
government rather than with the people on the village level, the
Point 4 program must be less effective than their own people-to-
people approach (forgetting, sometimes, that they themselves worked
in a country only with the approval of and under conditions laid
down by the central government).

Several agencies accepted contracts from Point 4 and enlarged
the programs to which they were committed. Of the agencies that
took this course some, in the judgment of a Point 4 official who
saw much of the overseas field work, did admirably, some moder-
ately well, some badly.[109] Other voluntary agencies hesitated to accept contracts lest, in becoming identified with Washington foreign
policy and bureaucracy, they forfeit the advantages their independent
and voluntary character gave them.

It is impossible in a brief account to present concrete examples
of all the positions and all the outcomes in the spectrum of govern-
ment-voluntary agency relations. But many of the basic issues can
be illustrated by reference to the experiences of four agencies.

The Near East Foundation, with its impressive record in education, sanitation, and agriculture, provided patterns which greatly
influenced the newly established Point 4 program. In several countries it had trained leaders and specialists indispensable to carrying
out an official American program. Yet, fearing that a close relationship with the United States government might curtail its freedom
and identify it in the minds of Near East people with official foreign
policy, the Foundation hesitated when the Point 4 administration
offered it a contract which provided government funds for enlarging
its own program. It finally accepted—with misgivings. Fortunately
these did not materialize. The Near East Foundation, thus involved
directly with two governments, that of Iran and that of the United
States, succeeded in working reasonably well with both. Supplementary support from the Ford Foundation enabled it to enlarge and
enrich its work still further. The program expanded from the five

---

[109] Mrs. Delia W. Kuhn, Point 4, to Merle Curti, August 14, 1961. I am indebted
to Mrs. Kuhn for some of the interpretations in this discussion.

original villages to almost five hundred, all of which were served by young men trained in one of its eighty schools. There were some failures, and what was done was, to be sure, little in terms of actual need. But given the difficulties imposed by thousands of years of tradition and problems inherent in changing basic customs in a culture very different from that of the United States, the Near East Foundation's record, expanded by new sources of support, including that of the United States Government, provided impressive evidence of possibilities.[110]

A project which the American Friends Service Committee undertook under a contract with the Technical Cooperation Administration provided another test of the advantages and limitations of cooperation between voluntary and government agencies. Like the Near East Foundation, AFSC had a fund of experience in rehabilitation through the self-help formula. To be sure, the Friends were not successful in every case in reaching the immediate goal of reconciling distrust and conflict through love, as the destruction of buildings and experimental plots in an agricultural-aid project during riots in Jordan in 1956 was to show. But they were not easily discouraged and, at the request of the Jordanian government, established a new program in 1960. The reputation of the Committee for wise and selfless giving as a testimony to human fellowship promised much in whatever was undertaken.[111]

These achievements included specific experience in India both in the emergency relief administered with British Friends in the Bengal famine during the Second World War and in the cooperative improvement projects initiated in India's Orissa and Madhya Pradesh regions to assist villagers organize ten-year community-wide programs in agricultural production, health, primary and adult education, and village industry.[112] After assuring itself that AFSC, though related to a church group, in no sense engaged in proselyting activities, the Technical Cooperation Administration asked it to undertake a program in India.

---

[110] *Technical Assistance Report,* 310; U. S. Operations Mission to Iran, *Annual Report,* June 30, 1956, 13; U. S., International Cooperation Administration, *Report of Regional Conference NEA Community Development, Tehran, Iran,* Nov. 27-30, 1954, 97; American Council of Voluntary Agencies for Foreign Service, *The Role of Voluntary Agencies in Technical Assistance,* 67-68, 106-07.

[111] American Friends Service Committee, *Annual Report,* 1956, 6.

[112] American Friends Service Committee, *Annual Report,* 1948, 16; 1949, 11; 1952, 4-5.

Like many voluntary agencies, the American Friends Service Committee had welcomed Point 4 since the needs of peoples overseas for technical assistance were far greater than nongovernment organizations could meet. The Committee hoped that the experience it had come by in working at the grassroot level might be useful in government programs. At the same time Committee officers expressed apprehension over the growing tendency of political and military considerations to affect foreign aid programs.[113] Moral conviction and love, not self-interest, were more likely, the Friends felt, to yield "the kind of projects that help people develop social sterngth." [114]

Up to this time the AFSC had not accepted government funds save in special circumstances and it now gave much thought to the matter of a contract with the Technical Cooperation Administration. It was an open question whether its freedom might not be unduly restricted and whether it might not be associated by those it was helping with the foreign and military policies of the United States government. In June, 1951, however, AFSC signed a contract with the Technical Cooperation Administration for rural demonstation and local worker-training projects in India, the government of which indicated a special preference for the AFSC. The contract which allocated $375,000 to the Committee, was renewed in 1954.

Aware from much experience of the importance of careful planning, the AFSC sent to India a survey team which took into account many factors relevant to the choice of areas in which to work. These included the attitudes, prejudices, and needs of the villagers. A rural sociologist who had been brought up in Orissa, which seemed to have special needs, found among the villagers fear, suspicion, and distrust toward the proposed project. Yet the difficulties and tensions that discouraged other agencies from choosing such a location were only a challenge to AFSC. The final choice was two areas, one in the Damodar area of Bihar and one in the Hirakud area of Orissa, comprising in all some fifty villages. Both Indians and Americans made up the AFSC field teams. These approached the task with imagination, flexibility, patience, and common sense. In training villagers

---

[113] Lewis M. Hoskins to Merle Curti, June 20, 1961; Lewis M. Hoskins to Henry G. Bennet, Administrator, Technical Cooperation Administration, June 22, 1951, in the files of the American Council of Voluntary Agencies for Foreign Service, New York, N. Y.

[114] Statement of Howard M. Teaf, Jr., U. S., Congress, Senate, Foreign Relations Committee, Subcommittee on Technical Assistance Programs, *Hearings, Technical Assistance Programs,* 84th Cong., 1st Sess., Feb. 24, 1955, 227 ff.

to guide the community in improving farming methods, health, and the crafts, every effort was made to work closely with Indian officials and with the villagers themselves. Pressure for quick results was resisted because the staff appreciated the fact that the villagers had never had any concept of change. One day a man in a village where an improved breed of cock had been distributed told a staff member that the eggs from his hens were infertile, but that if he could have another cock, he would try again. A visitor overhearing the remark observed that in his twenty-five years in India he had never known a villager to make such an open complaint or not to ascribe such a misfortune to a fate that made all his own efforts futile. "Incidents of this kind," said the visitor, "lead me to believe that the whole mentality of the peasants is changing and that they now believe that improvement can and must come." [115]

By 1956 a good deal had been accomplished. The AFSC appreciated the assurance of support over a period of time if a project were to have a fair chance of succeeding. It also appreciated the cooperative attitude of the officials in the Technical Cooperation Administration and its successor, the International Cooperation Administration. But in the autumn of 1956 the Committee expressed "profound disappointment" in being unable to continue its contractual relationship with ICA because of the latter's insistence that AFSC personnel be subject to a security check before appointment. This had not hitherto been required and the AFSC felt that it could not in conscience become part of the security check system, especially since the sources of derogatory information were unavailable to a candidate, who was thus unable to refute such information. The Committee did not dispute the right of the government to screen its own employees but it objected to the extension of the system to the voluntary agencies working under contract with government money. The AFSC was able to carry on with funds privately raised from the general public. [116]

The AFSC's misgivings about the association of technical aid with

[115] U. S., Congress, Senate, Foreign Relations Committee, Subcommittee on Technical Assistance Programs, *Hearings, Technical Assistance Programs*, 84th Cong., 1st Sess., Feb. 24, 1955, 229; Howard M. Teaf, Jr., "Origins of a Private Village Improvement Project," *Hands Across Frontiers: Case Studies in Technical Cooperation*, Howard M. Teaf, Jr., and Peter G. Franck, eds. (Ithaca: Cornell University Press, 1955), 65-125.

[116] Hoskins, *Annals of the American Academy of Political and Social Science*, 65; Lewis M. Hoskins, AFSC, to Charles Taft, Nov. 2, 1956, Advisory Committee Files.

foreign policy were shared by kindred agencies. In contrasting the impact of voluntary agencies with that of government-fostered programs, the director of the Heifer Project expressed the view that "foreign aid has become a tool in the fight against communism. Political groups abroad quickly learn that if there is no real communist threat in their countries they had better create one in order to qualify for American aid. Opposition groups in these same countries charge subservience to American desires and say we are buying friendship. . . . We also show a tendency to assist the countries that will align themselves with us militarily, thus giving our foreign critics an opportunity to say that we are primarily interested in recruiting front-line soldiers to defend American shores." [117]

The cooperation of government and voluntary agencies in technical aid was further tested in an educational project of the Unitarian Service Committee.[118] The Ministry of Education of the newly independent kingdom of Cambodia was seeking from the Foreign Operations Administration assistance in meeting the desperate need for extension and improvement of education in rural areas.[119] At this point the USC was asked to undertake a project under contract which would fit in with a program being initiated by Dr. Samuel Adams, chief of education in the United States Operations Mission (USOM) for Cambodia.

The period between an exploratory visit to Cambodia by Miss Helen Fogg of the Unitarian Service Committee and the actual signing of a contract some eight months later was one of frustration for the Committee. The document which finally emerged proved unsatisfactory when it was later subjected to rigorous interpretation after the establishment of a Contract Office in what had become the International Cooperation Administration. Before the Unitarian Service Committee could send a staff to Cambodia, there was also a serious problem of maintaining communication with USOM. Only a couple of months before the actual signing of the contract the

[117] Thurl Metzger, "Regarding Foreign Aid," *Christian Century* LXXV (Sept. 10, 1958), 1015.

[118] The following account is based on interviews with Miss Helen Fogg and Mrs. Curtice Hitchcock of the Unitarian Service Committee, June, 1960, and with Miss Joan Kain of the Advisory Committee, June, 1960, as well as on a letter from Mrs. Hitchcock to the author, May 29, 1961, and on the Unitarian Service Committee papers in the Advisory Committee Files.

[119] For a statement of American contributions, and especially of those of Dr. Samuel Adams of USOM, see John C. Caldwell, *Let's Visit Americans Overseas: The Story of Foreign Aid, The Voice of America, Military Assistance, Overseas Bases* (New York: Day, 1958), 45-46.

USC discovered that under pressure of the enthusiasm and impatience of the Cambodians, USOM had agreed to speed up the original program and to establish at once a new teacher-training institution, a task the USC had contemplated only at the end of a three-year buildup.

The contract was drawn between the Unitarian Service Committee and the Royal Government of Cambodia, a practice then in vogue in ICA but one that resulted in great difficulties for the USC. Construction of the buildings for the Center, including housing for the Americans, was to be the responsibility of the Cambodian Government, to be completed before the arrival of the USC staff. Several members of the USC staff had to devote the major part of their energies to the construction program, putting up meanwhile with interim housing which was very far from meeting minimum American standards. It was also because of this original contractual arrangement that the USC staff were at one point denied the medical services available at the Embassy to all official American personnel. Having no legal right to assistance in these matters, the Unitarian Service Committee at the same time had no way of enforcing its legal claims on the government of Cambodia. The first year was a tough experience for the staff in the field and for those in Boston who felt responsible for their trials. These frictions were eventually resolved.

But when an extended contract was made with ICA, it brought new problems. The complicated and rigorous procedures required when operating under a contract modeled on a commercial pattern, which ICA established in the interest of efficiency, took no account of the nonprofit nature of such a voluntary agency as USC. In the words of a staff member, it threatened "to destroy the spontaneity and the freedom and speed of action which should be one of the contributions a voluntary agency can make." A USC officer close to the whole experience wrote, "If another voluntary agency asked my advice about entering into a contract with ICA I don't know what I'd say but probably it would be: 'If you can stand frustration, if you can adapt to changes of plan in midstream without being consulted, if you can keep your temper when being unjustly blamed for delays and so forth, go ahead.' "

Such a spirit, a heritage from the early days of the Unitarian Service Committee and a continuing characteristic of its staff, figured in the success that was the final reward for refusing to give up to administrative snarls, misunderstandings, and unanticipated developments. In the estimation of seasoned American educators, the achievements of the Rural Education Demonstration and Training Center at Kampong Kantuot turned out to be impressive.[120]

Similar in many ways to antecedent agencies with technical aid programs, International Voluntary Services,[121] chartered in 1953, was in other respects unique. It was planned deliberately to align government effort in technical assistance with the experience and altruistic purposes of voluntary agencies. It operated on the conviction that well-trained and carefully supervised youth, dedicated to sharing their skills and experiences with people at the local level in underdeveloped countries, could contribute both to the welfare of these countries and to the broad purposes of American foreign policy.[122]

The Christian character of IVS was reflected in its original board of directors: a member was appointed from each of fifteen denominations (one Catholic and fourteen Protestant groups), all of whom were experienced in the administration of projects in underdeveloped countries. Proselytizing was, however, forbidden, and subsequently the board was enlarged to include personnel from the land grant colleges and from the World Federation of Country Women.

In addition to government funds provided by the Foreign Operations Administration and its successor, International Cooperation Administration, IVS drew support from the Ford Foundation, the Rockefeller Brothers Fund, Arabian American Oil Company, and World Neighbors. The sums designated for the various projects ranged from $400,000 for agricultural education, home child care, health, and sanitation in an Iraq area of 185 villages to the $12,500 earmarked for a low-cost housing project in Ghana which demonstrated the feasibility of using Cinva-Ram earth-cement building blocks. By 1960 projects had been completed in Egypt, Jordan, Iraq and Nepal. In the same year some 60 young workers, serving at

---

[120] Willard A. Hanna, "The State of the States of Indo-China," *Bungkarnos Indonesia: A Collection of 25 reports written for the American Universities Field Staff*, Willard A. Hanna, ed. (New York: American Universities Field Staff, 1960), 13-15.

[121] For the achievements of what was in some sense an early European counterpart, Le Service Civil International, with national branches which in Great Britain took the title International Voluntary Services for Peace, see Pacificus, "Manual Workers for Peace," *Contemporary Review* CLXXXVIII (Sept., 1955), 185-88.

[122] Technical Assistance Information Clearing House, *Directory of American Voluntary and Non-Profit Agencies Interested in Technical Assistance*, Wayland Zwayer, ed. (New York: American Council of Voluntary Agencies for Foreign Service, 1960), 131-32; J. S. Noffsinger, executive director of International Voluntary Services, to Merle Curti, July 10, 1961.

slightly more than maintenance costs, were working on the local level with natives of Ghana, Vietnam, and Laos. Commendation of the work done came from both voluntary agencies and from government officials.[123] An Arab leader in Jordan, to cite one example, felt that a single IVS team which developed a poultry farm to supply the Arabian American Oil Company—a project which cost roughly only $12,000 a year—contributed more to an understanding between the Near East and the West than the combined efforts of the UN and the ICA. Several factors seem to explain the success of IVS. It maintained its own identity as a voluntary agency, thus profiting from the reputation of these organizations for independence from official policy. At the same time it worked closely with ICA and other government agencies: on one occasion the anthropologist who evaluated its teams, citing proof of the success of official aid in Vietnam, refuted the charge of a Scripps-Howard reporter who had publicly condemned a project as an "outrageous scandal." [124] Also important in its success was the dedication and skill of the youth working in the overseas field. In providing an example and in arousing the interest of congressmen, International Voluntary Services contributed directly to the establishment of the Peace Corps in the early months of the Kennedy administration.[125]

Despite the vexing problems experienced by the Unitarian Service Committee and by the American Friends Service Committee, the partnership of the voluntary agencies and the United States government in technical assistance worked fairly well and proved mutually advantageous.[126] Government support enabled the voluntary agencies to accomplish a great deal more than would have been possible by relying on gifts alone. The advantage of having assurance through the duration of the contract of continuing support for a given project was also of great value. The record lends support to the point that the voluntary agencies had distinctive contributions to make in carrying through technical assistance projects: they could select personnel with more care than was possible in large government agencies; they could attract willing and dedicated men and

[123] *Technical Assistance Report*, 309 ff.
[124] *New York Times*, August 8, 1959.
[125] Dr. J. S. Noffsinger to Merle Curti, July 21, 1961; U. S., Congress, House, Committee on Foreign Affairs, *Mutual Security Act of 1960*, 86th Cong., 2d Sess., 1960, House Rpt. 1464, 28.
[126] Julius A. Elias, "Relations between Voluntary Agencies and International Organizations," *Journal of International Affairs* VII (1953), 30-34.

women of high professional competence who would have hesitated
for one reason or another to enter government service; and they generally developed friendly cooperation with local personnel by soften-
ing suspicions that technical aid was only another form of power
politics.[127]

Unlike some of the voluntary agencies, the foundations in general did not have financial support from the American government.
Their programs supplemented official undertakings of government
and intergovernment agencies. What the foundations did was, however, seldom initiated without the approval of Washington. In addition to other motives, the desire to help the uncommitted newer
nations withstand the blandishments of the Communist bloc and
move toward higher economic levels played a part in foundation ex-
terprises. It is likely that their trustees and executives would have
shared the satisfaction of H. Rowan Gaither, President of the
Ford Foundation, in pointing out that while the Foundation was not
the handmaiden of any government, it was of "special significance
that no statesman or official of government, either our own or of the
United Nations or of the countries where we have worked, have
ever differed with our major premises." [128]

The limitations of what the voluntary agencies and foundations
did in the all but boundless field of technical aid were clear enough.
With the meager resources in hand, achievements at best only
scratched the surface. In developing programs, the voluntary agencies
faced many of the same obstacles experienced by the much larger
official undertakings. These included the pull of ancient institutions and habits. It was all but impossible to measure progress in
acceptance of ideas and ways of life vastly different from those rooted
in a culture. Steps taken toward the solution of a problem often
raised other issues. Thus, after thirty years of experience in administering official and nonofficial famine relief in China and in promoting transportation and flood control, John Earl Baker sharply focused
a formidable problem during his association with the Joint Commission for Rural Reconstruction in Taiwan. Food production was
increased at the rate of 10 per cent a year; but the population was at

[127] The evidence for these points is impressive. See, for example, U. S. Congress,
Senate, *Foreign Aid Program: Compilation of Studies and Surveys prepared under the
direction of the Special Committee to study the Foreign Aid Program*, 85th Cong.,
1st Sess., 1957, Sen. Doc. 52, 1570, and Bock, *Fifty Years of Technical Assistance*, 12 ff.

[128] H. Rowan Gaither, Jr., "The Ford Foundation and Foreign Affairs: An Address
Delivered . . . at the Twenty-fifth Year Service Dinner of Dunwoody Industrial Institute, Minneapolis, May 3, 1956" (copy in the possession of the author).

the same time increasing 15 per cent a year. Taiwan officials, citing the doctrine of Sun Yat Sen to the effect that a nation's strength is its manpower, opposed birth control.[129]

Nor was it apparent, at least in the short run, that technical aid, even when offered and directed by nonofficial agencies, was helping very much in man's overarching problem—the East-West conflict. In taking steps in 1957 to develop the agricultural, medical, and biological sciences in Communist Poland and in facilitating an exchange of knowledge through fellowships to Polish scientists and scholars, the Rockefeller and Ford foundations did, to be sure, open a narrow door which held promise. But it was uncertain how much this might mean.[130]

At the same time it was also clear that technical aid under private auspices or in partnership with the government had won significant, if small, successes. It was also evident that, being regarded as largely disinterested altruism, voluntary services possessed many advantages over official programs. Even the most severe critics of foreign aid as it was exemplified in overseas fields did not include in their indictment privately supported agencies.[131] If the small funds and limited personnel of the voluntary agencies partly explained the better administrative record, the point is still important.

As the 1960's opened it seemed likely that technical assistance programs under the auspices of the governments of the United States and other countries, of the UN, and of the voluntary agencies were to be a part of the history of the decades to follow. It was less clear what role the American voluntary agencies would play. But on the record of their contributions it was reasonable to expect that they would find new and telling ways of helping underdeveloped areas and rising peoples create a world which shared some of the advantages of the industrialized nations—and quite possibly some of their problems.

---

[129] John Baker, Jr., to Merle Curti, July 17, 1961. See also John C. Caldwell, *Still the Rice Grows Green: Asia in the Aftermath of Geneva and Panmunjom* (Chicago: Regnery, 1955), 97, 102-03; Arthur F. Raper, *Rural Taiwan: Problems and Promise* (Taipei: Chinese-American Joint Commission on Rural Reconstruction in China, 1953), 61 ff., and George W. Barclay, *Colonial Development and Population in Taiwan* (Princeton: Princeton University Press, 1954), 255, 261-62.

[130] The initial Ford grant was $500,000, the Rockefeller, $475,000. The Polish government assured the foundations of their right to select beneficiaries for foreign study without Polish interference: *New York Times*, May 27, 1957, Nov. 2, 1957, Dec. 29, 1958.

[131] For examples, see the indictments of foreign aid, based partly on a commitment to American nationalism, in *National Review* II (June 6, 1956), 5-6; William J. Lederer, *A Nation of Sheep* (New York: Norton, 1961) and Thomas S. Loeber, *Foreign Aid: Our Tragic Experiment* (New York: Norton, 1961).

XX

Reflections and Implications

Proud of their record of private and voluntary giving at home and abroad, Americans often overlooked their indebtedness to the charity of the Old World. This debt has been both direct and indirect. Indirectly, Americans, in giving, responded to transmitted religious and humanitarian precepts. They adopted Europe's charitable trust and the common law and made use of the voluntarily supported permanent agency for the advancement of religion and knowledge, a model being the eighteenth-century British Society for the Propagation of the Gospel in Foreign Parts. The direct philanthropic debt of America includes private contributions from Europeans when catastrophes struck not only the relatively feeble colonies but well established communities in the nineteenth century and even in the early twentieth century. Far more important than such contributions in times of flood, fire, earthquake, and epidemic have been the private gifts from the Old World for founding and supporting schools, colleges, and learned societies in America. This story, which has been told only in fragments, needs to be kept in mind in the counterpart record of American giving to other peoples.

American philanthropy overseas falls into three main periods, each of which has much in common with the others. But each is also marked by special developments and characteristics related to a stage of economic growth, to the status of transoceanic transportation, and to America's role in world affairs at the time.

The first period began shortly after the founding of the Republic and spanned the nineteenth century. In general, each foreign disaster was met in a characteristically American *ad hoc* way: there was little formal or institutional connection between what was done on different occasions. To this generalization two important exceptions must be made. The foreign missionary movement, supported by permanent church organizations, raised funds not only for converting the "heathen" but for famine relief, for work projects enabling displaced persons to rehabilitate themselves, and for path-breaking clinics, hospitals, schools and colleges in the Near East, Africa, China, India, and Japan. By the 1890's the foreign missionary movement, largely supported by small donors, was a major philanthropic as well as religious enterprise. The other exception to the prevailing *ad hoc* character of American overseas philanthropy was the Red Cross, organized in 1882.

Even though each famine, earthquake, pestilence, and war required new organizations and appeals, the methods of fund raising continued to be similar to those established in the first national campaign for foreign relief in response to the Greek Revolution of the 1820's. These methods included the organization by chambers of commerce and boards of trade of committees for raising money and transporting food. Also of importance were the huge public meetings often initiated by the mercantile committees. At such meetings speakers graphically described the plight of the sore-pressed Greeks, or, later, of the famine-stricken peasants in Ireland and Russia and the persecuted Armenians in Turkey. On all these occasions churches also took up special collections. Sympathizers arranged musical and theatrical "benefits" and ladies' bazaars. Appeals from all these committees and public meetings, publicized by the press, led many farmers and millers to give corn, wheat, and flour. A new note was struck in the Irish famine of 1880 when the *New York Herald* initiated a special newspaper campaign for contributions. Even more impressive were the fund-raising campaigns of the *Christian Herald*, the most widely read religious newspaper in the world. It raised many millions of dollars chiefly through small contributions for disaster relief in various parts of the world and transported food in chartered vessels to the scene of suffering. These campaigns, in accustoming many Americans of all social and economic groups to the idea of giving for the needy across the seas, lent support to the thesis of Tocqueville that widespread American generosity reflected the absence of a sense of class barriers.

In view of the general reliance on voluntary organizations for accomplishing what in Europe was apt to be done by government, the role of the latter in overseas giving throughout the nineteenth century was understandably a minor one. Only once did Congress appropriate funds for the purchase of relief provisions, the occasion being the disastrous earthquake in Venezuela in 1812. Similar measures, introduced in 1847 and 1892 in behalf of overseas famine sufferers, were defeated on the ground that the Constitution did not give Congress power to use public funds for foreign relief. On several occasions Congress, under some pressure, did lend naval vessels to transport private gifts of food to Irish and Russian famine sufferers. These actions provided precedents for the later typically American cooperation of private and public agencies in overseas giving.

The second period of American overseas philanthropy, from the Spanish-American War to the end of the 1930's, differed from the preceding one in the greater magnitude of giving. This was to be expected in view of the economic growth of the country and the new role of America as a world power. The period was also marked by the larger role of government in overseas philanthropy. Government-owned food and other surpluses were allocated to private agencies for the relief of victims of the First World War. The larger role of government was also expressed, during the Spanish Civil War, in the federal registering and supervising of private overseas philanthropy in the interest of preserving American neutrality. In this period private philanthropy was used for almost the first time as an instrument of national policy.

The two older agencies for overseas relief (the Red Cross and the missionary organizations) were augmented in the first decade of the twentieth century by new agencies which came to be permanent. These included the American Jewish Joint Distribution Committee, the American Friends Service Committee, and Near East Relief. The newly organized Rockefeller Foundation, the Carnegie Corporation, the Phelps-Stokes Fund, the Rosenwald Fund, the Pilgrim Trust and the Commonwealth Fund devoted part of their resources to overseas philanthropies. This institutionalization meant, among other things, the development of the practice of using trained administrators and overseas field workers. Inspired by the phenomenal success of fund raising for charitable purposes in the great "drives" of the First World War, several campaigns for overseas relief in the 1920's made use of such professional organizations as Marts and Lundy and the John Price Jones Corporation.

Another innovation was the effort of relief agencies during the 1920's to attack the causes rather than simply the effects of endemic

famines in China. Work projects for flood control, irrigation, reclamation, and reforestation were instituted. These efforts, to be sure,
did not go very far, but, in view of the complexity and difficulties inherent in the situation, such a forerunner of the WPA, which was
.to come during the American depression of the 1930's, was notable.
At the same time the Near East Foundation, a successor of Near
East Relief, developed a remarkable program of rural reconstruction.
This was a modification of methods worked out at home to improve
rural life, such as the demonstration farm, the 4-H Club, the county
agent, and the Rockefeller Foundation's victory over hookworm
in the South. The Near East program stimulated self-help in improving agriculture, health, homemaking, and community recreation.
And during this period American missionaries in foreign countries
put greater stress on combining the testimony of the Word with the
Deed—especially on educational and health programs of long-range
significance.

All these tendencies became even more marked during and after
the Second World War, the third period of philanthropic endeavor.
While government support was given to the relief and health agencies of the United Nations, the precedent of providing public and
private aid within the context of national policy was carried further
than ever before. One example was the much more extensive use of
government surpluses by religious agencies and by such nonsectarian
groups as CARE in areas and under conditions stipulated by Washington. Another tendency in the recent period has been the increasing
emphasis on the development of self-help in the retraining and relocation of refugees and in economic and social reconstruction. The
technical assistance programs of the Rockefeller Foundation and
the Ford Foundation were cases in point though by no means the
only ones. The earlier support of scholarship and the arts through
international grants and fellowships, in which the Carnegie Corporation had led, continued as integral parts of the programs of several
foundations. In addition to the fuller development of earlier precedents and the impressive increase in the magnitude of overseas aid,
the recent period witnessed several innovations. One was the continuation of overseas philanthropies even after the immediate war
emergency abroad was surmounted, in contrast with the greatly
curtailed programs once the postwar crisis in Europe of the early
1920's was over. A second innovation has been the overseas philanthropic activities of labor organizations and of corporations in

business abroad, such as the United Fruit Company, Firestone, Creole, and the American Arabian Oil Company. Corporation giving, together with the growing practice of private disposition of government surpluses in a context of national policy, suggests that philanthropy for overseas relief and amelioration was not entirely altruistic. Indeed, as Emerson once wrote, "take egotism out, and you would castrate the benefactor." The point can be illustrated by examples from several levels of interest: the individual person, class and occupational groups, and the nation itself.

In each period personal factors and interests entered into overseas philanthropies. Some gave out of habit or in response to social pressure. Several native-born Americans of means who lived abroad contributed to some worthy cause in their adopted lands as an expression of appreciation of these countries. Sometimes such giving was highly creative as, for instance, when it provided for needed institutions unlikely otherwise to be established at the time. Examples are the munificent contributions to low-rent housing in London slums in the 1860's which made George Peabody an international figure; the hospital, school, and museum that Edward and Stella Tuck gave to a beloved community in France; the psychiatric research institute that James Loeb established in Munich; and the museum of Polynesian culture that Charles Bishop presented to Honolulu. Personal sentiment also explains contributions of Americans of foreign background to the country of origin. Carnegie, although the most munificent benefactor of his native land through the libraries and welfare institutions he founded, was by no means alone. The endowment of a Canadian university, the founding of an orphan asylum in Switzerland and a public library in Moravia, are merely illustrations that could be multiplied many times.

In some cases motives for giving were related to class and occupational considerations. The generous giving of nineteenth-century merchants to relief campaigns was in part related to their trade with the areas in distress. In sensationally publicizing the plight of sufferers from famine and pestilence and in collecting funds for relief, newspapers were not insensitive to the fact that such campaigns brought goodwill and increased sales. Occasionally the evidence for economic motivation is explicit. Thus the *Northwestern Miller*, a trade organ which inaugurated successful campaigns for getting flour to starving Russian peasants, observed that with the depressed prices associated with an oversupply of American grain, "philanthropy and business may properly walk hand in hand." Many Europeans felt that Hoover's famine relief program after World War I was designed to bolster the prices of surplus grain in the international market and thus to stave off or minimize an American agricultural depression. Such a consideration cannot be altogether ruled out of the picture. Finally, since 1945 the role of corporations in philanthropic giving to areas in which they do business is obviously related to the desire to develop good public relations and to reduce their tax bill through exemptions for contributions, as well as to genuinely humanitarian motives.

National pride also figured in a good deal of the giving. The fact that the Greek patriots first appealed for help to the transatlantic Republic was flattering to self-esteem and to the developing sense of an American mission to promote freedom in the world. This was to remain an important factor in many later crusades for overseas giving. Sensitive to slurs on the national character, unknown numbers of Americans gave in overseas causes as if to prove that they were in actuality less money-mad than foreign critics charged.

A feeling of special responsibility and a sense of guilt related to national policy and interest also played a part in seemingly altruistic behavior. In urging contributions to the Irish famine funds of 1847 and 1880, solicitors reminded the public of the brawn and sweat of the Irish workers who, at meager wages, had done the hard and dirty work of canal building and railroad construction in America. During the Civil War tens of thousands of Lancashire cotton workers lost their jobs as factories, unable to import American cotton by reason of the federal blockade of Southern ports, closed down. Despite heavy claims on giving for domestic war relief, Americans contributed to the substantial sums raised for these suffering Britons. Many decades later Americans contributed liberally to the sufferers in Japan from famine and earthquake, when reminded that of all foreign nations, Japan had given most generously to the victims of the San Francisco earthquake. In each period Americans were urged to give because their country, with its God-bestowed abundance, ought to be ashamed of indifference to the poverty, need, and suffering of peoples in less favored lands.

American contributions to the needs of peoples overseas were sometimes explicitly tied to national interest and policy. The use of the first public funds for overseas relief—in response to the Venezuela earthquake of 1812—was intended to prove the friendship of the United States for the rising Latin American republics and to stimulate commercial relations. Toward the end of the century, many, including President McKinley, gave for the relief of the reconcentrados in Cuba as a means of reducing popular pressure for armed intervention. During the years of neutrality in the First World War and in the following years, the government played a policy-oriented role in providing relief to the Allies and to Central and Eastern Europe in the dark time of starvation and pesitilence. Hoover thought in terms of national interest as well as in terms of humanitarianism. The relief and rehabilitation of Europe promised to insure future repayment of debts. It promised to open markets for American goods and to check the spread of communism. The intermingling of public and private giving during and since the Second World War has reflected an even more self-conscious awareness of national policy. Finally, relief was sometimes withheld as a measure of national policy. An example was the refusal of Franklin Roosevelt to countenance Hoover's urgent desire to campaign for gifts of food for countries occupied by Nazi Germany between 1939 and 1941.

Yet two closely interrelated motives overarched all others. One was related to Judeo-Christian teachings about the duty of compassion and charity. This duty was sometimes expressed in the doctrine of stewardship—that whatever of worldly means one has belongs to God, that the holder is only God's steward and obligated to give to the poor, the distressed, and the needy. From many diaries, letters, and other evidence it is clear that this factor was a dominant one in a great deal of giving. A second motive was humanitarianism, embracing the same conception of the brotherhood of man and of the duty of those who can help the needy to do so, but secular in character. It reenforced and supplemented the closely related Hebraic-Christian values.

The difficulties of administering relief stemmed in part from the simple fact that resources at hand were always inadequate to meet needs and in part from special circumstances. Sometimes, as in the case of the Greek struggle for independence and in the turmoil of China a century later, gifts intended for civilian relief were seized by pirates or diverted to the military. In the 1890's and in the period of World War I Turkish authorities threw many obstacles in the way of missionaries and the American Red Cross in their efforts to help the persecuted Armenians. After the First World War Soviet authorities suspected that desperately needed American relief was

intended to undermine the regime. This suspicion increased the difficulties of disbursement incidental to the breakdown of transportation
and the determination of the Americans that no one was to be deprived of help by reason of his religious or political opinions. The
diversion of American relief packages into the black market in the
years after the Second World War is still fresh in many memories.
These are only a few of the difficulties of administering philanthropy.

Shortcomings on the part of American overseas philanthropic endeavors often added to the difficulties inherent in the situation. Sometimes Americans gave what was neither wanted nor needed. Sometimes they attached unwise conditions to their gifts. On other occasions, they gave with a self-righteousness which militated against the
joy of giving and the joy of receiving. Understandably the British
regretted that American aid to the Irish famine sufferers was often
accompanied by denunciations of British ineptness, irresponsibility,
and downright callousness to the human suffering on their very
doorstep. Understandably the Irish were taken aback when Captain
Forbes, on presenting his cargo of supplies to the eager and responsive people of Cork, spoke of the great need of raising the Irish moral
standard.

Philanthropy itself of course implies an inequality between donor
and recipient, an implication which many Americans have tried to
minimize but not always successfully. The gulf between donor and
recipient was reflected, for example, in the feeling expressed by John
Dewey that our missions in China in the 1920's were training Chinese youth for minor roles rather than for positions of creative
leadership. On the other hand, American donors have been concerned
lest their gifts pauperize the nations receiving them as individual
bounty has sometimes pauperized the recipient. Two factors checked
this danger. One has been a growing concern with the causes rather
than the results of natural disaster, poverty, and ill health. The other
has been the increasing emphasis on helping those in need to help
themselves.

Before the Irish famine of 1880, little attention had been given in
American discussion and programs of action to the causes of famine,
pestilence, and other calamities. Slowly, with a good deal of trial
and error, much American philanthropy has moved in this direction.
In an effort to help remove the causes of poverty, Joseph Fels, an
ardent disciple of Henry George, financed single-tax campaigns and
projects in several countries. To cite another example, American

Jewish philanthropy contributed substantially not only to the creation of Israel but to the self-help projects which have developed its economy and improved its living standards. But the most impressive philanthropies designed to rise above the palliative level have been the increasingly emphasized programs of rural rehabilitation and reconstruction in many lands. At their best such approaches have provided not only the know-how for self-help, but moral leadership. This kind of giving, the most difficult of all benevolences, was expressed in Walt Whitman's lines:

> Behold, I do not give lectures or a little charity
> When I give myself.

But to give oneself has sometimes seemed to others to give what was not wanted. The point has often been made, but never more cogently than by John Dewey who, during his visit in the early 1920's to China, the country that had received the largest share of American overseas philanthropy, reminded his countrymen that charity might be used abroad to buy off resentment of a people suffering from profound need, rather than leave the way open for their own attack on their own problems in their own way.

Be that as it may, Americans in their overseas philanthropies have given what they themselves have most valued. These gifts included disaster relief and postwar rehabilitation of the maimed, the fatherless, and the displaced. Included also have been the worldwide attacks on death-causing diseases which those in other lands regarded as inevitable. It is possible that Herbert Hoover has overstated the American case in holding that in the last forty-five years American gifts to the starving and dying of the world have approximated $42,-200,000,000 and have saved a billion lives. Whatever the magnitude of the figures, few question the importance of giving to save lives.

American philanthropies abroad have transplanted, with varying degrees of success, such devices as the Eastman free dental clinics for children, aids to the blind and other physically handicapped, and such agencies of self-help as "Boys Towns" and 4-H Clubs and other agencies for improving agricultural, and, recently, industrial production. American donors, as individuals and as foundations, have contributed to the increase of knowledge regardless of national boundaries through subsidies to scientific research, through the reconstruction of libraries and laboratories in famous Old World universities, and through the rescuing of displaced scholars, writers, and artists. American philanthropy also established scores of educational institutions hitherto unknown in many lands, including schools and colleges for women. With peoples of other countries, Americans through their philanthropies have contributed to the internationalization of scholarship, science, and the arts.

Is the American self-conception of generosity, believed to have grown in part out of frontier experience of neighborly sharing and helpfulness, actually a distinctively American trait? We need to know whether Americans have, in relation to their resources, played the role of Lady Bountiful with a comparatively small hand. We need to know more about the impact of American giving on the American reputation and on the lives, institutions, and culture of recipients. These questions, on which this study has thrown some light, can be more fully answered when historians in many countries have thoroughly investigated the extent and character of giving in many lands to many peoples in other lands.

Efforts to improve the conditions that make living possible and desirable may create in nonindustrial societies some of the problems that beset industrialized nations. It is yet to be seen whether Toynbee will be regarded as an apt prophet in suggesting that the twentieth century will be remembered as that in which civilized man made the benefits of progress available to all humanity. If so, the American contributions, here presented for the first time in some detail, can be evaluated in a larger and more significant perspective.

Bibliographical Essay

Since the material on which this study is based is cited with considerable fullness at the appropriate places in the several chapters, it seems best in this essay to indicate, in broad strokes and with no effort at anything like completeness, the general character of the sources, secondary and primary.

No historian has hitherto written a documented and comprehensive account of American nonofficial contributions to the relief and rehabilitation of people in disaster-stricken areas overseas. Nor is there at hand an adequate account of American efforts to salvage refugees, or of what philanthropy did to strengthen the agencies and resources of cultural life in other countries or to promote the development of the less industrialized lands through technical assistance. Hermann Stöhr's *So half Amerika: Die Auslandshilfe der Vereinigten Staaten 1812-1930* (Stettin, 1936) is the only general account available, and it is at best a sketchy chronicle even within the time span covered. Secondary accounts of some of the relevant episodes and of a few of the voluntary agencies involved do, to be sure, exist. But with some exceptions these leave much to be desired. Few of them adequately relate to the broader contexts of which they are a part.

A few examples may illustrate what has been written about Old World contributions to disaster relief and to the agencies of cultural life in America—a largely untold story which needs constantly to be kept in mind in any study of American philanthropy overseas. Although written more than a century ago, Charles Deane's "The Irish Donation in 1676," *New England Historical and Genealogical Register* II (July, 1848), 245-50, (Oct., 1848), 398-99, might well serve as a model for describing the many Old World generosities to America. In the same category are Frank J. Klingberg's studies of the Society for the Propagation of the Gospel in Foreign Parts, of which *Anglican Humanitarianism in Colonial New York* (Philadelphia, 1940) is illustrative. A few competent studies of voluntary efforts of non-American agencies to relieve suffering beyond their own national borders have been written, an example of which is Norman De Mattos Bentwich's *They Found Refuge: An Account of British Jewry's Work for Victims of Nazi Oppression* (London, 1956).

American contributions to international efforts, official and unofficial, in refugee relief and rehabilitation are included in George Woodbridge's monumental and thoroughly documented *UNRRA: The History of the United Nations Relief and Rehabilitation Administration* (3 vols., New York, 1950), Jacques Vernant's *The Refugee in the Post-War World* (London, 1953), John Stoessinger's *The Refugee and the World Community* (Minneapolis, 1957), Malcolm Proudfoot's *European Refugees, 1939-1952; A Study in Forced Population Movement* (London, 1957), Louise Holborn's *The International Refugee Organization, a Specialized Agency of the United Nations: Its History and Work, 1946-1952* (London, 1956). Elfan Rees' *Century of the Homeless Man* (New York, 1957) and Robert Heilbroner's *Mankind's Children: The Story of UNICEF* (New York, 1959) are especially readable and dramatic.

Several useful secondary accounts of American private benevolence in particular overseas calamities are at hand. These include Frances Sergeant Childs, *French Refugee Life in the United States, 1790-1800* (Baltimore, 1940), Stephen A. Larrabee, *Hellas Observed: The American Experience of Greece, 1775-1865* (New York, 1957) and E. M. Halliday, "Bread upon the Waters," *American Heritage* XI (August, 1960), 62-69, 104-105, an account of American aid to Russian famine-sufferers in the 1890's. Several well-documented studies are available for American efforts in the famines and epidemics of the World War I period. Among these are Harold H. Fisher, *The Famine in Soviet Russia, 1919-1923: the Operations of the American Relief Administration* (New York, 1927), supplemented by Xenia Eudin and Harold H. Fisher, eds., *Soviet Russia and the West, 1920-1927: A Documentary Survey* (Stanford, 1957) and by Frank A. Golder and Lincoln Hutchinson, *On the Trail of the Russian Famine* (Stanford, 1927). A Master's essay by Charles Strickland, "American Aid for the Relief of Germany, 1919-1921" (University of Wisconsin, 1959), is excellent. Edward McSweeney's

American Voluntary Aid for Germany, 1945-1950 (Freiburg im Breisgau, 1950) and Albert Kohler's and Eugen Rendt's *Wir Danken Euch* (Mindelheim, 1949) are useful. Louis Lochner's *Herbert Hoover and Germany* (New York, 1960) adds some personal information to the detailed accounts Hoover himself has written of his outstanding contributions. John Van Gelder Forbes used the files of the American Friends Service Committee at Haverford for his unpublished manuscript of 1942, "A Short Account of the Collection, Distribution, and Administration and Relief for Spanish Civilians during the Spanish Civil War." Although this is a valuable study it needs to be balanced by Charles Wetzel's "American Relief to Spain during the Spanish Civil War, 1936-1939," a Master's essay presented at the University of Wisconsin in 1959.

The secondary material on overseas religious missions in general fails adequately to describe and evaluate contributions to education, health, welfare, relief, and rehabilitation. Much that is pertinent may, however, be found in Kenneth Scott Latourette, *A History of the Expansion of Christianity* (7 vols., New York, 1937-1945), John Lankford, "Protestant Stewardship and Benevolence, 1900-1941: A Study in Religious Philanthropy" (Ph.D. dissertation, University of Wisconsin, 1961), Alice H. Gregg, *China and Educational Autonomy: the Changing Role of the Protestant Educational Missionary in China, 1807-1937* (Syracuse, 1946) and the Commission on Appraisal, *Re-Thinking Missions: A Laymen's Inquiry after One Hundred Years* (New York, 1932). A recent evaluation is that in Harland Cleveland, Gerard J. Mangone, and John Clarke Adams, *The Overseas Americans* (New York, 1960). Also useful are the biographies of missionaries, examples of which are Francis Wayland, *A Memoir of the Life and Labors of the Rev. Adoniram Judson* (Boston, 1853), Frederick Wells Williams, *The Life and Letters of Samuel Wells Williams* (New York, 1889), William Elliott Griffis, *A Maker of the New Orient: Samuel Robbins Brown, Pioneer Educator in China, America, and Japan* (New York, Chicago, 1902), William Warder Cadbury, *At the Point of a Lancet: One Hundred Years of the Canton Hospital, 1835-1935* (Shanghai-Hong Kong, 1935), to cite only a few of the some two hundred biographical accounts examined. Nor should the lives of lay promoters of missions be forgotten: Chauncy J. Hawkins, *Samuel Billings Capen: His Life and Work* (Boston, New York, 1914), William Adams Brown, *Morris Ketchum Jesup: A Character Sketch* (New York, 1910), and Charles M. Pepper, *Life-Work of Louis Klopsch* (New York, 1910) are examples of a category of materials which, while often laudatory, contain indispensable information. In evaluating the impact of missions in the areas in which activities centered, institutional histories, some sketchy, others well-documented and objective, served useful purposes. A few examples of the large number of titles examined are Lotta Levensohn, *Vision and Fulfillment: The First Twenty-five Years of the Hebrew University 1925-1950* (New York, 1950), Charles B. Sissons, *A History of Victoria University* (Toronto, 1952), Mary Mills Patrick, *A Bosporus Adventure: Constantinople Woman's College 1871-1924* (Stanford, 1934), Stephen B. L. Penrose, Jr., *That They May Have Life: The Story of the American University of Beirut, 1866-1941* (New York, 1941), and the histories of St. John's University, Fukien University, Soochow University, Hangchow University, Shantung University, Ginling College and sister institutions, all sponsored by the United Board for Christian Colleges in China.

Several monographs and biographies give the main outlines of the nonsectarian educational and welfare overseas activities. These include Eugene E. Doll's account of the Carl Schurz Memorial Foundation, *Twenty-five Years of Service, 1930-1955* (Philadelphia, 1955), Perrin C. Galpin, *Belgian Higher Education and the Belgian American Exchanges between the Two Wars* (New York, ca., 1948), Louis E. Lord, *A History of the American School of Classical Studies at Athens* (Cambridge, 1947), Raymond B. Fosdick, *The Story of the Rockefeller Foundation* (New York, 1952) and *John D. Rockefeller, Jr., A Portrait* (New York, 1956) and Richard H. Heindel, *The American Impact on Great Britain, 1848-1914* (Philadelphia, 1940), to cite only a very few titles.

While no comprehensive studies exist of the over-all activities of voluntary agencies during and since the Second World War, a few studies are path-breaking. Special note should be made of Lewis M. Hoskins, "Voluntary Agencies and Foundations in International Aid," *Annals of the American Academy of Political and Social Science* CCCXXIX (May, 1960), 57-68, United States Displaced Persons Commission, *The DP Story. The Final Report of the United States Displaced Persons Commission*, August 15, 1952 (Washington: Govt. Printing Office, 1952), Jessie L. C. Adams, "Postwar Private Gifts to Foreign Countries Total $6 Billion," *Foreign Commerce Weekly* LVII (June 17, 1957), 13-15, and a series of articles without authors given, entitled "Doing Good Abroad" in *The Economist* CLXXXIX (Oct. 11, 1958), 141-42, (Nov. 15, 1958), 604-05, (Dec. 8, 1958), 895-96, (Dec. 27, 1958), 1158-60.

The voluntary agencies themselves have been the subject of several historical treatments. Especially useful are John D. Unruh, *In the Name of Christ: A History of the Mennonite Central Committee and Its Service, 1920-1950* (Scottsdale, Pa., 1952), Lorell Weiss, *Ten Years of Brethren Service* (Elgin, Ill., ca., 1952), Irvin B. Horst, *A Ministry of Goodwill* (Akron, Pa., 1950), Mary Hoxie Jones, *Swords into Ploughshares: An Account of the American Friends Service Committee, 1917-1937* (New York, 1937), and John Van Gelder Forbes, "Quaker Relief and Government" (Ph.D. dissertation, University of Pennsylvania, 1951). Richard W. Solberg's *As Between Brothers: The Story of Lutheran Response to World Need* (Minneapolis, 1957) should inspire other denominational agencies to sponsor historical accounts of their overseas activities.

Of the religiously oriented agencies, those of the Jews have received more historical recording than others. Mark Wischnitzer's *To Dwell in Safety: The Story of Jewish Migration since 1800* (Philadelphia, 1948) and *Visas to Freedom: The History of HIAS* (Cleveland, 1956) are well documented official histories. Moses A. Leavitt, *The JDC Story: Highlights of JDC Activities, 1914-1952* (New York, 1953) and Joseph C. Hyman's *Twenty-Five Years of American Aid to Jews Overseas: A Record of the Joint Distribution Committee* (New York, 1939) cut the path for a more detailed and much needed study in preparation. Herbert Agar's *The Saving Remnant: An Account of Jewish Survival* (New York, 1960), is one of the most moving of all accounts of American overseas efforts to relieve the sufferings of victims of persecution. The significant vocational training programs of a highly useful agency are described in American ORT Federation, *ORT: A Record of Ten Years of Rebuilding Jewish Economic Life* (New York, 1956). Several biographies of Jewish leaders interested in overseas philanthropy help explain the role of outstanding individuals. Among the more important are Cyrus Adler, *Jacob H. Schiff: His Life and Letters* (2 vols., Garden City, N. Y., 1928), Alpheus Mason, *Brandeis: A Free Man's Life* (New York, 1946) and Morris R. Werner, *Julius Rosenwald: The Life of a Practical Humanitarian* (New York, 1939).

The overseas activities of agencies with important domestic programs are indicated in greater or less detail in Herbert A. Wisbey,

Soldiers without Swords: A History of the Salvation Army in the United States (New York, 1955), in Maurice F. Egan and John B. Kennedy, *The Knights of Columbus in Peace and War* (New Haven, 1920), in Charles H. Hopkins, *History of the Y.M.C.A. in North America* (New York, 1951). *International Survey of the Young Men's and Young Women's Christian Associations: an Independent Study of the Foreign Work of the Christian Associations of the United States and Canada* (New York, 1932) is also helpful.

Several useful accounts have been written about secular agencies. These include International Social Service's publication *In a World They Never Made: The Story of International Social Service* (New York, 1957), Thaddeus Krysiewicz, "Polish Immigration Committee in the United States" (unpublished Master's essay, Fordham University, 1953), Bertha McCall, *History of the National Travelers Aid Association, 1911-1940* (New York, 1950), and James L. Barton, *Story of Near East Relief, 1915-1930* (New York, 1930). The as yet unpublished doctoral dissertation of Robert L. Daniel, "From Relief to Technical Assistance in the Near East: A Case Study: Near East Relief and Near East Foundation" (University of Wisconsin, 1953), goes far beyond the Barton account.

As might be expected, the history of the American Red Cross has been more thoroughly investigated and written about than that of any other agency. Several biographies of Clara Barton are available, but the official one by William E. Barton, *The Life of Clara Barton, Founder of the American Red Cross* (Boston and New York, 1922) is still useful by reason of the substantial extracts from the diary and correspondence of the first leader. *In The American Red Cross: A History* (New York, 1950), Foster Rhea Dulles summarized a number of carefully documented monographs on various aspects of the history of the organization, all of which are available in mimeograph form at the headquarters in Washington. Of those most useful in the present study mention should be made of Gustavus Gaeddert, "The Barton Influence," Mabel A. Elliott, "American National Red Cross Disaster Series, 1881-1918," Catherine Finnley, "American National Red Cross Disaster Series, 1918-1939," and Joseph Bykofsky, "Foreign Relief in the Post Armistice Period, 1918-1923." Dr. Clyde E. Buckingham kindly made available his unpublished manuscript, "The Golden Moment: Henry P. Davison and American Influence in the Founding of the League of Red Cross Societies" (1961).

The files of CARE in New York contain the manuscript history of the founding and early years of this important agency written by Charles Bloomstein. The most accessible account of CARE's achievements is in Section X of the *New York Times*, Feb. 10, 1957, under the title "CARE . . . A Report to the People."

In addition to information on nonofficial technical assistance available in some of the materials previously listed, the relations between voluntary and government efforts in this field are touched on in Merle Curti and Kendall Birr, *Prelude to Point Four: American Technical Missions Overseas, 1838-1939* (Madison, Wis., 1954). Dr. Wayland Zwayer has edited, for the Technical Assistance Information Clearing House of the American Council of Voluntary Agencies for Foreign Service, a list of agencies, with their sponsors, budgets, and programs under the title *Directory of American Voluntary and Non-Profit Agencies Interested in Technical Assistance* (New York, 1960). James G. Maddox, *Technical Assistance by Religious Agencies in Latin America* (Chicago, 1956), Harlan Cleveland and Gerard J. Mangone, eds., *The Art of Overseamanship* (Syracuse, 1957), Edwin A. Bock, *Fifty Years of Technical Assistance: Some Administrative Experiences of the United States Voluntary Agencies* (Chicago, 1954) are competent accounts.

Wherever possible, manuscript collections were searched for amplification and correction of published materials. The interest of mid-nineteenth-century merchant-philanthropists in overseas benevolence is reflected in the A. A. Lawrence Collection in the Massachusetts Historical Society. The William Lloyd Garrison papers in the Boston Public Library also provided useful information. Of special interest is the record of fund raising and relief administration in the papers of Charles P. Daly in the New York Public Library. Daly was deeply involved in Irish famine relief.

For overseas relief in the later nineteenth and early twentieth centuries the Herbert Welch Collection and the files of the Citizens Permanent Relief Committee [Russian Famine Correspondence], both in the Pennsylvania Historical Society, have a mine of otherwise inaccessible information. The Robert C. Ogden papers in the Library of Congress supplement the Philadelphia material. The T. De Witt Talmage papers, also in the Library of Congress, illuminate a worthy chapter in overseas famine relief history. Important beyond any of these collections are the Clara Barton diaries, journals, and correspondence in the same repository and at the headquarters of the American Red Cross. Indispensable, too, are the Carnegie papers in the Library of Congress. The George Washburn manuscripts, in the possession of Mrs. Basil Hall of Cambridge, Massachusetts, supplemented at many points the wide-ranging information about missionary activities available in published accounts. For the free dental clinics established in several European capitals the George Eastman collection at company headquarters in Rochester amplify the slender accounts available elsewhere.

For overseas Jewish philanthropy during and after the First World War the Julius Rosenwald papers at the University of Chicago and the papers in Mr. James N. Rosenberg's possession illuminate important movements.

American philanthropies in Germany, Russia, and other countries are reflected meaningfully in the Louis Lochner and Raymond Robins papers in the Wisconsin State Historical Society. The Baker Library in the Harvard Graduate School of Business Administration holds the files of the John Price Jones Corporation whose records of the fund-raising drives for overseas causes picture a development of importance. The researcher in this field is especially grateful for the fascinating manuscript of John Earl Baker, "Fighting China's Famine," which this remarkable man deposited in the University of Wisconsin Library in 1943.

On such matters as the nature and problems of the War Relief Control Board and United States policy toward refugees, materials in the Franklin D. Roosevelt Library at Hyde Park and in the Harry S. Truman Library at Independence proved useful.

Two major manuscript collections provide substantial and significant data for the analyses given in this study of overseas philanthropies during and since World War II. The American Council of Voluntary Agencies for Foreign Service in New York holds unpublished committee reports and correspondence with constituent members and with key figures in Congress and in the federal administration who were responsible for the cooperation of government and voluntary agencies in overseas relief, refugee aid, rehabilitation, and technical assistance. Some of the same material, and much in addition, is at hand in the files of the Advisory Committee on Voluntary Foreign Aid, an agency of the International Cooperation Administration in Washington. The Advisory Committee's files are useful for memoranda and other material relating to the administration and policies of the Committee as well as correspondence with voluntary agencies.

The record of appropriate Congressional committees, deposited in the National Archives, proved useful on minor points. So did the reports from overseas consular and diplomatic officials, since the archival records contain some information not included in the State Department's publications.

While the records of the voluntary agencies, committees, and foundations with overseas programs form, together with the auto-biographies, reminiscences, and reports of those concerned with overseas relief and reconstruction, the principal base for this book, published government documents, particularly in the last decades, were also used to advantage. It is impossible to list even a small fraction of these. Most helpful were the reports, hearings, and investigations of special subcommittees of various Congressional committees, *Papers Relating to Foreign Affairs, Department of State Bulletin* and *Press Releases*, the *Debates and Proceedings in the Congress* and its successors, *Register of Debates in Congress, Congressional Globe*, and *Congressional Record*, Richardson's *A Compilation of the Messages and Papers of the President* and the pertinent state papers of Hoover, Roosevelt, Truman, and Eisenhower. If, from the very extensive official published documents consulted, one were to select a few for special mention, these would certainly include Paul Dewitt Dickens and August Maffry, *Balance of International Payments in the United States in 1939*, Department of Commerce, Foreign and Domestic Commerce Bureau, Economic Series 8 (Washington, 1940) and subsequent similar reports, the War Relief Control Board's *Voluntary War Relief During World War II*, Department of State Publication 2566 (Washington, 1946), *Voluntary Foreign Aid: The Nature and Scope of Post-war Private American Assistance Abroad with Special Reference to Europe*, 80th Cong., 1st Sess., 1947 (a committee print of a special subcommittee of the House Committee on Foreign Affairs), *United States Foreign Aid: Its Purpose, Scope, Administration, and Related Information*, 86th Cong., 1st Sess., 1959, House Doc. 116, *Foreign Aid Programs*, 85th Cong., 1st Sess., 1957, Sen. Doc. 52, *Technical Assistance*, 85th Cong., 1st Sess., 1957, Sen. Rpt. 139, and *Final Report on Foreign Aid*, 80th Cong., 2d Sess., 1948, House Rpt. 1845. Special mention must be made of Arthur C. Ringland's "The Organization of Voluntary Foreign Aid, 1939-1953," *Department of State Bulletin* XXX (March 15, 1954).

Newspaper files were useful for data on fund-raising campaigns for overseas philanthropies and for information on policy problems of specific voluntary agencies. In all, over forty newspapers, representing major cities on the Atlantic and Pacific coasts and in the Middle West were consulted. Special use was made of the *New York Times*, especially for the period since 1914. It proved by far the most important newspaper source of information, as the annotation indicates. The London *Times*, a few Continental papers, and the *Japan Year Book* were also helpful on special points.

Even more important than newspapers were the almost countless articles with firsthand information on one or another pertinent subject. Periodicals of a general nature most frequently cited include the *North American Review, American Review, Atlantic Monthly, The Nation, Independent, Review of Reviews, World's Work, Harper's Weekly, Century, Forum, Colliers, Current Opinion, Outlook, Literary Digest, New Republic, Saturday Evening Post, Saturday Review, The Reporter, Life, Time, Newsweek,* and *Look.* British periodicals of general scope also proved useful, especially *The Economist, Spectator, Fortnightly Review, Nineteenth Century,* and *Contemporary Review.*

Periodicals dedicated to special interests yielded rich fruit. Representative of this category are *Commercial and Financial Chronicle, Business Week, Nation's Business, Fortune, Rotarian, Northwestern Miller, American Federationist, Survey, Scientific American, Public Opinion Quarterly, American Scandinavian Review, Slavonic and East Europe Review, Pacific Affairs, Asia,* and *Armerasia.* In the category of special interest periodicals the religious journals are by far the most important. It is hard to single out representative examples: they might be the *Congregationalist, Christian Herald, Christian Advocate, New York Observer, Lend a Hand, The Churchman, Christian Science Monitor Weekly Magazine, Catholic World, America, Commonweal, Commentary,* and *New Palestine.* The missionary journals are indispensable: of some fifty examined, the more important ones include *Chinese Repository, New York Observer, Home and Abroad, Baptist World, Heathen Woman's Friend, Spirit of Missions,* and *Missionary Review of the World.*

Published letters, diaries, autobiographies, and reminiscences of participants in and observers of American overseas benevolence and of the recipients of relief and rehabilitation provided a major source of information and understanding. Representative of this category of materials are Worthington C. Ford, ed., "Letters of Thomas Coram," Massachusetts Historical Society, *Proceedings* LVI (Oct., 1922), 15-56, Laura E. Richards, ed., *Letters and Journals of Samuel Gridley Howe* (2 vols., Boston, 1906-09), Samuel Gridley Howe, *An Historical Sketch of the Greek Revolution* (New York, 1828) and *The Cretan Refugees and Their American Helpers* (Boston, 1868), Mrs. Asenath Nicholson, *Ireland's Welcome to the Stranger* (New York, 1847), John Bigelow, *Retrospections of an Active Life* (5 vols., New York, 1909-13), E. B. Washburne, *Recollections of a Minister to France 1869-1877* (2 vols., New York, 1889), T. De Witt and Mrs. Talmage, *T. De Witt Talmage as I Knew Him* (New York, 1912), Francis B. Reeves, *Russia Then and Now, 1892-1917* (New York, 1917), *The Autobiography of Andrew D. White* (2 vols., New York, 1909), Frederick D. Greene, *The Armenian Crisis in Turkey* (New York, 1895), Helen B. Harris, *Letters from the Scenes of the Recent Massacres in Armenia* (New York, Chicago, 1897), Cyrus Hamlin, *My Life and Times* (Boston, Chicago, 1893), Daniel Bliss, *Reminiscences of Daniel Bliss* (New York, Chicago, 1920), Daniel McGilvary, *A Half-Century Among the Siamese and the Lao: An Autobiography* (New York, Chicago, 1912) and Justin Perkins, *A Residence of Eight Years in Persia* (New York, 1843). These volumes, a small fraction of those examined, are concerned with American overseas philanthropy in the first period of its history (1812-1897).

For the period from the Spanish-American War to 1930 this type of material proliferates. Examples are Ernest Bicknell, *Pioneering with the Red Cross* (New York, 1935), Ruth Gaines, *Helping France: The Red Cross in the Devastated Area* (New York, 1919), George B. Ford, *Out of the Ruins* (New York, 1919), John van Schaick, *The Little Corner Never Conquered: the Story of the American Red Cross War Work for Belgium* (New York, 1922), Grace H. Knapp, *The Tragedy of Bitlis* (New York, 1919), Clarence D. Ussher, *An American Physician in Turkey* (Boston and New York, 1917), Sam Higginbottom, *Farmer: an Autobiography* (New York, 1949), John R. Mott, *Five Decades and a Forward View* (New York, 1939), George Sherwood Eddy, *Eighty Adventurous Years* (New York, 1955), Nicholas Murray Butler, *Across the Busy Years: Recollections and Reflections* (2 vols., New York, 1939-40), Rufus M. Jones, *A Service of Love in War Time: American Friends Relief Work in Europe, 1917-1919* (New York, 1920), Frank A. Golder and Lincoln Hutchinson, *On the Trail of the Russian Famine* (Stanford, 1927), Henry Morgenthau, *All in a Life-Time* (Garden City, 1922), Henry R. Rosenfelt, *This Thing of Giving: The Record of a Rare Enterprise of Mercy and Brotherhood* (New York, 1924), and Joseph M. Proskauer, *A Segment of My Times* (New York, 1950). Other equally useful volumes are James N. Rosenberg, *On the Steppes: a Russian Diary* (New York, 1927) and Vernon Kellogg, *Fighting Starvation in Belgium* (Garden City, N. Y., 1918). The last volume is supplemented by George I. Gay and Harold H. Fisher, eds., *Public Relations of the Commission for Relief in Belgium* (2 vols., Stanford, 1929), and Allan Nevins, ed., *The Letters and Journals of Brand Whitlock* (2 vols., New York, 1936). Of special importance are Herbert Hoover's accounts of his relief activities in *An American Epic* (2 vols., Chicago, 1959-1960) and the *Memoirs of Herbert Hoover* (3 vols., New York, 1951-1952).

Cutting across this second period and the years between 1930 and our own time are many firsthand accounts. Representative examples include Howard E. Kershner, *Quaker Service in Modern War* (New York, 1950), Clarence Pickett, *For More Than Bread; an Autobiographical Account of Twenty-two Years' Work with the American Friends Service Committee* (Boston, 1953), and John Van Gelden Forbes, "The American Friends in Spain, 1937-1939," in *Administration of Relief Abroad: Recent Relief Programs of the American Friends in Spain and France,* ed. Donald S. Howard (New York: Russell Sage Foundation, 1943). The wealth of material on Jewish philanthropies is illustrated by such titles as Eli Ginzberg, *Report to American Jews on Overseas Relief: Palestine and Refugees in the United States* (New York, 1942), Cyrus Adler, *I Have Considered the Days* (Philadelphia, 1941), Charles Reznikoff, ed., *Louis Marshall: Champion of Liberty. Selected Papers and Addresses* (2 vols., Philadelphia, 1957) and Frieda Schiff Warburg, *Reminiscences of a Long Life* (New York, 1950). Of special note are the collected speeches of Herbert Hoover: *Addresses upon the American Road,* in three volumes for the period 1940-1948 (New York, 1941, 1946, 1949). The scope of activities in the recent period is further illustrated by such wide-ranging activities as those reflected in such titles as Gordon S. Seagrave, *Burma Surgeon* (New York, 1943) and *Burma Surgeon Returns* (New York, 1946), Victor George Heiser, *An American Doctor's Odyssey* (New York, 1936), *A Life for the Balkans. The Story of John Henry House of the American Farm School, Thessaloniki, Greece, as Told by His Wife to J. N. Nakivell*

(New York, 1939), Harold B. Allen, *Rural Reconstruction in Action. Experience in the Near and Middle East. Case Studies in Technical Assistance* (Ithaca, 1953) and Frank C. Laubach, who did so much to reduce the world's illiteracy through preparing teaching materials in many languages and dialects, *The World Is Learning Compassion* (Westwood, N. J., 1958). Murray D. Lincoln, *Vice President in Charge of Revolution* (New York, 1960) and Jonathan Bingham, *Shirt-Sleeve Diplomacy: Point Four in Action* (New York, 1954) include material on the technical assistance programs of voluntary agencies.

A basic source for this study has been the great body of reports of the committees formed to raise funds and supervise the administration of relief, rehabilitation and welfare activities. Some of these committees were of an *ad hoc* nature. Examples include *Address of the Committee Appointed at a Public Meeting Held at Boston, December 19, 1823, for the Relief of the Greeks* (Boston, 1823), American International Relief Committee for the Suffering Operatives of Great Britain, *Report, 1862-1863* (New York, 1864), John W. Hoyt, *Report of the Russian Famine Committee of the United States* (Washington, 1893), William C. Edgar, *The Russian Famine of 1891 and 1892* (Minneapolis, 1893), American Relief Committee at Rome, *Report of Funds administered for Relief of Earthquake Sufferers in Sicily and Calabria* (Rome, 1909), *Report of the Central China Famine Relief Fund Committee* (Shanghai, 1907), American National Red Cross, *The Report of the China Famine Relief* (Washington, 1922), Finnish Relief Fund, *Report to American Donors* (New York, 1940), and the reports issued during and at the end of World War II of the committees for the relief of France, Greece, Norway, Russia, Holland, Ireland, Britain, Italy, Poland, Korea and other countries. Another category in this general range of materials includes the reports of permanent organizations concerned with relief, refugee aid, and technical assistance, such as the American Friends Service Committee, which issues annual reports, and the Jewish organizations, such as Hadassah, HIAS, the Joint Distribution Committee, and ORT, for which reports are available and the activities of which, together with other Jewish overseas philanthropies, are summarized in the *American Jewish Yearbook*. Many agencies issue reports or other materials enabling the researcher to follow budgets, programs, and achievements: examples are Lutheran World Relief, Unitarian Service Committee, Catholic Relief Services and Catholic Bishops' Relief Fund, and Church World Service. Committee reports, issued during and since the Second World War, have been filed by both the American Council of Voluntary Agencies for Foreign Service in New York and the Advisory Committee on Voluntary Foreign Aid in Washington. In addition to the American Red Cross, agencies with special programs such as Heifer Project, Foster Parents Plan, Save the Children Federation, International Rescue Committee, and the International Committees of the YMCA and YWCA also issue reports.

The reports, yearbooks, and other releases of foundations with overseas philanthropic programs are generally available, most conveniently in the Foundation Library Center in New York. Major foundations with such programs include the Carnegie Corporation, the Carnegie Endowment for International Peace, the Carnegie Foundation for the Advancement of Teaching, and the British administered foundations endowed by Carnegie money, such as the Carnegie Dunfermline Trustees, the Carnegie Trust for the Universities of Scotland, and the Carnegie United Kingdom Trust. The Rockefeller Foundation and affiliated agencies, such as the Rockefeller Brothers Fund, provide reports and illustrative materials. The annual reports of the Ford Foundation, since 1951, are of special importance because of the magnitude and originality of many of its overseas programs. But use has also been made of the reports of smaller and less well-known foundations, such as the Kellogg Foundation, Tolstoy Foundation, Commonwealth Fund, Asia Foundation, Watumull Foundation, Near East Foundation, and Creole Foundation, to cite only a few. In addition to reports and public relations materials, occasional foundation-sponsored surveys were important. Especially notable were the African Education Commission's *Education in Africa* (New York, 1922), sponsored by the Carnegie and Phelps-Stokes Foundations, and William M. Hailey's *An African Survey* (New York, 1957).

These examples give, in brief compass, some indication of the widely diverse and abundant materials, secondary and primary, on which this study rests. In addition, numerous letters to the author, and interviews with leaders in various philanthropic endeavors provided information and insights not otherwise accessible. This material helped illuminate what, in the last twenty years, was done, why it was done, and what its importance and limitations were in the eyes of some of the participants.

Index

643

Index

645